The Economics of Work and Pay

THE ECONOMICS OF WORK AND PAY

Third Edition

DANIEL S. HAMERMESH
Michigan State University
and
ALBERT REES
Alfred P. Sloan Foundation

1817

HARPER & ROW, PUBLISHERS, New York
Cambridge, Philadelphia, San Francisco,
London, Mexico City, São Paulo, Sydney

Cover: The art appearing on the cover is a rendering of Figure 5.5 from page 129.

Sponsoring Editor: **David Forgione**
Project Editor: **Eleanor Castellano**
Designer: **Michel Craig**
Production Assistant: **Debi Forrest Bochner**
Compositor: Bi-Comp, Incorporated
Printer and Binder: R. R. Donnelley & Sons Company
Art Studio: Vantage Art, Inc.

The Economics of Work and Pay, Third Edition

Library of Congress Cataloging in Publication Data
Hamermesh, Daniel S.
The economics of work and pay.

Rev. ed. of: The economics of work and pay / Albert Rees. 2nd ed. c1979.
Includes index.
1. Labor economics. I. Rees, Albert, 1921– .
II. Rees, Albert, 1921– . Economics of work and pay.
III. Title.
HD4901.H18 1984 331 83-26650
ISBN 0-06-045355-9

Contents

Preface to the Student

This book is about labor economics—the branch of economic analysis that deals with topics such as the supply of labor, the allocation of labor among uses, the extent and incidence of unemployment, and the determination of wages. Two questions will help to define the field: Why is labor economics a separate branch of economics? How does labor economics differ from industrial relations?

The answer to the first question is that labor markets are very different from both commodity markets and markets for other factors of production. The employment of labor involves a continuing personal relationship between an employer and an employee; whereas, transactions in most other markets are by comparison brief and impersonal. Labor economics also involves the study of a major economic institution—the trade union—which is very different from the firm and whose behavior is not covered by the main body of economic theory.

Industrial relations has as its main focus the relation between an employer and the workers or their union in a particular establishment or firm, whereas, labor economics deals with larger aggregates. Because of its focus on smaller units, industrial relations is an interdisciplinary field that includes inputs from sociology, psychology, law, and personnel management as well as from economics. For much the same reason, industrial relations is largely an applied field, concerned with practice and the training of practitioners rather than with theory and measurement. It is thus related to the basic social sciences, including economics, as engineering is to the physical sciences or medicine is to the biological sciences.

This book does not pretend to cover industrial relations, although clearly no hard and fast line can be drawn to separate the fields. Rather, it concentrates on the application of economic theory and statistics to the problems of labor markets.

Nonetheless, we deal extensively with trade unions, discussing in detail economic theories of their behavior and analyzing their effects on particular labor markets and the entire economy.

In this volume we present recent data to illustrate how the theory of labor markets applies to contemporary economies. These data are important in their own right. Being familiar with them will enable you to develop a good sense of the way in which labor economics explains how modern labor markets function. In each chapter we present a number of policy issues—nearly 50 in the entire book—that are designed to illustrate the theoretical discussions after which they appear. These issues are also important because they deal with problems in labor-market policy that are continuously in the news. Along with each policy issue, which would be an excellent topic for a term paper, we provide references that can be used as background for such papers. Although most of these references are technical, some of them are summaries of the literature that you will find more accessible.

Throughout the text we assume only that you have had a yearlong course covering the principles of micro- and macroeconomics. Much of the theoretical development uses tools that are usually taught in courses in intermediate micro- and macroeconomics. In each case, however, we introduce these techniques anew here so that students who have not gone beyond courses in economic principles should be able to comprehend the theory of labor markets. Much of the research in modern labor economics is based on the use of statistical methods to analyze economic data. For the students who have not studied these methods we intersperse only the results of this research throughout the text to illustrate the theory. Those students who have studied statistics and econometric methods would benefit greatly from examining a few of the studies that we cite, in order to understand how the knowledge that underlies so much of the discussion in the text is obtained.

Preface to the Instructor

This volume is an expanded and revised version of the *Economics of Work and Pay,* 2d ed., by Albert Rees. In it we present modern theories covering all aspects of the economics of labor markets, both unionized and nonunionized. With each theoretical discussion, there is an examination of the data to which the theory applies and the econometric evidence that has been brought to bear upon the theory. The supporting evidence is mainly based on studies of the labor market in the United States, but in many cases, illustrations from research on other countries are used. Our desire to illustrate theory with empirical research leads to extensive use of the massive literature in this field that has been produced since the burgeoning of the field in the early 1960s. In all cases the empirical results are referenced specifically, as are the sources of data presented in the tables. However, if the study or data were produced by the U.S. Department of Labor, only a title reference is included.

Throughout the book we illustrate the theory with issues of labor-market policy. These are set apart from the body of the text, but they should be read in conjunction with the preceding discussion. The issues are designed to give students practice using the tools and analysis they have learned and to provide a sense of the many ways in which analytical labor economics is useful in the discussion of policy. The policy issues also make excellent topics for those instructors who choose to assign term papers, and the references upon which they are based provide good jumping-off points for students who are attempting to assemble a bibliography for such a paper.

Economics of Work and Pay assumes that the student has had only a yearlong course in economic principles and is able to handle graphical analysis. Virtually no math is used in the text, stemming from our belief that the concepts can be explained better graphically and that only a minute fraction of the students who are enrolled in labor economics courses have the background in mathematics that would enable them to go beyond the concepts conveyed in the graphs. In many cases the figures are original in this and in previous editions.

The book benefited greatly from the comments and criticisms of our colleagues and friends. One or more chapters of this or previous editions were read by Francine Blau, University of Illinois—Urbana-Champaign; George Borjas, University of California-Santa Barbara; William G. Bowen, Princeton University; Charles Brown, University of Maryland; Glen Cain, University of Wisconsin-Madison; Barry Chiswick, University of Illinois—Chicago; Henry Farber, Massachusetts Institute of Technology; T. Aldrich Finegan, Vanderbilt University; Alan Harrison, McMaster University; James Johannes, Michigan State University; George Johnson, University of Michigan; Duane Leigh, Washington State University; H. Gregg Lewis, Duke University; Jacob Mincer, Columbia University; George Neumann, Northwestern University; Ronald Oaxaca, University of Arizona; Sherwin Rosen, University of Chicago; Michael Taussig, Rutgers University; John Wolfe, Michigan State University; and Stephen Woodbury, Michigan State University.

None of these scholars is in any way responsible for our conclusions or our errors. To each, though, we are deeply indebted. We are also grateful to Gilbert Davis, who prepared the Index.

DANIEL S. HAMERMESH
ALBERT REES

one

LABOR SUPPLY

chapter 1

Labor-Force Participation

THE MEANING OF LABOR SUPPLY

In the writings of the classical economists of the eighteenth and nineteenth centuries, the discussion of labor supply concerned the forces that determine the size of the population of working age and, especially, the effect of changes in real wages on the growth of this population. Not much was said about the amount of work supplied by a population of any given size. There was no reason to consider this—everyone old enough and healthy enough to do any useful work toiled the entire day. More recently, labor economists have reversed this emphasis. We define the supply of labor as the amount of effort offered by a population of a given size. We pay only slight attention to changes in the size of the population, leaving the study of population dynamics to *demography.* This separate discipline which combines economics, sociology, and mathematics, has well-developed methods of its own for studying fertility, mortality, and migration flows that make up changes in population.

The amount of labor supplied by a given population can be broken down for convenience of exposition into four factors.

1. *Labor-force participation rate,* or the percentage of the population engaged in or seeking gainful employment. Labor-force participation has been studied extensively. Today we understand a great deal about why different groups are more or less likely to be working or seeking work, and how government programs affect participation. In this chapter we discuss these differences and effects.
2. *Number of hours* people are willing to work per week or per year while they are in the labor force. This aspect of labor supply is treated in Chapter 2.

3. *Amount of effort* workers put forth while at work. This is discussed in the last section of Chapter 2.
4. *Level of training and skill* that workers bring to their jobs. This important topic is the subject of Chapter 3.

Although we separate these four components of labor supply, they are not independent factors. Indeed, many of the same forces that affect any one of them affect each of the others. Together these components make up the amount of labor—work effort—that is available for the production of goods and services to be sold in the marketplace.

THE LABOR FORCE

The *labor force* is the number of people who work for pay or profit or who are unemployed during any part of some short period of time, usually a week. In the United States as of 1983, the employed are defined as those who worked 1 hour or more for wages or salary during the *reference week* (the week being studied), or did 15 hours or more of unpaid work in a family business or farm. Those absent from work because of vacation, illness, bad weather, or strikes and lockouts are also counted as employed, but in the separate subcategory "with a job but not at work." The unemployed are those who are on layoff from a job; who have no job but have looked for work during the preceding 4 weeks and were available for work during the reference week; or who are waiting to report to a new job within the next 30 days.

The labor force as defined in the United States is now limited to those persons who are 16 years of age and older; the small amount of labor supplied by those under 16 is not counted. Before 1967 the lower age limit for inclusion in the labor force was 14 years. The limit was raised to reflect the nearly universal requirement of compulsory education until age 16. However, being in school does not preclude someone 16 or over from being counted as in the labor force (as we see later in this chapter). Separate data on the *civilian* and the *total labor forces* have been kept; the latter adds resident military personnel to the civilian labor force. The discussion in this chapter analyzes the behavior of the civilian labor force only.

The labor force is measured every month. Following the reference week, the week containing the twelfth of the month, people in 60,000 households are interviewed by an employee of the U.S. Bureau of the Census. The households are chosen to reflect the principal characteristics of the population as measured in the most recent decennial census. These interviews form the Current Population Survey, the basis for the unemployment statistics and other labor-force statistics that are announced on the first Friday of the next month.

The questions asked by the interviewer enable the government analysts to determine the labor-force status of each civilian age 16 and over who is not in an institution. This is an all-or-nothing matter: For purposes of the survey, a person is either in or out of the labor force; by definition, one cannot be partly in the labor force and partly out. Because the interviewers also record the age, sex, race, and marital status of people in the households, the government publishes information on participation classified by these criteria. Special supplements to the survey each year

Table 1.1 CIVILIAN LABOR-FORCE PARTICIPATION RATES BY AGE AND SEX, 1982

Age	Males	Females
16–19	56.7	51.4
20–24	84.9	69.8
25–34	94.7	68.0
35–44	95.3	68.0
45–54	91.2	61.6
55–64	70.2	41.8
65+	17.8	7.9

Source: Employment and Earnings, January 1983, pp. 144–145.

provide additional information on participation rates classified by workers' education. Information on labor-force participation by detailed location is collected in the decennial census of population. Taken together, the information in the Current Population Survey and the census enables us to calculate labor-force participation rates for a variety of population groups and to examine their determinants.

Labor-force participation rates by age and sex for a recent year are shown in Table 1.1. Large variations in rates among the groups are immediately apparent. The participation rate is generally higher for men than for women, but within each sex there is substantial variation by age, and the age patterns for men and women are somewhat different. Participation rates also differ by race. Fewer black men 20 or over are in the labor force: In 1982 their participation rate was 74.7 percent as compared to 79.2 percent of white men. Among ethnic groups for which data from the Current Population Survey are published, Hispanic adult men were most likely to participate: 84.7 percent were in the civilian labor force in 1982. A somewhat higher percentage of adult black than white women were in the labor force: In 1982, 56.2 percent participated as compared to 52.2 percent of white women. Among Hispanic women, only 49.9 percent participated. To explain these patterns of participation we look at how decisions about the use of time are made within a household.

LABOR-FORCE PARTICIPATION DECISIONS

Each person in a household may be in or out of the labor force. The choice about whether to seek work is complex and is probably made in most households by a decision process that involves the entire household. Despite this, the case of a one-person household can be used to analyze the factors affecting decisions in larger households. The graphic presentation of the theory makes use of *indifference maps,* one of which is shown in Figure 1.1. Such maps are more commonly used to show a consumer's choice between two commodities. This one, however, is used to show a typical worker's choice between labor and leisure, where for brevity the term leisure is used to indicate all activity except market work. To make this map more like an ordinary two-commodity indifference map, we have measured hours of work from right to left along the horizontal axis. The scale has been arbitrarily cut off at the left

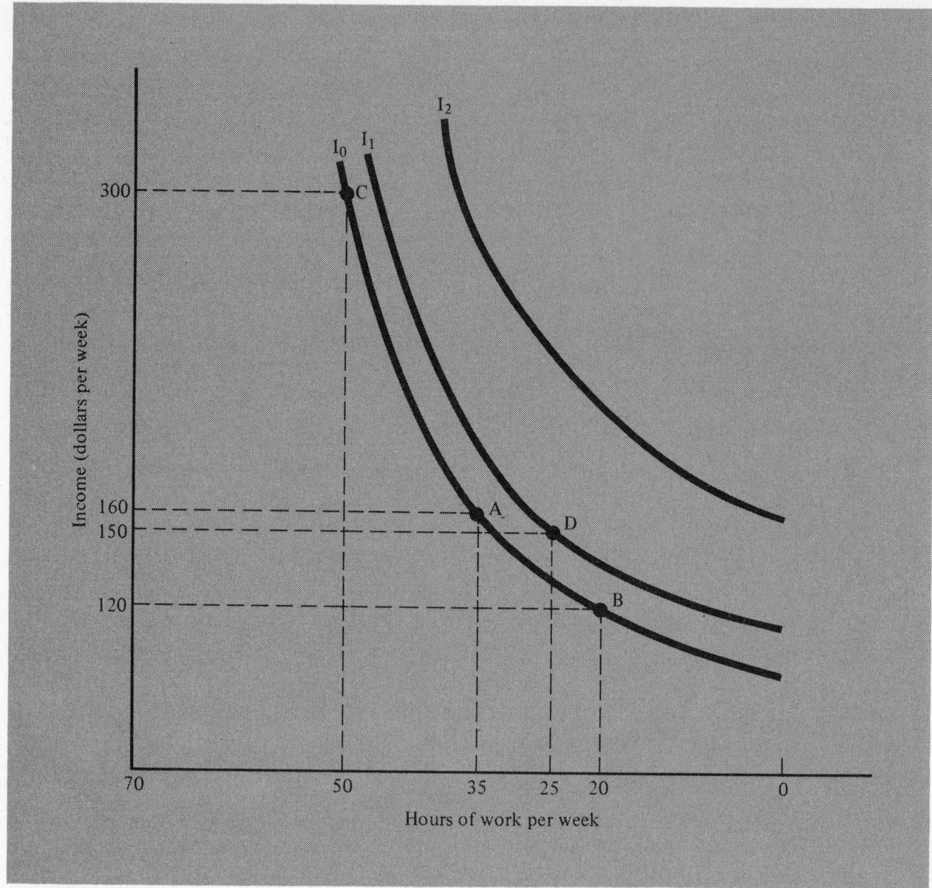

Figure 1.1 Workers' preferences for income and leisure.

at 70 hours per week, since very few workers choose to work more than 70 hours. Points like A and B along any one *indifference curve,* such as I_0, represent combinations of leisure and work (which produces money income or the ability to buy market goods) that give the worker equal satisfaction or *utility.* Workers like the person whose indifference map is shown in Figure 1.1 would be equally happy working 20 hours per week and enjoying an income of $120 per week, or working 35 hours per week and enjoying an income of $160 per week.

Indifference curves are convex to the origin. To maintain equal satisfaction when adding 15 hours to a 20-hour workweek, the individual whose tastes are depicted in Figure 1.1 requires only $40 more (the difference between $160 and $120). For this person to maintain the same satisfaction when the work schedule is increased by 15 more hours, from 35 to 50, an additional $140 dollars of weekly income is required. Workers must earn increasingly large amounts to be induced to give up their increasingly scarce leisure time. Indifference curves that lie above and to the right of I_0, such as I_1 and I_2, represent higher levels of satisfaction. Point D on indifference curve I_1 is preferred to all points on curve I_0. Even though more hours are worked than at point B, and less income is received than at point A, the combination of income and hours is such that point D is preferable to both A and B (and all other points along I_0). Indifferences curves cannot cross; if they did, the point where they cross would denote two different levels of utility, which makes no sense.

Figure 1.2 presents another indifference map characterizing the tastes of another worker, who has a nonlabor income of $100 a week. We assume for the moment that workers like this one are free to choose as many hours as they want at a constant hourly wage rate. One such wage rate, $2 per hour, is represented by the slope of the line moving left from A to B. Working 70 hours per week yields earnings of $140. The height of the line above any point on the horizontal axis measures the income in dollars per week earned by working that many hours plus nonlabor income of 0A.

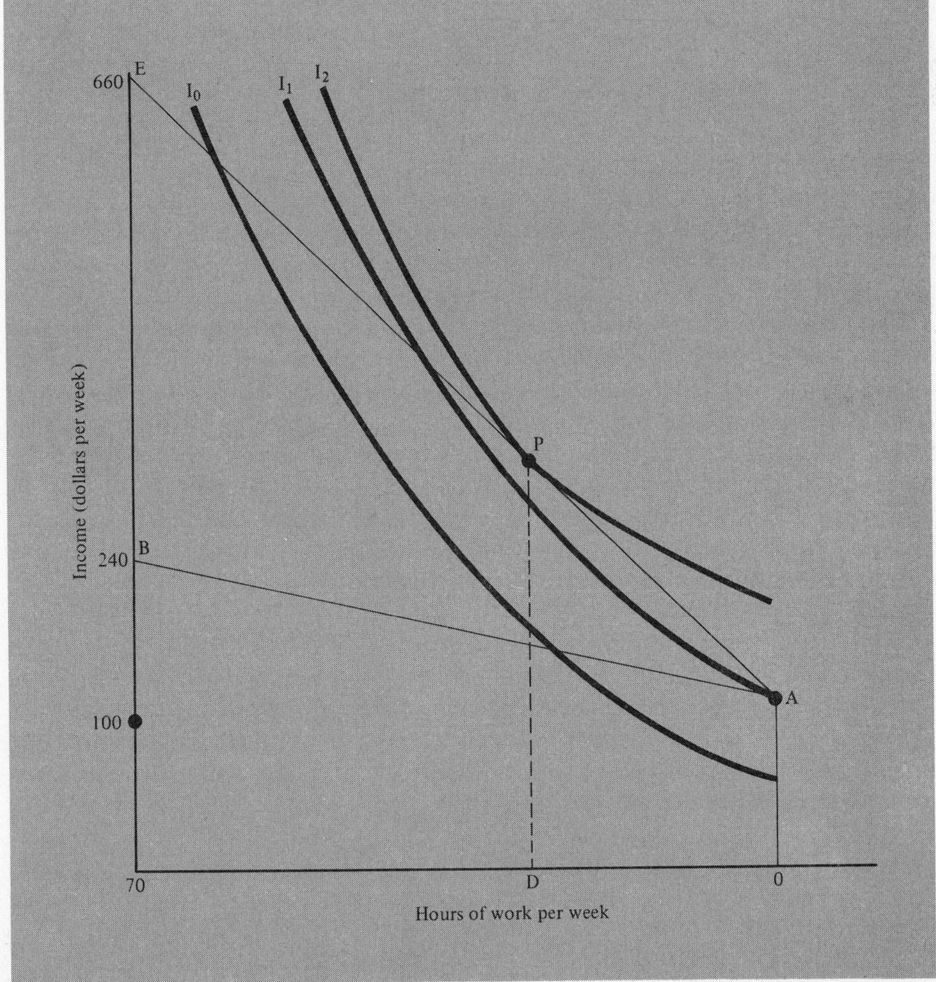

Figure 1.2 The choices of participating in the labor force.

Will workers be better off doing some work rather than devoting all their time to leisure? Remember that in Figure 1.2 the worker shown receives nonlabor income of 0*A* even if no hours of work are supplied to the market. (This could be investment income, charity, some public support program, or the earnings of others who might provide support.) Some things can thus be bought without working. Workers seek to find that combination of income and leisure that gives the greatest satisfaction. This combination is the indifference curve that is farthest to the right in Figure 1.2 that they can get to. They can do better than I_0, but they cannot improve upon I_1. Any better indifference curve simply is unavailable to those with this wage rate and nonlabor income. The best they can do is earn nothing, spend all their time enjoying leisure, and not participate in the labor force. Point A in the figure indicates this combination of leisure and income.

At point A the slope of indifference curve I_1 shows how much extra earnings the workers would require to be induced to give up 1 hour of leisure. This amount of extra earnings is called the *reservation wage*.[1] The reservation wage is the value of leisure if the person is not working in the market (is out of the labor force). As the figure is drawn, the reservation wage exceeds the market wage. (Curve I_1 is steeper than the line AB.) What will induce them to enter the labor force—to cut leisure time below the maximum possible? If the wage rises to $8 per hour, so that the line AB rotates clockwise to AE, it will exceed the reservation wage. (A shift like this occurred during World War II, as job opportunities for women expanded rapidly.) Market work then pays more than the value of an hour of leisure. People will enter the labor force, working D hours. (The highest attainable indifference level is now I_2; they choose point P.) In other words, people will be in the labor force whenever their wage rate exceeds their reservation wage. People with high (potential) wage rates, abstracting from differences in reservation wages, will more likely be in the labor force. Groups of such people will have higher labor-force participation rates.

At a given wage rate a person with a lower reservation wage will more likely be in the labor force. That the reservation wage is low suggests the person does not value time spent at leisure very highly. A "workaholic" has a low reservation wage; people with many hobbies or other outside interests place a higher value on their leisure time (have a higher reservation wage) and will less likely be in the labor force. These differences in tastes will be reflected in the shapes of the individuals' indifference maps.

Let us now consider households with more than one person. (Despite the stories on the "decline" of the family unit, families—households with people related by blood or marriage—contained 88 percent of the U.S. population in 1980.) The presence of other family members, their earning power and requirements for support, will affect each person's reservation wage and thus each person's choice about whether or not to participate in the labor force. The precise effect will depend

[1] This concept goes back at least as far as Jacob Mincer, "Market Prices, Opportunity Costs, and Income Effects," in Carl Christ (ed.). *Measurement in Economics,* Stanford University Press, Stanford, Calif., 1963. This approach to analyzing participation decisions was developed and placed in a framework that allows one to infer the value of the reservation wage by Reuben Gronau, "The Intrafamily Allocation of Time: The Value of the Housewives' Time," *American Economic Review* (63): 634–651 (1973), and James Heckman, "Shadow Prices, Market Wages and Labor Supply," *Econometrica* (42): 679–694 (1974).

on how decisions are made in the household. Whether the members of the household make these decisions collectively or individually, or whether the head makes them for the whole household, need not concern us here. Presumably there are households that make their decisions in each of these ways.

The addition of a young child to the household affects the reservation wages of the adults by sharply increasing the value of their time spent at home. Because of this increase one of the adults who had been in the labor force may drop out: The value of his or her time at home suddenly exceeds the market wage. As children grow up they require fewer hours of care, so the value of the adults' time at home decreases. It is likely that an adult who had left the labor force will then return to it. Historically in the United States and in most industrialized countries, the wife's behavior has been most affected by the birth of a child, and she has left the labor force. This is partly a cultural phenomenon; as attitudes change, and if the market wages of women approach those of men, we should expect to see more men leaving the labor force to care for children.

The reservation wage when young children are present is also affected by the availability of substitutes for the adults' time spent caring for the children. The presence of a grandparent to do baby-sitting, the availability of inexpensive and convenient day-care centers, and inexpensive domestic help all reduce the likelihood that one spouse will be out of the labor force to care for small children. The existence of convenient and inexpensive substitutes for time spent in household chores will also lower the reservation wage and increase the likelihood of participation. Automatic washing machines, food processors, and fast-food restaurants are all substitutes for time spent working in the household.

An increase in the household's resources, unaccompanied by any other change in opportunities—such as an inheritance that substantially increases nonlabor income—will usually reduce total labor supply. Thus it might lead the family to decide that a teenage son should stay in school longer, that an elderly grandfather should retire earlier, or that a working spouse should become a full-time homemaker. Underlying the expectation that a rise in nonlabor income tends to reduce participation in the labor force is the assumption that, for at least some members of most households, the ability to buy more goods raises the value of their leisure and thus their reservation wage. All that can be predicted is that the likelihood of nonparticipation by some household members increases when nonlabor income rises. Leisure is not usually an *inferior good,* one whose consumption falls when income rises. Which members leave the labor force, though, will depend on whose leisure is most greatly increased in value by the extra goods the household can now purchase.

The values attached to other nonmarket alternatives also affect the household's decisions. If a spouse or a teenage son must work to maintain the family's customary living standard, and if both could earn the same market wage, then the extent to which the son's additional schooling would augment his earnings in the future must be weighed against the costs of the spouse's absence from the home now.

This entire discussion has proceeded as though workers could freely choose to work as many or as few hours as they wish if they participate in the labor force. Although there is much more flexibility in hours worked than is commonly believed (see Chap. 2), complete freedom to choose work hours is an extreme assumption. The other extreme assumption is that there is no choice; as in Figure 1.3, workers are offered the choice of working, for example, 40 hours, or not working at all. Those workers with a low market wage have the choice of not working (point A) or working and earning an amount FG. (In this and subsequent figures like it, we do not label the vertical axis with specific dollar figures; still, the slopes of lines such as AB indicate the wage rates the workers can obtain.) Since indifference curve I_0 is the highest they can attain, they choose not to participate in the labor force. Workers with a higher wage rate have a choice between not working (point A) or working and earning an amount FH. As shown in Figure 1.3, they will choose to participate by working 40 hours, for I_1 is the highest indifference curve they can attain. Thus as in Figure 1.2, an increase in the market wage rate increases the likelihood of participation. So, too, anything that increases the reservation wage (makes the indifference curves steeper at zero hours of labor supplied) reduces the likelihood that people will choose to participate. The general outlines of the theory of labor-force participation change

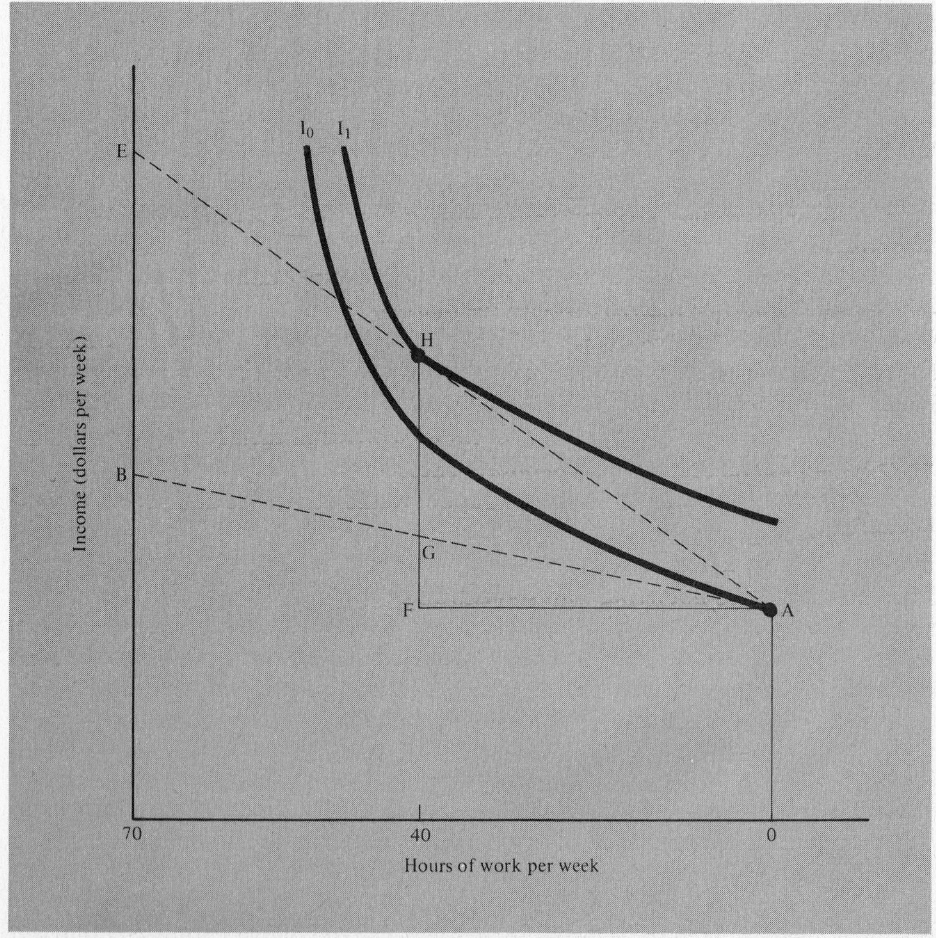

Figure 1.3 Labor-force participation with fixed hours of work.

little when the assumptions underlying the range of choices open to workers are varied.

PARTICIPATION RATES—THE EFFECT OF AGE, SEX, AND RACE

Adult Men, Ages 20 to 54

If a household includes an ablebodied male who has completed his formal schooling and not yet reached the age of retirement, it is taken for granted in our society that he will be a member of the labor force. In the Current Population Survey of March 1979, the labor-force participation rate of married men (with wife present) between the ages of 30 and 34 was 97.8 percent. Presumably most of the remaining 2.2 percent were disabled. Even a married man with enough income from property to escape the necessity of working would undoubtedly have reported himself as employed in the management of his own investments.

Although the labor-force participation rate of married men in the prime age groups is very high, it is still possible to find and explain differences in the rates for different population categories. For example, one study reports that the participation rate is lower for nonwhites than for whites and that for both groups it rises with the number of years of school completed.[2] Both of these effects correspond to differences in market wages, which are higher for whites than for nonwhites and rise with education in both groups.

A single man does not have a spouse on whom he can rely to take care of domestic responsibilities. His reservation wage is likely to be greater than that of an otherwise identical married man, for he must arrange for cooking, cleaning, and so on. Also, the compulsion of the social role of breadwinner does not have so much force for the unmarried man as it has for the married man. In the Current Population Survey of March 1979, the labor-force participation rate of men between the ages of 25 and 54 who were widowed, divorced, separated, or never married was 88.2 percent. The data also show that the participation rates for these groups are less than those for married men who were living with their wives in each 5-year age range in the 25 to 54 interval considered separately. These facts do not necessarily imply that being single causes a lower rate of participation. Rather, the same underlying factors that led some single men to drop out of the labor force might have contributed also to their decisions not to marry or to the dissolution of their marriages. The 12 percent of those men who were not living with spouses and who in any 1 week were not in the labor force in 1979 were not all permanently out of it, though. These figures no doubt reflect the behavior of a larger fraction of the total population of single men, whose freedom from family responsibilities permits an alternation of periods of work with periods of nonmarket activities of one kind or another.

Adult Women

The single most important development in the labor market since World War II has been the growth in the percentage of adult women who are working or seeking work.

[2]William Bowen and T. Aldrich Finegan, *The Economics of Labor Force Participation*, Princeton University Press, Princeton, N.J., 1969, p. 45.

Table 1.2 FEMALE LABOR FORCE PARTICIPATION, 1955–1982, WOMEN 20–54

	Age			
Year	20–24	25–34	35–44	45–54
1955	45.9	34.9	41.6	43.8
1960	46.1	36.0	43.4	49.8
1965	49.9	38.5	46.1	50.9
1970	57.7	45.0	51.1	54.4
1975	64.1	54.6	55.8	54.6
1980	69.0	65.4	65.5	59.9
1982	69.8	68.0	68.0	61.6

Source: Employment and Training Report of the President, 1981, Table A-5; and *Employment and Earnings,* January 1983, p. 145.

As Table 1.2 shows, in every age category, this growth has been tremendous, leading to what one author has called "the subtle revolution."[3] Despite this enormous change, the labor-force participation rates in Table 1.2 are still well below those of men in the same age categories. Why?

There is a very strong positive relation between educational attainment and the likelihood of being in the labor force for married women. This relation reflects the higher market wage available to more educated workers; this makes it less likely that they will choose to be at a point such as point A in Figure 1.2. Also, the more educated worker has access to more interesting and challenging jobs. Yet women in the United States receive only slightly less formal education than do men: Among women aged 25 or over in 1979, the median educational attainment was 12.4 years; among men, it was 12.6 years.

The answer lies in current Western attitudes about responsibilities for domestic chores: The wife is generally expected to bear most of the burden of child care and household maintenance, even if she is working. The value of her output at home is very large: One study estimates that in 1973 the value of the services produced in the home, mostly by housewives, exceeded two-thirds of the family's after-tax money income.[4] In 1965, for example, employed married women worked a total of 69 hours per week, of which 34 were in the home; employed married men worked 61 hours, of which only 13 were in the home. By 1976, total hours had approached equality for employed married men and women, 58 and 59, respectively; but employed women still did twice as much of the housework, including caring for children.[5] With the attitudes implied by these figures, we should not be surprised that changes in domestic circumstances, including the spouse's income, have far greater effects on women's labor-force participation than on men's.

This is exactly what we observe. As far back as the 1930s it was shown that in cities where male earnings are higher than elsewhere, women were less likely to be in

[3]Ralph Smith (ed.), *The Subtle Revolution: Women at Work,* Urban Institute, Washington, 1979.

[4]Reuben Gronau, "Home Production: A Forgotten Industry," *Review of Economics and Statistics* (72): 412 (1980).

[5]Frank Stafford and Greg Duncan, "The Use of Time and Technology by Households in the United States," *Research in Labor Economics* (3): 335–375 (1980), and Kathryn Walker and Margaret Woods, *Time Use: a Measure of Household Production of Family Goods and Services,* American Home Economics Association, Washington, 1976, used in calculations by Clair Vickery, "Women's Economic Contributions to the Family," in Ralph Smith, op. cit., p. 194.

the labor force.[6] In 1950 this was no longer true; but among women with the ability to earn the same wage, those whose husbands earned more were less likely to be in the labor force.[7] More recently, data on married women from the Current Population Survey in 1967 show that, adjusted for numerous other factors, the participation rate of women whose husbands earned 10 percent more than the average was 7 percent below the average participation rate.[8]

Additional children in the home raise the wife's reservation wage and lower her likelihood of being in the labor force. Data for 1976 showed that having a child under age 6 reduces the wife's likelihood of being in the labor force by nearly 20 percent, once other factors are accounted for. The more educated the wife is, the less likely will young children appear to deter her from participating in the labor force. Either her education makes her a more efficient household worker, thus lowering her reservation wage, or her higher market wage enables her to purchase substitutes for her own time at home. The presence of children age 6 or more has only a tiny impact on labor-force participation rates, apparently less than it had before the 1970s.[9] When the price of domestic help, a substitute for housewives' time, is lower, married women are also more likely to be in the labor force; having a relative who is not part of the nuclear family who is living in the household also raises the wife's likelihood of participating.[10] Husbands' labor-force participation is far less sensitive to differences in wives' market wages, or to the presence of young children. As we have seen, the participation rates of married men above age 25 and not yet close to retirement age are nearly 100 percent, and therefore cannot differ greatly with family circumstances.

We have also noted that black women are somewhat more likely to be in the labor force than are white women. The difference is partly explained by the difference in their husbands' incomes. The lower-wage rates available to black men reduce their wives' reservation wages and increase their labor-force participation rate. The greater prevalence of extended-family living arrangements also provides more black women with a ready source of child care in the form of grandparents who are living at home. That Hispanic women are less likely than other whites to participate may in part reflect the very high labor-force participation of Hispanic men.

What explains the tremendous growth in participation among women? Educational attainment has increased since the 1950s: Median years of education of women 25 or over rose from 9.6 in 1950 to 12.4 in 1979. The most rapid growth,

[6] See Erika Schoenberg and Paul Douglas, "Studies in the Supply Curve of Labor," *Journal of Political Economy* (45): 45–70 (1937), and Clarence Long, *The Labor Force Under Changing Income and Employment,* Princeton University Press, Princeton, N.J., 1958, pp. 54–81. These studies analyze participation rates for both sexes, but the results for women have received the most attention from later writers.

[7] Jacob Mincer, "Labor Force Participation of Married Women," in H. Gregg Lewis (ed.). *Aspects of Labor Economics,* Princeton University Press, Princeton, N.J., 1962.

[8] Calculated from Giora Hanoch, "A Multivariate Model of Labor Supply: Methodology and Estimation," in James Smith (ed.). *Female Labor Supply: Theory and Estimation,* Princeton University Press, Princeton, N.J., 1980, p. 284.

[9] Calculated from John Cogan, "Labor Supply with Costs of Labor Market Entry," in James Smith, op. cit., p. 348.

[10] Orley Ashenfelter and James Heckman, "Estimating Labor Supply Functions," in Glen Cain and Harold Watts (eds.). *Income Maintenance and Labor Supply,* Markham, Chicago, 1973, and James Heckman, "Effects of Child-Care Programs on Women's Work Effort," *Journal of Political Economy* (82): S136–S163 (1974).

though, was before 1970, whereas participation has risen most rapidly since 1970. Changes in the amount of education are not a very likely explanation for the rapid rise in participation. Changes in husbands' incomes are a better candidate. As Table 1.2 shows, the biggest increases in participation rates since 1955 have been among women aged 25 to 34, with the sharpest increase coming since 1975. This is precisely the period when the earnings of young husbands have grown most slowly in real terms.[11]

The decline in birthrates of the late 1960s and 1970s has also made it much easier for married women to participate. With the adjusted lifetime fertility rate per adult female down from 3.7 children ever born in 1955 to 1959 to 1.9 in 1979, it is not surprising that more women in their childbearing years are participating in the labor force. Perhaps, though, the causation has gone the other way; perhaps women are having fewer children because of an increased commitment to the labor market. Undoubtedly some of this reverse causation has occurred; but the evidence suggests that, even when the reverse causation is accounted for, there is a powerful effect of the number of children born on women's labor-force participation.[12]

In a sample of 30- to 34-year-old married women in 1967, the participation rate was 40 percent; in another sample of 30- to 34-year-old married women in 1978, the participation rate was 54 percent. Of this 14 percentage point change, only half could be accounted for by changes in educational attainment, number of young children, and other easily measurable characteristics that we have seen affect the labor-force participation of married women.[13] Other, less easily quantified factors may have accounted for the rest of the change. Technological changes have led to the expansion of industries and occupations that have historically provided most of the jobs that women have held. The standard workweek has been shortened, and the availability of products that reduce the amount of household work, such as washing machines, clothes dryers, and frozen foods, may have made it easier for a wife both to hold a job and care for a house. In addition, a more positive attitude among women toward careers and new legislation against sex discrimination could have contributed to the rise in women's participation rates.

POLICY ISSUE—DAY CARE AND THE COSTS OF WORK

That young children deter labor-force participation by married women is partly due to the cost of finding alternative providers of child care. Just to work 1 hour per day a mother of a young child must arrange for someone to come to the home, or must take the child to an alternative provider of care. The effect of this necessity on labor-force participation is shown in Figure 1.4, a modified version of Figure 1.2. The distance AC is the sum of

[11] Richard Freeman, "The Effect of Demographic Factors on Age-Earnings Profiles," *Journal of Human Resources* (14): 289–318 (1979), and Finis Welch, "Effects of Cohort Size on Earnings," *Journal of Political Economy* (87): S65–S98 (1979).

[12] Glen Cain and Martin Dooley, "Estimation of a Model of Labor Supply, Fertility, and Wages of Married Women," *Journal of Political Economy* (84): S179–S200 (1976); Belton Fleisher and George Rhodes, "Fertility, Women's Work Effort and Labor Supply," *American Economic Review* (69): 14–24 (1979); and Mark Rosenzweig and Kenneth Wolpin, "Life Cycle Labor Supply and Fertility," *Journal of Political Economy* (88): 328–348 (1980).

[13] David Shapiro and Lois Shaw, "Growth in the Labor Force Attachment of Married Women: Accounting for Changes in the 1970's," *Southern Economic Journal* (50): 461–473 (1983).

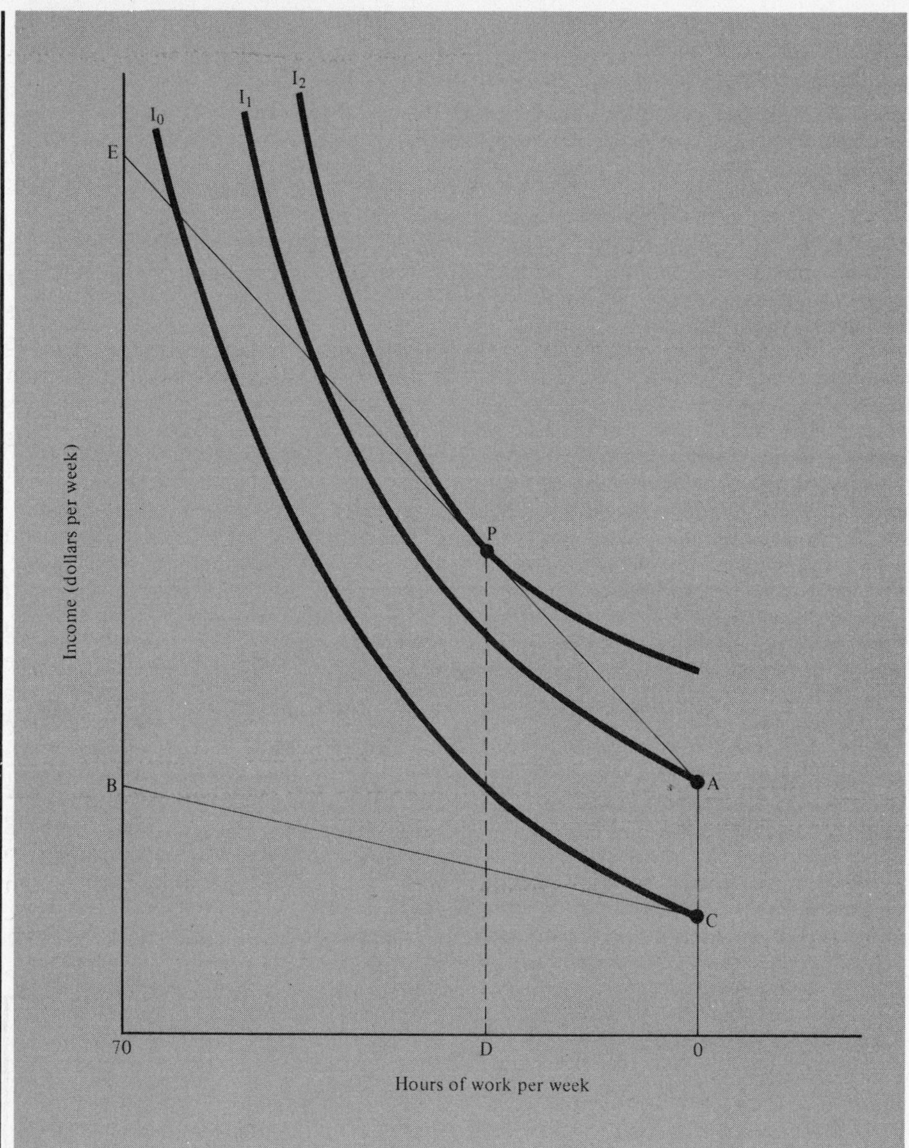

Figure 1.4 Costs of work and labor-force participation.

such *fixed costs* of child care. Even if the woman works just 1 hour per day she must incur the costs of, for example, transporting the child to a baby-sitter or child care facility. Thus if she works only a little bit, her net income drops from 0A, if she did not work, to 0C. Moreover, the more she works, the more she must pay for child care. Many baby-sitters charge by the hour and child care facilities too charge more, the longer the child is left there. Her net wage per hour is reduced, so that her market wage is now shown by the slope of CB; this is less than the wage implied by the slope of AE. This reduction represents the *variable costs* of child care. In this situation, I_1 is the highest indifference curve she can attain, and thus she will not participate in the labor force.

The fixed costs of work are not insubstantial: One study estimated these costs as $1000 per year in 1976.[14] A woman would have had to work over 5 hours per week at the average wage just to make enough money after taxes to cover the fixed cost of work. Moreover, tax rates have risen in the United States and elsewhere in the past 30 years, reducing take-home pay as a fraction of total pay, and thus reducing the incentive to participate in the labor force.

Free day care changes the situation. The fixed costs of entering the work force are, to simplify, removed; and the net wage rises because child care is free. The woman can now earn the full hourly wage rate, shown by the slope of AE; her opportunities now lie along the line segments 0AE. In the example shown in Figure 1.4 she is better off participating—choosing to work D hours—than not participating, for she attains the highest indifference level along I_2 at point P.

Although day care is rarely free, day-care programs have expanded greatly in the United States. In 1977, 407,000 children were enrolled in day-care centers that received at least partial government funding. Also, since the middle 1970s in the United States, couples with both spouses working have been able to credit up to 20 percent of child care expenses against their income tax liabilities. One study that used data on women aged 30 to 44 in 1966 to estimate how sensitive their participation decisions are to the cost of child care found that doubling the price of child care reduced the average married woman's likelihood of participating by 14 percent.[15] This result suggests that subsidizing day care can have an effect in inducing women with young children to leave home and work for pay.

Differences by Age—Youths and Older People

Table 1.1 showed large differences in labor-force participation by age group. Among men and, to a lesser extent, among women, too, the pattern of participation rates by age is shaped roughly like an upside-down U. The *life-cycle theory* of labor supply leads us to expect this. When people are young and inexperienced, their market wage is likely to be low, providing little incentive to participate in the labor force.[16] Also, the major alternative to work—school—will raise their wage throughout their lives, including a working life that could last 50 years. It therefore makes sense for most people to postpone labor-force entry and go to school even after the age of compulsory school attendance. At the other end of the life cycle, people's market wages are likely to be declining or growing very slowly. Moreover, the wealth they have accumulated during their working lives by saving and through Social Security and other retirement plans raises the value of that leisure, and thus their reservation wages. For these economic reasons alone we should expect older people to have lower labor-force participation rates than people in their thirties and forties.

Labor-force participation rates among 16- to 24-year-olds are strongly influenced by decisions about the age at which a youth leaves school. Thus as the last two columns in Table 1.3 show, among youths aged 16 to 19 and 20 to 24 who are not enrolled in school, the overwhelming majority participate in the labor force.

[14] Cogan, op. cit., p. 354.

[15] James Heckman, "Effects of Child-Care Programs . . . " loc. cit.

[16] The details of this argument are set out in a fairly complex fashion by Gilbert Ghez and Gary Becker, *The Allocation of Time and Goods over the Life Cycle,* Columbia University Press, New York, 1975 and Thomas MaCurdy, "An Empirical Model of Labor Supply in a Life-Cycle Setting," *Journal of Political Economy* (89): 1059–1085 (1981).

Table 1.3 LABOR FORCE PARTICIPATION OF YOUTHS, BY AGE, SEX, AND ENROLLMENT STATUS, 1955–1980

	In school				Not in school	
	Males		Females		Both sexes	
Year	16–19	20–24	16–19	20–24	16–19	20–24
1955	39.2	41.7	22.9	42.0	71.9	67.1
1960	34.6	44.2	26.5	40.6	71.1	69.3
1965	36.8	49.0	26.9	39.6	71.8	69.8
1970	40.5	51.2	34.8	50.5	70.4	74.1
1975	41.9	51.2	40.3	55.1	74.8	78.9
1980	45.2	55.3	42.5	59.0	77.6	83.0

Source: Calculated from *Employment and Training Report of the President*, 1981, Table B-9.

Even among those who are still in school, there is substantial participation on a part-time and part-year basis (after school, on weekends, and during vacations). Over one-third of the students aged 16 to 19 are in the labor force as compared to over half the students aged 20 to 24. These participation rates reflect averages over the calendar year that include high participation in the summer and lower participation during the school year. Thus in July 1982, 65.7 percent of youths aged 16 to 19 participated, whereas in April 1982 only 49.3 percent participated. One might expect lower participation rates by students from higher-income families, since they may be better able to afford to devote full time to their studies. Data for 1973 for students 19 or 20 years old support such a view. They show that weeks worked, and presumably also participation rates for students, were lower among those from upper middle-income families than from low-income families, after adjustment for differences in race, high school achievement, and other effects.[17]

As Table 1.3 shows, there has been a very sharp upward trend since 1960 in the participation rates of youths still in school. (The trend among out-of-school youth reflects chiefly the trends in the participation of young women, which we have already noted.) This trend is especially strong among college-age youths. What explains this? Better market opportunities do not provide an answer: The usual weekly earnings of a full-time worker aged 16 to 24 fell between 1967 and 1978 from 80 to 71 percent of the economywide average, suggesting that postponing entry into the labor force would be a better choice. Also, the unemployment rates among youths rose dramatically during this period, implying market opportunities were decreasing. The answer lies on the reservation-wage side of the participation decision, and with other factors. Smaller family sizes since the early 1970s mean that fewer teenagers and young adults must stay home after school to help care for younger children in the household. Greater flexibility in the scheduling of classes and the increased possibility of being a part-time student also make it easier for youths to work and remain in school. The abolition of the military draft removed the incentive for young men to attend school full-time as a way of obtaining deferments that kept

[17] Robert Meyer and David Wise, "High School Preparation and Early Labor Force Experience," in Richard Freeman and David Wise (eds.). *The Youth Labor Market Problem: Its Nature, Causes and Consequences,* University of Chicago Press, Chicago, 1982, Table 9A.1.

them out of the military. Rapid rises in the costs of attending college, increases that have outpaced inflation, may also have induced more students to work part-time to finance their education.

Table 1.1 shows that participation rates drop sharply at age 65, and decline somewhat as people approach their late fifties. A major contributing factor to the sharp drop is the spread of pension plans that offer substantial incentives to retire, often at age 65. Eligibility for a pension raises the reservation wage by providing an alternative source of income. Even among people who are eligible for pensions, though, other factors affect the reservation wage and thus change the likelihood of labor-force participation. The most important of these is the person's education. Among men ages 62 to 64 who were interviewed in the March 1973 Current Population Survey, each extra year of schooling increased the likelihood of being in the labor force by 1 percentage point, after adjustment for numerous other differences. The effect was even more pronounced, 2 percentage points, among men aged 65 to 70.[18] College graduates are close to the peak of their earning power after age 55, whereas the earnings of those with little education that are more dependent on physical strength and stamina are therefore more likely to have declined. Bad health also reduces participation rates among older people by reducing market wages. Among men aged 48 to 62 in 1969 who died within the next 7 years, the 1969 participation rate was roughly 20 percentage points below that of otherwise comparable men.[19]

An intriguing puzzle is whether older men with working wives will be more or less likely to work. If the wife works, the older husband may have to bear more of the burden of household chores. The greater usefulness of time spent at home should reduce his likelihood of being in the labor force. On the other hand, he may find that time spent at home when the wife is away is not very enjoyable. This would lower his reservation wage. The evidence on this issue shows that an older man is less likely to be working if his wife is not in the labor force.[20] The leisure time of an older husband and that of his wife turn out to be *complements*—they are consumed together. Presumably their complementarity at least partly reflects labor-force decisions that are made jointly by the husband and wife.

Women ages 55 to 64 have been participating in the labor force at an increasing rate (see Table 1.4). This probably reflects a carryover into later life of the work habits acquired by women during their earlier work life. Among women above age 65, though, and especially among men above age 55, there has been a sharp downward trend in participation rates. Older men are the only major demographic group in the United States whose participation rate has declined sharply since World War II. In some ways this is quite puzzling. Many of the factors that make it more likely in the *cross section* (at a point in time) that older men participate in the labor force have changed in such a way as to increase the participation rate among older males. Their

[18] Anthony Pellechio, "Social Security and the Decision to Retire," Working Paper No. 734, National Bureau of Economic Research, Cambridge, Mass., 1981.

[19] Donald Parsons, "The Decline in Male Labor Force Participation," *Journal of Political Economy* (88): 117–134 (1980).

[20] Ibid. and "Health, Family Structure and Labor Supply," *American Economic Review* (67): 703–712 (1977).

Table 1.4 LABOR-FORCE PARTICIPATION OF OLDER PERSONS, 1955–1982

	Age and sex			
	Men		Women	
Year	55–64	65+	55–64	65+
1955	87.9	39.6	32.5	10.6
1960	86.8	33.1	37.2	10.8
1965	85.6	28.0	41.1	10.0
1970	83.0	26.8	43.0	9.7
1975	75.8	21.7	41.0	8.3
1980	72.3	19.1	41.5	8.1
1982	70.2	17.8	41.8	7.9

Source: Employment and Training Report of the President, 1981, Table A-5; and *Employment and Earnings,* January 1983, pp. 144–145.

real wages have increased, and have increased relative to those of the average male. Partly this is the result of the greater educational attainment of older men today as compared with men in their fathers' generation at the same age. (In 1950 the average male aged 55 to 64 had attained only 8.4 years of schooling; in 1979 the average was 12.3 years.) The downward trend has also not been caused by declining health: Life expectancy among males age 55 increased from 16.9 years in 1950 to 20.9 years in 1980. Today's older male can look forward to a longer and healthier future than could older men in previous generations.

One factor that reduces participation of older workers in the cross section has changed dramatically in a direction that would have reduced participation among older men. In 1950, 26 percent of private workers were covered by a pension plan other than Social Security; in 1975 the figure was 46 percent. The rise in coverage by pensions partly reflects workers' desires for income support during the retirement that an increasing number expect to enjoy fully because of improved health status during early old age. Although good health makes otherwise identical men less likely to retire, improvements in health may have encouraged people to seek better pension coverage, which in turn has led to reduced participation.

Social Security retirement benefits have been liberalized substantially since the inception of the program in the 1930s, and an increasing fraction of older workers have become eligible for benefits. Covered workers aged 65 and over have been eligible for benefits throughout the life of the program, but in 1956 women workers age 62 (men in 1961) also became eligible for (somewhat reduced) benefits. To what extent the expansion of Social Security retirement benefits has spurred early retirement is currently a controversial topic among economists, with some studies indicating very large effects, others showing small effects or even none.[21] The most reasonable conclusion is that although Social Security does induce retirement (especially among people 65 and over), its contribution to the downward trend in labor-force participation among older people is smaller than that of the growth of private pension plans.

[21] Pellechio finds substantial effects of Social Security, whereas Roger Gordon and Alan Blinder, "Market Wages, Reservation Wages and Retirement Decisions," *Journal of Public Economics* (14): 277–308 (1980), find very small effects.

POLICY ISSUE—DISABILITY INSURANCE

Since 1960 people of any age who are disabled have been eligible for benefits under the Social Security system. These Disability Insurance payments, totaling $16 billion in 1982, are administered under strict standards. The applicant must be certified as disabled by a state agency, must not have worked in the last 5 months, and must engage in no gainful activity (defined in 1983 as earnings above $300 per month) while drawing disability benefits. Certifications of disability are often for an "occupational disability," implying the workers are no longer physically able to work in their previous occupations. The level of benefits is related to the Social Security retirement benefit that the person would receive were he or she of retirement age. The benefit is a smaller fraction of the worker's full-time wage, the higher the wage is. The benefits are not subject to federal or state income taxes.

The effect of Disability Insurance on the choice whether or not to participate is shown in Figure 1.5. In the absence of disability benefits partly disabled workers, who can

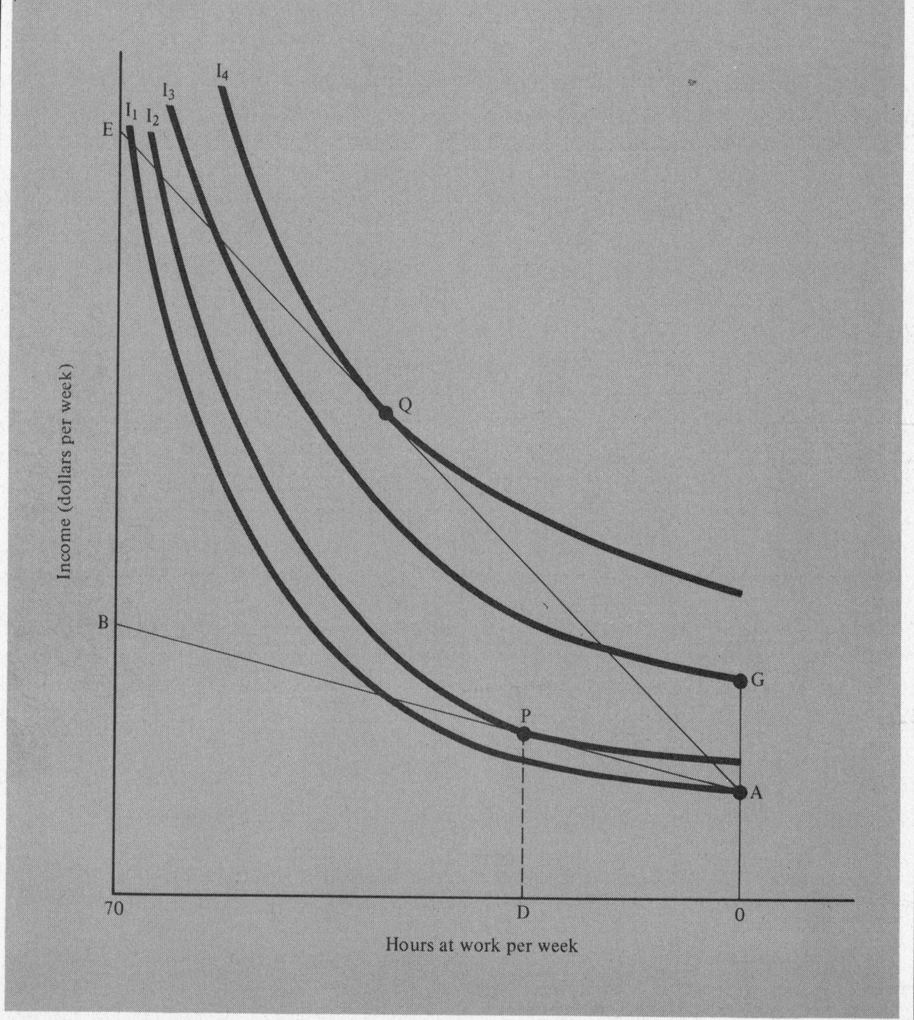

Figure 1.5 The effect of disability benefits on participation.

earn a wage shown by the slope of the line AB, will choose to work D hours. Participation in the work force is the best choice: point P, on indifference curve I_2, yields the highest level of satisfaction. Although they would like to stay at home, their nonlabor income 0A is insufficient to raise the reservation wage above the market wage. (I_1, which passes through A, yields lower satisfaction than I_2.) Instituting a Disability Insurance program (which, we assume for simplicity, forbids beneficiaries from earning anything) gives an additional AG of nonlabor income, *but only if the person leaves the labor force.* Should the people drop out? For people whose situation is shown in Figure 1.5 the answer is, yes: They achieve a higher level of satisfaction at point G on I_3 than by working D hours. Disability benefits make participation less attractive.

This simplified diagram appears to describe the program's actual effects fairly well. Estimates of the impact of disability benefits on labor-force participation range from a small, but significant effect, to an impact so large as to be able to account completely for the downward trend in participation among men 45 to 54. The effects are more pronounced among workers who earned low wages when they worked.[22] Figure 1.5 leads us to expect this result: If the wage rate is sufficiently high, as shown by the slope of AE, people who are eligible for benefits would be better off working than not participating, for they can achieve an indifference level of I_4 at point Q as compared to I_3 at point G if they do not work.

PARTICIPATION RATES—THE OVERALL TREND, AND SOME INTERNATIONAL COMPARISONS

Combining all demographic groups, including those not previously mentioned separately, we find that labor-force participation rates were basically unchanged between 1950 and the late 1960s, as the increases for women roughly offset the decreases for men. As Table 1.5 shows, though, since the late 1960s the more rapid upward trend in female labor-force participation has dominated the declining participation of older men. Overall, the civilian labor-force participation rate for both sexes has risen from 59.2 percent of the noninstitutional population in 1950 to 64.0 percent in 1982.

Many of the trends and demographic differences we have noted in the United States are also present in other developed countries. As Table 1.6 shows, most such nations have also had an increase in female labor-force participation. This is not surprising: Fertility has declined in these nations as well, and people have access to much the same labor-saving household devices as in the United States. Only in

Table 1.5 CIVILIAN LABOR FORCE PARTICIPATION RATE, 1950–1982

Year		Year	
1950	59.2	1970	60.4
1955	59.3	1975	61.2
1960	59.4	1980	63.8
1965	58.9	1982	64.0

Source: Economic Report of the President, 1983, Tables B-29, B-33.

[22] Robert Haveman and Barbara Wolfe, "Disability Transfers and Early Retirement," unpublished paper, University of Wisconsin, 1982; Jonathan Leonard, "The Social Security Disability Program and Labor Force Participation," Working Paper No. 392, National Bureau of Economic Research, Cambridge, Mass., 1979; and Parsons, loc. cit.

Table 1.6 LABOR-FORCE PARTICIPATION RATES, EIGHT COUNTRIES, 1968 AND 1980, PERSONS 15–64[a]

	Year and group			
	Total		Females	
Country	1968	1980	1968	1980
United States	67.1	72.4	46.9	59.7
Canada	64.2	71.8	41.7	57.3
United Kingdom	72.4	73.5	50.0	57.6
West Germany	66.8	65.4	47.7	49.3
Italy	60.4	60.9	33.6	39.8
Sweden	73.5	81.0	56.6	74.1
Australia	69.5	70.5	44.2	52.6
Japan	72.4	71.8	56.1	54.9

[a]Except 14–64 for Italy.

Source: Organization for Economic Cooperation and Development, *Labor Force Statistics,* 1968–1979 and 1969–1980.

Japan, which had one of the highest female participation rates after World War II, has the increase not been observed. This may be because the early postwar period saw a tremendous shortage of male labor that led to an early rise in market opportunities for adult women, accompanied by a decline in their participation as self-employed workers and as unpaid employees in family businesses.[23]

Despite the similar trends in female participation, there is little sign of a convergence in participation rates across developed economies. The range in aggregate participation rates in 1980 across countries, shown in the second column of Table 1.6, is very large. The addition of still more nations would not greatly change this impression. Part of this diversity is due to differences in the age structure of the populations; countries with relatively few youths exhibit higher participation rates. Also, differences in survey procedures and completeness produce differences in reported participation (e.g., Italy's large underground economy may produce an underreporting of labor-market activity). Despite these considerations, though, the great diversity in the face of often similar trends and cross-section differences suggests the importance of various cultural (taste) factors that affect participation.

THE DYNAMICS OF PARTICIPATION

The discussion of cross-section differences and trends may give the impression that participation rates apply to individuals. For example, does a 68 percent participation rate for females aged 25 to 34, for example, mean that each woman in this age group will be in the labor force 68 percent of the time? Or does it mean that 68 percent of women in this age group are in the labor force all the time while the other 32 percent never participate? The correct answer lies somewhere between these two extremes. In a sample of married women aged 30 to 44 in 1968, only 38 percent were in the labor force in all 3 years, 1968, 1969, and 1970. Nevertheless, 62 percent were in the labor force in at least 1 of those 3 years. The average participation rate for this group in any particular year was only 49 percent. Among women aged 45 to 59 in 1968, 39

[23]M. Anne Hill, "A Comparison of Economic Models and Empirical Results for Female Labor Force Participation in Japan and the United States," Discussion Paper No. 415, Yale University Economic Growth Center, New Haven, Conn., 1982.

percent participated in the labor force in all 3 years, and 56 percent participated in at least 1 year. The average participation rate in each year was 48 percent.[24] Some people are always in the labor force; others never participate; and still many others are in at some times and not at others.

The magnitude of these flows into and out of the labor force is even more striking when one considers the entire population. In a typical month in 1978 in the United States, only 63 percent of the population 16 and over was in the labor force. But fully 73 percent of the population 16 and over was in the labor force at some time during that year! The difference results from the large flows of workers into and out of the labor force that occur during the course of the year. Partly these flows reflect the behavior of seasonal workers and students who enter and leave the labor force on a regular basis. Partly, however, they reflect changes in the reservation wages and other variables that affect decisions of nonseasonal workers. Even among adult males, 1.4 percent of those employed left the labor force during a typical month in 1973, whereas 18 percent of those few adult men not in the labor force chose to reenter it.[25] Merely looking at participation rates for entire demographic groups masks the dynamics of participation within these groups. Underlying the broad averages is a substantial commitment to the labor market by many people who may not be in the labor force in one particular month.

THE EFFECT OF CHANGES IN DEMAND

We now turn to the effect of variations in the strength of the demand for labor as a factor affecting the measured participation rate. Discussion of this topic began in the 1930s with the emergence of the so-called *added-worker hypothesis*. This view held that when the usual breadwinner was unemployed and seeking work, additional members of the household would enter the labor force in an effort to maintain the family income; thus labor-force participation rates would rise as unemployment rose. The added-worker hypothesis, which argued that during a depression the labor force would be above the long-term trend, therefore implies that unemployment is overestimated, in the sense that creating one new job might reduce the number of unemployed by two people.

The contrary view, which has come to be called the *discouraged-worker hypothesis*, is that looking for work in conditions of general unemployment becomes so disheartening that some of the unemployed give up and withdraw from the labor force and that some people who would ordinarily enter the labor force do not do so. The size of the labor force therefore varies in the same direction as demand rather than in the opposite direction. With unemployment measured in the Current Population Survey as the number of people who report themselves as seeking work, the discouraged-worker hypothesis implies that unemployment is underestimated. It implies that we should add to those enumerated as unemployed another group, the *hidden unemployed*, who would be looking for work if they did not regard the search

[24] Calculated from James Heckman, "Heterogeneity and State Dependence," in Sherwin Rosen (ed.). *Studies in Labor Markets*, University of Chicago Press, Chicago, 1981, p. 106.

[25] These are the probabilities that would exist if all labor-market conditions facing a sample of persons in Denver remained unchanged, as shown in Nicholas Kiefer and George Neumann, "Wages and the Structure of Unemployment Rates," in Martin Baily (ed.). *Workers, Jobs and Inflation*, Brookings, Washington, 1982, p. 345.

as hopeless. Even in boom times enough people in the Current Population Survey say they have ceased looking for work because they cannot find any that, if added to the unemployed, they would raise the unemployment rate by 0.5 percentage points.

Reduced demand for labor thus has two effects on the worker's choice about whether or not to participate. The added-worker hypothesis implies that reduced aggregate demand lowers the income of other family members (those who lose their jobs or are put on short workweeks). In terms of Figure 1.2 this is a reduction in the nonlabor income available to people who are not currently in the labor force. This reduction lowers their reservation wages, for there is now less income from other sources to support the household. If all families had large holdings of liquid assets or could borrow easily at the going rate of interest, a temporary reduction in earned income might have only negligible effects on labor-force participation. The family's usual standard of consumption could be maintained by drawing down assets or by borrowing. The typical working-class family, however, has only a small amount of liquid assets and limited ability to borrow. Rates of interest on cash loans to such families, when they are available, are typically 18 percent per year or higher. Unemployment insurance benefits, for those eligible to receive them, often cover only half the income loss. Under these conditions, an increase in labor-force participation of other family members is an important alternative means of adjustment to unemployment even when it is expected to be temporary.

The discouraged-worker hypothesis can be viewed as stressing the importance of the reduction in market opportunities for people who are in the labor force even in good times. The jobs still available are likely to be lower paid or less attractive than before, and they can be found, if at all, only after longer and more costly search. For some of those deciding whether to stay in school or to leave, or whether to remain full-time housekeepers or to seek employment, this will tip the scales in favor of the nonmarket activity. Elderly workers who lose their jobs when unemployment rates are high are also more likely to settle for early retirement than they would if the chances of finding suitable new positions were better.

Clearly, both the added-worker and the discouraged-worker effects can be present at once for different households, so that the question to be decided by the evidence is which effect predominates. This is not merely an academic debate: In most recessions, liberal groups point to the discouraged-worker phenomenon and argue that the unemployment rate based on the Current Population Survey understates the severity of the recession. Because of the understatement of unemployment, they argue that macroeconomic policy tends to be too restrictive if based on the measured unemployment rate. Conservatives, on the other hand, downplay the discouraged-worker effect and point to the added-worker effect. They view macroeconomic policy as too stimulatory if it is guided by the measured unemployment rate, for they believe the measured rate overstates the severity of the recession.

One study does show that, among households in which the husband has been unemployed, wives are more likely to be in the labor force.[26] On the other hand, the cross-section evidence is very clear that, in cities where unemployment is more severe, participation rates are lower. Table 1.7 shows one set of estimates of the sensitivity of labor-force participation rates to unemployment for males and for

[26] Mincer, "Labor Force Participation . . . ," pp. 78–80.

Table 1.7 ESTIMATED SENSITIVITY OF LABOR-FORCE PARTICIPATION TO UNEMPLOYMENT (FROM INTERCITY REGRESSIONS FOR CENSUS WEEK OF 1960)

Males		Married women, husband present	
Age group	Sensitivity[a]	Age group	Sensitivity[a]
16–17	−5.6	14–19	−5.3
18–19	−2.0	20–24	−3.1
20–24	−0.4	25–29	−3.6
25–34	−0.3	30–34	−2.8
35–44	−0.4	35–39	−3.1
45–54	−0.6	40–44	−2.7
55–64	−1.5	45–54	−2.8
65 and over	−4.4	55–64	−3.6
		65 and over	−3.5

[a]The estimated sensitivity is the percentage change in the labor-force participation rate associated with a 1 percentage point increase in the overall unemployment rate.

Source: William Bowen and T. Aldrich Finegan, *The Economics of Labor Force Participation,* portions of Table 15-1, p. 482. Copyright © 1969 by Princeton University Press. Reprinted by permission of Princeton University Press.

married women as estimated across cities for 1960. A difference of 1 percentage point in the overall unemployment rate causes more than a 1 percent decline in the participation rate for all groups except males between 20 and 54. Negative sensitivities (not shown here) were also estimated for five of eight groups of women who were not living with their husbands. The table makes clear that the responsiveness to differences in demand conditions across cities is greatest in those population groups whose normal participation rates are low.

In Table 1.8 we present cyclical changes in participation rates for three large demographic groups. Because there are trends in these rates over time, the data for

Table 1.8 CYCLICAL VARIATIONS IN SEASONALLY ADJUSTED LABOR-FORCE PARTICIPATION RATES, 1957–1982

Business-cycle peaks and troughs	Teens	Women 20+	Men 20+
8/57 peak	48.4	36.4	86.7
4/58 trough[a]	48.1	36.8	86.7
4/60 peak	48.5	37.6	86.1
2/61 trough[a]	46.5	37.9	86.1
12/69 peak	50.4	42.9	82.6
11/70 trough[a]	49.0	42.5	82.8
11/73 peak	55.1	44.9	81.3
3/75 trough[a]	53.6	44.5	80.8
1/80 peak	57.6	51.3	79.6
7/80 trough	57.4	51.4	79.4
7/81 peak	54.5	52.3	78.9
11/82 trough[b]	54.5	52.8	78.9

[a]Adjusted for peak-to-peak trends.
[b]Approximate date of cyclical trough.
Source: CITIBASE data file, and *Employment and Earnings,* December 1982, Table A-33.

each cyclical trough through 1975 are adjusted to account for these trends and highlight the cyclical changes in participation. Although the effects are much smaller than those implied by the cross-section sensitivities in Table 1.7, the data in Table 1.8 give a picture that is qualitatively similar. Among adult males, the cyclical changes are tiny, even though in the 1973 to 1975 recession, and in the long decline from early 1980 through late 1982, the discouraged-worker effect predominated for this group. Among adult women and especially among teens, the discouraged-worker effect predominates in the recessions up through the 1970s.[27] In the shallow recession of 1980, and in the long decline from early 1980 through late 1982, the evidence is less clear, perhaps because it is difficult to extricate cyclical effects from trends in the participation rates over this period of time.

For the labor force as a whole the discouraged-worker effect is probably dominant. This conclusion is strengthened by additional evidence from the Current Population Survey on the number of people who say they have not looked for work, and thus are not counted in the labor force, because they believe there are no jobs to be found. During the 1973 to 1975 recession, between the second quarters of these years, this number rose from 0.5 to 0.7 percent of the population 16 and over. In the long economic decline from early 1980 to late 1982, the increase was from 0.5 to 1.1 percent. However, between 1967 and 1977 the change in this number was very small as compared to changes in the measured unemployment rate.[28] This evidence thus suggests that changes in the measured unemployment rate do understate increases in the true unemployment rate during a recession, although probably not by very much.

POLICY ISSUE—UNEMPLOYMENT AND THE VOLUNTEER ARMY.

With the abolition of the military draft in the early 1970s, military personnel have been induced to enter and remain in the armed forces of the United States by economic incentives and appeals to pride and patriotism. Although enlistments and reenlistments in the late 1970s fell below targets, in the early 1980s the targets were met. Secretary of Defense, Caspar Weinberger, attributed the military's success in recruiting to higher military pay and a trend toward greater patriotism, arguing, "I don't believe that the recession [of the early 1980s] is the major factor."[29]

Higher military pay will induce greater enlistments, for the economic alternative of military employment is made more attractive relative to civilian employment. In one study a 10 percent increase in military pay relative to civilian wages was shown to induce an increase of 8 percent in the enlistment rate.[30] So, too, increased patriotism can be viewed as a shift in preferences that leads to higher enlistment rates at any given relative pay between the military and civilian sectors. However, higher unemployment also makes the military a more attractive option for young people. During recessions the military

[27] However, Olivia Mitchell, "Labor Force Activity of Married Women as a Response to Changing Jobless Rates," *Monthly Labor Review* (103): 32–33 (1980), finds a net added-worker effect among married women in time-series data covering 19 standard metropolitan statistical areas from 1968 to 1975.

[28] T. Aldrich Finegan, "Discouraged Workers and Economic Fluctuations," *Industrial and Labor Relations Review* (35): 88–102 (1981).

[29] *Wall Street Journal,* October 19, 1982, p. 4.

[30] Anthony Fisher, "The Cost of the Draft and the Cost of Ending the Draft," *American Economic Review* (59): 239–254 (1969). See also the studies by Alan Fechter, David Grissmer, and Glenn Withers in Richard Cooper (ed.). *Defense Manpower Policy,* RAND, Santa Monica, Calif., 1979.

provides a secure job at a time when young workers especially are likely to have difficulty finding work. Indeed, each doubling of the unemployment rate appears to raise the enlistment rate by 35 percent.[31] With the unemployment rate nearly twice as high in 1982 as in 1979, it is not surprising that the enlistment rate jumped sharply during this period. By providing an outlet for youths who have difficulty finding work and might become discouraged workers, the volunteer armed forces keep total labor force participation from falling in a recession as much as it would otherwise.

SUMMARY

Labor-force participation—the choice of whether or not to do or seek market work—is always based on a comparison of market opportunities and the benefits of staying at home. We have analyzed this choice by reducing it to a comparison of one's market wage with one's reservation wage. Using this framework, we can explain a number of cross-sectional differences in labor-force participation rates (the fraction of persons 16 and over in a particular demographic group who are in the labor force). These include: (1) why women with young children, especially those who lack access to child care facilities or who have less education, are less likely to be in the labor force; (2) why youths who are in school are less likely to be in the labor force; (3) why there is a very sharp decline in participation rates at age 65; and (4) why participation rates are higher among the better educated. This approach explains the major labor-force trend of the past 30 years in the United States, the increase in female labor-force participation. This trend results from a lowering of the reservation wages of married women, due to the decline in birthrates (and thus the number of young children), and to the growth of good substitutes for housewives' time at home.

This approach to participation also enables us to understand the effects of several government policies. Subsidies for day care, for example, are clearly designed to increase participation. Numerous programs that transfer unearned income to recipients, of which Disability Insurance is a good example, can also affect participation rates. The actual effects of each policy must be carefully and specifically evaluated; but the basic framework we have outlined should underlie any such evaluation.

APPENDIX: Combining Income and Leisure

The analysis of labor-force participation in this chapter and that of hours of work in Chapter 2 follows the traditional approach of dividing activity into market work and all other activity, which can be called "leisure" for convenience. An alternative approach that gives greater generality at the cost of greater complexity notes that both productive activities and consumption take time.[32] Things from which people derive satisfaction can be called *commodities,* produced by a combination of two inputs, time and purchased goods. Commodities can then be classified by whether they are relatively time-intensive or goods-intensive, and work

[31] Fisher, Fechter, Withers, loc. cit.

[32] Gary Becker, "A Theory of the Allocation of Time," *Economic Journal* (75): 492–517 (1965).

can be viewed as a particular commodity that yields more goods than it uses and sometimes involves more negative than positive direct satisfaction. The outcome of such events as a rise in wages can then be analyzed in terms of their effects on time-intensive and goods-intensive activities, rather than simply on the amount of labor and leisure.

Classifying commodities into those that are relatively time-intensive and those that are relatively goods-intensive is not so easy as it might appear at first. Narrowly defined commodities are fairly easy to classify; listening to Beethoven's Ninth Symphony takes 1 hour (there is no satisfactory way of listening to it more quickly) and requires the purchase of a recording, costing less than $10. (Moreover, the recording can be reused many times, thus amortizing its money cost per hearing down to mere pennies.) Conversely, automobiles can be quite goods-intensive: One young tennis star recently admitted to owning seven luxury automobiles at the same time! When it comes to broader commodities, though, the classification is less clear. Is a 1-week vacation relatively time- or goods-intensive? It is time-intensive if you spend it tenting at a lake in a nearby park. It may be relatively goods-intensive if you spend it flying to Paris, staying at luxury hotels, and eating at three-star restaurants.

Despite this potential ambiguity, this extension of the standard theory of choice between working and not working provides certain implications that do not emerge from traditional theory. Consider, for example, the effect of a rise in wages offset by a lump-sum tax. Traditional theory predicts only that this would induce more labor-force participation, since the marginal return to work (or the "price of leisure") is increased while income is unchanged. The extension of standard theory allows us to examine the effects of this change on the activities workers undertake. The change in circumstances will encourage reductions in all time-intensive activity, not just the broad category "leisure"; that is, it will presumably lead to a substitution of activities that use more market goods for such activities as walking in the park and weeding one's own garden. Compare two people with the same income, one of whom lives off an inheritance, the other of whom is a high-paid executive. The executive will consume goods-intensive commodities; the wealthy person will consume time-intensive commodities.

A few attempts have been made to discern which among broad categories of goods are complements to (consumed with) leisure, and which are *substitutes* for (less likely to be consumed with) leisure. The ownership of durable goods is a relatively goods-intensive commodity, as the behavior of the tennis star would lead us to suspect. Obversely, the services of housing are complementary with leisure: Owning a house is a relatively time-intensive commodity, as anyone who has ever spent an afternoon trying to fix a clogged drain will attest. Beyond these two broad examples the rest of the effects are less clear, with no ready classification of such other items as food, purchased transportation services, clothing, and other nondurable goods.[33]

This extended theory has very interesting implications for people's behavior as the value of their time increases. With higher and higher earned incomes, and thus command over more goods, yet with no more time available to spend their incomes, they will try to cut corners on the consumption of time-intensive commodities. In an entertaining popular account of these effects, one author has referred to them as problems of *The Harried Leisure Class.*[34]

[33] Michael Abbott and Orley Ashenfelter, "Labour Supply, Commodity Demand and the Allocation of Time," *Review of Economic Studies* (43): 389–412 (1976).

[34] Staffan Linder, *The Harried Leisure Class,* Columbia University Press, New York, 1970.

chapter 2

Hours of Work and the Supply of Effort

VARIATION IN HOURS OF WORK

The amount of labor that workers supply depends on the number of hours per week they are willing to work as well as on the number of people in the labor force in a given week. It is necessary to distinguish among three concepts of hours supplied: (1) hours paid for; (2) hours spent at the workplace; and (3) hours spent actually working. It is the amount of time on the job actually spent working rather than preparing to work or relaxing that determines the amount of labor available for production. The supply aspects of hours spent at the workplace have been widely studied; unfortunately, the study of effort while on the job is much less well developed.

Before turning to the theory of hours of work, let us look at a few salient facts. First, there clearly has been a long-term decline in average hours at the workplace. The data in Table 2.1 show this decline was very rapid between 1900 and 1940, due mainly to reductions in the length of the standard workweek. Since 1940 the standard workweek has not been reduced significantly; but average hours at work have continued to fall, though more slowly. Taking years of roughly comparable demand pressures, we find that data from the Current Population Survey show that in May 1961 the average workweek (among all workers) was 40.4 hours in the survey week; in May 1975 the average workweek was 39 hours, and in May 1982 only 38.2 hours. Thus at the turn of the century most industries had an average workweek of more than 50 hours, whereas now the average workweek is under 40 hours.

The second important fact is that the level and trend of hours (both hours paid for and hours spent at work, which exclude paid holidays and vacation time) in the United States are similar to those of other developed nations. Table 2.2 shows that

Table 2.1 AVERAGE FULL-TIME HOURS OF WORK PER WEEK IN MANUFACTURING AND PRIVATE NONFARM INDUSTRY, SELECTED YEARS, 1900–1969

Year	Manufacturing[a]	Private nonfarm industry[b]
1900	55.0	58.5
1910	52.2	55.6
1920	48.1	50.6
1930	43.6	47.1
1940	37.6	42.5
1950	38.7	41.1
1960	38.1	41.0
1969	38.3	—

[a]Average of hours per week *actually* spent at the workplace (not hours paid for) so that an increase in paid leave time such as holidays and vacations results in a reduction of the average workweek as measured in this series.

[b]Average hours per week paid for.

Source: Ethel B. Jones, "New Estimates of Hours of Work per Week and Hourly Earnings, 1900–1957," *Review of Economics and Statistics* (45): 375 (1963), and Thomas Kniesner, "The Full-time Workweek in the United States," *Industrial and Labor Relations Review* (30) (1976), Tables 1, 3.

for several countries with comparable data, workweeks of about 40 hours are fairly typical. In other countries as in the United States, there has been a trend even recently toward somewhat shorter workweeks. Whereas the trend here and abroad is clear, it is much less clear what the roles of supply forces, demand forces, and institutional changes have been in causing this trend. We shall return to this subject later.

The third important fact is that at any given time there is substantial variation in the hours worked by different members of the work force. Table 2.3 gives the percentage distributions of hours worked at all jobs in May 1982. Although 44 percent of those at work outside agriculture reported working exactly 40 hours, the prevailing standard workweek, many people worked much less or much more. Within this tremendous diversity there is an interesting trend: Comparing 1961 and 1982, both recession years, there has been a movement over time toward more part-time work (less than 35 hours per week) and toward fewer people working long hours (41+).

The common view is that employers establish hours and that workers must accept them if they are to have jobs. This demand-dominated view contains an

Table 2.2 HOURS PAID FOR IN MANUFACTURING, INTERNATIONAL COMPARISONS, 1973 AND 1979

	1973	1979
United States	40.7	40.2
West Germany	42.8	41.6
Netherlands	43.1	41.1
Canada	39.6	38.8

Source: International Labor Organization, *Yearbook of Labor Statistics, 1981,* Table 12.

Table 2.3 PERCENT DISTRIBUTION OF HOURS OF WORK PER WEEK, MAY 1961 AND MAY 1982, NONAGRICULTURAL INDUSTRIES

Hours of Work	May 1961		May 1982	
1–14	6.5		5.6	
15–29	8.4	19.1	12.4	25.2
30–34	4.2		7.2	
35–39	6.5	50.2	7.8	52.3
40	43.7		44.5	
41–48	14.3		8.9	
49–59	8.2	30.5	8.0	22.6
60 and over	8.0		5.7	
Total at work	100.0		100.0	

Source: Employment and Earnings, June 1961, Table A–15; June 1982, Table A–26. The figures are obtained from household interviews in the Current Population Survey. Detail may not add to total because of rounding.

important element of truth, but the reality is more complicated. Part-time work illustrates the importance of supply forces. Many people want to work only part time because of commitments at home or at school, and many succeed in finding regular part-time jobs. In some cases workers may take full-time jobs because they cannot find part-time jobs. In other cases employers create part-time jobs when they cannot find full-time employees; for example, they fill one full-time position with two halftime workers.

Just as there are people who want to work less than the standard workweek, there are others who want to work more. Those who want more income than they can get from a single job can hold two or more jobs at once. In Table 2.3 multiple jobholders are included among those working long total hours.

We return to a detailed analysis of the determinants of these variations from the standard workweek later in this chapter. But first we consider the forces that influence the length of the standard itself. These include market forces on the supply and demand sides as well as legislation and collective bargaining. We deal with the supply forces in this chapter.

THE THEORY OF CHOICE OF HOURS OF WORK

In Chapter 1 we explained a way of analyzing how a rational decision maker chooses *whether or not* to participate in the labor force—to supply some positive number of hours to the labor market. Here we use a similar mechanism to analyze how such a decision maker chooses *how many* hours to supply. As in the discussion of labor-force participation, we assume that workers can earn some fixed wage rate for each hour they choose to work and that the number of hours chosen is entirely at their discretion. Later on we relax these assumptions when we discuss overtime work and moonlighting.

Consider people whose opportunities are depicted in Figure 2.1. With a wage rate of w_1 per hour, they are free to choose any combination of hours and income

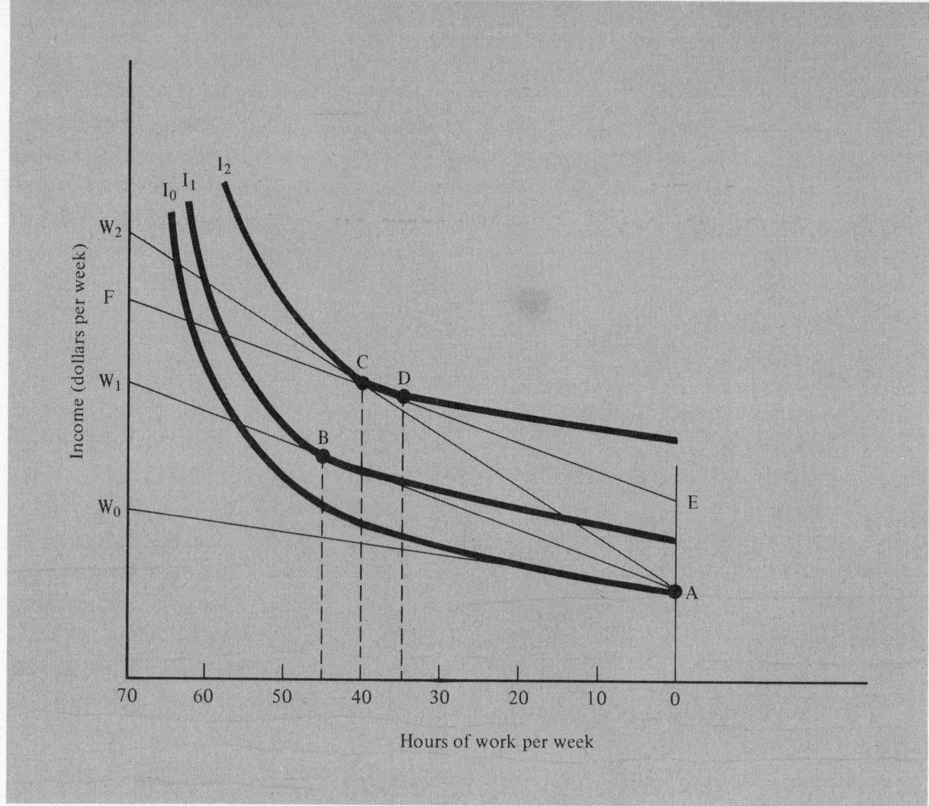

Figure 2.1 The choice between hours of work and hours of leisure.

along the line $0AW_1$. Individuals whose indifference maps are shown would maximize utility at B, where AW_1 is tangent to I_1, at 45 hours of work a week. Any other point on AW_1 that they might choose lies on a lower indifference curve and therefore represents a less satisfactory position. If the wage rate then rises to w_2, so people can choose points along $0AW_2$, the new optimum is at C, where AW_2 is tangent to the higher indifference curve I_2. The number of hours they would choose to supply is reduced to 40. If the wage rate were as low as w_0, hours supplied would be still different. At w_0 the people choose to supply zero hours—would be out of the labor force—for the most desirable combination of income and leisure would be at point A.

An individual's supply curve of hours in terms of wage rates cannot be read directly from Figure 2.1, but we can use the results of Figure 2.1 to find that supply curve. We know that at a wage rate of w_0 the person supplies zero hours; at w_1, 45 hours are supplied; and at w_2, 40 hours are offered. Had we drawn a different line for each wage rate starting at zero, we could have derived the number of hours offered at each wage. Taking the three combinations of wage rates and hours that we have derived, and assuming that we had derived the other intermediate combinations, we find that the labor-supply curve based on Figure 2.1 would look like that shown in

Figure 2.2. This supply curve implies that the person offers more hours as the wage rate rises up to, or slightly beyond, w_1. Further increases in the wage rate decrease the number of hours offered.

The supply curve in Figure 2.2 may seem strange, since most supply curves have a positive slope throughout. Why is this one different? The answer to this question can be seen if we decompose the effect of the increase in the wage rate from w_1 to w_2 in Figure 2.1. This is done by drawing the line parallel to AW_1 that is tangent to I_2 at D, line EF. The height of this line above AW_1 is the amount of nonlabor income that would be needed to make workers as well off as they are after the wage increase, without any change in the relative prices of labor and leisure. Since AW_2 is steeper than AW_1, which makes leisure more expensive in terms of earned income, D must lie to the right of C. As the figure is drawn, the wage increase reduces hours supplied from 45 to 40; the equivalent increase in nonlabor income would reduce them to 35. The supply curve of labor (the demand for leisure) can have a negative slope because a rise in the price of leisure (the wage rate), which would make workers consume less leisure, also raises their incomes, which may lead them to consume more leisure.

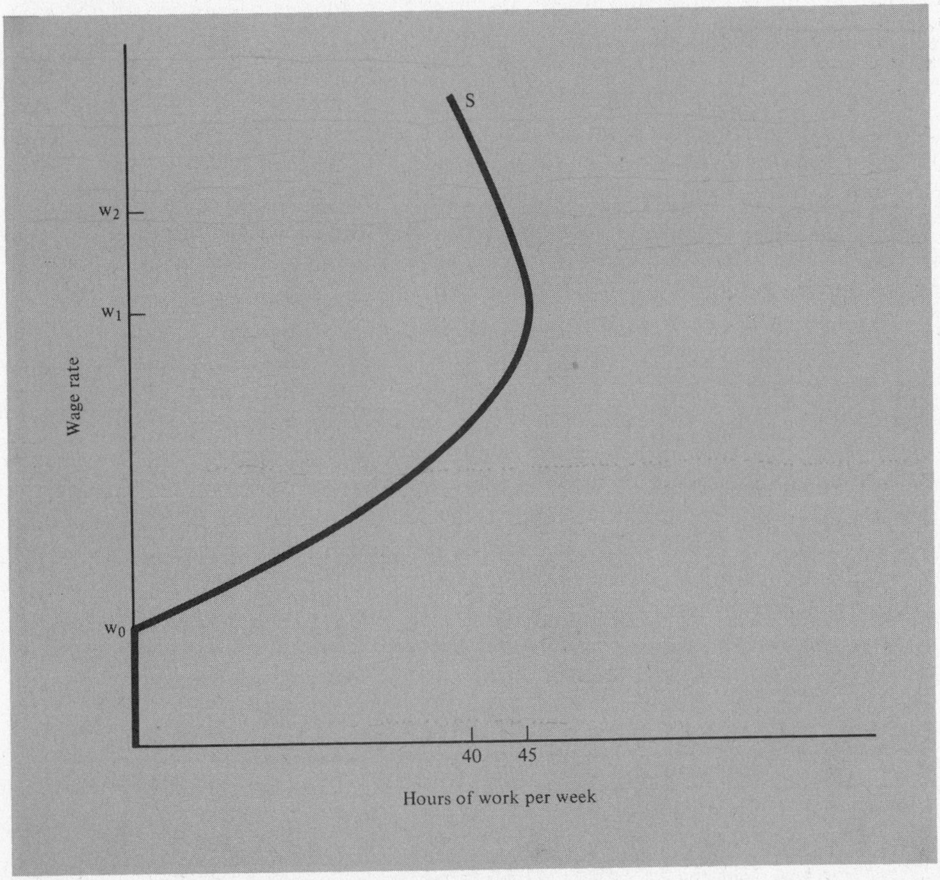

Figure 2.2 A supply curve of hours of work per week.

The horizontal distance from B to D, moving to the right, is the *income effect* of the wage change on hours of work. An income effect shows the response of hours worked to an increase in income that occurs at an unchanged wage rate (perhaps from receipt of a bequest or a gift). In this example it is −10 hours per week. The horizontal distance from D to C moving to the left, is the *substitution effect*. The substitution effect shows the change in hours that occurs when wage rates change, but workers' income is changed so as to keep their utility constant (keep them on the same indifference curve). In this example it is +5 hours per week. Their sum, the horizontal distance from B to C, moving to the right, is the total effect of the wage change on hours of work.

The substitution effect must be positive. By assumption workers are compensated by having enough income taken away to keep them on the same indifference curve (I_2); since the higher wage implies that the line EF rotates around point C to AW_2, hours worked must increase. The income effect can be negative; it is negative in Figure 2.1 by an amount large enough to dominate the substitution effect. The people whose choices are shown here value leisure so much that the extra purchasing power generated by a rise in the wage rate from w_1 to w_2 more than offsets the incentive that the increased wage rate gives to reduce consumption of the now higher-priced leisure.

There is no necessary relation between the positions of either C or D and B. Placing D to the right of B involves the plausible assumption that leisure is a *normal good* (as distinguished from an inferior good), so that more of it is consumed when income rises and relative prices are unchanged. Placing C to the right of B involves the much stronger assumption that the income effect of the wage increase is larger than the substitution effect. Nothing requires that the curves be placed so that this condition is satisfied. Whether the income effect is actually negative, and whether it is big enough to offset the positive substitution effect, are empirical issues.

These are issues to which labor economists have paid a good deal of attention. Table 2.4 summarizes the results of a large number of studies of labor-supply decisions as they are affected by changes in wage rates when other factors are held constant. The ranges of estimates are presented as *elasticities*, percentage responses of hours to 1 percent increases in wages or nonlabor income, to make them comparable to each other. As the table indicates, there is a wide range of variation in the estimates, stemming from differences in the data underlying the studies, in the ways in which the effects are estimated, and in the demographic composition of the groups being studied. With the exception of a few studies that have found theoretically implausible negative elasticities, empirical studies of hours of work find that the substitution effect is positive. As the final column of Table 2.4 shows, income effects are negative; for most people leisure is a normal good. The total elasticity of labor

Table 2.4 ESTIMATES OF LABOR-SUPPLY ELASTICITIES OF MEN AND WOMEN

	Total elasticity	Substitution elasticity	Income elasticity
Men	−0.40 to 0.30	−0.10 to 0.96	−0.33 to 0
Women	−0.07 to 0.90	0.10 to 2.00	−0.75 to −0.10

Source: Mark Killingsworth, "A Survey of Labor Supply Models," *Research in Labor Economics* (4) (1981), Tables 1–4.

supply is the sum of the substitution elasticity and a fraction (dependent on how much of the available time the person works) of the income elasticity.

Empirical elasticities of hours supplied differ significantly by sex. Income elasticities of women's labor supply are more negative than men's, whereas substitution elasticities are more positive. (These facts are consistent with the observation in Chapter 1 that women's labor-force participation is more responsive to economic and demographic factors than is that of men.) The total elasticity of hours supplied by men is approximately zero. This means that for the average man the supply curve in Figure 2.2 would be nearly vertical around the going wage rate.[1] Among women the total elasticity is positive but not very large, implying that for the average woman the supply curve would have a positive slope. As with differences in the determinants of labor-force participation, we should expect the differences in these elasticities between the sexes to decline over time as women become more attached to the labor force.

The ranges of estimates may give the impression that an increase in the wage rate or in nonlabor income produces an immediate change in hours supplied of the size shown in Table 2.4. This is quite wrong. People's labor supply, like much other behavior, is based partly on habit. A change in stimulus in the form of a change in the regular hourly wage rate affects their behavior only slowly; it takes time before people realize that a wage is permanent, and more time to adjust to the new set of circumstances facing them. One study estimates that it takes 2.5 years before half the eventual response of labor supply to a change in wage rates occurs; another finds it takes 4 years.[2]

POLICY ISSUE—WILL LOWERING TAX RATES RAISE PRODUCTION?

In 1981 the U.S. Congress passed, and President Reagan signed, a bill authorizing a 25 percent cut in tax rates spread over a 3-year period. A major economic rationale for this legislation was that it would increase the supply of savings to be used to finance new capital investments and increase the supply of labor by raising the after-tax return to working outside the home. An increase in the supply of labor, so the argument went, would increase GNP (the production of goods and services), since more people would be employed for more hours. Some proponents of this version of supply-side economics went so far as to claim that the tax cut would actually increase total tax revenues, for the increase in *total* hours worked would more than offset the decrease in taxes received *per hour* worked because of the cut in tax rates.[3] Others argued that the tax cut would produce only small increases in the total number of hours supplied to the market, and therefore would not increase total tax revenue.

[1] Even very sophisticated models that account for the interaction between husbands' and wives' labor-supply decisions produce results that are little different from those summarized in Table 2.4. One of these, Jerry Hausman, "Income and Payroll Tax Policy and Labor Supply," in Laurence Meyer (ed.), *The Supply-Side Effects of Economic Policy,* Kluwer-Nijhoff, Boston, 1981, p. 190, finds a zero substitution effect and an income effect of only −0.18 for husbands.

[2] Richard Freeman, "Employment and Wage Adjustment Models in U.S. Manufacturing, 1950–1976," *Economic Forum* (11): 1–27 (1980), and Edward Kalachek, Fredric Raines, and Donald Larson, "The Determination of Labor Supply: A Dynamic Model," *Industrial and Labor Relations Review* (32): 371 (1979).

[3] This is the so-called Laffer curve, a hypothetical inverse U-shaped relation between tax revenues and tax rates. A formal statement of this hypothesis is given by Victor Canto, Douglas Joines, and Arthur Laffer, "Tax Rates, Factor Employment and Market Products," in Meyer, loc. cit.

Our discussion of elasticities of hours supplied enables us to make fairly safe predictions about the probable impact of the tax cut on people already in the labor force. If typical workers pay a federal tax of 24 percent of each extra dollar earned, they retain 76 cents of that dollar (ignoring other taxes). The 25 percent tax cut lowers the tax rate to 18 percent, allowing them to retain 82 cents of each extra dollar of earnings. The return to additional work is increased by 6 cents per hour, or roughly 8 percent. The estimates in the first column of Table 2.4 suggest that for men the *maximum* impact could be an increase in hours worked of 2.4 percent (8 percent times an elasticity of 0.3); for women the *maximum* could be 7.2 percent (8 percent times an elasticity of 0.9). These calculations are admittedly rough, but they are based on a wide range of available estimates. They imply that the increase in hours supplied by today's workers will be small. Although labor-force participation rates may increase, especially among married women with children, other effects would tend to reduce the total supply of labor to the market. To the extent taxes on nonlabor income, such as capital gains, dividends, and interest, are cut, they will induce an income effect that reduces hours of work and raises the reservation wage of persons not currently in the labor force. In sum, the effect on total labor supply and thus on total GNP, is probably very small. It will certainly be insufficient to generate an actual increase in tax revenues.

A proponent of supply-side economics might argue that these estimates are not applicable, for they are based on elasticities showing the response of hours to changes in wage rates, not taxes. Several studies have examined whether labor supply responds to changes in taxes any differently from how it does to equal cost changes in wage rates. The answer is generally, no. Within the range of taxes in effect in most Western countries in the 1980s, the evidence shows that lower taxes will not lead to a large increase in labor supply that would increase output greatly.[4]

So far we have not made much use of the decomposition of changes in labor supply into substitution and income effects. Yet this decomposition is not merely an expositional device: It allows us to examine both general economic issues and specific policy matters. Many states offer grand prizes in the state lottery that pay the winners substantial sums each year for life. These represent a large addition of unearned income to the person's resources. With the negative income effects that the estimates in the third column of Table 2.4 suggest exist, typical workers will reduce their supply of hours. If the income elasticity is sufficiently large, or the lottery prize is very generous, they may drop out of the labor force. (That would be the same response we saw in Figure 1.5 in Chapter 1 when eligible workers received a disability benefit that was only loosely based on their earning ability.) For some people, though, income effects are small enough that even extremely large increases in

[4]Hausman, loc. cit.; Harvey Rosen, "Taxes in a Labor Supply Model with Joint Wage-Hours Determination," *Econometrica* (44): 485–507 (1976); and Jane Leuthold, "The Effect of Taxation on Hours Worked by Married Women," *Industrial and Labor Relations Review* (31): 520–526 (1978), all show that changes in take-home pay resulting from tax changes induce effects that are similar to those stemming from changes in hourly wage rates. At least among married women, any tax-induced reduction in market hours is partly offset by an increase in household production, not leisure; thus the true loss to society is smaller than the loss in GNP. See Janet Hunt, Charles DeLorme, and R. Carter Hill, "Taxation and the Wife's Use of Time," *Industrial and Labor Relations Review* (34): 426–432 (1981). Where marginal tax rates are very high, though, the conclusion may be different. Charles Stuart, "Swedish Tax Rates, Labor Supply, and Tax Revenues," *Journal of Political Economy* (89): 1020–1038 (1981), claims that the average marginal tax rate in Sweden is 80 percent, and the country is on the downward-sloping portion of its Laffer curve.

unearned income do not reduce hours of work to zero; for example, some winners of lottery grand prizes do not drop out of the labor force entirely.[5]

Another issue to which this analysis has been applied fruitfully is the proposal for a *negative income tax.* In response to rapidly expanding welfare costs in the 1960s, there was widespread political interest in alternatives to welfare. These alternatives were designed to reduce the penalty on work effort by welfare recipients. In some states the statutory requirements at the time allowed a welfare mother to keep none of her extra earnings above a certain low level. Even with changes in the laws effective in 1969, only one-third of each dollar of earnings beyond a low amount was supposed to be retained by a welfare recipient. The negative income tax would have offered people income supplements whether or not they worked and even if they had no dependent children. A national program of this sort was proposed by President Nixon in 1969 and was passed by the House of Representatives, but not by the Senate.[6] Modified versions were proposed by both Presidents Ford and Carter during their terms in office. Such programs would offer each household a *guarantee* even if they have no earnings; the amount paid is reduced by some fraction (the *tax rate* in the program) of each dollar earned. Thus, for example, each household might receive $3600 if it had no earnings; if its earnings were $2000, and the program's tax rate was 50 percent, it would receive only $2600 from the government, for a total income of $4600.

Because the program was to be integrated into the tax system, it would have affected welfare recipients and low-wage earners who were not on welfare. Figure 2.3 shows the effects on hours of a program in which someone with no earned or other nonlabor income is eligible to receive a payment equal to AE, and the payment is reduced by 50 cents for every dollar earned. Therefore when earned income is twice the amount of AE or more, no payment is made. The point at which this occurs (the *breakeven point*) is marked F.

Initially workers are in equilibrium at point B on I_1, exactly as in Figure 2.1. When the program is in effect, they choose point C on I_2 at which they work fewer hours but have a higher total income. We can again decompose this move into an income effect and a substitution effect by constructing the line beginning at G, parallel to AW_0 and tangent to I_2 at D. The horizontal distance from B to D is the income effect, that is, the effect on hours of the higher level of nonlabor income represented by the shift from I_1 to I_2. The horizontal distance from D to C is the substitution effect, representing the lower relative price of leisure. The price of leisure has fallen because, if the workers choose to work fewer hours, they gain a dollar of government payments for every $2 they lose in wages. Note that in Figure 2.3, unlike Figure 2.1, the income and substitution effects both work in the same direction—toward shorter hours of work. The guarantee is an increase in nonlabor income; the 50 percent tax rate on earnings reduces the return to an extra hour of work at a fixed level of utility.

[5] A vice president of a large international union planned to use the $448,000 he won in 1979 for his children's education and for charity; he made no mention of retiring. *New York Times,* October 18, 1979, p. 3.

[6] For a complete account, see Daniel P. Moynihan, *The Politics of a Guaranteed Income,* Random House, New York, 1973.

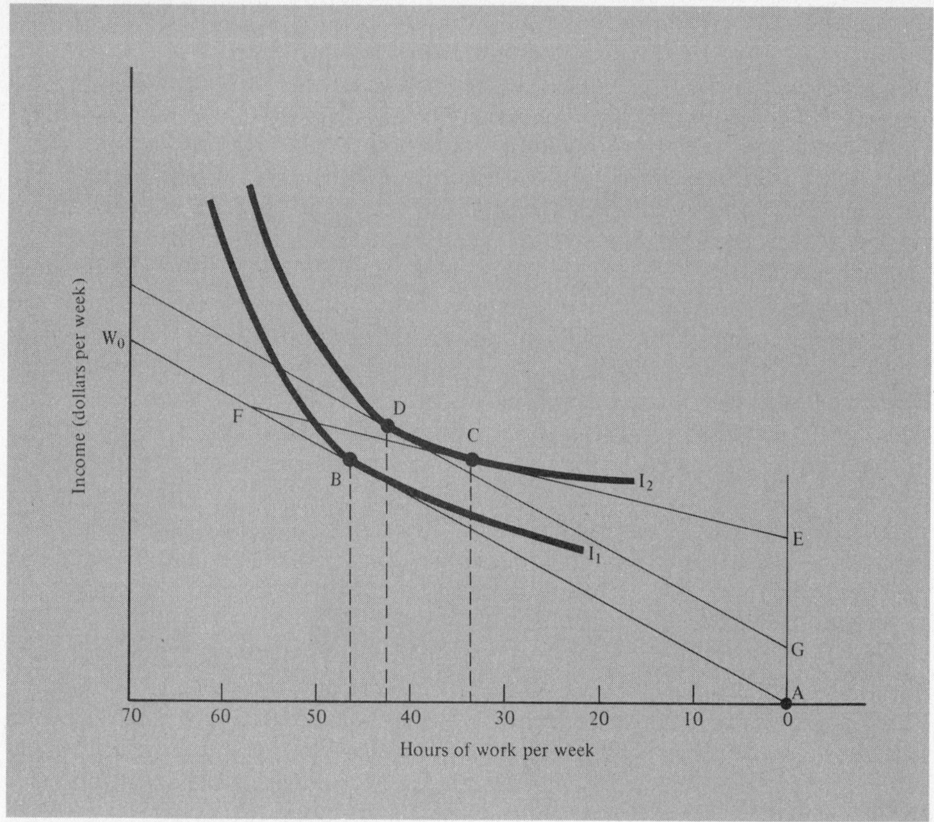

Figure 2.3 The effect of a negative income tax on labor supply.

Its proponents hoped that this negative effect of the program on hours supplied by low-wage workers who were previously not on welfare would be offset by a positive effect on the supply of hours and labor-force participation of former welfare recipients. Able to keep 50 cents of each dollar earned, rather than the one-third or less that they had previously kept, they would supply more hours so long as their total supply elasticity was positive. Since the evidence indicates that supply elasticities are quite large for low-wage women, including mothers who are receiving welfare payments because they have dependent children, the positive effect on total hours could have been quite substantial.[7]

To estimate the effect of the program on the hours of people not receiving welfare, experiments were conducted that made such payments for several years to one part of a randomly chosen sample. The payments had significant although small negative effects on the hours of work per week of married men and on the labor-force

[7]Daniel Saks, *Public Assistance for Mothers in an Urban Labor Market,* Princeton University Industrial Relations Section, Princeton, N. J., 1975, p. 73, and Danny Steinberg and Jane Kulik, *Implicit Taxes, Wages and Labor Supply in a Welfare Population,* Abt Associates, Cambridge, Mass., 1981, p. A-6.

participation rate of married women.[8] Assuming no changes were to occur in other income transfer programs, one study summarized the impact of a plan that would offer unearned income AE equal to two-thirds of the official poverty level. It estimated that the plan would induce a 4 percent drop in hours worked by participating husbands; a 27 percent drop by wives; and a 16 percent drop by female heads of households.[9] Given the relatively small number of people who are eligible to participate, and the small fraction of hours they supply as compared to the entire labor force, the reductions in their labor supply probably imply some small cost to the program, and thus also to the economy's GNP.

Partly because of these findings there has been less interest in starting a negative income tax in the last 5 years than in the preceding decade. Also, detailed research on actual welfare benefits received has shown that welfare mothers are able to retain 50 percent or more of each dollar earned, a percentage that has increased over time (especially since the one-third rule became effective).[10] Offering them a negative income-tax scheme like that described in Figure 2.3 as a substitute for welfare would not be so helpful as people initially thought. Finally, since 1978 every low-income household in the United States, regardless of its demographic makeup, has been eligible for an allotment of food stamps that has most of the characteristics of a negative income tax: Some income is guaranteed, and recipients may keep 20 percent of each extra dollar of earnings.[11]

POLICY ISSUE—THE EARNINGS TEST FOR SOCIAL SECURITY

We saw in Chapter 1 how the provision of Disability Insurance benefits provides workers an incentive to retire earlier than they otherwise would. In discussing that issue we simplified matters by assuming that nothing could be earned without reducing the benefits received. That assumption is not unreasonable under Disability Insurance, in which only $300 per month ($3600 per year) could be earned in 1983 without disqualifying the worker from the program. Under the Social Security retirement program, though, the exemption cannot be ignored: In 1983 eligible workers could earn $6600 per year without losing any retirement benefits, and had to give up only 50 cents of each dollar earned beyond that. (After the seventieth birthday the workers' benefits are unaffected by their earnings.)

How does this *earnings test* affect the supply of hours and the choice of whether or not to participate in the labor market? In the absence of Social Security workers' budget lines are like $0AW_1$ in Figure 2.4. With the provision of benefits and the application of the earnings test, the budget shifts to $0CDEW_1$. The segment CD is parallel to AW_1, because workers can earn income at their usual wage rate w_1 and keep each dollar earned. To the

[8] See Harold Watts and Albert Rees (eds.). *The New Jersey Income Maintenance Experiment,* vol. 2, Academic Press, New York, 1977, chap. 1, and Robert Moffitt, "The Effect of a Negative Income Tax on Work Effort: A Summary of the Experimental Results," in Paul Sommers (ed.). *Welfare Reform in America: Perspectives and Prospects,* Kluwer-Nijhoff, Boston, 1981.

[9] Moffitt, op. cit., p. 223.

[10] Saks, op. cit., p. 59, found that the true tax rate on welfare mothers' earnings in New York City before 1969, when the one-third rule went into effect, was only 0.67. Steinberg and Kulik, op. cit., p. B-9, show that the tax rate on earnings of welfare mothers in Minnesota in 1979 was only 28 percent. Robert Hutchens, "Changes in AFDC Tax Rates, 1967–1971," *Journal of Human Resources* (13): 60–74 (1978), shows that the effective tax rate nationwide in 1967 (before the one-third rule) was 65 percent but that it had dropped to 37 percent by 1971.

[11] William Albrecht, "Welfare Reform: An Idea Whose Time Has Come and Gone," in Sommers, loc. cit., makes this point very forcefully.

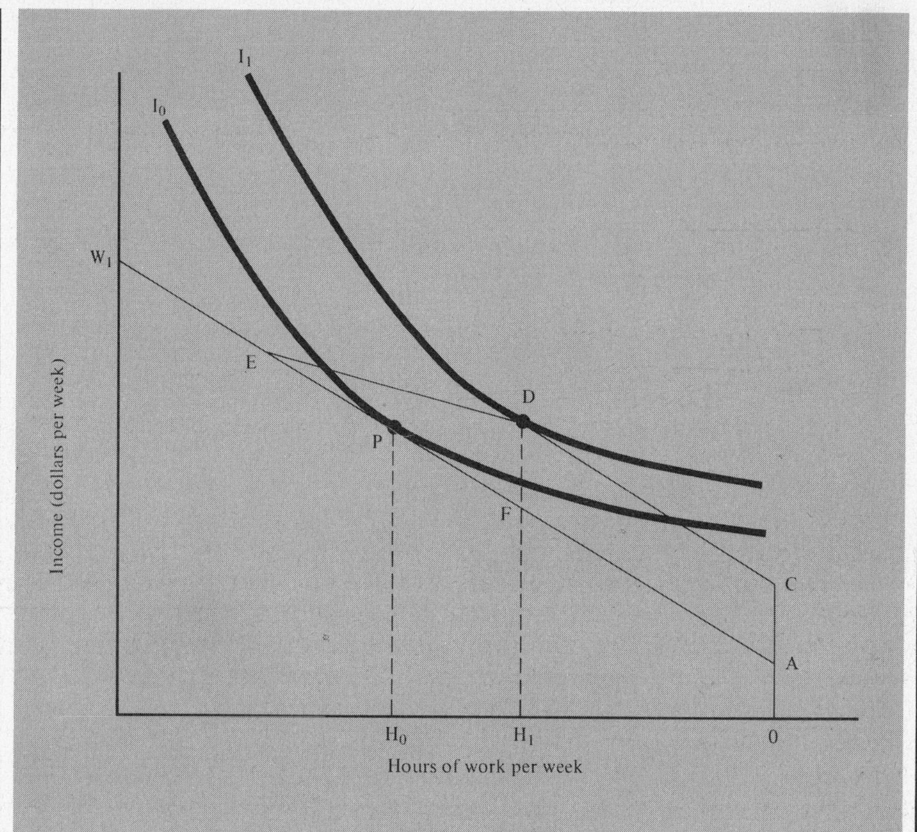

Figure 2.4 The effect of the social security earnings test.

left of point D workers' earnings exceed $6600; each additional dollar earned yields only 50 cents of income, reducing the slope of DE to half that of AW_1 or CD. To the left of point E the worker earns more than $13,200 (twice $6600) and receives no benefits. People who achieve the highest indifference level at point P along I_0 will be induced to change their behavior by the presence of the earnings test when they become eligible for benefits. The return to extra hours of work beyond H_1 is cut in half, and their incomes are also higher because of the benefits DF paid if they work only H_1 hours. The first change induces a substitution effect that reduces work hours; the second induces an income effect in the same direction. Together they lead workers to their highest indifference level, I_1; they are better off than before, but they work fewer hours. One set of estimates indicates that, among workers who in the absence of the earnings test would work at least H_1 hours, work time is cut by 25 percent. This is a very large impact. The impact on the entire retired population is small, though, for only 12 percent of retirees would work more than H_1 hours if there were no earnings test.[12] Among the provisions of the Social Security program that may reduce the supply of labor to the market, the earnings test does not loom very large.

[12] Gary Burtless and Robert Moffitt, "The Effect of Social Security Benefits on the Labor Supply of the Aged," in Henry Aaron and Gary Burtless (eds.). *Retirement and Economic Behavior,* Brookings, Washington, 1984.

THE OPTIMAL LENGTH OF THE WORKWEEK

Let us now use the apparatus described in the last section to see how the length of the workweek might be determined in a competitive economy. Under certain assumptions that are an oversimplification of reality, Figure 2.1 could completely explain this determination. These assumptions are:

1. Labor and product markets are competitive.
2. All workers have the same unchanging set of preferences concerning the choice between income and leisure.
3. There are no costs of employment other than hourly wages.[13]
4. The productivity of all workers in each hour is independent of the length of the workweek, and workers have the same productivity.

Assumptions 3 and 4 taken together make employers indifferent to the number of hours worked per worker and to which worker is performing a particular task. They would as soon have one worker working 70 hours a week as two workers working 35 hours each. Under these assumptions the demand for hours cannot be decomposed into a demand for workers and a demand for hours per worker.

Assumptions 1 and 2 assure that, given the competitively determined wage, employers who select a workweek other than the preferred one will be at a competitive disadvantage and will be unable to attract labor. They are selecting a position in Figure 2.1 on AW_1 to the right or left of B, a position that for all workers lies on an indifference curve lower than I_1. If these employers attempt to offset their undesirable choice of hours by offering a higher hourly rate, their costs will rise and they will suffer losses, since they must still charge the competitive market price for their product. Under these conditions the history of hours of work, as real wages per hour rose through time, would trace out a series of points such as B and C, which are entirely determined by workers' preferences.

If we relax assumption 2, that all workers have the same preferences, then there will be dispersion in the workweeks set by different employers. Some employers will offer long workweeks to attract the workers with the strongest preferences for money income, whereas others will offer shorter workweeks to attract workers with the strongest preferences for leisure. To the extent their production techniques permit, some employers may offer workweeks of differing lengths to workers in their plants whose preferences differ. If there is an oversupply of workers with a given set of preferences, employers who offer the corresponding numbers of hours will be able to hire labor at less than the prevailing wage (or to hire superior workers at that wage), and they will therefore have a competitive advantage. This will induce other employers to alter their workweeks so as to eliminate the excess supply or the below normal wage at this number of hours. Hours of work, although no longer uniform, will still be entirely supply determined.

The fact that the labor force is not homogeneous in terms of age and sex is sufficient to ensure that preferences for hours will not be uniform. Students, people

[13] This assumption, although needed here, will not be discussed until Chapter 5, when the employer's choice between more hours and more workers is considered.

with young children, and the elderly can be expected to prefer shorter hours, either because of their commitments to nonmarket work or because they are physically less vigorous than prime-age workers. If people cannot borrow freely against their future earnings, some young husbands or wives who wish to acquire houses, cars, or household appliances will seek to work longer hours as an alternative to borrowing at high interest rates or to deferring consumption if they cannot borrow at all.

Additional interesting possibilities are opened up by relaxing assumption 4. Workers with higher productivity will receive higher wage rates. Even if all the other assumptions hold they will wish to supply more or fewer hours (depending on the shape of the supply curve in Figure 2.2), and employers will set workweeks of differing lengths. If each worker's productivity per hour varies with the length of the workweek, there should be some relation between output per hour and the number of hours per worker at any particular place and time. Up to some point this relation is linear, as productivity, and thus the wage rate employers are willing to offer is unchanged. In Figure 2.5 this is true from 0 up to 40 hours per week; workers can earn a wage rate of w_1 per hour, choosing points on that part of the income line $0AW_1$ to the right of G. Beyond 40 hours the worker's additional output may fall, and even become zero or negative. Employers will be unwilling to offer a wage as high as w_1. Beyond 60 hours of work per week, they will be unwilling to offer anything, for the worker is subtracting from the firm's output. At that point the worker's income will decrease with more hours at work. If the drop in productivity shown in Figure 2.5 exists, nobody will seek to supply more than 60 hours per week; to do so would lower

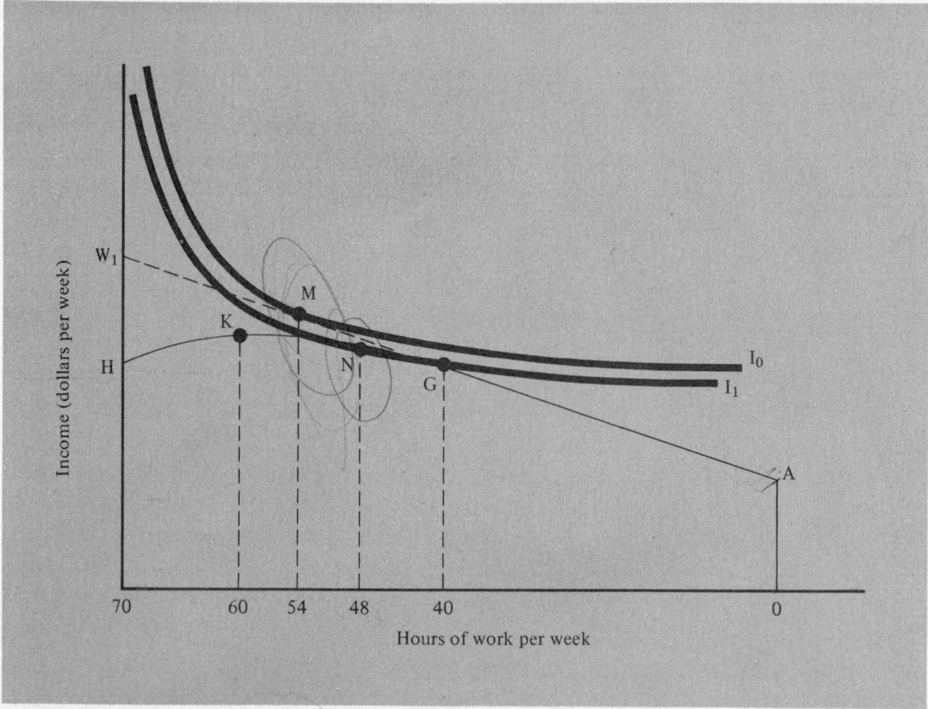

Figure 2.5 The choice of hours of work when productivity decreases as the workweek lengthens.

income and require a reduction in leisure as well. Assuming labor supply decreases when the wage rate is reduced, this sort of productivity effect would reduce the supply of labor. In terms of Figure 2.5, workers who would maximize utility by choosing to supply 54 hours of work per week (point M along $0AW_1$) would choose to supply only 48 hours per week (point N along 0AH) if the wage rate they could receive falls after 40 hours because their productivity falls.

It is often alleged that in the early days of the Industrial Revolution employers chose such a long workweek that total weekly output per worker could have been increased by shortening it (that the typical worker was to the left of point K in Figure 2.5).[14] If this had been true, employers could have increased both the satisfaction of their workers and output at no cost, by requiring shorter work hours and holding the weekly wage constant. They would then presumably have had a competitive advantage that would have forced other employers to follow them. Collusion among employers is not sufficient to rationalize this view, since they would have been colluding against their own interests, whether viewed individually or collectively. The argument requires that all employers be either ignorant or shortsighted. One explanation for the allegation is that the beneficial effects of shorter hours on output are felt only after the passage of some time and that no employer is willing to try the experiment of shortening hours for a long enough period to observe these effects.[15]

The possibility cannot be ruled out that, at very low real wages, the optimum position of workers lies quite far to the left in Figure 2.1 and that with habituation and a less intense pace of work, output could continue to rise with increases in the workweek well beyond any number of hours we would now regard as reasonable. Much of the empirical evidence usually cited to show the adverse effect of long hours on output comes from studies of abnormally long hours in wartime. These hours were worked by workers who were either accustomed to shorter hours or were new wartime recruits to the labor force, unaccustomed to industrial work. They worked long hours at high money wages at a time when there was a severe shortage of consumer goods. In these circumstances the number of hours that would maximize output may well have been in the neighborhood of 54 hours per week, with extensions beyond this offset by a slower work pace and more absenteeism and tardiness. This evidence is not inconsistent with an output-maximizing figure of 60 or even 72 hours a week a century earlier.

To the right of point K in Figure 2.5, at which longer hours reduce output, abandoning the assumption of competition could clearly make it possible to frustrate the influence of worker preferences on hours of work. By custom or agreement, employers could keep to a workweek that was too long (to the left of N in Figure 2.5) and confront most workers with the choice of working too much or not at all. In these circumstances, legislation or trade-union action would be needed to reduce the workweek.

The possibility of impediments to the working of competition in reducing hours, at least in the short run, is increased by the lumpiness of some decisions to

[14] For a good example of this view, see Kurt Rothschild, *The Theory of Wages,* 2d ed. Blackwell, Oxford, 1965, pp. 50–55. The point of maximum output is sometimes called the point of optimum hours, which is a usage of the word optimum different from that in the text.

[15] Ibid., p. 55.

change hours, especially in continuous-process industries. For example, the American steel industry in 1923 moved in one jump from the 12-hour day to the 8-hour day by adding a third shift. Such a choice may mean moving initially from a workweek that is "too long" to one that is "too short," which helps to explain why steel lagged far behind other industries in shortening the workweek.

Even if average hours are strongly influenced by workers' preferences, the possibility remains that particular workers with preferences differing from the average may not be able to find jobs with the schedule they prefer. Thus a young parent with a large family who would like to work regularly for 48 hours a week may be able to find only a job with a 40-hour regular workweek and occasional opportunities for overtime. Someone with school-age children who would like to work from 9:00 A.M. to 3:00 P.M. may have to choose between working from 9:00 to 5:00 or not working at all.

Up to this point our discussion of hours of work has been entirely in terms of the number of hours per week. In the years since World War II, however, reductions in the length of the work year have largely taken a different form, that of increases in paid vacations and holidays. As Table 2.5 shows, paid vacations and holidays were essentially unknown in the 1920s. Even in 1961, time paid for but not worked equaled only 7.1 percent of wage and salary costs; by 1981 it was 10.0 percent of those costs. The change since 1961 alone is sufficient to produce a decline of 1 hour per week at the workplace.

There is good reason, after the workweek has reached reasonable levels, that further decreases in time spent at the workplace should take the form of more vacations and holidays rather than shorter hours in each workday. Vacations and holidays, especially holidays falling on Monday or Friday, create blocks of free time that can be used for trips or for substantial projects of work in the household. They reduce the fixed costs of getting to work as well as working time, so that more time is saved for recreation or for household work than is lost at the job. With a 40-hour week, if the time involved in an extra week of paid vacation were spread across each of 240 working days in a year, it would amount to only 10 minutes a day, a change so slight that the worker would derive little benefit from it.

Recently there have been some experiments with regular 4-day weeks, which may or may not involve a reduction in total hours. For example, a week of five 8-hour days could be changed to four 10-hour days. This not only cuts total commuting time, but makes it possible for workers to commute at hours when there

Table 2.5 PAID TIME NOT AT WORK AS A PERCENT OF WAGE AND SALARY COSTS

	1929	1951	1961	1971	1981
Vacation	0.3	3.0	3.8	4.3	5.1
Holidays	0.3	1.8	2.4	2.9	3.4
Sick leave	0.1	0.6	0.8	1.0	1.3
Other time paid but not worked	0	0.1	0.1	0.2	0.2

Source: U.S. Chamber of Commerce, *Employee Benefits, 1981,* Chamber of Commerce, Washington, 1982, p. 30.

is less congestion on highways or transit systems. A number of firms report general satisfaction with such work patterns, including higher productivity and decreased absenteeism. However, it reduces workers' flexibility in scheduling activities on the 4 days, which may be a particular problem for people with some child care responsibilities. At this point it is too soon to say whether a 4-day workweek will become common. In 1979, however, only 2 percent of full-time employees (those working 35 or more hours per week) worked fewer than 5 days a week.

Even accounting for the increase in paid leisure time, there was a clear break sometime between 1935 and 1950 in the trend toward shorter hours. It may be that we have reached the point where the long-term income and substitution effects of rising real wage rates are in balance, or the income effect is just slightly greater than the substitution effect. It may be, though, that other changes have occurred outside this simple framework that have caused the decline in hours worked to decelerate. One study points to the increased amount of leisure consumed late in life in the form of earlier retirement, which may have induced people to put in longer weeks while at work.[16]

SHIFT TIME, OVERTIME, MOONLIGHTING, AND PART-TIME WORK

We have been discussing cases in which all hours per week are paid at the same rate. However, it has now become almost universal practice to pay blue-collar and many clerical workers for hours beyond the standard workweek at higher rates, which can be viewed as premium rates if the emphasis is on the supply response, or as penalty rates if one focuses on the demand side, as we do in Chapter 5. In the United States, overtime is almost always paid at 1.5 times the straight-time rate; practice varies more in Britain, where 1.25 and 1.33 times the straight-time rate are often used.

Figure 2.6 shows the response to overtime premiums. Workers can earn a straight-time wage w_0 for each hour worked, shown by the slope of AW_0. Let us assume that if no overtime were paid, workers would achieve the greatest satisfaction along I_0, at point D, working 40 hours per week. If an overtime premium of time and a half beyond 40 hours is introduced and overtime work is freely available, they could choose any combination of income and leisure along the lines 0ADB. They would then choose the position E on indifference curve I_1, which is higher than the indifference curve I_0. Hours of work now rise from 40 to 50. Premium pay for overtime will call forth more hours of work from anyone who initially chose to work exactly the standard workweek. A very small increase in the premium above the standard rate produces only a positive substitution effect on hours supplied.

Overtime work is important to many people: In May 1978, 12 percent of all full-time workers received premium pay for overtime.[17] There are substantial differences by occupation and demographic group in the amount of overtime worked.

[16] See Richard Burkhauser and John Turner, "A Time-Series Analysis of Social Security and Its Effect on the Market Work of Men at Younger Ages," *Journal of Political Economy* (86): 701–716 (1978).

[17] Bureau of Labor Statistics, *Long Hours and Premium Pay,* May 1978, Special Labor Reforce Report No. 226, p. 41.

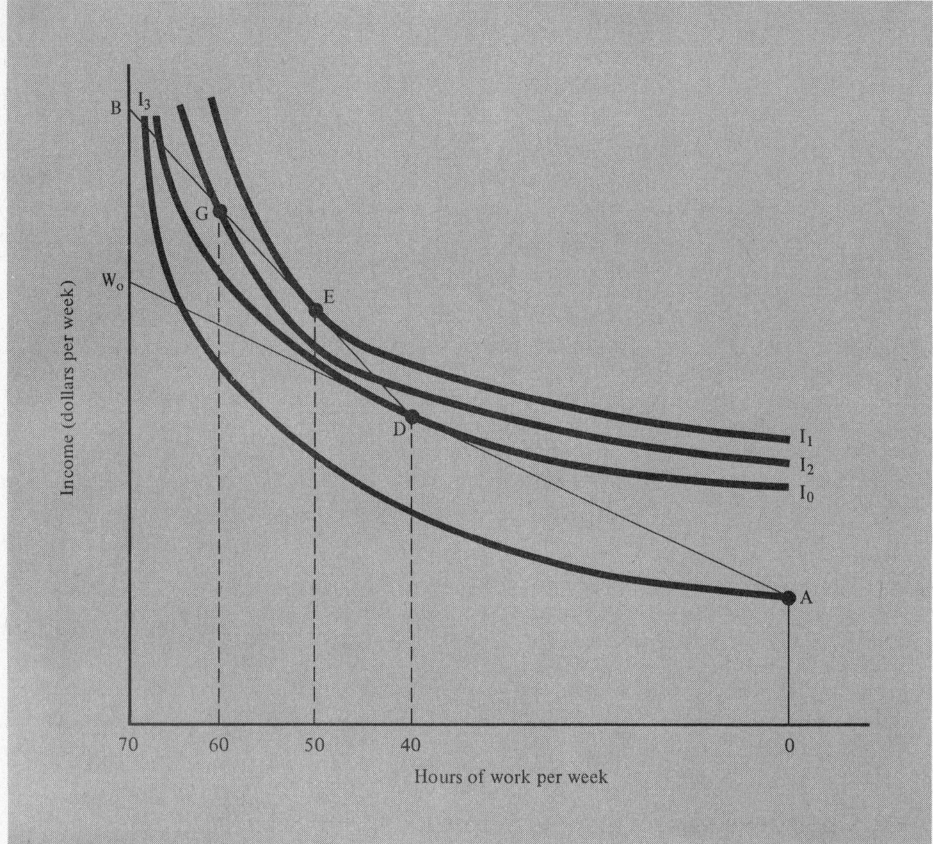

Figure 2.6 The choice of overtime hours.

Other things equal, unionized workers are less likely to work overtime than are other manufacturing workers. In larger plants, overtime work is also more prevalent, perhaps because of the need to use workers with substantial skills along with the greater amount of capital available per worker in such plants.[18]

In addition to these effects, the overtime premium and other factors will affect the amount of overtime employers wish to schedule. (We discuss some of these effects in Chap. 5.) In most cases it appears that worker preferences are such that more overtime hours would be worked at time and a half were they available. This scarcity requires that overtime work be rationed by seniority and suggests that overtime premiums are usually larger than are needed to call forth the extra hours that are demanded. In other words, the effect of paying time and a half beyond 40 hours is largely that of a penalty rate to discourage employers from using regular overtime schedules. Of course, the willingness of workers to work overtime at premium rates does not imply that standard hours are too short. To show this, one would have to show that workers wanted to work more hours at straight-time rates.

[18] Ronald Ehrenberg and Paul Schumann, *Longer Hours or More Jobs?* New York State School of Industrial and Labor Relations, Ithaca, N.Y., 1982, p. 143.

POLICY ISSUE—THE ABOLITION OF MANDATORY OVERTIME

In 1979 and 1981, bills were introduced in the U.S. House of Representatives requiring that employers obtain the consent of employees before they assign overtime work.[19] The impetus for this proposal (one of several proposals dealing with the overtime provisions of the Fair Labor Standards Act, the legislation governing overtime and minimum wages) was from workers in industries in which employers want large amounts of overtime work, even more than workers are willing to supply. Although the incentive of premium pay will induce workers to offer more than 40 hours per week, it may not be enough to elicit all the overtime the employer wishes to obtain. The best known case is that of the 6-day week sometimes worked in automobile assembly plants.

Why this reluctance on the part of workers, this implied unwillingness to increase their earnings? Figure 2.6 showed that workers who are free to choose overtime hours will supply 50 hours per week (40 at straight-time pay, 10 at time and a half). But the employer may require them to work 60 hours as a condition for retaining their jobs. The workers are faced with the choice of working the 60 hours, at point G in the figure, or losing the job and not working, point A in the figure. The level of satisfaction at point G is indicated by indifference curve I_2; that at point A is indicated by indifference curve I_3. Clearly the workers are better off working the 60 hours than refusing the assignments and losing their jobs. Even if they can obtain other jobs, those may pay lower straight-time wages. They are worse off, though, than if they could choose their overtime hours freely: The indifference level I_2 is below that, I_1, attainable at point E when they work only 50 hours per week. The workers value the extra 10 hours of leisure that they must forego when they are forced to work 60 rather than 50 hours, even more than they value the premium wages they earn for those extra 10 hours.

The proposals to abolish mandatory overtime did not achieve much success. With reduced labor demand in the early 1980s, and thus less overtime being required by employers, unions' interest in pressing for such legislation waned. Nonetheless, it is likely to become an issue whenever labor markets are tight and overtime hours are required of more employees. It could be dealt with by legislation such as that proposed in 1979 and 1981; it could also be handled through collective bargaining or individual negotiation in nonunionized plants. To some extent it is already taken care of by collective bargaining: Unionized workers who are required to work mandatory overtime hours receive a straight-time wage that is 2 percent higher than that received by otherwise identical unionized workers who do not face this requirement. Nonunion workers required to work overtime do not receive a higher straight-time wage than other nonunion workers. This suggests they will obtain compensation for the disutility of mandatory overtime work only with the aid of legislation.[20]

The supply of hours depends not only on the length of the workweek but also on the pattern of hours during the week. As production becomes more capital-intensive, there is a growing incentive for management to operate facilities with more than one shift. In continuous-processing operations, such as steel mills and petroleum refineries, it is necessary for the plant to operate 168 hours a week. Yet workers are in general reluctant to work night shifts or on weekends. Another undesirable working pattern is the split shift, often needed in urban and suburban transportation, in which a worker works 4 hours during the morning rush and another 4 hours during the evening rush.

[19]This proposal, H.R. 1784, 96th Congress, and H.R. 1784, 97th Congress, was introduced and reintroduced by Representative John Conyers of the auto-producing state of Michigan.

[20]Ehrenberg and Schumann, op. cit., p. 130.

Such strange work schedules are much more common than one might suspect. In 1978 only 84 percent of full-time nonfarm wage and salary workers were on day shifts. Eight percent reported working an evening shift; 3 percent worked a night shift; and 5 percent worked miscellaneous shifts. In some cases this pattern of labor supply may accord with workers' preferences. In others, the need for shift work occasioned by employers' requirements can be dealt with through either the rotation of shifts or payment of premium rates for undesirable shifts. In the United States, these premiums (unlike overtime premiums in most industries) are generally set too low to overcome worker aversion to night and split shifts; thus in the absence of rotation, these shifts are worked by the workers with least seniority or those at the greatest disadvantage in the labor market. It is not at all clear why unions have not made higher shift premiums a more important goal in bargaining or why employers have resisted offering them as a way of inducing more skilled workers to work the less desirable shifts.

Working the standard workweek or more on the same job is the apparent preference of the majority of labor-force participants. As Table 2.3 showed, though, a large and increasing fraction of them works less than the 35 hours per week that form the minimum standard workweek in the United States. Of the 24.3 million people who worked part-time in May 1982, 11.9 million usually worked part-time and did not want or could not accept full-time jobs. Thus 11 percent of the labor force (which was 109.9 million people in that month) voluntarily chose work hours less than the standard workweek. Of the remaining 12.4 million part-time workers, only 2.3 million wanted a regular full-time job but could only find a part-time job. Most of the rest were regular full-time workers who worked short hours in that particular week for reasons such as illness or temporary slack work.

The part-time work force consists disproportionately of women with young children, teenagers, and older women. Relatively few married men or prime-age (25 to 54 years old) women without young children are part-time workers.[21] These demographic differences in the incidence of part-time work are important.[22] Yet even accounting for their impact, purely economic forces play a major part in the choice of whether to work part- or full-time. One study suggests that a 1 percent increase in the wage paid for an hour of part-time work will induce a 5 percent increase in the supply of part-time workers relative to the number of full-time workers. Another finds that the total elasticity of hours supplied is twice as large for married women in part-time work as it is for those in full-time jobs.[23] These responses seem large; they reinforce the observation that the supply of hours of people with a relatively loose attachment to the labor force is quite responsive to changes in the returns to work.

Whereas some people want to work less than the standard workweek, others want to work more. Some of these work on two jobs because they do not value leisure

[21] John Owen, *Working Hours,* Heath, Lexington, Mass., 1979, p. 67.

[22] One bank recently took advantage of these differences in preferences by offering jobs that were shared between college students and mothers of school-age children; the mothers worked from September to June, the students from June to September. *Wall Street Journal,* February 8, 1983, p. 1.

[23] Owen, op. cit., p. 84; Richard Morgenstern and William Hamovitch, "Labor Supply of Married Women in Part-Time and Full-Time Occupations," *Industrial and Labor Relations Review* (30): 59–67 (1976).

very highly and cannot work as long as they would like at their main job. If people whose behavior is described in Figure 2.7 could choose their hours freely at the wage on their main jobs, they would be able to choose any point along the line $0AW_2$. Given their preferences, the highest indifference level attainable is at point P along indifference curve I_2. If their employers do not offer more than 40 hours of work, the best they can do on their current jobs is to work 40 hours, attaining a level of satisfaction indicated by indifference curve I_0. What if second jobs become available that offer them as many hours per week as they wish, but at wage rates w_1, lower than the rates w_2 that they receive on their primary jobs? The set of choices then becomes the line $0AFW_1$; the segment FW_1 has a smaller slope than FW_2, because the wages on the jobs they are offered are less than the wages on their primary jobs. To achieve the highest satisfaction, individuals whose preferences are depicted in Figure 2.7 will choose point Q and attain an indifference level, I_1, above what they could have achieved without moonlighting. Although they are not so well off as if their primary employers allowed them to work 55 hours at the regular straight-time wage rates, their weak desire for leisure makes them better off moonlighting than not doing so. Other individuals who would work 55 hours if they could obtain a wage w_2 will not offer more than 40 hours if they can only obtain w_1. The inability to earn as high a wage on the second job adds to the clustering of hours worked around 40 that we observed in Table 2.3.

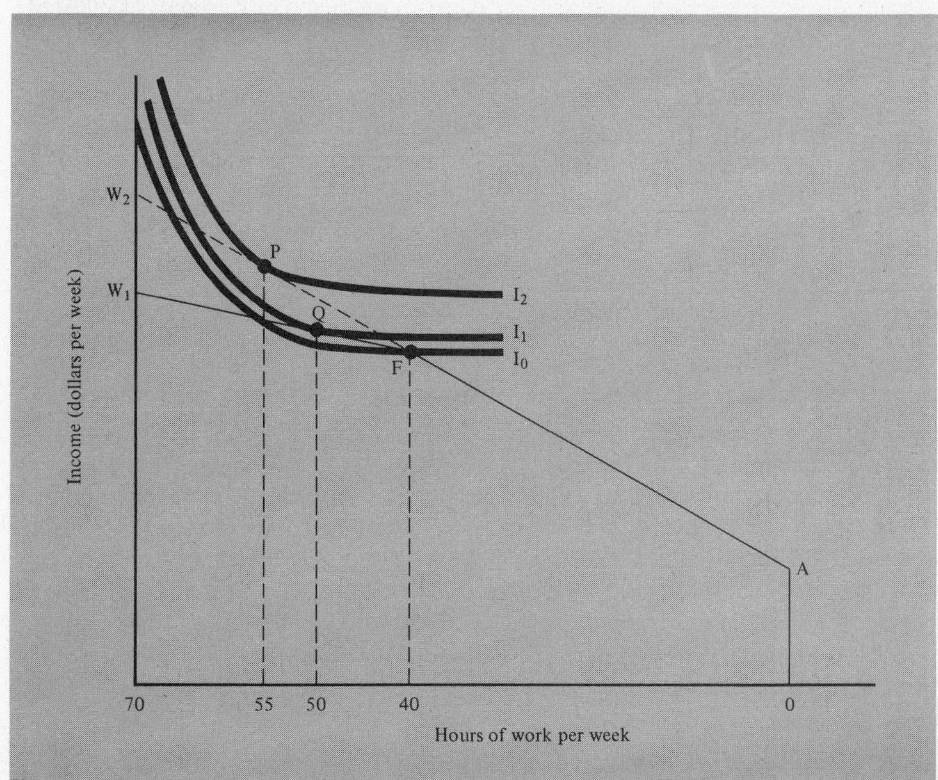

Figure 2.7 The decision to moonlight.

Table 2.6 MULTIPLE JOB HOLDING RATE, SELECTED YEARS, BY SEX AND RACE

	Total	Men	Women	Whites	Nonwhites
May 1963	5.7	7.4	2.4	5.7	5.2
May 1975	4.7	5.8	2.9	4.8	3.7
May 1978	4.8	5.8	3.3	5.0	3.1

Source: Bureau of Labor Statistics, *Multiple Jobholders in May 1978,* Special Labor Force Report No. 221, p. 59.

The situation facing people described in Figure 2.7 is not unusual among people in the labor force in the United States. As Table 2.6 shows, nearly 5 percent of workers moonlight in any particular week. The incidence of moonlighting is much higher among men than among women and is higher for whites than for nonwhites. In 1978, 8.3 percent of employees in education, 9.1 percent of postal workers, 9.3 percent of state and local government employees, and 11.9 percent of male protective service workers, largely police and guards, held second jobs. Even accounting for demographic and occupational differences, though, economic factors do affect the amount of moonlighting. Data for 1969 show that the wage rate on the second job was 6 percent below that on the primary job. Presumably the wage rates on other jobs that those who chose not to moonlight could have obtained were even further below their primary wage rates. A lower wage rate on the second job, a higher wage rate on the primary job, and higher nonlabor income all decrease the number of hours of moonlighting work.[24] Each of these three effects is predicted by the analysis in Figure 2.7. (For example, higher nonlabor income produces a negative income effect that lowers hours of work.)

Comparing 1963 and 1978, Table 2.6 shows that the incidence of moonlighting has decreased in total, even though it has increased among women. This reflects the overall trend toward increased demand for leisure, as well as the increased commitment of women to the labor market. Moonlighting decreases during recessions, as the data for May 1975 show. This suggests that moonlighting is partly determined by employers' demand for labor as well as by workers' preferences for scheduling their work hours.

THE SUPPLY OF EFFORT

All this discussion of the supply of hours has referred to scheduled hours (hours paid for) or to hours spent at the workplace. Each hour at work has been treated as if it measured the same amount of effort being offered, and thus the same *effective supply* of labor. In reality this may not be the case. If workers are erratic in their attendance at the workplace, their productivity per hour on the job will be less than that of otherwise identical workers, and their cost to their employers may be greater, too. The employer may be forced to maintain a larger work force merely to prevent operations from being slowed down by an unexpectedly large number of absentee workers on a particular day. Table 2.5 showed that sick leave accounted for over 1 percent of wage and salary costs; another estimate puts total absenteeism (both paid and unpaid) in 1976 at 3.5 percent of scheduled work hours.[25]

[24] Robert Shishko and Bernard Rostker, "The Economics of Multiple Job Holding," *American Economic Review* (66): 306 (1976).

[25] Janice Hedges, "Absence from Work: Measuring Hours Lost," *Monthly Labor Review* (100): 16–23 (1977).

Illness and pressing personal business are common reasons for absenteeism. In a sample of workers in 1972, those whose health was worse were more likely to be absent; and the requirement of a fixed work schedule was also associated with a greater likelihood of being absent. Economic factors are important as well. To the extent that the supply curve of labor is upward-sloping, we should expect absenteeism to be lower where the wage rate is higher. Accounting for the presence of paid time off, and holding skill level constant, the absentee rate decreases by 5 percent for each 10 percent increase in the wage rate.[26]

While at work effort need not be the same among otherwise identical workers, and it may vary with the length of the workday itself. The pace of work should be faster where hours are short than where they are long, since a worker cannot sustain an intense pace for long periods. There should also be an increase, within some range, in the intensity of work as real wages rise. Where real wages are very low, a wage increase may call forth a greater supply of effort simply because better paid workers will have a more adequate diet and better medical care, and will therefore, for essentially biological reasons, be able to work harder.[27] This effect can no longer be of any appreciable importance in developed countries, where the wages of almost all fully employed workers permit an adequate, if not necessarily an appealing diet.

For developed countries the main effect of the level of wages on the supply of effort probably operates through the kind of supervision exercised by management. If labor is cheap, the costs of a leisurely work pace are not too great. If labor is expensive, the employer will take greater care to see that it is not wasted. However, the extent to which the pace of work can be controlled by supervision is limited by custom and the protective role of the trade union. Attempts to force a pace of work that workers regard as unreasonable, even though it is one that has been achieved elsewhere, can lead to resistance of various forms, including failure to carry out the work properly. This is true in nonunion as well as unionized establishments.

The pace of work can also be influenced by the use of piecework or other incentive payment schemes. Where the pace of work is under the control of the individual worker, as in sewing garments or picking fruits and vegetables, individual piece rates are frequently used. Where cooperation among workers is important, various kinds of group incentives covering departments, establishments, or whole enterprises may be used. Piece-rate payment mechanisms do seem to elicit more output. Some estimates indicate that piece-rate workers receive between 7 and 15 percent higher pay than their otherwise identical time-rated counterparts in the same occupation and industry; another study showed that their output per hour is about 15 percent higher.[28] Whether these differences really arise from greater effort by those workers who are paid on a piece-rate basis, or because the more able and energetic workers choose jobs in plants that offer piece-rate pay, is unknown. What is clear, though, is that piece-rate pay schemes have been of declining importance in those

[26]Steven Allen, "An Empirical Model of Work Attendance," *Review of Economics and Statistics* (63): 77–87 (1981).

[27]The relation of this case to the demand for labor is considered in Chapter 5.

[28]John Pencavel, "Work Effort, On-the-Job Screening, and Alternative Methods of Remuneration," *Research in Labor Economics* (1): 245 (1977); Eric Seiler, "Piece Rate vs. Time Rate: The Effect of Incentives on Earnings," Working Paper No. 879, National Bureau of Economic Research, Cambridge, Mass., 1982; John Cable and Felix FitzRoy, "Productive Efficiency, Incentives and Employee Participation: Some Preliminary Results for West Germany," *Kyklos* (33): 100–121 (1980).

industries where they have been used.[29] This may reflect the increased difficulty of identifying an individual worker's contribution to output as production processes become more capital-intensive.

It is true that the distribution of total earnings is much wider within a narrow industry among workers who receive incentive pay than among those paid by the hour.[30] Even this greater dispersion, however, may be less than what would arise if each worker were free to respond to purely monetary incentives. The supply of effort is generally regulated by the work group in both union and nonunion situations.[31] This regulation arises from the desire to prevent less able workers from being shown up as inadequate or lazy and to prevent the employer from making the achievements of a few into a standard for all. The control often takes the form of a quota of work or *bogey* that no one is to exceed; those who do may be ostracized or even threatened with physical harm. Workers who have completed their quota may appear to keep busy at work or may be permitted to play cards or take other forms of leisure on the job, such as long coffee breaks. If technical change makes a job easier, traditional work quotas can become unreasonably low. In such circumstances the employer often attempts to renegotiate the effort bargain by offering other advantages in return for a more reasonable work pace.

Group restrictions on the pace of work can also be present when payment is according to time worked and not directly related to output. In such cases the motive may be the fear of using up the available work too quickly and working oneself out of a job. Restrictive practices arising from this kind of fear should diminish under sustained full employment.

The presence of leisure on the job illustrates the difficulty of making a strict separation between working time and nonworking time. Those inclined to be indignant about the restriction of output by manual workers should remember that every occupational group has its own way of combining work and leisure. Data on time use while at work in 1976 show that 69 percent of workers reported taking some time in unscheduled breaks, including long lunch hours, socializing on the job, and so on; and the average length among those reporting this form of on-the-job leisure was 27 minutes per week. By occupation group, however, professionals and managers were most likely to take some amount of informal break time, although their breaks were shorter than those of skilled craft workers. Unskilled workers were least likely to take breaks, and those who did spent less time on break.[32]

SUMMARY

Hours of work in developed nations have been decreasing since 1900, even though the rate of decline has been slower since World War II. This decrease reflects the predominance of the income effect of higher wage rates on the demand for leisure

[29] Norma Carlson, "Time Rates Tighten Their Grip on Manufacturing Industries," *Monthly Labor Review* (105): 15–22 (1982).

[30] Seiler, loc. cit.

[31] For a classic study of such restriction, see Stanley Mathewson, *Restriction of Output Among Unorganized Workers,* Viking, New York, 1931.

[32] Frank Stafford and Greg Duncan, "The Use of Time and Technology by Households in the United States," *Research in Labor Economics* (3): 346 (1980).

over the substitution effect. At a point in time, though, higher wage rates do elicit a greater supply of hours from most workers. This is especially true among married women with young children and among younger workers and workers nearing retirement. For these groups both income and substitution effects seem to be quite large, with the substitution effect being the bigger of the two. Among prime-age males and females without children, the income and substitution effects of higher wage rates are roughly offsetting.

Fewer than half of all workers in the United States work a 40-hour per week schedule. Part-time work and moonlighting are widely prevalent, and the number of workers who do not work the standard workweek is quite sensitive to the wage rates paid for part-time work or for second jobs. Among those with a scheduled standard workweek, many work overtime, with more workers seeking such extra hours, the greater is the premium paid for them. Absenteeism and unscheduled work breaks increase the difference between reported and actual hours and widen the diversity in hours supplied within the employed population.

chapter 3

The Supply of Skill: Investment in Human Capital

AN OVERVIEW

In addition to their mere presence at the workplace and willingness to work, almost all workers bring to their jobs some skill and experience. Skills are acquired through either schooling or experience, accompanied by formal or informal on-the-job training; both schooling and on-the-job training are forms of investment in *human capital.* Human capital can be defined as all acquired characteristics of workers that make them more productive. Other forms of investment in human capital include expenditures to improve workers' health, time spent acquiring information about jobs, and the costs of migration to a labor market where employment opportunities are better. The first of these will not be considered explicitly; treatment of the others is deferred to Chapters 6 and 7.

In most of the discussion we equate schooling with the acquisition of skills. Whether this equation is correct is the subject of much debate to which we turn later in the chapter. Even if it is only partly valid, it suggests the importance of analyzing investment in human capital to help determine how much of its resources a society should devote to schooling and training relative to investment in other areas such as research and development or physical capital (structures and machines). The analysis helps us consider who should pay for investment in schooling—the students and their parents, or society. Also, it enables us to understand some of the causes of differences in wage rates among workers.

The importance of historical changes in skill levels is suggested by the changes in the occupational distribution shown in Table 3.1. Since 1900 there has been a sharp decline in the proportion of the work force who are farm workers or nonfarm laborers and a striking growth in the number of workers in white-collar occupations, especially professional, technical, and clerical workers. The proportion of males who are skilled craftsmen has also grown.

Table 3.1 PERCENTAGE DISTRIBUTION OF WORKERS BY MAJOR OCCUPATION GROUP, 1900, 1950, and 1982[a]

	1900	1950	1982
Males			
White-collar workers			
Professional and technical workers	3.4	7.2	16.5
Managers, proprietors, and officials	6.8	10.5	14.7
Clerical workers	2.8	6.4	6.3
Sales workers	4.6	6.4	6.4
Blue-collar workers			
Craft and kindred workers	12.6	19.0	20.3
Operatives	10.3	20.6	15.4
Nonfarm laborers	14.7	8.8	7.1
Service workers			
Private household workers	0.2	0.2	0.1
Other service workers	2.9	6.0	9.2
Farm workers			
Farmers and farm managers	23.0	10.0	2.3
Farm laborers and supervisors	18.7	4.9	1.7
Total	100.0	100.0	100.0
Females			
White-collar workers			
Professional and technical workers	8.2	12.2	17.7
Managers, proprietors, and officials	1.4	4.3	7.4
Clerical workers	4.0	27.4	34.4
Sales workers	4.3	8.6	6.9
Blue-collar workers			
Craft and kindred workers	1.4	1.5	2.0
Operatives	23.7	20.0	9.6
Nonfarm laborers	2.6	0.9	1.2
Service workers			
Private household workers	28.7	8.9	2.3
Other service workers	6.7	12.6	17.3
Farm workers			
Farmers and farm managers	5.9	0.7	0.4
Farm laborers and supervisors	13.1	2.9	0.7
Total	100.0	100.0	100.0

[a]The base of these percentages differs for each year. In 1900 it is all gainful workers (those having a usual occupation); in 1950 it is the labor force 14 years of age and older, which includes the employed and the unemployed; in 1982 it is employed workers 16 years of age and older. These changes in the base are not large enough to affect the major trends appreciably.

Source: Gertrude Bancroft, *The American Labor Force: Its Growth and Changing Composition*, Wiley, New York, 1958, Table D-2, and *Employment and Training Report of the President*, 1981, Table A-19. *Employment and Earnings*, January 1983, p. 157.

Table 3.2 MEDIAN YEARS OF SCHOOL COMPLETED BY THE CIVILIAN LABOR FORCE, SELECTED DATES 1952–1980

	Both sexes	Male	Female
October 1952[a]	10.9	10.4	12.0
March 1962[a]	12.1	12.0	12.2
March 1972[b]	12.4	12.4	12.4
March 1980[b]	12.7	12.7	12.6

[a]Data relate to people 18 years old and over.

[b]Data relate to people 16 years old and over. Figures for March 1972 are available on both bases; they differ by only 0.1 years for females and for both sexes, and are identical for males.

Source: Employment and Training Report of the President, 1981, Table B-14.

A second way of looking at the growth of skills is illustrated in Table 3.2, which gives the median educational attainment of the labor force, and thus provides a measure of the average level of schooling brought to the workplace. These data are available on a consistent basis only for the years since 1952. The average member of the labor force in 1980, however, had completed almost 2 more years of school than had his or her counterpart in 1952; for males alone the gain was more than 2 years.

This rapid increase in educational attainment has not been uniform across the work force. Among white males, the increase between 1962 and 1980 was only 0.6 years of schooling; among black males, the difference was an astonishing 3.3 years. The figures for females are also strikingly different: Among whites, an increase of 0.4 years on average; among blacks, an increase of 1.9 years. Although separate data on Hispanics as compared to other whites do not extend back beyond 1970, the increase in median years of schooling attained by Hispanics between 1970 and 1980 was at least 1.5 years, far larger than that achieved by other whites. In the 1960s and 1970s in the United States, there was a very rapid convergence in educational attainment by race and ethnic origin. This occurred because young, better educated blacks and Hispanics took the place of their poorly educated elders who retired from the labor force.

The proposition that a trained worker, like a machine, represents a valuable investment is an old one in the history of economics, going back to the eighteenth century. The point was best expressed by Adam Smith, who wrote:

> When any expensive machine is erected, the extraordinary work to be performed by it before it is worn out, it must be expected, will replace the capital laid out upon it, with at least the ordinary profits. A man educated at the expense of much labor and time to any of those employments which require extraordinary dexterity and skill, may be compared to one of those expensive machines. The work which he learns to perform, it must be expected, over and above the usual wages of common labor will replace to him the whole expense of his education, with at least the ordinary profits of an equally valuable capital. It must do this too in a reasonable time, regard being had to the very uncertain duration of human life, in the same manner as to the more certain duration of the machine.[1]

[1]Adam Smith, *The Wealth of Nations,* Random House, New York, 1937, bk. 1, chap. 10.

Both in the case of a worker and of a machine, making the investment requires a sacrifice of current consumption in order to increase future output. More precise analysis of the nature and role of human capital is quite recent.[2]

The market for human capital differs from that for physical capital in that human capital is always rented rather than sold (except, historically, for slave economies). The market is for the services of the capital rather than for the capital stock or capital goods. This is the major reason that most of the investment in schooling is made by students or their families and much of the rest is made by governments or such nonprofit institutions as foundations and universities. Commercial interests invest very little in schooling, although in the United States there has been a recent growth in bank loans to finance college education, partly because the federal government subsidizes the interest on them. It is sometimes asserted that the nontransferability of property rights in human capital (i.e., the prohibition of slavery) inhibits the development of a commercial market for investment in people. This suggests that losses through default are expected to be higher on loans without collateral to finance college education than on loans with physical or financial collateral, although there does not appear to be any evidence that they actually are higher. No stock market for investment in people has developed. Such investment would take the form of loans to students, which would be repaid, not in the form of principal plus stated interest but as some fraction of the students' earnings after graduation. The difficulty confronted by such a plan if it is voluntary is that those students who expect high earnings will choose to take conventional loans, and thus the plan faces an adverse selection of entrants.[3]

Skills acquired by schooling beyond the legally required minimum are supplied by people who voluntarily take additional schooling at a cost to themselves in return for higher money income or satisfaction in later years. Increasing the supply of skills acquired through schooling requires that private costs be lowered, that the extra earnings of those who have attained extra schooling be increased, or that there be other improvements in the prestige or satisfactions of skilled work.

SKILLS ACQUIRED AT SCHOOL

Private Monetary Incentives to Invest

In order to study the effect of investment in schooling on earnings we make use of age-earnings profiles, which show the average hourly or annual earnings in a cross

[2] See especially T. W. Schultz, "Investment in Human Capital," *American Economic Review* (51): 1–17 (1961), and Gary Becker, *Human Capital: A Theoretical and Empirical Analysis, with Special Reference to Education,* National Bureau of Economic Research, New York, 1964.

[3] Despite this difficulty, at least one university established such an arrangement. In 1971 Yale University offered students a chance to defer tuition, with each $1000 of tuition deferred repayable by 0.4 percent of the student's annual earnings from graduation until death. The economics of this type of plan are analyzed by Karl Shell, Franklin Fisher, Duncan Foley, and Ann Friedlaender, "The Educational Opportunity Bank: An Economic Analysis of A Contingent Repayment Loan Program for Higher Education," *National Tax Journal* (21): 2–47 (1968), and by Marc Nerlove, "Some Problems in the Use of Income-Contingent Loans for the Finance of Higher Education," *Journal of Political Economy* (83): 157–183 (1975). The idea stems from Milton Friedman, "The Role of Government in Education," in Robert Solo (ed.). *Economics and the Public Interest,* Rutgers, New Brunswick, N.J., 1955.

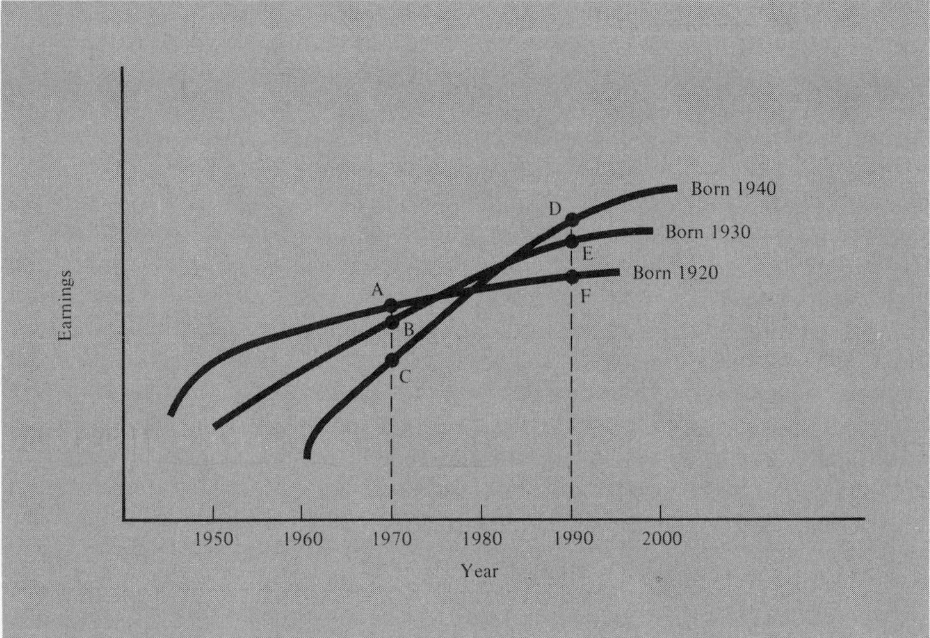

Figure 3.1 Cohort age-earnings profiles.

section of people of different ages who have had the same amount of schooling. Such profiles typically show that both hourly and annual earnings are lowest among young workers, highest among workers in middle life, and somewhat lower among older workers. Those approaching retirement may also have lower annual earnings because they choose to work fewer hours per year.

We are not suggesting that the earnings of a given *cohort* of individuals (a group of workers born in the same year) decline through time after middle age, but only that they are less than those of the next younger cohort. This process is depicted in Figure 3.1 for three cohorts of workers born in 1920, 1930, and 1940. This figure is a stylized version of the patterns of growth in earnings that have been observed over shorter periods of time for different cohorts in the United States.[4] As the figure shows, earnings rise throughout the work life of each cohort. Viewed in 1970, the members of the oldest cohort earn A, which exceeds B and C that are earned by the younger cohorts. This is consistent with the data in Table 3.3, showing higher earnings for 50-year-olds than for 40- and 30-year-olds. In 1990, even though each worker's earnings have risen through time, workers in the youngest (1940) cohort earn D, more than E earned by those in the 1930 cohort, and more than F earned by those in the 1920 cohort. In 1990, 50-year-olds earn more than 60-year-olds who earn more than 70-year-olds; this, too, is roughly consistent with the observation that age-earnings profiles at a point in time are shaped like an inverted U. Note that we deal here

[4]See Nancy Ruggles and Richard Ruggles, "The Anatomy of Earnings Behavior," in F. Thomas Juster (ed.). *The Distribution of Economic Well-Being,* Ballinger, Cambridge, Mass., 1977.

Table 3.3 MEAN EARNINGS OF MALES, YEAR-ROUND FULL-TIME WORKERS, BY AGE AND EDUCATIONAL ATTAINMENT, 1980

	Years of school completed				
Age in 1980	8	12	College 1–3	College graduate	Professional or graduate degree
18–24	$ 9,892	$12,527	$12,888	$14,182	—
25–29	12,190	16,339	16,858	18,692	$20,007
30–34	13,355	18,611	19,889	22,902	25,541
35–39	15,269	20,124	23,478	27,878	31,809
40–44	15,586	20,916	23,243	30,078	34,045
45–49	15,792	21,307	25,429	32,266	38,317
50–54	16,594	21,171	25,147	34,452	36,788
55–59	15,504	20,912	24,257	33,982	36,103
60–64	14,451	18,834	23,039	31,229	37,449
65+	12,918	14,594	16,866	30,026	31,591

Source: U.S. Bureau of the Census, *Money Income of Persons and Families in the United States, 1980,* Current Population Report, P-60, No. 132, Table 52.

and throughout with changes over the lifetime in *real earnings;* inflation-induced changes are assumed to be removed from all the effects we discuss.

Age-earnings profiles for five levels of schooling are shown for 1980 in Table 3.3. These are for year-round full-time workers only, so that any effect of education on the fraction of time spent not working, through differences in labor-force participation or time spent unemployed, is excluded. In other words, these are pure effects on wage rates. Notice that the mean earnings at each age increase with educational attainment. Moreover, the differences between education groups "fan out" as people age: The ratio of earnings of a college graduate to those of a high school graduate is much higher when they are both 50 than when they are 25 (1.62 versus 1.14). Finally, among all but the most educated group, full-time earnings are lower for people above age 59 than for those 55 to 59.

These facts and the process of investment in schooling are illustrated in Figure 3.2 for the case of a decision about attending college for 4 years. The figure is drawn for people in one age cohort; but the age-earnings profiles are based on cross-section profiles like those in Table 3.3. Money earnings and the out-of-pocket costs of education to the individual (tuition, books, and so on) are measured on the vertical axis; age is measured on the horizontal axis. (For clarity, the scale for the college years, 18 to 22, is twice as large as it should be relative to the length of working life after college.) Curves A and B are the age-earnings profiles of two workers. Worker B enters the labor market at age 18 on graduation from high school and works until retirement at age 65. Worker A attends college, incurring out-of-pocket costs for 4 years. These costs are shown by the position of the left end of curve A, which lies below zero on the vertical axis. In addition, A forgoes the earnings made by B, which A could have earned from the time of labor-force entry at 18. Areas 1 and 2 are the sum of the actual dollars of forgone earnings and the out-of-pocket costs; they are the cost of the investment in college education. In practice, earnings from jobs during vacations and part-time jobs during the school year may offset part of the out-of-

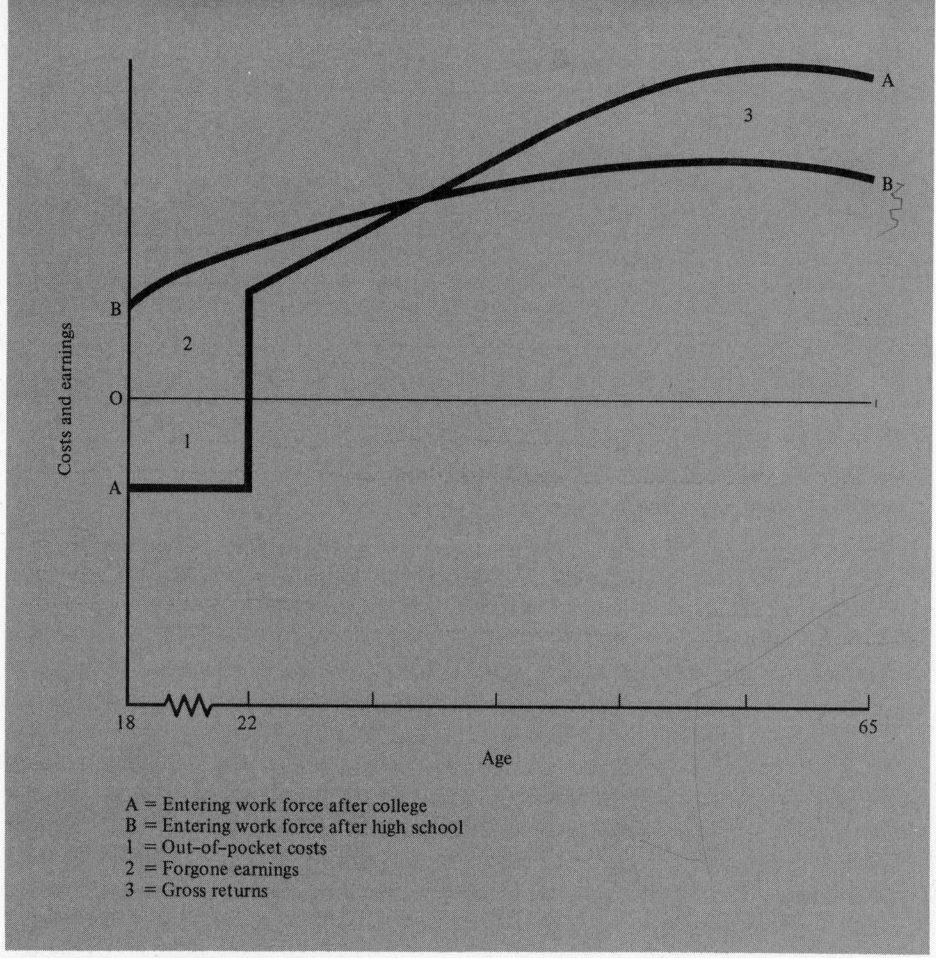

Figure 3.2 Investment in schooling.

pocket costs. The cost of subsistence while in school should not be included, unless subsistence is higher in college than while not enrolled. To count both subsistence, and forgone earnings would be double counting, since B also has costs of subsistence, which are paid out of earnings.

In general, forgone earnings represent a much larger part of the *private costs of education* (those incurred by students and their families) than do out-of-pocket costs. In the early 1980s, the annual cost of books, tuition, and other requirements of attending public universities in the United States rarely exceeded $3000, whereas the average annual earnings of high-school graduates aged 18 to 24, which represent forgone earnings to a college student, were $8400 in 1980. (Among full-time year-round workers aged 18 to 24 who were high school graduates, average earnings were $12,500.) Even for students attending the most expensive private colleges and universities the direct costs are no larger than the forgone earnings. These observations imply that differences in the direct cost of attending college will not have a very large effect on people's decisions about going or not going to college. One study showed that doubling tuition reduces the likelihood of attending college, but only by 14 percent; doubling the cost of travel to college and of room and board reduced college attendance by only 5 percent.[5]

POLICY ISSUE—GUARANTEED LOANS FOR COLLEGE STUDENTS

The small effects of higher tuition and costs of travel and room and board on decisions about attending college indicate that it would be necessary to provide stipends or grants to college students to replace forgone earnings in order to induce sharply increased enrollment. The federal government does not provide such grants in the United States (although national governments do in many other developed countries). Instead, it guarantees loans by private lenders, essentially providing students a subsidy in the form of an interest rate lower than the market is charging for equally risky loans. From 1981 to 1982 private lenders made $6.1 billion worth of student loans, aiding 2.8 million students.

To recipients of this federal largesse, no doubt it seems a wise policy. As usual, however, there are both efficiency and equity considerations. Do the loans enable students to attend college who otherwise would not? There is evidence that loans allow students to spend less time working for pay; this should enable them to learn more and complete their studies more rapidly.[6] To the extent society gains from the students' accomplishing this (which we discuss later in this section), the student loan program adds to economic efficiency. The equity effects may be less favorable to the program. State-supported higher education may have regressive effects on the distribution of real income. Most of the evidence suggests that the benefits to higher-income families—parents and the children who themselves will be in the upper part of the distribution of income—are more than proportional to their share of taxes that finance the cost of higher education.[7] Although federal taxes are more progressive than state taxes, it is likely that they too do not compensate for the higher propensity of children of more affluent families to attend college and avail themselves of subsidized student loans. As is often the case, there is a trade-off between equity and efficiency. The Reagan administration's stringent requirements for borrowing by students whose family incomes are above $30,000 may have removed some of the program's tilt in favor of higher-income families.

As Figure 3.2 is drawn, A's earnings on entering the labor market do not immediately equal B's. B has meanwhile been receiving on-the-job training, which, as we discuss later in this chapter, also affects the age-earnings profile. The forgone earnings associated with attending college thus extend beyond the actual period of attendance. This is not a necessary feature of the diagram; it could have been drawn so that A's earnings were greater than or equal to B's earnings from the time of A's entry into the labor force.

At some time after entry into the labor force A's earnings catch up and overtake B's, and remain higher from then on. Area 3, lying below A's profile and above B's, to

[5]John Bishop, "The Effect of Public Policies on the Demand for Higher Education," *Journal of Human Resources* (12): 285–307 (1977).

[6]Thomas Johnson, "Time in School: The Case of the Prudent Patron," *American Economic Review* (68): 862–872 (1978), demonstrates this on a small sample of persons who graduated from high school in 1971.

[7]For results from Florida, see Douglas Windham, *Education, Equality and Income Redistribution*, Heath, Lexington, Mass., 1970; for a study using data from California, which has the largest system of public higher education in the United States, see W. Lee Hansen and Burton Weisbrod, *Benefits, Costs and Finance of Public Higher Education*, Markham, Chicago, 1969.

the right of the point where they cross, is the *gross return* on college education, the excess of the actual dollars earned by A. It might be more realistic to assume also that the person with more education will retire later (see Chap. 1). However, the added earnings would come at the end of working life and would be so distant as to have little effect on decisions at age 18 about how much education to acquire. Nonetheless, with a sufficiently large change in the length of the expected work life, people's willingness to invest in skills through formal education will be affected. When the average teenager did not expect to live beyond age 50, there was a much shorter period over which to reap the benefits of spending 4 years in college. With the extensions of longevity that have occurred in the past 50 years, the expected work life of young adults has increased. In developing countries this extension has been especially pronounced and seems to have contributed to a rapid expansion in the demand for investing in human capital through schooling.[8]

There are two principal methods of deciding from profiles like those in Figure 3.2 whether investment in college education is economically productive. If a student can borrow to finance an education at a known interest rate, both the costs and gross returns can be discounted back to age 18 at this interest rate to calculate the *present value* of the investment at that age. In choosing between two investment programs, an individual who seeks to maximize the economic return on investment will choose the program with the highest present value. An investment program might consist of entering the labor market after graduating from high school or of completing 4 years of college instead and then entering the labor market. The present-value formula in this case is

$$V = \sum_{i=18}^{65} \frac{Y_i^C - Y_i^H}{(1 + r)^{i-18}}$$

where V is the present value at age 18, r is the market rate of interest, and i designates age. The stream of earnings Y^C is received if the person goes to college. It is net of the cost of tuition, books, and so on; these costs may make Y^C negative during the college years. Y^H is earnings if the person goes to work full time at age 18. The difference $Y^C - Y^H$ will probably be negative, showing the cost of the investment (that profile B lies above profile A in Fig. 3.2), at least at ages 18 to 22. V is equal to the sum of discounted differences in the monetary returns from going to college as opposed to entering the labor market after high school at age 18. Calculating V allows the comparison of dollars today with dollars in the future. To be comparable to a dollar today more than $1 is required in the future. Even after accounting for inflation, one must make up for the interest one can earn if today's funds are invested in alternative ways. The higher the interest rate is, the smaller will be the present value of investing in college. Indeed, V can be negative at high interest rates even if total costs are smaller than gross returns (as they are in Fig. 3.2); the costs are all incurred before the returns begin, so the returns are discounted more heavily. Some evidence indicates that V was negative for blacks in the 1950s.[9]

[8] Rati Ram and T. W. Schultz, "Life Span, Health, Savings and Productivity," *Economic Development and Cultural Change* (27): 399–422 (1979), discuss this phenomenon in the experience of India in the past 50 years.

[9] Giora Hanoch, "An Economic Analysis of Earnings and Schooling," *Journal of Human Resources* (2): p. 322 (1967).

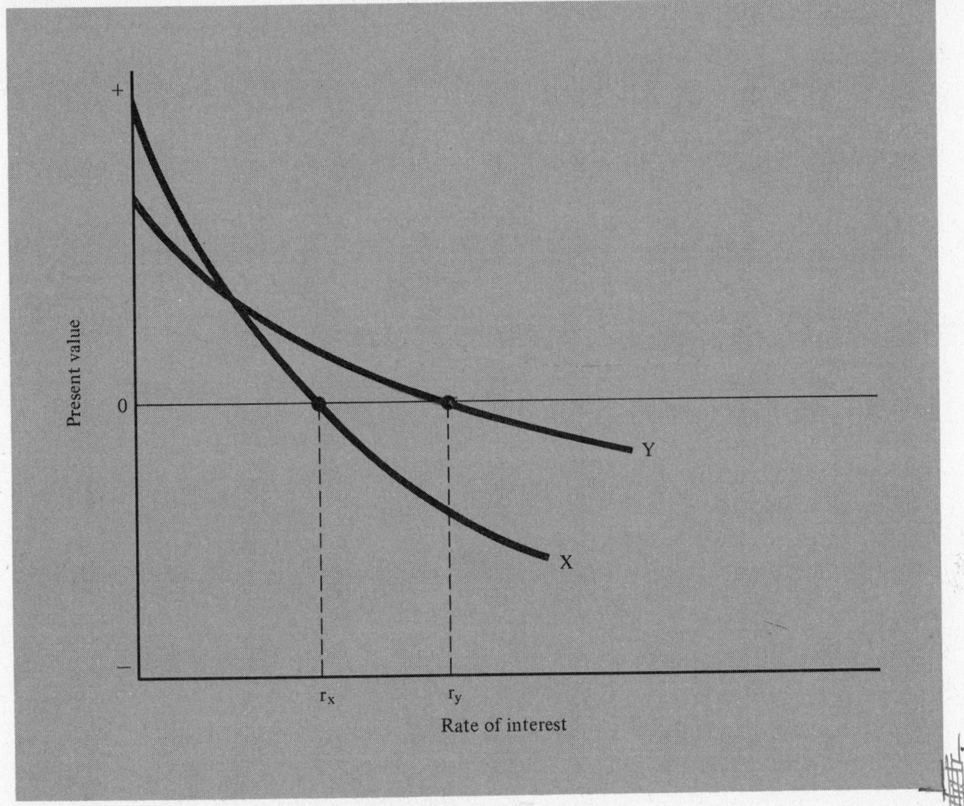

Figure 3.3 Present values of two investments.

The alternative method of calculation is to compute a rate of interest at which the present value of the investment is zero because the costs and returns are exactly equal when discounted back to age 18 at this rate. Such a rate is known as an *internal rate of return.*[10] The relation between present values and internal rates of return is shown in Figure 3.3, in which X and Y are two investment programs. The curve X might represent a 7-year college and law school program, where the alternative is high school only; curve Y might represent 4 years of college, where the alternative is high school only. On the vertical axis the intercept of the curve is the excess of undiscounted returns over undiscounted costs, since the interest rate at the vertical axis is zero. The points at which each of the curves crosses the horizontal line indicating zero present value give the two internal rates of return, r_x and r_y. The example has been chosen to illustrate the possibility that the curves can cross because of differing time patterns of costs and returns. Investment program X, with higher undiscounted net returns, has a lower internal rate of return because more of the benefits lie in the distant future. Two competing programs of investment in human capital may have internal rates of return far above the prevailing rates of return on

[10] There is no unique internal rate of return; rather, there are as many values r that make $V = 0$ as there are periods in the stream of costs and returns. Usually, though, only one calculated rate of return is economically reasonable.

investment in physical capital. Because it is hard for people to borrow to finance investment in human capital, this is quite possible. In that case the best decision is based on a comparison of their present values, V, evaluated at the market rate of interest on equally risky investments in physical capital. This is because the alternative investment to either program is to invest in physical capital yielding a market rate of return. For the average individual, this means buying assets that represent ownership of physical capital, such as shares of stock.

Investment in schooling is not always made early in life; some people go back to school toward the middle of their working lives. However, investments in human capital made late in life, whether in schooling or anything else, tend to have lower rates of return than investments made in youth. There is less working life left in which they can yield benefits, and the amount of income lost during a year spent in school is higher. Therefore, only in rare cases does an investment in the middle of one's work life yield a satisfactory rate of return. (A 27-month M.D. degree program that one American medical school offers to scientists who already have a Ph.D. is an example of such an investment opportunity.) Nevertheless, rapid technological progress in any field can make original investments in schooling obsolete by reducing the returns on past investments. With a sufficient reduction in the value of their present skills, skilled workers will seek to learn new techniques, many by going back to school in middle age.

We have treated investment in college as if it were an all-or-nothing proposition. Although students are free not to finish college, and too many exercise that choice, that decision is in most cases not a wise one. One study estimated that the return to college education as a whole is 18 percent; but the rate of return to finishing a 4-year program, if 3 years have already been completed, is 39 percent. The return to completing the third year considered alone was only 9 percent.[11] It seems unlikely that the amount actually learned increases in the fourth year; it would be more logical to expect diminishing returns to successive years in a program. The bonus for completion of a program is more likely to reflect a personal attribute, such as the determination needed to finish tasks undertaken, that is valued by employers and is more likely to be present among graduates than among dropouts. The effects of such personal attributes on the true rate of return to education are discussed later in this chapter.

Just as the returns to different years of college differ, the rate of return to college as a whole can vary over time. This requires students making decisions about whether or not to invest in education to estimate from present conditions the returns that will actually be received at some time in the future. Thus a high rate of return on college education could attract many new entrants to college, and this increased supply of college graduates would eventually eliminate the potential returns that gave rise to it. Conversely, a low rate of return deters many potential entrants from undertaking a college education. This rational response to changes in the rate of return describes the supply curve S_{1955} in Figure 3.4, relating the number of college graduates to the rate of return to college education. Corresponding to this

[11] Richard Raymond and Michael Sesnowitz, "The Returns to Higher Education: Some New Evidence," *Journal of Human Resources* (10): 149 (1975). The rate of return to the first 2 years of college was 17 percent. The fact that it is higher than the return to the third year undoubtedly reflects the completion of 2-year degree programs by a large fraction of people with just 2 years of college.

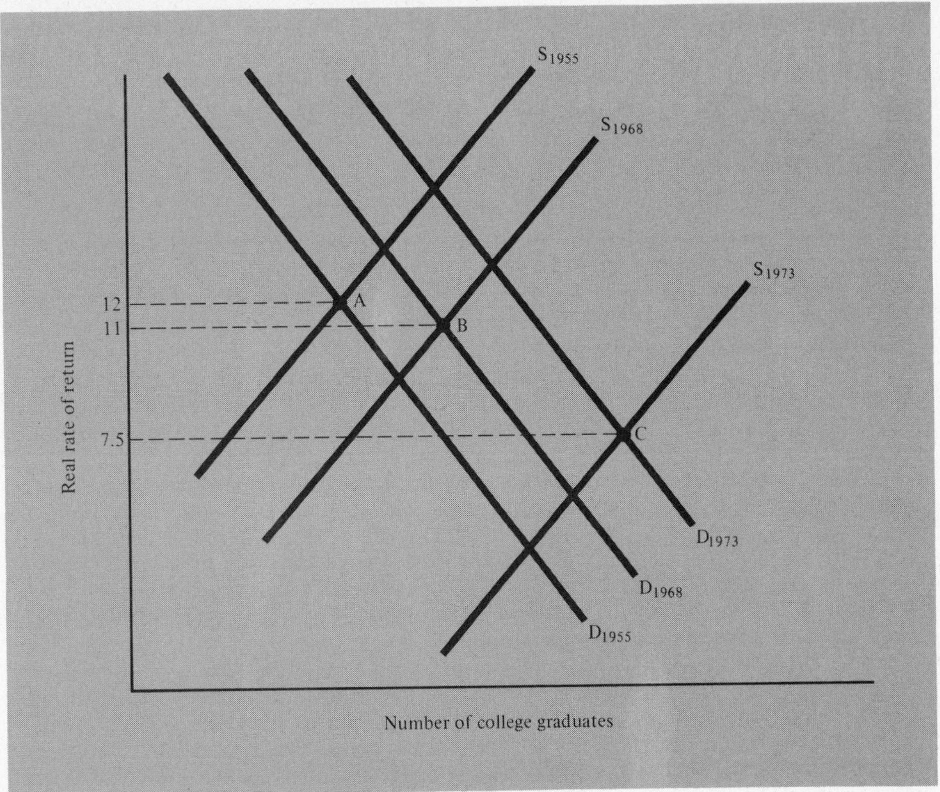

Figure 3.4 Supply and demand for college graduates.

supply curve is the demand curve D_{1955}, describing employers' desires for educated workers. For reasons to be discussed in Chapter 4 on the demand for labor, this curve slopes downward. Other things being equal, when the rate of return to schooling, which partly reflects the extra wages paid to college graduates, is higher, employers prefer to use fewer educated workers.

Point A describes the equilibrium rate of return in the United States in 1955. The rate of return for that period has been estimated at between 12 and 14 percent. Moreover, it appeared to have been roughly unchanged since the 1930s; although the supply of college graduates shifted rightward rapidly during the 1940s and 1950s, the demand shifted rightward just as fast.[12] Even with the tremendous growth of higher education during the 1960s, the rate of return was perhaps 11 percent around 1968. As shown by the intersection of S_{1968} and D_{1968}, this represented only a slight drop from earlier rates. With the continued expansion of higher education in the 1970s, though, the return fell, shown by the intersection at point C in Figure 3.4. The demand shifted outward far less rapidly than the supply, to such an extent that one observer places the rate of return only at 7.5 percent in 1973.[13] Whether the rate of

[12] Becker, op. cit., p. 128.

[13] Richard Freeman, "The Decline in the Economic Rewards to College Education," *Review of Economics and Statistics* (59): p. 28 (1977).

return has continued to drop or has leveled off in the past 10 years is unclear, but it seems unlikely that it has returned to its high level of the 1960s. Although the average American may not be overeducated, investment in a college education no longer yields a real rate of return (actual rate of return minus the rate of inflation) very far above that of corporate bonds whose return is as risky as the return to a college education.

POLICY ISSUE—HOW TO VALUE A LIFE

Late in December 1980 27-year-old Mrs. Smith left a bar in a midwestern city, walked in a stupor onto a major highway and was killed instantly. Under the "dram shop" law the bar owner was liable for damages because he had served Mrs. Smith after it was apparent she was no longer fully in control of her faculties. In assessing the damages an economist was consulted to calculate both the *earnings loss* incurred by her family as a result of her death, and the loss in the value of her services in the home.

Mrs. Smith earned $200 per week at the time of her death, but had not been working long. If we assume she had not planned to work much longer, the total loss is the value of her services at home—child care, household maintenance, and so forth. For a woman like Mrs. Smith with two small children the annual cost of replacing these services in 1980 was $11,000; the present value of the cost of replacing her services until her children are grown is $104,000.[14] This may seem like a large sum, but with young children it is only enough to pay housekeepers until the children reach age 18.

If Mrs. Smith were to have continued working until age 65, she would have contributed to the family's income over many years. She earned $10,000 in 1980; the present value of her earnings was $181,000. We saw in Chapter 1 that working wives do not work as many hours in the home as nonworking wives. Nonetheless, they do spend substantial amounts of time in child care. The present value of the cost of replacing her services at home in this case was $74,000. Assuming she would have worked until age 65, the damages resulting from her death totalled $255,000 ($181,000 plus $74,000).

Whether to assess damages of $104,000 or $255,000 has to be settled by lawyers or by the judge and jury that hear this case. The economist's role, one that is filled in many such cases each year, is to make the best estimate of the size of the loss, based on knowledge of the earnings of people with comparable skills and the evaluation of the costs of replacing services the deceased person provided at home.

Within these trends there are cycles that affect the rate of return to schooling and hence the number of high school graduates who decide to go to college. When jobs are scarce the burden falls most heavily on those with less education. The chance of unemployment becomes relatively greater for a high school than a college graduate, making the potential job security offered by a college degree more attractive. Also, the forgone earnings of attending college drop, for the high school graduate's alternatives worsen. For both those reasons the rate of return to schooling rises in recessions. That this higher return affects the supply of skill is shown by the higher enrollments typically reported at all but the most selective colleges during recessions. These indirect effects of high unemployment are reinforced by addi-

[14] Calculated from William Gauger and Kathryn Walker, *The Dollar Value of Household Work,* Cornell University College of Human Ecology, Ithaca, N.Y., 1980.

tional, direct effects, as risk-averse students stay in school when jobs become scarce.[15] Because of these cyclical factors, the high unemployment of the early 1980s should lead to at least a temporary mitigation, if not reversal, of the trend toward the decline in the rate of return to college that we described in Figure 3.4.

Private Nonmonetary Incentives to Invest

So far we have described the value of the skills acquired in school solely in monetary terms. There may also be nonmonetary returns that make schooling even more attractive and that enhance the importance of those skills. More education permits workers to avoid repetitious and physically dangerous work; but the more attractive working conditions available to the more educated worker are obtained at the price of a somewhat lower wage rate, and thus a somewhat lower monetary return to schooling than would otherwise be obtained (see Chap. 12). Accounting for the better conditions on the job obtained by more educated workers raises the rate of return to schooling by over 1 percentage point at today's rate of return on schooling.[16] So, too, more education should lead to better health and thus greater longevity, as better educated people are more aware of the kinds of behavior that contribute to good health. Death rates are slightly lower among more educated older people, independent of any effects of higher income.[17] Although no monetary value can be placed on the improved health implied by this effect, it clearly indicates that concentrating on the monetary return to schooling leads one to underestimate its total benefit to the individual.

Social Incentives to Invest and the True Return to Education

The analysis of the private rate of return can be modified to deal with social or government decisions on investment in education. Government planners would not make the same calculations that we have presented in deciding whether society should devote more resources to education. Instead, they would calculate the gross returns without deducting income and payroll taxes, since society as a whole benefits from the services bought with these taxes. The costs include expenditures on education by governments and nonprofit institutions as well as expenditures by students and their families. Comparing these gross returns to the costs yields an estimate of the *social rate of return* to the investment. Standard calculations of the

[15] Thomas Kniesner, Arthur Padilla, and Solomon Polachek, "The Rate of Return to Schooling and the Business Cycle," *Journal of Human Resources* (13): 274–275 (1978), and J. Peter Mattila, "Determinants of Male School Enrollment: A Time-Series Analysis," *Review of Economics and Statistics* (64): 242–251 (1982).

[16] Robert E. B. Lucas, "Hedonic Wage Equations and Psychic Wages in the Returns to Schooling," *American Economic Review* (67): 549–558 (1977).

[17] Using data from the March 1973 Current Population Survey matched to subsequent Social Security records, Sherwin Rosen and Paul Taubman, "Changes in the Impact of Education and Income on Mortality in the U.S.," in U.S. Department of Health, Education and Welfare, Social Security Administration, *Statistical Uses of Administrative Records,* Washington, 1979, demonstrate this relationship. The effect is clearer when one makes some standardization for ability, as Michael Grossman, "The Correlation Between Health and Schooling," in Nestor Terleckyj (ed.), *Household Production and Consumption,* Columbia University Press, New York, 1975, shows.

social rate of return to college education suggest it is several percentage points higher than the *private rate of return* we have discussed so far.[18] This is partly because the progressive income tax causes the additional returns to society—in the form of higher taxes—to be a greater proportion of the total returns, the more education is attained, and the higher pretax earnings are as a result.

In viewing social decisions one should also take into account that education may produce better informed and more responsible citizens, as well as simply producing better workers. Such arguments suggest that the return on education calculated from earnings is a minimum return—the lower bound of a true overall return. This implies that educational programs whose calculated return is very low should not necessarily be discontinued. An extreme case is offered by a few long programs of training for occupations with low earnings, such as the ministry. For training in theology, calculated present values based on monetary rewards are substantially negative, but substantial nonpecuniary benefits may be involved.[19] They may make the true rates of return, both social and private, positive.

Critics of the calculation of the social rate of return on education from subsequent earnings argue that not all the higher earnings of educated people represent their higher productivity. One argument is that a diploma, especially one from a school or college with high prestige, is simply a way to get a preferred place in the queue for scarce, highly paid jobs. It is argued that the successful applicants are selected by previous graduates of the same schools or similar ones on the basis of loyalty and friendship rather than on the basis of performance. If this *old-school tie hypothesis* were a good description of reality, the true social rate of return on higher education would be negative. Costs are incurred by society, but there is no gain in productivity or in employers' ability to find the workers who are inherently more able.

A more important criticism is that schooling is merely a way in which individuals with traits that employers find attractive are sorted into those jobs that pay higher wages. Four years spent in college may be a way of demonstrating to employers that the graduates have the self-discipline, the motivation, and the ability to perform well on the job. If this is true, the resources devoted to investment in that education may produce a high private rate of return, for the investment enables those who acquire the schooling to reap high earnings later in life. The social rate of return, though, may be negative: The only socially productive function of schooling in this case is to provide information to employers about which young people will make good workers.

A variant on the *screening hypothesis* points out how students' decisions about attending college are affected by employers' willingness to pay more to workers who have jumped the educational hurdle.[20] In this view, education functions as an acquired *signal* to employers of people's inherent ability. Consider a world in which there are two equal-size groups of workers, one of which (Dull) is naturally less productive than the other (Bright). The dull workers will produce an amount that

[18] Freeman, op. cit., p. 28.

[19] See David Stager, "Monetary Returns to Post-Secondary Education in Ontario," doctoral dissertation, Princeton University, Princeton, N.J., 1968.

[20] Michael Spence, *Market Signaling,* Harvard University Press, Cambridge, Mass., 1974.

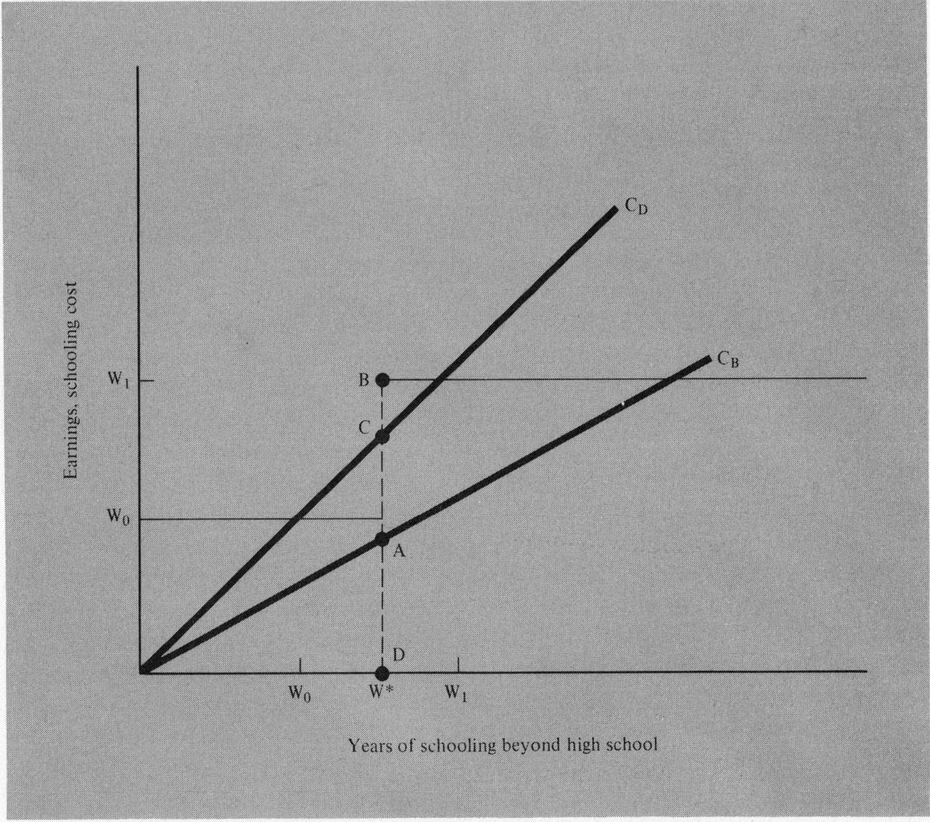

Figure 3.5 Educational signaling.

would justify a wage of W_0 in Figure 3.5; the bright workers will produce an amount justifying a wage W_1, twice W_0, because they are inherently that much more productive. If employers cannot distinguish between workers of the two types, there is no way to keep the less productive workers from obtaining the high-paying jobs that only the more productive workers would obtain if the employer could monitor individual workers' productivity.

If it takes the dull workers more effort to succeed in school (the costs, psychic and monetary, of schooling are greater for them), it pays the bright workers to use education as a signal that separates them from the less productive workers. Assume that the dull workers' cost of acquiring schooling is denoted by C_D in Figure 3.5, and the bright workers' by C_B. Assume the years of schooling beyond high school cost just what they return in discounted lifetime earnings. If employers set a hiring standard of W* and only offer high-paying (wage rate of W_1) jobs to workers who attain this level of schooling, the market for education will be in equilibrium. Dull workers will obtain no post-high school education; their net return is then W_0. If they obtain W* years of schooling, they receive a wage of W_1, but they incur a cost of CD. Since the difference between returns and costs is BC, which is less than W_0, they will not bother with further schooling. The bright workers can acquire W* years of extra schooling at a cost only of AD. If they do so they earn a gross wage of W_1; their net wage is the difference between that and the costs, or BA. Since this exceeds W_0, it pays them to make the investment in education.

In the world described by Figure 3.5, and by the screening hypothesis more generally, education merely enables employers to separate out productive from unproductive workers and prevent the unproductive ones from obtaining jobs that would pay them more than the value of what they produce. Education is productive in that it adds to the efficiency of the *market* by sorting workers into jobs. It is not productive in the way implied by human capital theory, for it does not add to the ability of an *individual worker* to produce more. Whether formal education is a sufficiently efficient signal to justify all the resources devoted to it is not clear.

If the most able people also get the most education, some part of the estimated return to education is in fact a return to ability. Colleges use such criteria as high school grades and scores on the Scholastic Aptitude Test in deciding which applicants to admit. The successful applicants might be those who would have earned higher incomes because of their intelligence even if they had never gone to college. If all people with average SAT scores over 500, and only such people, went to college, we would be unable to distinguish between the hypotheses that there is a positive rate of return to college education and that there is a positive return to ability as measured by SAT tests. In fact, however, the problem is not nearly this bad, because the correlation between ability measures and years of schooling is far from perfect. Some very able high school students do not go to college and some who are not so able do go.

Not surprisingly, given the importance of this issue for educational policy, substantial effort has been devoted to using data on individuals' earnings, schooling, and intelligence test scores to discover how the correlation of ability and education affects the measured rate of return. Estimates of the upward bias in the real rate of return range from nearly 0 up to as high as 50 percent in one very special sample of workers. The best estimate is that for the average worker the private real rate of return, adjusted for differences in ability, is 1 to 2 percentage points lower than the range of 7.5 to 12 percent presented in Figure 3.4.[21]

Additional light is shed upon the screening hypothesis by looking at the schooling decisions of the self-employed, people who presumably do not need to use education as a screening device, because they can assess their own capabilities. The average self-employed person acquires three-fourths as much education beyond high

[21] The very high estimate is for younger people who had been poor students, from W. Lee Hansen, Burton Weisbrod, and William Scanlan, "Schooling and Earnings of Low Achievers," *American Economic Review* (60): 409–418 (1970). Estimates within the range of a 0 to 20 percent bias are found by John Hause, "Ability and Schooling as Determinants of Lifetime Earnings, or If You're So Smart, Why Aren't You Rich?" in F. Thomas Juster (ed.). *Education, Income and Human Behavior,* McGraw-Hill, New York, 1975, pp. 123–149. Similar results are found by Lee Lillard, "Inequality: Earnings vs. Human Wealth," *American Economic Review* (67): 47 (1977) and by Zvi Griliches and William Mason, "Education, Income and Ability," *Journal of Political Economy* (81): S74–S103 (1973). See also Paul Taubman and Terence Wales, "Higher Education, Mental Ability and Screening," *Journal of Political Economy* (81): 28–55 (1973). More favorable evidence for the screening hypothesis is provided by John Riley, "Testing the Educational Screening Hypothesis," *Journal of Political Economy* (87): 227–252 (1979).

school as does the average salaried employee.[22] Assuming people expect to be self-employed at the time they decide how much schooling to acquire, this evidence suggests that self-employed individuals view the acquisition of at least some college education as providing direct benefit to them, and not indirectly through an employer. Their somewhat lower educational attainment does imply, though, that schooling does play some role in screening salaried employees. Also, a study of employees within one large corporation found, after adjusting for the selectivity of the colleges the employees attended and for the level of degree attained, that those who achieved a higher grade-point average obtained more rapid rates of salary increase from the firm and received higher job-performance ratings from their supervisors.[23] Assuming the higher grade-point average reflects more learning, this is further evidence against the screening hypothesis. Yet another study that adjusted for differences among workers in psychological traits such as self-restraint, sociability, emotional stability, and so on found that the rate of return to college education is only slightly affected by these characteristics.[24] All this evidence implies that education is doing more than merely sorting people with desirable characteristics into higher-paying jobs.

When all the adjustments are made, we still find education produces a reward in the workplace that makes it an investment that is very competitive with investments in physical capital. Formal education does provide skills that add to productivity, so we are correct in equating the growth in educational attainment with an increase in the supply of skill per hour supplied or per labor-force participant. Are potential investors aware of this though; that is, are the supply curves in Figure 3.4 fairly flat, or are they nearly vertical? The answer is pretty clear: Students' choices about the amount of education they obtain are sensitive to the returns on education, to both its costs and the incremental earnings it produces. Indeed, one study that accounted for differences in ability and a wide variety of measures characterizing family background found that each 10 percent increase in the rate of return induced nearly a 20 percent increase in college enrollment. A recent nationwide survey of college freshmen found 70 percent stating that to "make more money" was a reason "very important in deciding to go to college."[25] Educated labor is an economic good in that it is scarce; and like other economic goods, its supply is responsive to its price. It seems reasonable to conclude that the long-run supply curve of educated labor is nearly horizontal around a rate of return that depends on the risks of investment in schooling and on people's attitudes toward bearing those risks.

[22] Kenneth Wolpin, "Education and Screening," *American Economic Review* (67): 956 (1977).

[23] David Wise, "Academic Achievement and Job Performance," *American Economic Review* (65): 350–366 (1975). Interestingly, the benefits of going from the lower to the higher part of one's graduating class are greater, the greater the selectivity of the undergraduate college is.

[24] Randall Filer, "The Influence of Affective Human Capital on the Wage Equation," *Research in Labor Economics* (4): 367–409 (1981), examines the effect of personality traits.

[25] Numerous American studies of the relation between the demand for college education and its costs and benefits are summarized by Leonard Miller, "Demand for Higher Education in the United States: A Second Progress Report," in Joseph Froomkin, Dean Jamison, and Roy Radner (eds.). *Education as an Industry,* Ballinger, Cambridge, Mass., 1976. A British study is Christopher Pissarides, "From School to University: The Demand for Post-Compulsory Education in Britain," *Economic Journal* (92): 654–667 (1982). The specific effect cited in the text is from Robert Willis and Sherwin Rosen, "Education and Self-Selection," *Journal of Political Economy* (81): S32 (1979). The survey results are reported in the *New York Times,* January 29, 1983, p. 9.

POLICY ISSUE—COMPULSORY SCHOOL ATTENDANCE LAWS

In the United States, as in most developed countries, children must attend school until they attain a certain age. Whereas most states in 1981 required attendance until age 16, four allowed students to leave before their sixteenth birthday, and nine required attendance until the seventeenth or eighteenth birthday. Do these laws affect the amount of schooling obtained, and should they be continued? Perhaps everyone would attend school until age 16 or later even without compulsory attendance laws. Accounting for many other differences across states, however, one finds that enrollment of male 16- and 17-year-olds is substantially higher in states that require attendance beyond age 16, and slightly higher among females ages 16 and 17.[26] That the laws have a larger effect on the schooling decisions of males than of females is to be expected: The full-time wage rate of teenage boys is higher than that of teenage girls, making the cost of schooling higher and dropping out more attractive to boys.

This evidence suggests that the law is effective; but whether it increases the level of skill embodied in the work force is another issue. As we have seen, part of the social return to schooling is a more informed citizenry; requiring teenagers to stay in school could increase this return. On the other hand, students who are kept in school only by the compulsory attendance law may not be learning anything and may be detracting from their classmates' ability to learn. Voters and legislators need better information about these effects in order to assess the appropriate trade-off.

SKILL ACQUIRED ON THE JOB

If schooling were the only form of investment in human capital that affects earnings, we could not explain the higher earnings of older cohorts that occurs up through age 54 in the data in Table 3.3. Formal education usually stops by age 25, so that earnings would remain constant across age groups after that age if schooling alone raised the college graduate's productivity. Indeed, because of the obsolescence of skills acquired at school, earnings would probably drop after age 25: There is good indirect evidence that the stock of human capital acquired through formal schooling does depreciate over time.[27] Because of *investment in on-the-job training,* though, the age-earnings profile slopes upward through much of the work life.

On-the-job training offered by employers varies from formal programs that are not unlike those conducted by educational institutions to the simplest forms of learning by doing, observing others, and being reprimanded for mistakes. Since there are substantial economies of scale in conducting formal training programs, they tend to be run mainly by larger employers. On-the-job training of a less formal nature takes place in all work environments, though.

Training within a firm is undertaken at a cost. Where the training is clearly a separable activity, these costs can be identified quite precisely. For example, training an airline pilot to fly a new type of aircraft involves costs that include the pay of the instructor and the trainee, the operating and capital costs of the aircraft, and perhaps the cost of special materials or equipment that are used in training, such as flight

[26] Linda Edwards, "The Economics of Schooling Decisions: Teenage Enrollment Rates," *Journal of Human Resources* (10): 165 (1975).

[27] Thomas Johnson, "Returns from Investment in Human Capital," *American Economic Review* (60): 556–557 (1970).

simulators. Where training takes place concurrently with production, the costs, although of the same general kind, may be more difficult to measure. Some of the trainees' time and that of their supervisors or coworkers is used in training; output is therefore less than it would be if all workers were fully trained. For the same reason, capital costs per unit of output may be higher than normal. Materials may be wasted in scrap or defective products owing to the trainees' inexperience.

Whether employers or workers actually bear the cost of the training depends on the nature of the training opportunity. But employers will not incur these costs unless they expect enough extra output in the future to provide a rate of return equal to that obtainable on competitive investments. So, too, workers will not wish to sacrifice any pay while being trained unless they can be assured of a higher wage later on. To the extent that these costs are expected to produce enough future benefits to provide a competitive rate of return, employers will offer training, and workers will seek training opportunities.

When and where will this training take place? If employers expect workers to stay with the firm for a long time, they will be more willing to offer training, for there is a longer payout period on the investment. Workers will also be more willing to accept training if they expect to stay with the firm longer, or if they are younger: In both cases they too have a longer time over which to reap the returns on the investment. These considerations suggest that the fraction of time on the job that workers spend learning will be highest right after they complete their formal education, and will decline thereafter. At some time late in the work life it will neither pay for them to accept nor for their employers to offer any more training, for there is not sufficient time left in the work life to make the investment pay off. These considerations suggest that the optimal pattern of investment in on-the-job training over the work life is described by a curve like AA in Figure 3.6. This graph is drawn for college graduates starting work at age 22; a qualitatively similar one could be drawn for high school grads starting at age 18.

This pattern of declining investment in on-the-job training during the work life carries specific implications for the age-earnings profile observed at one point in time. Early in the work life the workers' earnings capacities and earnings are rising rapidly because of the large investment in on-the-job training being made. This is shown by the rising left portion of the age-earnings profile BCB in Figure 3.6. Their stock of human capital is depreciating all the time, however. At point C their earnings begin to decrease below those of slightly younger people. Even though they are still investing in training, the negative effect of the depreciation of the stock of skills begins to outweigh the positive impact of the diminished additional investment in additional skills. Earnings drop more rapidly still near the end of the work life, when the stock of skills is still depreciating and is no longer being augmented by additional investment in training on the job. Had Figure 3.6 been drawn for a cohort rather than for workers of different ages at one point in time, BCB would look like the curves in Figure 3.1.

This view of workers and firms choosing to invest in on-the-job training provides a unified explanation of the shape of the age-earnings profiles presented in Table 3.3. Assuming that experience reflects the accumulation of on-the-job training, one can infer (from the age-earnings profiles themselves) that the equivalent of

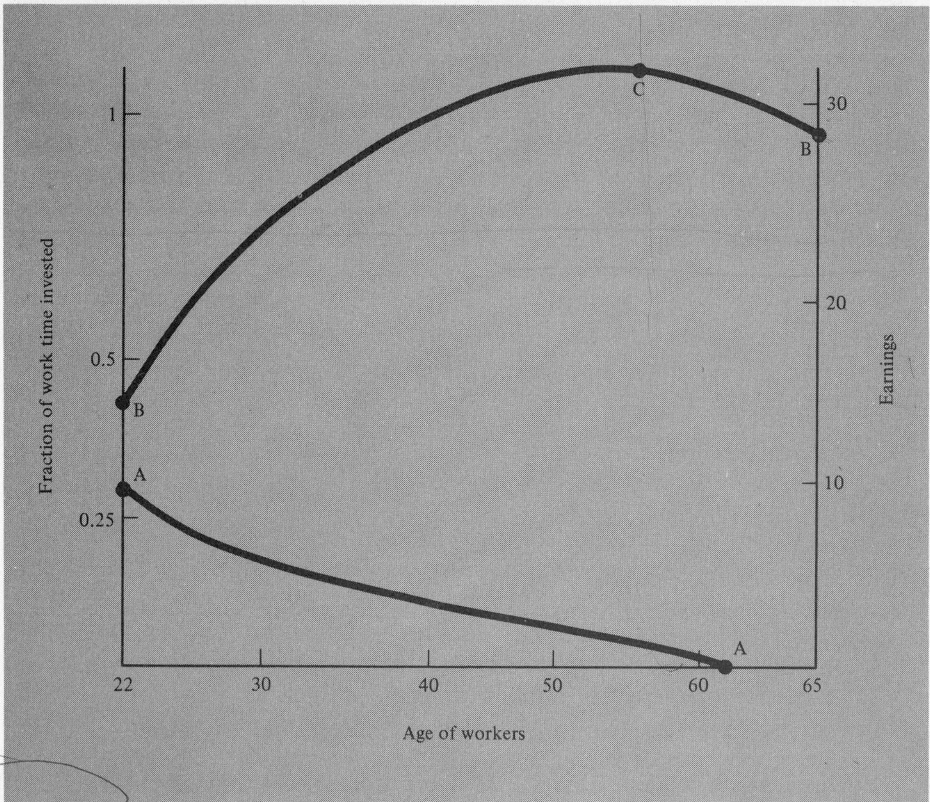

Figure 3.6 Earnings and time spent learning on the job.

2.5 to 4 full years on the job are spent learning skills that augment future earnings.[28] The amount of time spent investing on the job differs somewhat by educational attainment. The monetary value of that time differs greatly, though, because the opportunity cost of the more educated worker's time is greater. The total cost of investing is therefore higher for more educated workers, and the returns, in the form of additional earnings, must also be higher. This explains the "fanning out" of age-earnings profiles we noticed in Table 3.3: The profiles fan out because highly educated middle-aged workers have also made more costly investments in skills on the job than their less-educated counterparts.

Additional insight into the training process is gained by distinguishing between *general* training and training that is *specific* to the firm offering it.[29] General training develops skills of equal value both in the organization that gives the training and elsewhere. Specific training is training in skills that are of value only to the employer who gives the training, either because the employer is a monopolist or because of special methods, routines, and equipment with which newcomers must become familiar.

[28] Jacob Mincer, *Schooling, Experience and Earnings,* National Bureau of Economic Research, New York, 1974, p. 73.

[29] Becker, op. cit., pp. 8–28.

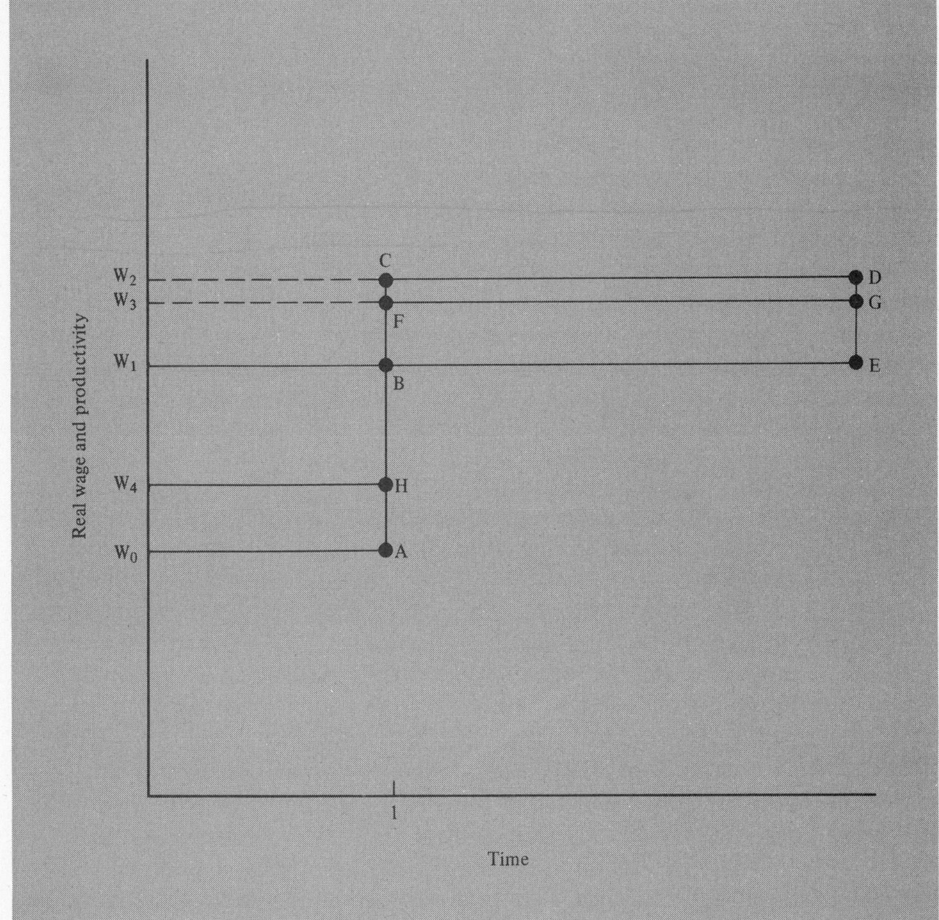

Figure 3.7 Wages and the type of training.

This distinction allows us to predict whether the employer or the worker will bear the cost of training. Whichever party bears the cost must also expect to receive the return, or there will be no incentive to invest. Assume that workers would receive a wage rate W_1 in Figure 3.7, equal to their productivity if they received no training. Assume further that training takes place only during the first year on the job. During training, workers' productivity is lower and out-of-pocket training costs are incurred, so that the net value of workers' services during training is only W_0. If the training is entirely general, employers would be willing to pay workers only W_0 during training. If they paid more than that, they would have to receive some return on their investment, a return in the form of an excess of the workers' productivity (W_2) over their wage after training. If employers pay less than W_2, workers will simply seek another job paying W_2. Since the training is general, other employers will be willing to offer W_2. That being the case, the current employer must pay W_2, and will only be willing to do so if the wage W_0 has been paid throughout the training period. Thus general training will be financed entirely by workers. Ignoring discounting, in equilibrium the value of the costs, the rectangle W_0W_1BA, will equal the value of the returns, BCDE.

If training is firm-specific, employers could be willing to bear the entire cost of the investment. The best the workers could do after training if they left the firm is W_1. If they stay in the firm, the employer can pay them one penny more than W_1 throughout their working lives. The employer would then reap an excess of productivity over the wage in the amount $W_2 - W_1$ per time period; the employer would pay for this during training by paying the worker a wage of W_1 and accepting productivity of only W_0. If trained workers move only if the alternative wage is higher than the current wage, employers who pay one penny above W_1 will retain all the workers in whose specific training they have invested. In exact opposition to the allocation of the costs and returns to general training, if the assumptions about workers' decisions about moving are correct, the costs and returns to specific training will be born entirely by the employer.

Workers do leave jobs, however; and although the reasons for quitting are often noneconomic, the likelihood of leaving is affected by the wage received (see Chap. 7). The smart employer will offer a wage above W_1, perhaps W_3, after the training is completed. This will induce the trained worker to stay with the firm, since W_3 is well above W_1, the highest wage attainable elsewhere. Because of this higher wage, the employer's returns on the training investment are only CDGF. The reduced returns make the investment profitable to the employer only if the costs are also reduced; and costs can be reduced only if the employee shares them by accepting a lower wage, W_4, during training. The employer's costs are then W_0W_4HA, equal to the returns. The employee's costs are W_1W_4HB, the forgone wages during training; they are equal to the extra wages, BEGF, received after the training is completed. The chance that workers will quit, destroying the value of their firm-specific training, induces employers to require that the costs and returns of such training be shared.

General and specific training are best regarded as the ends of a continuum rather than as alternatives. In most cases a new worker simultaneously acquires some skills that are general and some that are specific to the firm. Despite our inability to separate out the two types of training, the distinction is important for several reasons. It points out that the supply of skill may consist of components that are not generally useful in the economy as a whole; it provides a reason (firm-specific investment) for different patterns of workers' attachment to their employer by age, industry, and occupation; and it has implications for the pattern of wage differences among workers. This last effect can be seen by considering workers who have held several jobs. Any general training that accompanied experience with their previous employers will by definition be of use on their current jobs; but any firm-specific training acquired elsewhere does not raise their productivity with current employers. Additional experience raises earnings, as the age-earnings profiles in Table 3.3 made abundantly clear. Additional tenure with the current employer should have an especially large impact, for its effects on wages reflect the returns to both general and firm-specific training. Similarly, any formal company training program undertaken in the current job will have a bigger effect on wages than a similar program undertaken before the worker started with the current employer.

The added importance of tenure in the current job is demonstrated by the data. Among adult men in the United States in 1976 a year of experience with the current employer added 37 percent more to earnings than a year of experience in jobs held before the current one. Similar extra effects of experience with the current employer have been observed in Mexico too.[30] More direct evidence is provided by a sample of workers aged 50 to 64 in 1971. Adjusting for occupational and demographic differences, those nonunion workers who had participated in a formal company training program received 17 percent higher wages than those who had never been in any formal training program; workers who had taken part in a formal training program outside the company received only 5 percent more than workers who had not been in any program.[31]

The theory of on-the-job training elegantly describes the optimizing behavior of both workers and employers. Its predictions about age-earnings profiles fit the observed data well, and the distinction between general and firm-specific training leads to predictions that are supported by data on differences in earnings. But just as some observers have objected to the theory of investment in schooling, others have objected to this theory. They argue that the age-earnings profile cannot reflect the effects of productive investment, for experience does not seem to be related to workers' performance as measured by supervisors' assessments. If this is true, we cannot claim that differences in work experience represent differences in the amount of skill supplied to employers. At one large company the relationship was actually negative among a group of workers with experience covering the entire range; adjusting for differences in schooling, those workers with more experience in a job category actually received worse evaluations than their less-experienced coworkers. This relationship may be spurious; those who stay in a category longer may be less able workers. The good workers would have less experience in each job, because they rose through the ranks more rapidly. In any case, another study found that the productivity of new workers did increase as they acquired more experience.[32]

At this stage it seems best to accept the notion that additional experience on most jobs does represent additional skill. One should recognize, however, that there are problems with this assertion that can only be solved by better observation of the learning process within the workplace. Until more such observations are made, the conclusion of a direct relation between experience and productivity must remain tentative.

[30] Calculated from Jacob Mincer and Boyan Jovanovic, "Labor Mobility and Wages," in Sherwin Rosen (ed.). *Studies in Labor Markets,* University of Chicago Press, Chicago, 1981, p. 41. Somewhat larger effects are implied by estimates in Albert Rees and George P. Shultz, *Workers and Wages in an Urban Labor Market,* University of Chicago Press, Chicago, 1970, pp. 152–156. See also Richard Miller and Mahmood Zaidi, "Human Capital and Earnings: Some Evidence from Brazil and Mexico," *Industrial Relations Research Association Proceedings* (34): 207–214 (1981).

[31] Gregory Duncan and Duane Leigh, "Wage Determination in the Union and Nonunion Sectors: A Sample Selectivity Approach," *Industrial and Labor Relations Review* (34): 29 (1980). The difference in the unionized sector is smaller but in the same direction as that in the nonunionized sector.

[32] James Medoff and Katharine Abraham, "Are Those Paid More Really More Productive? The Case of Experience," *Journal of Human Resources* (16): 186–216 (1981); John Bishop and Stanley Stephenson, "Productivity Growth and Tenure: A Test of OJT Theories of Wage and Productivity Growth," Unpublished Paper, Ohio State University, 1982.

POLICY ISSUE—SUBSIDIZED ON-THE-JOB TRAINING

In most developed countries the national government offers employers subsidies to cover some of the costs of on-the-job training. These may take the form of lump-sum grants to employers; in other cases they are paid as wage subsidies during an employee's early years with the employer, in recognition of the fact that much training is received early in one's tenure in a job. For most of the time since 1962 the federal government has offered employers subsidies to defray the costs of training new workers, by either direct subsidies or, under CETA, the Comprehensive Employment and Training Act of 1973, payments channeled through local agencies.[33] The government subsidy is targeted to the training of unemployed or very low-wage workers, those whose prior work record indicated they had not accumulated the skills that would guarantee them stable employment at a decent wage.

Have these subsidies increased the amount of human capital that is embodied in the work force? The argument for such subsidies rests on several grounds. Unless unemployment is very low, firms are unlikely to provide training to the most disadvantaged, least educated younger members of the work force. Subsidized training of such persons could give them an entrée into training opportunities they would not otherwise receive, enabling them to launch themselves on a path of steady earnings over the rest of their work lives. With difficulties in borrowing and with the riskiness of investments in training, these workers cannot finance the training opportunity themselves; they need government inducements to get employers to offer the training to them. The second argument is that the social return to such training exceeds the private return. Because of the training and the stable employment it will engender, antisocial behavior by an alienated segment of the work force may be reduced.

The counterargument also has several bases. Those who are offered subsidized training may merely *displace* other workers with similar backgrounds who would have received the training. Whereas the private return to those receiving the training may be large, the social return is small, because there is little net addition of skills in the work force. The program, in this view, only shuffles training opportunities around within the low-skilled work force. The second counterargument is that the training will have little value if aggregate demand is insufficient to provide steady jobs for the workers after they are trained. This line of attack suggests that the government would increase the skill level of the population more if it maintained high aggregate demand and thus tried to create jobs directly.

The relative merits of these arguments cannot easily be discerned in the real world. Economists have been reduced to attempting to answer the narrower question, namely, whether those who do receive subsidized training earn a sufficient amount more thereafter to justify the government's investment. Substantial effort has been devoted to measuring the rate of return on training, an exercise that falls under the general rubric of benefit-cost analysis. One study dealt with a program that operated from 1968 through 1973. It indicates that the program was fairly successful in yielding higher posttraining earnings for participants. Among males the program produced a small gain in earnings, although this stemmed solely from an increase in hourly wages. The fraction of time spent working actually decreased slightly. Much larger earnings gains were obtained by female trainees, due both to higher hourly wages and increases in the amount of time spent employed.[34] Because the programs change so frequently, it is very risky to use evaluations of previous

[33] A thorough description of employment and training programs in the United States is provided in Sar Levitan, Garth Mangum, and Ray Marshall, *Human Resources and Labor Markets,* Harper & Row, New York, 1981.

[34] Nicholas Kiefer, "The Economic Benefits from Four Government Training Programs," *Research in Labor Economics* (Suppl. 1): 173, 175 (1979).

subsidized on-the-job training programs as a guide to the success of current or future programs. These results suggest, though, that the private rate of return to this form of subsidized training is well above zero. Whether the social rate of return is positive is unclear.

OCCUPATIONS-AGGREGATES OF SKILLS

It is useful to distinguish between a skill and an occupation. A *skill* may be defined as the ability to perform a particular task well. An *occupation* is a line of work whose practitioners use a particular combination of skills, or one of a related set of combinations, to contribute to the production of some marketable good or service. Some skills, when not pursued entirely as a hobby, are useful in only one occupation and are the principal requirement for following that occupation (e.g., cutting hair or flying an airplane). We call these *occupation-specific* skills. Others are useful in a wide variety of occupations, although they may be the principal requirements for some (e.g., writing good prose). Students who have not yet developed a strong preference for a particular occupation or who are uncertain about their prospects in various occupations can hedge by investing in skills with multiple uses.

The extent of occupation-specific training required to perform well varies among occupations in ways that one would expect. Table 3.4 presents estimates by the U.S. Department of Labor of the amount of vocational preparation required for a number of occupations. It shows that the amount of occupation-specific training for some specialities is as much as 9 years; for others, it may be as little as 2 years.

Since we cannot directly observe the earnings produced by having particular skills, we must use data on earnings by occupation to measure the returns to choices of kinds of skill (as distinguished from length of schooling). The earnings profiles of Figure 3.2 can be modified for this purpose so that each profile represents an occupation. The periods of training could coincide in whole or in part but could differ in cost because of differences in tuition rates, in the availability of scholarships

Table 3.4 SPECIFIC VOCATIONAL PREPARATION REQUIREMENTS, IN YEARS, 1977

Occupation	Years required
Newspaper editor	9
Stereotyper	8
Mechanical engineer	8
Tax accountant	8
Cheesemaker	7
Insurance agent	6
Stenographer	5
Leather stitcher	4
Airplane flight attendant	3
Telephone solicitor	3
Charge-account clerk	2

Source: Selected Characteristics of Occupations Defined in the Dictionary of Occupational Titles, 1981.

or fellowships, or in the amount of specific vocational preparation required. Examination of age-earnings profiles for different occupations reveals the expected relationship between the amount of training and the shape of the profile. In those occupations in which more skill is acquired, through both formal schooling and on-the-job investment, the age-earnings profile is both higher on average and much steeper. Earnings of professionals and managers rise very rapidly during the first 10 years of their work lives; those of semiskilled operatives rise much more slowly. Comparing male professionals aged 25 to 34 in 1959 with male professionals aged 35 to 54 in 1969, earnings increased 135 percent; among operatives, the increase in this cohort between 1959 and 1969 was only 77 percent.

Young people trying to decide which of two occupations to enter would tend to choose the one where the present value of the income stream is higher. Such comparisons are not intended to suggest that these calculations are made explicitly or that they dominate decisions on occupational choice or the kind of training to undertake. Personal tastes and interests and the influence of parents, teachers, and friends play major and often controlling roles. Yet for many students, tastes and advice are not decisive. For them the influence of economic rewards is probably important; and since tastes change more slowly than economic factors, the latter will be especially important in changing career choices. In the field of law, for example, a 10 percent increase in the earnings of lawyers relative to earnings of other professionals "raises the number of first-year law students by about 10 percent in a year and 30 to 40 percent over the long run."[35] Even in a field requiring as much specialized talent as physics, the supply of juniors majoring in the field is highly responsive to the salaries physicists are currently receiving.[36]

The age-earnings profile for an occupation shows only the mean earnings of its practitioners and not the dispersion of earnings. But dispersion also influences occupational choices. Adam Smith argued that where many of those who trained for a profession will not succeed in it, the returns to those who do succeed should balance the costs of those who fail. He also felt that the presence of a few conspicuously high rewards in a profession, like high prizes in a lottery, would attract a number of entrants out of proportion to the true expectation of success.[37] But if some students are risk lovers in their choice of careers, others are risk averters; risk averters may be attracted to a career like teaching, despite the absence of large prizes, for the security it offers as compared to most other occupations. In professional occupations, the riskier the income is the higher will be the average income in the profession.[38] This implies that the marginal worker who is drawn into the occupation must be risk averse and has to be induced to enter the occupation by the expectation of higher earnings than might be achieved in a less risky field.

The kind of analysis used for occupations where training takes place in schools

[35] Richard Freeman, *The Overeducated American,* Academic Press, New York, 1976, p. 120.

[36] Richard Freeman, "Supply and Salary Adjustments to the Changing Science Manpower Market: Physics, 1948–1973," *American Economic Review* (65): 33 (1975).

[37] Smith, loc. cit.

[38] Allan King, "Occupational Choice, Risk Aversion, and Wealth," *Industrial and Labor Relations Review* (27): 586–596 (1974); Richard Evans and Robert Weinstein, "Ranking Occupations as Risky Income Prospects," *Industrial and Labor Relations Review* (35): 252–259 (1982); and William Johnson, "Uncertainty and the Distribution of Earnings," in Juster, *Distribution* . . . .

or colleges can be extended to other kinds of training, such as apprenticeship. At one time apprenticeship often involved the payment of money by a boy's family to a master craftsman in return for the training the craftsman would provide. Less explicit costs are involved where apprentices work for less than the wage they could have earned in an alternative occupation. Over the years, as training for the crafts has shifted in part from training by employers and journeymen to training in secondary schools, periods of formal apprenticeship have tended to begin later and become shorter, and wages of apprentices may even exceed those of operatives of the same age. In such cases, apprenticeship for a well-paid craft may have little or no economic cost to the apprentice and large returns, so that there is an excess supply of workers seeking apprenticeship. Access to apprenticeship programs has to be rationed, for example by admitting only the relatives of journeymen.

POLICY ISSUE—OCCUPATIONAL LICENSING

In many occupations the rationing of entry will not work, for there is no centralized way of ensuring that local groups abide by agreements to limit entry into the occupation. Organized attempts to limit entry often will not succeed without some external agent enforcing compliance on the part of participating groups that are capable of providing the training. This enforcement often takes the form of state occupational licensing laws. To receive a license, the practitioner must meet certain standards set by the state licensing board for the particular occupation. The gamut of licensed occupations is wide, and the requirements for licensing are often unusual. In Michigan in 1982, for example, hearing-aid dealers had to be licensed; to acquire a license a would-be dealer must have worked for another licensed hearing-aid dealer for at least 1 year. A licensed barber had to serve a 100-week apprenticeship or spend 5 years combined in an apprenticeship and a barber college.

The effect of occupational licensing is to limit entry into the occupation. This restriction, like any constraint on supply, can help to maintain rates of return above those that would be generated in a competitive market. The average income in the profession is associated with the severity of the restrictions. Average professional incomes are lower among lawyers and dentists in states that pass more applicants for licenses to practice in these professions; stricter educational requirements for barbers reduce the number of practicing barbers; and requirements that hospital lab personnel have college degrees raised earnings in that occupation.[39]

Occupational licensing is almost always depicted as an attempt to preserve reasonable standards of competence in the craft or profession and as a way of protecting the public's health and safety. Occupational licensing legislation, though, raises the problem of distinguishing reasonable standards from unreasonable barriers whose main purpose is to restrict entry. In recent years the trend in the United States toward deregulation of markets has resulted in the easing of occupational licensing laws in many states. That this trend will lower the returns to professionals in the deregulated occupations is not in doubt. The potential negative effects on the public's health are less clear, but in many occupations, such as barbering, they must be small indeed.

[39] Arlene Holen, "Effects of Professional Licensing Arrangements on Interstate Labor Mobility and Resource Allocation," *Journal of Political Economy* (73): 494 (1965); Robert Thornton and Andrew Weintraub, "Licensing in the Barbering Profession," *Industrial and Labor Relations Review* (32): 242–249 (1979); and William White, "The Impact of Occupational Licensure of Laboratory Personnel," *Journal of Human Resources* (13): 91–102 (1978). See also Simon Rottenberg, "The Economics of Occupational Licensing," in H. Gregg Lewis (ed.). *Aspects of Labor Economics,* Princeton University Press, Princeton, N.J., 1962.

SUMMARY

Increases in the supply of skill increase the effective supply of labor by making workers more productive. Skill can be acquired formally through education or training programs, or informally on the job. All indicators of the skill of the work force, including its occupational mix and the level of education attained, show that the average skill level in the United States has increased in the past 30 years.

The acquisition of skills in free-market economies is in large part the result of optimizing decisions made by current and potential labor-force participants. The theory of investment in human capital relates individuals' decisions to the costs (forgone earnings and direct costs) and the benefits (higher future earnings) that the investment can be expected to generate. Substantial evidence indicates that young people are more likely to acquire one form of human capital, formal education, when the costs are lower and the relative earnings of college graduates are higher. Even though the rate of return to investment in college education has fallen since the 1960s, it is still highly competitive with rates of return on physical capital.

Another type of investment in human capital is in skills acquired on the job. Because there is a longer work life over which to amortize the investment, most of the costs of training will be incurred early in the work life. This pattern of investment produces the inverse U-shaped profile that characterizes the relationship between age and earnings. Age-earnings profiles have this shape whether we classify workers by level of formal education or by occupation; and occupational choice is partly motivated by the same considerations of cost and returns to the investment in occupation-specific skills.

APPENDIX: The Supply Curve of Labor: A Synthesis

As we noted at the outset of the discussion of labor supply, decisions on labor-force participation, hours of work, and investment in human capital are interrelated. For example, individuals who expect to be in the labor force all their lives have a stronger economic incentive to invest in education than those who do not. People investing in on-the-job training may work longer total hours than others who regard their training as completed. Workers who have a large investment in human capital are less likely to retire early than those who do not. All these many interrelated decisions will be influenced by prevailing wages, costs of training, taxes on earned income, and the income from property or transfer payments that are available to those who do not work.

We can conclude and summarize our discussion of the supply of labor with a few remarks about supply schedules. The long-run supply curve of employee hours to the economy as a whole, in Figure 3.8, will probably be backward-sloping at the average real wage levels of developed countries. With permanent increases in the real wage, from W_2 to W_3, hours of work supplied by a fixed population will decline. The backward slope arises from the tendency in developed countries for hours actually worked per year to be reduced as real income rises over time while the overall rate of labor-force participation for all groups in the population taken together remains roughly constant or rises slightly. In developing countries, hours may increase, as the wage rises from W_0 to W_1. A different picture emerges if we look at short-run supply curves of labor in different countries. Because of discouraged-worker phe-

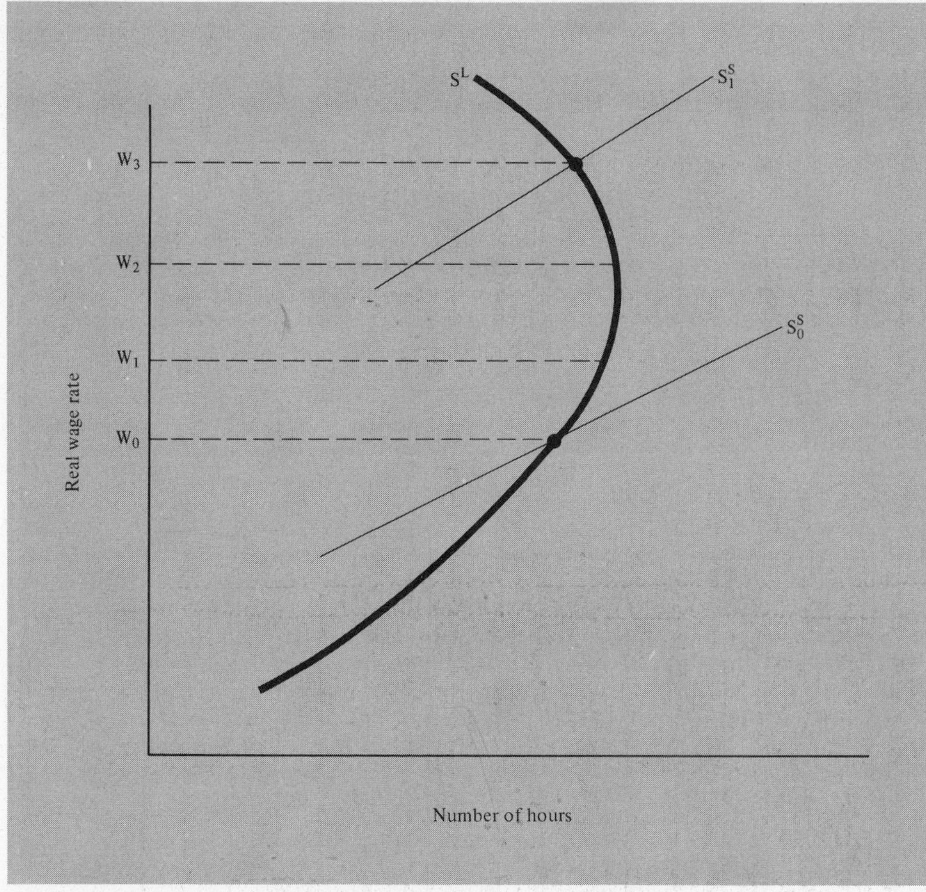

Figure 3.8 The short-run and long-run supply of labor to the economy.

nomena and the tendency to supply labor at those times in one's life when the returns to work are highest, short-run supply curves like $S_0{}^s$ and $S_1{}^s$, slope upward. Temporary increases in real wages elicit a greater supply of labor.

If we relate individuals' average real wage rates to their annual or lifetime labor supply, we find the usual effects. For all but the highest wage groups the supply curve will be positively sloped. An increase in the returns to work will elicit more work effort, through more hours per year, a greater likelihood of supplying at least some hours, and greater effort per hour on the job.

Both short- and long-run supply curves of labor to any particular occupation, industry, or area must necessarily slope upward when measured against the wage for this employment relative to wages elsewhere. This will be true whether the supply is measured in number of workers or in number of hours. Such curves, shown in Figure 3.9, slope upward because the higher relative wage attracts labor to this activity or area at the expense of others. The supply of labor to unskilled occupations is determined in part by the mobility of mature workers; the supply curve could be quite flat even in the short run because of the ease of entry into the occupation. For occupations using specialized skills requiring a long period of training, the short-run supply curve might be almost vertical, like S^5 in Figure 3.9. A pronounced flattened

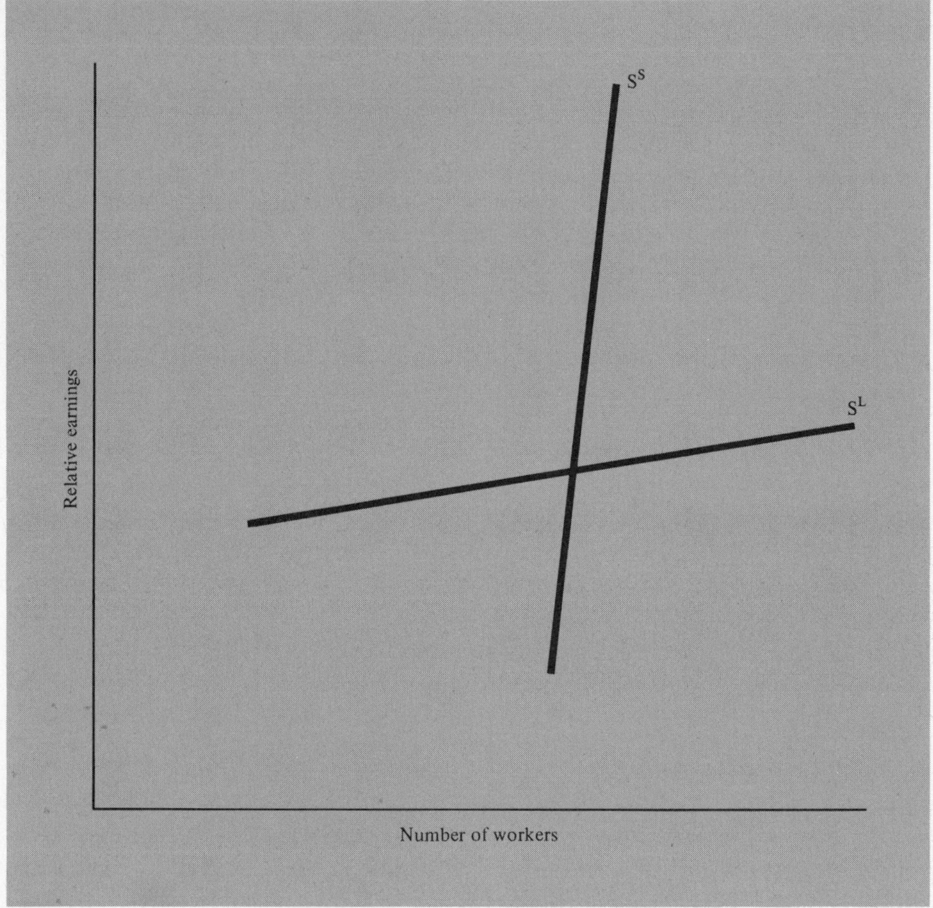

Figure 3.9 The short-run and long-run supply of labor to an occupation.

curve would emerge only after a change in relative wages had produced a response through changes in the number of those acquiring skills that are specific to the occupation. Such a long-run response would be absent only if the number of training places were somehow rigidly fixed or if decisions on career choice were based entirely on nonmonetary factors. Neither of these conditions is likely to be met. Another improbable requirement also must be met for the long-run supply curve of labor to a particular use to be completely vertical: The rate of retirement and of transfer out of this employment in midcareer would have to be completely unaffected by the relative wage.

At the same time, there is good reason to believe that the supply of labor to an occupation will not usually be horizontal (perfectly elastic) even in the very long run. Rather, the typical long-run supply curve of labor to an occupation will look like S^L in Figure 3.9. It intersects S^S at the point from which some initial change in demand in the occupation causes wages to change. The long-run supply would be perfectly elastic if occupations differed only in the cost of the training needed to enter them. Each occupation would then be able to attract an unlimited number of entrants by offering average annual earnings that exceeded the average earnings of an occupation requiring no training by a margin that, when discounted at the prevailing rate of interest, fully covered private training costs. Occupations differ, however, not only in the amount of training they require, but also in the extent to which they call upon scarce innate talents and in the nonpecuniary advantages and disadvantages of working in them. These advantages and disadvantages will be evaluated differently by different people, which is sufficient to give the long-run supply curve an upward slope. To the extent that the disadvantages lie in the difficulty of doing work, they will seem least important to those people who have the relevant innate talents. As an occupation continues to expand, it must eventually recruit more people who do not find it congenial and who will therefore insist on a higher return for entering it. This will cause S^L to slope upward at least slightly.

two

LABOR DEMAND

chapter 4

The Demand for Labor in Competitive Markets

THE NATURE AND USES OF A THEORY OF THE DEMAND FOR LABOR

The basic purpose of a theory of the demand for labor is to determine how much labor employers will want to employ at different wage rates. Answers to this question are important in a variety of contexts. For example, if the government raises the minimum wage, will many fewer low-wage workers be employed or about the same number as before? If a union wins a wage increase in collective bargaining, will its members therefore have fewer hours of work than they had previously? If so, how many fewer? If the government offers employers a subsidy to increase employment, how many more workers will be employed? Many similar examples can easily be imagined.

Where wages are determined in the market rather than by law or collective bargaining, the theory of demand for labor has an important additional purpose—it becomes a major component of a theory of wage determination. To some extent, though less directly, it is also a component of the theory of wage determination under collective bargaining. However, as we shall see, the theory of demand cannot comprise the whole of a theory of wage determination under any set of institutions.

The demand for labor is almost always a *derived demand:* It stems from the consumer's desire for some product or service. In many cases the derivation is quite indirect. The particular kind of labor is used in combination with many other inputs to produce a complex product or service, such as an automobile or a television broadcast.

The theory of the demand for labor has changed little since the beginning of this century. It is an application of the *marginal productivity theory* of the demand for any input into production—*factor of production*—in processes where two or more factors cooperate.[1] The theory has been severely attacked by institutional labor economists, and by theories of segmented markets. It survives the attacks both because the critics have often misunderstood it and because they have failed to develop as useful an alternative theory to put in its place.

Much of the misunderstanding of marginal productivity theory is summed up in the single unfortunate term "the marginal productivity theory of wages." This term makes no sense. A demand schedule is a relation between a price (in this case, a wage, the price of labor services) and the quantity demanded. This relation does not uniquely determine the wage except in the highly unusual cases in which supply is perfectly inelastic, that is, where the supply curve is vertical. The demand schedule has no effect whatever on the wage in the cases at the other extreme of possible supply conditions, in which the supply curve confronting an employer is perfectly elastic, that is, when the supply curve is horizontal. These cases include both the decisions of the individual firm under perfect competition and circumstances in which employers are required by legislation or by trade union action to pay a wage higher than they otherwise would. In these cases, the demand schedule determines only the amount of labor employed. In all intermediate cases, wages and employment are jointly determined by supply and demand. Change in supply or demand will change both wages and employment. To speak of "the marginal productivity theory of wages" is analogous to speaking of "the demand theory of prices," a term so ridiculous on its face that it is not used.

The discussion in this chapter retains two simplifying assumptions that were introduced in Chapter 2: (1) There are no costs of employment other than hourly wages. (2) The productivity of labor is independent of the length of the workweek. These assumptions permit us to express the quantity of labor demanded as employee hours without worrying about the split between hours per week and the number of employees. Thus we again assume that the employer is indifferent between one worker working 70 hours per week and two workers each working 35 hours, provided that in both cases the capital equipment is working 70 hours. Variations in the length of time per week that the capital is working (say, by adding a second or third shift) as ways of altering the ratio of inputs are not considered.

The basic theory of the demand for labor in competitive markets is considered in this chapter. Chapter 5 examines departures from competition and some other extensions. Among these, we introduce the fixed costs of employment and discuss the separate demands for hours and for employees.

THE SHORT-RUN DEMAND SCHEDULE

Figure 4.1 illustrates the production choices facing a typical firm that combines the services of capital with worker hours to produce output. The technological relationship that determines the most that can be produced with each combination of capital

[1]For a good brief account of the historical development and criticism of marginal productivity theory, see Allan Cartter, *The Theory of Wages and Employment,* Irwin, Homewood, Ill., 1959, chaps. 2–4. More recent criticism, from the perspective of students of segmented labor markets, is presented by Glen Cain, "The Challenge of Segmented Labor Market Theories to Orthodox Theory," *Journal of Economic Literature* (14): 1215–1257 (1976).

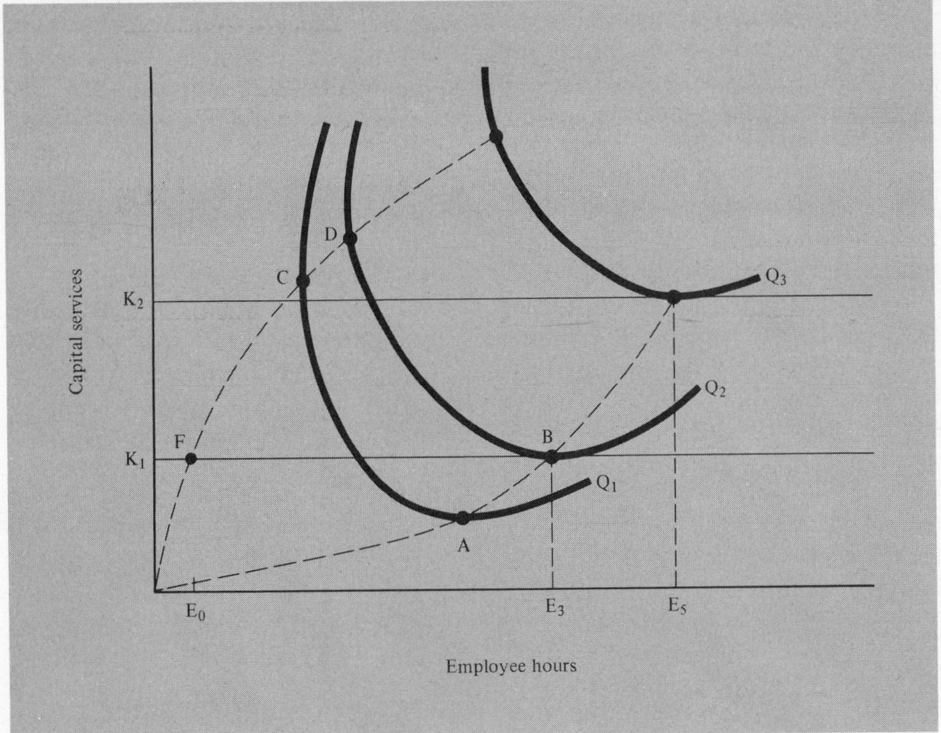

Figure 4.1 Production using capital and labor.

services and worker hours is the firm's *production function.* It represents for an unchanging technology the output associated with each possible combination of factor inputs (not all of which may be currently in use anywhere). Hours of homogeneous labor per period of time are measured on the horizontal axis; units of capital services (machine-hours, if one likes) on the vertical axis. The main reason for measuring capital inputs as a flow of services rather than as a stock is to allow for differences in the life of capital equipment. A machine costing $10,000 and lasting 5 years is furnishing services that cost $2000 a year through depreciation, in addition to the cost of actual or imputed interest on its value. A machine of the same cost that lasted 10 years would be furnishing services corresponding to depreciation at only half this rate.

Output per period of time is measured as the vertical distance above the plane defined by the axes in Figure 4.1. The curved lines labeled Q_1 and Q_2 are *isoquants,* or sets of all points at which output is equal. Thus at all points on Q_2 output is greater than at all points on Q_1; on all points on Q_3 output exceeds that at all points on Q_2. The amount of output represented by each can be specified, so the resulting diagram of the *production surface,* the vertical distance above the axes, is analogous to a relief map. The isoquants can be drawn as densely as one likes. They cannot cross, though; if they did, one point would represent two different outputs, which is not possible if, as the production function implies, the firm is using its factors of production efficiently.

The isoquants are bowed inward; that is, they are convex to the origin. This represents the principle of the *diminishing marginal rate of substitution* in production—the higher the proportion of one factor in the input mix is, the more of it the employer would have to add to make up for the loss of one unit of the other factor. For example, with a few microwave ovens and many workers, owners of a fast-food restaurant cannot maintain their output of hamburgers when one oven breaks down without hiring many more workers to engage in activities that would economize on time in the few remaining ovens. If there were many ovens, burger output could be maintained with just a few more worker-hours spent preparing raw burgers.

By definition the *short run* is that period of time during which one of the firm's factors of production is fixed. For simplicity we assume that the amount of capital services is fixed at K_1. Because of delivery and installation lags, lack of access to funds to buy machines, or because the rate of return on adding capital equipment will be too low, the firm cannot increase its use of capital services beyond K_1.

The height of the production surface above the line K_1 initially increases as we move to the right; it measures the amount of *total product* as a function of the quantity of labor employed. The total product when K_1 units of capital services are used is shown in Figure 4.2 as TP_1. The slope of this total product curve is the short-run *marginal product* schedule of labor; it is shown in Figure 4.3 as MP_1. In other words, the marginal product schedule shows the addition to total output obtained by using an additional hour of labor input, with inputs of capital services

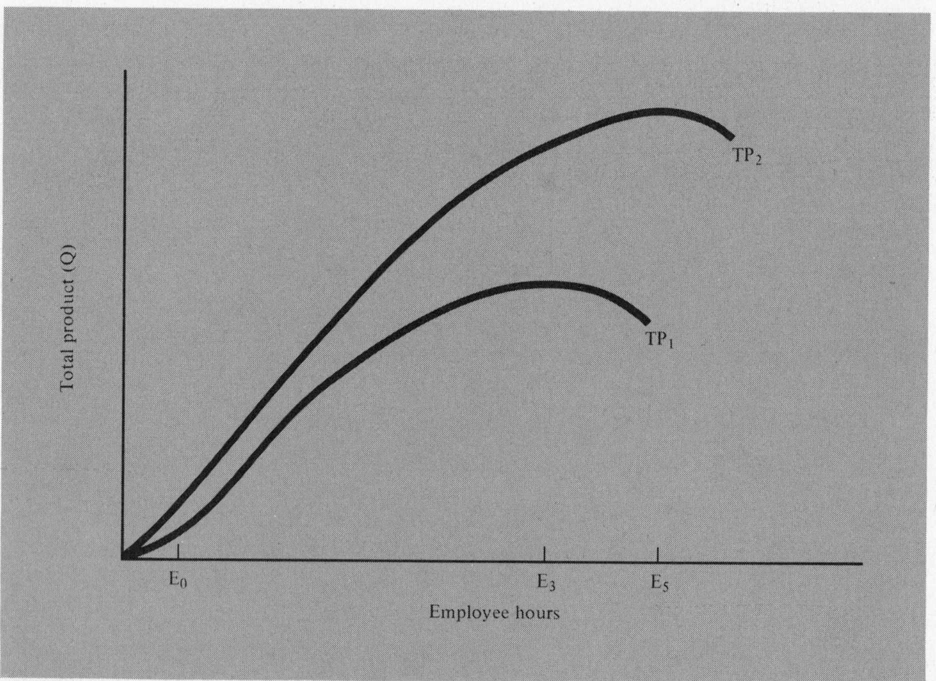

Figure 4.2 The total product of labor.

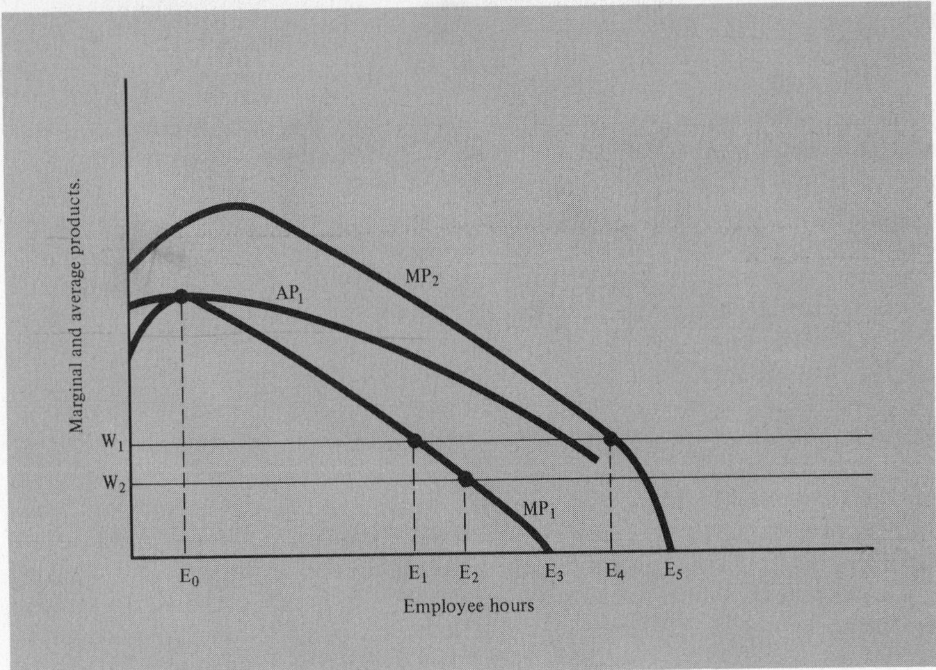

Figure 4.3 Labor productivity schedules.

constant. MP_1 is declining beyond E_0 because the slope of TP_1 in Figure 4.2 is declining; MP_1 is zero at E_3 because TP_1 reaches its maximum at E_3.

Point B in Figure 4.1, at which the line from K_1 is tangent to an isoquant, is the point at which total product is at a maximum for the given capital input; at this point the marginal product of labor is zero. Beyond E_3 so much labor is being used relative to the fixed amount of capital services that output could actually be increased by reducing labor inputs. Beyond E_3 in Figure 4.2 the total product begins to decline. In the example of the fast-food restaurant, there are so many workers behind the counter that they are getting in each other's way and actually decreasing the number of burgers produced each hour. Employers who want to maximize short-run profits and who have only K_1 units of capital services will never use more than E_3 hours of labor. They would use exactly E_3 only if labor were free.

The set of points such as A and B that are the lowest points of isoquants is shown by a dash line in Figure 4.1. This is sometimes called a *ridge line,* because as one moves horizontally to the right it marks the point at which the production surface begins to slope downward (at which total product curves decline). The corresponding line through C and D is the ridge line defined by moving vertically upward, with the number of hours of labor fixed. Beyond it, for any fixed labor input, output cannot be increased by adding capital services. If we move from left to right along the line at K_1, we start to the left of the upper ridge line. Point F is where the average product of labor (output per hour), AP_1 in Figure 4.3, is at a maximum. No profit-maximizing entrepreneur would knowingly operate to the left of this point, since output could always be increased without any more labor just by not using all the available inputs of capital.

The peak of the marginal product schedule in Figure 4.3 lies to the left of the point corresponding to the upper ridge line. When the average product is rising, marginal product must lie above it; that is, each additional employee hour must be pulling up the average product. The marginal product schedule, MP_1, therefore slopes downward throughout the relevant range of input combinations between the two ridge lines. This downward slope represents the *law of variable proportions*, sometimes called the *law of diminishing returns*. This states that as one adds units of one factor to a fixed input of the other, the increments to the product will diminish. With a fixed number of microwave ovens, each additional worker behind the counter adds less and less to the output of burgers.

The discussion of this section up to this point can be clarified by referring to Table 4.1, which shows a hypothetical example of total, average, and marginal product schedules. For convenience, the labor input is measured in number of workers rather than in hours. Reading down the table is equivalent to moving across the horizontal line beginning at K_1 in Figure 4.1. The portion of this line that lies to the left of the upper dash line in Figure 4.1 is represented by the first four workers employed; as each of these workers is added, the average product rises until it reaches its maximum when employment is 4. From this point to the point at which employment is 10, total product is rising, but average and marginal product are falling. This part of the table corresponds to the part of the horizontal line at K_1 between the two dash lines. When more than 10 workers are employed with the capital input held constant at K_1, output is reduced, and accordingly marginal product is negative. This corresponds to the part of the horizontal line at K_1 that lies to the right of point B.

What happens if the firm can somehow add more pieces of equipment, and

Table 4.1 HYPOTHETICAL TOTAL, AVERAGE, AND MARGINAL PRODUCT SCHEDULES

	Output per hour		
Number of workers	Total product (output)	Average product	Marginal product
0	0	0	—
1	5	5.0	5
2	12	6.0	7
3	20	6.7	8
4	28	7.0	8
5	34	6.8	6
6	39	6.5	5
7	42	6.0	3
8	44	5.5	2
9	45	5.0	1
10	45	4.5	0
11	44	4.0	−1
12	42	3.5	−2

thus increase capital services? In Figure 4.1 the fixed amount of capital services rises to K_2. With more capital, output is higher at each input of labor. The total product curve rises to TP_2 in Figure 4.2. Nonetheless, there is still some labor input, E_5, beyond which additional employee hours actually reduce output (TP_2 declines). What is crucial, though, is that at any input of labor the marginal product of an additional hour is higher than when the firm only had access to K_1 units of capital services. The slope of TP_2 exceeds that of TP_1 so that the marginal product of labor is higher. In Figure 4.3 MP_2, the slope of TP_2, always lies above MP_1. With the increase from K_1 to K_2, each worker has more capital with which to work, and is therefore able to produce more. The addition of more input of one factor raises the marginal product of the other. If there are only two factors of production, this will generally be true.

We can use the marginal productivity schedules to show how the employer's production process determines the quantity of labor demanded in the short run. Assume again that the firm only has access to K_1 units of capital services, so it faces the marginal productivity relation MP_1. We can express marginal productivity in monetary terms, as the *value of marginal productivity* (VMP), by either of two devices. The marginal product can be converted to the value of marginal product by multiplying it by the price of output per unit (where output is sold in a competitive market). Alternatively, one can imagine labor being paid in kind in output units, although this is unrealistic in a modern economy. Most workers prefer monetary payments, since it is hard for them to barter their output for the other goods they wish to consume. In either case the VMP shows how adding another worker or another hour of labor affects the employer's revenue.

The marginal productivity schedules in Figure 4.3 can thus be redrawn in Figure 4.4 as showing the value of marginal product. If the firm is confronted with the market wage W_2, it will employ E_2 hours of labor. The firm will not use more than E_2 hours, because beyond this point the wage paid to hire another hour of labor exceeds the value of its product; therefore adding labor reduces profits. The value of total output is the area under the value of marginal product curve up to E_2. This whole area is divided into two parts: the *wage bill,* the wage rate times the number of hours used (the rectangular area OW_2AE_2), and payments for capital services (the irregular area W_2BA). Payments for capital services include depreciation charges, interest, and profit. In the case of fixed capital inputs, however, depreciation charges and interest charges will be insensitive to changes in wages or the amount of labor used; thus changes in the area representing payments to capital services can be viewed as changes in profit (i.e., return on equity capital).

If the wage that the firm must pay rises to W_1 (because of collective bargaining, government decree, or the workings of the market), the employer will make the highest profits at point C. The number of hours demanded will fall to E_1. The extra hours of labor between E_1 and E_2 do not add enough to the firm's revenues to justify their now higher cost. Whether the reduction in labor input is accomplished by layoffs, failure to fill vacancies, or reduced weekly hours will depend upon considerations such as fixed employment costs, which we leave until the next chapter. But if the value of marginal productivity schedule slopes down, the profit-maximizing employer will make some adjustment that reduces labor input.

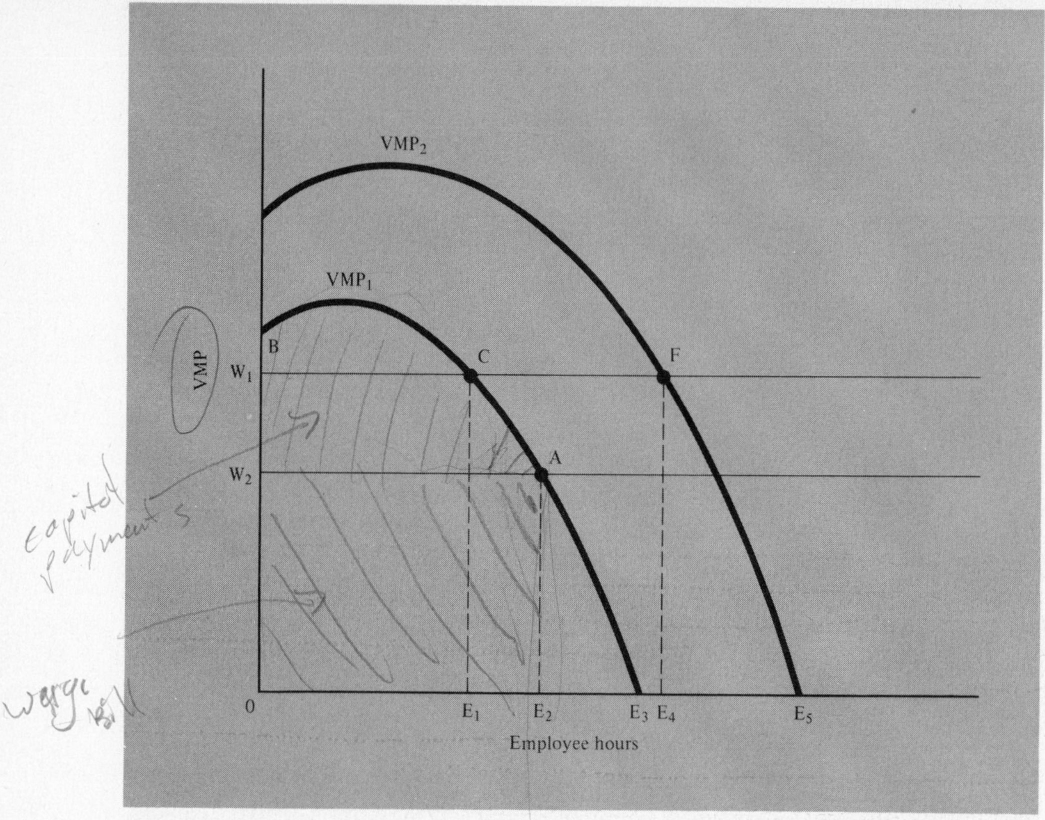

Figure 4.4 Determining demand for labor.

Assume the firm's fixed amount of capital services rises to K_2, so that the value of marginal productivity of labor is now depicted by the curve VMP_2. With the firm required to pay a wage W_1, it will again employ all labor hours that add at least W_1 to the value of sales. This means that it will maximize profits at point F, employing E_4 worker-hours. Because there is more capital, each hour of labor is more productive. Greater productivity justifies using more hours when the wage is W_1 than it did when there were only K_1 units of capital.

For a fixed amount of capital services, say, K_1, we have derived the amount of labor the employer wishes to use at various wage rates. This relation must be the employer's demand curve for labor in the short run. It is a relation between the price of labor services (the wage rate) and the quantity of labor services desired. The value of marginal productivity schedule is thus the employer's short-run demand curve for labor. With a greater fixed amount of capital services, the value of marginal productivity is higher at each labor input, and the employer's short-run labor demand curve is therefore higher as well. The market demand curve is the horizontal sum of all individual demand curves in the particular labor market, occupation, or industry. Since the curve for each firm slopes downward, the market demand curve must also slope downward.

DO LABOR DEMAND SCHEDULES REALLY SLOPE DOWN?

It should not be imagined that employers make explicit estimates of marginal product every time they hire a worker. Of course they do not. Most employers are not familiar with the term "marginal product." Yet they do make judgments about whether or not new employees are likely to be worth as much as they will cost, and many describe their decisions in these terms, which comes to very much the same thing.

Professor Fritz Machlup has suggested an analogy that is useful in this context. Imagine a driver deciding whether it is safe to pass a truck on a two-lane road when a car is approaching in the opposite lane. A formal model of the decision involves several different elements, including the speed of the approaching car, how far away it is, the speed of the truck, the rate at which the driver's car can accelerate, and the condition of the road. The driver has neither the ability nor the time to estimate each element separately and to combine them in a formal analysis. Yet millions of such decisions are made intuitively every day—fortunately, correctly in the majority of cases. Moreover, a formal model of the process might assist an analyst who was trying to design safer highways, even though it might not be a descriptively correct picture of the driver's conscious thoughts.

Critics of marginal productivity theory often assert that in the short run capital-labor ratios are fixed by technology, so that the short-run marginal product schedule is vertical, and raising wages will therefore not reduce the use of labor. No doubt there are cases where this is true, but there are also many where it is not. If one is using hand labor to dig a ditch and has only five shovels, each of which can be used by only one worker at a time, it does not follow that the marginal product of a sixth worker is zero. It has been fancifully suggested that the sixth worker could contribute to output by bringing water for the other five. More realistically, the sixth could add to output by relieving each of the others for 5 to 10 minutes each hour, so that the shovels would always be in use while the workers all rested regularly. Similarly, the speed of an automobile assembly line can be increased after relatively minor changes in equipment by adding more work stations and providing more relief workers to back up the line when the line workers fall behind or need to rest.

There is little direct empirical evidence on the slope of the labor demand curve for an individual firm. However, many economists have examined the demand for labor in a single large industry or in the entire manufacturing sector. The crucial parameter of interest is the *elasticity of labor demand*—the percentage change in employment in response to a 1-percent increase in the real wage. A summary of 14 studies of this parameter in the United States, shown in Table 4.2, finds that a medium estimate is −0.32 in the short run. This effect is composed of an output

Table 4.2 ESTIMATES OF 1-YEAR LABOR DEMAND ELASTICITIES

	Total elasticity	Output elasticity	Substitution elasticity
Medium	−0.32	−0.17	−0.15
High	−0.62	−0.27	−0.35
Low	−0.09	−0.04	−0.05

Source: Adapted from Daniel Hamermesh, "Econometric Studies of Labor Demand and Their Application to Policy Analysis," *Journal of Human Resources* (11): 519 (1976).

elasticity, reflecting the movements between isoquants that we have been discussing, and a substitution elasticity, reflecting movements along isoquants as the amount of capital changes, too (see the next section).[2] Within 1 year after a 1-percent rise in the real wage that manufacturing employers must pay, they will use 0.3 percent fewer worker-hours if technology has remained the same. A study of the short-run labor-demand elasticity in nine other developed countries found it to be negative in the postwar period in all but one, with a median value of -0.2. Other examples are estimates of -0.25 for iron and steel in West Germany and -1.06 for public education in the United States.[3]

POLICY ISSUE—CARTER AND BENTSEN ON WAGE SUBSIDIES

In 1977 the newly elected President Carter proposed stimulating the economy by giving employers a general tax credit, a reduction in the tax on their profits, equal to 4 percent of their Social Security taxes. The proposal would have reduced payroll costs by only 0.2 percent (since Social Security taxes accounted for 6 percent of payroll cost). This was hardly a major cut in the cost of hiring another worker. The extent to which it would have achieved its goal, stimulating employers to increase their input of labor, depends on the elasticity of labor demand. In terms of Figure 4.5, the tax credit is equivalent to a cut in the wage rate that the employer must pay, from W_0 to W_1. Like any other such cut, it stimulates an expansion in the amount of hours demanded, from E_0 to E_1.

This wage subsidy would have added $E_1 - E_0$ employee hours in the typical firm, a clear gain to the economy. But to do so the government would be subsidizing employers on *every hour* of labor they used. To lower the cost of labor to W_1, and to induce the small expansion in jobs, the government would have to incur a cost equal to the rectangle W_0W_1BC in Figure 4.5. Most of the subsidy goes to *inframarginal employment,* the E_0 hours that would be demanded even without the subsidy. In recognition of this cost, and the small "bang for the buck" it implied, Senator Lloyd Bentsen of Texas introduced a *marginal employment tax credit.* As a simplified description, no credit was to be given for any employment below what the firm had used the previous year; in Figure 4.5, this means that employers paid the full cost, W_0, on all hours up to E_0. On any new jobs created a very large subsidy in the form of a tax credit of as much as 50 percent of the hourly wage was given. If the firm increased employment beyond E_0, it had to pay only W_2 per hour out of its own funds. In firms whose labor demand curves remained unchanged, this scheme meant that it paid to expand employment from E_0 to E_2, a much larger expansion than under the Carter proposal. Moreover, the cost to the government is shown by the rectangle AHFG. It is far less per job created than under the Carter proposal, because the subsidy is not being wasted on jobs that would have existed anyway.[4]

[2] Daniel Hamermesh, "Econometric Studies of Labor Demand and Their Application to Policy Analysis," *Journal of Human Resources* (11): 509–525 (1976).

[3] Allan Drazen, Daniel Hamermesh, and Norman Obst, "The Variable Employment Elasticity Hypothesis: Theory and Evidence," *Research in Labor Economics* (6) (1984); Christoph Kollreuter, "Recent and Prospective Trends of the Demand for Labor in the Federal Republic of Germany," in Edmond Malinvaud and Jean-Paul Fitoussi (eds.). *Unemployment in Western Countries,* St. Martin's: New York, 1980, p. 332; and Orley Ashenfelter and Ronald Ehrenberg, "The Demand for Labor in the Public Sector," in Daniel Hamermesh (ed.). *Labor in the Public and Nonprofit Sectors,* Princeton University Press, Princeton, N.J., 1975, p. 71.

[4] John Bishop, "Employment in Construction and Distribution Industries: The Impact of the New Jobs Tax Credit," in Sherwin Rosen (ed.). *Studies in Labor Markets,* University of Chicago Press, Chicago, 1981, and Jeffrey Perloff and Michael Wachter, "The New Jobs Tax Credit: An Evaluation of the 1977–78 Wage Subsidy Program," *American Economic Association, Proceedings* (69): 173–179 (1979).

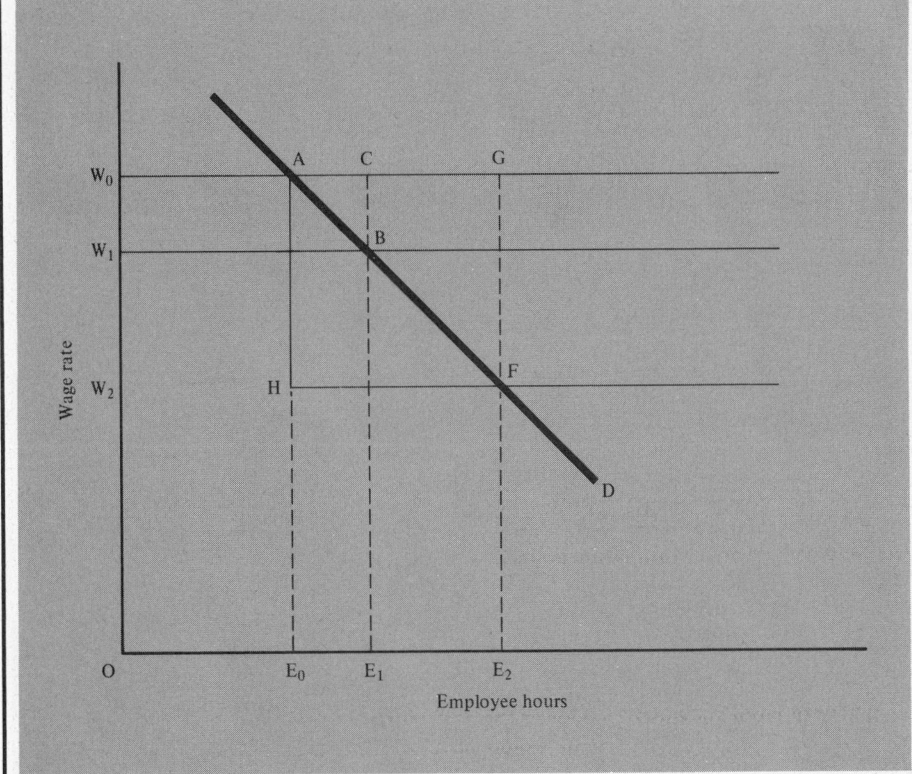

Figure 4.5 The effect of wage subsidies.

The Carter proposal was quickly dropped; the Bentsen proposal became law, and was in effect from mid-1977 until the end of 1978. Was it effective? This is an important question, insofar as it cost the U.S. Treasury $4.8 billion in corporate income tax credits. One study shows that one-third of the expansion in retail and construction employment that occurred during the period that this New Jobs Tax Credit was in effect stemmed from the credit. Another indicates that employers who knew about (and presumably used) the tax credit added 3 percent more worker-hours during 1977 to 1978 than did otherwise similar employers who did not know about the credit.

THE DEMAND FOR LABOR IN THE LONG RUN

Even after a time as short as 1 year, employers will begin to shift the amount of capital they use in response to a change in the price of labor. We can describe this process by redrawing the firm's isoquant map to derive the long-run demand for labor in a production method when technology is constant but the amount and nature of capital services used can be varied. The diagonal line CD, tangent to the isoquant Q_1 at A in Figure 4.6, is a budget constraint representing a given sum to be spent in buying inputs. Its slope is determined by the ratio of the price of labor services to the price of capital services. With a fixed budget, an increase in the wage rate would reduce the maximum amount of labor that could be hired, moving the

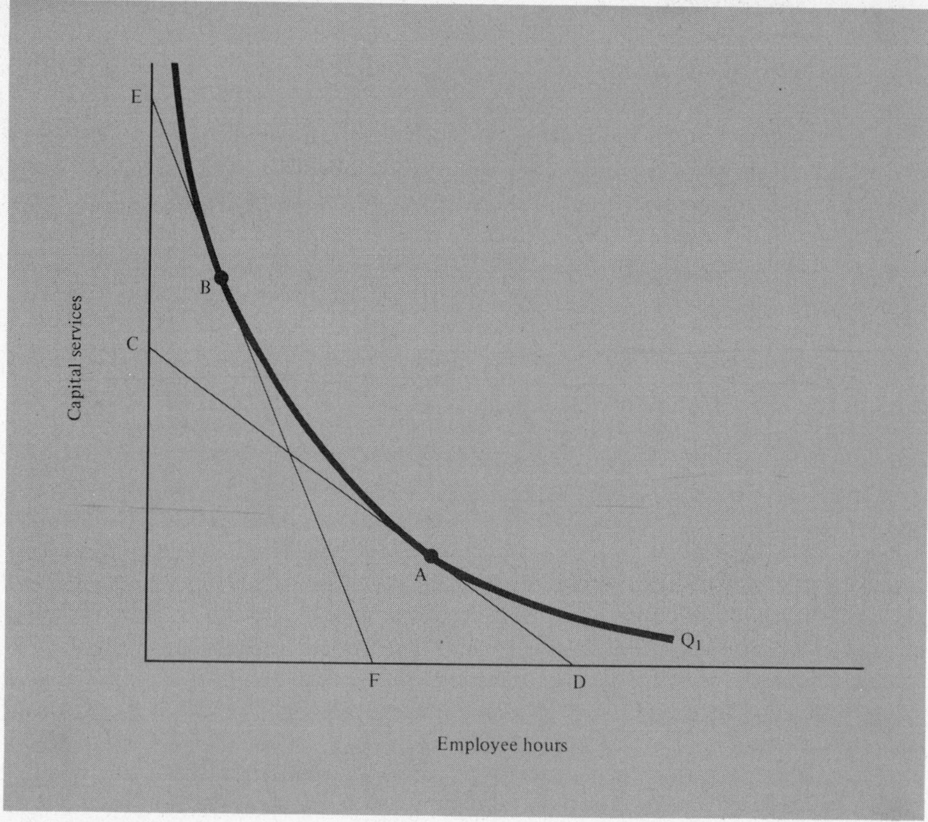

Figure 4.6 The standard case of labor-capital substitution.

CD line left from D along the horizontal axis. Conversely, the more expensive capital services relative to hours are, the more horizontal the constraint becomes. The intercepts on the two axes show how much of each factor could be bought if the whole budget were devoted to buying that factor. The tangency at A indicates the long-run position of cost-minimizing producers—at this point they get the largest possible output for the fixed expenditure on inputs. Note that the condition that the producers be cost minimizers is much weaker than the condition that they be profit maximizers. It can reasonably be assumed that even organizations that are not motivated by profits, such as government agencies or nonprofit institutions, will try to the best of their ability to minimize the costs of producing a given output.

Consider the case in which the price of labor is increased (with the price of capital services unchanged), and the budget is also increased to permit the production of the same output as before. The new budget constraint line, EF, is still tangent to Q_1 but cuts the horizontal axis farther to the left. Its slope is steeper and the tangency lies farther to the left, at point B. As equipment wears out, the producer will replace it with equipment designed to use less labor per unit of capital services. In the long run it is possible to substitute capital for labor through changes in the amount and kind of capital equipment. (How easy this is depends on the *elasticity of*

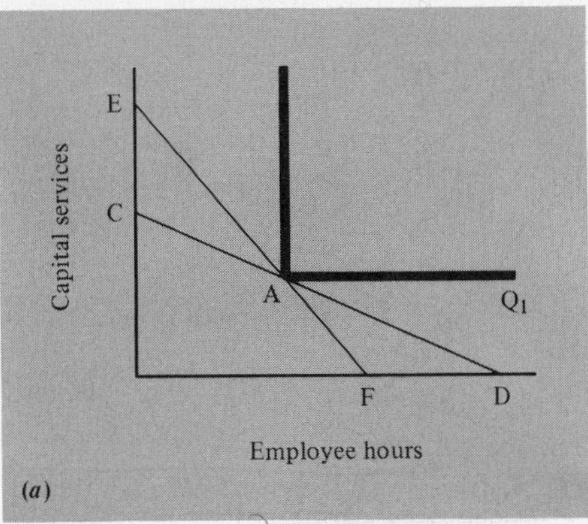

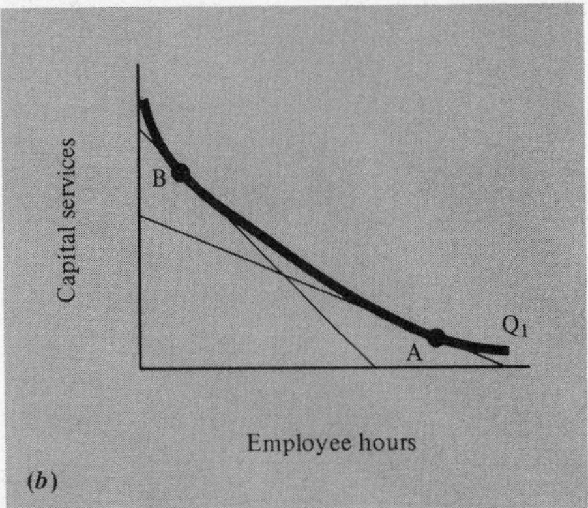

Figure 4.7 (a) No capital-labor substitution; (b) strong capital-labor substitution.

substitution, which is related to the extent of curvature of the isoquant.) The long-run demand curve for labor must be more elastic than the short-run demand curve.

The example in Figure 4.6 is only one of many possible cases illustrating entrepreneurs' responses to changes in the relative prices of labor and capital services. Although it is the standard one, some extreme cases also merit consideration. It is possible, though very rare, that even a large change in the relative prices of capital and labor will not change firms' labor input (e.g., it takes the labor of four people and the capital services of two violins, a viola, and a cello to produce a string quartet). With the budget constraint CD and the typical isoquant Q_1 in Figure 4.7(a), the entrepreneur will produce at point A. Even if labor becomes relatively much more expensive, though, the cost-minimizing employer will not change the mix of capital services and hours. In this case the elasticity of substitution between capital and labor is zero; each output can be produced by only one combination of labor and capital. It would never pay to produce the output Q_1 other than at point A: Additional labor inputs would not allow any saving on capital inputs, and vice versa. In this situation demand for labor at a given level of output is completely inelastic.

A nearly opposite case, of very easy capital-labor substitution (a very high elasticity of substitution), is shown in Figure 4.7(b). After the budget constraint tilts from CD to EF, it pays the firm to shift its production of Q_1 from A to B. A small change in relative input prices induces a very large change in relative factor utilization. Labor and capital are very close substitutes; and the long-run demand curve for labor is very elastic.

Do firms really do this? Anecdotal evidence suggests they do. In the United States, a truck that delivers soft drinks to stores is usually operated by one person. In India, similar trucks are said to have a crew of four—a driver, a manager who keeps the records, and two porters who carry the cases into the store. The relatively more expensive truck spends less time at each stop. This may well reflect appropriately the differences in the relative prices of labor and capital in the two countries. In China, large rugs are woven on very simple looms by weavers who spend months making one rug. In the United States, the process is mostly mechanized and is much more rapid.

Statistical evidence also confirms the existence of capital-labor substitution. There is an emerging consensus that a 1-percent change in relative factor prices induces about a 0.75-percent opposite change in relative factor demands, at a constant output (that the elasticity of substitution of labor for capital is 0.75). This estimate characterizes developed economies fairly well. Clearly, this is not a precise figure and has been the topic of substantial debate. Moreover, the extent of substitution differs among firms and industries.

Throughout the discussion we have assumed that technology is unchanged. In the very long run, however, one must abandon the assumption that the technology embodied in the production function is constant and unaffected by the wage rate. The direction of technological change can also be influenced by relative factor prices, with the greatest efforts being made to devise technologies that save the scarcest and most expensive inputs. This increased effort further raises the long-run elasticity of labor demand.

POLICY ISSUE—SHOULD DEVELOPING COUNTRIES USE WESTERN TECHNOLOGY?

During the 1950s and early 1960s the United States helped finance the export of American technology to developing nations through its programs of foreign assistance. Methods of production that worked well in the United States, in the sense of being able to produce output competitively, were instituted with U.S. aid in countries where real wage rates were far below those in the United States, but capital was at least as costly. Large-scale steel manufacturing plants were put in place in Pakistan and other less-developed countries with the encouragement of the U.S. Agency for International Development. The same agency encouraged agricultural planners and eventually, farmers themselves in West and East Africa to adopt mechanized methods of production, including the use of tractors, combines, and so forth. Did these exports of capital-intensive technologies improve productivity and raise output in the industries that the United States had "aided"?

Given the vast differences in relative factor prices between the United States and developing countries, it is not surprising that these exports of subsidized technology often did not produce the desired results. Local entrepreneurs, recognizing these difficulties, regularly switched back to older methods that accounted for the relative costs of capital and labor more accurately. For example, in Sierra, Leone bakers abandoned electric ovens in favor of wood-fired ones; and clothing firms that used large-scale, capital-intensive technology reported much lower rates of profit than did firms that relied on workers using simple sewing machines.[5] These findings suggest that policymakers may do their citizens no favor by importing technology that looks impressive but is inappropriate because of factor prices that differ from those for which the technology was designed.

THE DEMAND FOR SEVERAL TYPES OF LABOR

We have treated the employer's decisions as being limited to choosing between two factors, capital services and employee hours. This is clearly an inadequate description of the real world, for there is tremendous heterogeneity within capital services

[5]Enyinna Chuta and Carl Liedholm, "Employment Growth and Change in Sierra Leone Small-Scale Industry, 1974–1980," *International Labor Review* (121): 108 (1982), and Enyinna Chuta, "Techniques of Production, Efficiency, and Profitability in the Sierra Leone Clothing Industry," *Rural Africana* (6): 121 (1980).

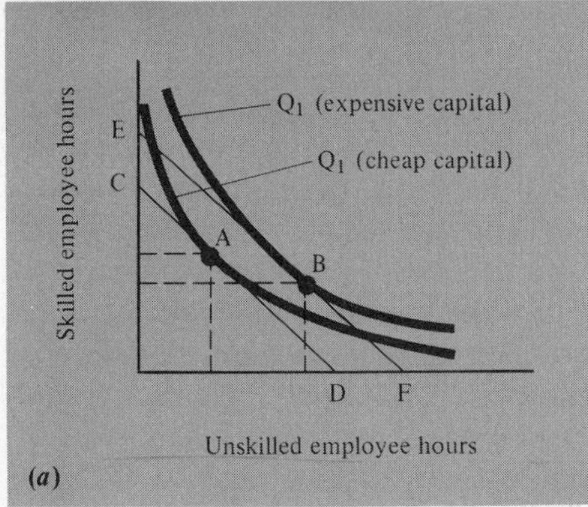

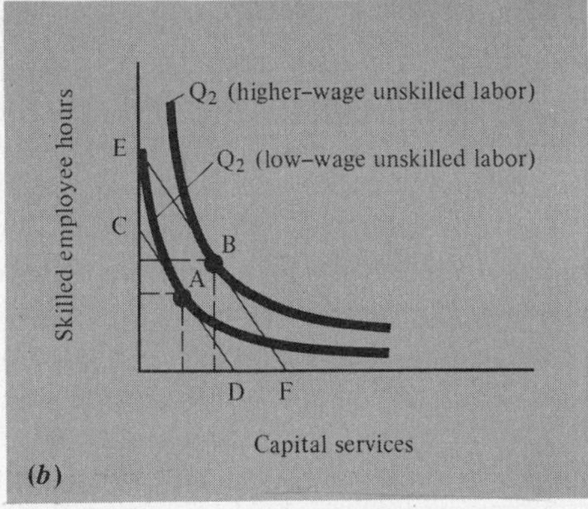

Figure 4.8 (a) Skilled labor and capital are complements; (b) skilled and unskilled labor are substitutes.

and among the various members of any work force. Some workers are skilled, others are less so; some are old, others are young. It is an oversimplification to aggregate workers into one lump, since employers do not set their employment this way, and many issues of public policy revolve around employers substituting workers of one type for those of another.

Consider the simplest extension of the two-factor case, a world in which firms use capital services and the hours of skilled and unskilled workers. The employer's decision about how many hours of skilled and unskilled labor to use is shown, as in the previous section, by the tangency of the budget constraint CD in Figure 4.8(a), with the isoquant Q_1 at point A. This isoquant differs from those we drew in the previous section, since along it the amount of capital being used is assumed to be constant. We also assume that the price of capital services is low and label the isoquant accordingly. With capital services cheap, the firm will use a lot of those services; thus by assumption at point A the skilled and unskilled workers have a lot of equipment with which to work.

What if the price of capital services rises? We know that the use of any factor will decrease when its price rises, so the firm will use less capital. In order to hold production at Q_1 the firm must increase its use of skilled or unskilled labor, or both. In fact, a large amount of research indicates that the typical firm will behave as depicted in Figure 4.8(a).[6] The isoquant for output Q_1 will *shift* out when capital becomes expensive and less capital is used, but it will also *tilt* as shown in Figure 4.8(a). With the relative prices of skilled and unskilled labor unchanged, the firm will minimize costs by producing Q_1 at point B. It will cut its demand for skilled labor and capital services when the price of capital services rises. It will maintain production by increasing its use of unskilled workers. Capital and skilled labor are thus *complements* in production. They are used together, and when the price of one of them rises,

[6] The initial work is by Zvi Griliches, "Capital-Skill Complementarity," *Review of Economics and Statistics* (51): 465–468 (1969); the large literature that followed is summarized by Daniel Hamermesh and James Grant, "Econometric Studies of Labor-Labor Substitution and Their Implications for Policy," *Journal of Human Resources* (14): 518–542 (1979).

firms' use of both declines relatively. Each is a *substitute* for unskilled labor; when their prices rise, firms expand their use of unskilled labor.

The point can be illustrated slightly differently by considering Figure 4.8(b). The lower Q_2 isoquant shows the combinations of skilled hours and capital services that will produce Q_2 when a lot of unskilled labor is used (when unskilled labor is cheap). Given the relative prices of skilled hours and capital services, denoted by the budget line CD, the firm minimizes costs at point A. When unskilled workers' wage rates rise, the employers cut back their use of unskilled hours. To maintain output at Q_2 the isoquant in Figure 4.8(b) must shift out. The budget constraint EF shows the same relative price of skilled hours and capital services; but with fewer unskilled hours being used, the firm will use more of both skilled labor and capital. They are joint substitutes against the now more expensive unskilled labor.

The fact that capital and skilled workers are complements has important implications for a number of issues in public policy and for understanding economic development. It suggests, for example, that investment tax credits and other subsidies for capital investment will stimulate job creation but that most of the jobs created will require skilled workers. The subsidies will not help unskilled workers on the whole. The ever-increasing mechanization of production that has accompanied economic development has required the simultaneous investment of resources in the development of human capital. Without this investment it seems unlikely that the rising living standards that have accompanied mechanization could have occurred. Investment in human capital would otherwise have placed a constraint on the returns to investment in physical capital.

Less is known about substitution among workers of different educational attainment. Perhaps not surprisingly, since greater educational attainment indicates more skill, educated workers appear to be substitutes for uneducated labor and are complements with capital services. Employers also seem to substitute younger workers for older ones when the relative wage of young workers declines.[7]

POLICY ISSUE—HAVE WOMEN BEEN "TAKING JOBS AWAY" FROM YOUTHS?

As we saw in Chapter 1, the increased labor-force participation of women represents a fundamental change in the labor market in the United States since 1945. The sharpest increase, between 1960 and 1980, occurred exactly when the number of young people entering the labor force expanded rapidly as the "baby-boom" generation matured. Between 1960 and 1980 the unemployment rate of youths 16 to 19 rose from 14.7 percent to 21.6 percent. Was this due in part to the growth in the adult female labor force? Were the adult women competing with teenagers for the same jobs?

The evidence shows that employers do treat women and youths as substitutes in production: If the wages of each group do not change, increased availability of one group reduces employers' demands for members of the other group. In that sense they do compete for the same positions.[8] If wages could never adjust to reflect changes in supply, such as the entrance of the baby-boom workers, then the increase in female labor-force

[7] Ibid. For the United Kingdom, see Richard Layard, "Youth Unemployment in Britain and the United States Compared," in Richard Freeman and David Wise (eds.). *The Youth Labor Market Problem: Its Nature, Causes and Consequences,* University of Chicago Press, Chicago, 1982, p. 524.

[8] This discussion stems from James Grant and Daniel Hamermesh, "Labor-Market Competition Among Youths, White Women and Others," *Review of Economics and Statistics* (63): 354–360 (1981).

participation would certainly have taken jobs away from the youths and contributed to the higher youth unemployment rates. Relative wages do adjust, though: Between 1960 and 1978 the wage of full-time year-round young workers fell from 80 to 70 percent of the average full-time year-round wage of workers of all ages.[9] Most of this decline was undoubtedly due to the growth in the number of young workers. Partly, however, it resulted from competition with the increased number of adult female workers. The competition from adult women did not itself increase the rate of unemployment of youths. It did, though, mean that the relative wages of young workers fell farther than they would have if the influx of adult women into the labor force had not occurred. So, too, the competition from young workers caused the wages obtained by these new women workers to be somewhat lower than they would have been if the youth and adult female work forces had not grown simultaneously.

THE EFFECTS OF THE MINIMUM WAGE

The discussion of the policy issue on substitution between youths and adult women makes it clear that relative wages are not fixed, but instead, can adjust to changes in relative demand and supply. This will be generally correct, so long as some external force is not preventing the adjustment toward an equilibrium of supply and demand from taking place. One such force that might produce a prolonged disequilibrium in the labor market is the imposition of a legal minimum wage above the equilibrium wage. The theory of competitive labor markets predicts that such an effective minimum wage will reduce employment, as illustrated by the analysis of Figure 4.9. For ease of exposition, in this figure, employment is measured in workers rather than hours; the analysis would be unchanged if hours were used instead. If the labor market were not competitive, a case we discuss in Chapter 5, the analysis would be much different.

The market demand curve is DD and the market supply curve is SS. Their intersection determines the competitive wage, W_c, at employment E_0. If a legal minimum wage is set at W_m, employment is reduced to E_1. The reduction in employment is smaller than the excess supply of labor at the minimum wage (AC); the excess supply includes a second component consisting of workers who would like to work in this market at the new wage but are not hired. Some of these workers may be unemployed or out of the labor force; others may be employed in markets where the minimum wage does not apply. In the diagram the two components are shown by the horizontal distances AB and BC. The sizes of the two components depend on the slopes of the demand and supply schedules.

It should be noted that in the long run some of the reduction in employment may result from a reduction in the number of firms in the market rather than from changes in the number of workers employed by each firm. Such cases might occur where the firms in question competed in the product market with firms in other labor markets paying wages higher than W_m for superior labor. The minimum wage would then raise wages in the low-wage market without improving the quality of its labor. If the firms in question had been competing on even terms before the minimum-wage

[9] This calculation is based upon various issues of U.S. Bureau of the Census, *Current Population Reports, Consumer Income,* and upon unpublished data supplied by the U.S. Bureau of Labor Statistics.

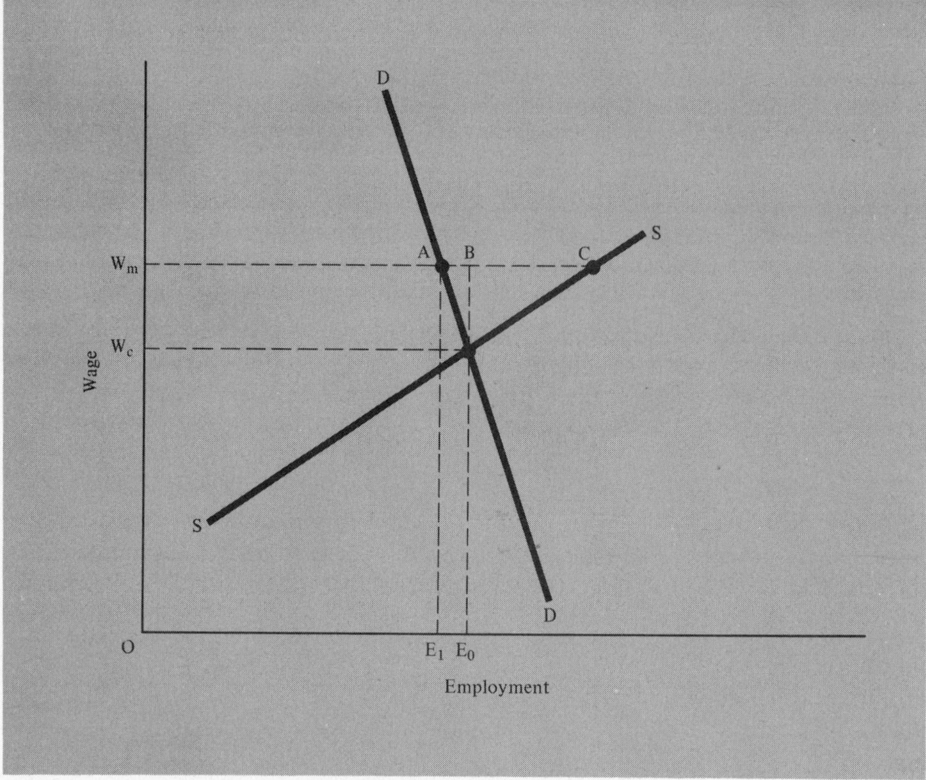

Figure 4.9 The effects of a legal minimum wage in a competitive market.

law, they would now be at a disadvantage and might have to move out of the local labor market or go out of business.

The legislated minimum wage will affect employment only if it is above the equilibrium wage, and only if it applies to the labor market one is examining. As column (1) of Table 4.3 shows, the statutory minimum wage has risen, albeit in fits and starts, over the past several decades. It has been increased sporadically from the $0.25 per hour rate that was set when the Fair Labor Standards Act of 1938 instituted a national minimum wage policy in the United States. Column (2) shows, though, that the minimum wage really has not changed much relative to the average wage. To the extent the average wage measures the equilibrium wage in the typical labor market to which the minimum wage applies, this means that the relative size of the horizontal distance AB in Figure 4.9 probably has not been increasing in markets to which the policy has applied since its inception. The major change in the impact of minimum wages has come from the expansion of its coverage to previously unaffected sectors. As column (3) shows, the fraction of nonsupervisory employees whose jobs are covered by the minimum wage (whose employer is required by law to pay them at least the minimum) more than doubled in 20 years. This expansion of coverage to additional firms accounts for the sharp rise in the minimum wage index in column (4). This measure, derived by multiplying column (2) by column (3),

Table 4.3 MINIMUM WAGE AND RELATED TIME SERIES, PRIVATE NONFARM EMPLOYMENT, SELECTED YEARS, 1960–1982

Year	Yearly average minimum wage (1)	Relative minimum wage (2)	Coverage ratio (3)	Minimum wage index (4)
1960	1.00	0.465	0.389	0.181
1962	1.15	0.520	0.538	0.280
1965	1.25	0.523	0.519	0.272
1967	1.39	0.517	0.676	0.350
1969	1.60	0.537	0.735	0.395
1972	1.60	0.482	0.741	0.357
1974	1.87	0.484	0.760	0.367
1975	2.10	0.515	0.756	0.389
1976	2.30	0.531	0.783	0.416
1977	2.30	0.502	0.819	0.412
1979	2.90	0.542	0.839	0.445
1980	3.10	0.536[a]		
1981	3.35	0.532[a]		
1982	3.35	0.501[a]		

[a]Estimate based on growth of private nonfarm earnings.
Source: Minimum Wage Study Commission, *Report, Volume 1,* 1981, p. 36.

shows the overall potential impact of the policy. In sum, the gap between the minimum wage rate and the equilibrium wage may not have increased in markets that were covered by minimum wage policies before 1960; but the number of markets affected has risen dramatically.

Has this expansion really resulted in the loss of employment suggested by the analysis in Figure 4.9? One can easily see that the effects will be confined to certain parts of the work force. A bricklayer earning $10 per hour will not be thrown out of work because the minimum wage is raised from $3.10 to $3.35. A worker who was getting $3.20 per hour before the increase may well be out of work after the increase. Even more likely in view of the costs of hiring workers (the fixed employment costs we shall deal with in Chap. 5), a worker who would have been hired for $3.20 will not be hired if the employer must offer a wage of $3.35. We should expect the market for low-skilled, inexperienced workers to have an equilibrium wage rate below the minimum wage.

This expectation has led research on the effects of the minimum wage on employment to focus on the demand for teenage workers. This is a group that has not acquired much experience, is not yet well educated, and thus whose equilibrium wage rate may be below the minimum. The evidence is overwhelming that a higher effective minimum wage has reduced employment among people aged 16 to 19 in the United States, and there is some evidence that greater coverage of that minimum has had the same effect.[10] The estimates vary, but they cluster around a reduction in teen employment below what it would otherwise be of between 1 and 2 percent for

[10]Robert Goldfarb, "The Policy Content of Quantitative Minimum Wage Research," *Industrial Relations Research Association Proceedings* (27): 261–268 (1974), and Charles Brown, Curtis Gilroy, and Andrew Kohen, "The Effect of the Minimum Wage on Employment and Unemployment," *Journal of Economic Literature* (20): 487–528 (1982).

each 10 percent increase in the minimum wage index shown in column (4) of Table 4.3. Not surprisingly, since their equilibrium wage is somewhat higher, employment of 20- to 24-year-olds is less adversely affected by increases in the minimum. Similar effects have been found in Quebec, Canada, and in France.[11]

Even though the employment effects of the minimum wage have been clearly documented, we cannot infer from them that the minimum wage has contributed to higher unemployment rates among young workers. We showed in Chapter 1 that the labor-force participation rate of teenagers is quite responsive to changes in their job opportunities. Those teenagers who do not find work because of the effects of the minimum wage on employers' demand for their labor may drop out of the labor force rather than continue looking for work. This seems to be what happens. In the United States between 1954 and 1969, each 10 percent increase in the minimum relative to the average wage lowered the participation rate of white teenagers by 1.6 percent; among nonwhites the effect was even larger, a 3.7 percent decline. In Canada between 1956 and 1975, each 10 percent increase resulted in a 1.3 percent drop in the participation rate of young people.[12] Given the size of the employment effects, the magnitude of the declines in participation is such that the minimum wage has not caused much change in the unemployment rate of teenagers. Instead, it has reduced their employment and increased their rate of nonparticipation in the labor force.

An additional argument against the minimum wage is that it reduces investment in on-the-job training. As we saw in Chapter 3, workers pay the cost of such training by accepting low wages early in their tenure on the job. With the imposition of the minimum wage, there is a floor to the wage they can be offered. This forces employers to bear more of the cost of training, which they will not do if the training is general. There is some evidence that the amount of training on the job is reduced by increases in the minimum wage. On the other hand, human capital acquired through education expands: More youths enroll in school when the minimum wage increases, probably because the attractiveness of schooling is enhanced when employment opportunities are restricted by the higher minimum.[13]

The conclusion that a minimum-wage law will reduce employment and on-the-job training does not dictate the judgment that such a law is undesirable. Indeed, one of the goals when the law was enacted was, "to reduce youth employment and limit their competition with adults."[14] If taking jobs away from young

[11] Pierre Fortin, "L'Effet du Salaire Minimum sur les Prix, L'Emploi et la Repartion des Revenus: Le Cas du Quebec," *Relations Industrielles* (34): 660–672 (1979), and Organization for Economic Cooperation and Development, Economic Policy Committee, *Effects of the Minimum Wage on Youth Employment and Unemployment: A Review of the Recent Literature Together with a Study of the French Experience,* OECD, Paris, 1981.

[12] Jacob Mincer, "Unemployment Effects of Minimum Wages," *Journal of Political Economy* (84): S104 (1976), and Robert Swidinsky, "Minimum Wages and Teenage Unemployment," *Canadian Journal of Economics* (13): 168 (1980).

[13] Jacob Mincer and Linda Leighton, "Effects of Minimum Wages on Human Capital Formation," in Simon Rottenberg (ed.). *The Economics of Legal Minimum Wages,* American Enterprise Institute, Washington, 1981; Masanori Hashimoto, "Minimum Wage Effects on Training on the Job," *American Economic Review* (72): 1070–1087 (1982); J. Peter Mattila, "Youth Labor Markets, Enrollments and Minimum Wages," *Industrial Relations Research Association Proceedings* (31): 134–140 (1978).

[14] Paul Osterman, *Getting Started: The Youth Labor Market,* MIT Press, Cambridge, Mass., 1980, p. 84.

workers means giving them to adults who have more family responsibilities, that may be a reasonable argument for the minimum wage. So, too, raising the minimum wage may raise the incomes of some workers who are in lower-income households and who manage to retain their jobs. To the extent that a more equal income distribution is desirable, the minimum wage contributes to this goal if people who work at the minimum wage are disproportionately in low-income households. Unfortunately, there is little relation between a household's income and the chance of it containing a worker who is earning just the minimum wage, because many teenagers earning the minimum live in middle-income households.[15]

POLICY ISSUE—WOULD A YOUTH SUBMINIMUM WAGE DISPLACE ADULT WORKERS?

The evidence that higher minimum wages and expanded coverage of minimum wage legislation have restricted the employment of teenagers has led to a search for alternatives. One such alternative is a subminimum wage rate that is applicable only to youths. For example, employers might be required to pay workers aged 16 to 19 only 75 percent of the legislated minimum wage required for adult workers. Such a proposal was debated in Congress in 1974, came within one vote of passage in the House of Representatives in 1977, and has been at the center of discussion of minimum wage policy since then. Proposals that would offer tax credits to firms that hire young workers are designed to have effects similar to those of the subminimum wage.

As the evidence on labor demand elasticities indicates, the subminimum wage would clearly generate additional employment for teenagers. But would that employment come at the expense of adult workers? That is, what would be the displacement effect of a subminimum wage for youths? The answer depends partly on the extent to which employers react to the decline in the wage of young workers relative to that of adults by substituting youths for adults. It will also be affected by the amount of additional product that can be sold as competitive employers, seeing reduced unit costs when they can pay a lower minimum wage, lower their selling prices and find their output expanding as customers buy more.

The extent of displacement is clearly not one adult job for each additional youth employed. Current estimates suggest that somewhere between three and nine youths would be employed at the expense of one adult worker. The adult workers are most likely to be people whose wages are barely above the minimum wage.[16] Whether one adult worker who is not employed is too high a price to pay for three, or even nine additional employed teens is a very difficult and essentially noneconomic question. All that labor economists have shown is that the trade-off resulting from a subminimum wage is much more favorable than one adult job for each teenage worker employed. The results also suggest that some of the displacement can be avoided if the subminimum applicable to more experienced teens is closer to the minimum wage for adults. A program such as that in the United Kingdom that sets higher youth wage rates for each older group of young workers would accomplish this purpose. By legislating a higher minimum for such workers, Congress would prevent them from gaining an unfair advantage over slightly more experienced young adults who are not eligible for the subminimum wage.

[15] Edward Gramlich, "Impact of Minimum Wages on Other Wages, Employment and Family Incomes," *Brookings Papers on Economic Activity:* 409–451 (1976), and William Johnson and Edgar Browning, "The Distributional and Efficiency Effects of Increasing the Minimum Wage," *American Economic Review* (73): 204–211 (1983).

[16] Daniel Hamermesh, "Minimum Wages and the Demand for Labor," *Economic Inquiry* (20): 365–380 (1982), and Peter Linneman, "The Economic Impacts of Minimum Wage Laws: A New Look at an Old Question," *Journal of Political Economy* (90): 443–469 (1982).

THE ROLE OF THE DEMAND FOR THE FINAL PRODUCT

Although we began the discussion of the demand for labor in terms of the substitution between factors in production, that is by no means the only force involved. Since the demand for labor is derived from the demand for the products or services it produces, the nature of the demand for these final products or services is also of great importance. A shift in the demand for the final product will produce a shift in the same direction in the demand for the labor input, where a shift means a movement of the whole demand schedule to the right or left.

More interesting problems are presented by an increase in the wage of labor used in a particular industry relative to wages elsewhere. Frequently such wage increases occur where certain occupations are specialized to an industry, or where all the firms in an industry are covered by one collective bargaining agreement or by separate agreements with the same union. The impact of the wage increase on costs per unit of output will be minimized by substitution in production, but this will not ordinarily prevent some rise in unit costs, especially in the short run, when substantial changes in the input mix are seldom feasible. For a given wage increase, the size of the increase in unit costs depends on the importance of labor in the input mix as well as on the ease of substitution; the larger the ratio of labor cost to other costs, the greater will be the increase in total unit costs. In a competitive industry in the long run all firms are earning zero economic profits (just covering the opportunity cost of all inputs). Thus none of the increase in total unit costs can be absorbed by profits; it will all be passed on in product prices. The impact of this price increase on the quantity of labor demanded will depend on the elasticity of demand for the final product.

Where the price elasticity of demand is small, the reduction in output and in the amount of labor demanded will also be small. Price elasticity reflects the possibility of substitution in consumption. Like substitution in production, this is usually less important in the short run than in the long, because substitution involves learning and may involve changes in capital equipment. Thus an increase in the relative wages of coal miners, passed on in the price of coal, would not immediately induce much change in the pattern of fuel consumption, since few users are equipped to burn more than one fuel. Over time, however, it would influence the type of fuel chosen for new installations and for the replacement of those that become obsolete.

Alfred Marshall summarized the determinants of the elasticity of factor demand in four *laws of derived demand.* The first two follow from the discussion thus far: The demand for labor will be less elastic: (1) the harder it is for firms to substitute labor for capital at a given output (i.e., the production process is more like the isoquant in Figure 4.7(a) and less like that in Figure 4.7(b)); and (2) the smaller the elasticity of demand is for the final product (so that any wage increase can be passed on to consumers with little loss in the demand for output, and thus for labor). The third law states that the demand for labor will be less elastic, the smaller the initial ratio of labor cost is to other costs.[17] This may not be intuitively obvious. Suppose,

[17] J. R. Hicks, *The Theory of Wages,* 2d ed., Macmillan, London, 1964, pp. 241–246, demonstrates that this law may be reversed. If the ease of substituting along an isoquant exceeds the elasticity of demand for the product, then the elasticity of demand for labor will be smaller, the *larger* the ratio of labor

though, that the wages of barbers comprise 80 percent of the total costs of a haircut, and the wages of motion picture projectionists make up 5 percent of the total costs of a motion picture theater. Suppose further that wages in both occupations rise 10 percent with other wages remaining constant. The cost of a haircut will tend to rise by about 8 percent and that of attending a motion picture by about 0.5 percent. For equal elasticities of demand for the final output, the 10 percent wage increase is likely to cause a far greater reduction of employment among barbers than among projectionists. The fourth law is that the demand elasticity will be lower if the supply of other factors is less elastic. If the wage falls, employers will, as we have seen, seek to expand output by passing on some of the lower costs to the consumers in the form of lower prices. If the supply of other complementary factors of production, such as capital, is very inelastic, however, additional workers will not produce much, for they will have little additional machinery with which to work. That being the case, the employer's incentive to expand production, and thus to hire more labor, will be reduced.

The usefulness of these laws becomes clear when we examine the probable success of unions in achieving wage increases without causing a substantial loss of employment for their members. The laws are also helpful in constructing wage subsidies designed to stimulate employment, particularly if those subsidies are to differ by industry, occupation, or geographic area. Indeed, in any case in which the wage of a particular group of workers is to be altered, these laws aid in identifying those characteristics that will strengthen or mitigate the effect on employment.

We saw that in the short run the elasticity of demand for labor in response to wage changes is below the long-run elasticity and is far below one. The demand for labor is far more responsive in the short run to shifts in demand for output than to changes in wage rates.[18] This observation has led economists, especially those in planned economies, to use techniques designed to make predictions of *employment requirements* based only on shifts in final demand and in the ratio of worker-hours to output, although these techniques are clearly incorrect.[19] The assumptions underlying any application of these techniques are: (1) *returns to scale* are constant: doubling output requires doubling all inputs; and (2) relative wage rates are not affected by shifts in demand. A simple application of the technique is shown in Figures 4.10(a) and (b). Suppose the economy produces output by using trained workers. Initially 50 workers produce 100 units of output (at point A in Figure 4.10(a)). Because of wartime demands for production, output must quickly double to 200 units. This requires a doubling of the trained work force to 100 workers, as shown at point B in Figure 4.10(a). Workers are not born trained, however. Trained workers are produced by a combination of their time and that of training instructors. As point C in

---

cost is to other costs. In other words, when the producer can substitute more easily than the consumer, it is an advantage to labor to have a large share in the initial input mix. In this case the use of labor is not much reduced by a rise in the product price, and substitution in production will be more difficult and expensive, the larger the amount of labor is that needs to be replaced. The laws are presented in Alfred Marshall, *Principles of Economics,* 8th ed., Macmillan, London, 1923, pp. 383–388.

[18] Hamermesh, "Econometric Studies . . . ."

[19] See, for example, the studies in Organization for Economic Coorporation and Development, *Econometric Models of Education,* OECD, Paris, 1965.

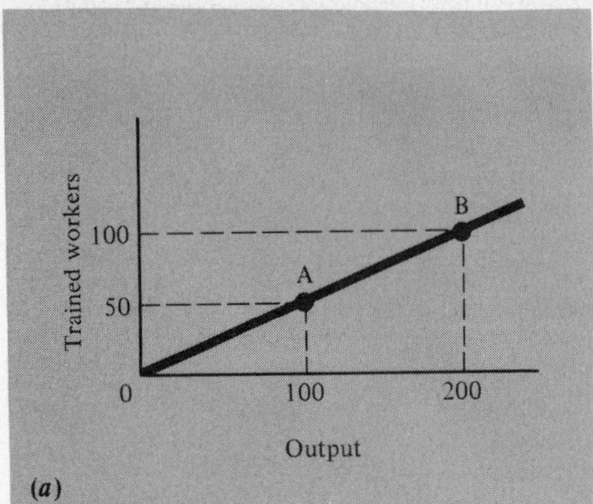

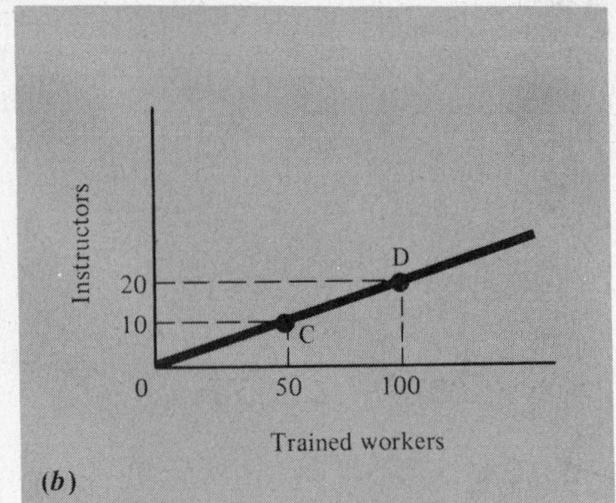

Figure 4.10 (a) Employment requirements, production sector; (b) employment requirements, training sector.

Figure 4.10(b) shows it takes 10 training instructors to keep 50 trained workers on the job. If the economy needs 100 trained workers, it must also produce an extra 10 instructors (point D in Figure 4.10(b)). If people involved in planning in this economy do not expand the number of instructors, they will find themselves unable to meet the requirement for trained labor that is dictated by the need to double output.

So long as the increase in output does not change the relative wage of trained workers and training instructors, this simple approach will predict employment requirements very well. Especially for unexpected, rapid increases in output, while custom and lags in perception hold relative wages roughly constant, employment planning using complex versions of the apparatus developed in Figures 4.10(a) and (b) will give a good approximation to the optimal allocation of workers by occupation or skill level. In such cases it will be a helpful technique for planners in developing economies, or for corporate managers who must integrate planned expansion in one sector of the corporation with the needs for inputs of labor from other sectors.

THE DEMAND FOR LABOR IN THE ECONOMY AS A WHOLE

Having looked at the demand for labor in a firm and in an industry, we can now venture further and ask what the aggregate demand schedule for labor might look like—the curve showing the demand for labor in the economy as a whole. To construct such a curve, we must assume that all wages change in a constant proportion relative to other input prices.

We assume that the aggregate demand for all factors taken together remains unchanged. For example, this could happen if the change in relative factor prices consisted of an absolute increase in the money wage and an absolute decrease in other factor prices, such that the increased spending by wage earners was just matched by the decreased spending of owners of other factors. Alternatively, one could think of the net effect on aggregate demand of a shift in relative prices as offset by a change, for example, in the level of government spending. This case should be contrasted with the usual case in macroeconomics in which an increase in the general level of wages is assumed to increase aggregrate demand.

The earlier discussion of substitution in consumption was based on a rise in wages in one industry only. This might lead one to think that if all wages rise together, there will be no substitution in consumption. This conclusion is not correct. Consider an example in which all wages rise by 10 percent and wages make up half the total costs of production in the coal industry, but only one-fifth of the total costs of production in the petroleum industry. If cost increases are fully passed on in prices in the long run, the price of coal would rise 5 percent and that of fuel oil only 2 percent, leaving an incentive to use more fuel oil. (This calculation ignores the labor cost component in the price of capital goods. To include it would alter the numbers but not the conclusion.)

The argument of the last two paragraphs suggests that when all wages rise together, the force of substitution in both production and consumption is attenuated but still present. The aggregate demand curve for labor will therefore still slope downward, although it will be less elastic than the demand curves for the great majority of firms, industries, occupations, or demographic groups.

The aggregate demand curve for labor is derived, like the labor demand curve for each industry or market, under the assumption of constant technology. Technology is continually changing, though, and generally in the direction of increasing the amount of output each worker can produce. In the United States from 1948 to 1975, output per hour of all people engaged in production in the private business sector rose at the average annual rate of 2.7 percent. Output per hour was 2.1 times as large in 1975 as in 1948. Even during the 7 years of slow growth between the recessions of 1975 and 1982, output per hour grew at an annual rate of 1.2 percent, so that output per hour in 1982 was 2.3 times as large as in 1948.

Growth in output per hour shifts the aggregate demand schedule outward. At any wage rate employers seek to use more labor because labor is more productive. Improved technology usually means increased automation. Within an individual industry, automation may mean that fewer workers are required; because of the complementarity of capital and skilled labor, the workers who are no longer employed are especially likely to be low-skilled. In the economy as a whole, however, automation and labor-saving technical progress produce higher real wages and profits, and thus greater spending on goods and services. Since the demand for labor is derived from the demand for final output, the aggregate demand schedule shifts out even though some individual industries use less labor. The best illustration of this argument is that real wages were 58 percent higher in 1979 than in 1949, due to the improvements in technology; yet unemployment rates in the 2 years were 5.9 and 5.8 percent, respectively. Aggregate labor demand shifted out rapidly enough, because of the increase in consumer spending, to absorb the additional output generated by the increase in labor productivity.

SUMMARY

Individual employers' labor demand schedules are downward-sloping. As the wage the employer must pay drops, the extra output of additional workers becomes profitable. The demand for entire groups of workers is also somewhat elastic. When the wage of one group rises, employers substitute capital or the hours of workers in other groups for the services of workers who have become more expensive. Even in the economy as a whole the demand for labor is downward-sloping, although not so sharply as for any individual firm, industry, labor market, or group of workers.

That labor-demand schedules slope downward must be remembered whenever we examine the effects of imposing a change in the wage rate of a group of workers or in a particular industry. Wage subsidies, changes in minimum wage rates, higher payroll taxes and union-imposed wage increases will all affect the quantity of labor that employers want to use. The magnitude of the effects depends upon a host of considerations. The ease with which employers can substitute against any group of workers whose wage rate is increased, and the ease with which consumers can switch their demands away from employers who attempt to pass the increased wage costs forward through increases in product prices, are major determinants of the size of these effects.

chapter 5

The Demand For Labor: Some Extensions

THE DEMAND FOR LABOR IN NONCOMPETITIVE PRODUCT MARKETS

The preceding chapter reviewed the theory of the demand for labor in perfectly competitive markets. In this chapter some of the assumptions of that discussion are relaxed to obtain propositions about demand in other circumstances. We first examine the demand for labor in markets that are not perfectly competitive.

The simplest way to extend the competitive theory is to drop the assumption of perfect competition in product markets. Without perfect competition the firm faces a downward-sloping demand curve for its product. If it employs more labor, it must lower its product price to sell the additional output. In this case the demand curve for labor is not the value of the marginal product (marginal physical product multiplied by the product price), but is the *marginal revenue product, MRP* (marginal physical product times the marginal revenue). Indeed, it is really the general case that labor is demanded up to the point where its wage is equal to the marginal revenue product, and perfect competition in product markets is a special case—in which marginal revenue product (MRP) equals the value of the marginal product (VMP). Since in product markets that are not perfectly competitive marginal revenue is always less than price, the marginal revenue product must always be less than the value of the marginal product, as in Figure 5.1, and will fall more rapidly as employment is increased.

A profit-maximizing employer who has some control over product price (a price-setter), but who is confronted with a fixed wage, will employ labor up to the point where the cost of another hour of labor is equal to the marginal revenue product. In Figure 5.1 this is shown where the MRP curve cuts the wage, W_0, determining employment E_0. Beyond this point, using another hour would increase

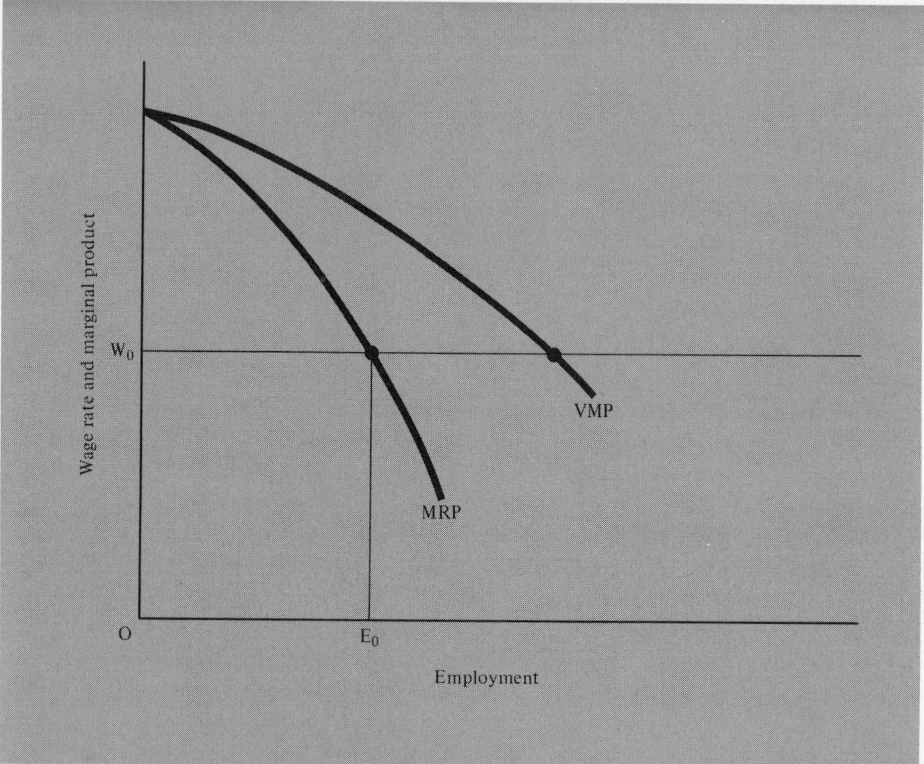

Figure 5.1 The demand for labor in a noncompetitive product market.

the wage bill more than it would increase total revenue, and would therefore reduce profits. The number of hours of labor used will be less than in a competitive product market. Although labor will receive a wage that is equal to its marginal value to the firm, it will receive less than the value of the output to society, the marginal social product. This is not because its wage is lower than the wages of similar labor elsewhere; rather, the restriction of output to maximize profits has raised the marginal social product of labor in this use above what it would be in a competitive product market. This is equally true of other factor inputs utilized by such firms.

Although the analysis of the demand for labor by a profit-maximizing price-setter is a simple extension of marginal productivity theory, one may question whether real-world price-setters are typically profit maximizers in the short run. They may be under a variety of political and public relations pressures to stabilize employment, to restrict profits to reasonable amounts, to restrain increases in product prices, and not to enlarge their share of the product market unduly. The penalty for not complying, or at least seeming to comply, with these pressures could be government intervention to diminish or regulate their market power. As a result, the management of a firm with some market power could choose to devote profits to paying higher wages than the labor market requires or to using more labor than a profit maximizer would. In this case, high profits that might otherwise invite government intervention are used to buy a more contented work force or stave off unionization.[1] There is evidence that firms that produce in markets characterized by little competition do pay wages higher than workers would get in competitive industries, but the effect seems to be fairly small.[2]

A firm with some product-market power may be restrained in its ability to make the maximum use of this power by the presence of some form of government regulation. Among public utilities in the United States, such as power and telephone companies, this regulation takes the form of state and federal commissions that must approve price increases. Commissions seek to ensure that firms' return on their invested capital does not exceed certain limits. The firm seeks to maximize profits; the commission limits only its *rate of return,* the ratio of profits to its rate base (which we take here as being identical to its capital stock). The regulated company thus faces different incentives from the typical competitive firm when deciding what technology to use, given the relative prices of capital and labor.[3] Although labor-intensive technology may be the best choice given factor prices, adding labor instead of capital does not add to the rate base. If the choice of technology reduces costs and increases profits, the regulatory commission will force the firm to reduce prices to prevent the rate of return from rising. Choosing a more capital-intensive technology has the advantage of increasing both profits and the rate base, and thus not necessarily producing an increase in the rate of return, which might be disallowed. Since firms facing this type of regulation tend to choose more capital-intensive technologies, a fall in the relative price of labor will induce a different rate of substitution of labor for capital than would be undertaken by the typical firm that is free to maximize profits, if the elasticity of substitution is not constant along an isoquant.

In many firms the profit motive is completely absent. Universities, many hospitals, charitable organizations, governments, foundations, and other institutions all hire workers without any profit motive in mind. To the extent they seek to minimize costs, though, their demand for labor will be like that of the competitive firm. The analysis of the competitive firm rested solely on cost minimization; it did not require the employer to maximize profits. If the nonprofit firm does not minimize costs, however, things are not so straightforward. A government official who makes employment decisions may try to maximize the chance of remaining in office.[4] Not reducing employment after wages increase may be consistent with this goal. A university administrator may seek to maintain some traditional balance between junior and senior faculty regardless of changes in the relative costs of employing them. The evidence shows, though, that governments and universities do

[1] For an elaboration of this point, see J. R. Monson, Jr. and Anthony Downs, "A Theory of Large Managerial Firms," *Journal of Political Economy* (73): 221–236 (1965).

[2] See Leonard Weiss, "Concentration and Labor Earnings," *American Economic Review* (56): 96–117 (1966); Wallace Hendricks, "Labor Market Structure and Union Wage Levels," *Economic Inquiry* (13): 401–416 (1975); James Dalton and E. J. Ford, "Concentration and Labor Earnings," *Industrial and Labor Relations Review* (31): 45–60 (1977); and Wesley Mellow, "Employer Size and Wages," *Review of Economics and Statistics* (64): 494–501 (1982).

[3] This argument was first made by Harvey Averch and L. L. Johnson, "Behavior of the Firm Under Regulatory Constraint," *American Economic Review* (52): 1053–1069 (1962).

[4] Melvin Reder, "The Theory of Employment and Wages in the Public Sector," in Daniel Hamermesh (ed.). *Labor in the Public and Nonprofit Sectors,* Princeton, Princeton, N.J., 1975, discusses this and other motivations that might distinguish the labor demand of a governmental unit from that of a private firm.

respond to changes in the price of labor by reducing the amount demanded and do substitute one type of labor for another when their relative wages change.[5] This is probably true for other nonprofit employers as well.

Not all firms maximize profits, but other motives are equally consistent with the predictions of the theory of demand for labor. This means that we can safely assume that an increase in the wage rate facing most employers, regardless of the industry in which they operate or the structure of the firm, will eventually make the amount of labor they use less than it would otherwise have been.

MONOPSONY IN LABOR MARKETS: THE FORMAL MODEL

From the point of view of the theory of labor markets, it is more interesting to abandon the assumption of competition in the labor market, restoring for simplicity the assumption of competition in product markets. Price-setters in the product market are confronted directly by the downward-sloping demand curve for their products rather than by prices set in a competitive product market. Similarly, labor *monopsonists* are confronted directly by an upward-sloping supply curve of labor in their markets rather than by a wage set in a competitive labor market. Literally speaking, the term *monopsony* refers to a market in which there is only one buyer. However, we will use it here to include cases in which there are only a few employers of labor in a labor market or in which employers collude in setting wages.

Figure 5.2 shows the relevant schedules for a labor market monopsonist. The downward-sloping curve VMP is the value of the marginal product. The upward-sloping curve S is the supply curve of homogeneous labor, which in this case is measured in number of employees rather than in hours. (The assumption that all employees work the same number of hours avoids unnecessary complications in the subsequent discussion.) The steeper upward-sloping curve MLC is *marginal labor cost,* which measures the addition to the wage bill that results from employing an additional worker when all workers employed get the same wage (the case known as *nondiscriminating monopsony*). The upward-sloping supply curve indicates that new workers can be hired only at wages that are higher than the wages paid to those already employed. The cost of hiring an additional worker therefore includes both the wage of the new worker and the cost of bringing the wages of everyone previously employed up to the new level. For high levels of employment, the second element of this marginal cost can easily exceed the first. The profit-maximizing employment, E_0, is given by point A, where MLC and VMP are equal. Beyond this, employing another worker adds more to total labor cost than it adds to total revenue. The wage corresponding to E_0, which is W_0, is given by the height of supply curve at B, *not* the height of MLC at A (since the supply curve, not the MLC, shows the available combinations of workers and wages).

Although Figure 5.2 is an extension of marginal productivity theory because the value of marginal product is one of the elements that determine the wage, the VMP curve in this case is not a demand curve for labor. Monopsonists have no

[5] See Orley Ashenfelter and Ronald Ehrenberg, "The Demand for Labor in the Public Sector," in Hamermesh, op cit., p. 71, and William King, *A Multiple Output Translog Cost Function Estimation of Academic Labor Services,* Doctoral Dissertation, Michigan State University, 1980.

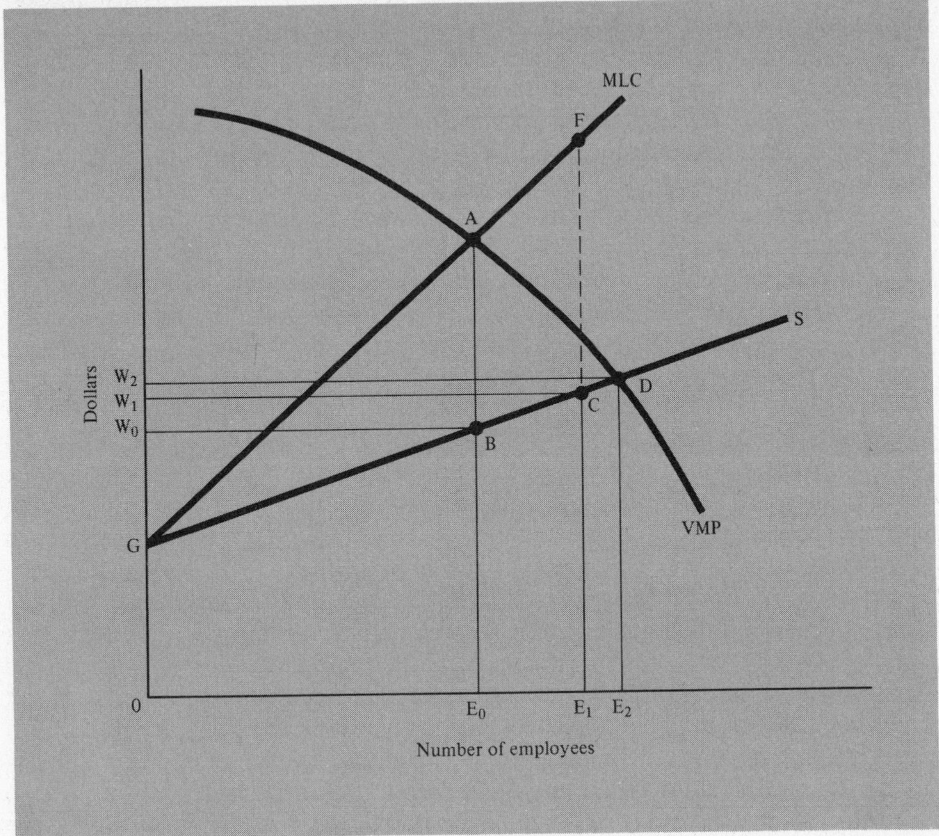

5.2 The wage-employment position of a monopsonist.

MLC
S = Monopsonist
VMP
No Demand Curve

demand curve for labor, in the sense of a simple relation in which quantity demanded depends on the wage, for exactly the same reason that product market monopolists have no supply curve for their products. The number of workers demanded depends not only on the height of the supply curve at any employment but also on its elasticity. Imagine another supply curve that also passes through B but slopes upward more steeply than S. The marginal labor-cost curve corresponding to such a supply curve would lie above the one shown on Figure 5.2; employment would be lower than E_0, and the profit-maximizing wage would be determined at a point below W_0 on the new supply curve.

In a labor market characterized by competition among employers for workers, or by a union-imposed wage rate, the marginal product of labor will equal the wage rate. This is not true in a labor market characterized by monopsony. In Figure 5.2, the value of the marginal product is indicated by the height of the VMP curve at A; the wage rate is only W_0. In such markets the employer or colluding employers are exploiting the workers, in the sense that the workers receive a wage less than the value of the marginal product (by an amount equal to vertical distance AB). Without the collusion among employers that can produce a monopsonized labor market there would be no divergence between wage rates and the value of the marginal product.

Figure 5.2 can be used to show that imposing a legal minimum wage on a monopsonist can sometimes increase employment. Suppose that the minimum wage is set at W_1. Marginal labor cost is equal to W_1 up to C, where W_1 crosses the supply curve. Up to that point additional workers can be hired at the wage already being paid, and hiring them will add only their own wage to the wage bill. But at C marginal labor cost jumps upward to F on the old MLC curve, as shown by the dash line. The next worker hired must be paid more than the minimum wage; if the worker is hired, everyone previously employed must be paid more as well. If, as in this case, the VMP curve passes through the dash segment CF, profit-maximizing employment will be E_1. By the same reasoning one can show that an increase in the minimum wage from W_1 to W_2 would increase employment from E_1 to E_2. A minimum wage increase above W_2 would decrease employment as in the competitive case, for the minimum would intersect the VMP curve to the left of D. Indeed, if the minimum wage were raised above A, employment would be reduced below E_0. Since the evidence in Chapter 4 made clear that on balance an increase in the minimum wage reduces employment, we may conclude that either monopsony characterizes relatively few labor markets or the minimum wage is typically above W_2.

The employment of a *perfectly discriminating* monopsonist would be quite different from that of a nondiscriminator. By perfect discrimination we mean that the monopsonist is able to hire each worker at the worker's own supply price, thus paying unequal wages for equal work. Such an employer would maximize profits at D, with employment of E_2, which, of course, would also be the equilibrium employment of a perfectly competitive industry with the same supply and productivity conditions. But although the allocation of resources is the same in the two cases, the distribution of income is very different. In the competitive case the wage bill is the rectangle OW_2DE_2. In the case of the discriminating monopsony, the triangular portion (W_2GD) of this rectangle lying above the supply curve is part of profit rather than part of the wage bill.

The possibilities for paying different hourly wages, except through an incentive pay or piecework system, to different individuals doing the same work are probably quite limited for manual workers. There is among manual workers a strong tradition of concern about interpersonal equity, as well as a general knowledge of rates of pay. Discriminating monopsony may be more possible for professional and managerial workers, where the tradition has been that salaries are confidential and related to individual merit, although this tradition may be beginning to break down. Where classes of equally productive workers, such as men and women, have different supply schedules, more limited kinds of discrimination are feasible. This problem, however, goes beyond the case of monopsony; it will be considered at length in Chapter 13.

POLICY ISSUE—MONOPSONY IN PROFESSIONAL SPORTS

Until 1977, professional baseball players worked under the *reserve clause;* they sold their services in a monopsonistic labor market. The team that initially engaged them reserved the right to pay them what it wished, to trade them to another team, or to urge them to leave professional baseball. The player always had the choice of leaving organized baseball, and that was his main bargaining weapon; he had no choice about where he would play. This gave the team owners the means to exploit the players by paying them salaries below what the players would add to the teams' revenues. One study compared player salaries to their marginal revenue products, derived as the amount each extra point in a batter's slugging average (total bases per time at bat), or in a pitcher's strikeout-to-walk average, added to team revenues.[6] Star players received only 15 percent of their marginal revenue products, and average players received only 20 percent. The reason is clear: Even this small fraction of their marginal revenue product far exceeded what they could earn through their only alternative, leaving baseball. There was no exploitation of mediocre players; they were paid relatively little, roughly equal to what they added to their team's revenue and what they could get if they left baseball. They could not be exploited, for any attempt to do so would have driven them out of the profession.

Part of the monopsony profits from major league teams undoubtedly went into the team owners' pockets. Part was also used to finance a large network of so-called minor league teams. Their substantial losses, covered by the excess profits from the majors, were the teams' investment in developing the training that converted a talented teenager into a baseball star. This investment was specific to the team. Because the minor league player had to remain with the team when he got to the major leagues, an otherwise general investment in baseball skill became firm-specific. As we would expect, the specific investment was paid for by the team, and the team reaped the returns to this investment in the form of marginal revenue products in excess of most major league players' wages.

Since 1977, following a federal court decision, each experienced player has had the right to sell his services to the highest bidder. This has resulted in a sharp rise in average salaries (a 144 percent increase between 1977 and 1981 alone, compared to only 51 and 44 percent increases among professional football and basketball players, respectively, in the same period).[7] A large part of this increase was due to bidding wars for star players: A $400,000 salary was the highest in 1977; in 1982, the highest was $2.5 million. The stars, who were most exploited under the monopsonistic system, received the greatest gains when it was ended.

Wiping out the owners' monopsony profits has also changed the economics of training in the industry. Major league owners, no longer able to finance training themselves, are abandoning their system of minor league teams. The Detroit Tigers, as a typical example, had 14 such teams in 1949; today they have only five. Increasingly, training that is general to all (baseball) firms is being obtained in schools where general training in many fields is acquired; the baseball teams are recruiting an increased fraction of their players from colleges.

How did the court decision affect the consumer? This is a difficult question to answer, but recent consumer behavior gives some clues to it. In 1982 attendance at major league baseball games reached an all-time high, despite the decline in personal income that accompanied the severe recession of that year. The game's appeal does not seem to have been greatly damaged.

MONOPSONY IN LABOR MARKETS: AN INTERPRETATION

Before employers can be discriminating monopsonists, they must first of all be monopsonists. This takes us back to the question of how prevalent monopsony in labor markets actually is. There is some reason to think that the monopsony case has been given more attention in textbooks and the economics literature than its actual importance would warrant.

The simplest case of monopsony is the company town with only one employer,

[6] Gerald Scully, "Pay and Performance in Major League Baseball," *American Economic Review* (64): 915–930 (1974).

[7] Glen Waggoner, "Money Games," *Esquire* (97): 57 (June 1982).

a situation that was once common in the American textile and mining industries.[8] Today the importance of such cases is diminishing, both because they are found largely in declining industries and because better roads and the low cost of serviceable used cars have reduced the isolation of company towns. It is now practical and common for American workers to commute up to 25 miles to work, and very few employers provide the bulk of employment within a 25-mile radius of their establishments. The cost of commuting long distances leaves some residual monopsony power to isolated employers, but less than when commuting was impossible.

The other possibility is collusive monopsony resulting from agreements among employers not to raise wages individually or not to hire away each other's employees. There is indeed evidence that some such agreements exist.[9] However, these agreements must be very difficult to enforce. They are not needed in loose labor markets, when there is no shortage of labor or upward pressure on wages. When labor markets become tight, the temptation for the parties to collusive agreements to violate or evade them probably becomes irresistible. Once labor is scarce, it is in the interest of all employers to seek to raise the compensation of their workers relative to compensation elsewhere (e.g., by allowing earnings to rise through upgrading, paying for unnecessary overtime, and similar devices), although they might maintain the agreed basic scale. Collusion among small numbers of employers is, of course, easier to establish and maintain than collusion among large numbers.

The employer who uses highly specialized workers is often the only employer in a labor market who employs workers in certain occupations. In this case, however, the monopsony power is bilateral. The workers have nowhere else to go without leaving the area, but the employer has no local labor supply beyond present employees. Attempting to exploit this position beyond obtaining a fair return on investment in specialized training will increase the movement of workers to other areas and could produce losses on past investment in them.

Let us now return to the case in which an employer can hire workers at the same wage, but let us abandon the assumption that they are all of equal quality and work equally hard. Instead, assume that the employer can rank workers from best to worst and that increasing the work force would mean adding workers less able than any now employed. The best workers would be the first hired and the last to be laid off. The short-run marginal revenue product schedule drawn on these assumptions would be MRP_1, in Figure 5.3; it is more steeply sloped than the standard curve, MRP_0, that assumes homogeneous labor. Adding workers to the fixed input of capital now involves both raising the ratio of labor to capital inputs and lowering the quality of labor at the margin. Both forces work in the same direction. An increase in wages from W_0 to W_1 will still generally cause a reduction in employment. The cutback will be from E_0 to E_1, smaller than in the standard case, though; MRP_1 is steeper than MRP_0, and thus demand is less elastic.

[8]There has been very little study of the amount of employer concentration in labor markets. One work is Robert Bunting, *Employer Concentration in Local Labor Markets,* University of North Carolina Press, Chapel Hill, 1962. Another, Robert Baird and John Landon, "The Effect of Collective Bargaining on Public School Teachers' Salaries," *Industrial and Labor Relations Review* (25): 410–416 (1972), provides some evidence that monopsonistic exploitation exists where there are fewer school districts within a geographic area.

[9]See, for example, Richard Lester, *Adjustments to Labor Shortages,* Princeton University Industrial Relations Section, Princeton, N.J., 1955, pp. 46–49.

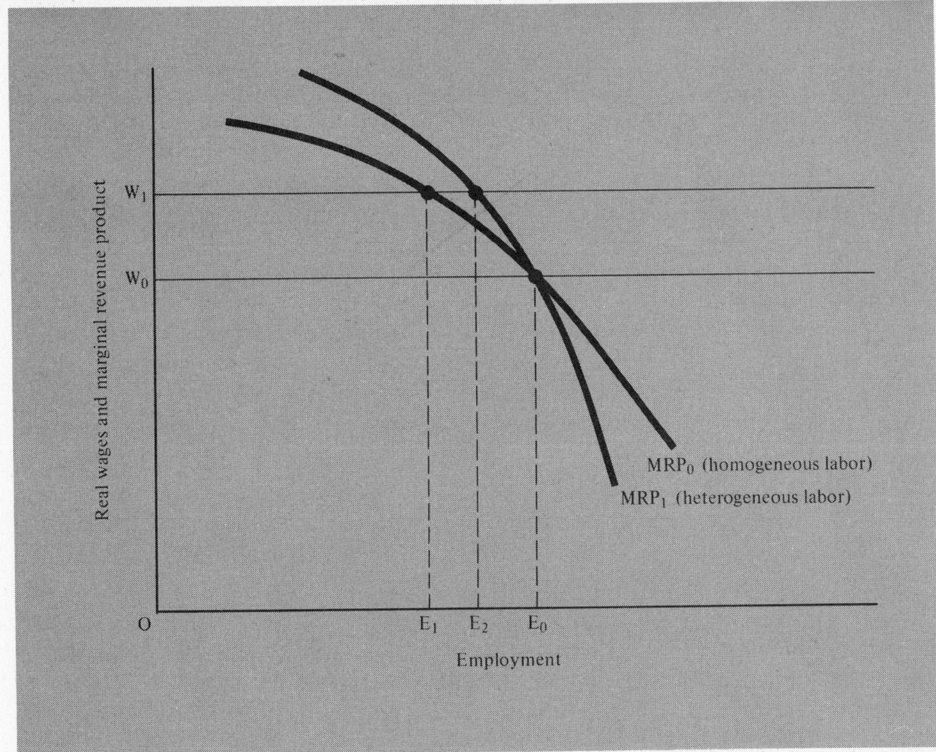

Figure 5.3 Demand for homogeneous and heterogeneous labor.

This extreme case assumes a total lack of competition in the market for ability and thus a total lack of bargaining power on the part of the superior workers. Their added ability or effort should command a premium over the wage of their less able or less energetic colleagues; the example assumes that the employer succeeds in capturing this rent. Under fully competitive conditions all employers would be able to identify the abler workers and the competition for them would raise their pay. This is what Marshall meant in arguing that competition would equalize *efficiency wages*—wages relative to abilities and efforts—within an occupation.[10] The tendency toward this result will be weaker, the greater are the barriers to mobility and the greater the importance of seniority rules are.

INTERDEPENDENCE BETWEEN WAGES AND PRODUCTIVITY

One of the assumptions involved in stating that wages are determined by the intersection of a supply curve with a demand curve based on marginal productivity is that the demand schedule is independent of the wage. If it were not, an upward shift of the supply schedule or an imposed increase in the wage rate would shift the

[10] Alfred Marshall, *Principles of Economics,* 8th ed., Macmillan, London, 1923, p. 547. For an attempt to measure the relation between individual wages and ability, see Albert Rees and George P. Shultz, *Workers and Wages in an Urban Labor Market,* University of Chicago Press, Chicago, 1970, pp. 88–90, and the discussion of this issue in Chapter 3.

position of the demand schedule and the new equilibrium position would not lie on the old demand schedule. This assumption of independence has frequently been attacked by critics of marginal productivity theory. The criticism can be considered under two heads—cases in which wage increases raise the efficiency of workers and cases in which wage increases improve the efficiency of management. The first is sometimes called the *economy of high wages* and the second is sometimes called *shock theory.* The possible relation between wages and the supply of effort by way of better nutrition and health was mentioned in Chapter 2, where we suggested that the effect is probably not of any substantial importance in developed countries. However, the analysis may be of practical importance in developing countries. Although the evidence does not completely support the assertion that better nutrition improves productivity in developing countries, most research indicates this is the case. One especially detailed study showed that improved nutrition, which presumably is purchased with higher wages, resulted in higher output by ditchdiggers in Kenya.[11] It is thus worthwhile to construct a demand schedule under these assumptions. This is done in Figure 5.4, which shows the demand for labor by a firm.

The analysis assumes that instead of a single marginal productivity curve there is a family of such curves, one for each wage, with higher wages corresponding to higher marginal productivity schedules. The demand curve D then connects the points at which each wage crosses its own marginal productivity schedule, at points such as A, B, and C. The demand curve is steeper than any of the marginal productivity curves at the points where it crosses them. The marginal productivity curves for higher wages lie above those for lower ones because by assumption a higher wage makes workers more productive. Thus under conditions where productivity increases with the level of wages, the reduction in employment induced by wage increases will be smaller than it would be along a demand curve based on a single marginal product schedule.

The wages chosen for illustration in Figure 5.4 differ by constant amounts. The corresponding increments in product have been drawn so that they are always smaller than the increments in wages.[12] This assumes that the worker is not a perfectly efficient machine for converting higher wages into added product, if only because wages are normally shared with the worker's family and are not all spent on consumption that raises the worker's efficiency. An employer would not continue a situation in which output could be increased more than proportionately by increasing wages unless this was done from ignorance. Even a slave owner would spend more in feeding slaves if it was known that their product would rise by more than the added outlay.

[11]Carl Stevens, "Health and Economic Development: Longer-Run View," *Social Science and Medicine* (11): 809–817 (1977), and R. M. Brooks, M. C. Latham, and D. W. T. Crompton, "The Relation of Nutrition and Health to Worker Productivity in Kenya," *East African Medical Journal* (56): 413–422 (1979).

[12]In terms of the diagram, this requires that the area between two marginal product curves up to any given employment must be less than the area between the corresponding wage levels. This condition is ordinarily sufficient to ensure that the demand curve slopes downward. The condition is violated in Harvey Leibenstein, "The Theory of Underemployment in Backward Economies," *Journal of Political Economy* (65): 91–103 (1957), one of the earliest and most complete discussions of the economy of high wages.

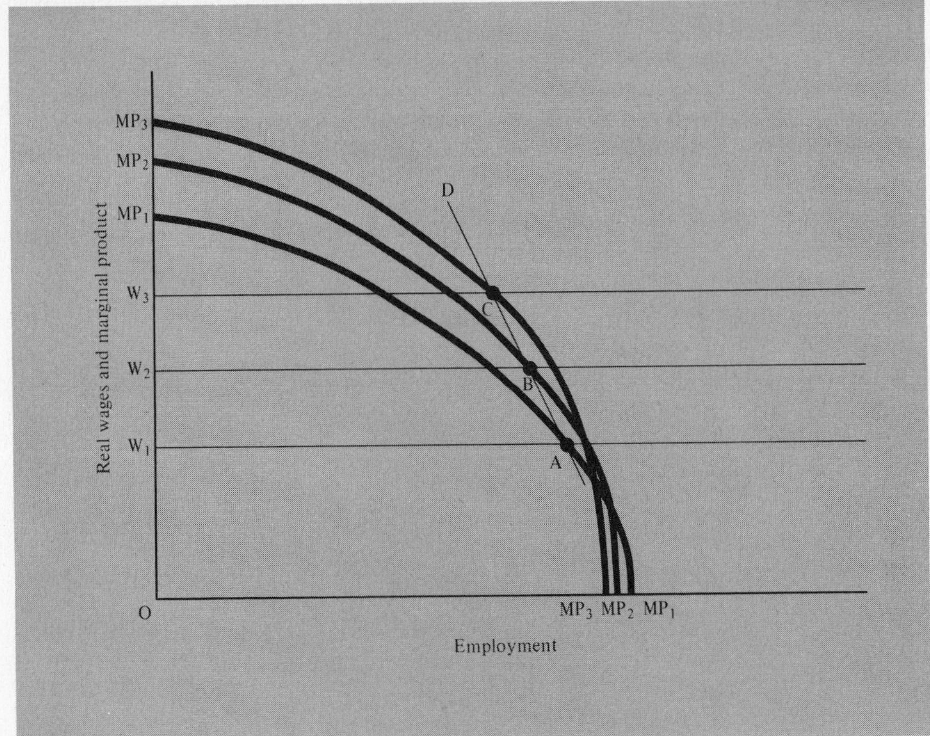

Figure 5.4 The economy of high wages.

The vertical distance between successive marginal product curves in Figure 5.4 decreases as wages rise, indicating that successive increments in wages have diminishing returns in added product. This is consistent with the argument that this analysis is most applicable to economies where living standards, and wages, are initially at very low levels. The marginal product curves also converge as employment increases, and eventually they cross. This shows that, with the quantity of other factors fixed, the amount of labor (in efficiency units) needed to bring total product to a maximum (and thus marginal product to zero) is embodied in a smaller number of workers when the wage is high. If we assume, for example, that 10 poorly paid workers working for a week could cultivate a field so thoroughly that further cultivation would not increase its output, the same point might be reached in a week by 8 well-paid workers.

The analysis of shock theory is not unlike that of the economy of high wages, except that it is management's productivity that is said to increase with the wage rate. This difference makes the shock theory applicable to developed countries. The theory is often used to argue that there need be no reduction in employment in response to a wage increase; that is, the demand curve for labor is vertical. The large wage increases, or shocks, are contrasted with the more gradual changes in wages that might be required by the tightening of a competitive market.

The basic premise of shock theory is that any organization operates with some slack or inefficiency and that this inefficiency can be reduced when the organization is seriously threatened. This will produce a higher marginal productivity schedule for labor in response to a sudden wage increase, since special attention will be given to eliminating inefficiency in the use of the factor whose price has suddenly increased.

It is important to note that one cannot confirm shock theory merely by observing that the result of a wage increase is the use of more or newer machinery per unit of labor. Such changes are exactly what is predicted by the marginal productivity explanation of demand, in particular by capital-labor substitution along an isoquant. Shock theory requires that the isoquant associated with any particular output level shifts inward (requires less capital and/or labor) because of innovations in technique or organization that are induced by the increase in wage rates.

Shock theory is most plausible as applied to the unionization of a previously nonunion enterprise. In most cases this will produce both a substantial wage increase and a simultaneous challenge to the unlimited authority of management and its ways of doing things, which could well inspire management to reexamine its methods and procedures with some care. The cost saving could enable the firm to hold its product prices in line with those of nonunionized competitors, thus maintaining output and employment. Whether this occurs is part of the more general issue of management behavior in the presence of unionism, which we discuss in Chapter 11. It is much harder to imagine repeated waves of successful innovation in response to annual wage increases that are negotiated with an established union. Such negotiated wage increases will themselves become routine, and a complacent organization can deal as inefficiently with them as with other aspects of its activity.

Shock theory is also used to justify the notion that the imposition of a higher minimum wage will not cause affected employers to reduce employment. This argument is not very credible on theoretical grounds for the same reason that routine negotiated wage increases are unlikely to produce a shock effect: Increases in the minimum wage have come quite often, and although they are not regular, they are not entirely unexpected. On empirical grounds, the evidence that the minimum does reduce employment indicates that if the shock effect exists, it is outweighed by the more conventional effects induced by a downward-sloping labor demand schedule.

FIXED COSTS OF EMPLOYMENT

So far in the discussion of demand we have been assuming that the cost of labor to the employer consists only of an hourly wage. We now drop that assumption and recognize that there are also fixed costs of employment.[13] These fixed costs have important implications for the incidence of unemployment by skill level, for the dynamics of employment demand and for the employer's choices between changes in numbers of workers and changes in hours of work.

Broadly defined, fixed costs of employment are any costs that vary less than proportionately with the hours worked by an individual employee. These costs are of two general types. The first are turnover costs—the costs incurred when employees are hired, laid off, or discharged. These include the costs of recruitment, screening,

[13] One of the earliest and best discussions of the issues treated in this section is Walter Oi, "Labor as a Quasi-Fixed Factor," *Journal of Political Economy* (70): 538–555 (1962).

and initial training, as well as such terminal costs as severance pay and increases in taxes for unemployment insurance. The second type of fixed costs consists of costs that occur throughout the period of employment but are not related (or not fully related) to hours of work. A tax on employment based on numbers of employees rather than on wages or hours of labor, or any payroll tax whose tax base has an annual earnings limit, such as social security and unemployment insurance taxes in the United States, falls in this category, as would similarly based contributions to private pension and welfare plans.

All fringe benefits are not fixed costs; whether they are or not depends on the details of how they are calculated. For example, contributions to a health and welfare fund stated in dollars per employee per month involve an element of fixed costs, since they are not increased by overtime work. Contributions stated as a percentage of payroll, including overtime pay, would have quite an opposite effect. If overtime were paid for at premium rates, the contribution would in effect also be paid at premium rates. The neutral case is that in which the contribution is paid at the same rate for standard and overtime hours.

For several reasons turnover costs rise as a proportion of total labor cost with the skill level of the employee. Much more intensive effort is devoted to hiring highly skilled employees such as professionals or executives than to hiring unskilled workers, because in jobs that involve great responsibility mistakes in staffing can be costly. Expenses for recruiting, including agency fees or advertising, and for screening, will be higher for the skilled employee. Expenses for travel to interviews may be paid; references will be checked more carefully; more expensive management time will be used in interviewing. Although there are few data available on the costs of hiring, those shown in Table 5.1 do support the belief that hiring costs increase with skill level. The few other surveys that are available corroborate this conclusion.[14]

Training costs as well as hiring costs usually vary with skill level since the period of induction or specialized on-the-job training needed before the new employee reaches full usefulness will usually be longer for more skilled workers. A new janitor might be fully effective in 2 or 3 days in the job; a new executive might need months to learn how an organization functions. This expectation is supported by data from the survey that forms the basis for Table 5.1; employers reported training costs for professional, managerial, and technical occupations that were triple those reported for an average of all occupation groups.

Differences in fixed costs by level of skill imply that employers will be more reluctant to lay off skilled than unskilled employees, especially in response to a drop in demand that is expected to be temporary. The longer an employee remains with an employer, the longer the period will be over which the initial fixed costs can be amortized. To lay off a skilled employee in response to a temporary reduction in demand frequently involves incurring new fixed costs when demand revives, for the employee on layoff may find suitable work elsewhere and not be available for recall. Between the peak in 1981 and the approximate trough of the 1982 recession employment of white-collar workers actually rose 3.6 percent; that of blue-collar

[14] Peter Doeringer and Michael Piore, *Internal Labor Markets and Manpower Analysis,* Heath, Lexington, Mass., 1971, p. 116.

Table 5.1 AVERAGE HIRING COSTS BY OCCUPATION AND INDUSTRY, MONROE COUNTY, NEW YORK, 1965–1966, IN 1982 DOLLARS[a]

Occupation group	Manufacturing	Nonmanufacturing
Professional, managerial, and technical	$3435	$881
Clerical	452	392
Skilled manual	1620	311
Semiskilled and unskilled	277	284
All occupations	670	416

[a]The data were obtained from a survey of 17 employers in the Rochester, New York, area.

Source: Based on John Myers, *Job Vacancies in the Firm and the Labor Market,* National Industrial Conference Board, New York, 1969, Table 3-1.

workers fell 8 percent. Unemployment rates in the two groups of occupations were 5.6 and 16.5 percent, respectively, at the cyclical trough. The existence of fixed costs in large part explains the greater stability of employment and the lower unemployment of skilled workers.

The most conspicuous distinction in the stability of employment is that between manual and white-collar workers. The former are usually hired by the hour and the latter by the month or year, and longer notice of layoff or dismissal is typically given to white-collar employees. If demand falls, all white-collar employees may be permitted to continue to work at a less intensive pace, whereas some blue-collar employees are usually laid off. Some of this difference may be due to the failure of required paperwork to decline proportionately with physical output. Since on average the white-collar employees have a higher level of skill, though, the fixed cost concept may also have some relevance to these differences in treatment. Despite these arguments, there is much overlap in levels of skills between the two broad classes of workers. For example, skilled craft workers are better paid and have a longer period of training than many clerical workers. In 1969, 39 percent of full-time blue-collar workers in manufacturing earned less than $6000, but so did 33 percent of white-collar workers. On the other hand, 34 percent of white-collar workers earned more than $10,000, but so did 20 percent of blue-collar workers. Undoubtedly some higher-level white-collar skills are very specific to particular firms. The large overlap in the distribution of skills among white- and blue-collar workers generally suggests, however, that other factors also help explain the differences in unemployment between manual and white-collar workers—factors rooted more in the concept of social class than in the economics of overhead costs.

When despite a drop in product demand workers are retained because of the employer's substantial investment in their firm-specific training, the employer may be paying them more than their *current* marginal product. The decision to retain workers involves the judgment that over some longer period their marginal product will again exceed their wage, even though it is lower at the moment, and that the wage will not fall. The VMP must exceed rather than equal the wage because the current deficit must be made up. It is irrelevant, however, whether or not the initial investment in the workers has been fully amortized. The initial investment is now a sunk cost, and unless in the future the workers' marginal products are expected to exceed their wages, unrecovered initial investment is lost whether they are dismissed or retained. Clearly, the longer a drop in demand lasts, the more convinced employers become of its permanence. With this belief it becomes less likely that the workers' marginal products will eventually exceed their wages by a sufficient amount. Thus in a long recession even skilled workers will be laid off.

Lags in changing employment are also produced by profit-maximizing employers' responses to the *structure* of fixed costs. Table 5.1 lists average costs of hiring, but these average costs are not likely to be constant no matter how many new employees are being added. If a firm seeks to add an extra 1 percent to its work force each month, and it has been doing so for many months, the hiring costs should not be very great. Work processes are designed to absorb these new workers, and personnel offices are set up to handle them. If such a firm suddenly tries to expand by 10 percent, the per worker costs may rise substantially. Production may be partly disrupted, as many new workers must be instructed in the plant's operation; and the efficiency of the suddenly overloaded personnel office may decline. The employer's per worker cost of laying off an unusually large number of people may also be higher than it is when layoffs are a smaller fraction of the work force. An unusually large reduction in force may leave the production process understaffed and result in a lower output per worker remaining.

These arguments imply that the average cost of adjusting the size of the work force rises with the size of the adjustment. Consider how this affects profit-maximizing employers, such as the one in Figure 5.5(a), who are confronted with a drop in the wage rate they must pay from W_0 to W_1. The static theory of labor demand we presented in Chapter 4 shows that it would pay to expand employment from E_0 to E_1, where the VMP equals the new, lower wage rate. Adding $E_1 - E_0$ workers produces hiring costs, though. Our argument suggests, as shown in Figure 5.5(b), that the average hiring cost is higher the larger the change in employment is in each time period. If the firm hires all $E_1 - E_0$ workers at once, the per worker hiring cost is denoted in Figure 5.5(b) by the vertical distance OD. Total costs of adjustment are thus the whole rectangle OAFD.

Consider what happens if employers make only half the adjustment between A and B in Figure 5.5(a) immediately and wait a month to make the rest. They will not be setting VMP equal to the new wage, W_1, if they only expand employment to E_2.

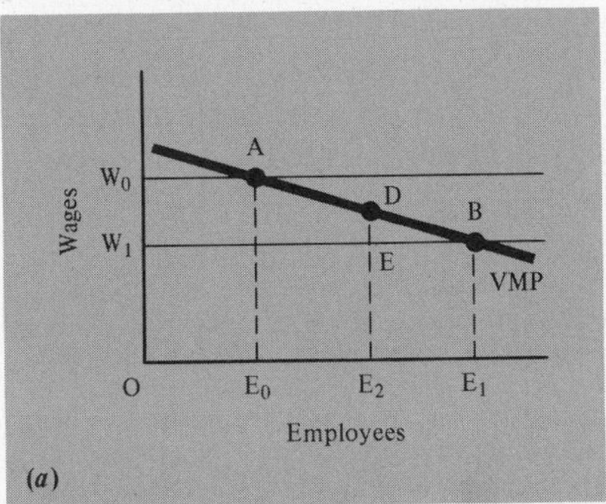

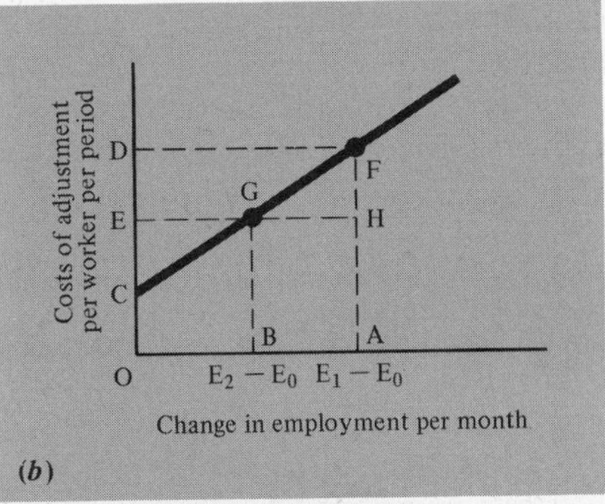

Figure 5.5 (a) A two-step change in employment; (b) costs of adjusting employment.

This will cost them some potential profits, for they could employ workers whose VMP exceeds W_1. The amount of forgone profits is indicated by the triangle DEB; the vertical distances in this triangle are the excesses of VMP over W_1 for each worker not hired. The hiring cost per worker is the vertical distance OE in Figure 5.5(b); total hiring costs initially are OBGE. When the adjustment from E_2 to E_1 is made next month, the firm again incurs hiring costs of OBGE. Since E_2 represented half the total change between E_0 and E_1, the rectangles OBGE and BAHG are equal. Together, though, they are less by an amount EHFD than the hiring costs would have been if the adjustment had been made all at once.

Should the firm make the entire adjustment immediately, or should it change employment in two equal monthly increments? The cost savings from waiting are EHFD; the forgone profits are DEB. As the figures are drawn, it pays to wait. Average hiring costs that rise with the number hired make it optimal for the firm to change employment slowly when factor prices or product demand change.[15] The more rapidly such costs rise with increases in employment (the steeper the slope of the line CF in Figure 5.5(b)), the more profit-maximizing employers will spread out the expansion of employment.

Employers do take these costs into account when they wish to change the size of their work force. Only half the eventual adjustment to an increase in product demand is accomplished in the first 3 months after product demand increases. The response to a decrease in the real wage rate is even slower. Moreover, these responses are all slower where hiring costs are higher.[16]

To avoid incurring at least some of the costs of adjustment (those associated with recruiting efforts), the employer can change hours of work rather than change employment. The choice between adding workers and adding hours also depends on the quality of the workers available in the market and depends heavily on how long the increase in demand is expected to last. If the increase is expected to be temporary, the cost of hiring workers, and laying them off again will usually be viewed as prohibitive, and weekly hours will be increased. Some aspects of these costs may be quite indirect. Employers whose employment is unstable may acquire a bad reputation that could hamper recruitment or even hurt sales. Employers with a strong social conscience might incur psychic costs in choosing an unstable employment strategy.

The longer the increase in demand is expected to last, the smaller the fixed costs become and the stronger is the case for adding workers. This reasoning explains the consistent tendency of changes in hours of work to occur before changes in employment at cyclical turning points. Hours are increased or decreased when employers

[15] The importance of increasing average costs of adjustment was first pointed out by Charles Holt, Franco Modigliani, John Muth, and Herbert Simon, *Planning Production, Inventories and Work Force,* Prentice-Hall, Englewood Cliffs, N.J., 1960. The general theory of adjustment costs is presented in Frank Brechling, *Investment and Employment Decisions,* Manchester University Press, Manchester, Engl., 1975.

[16] The sizes of the lags in changes in employment behind changes in product demand and wages are shown *inter alia* by Daniel Hamermesh, "Subsidies for Jobs in the Private Sector," in John Palmer (ed.), *Creating Jobs* Brookings, Washington, 1978, p. 113, and the relation of these lags to industry differences in variables representing hiring costs is shown in Daniel Hamermesh, "A Disaggregative Econometric Model of Gross Changes in Employment," *Yale Economic Essays* (9): 127 (1969).

Table 5.2 ANNUAL PERCENTAGE CHANGES IN LABOR PRODUCTIVITY IN THE NONFARM BUSINESS SECTOR, BEFORE AND AFTER BUSINESS-CYCLE TROUGHS, 1961–1980

	Twelve months before trough	Twelve months after trough
1961, first quarter	1.1	4.8
1970, fourth quarter	1.7	4.0
1975, second quarter	1.7	4.5
1980, third quarter	0.2	0.9

Source: Unpublished data, Bureau of Labor Statistics, for 1961; Bureau of Labor Statistics, *Employment and Earnings,* June 1972, Table C-10; December 1976, Table C-11; April 1982, Table C-11.

are still uncertain about the strength of changes in demand; employment is changed in the same direction once the importance of the demand shift has become clear.[17]

During a recession another response to the existence of fixed costs is to *hoard* labor. Even though there is little need for workers to produce as much output as in good times, the employer who does not wish to lose past investments in specific training or to incur hiring costs when the recession is over may not cut hours or employment as much as short-term profit maximization would dictate. Trained workers can be kept busy repairing machinery or cleaning and painting the plant; they can also be allowed to work a little less hard than when product demand is high. This long-run profit-maximizing behavior means that worker-hours paid for and hours spent at the workplace during recessions will overstate the number of worker-hours actually spent producing current output. Labor productivity, conventionally measured as output per hour paid for, will thus fall, or at least will not rise so rapidly as otherwise, during a recession. When the recession is over, the opposite effect will occur: Employers will be able to expand output for a while without increasing the hours they must pay for.

The fact that this effect occurs is shown by the data in Table 5.2. During the 12 months before business-cycle troughs output per worker-hour grew far more slowly than in the 12 months after the business cycle reached bottom. Fixed costs clearly dictate the sequence of employers' profit-maximizing responses to a change in product demand: First, change the amount of effort per worker-hour devoted to actual production; then, change hours per worker; finally, change the number of workers.

The increasing importance of fixed costs of employment also helps to explain the rapid growth in recent years of temporary help agencies. Such agencies provide employers with clerical workers or laborers on a day-to-day basis to meet unusual needs or to replace workers who are absent. The employer pays an hourly rate above that prevailing for permanent employees but bears none of the costs of recruiting, screening, payroll accounting, and payroll taxes—all of which are paid by the agency. The worker gets a substantially lower wage rate than that paid by the

[17]For evidence of this, see Gerhard Bry, *The Average Workweek as a Economic Indicator,* National Bureau of Economic Research, New York, 1959.

employer, with the difference providing for the fixed costs and the agency's profit margin. Working for temporary help agencies is especially attractive to workers who for some reason are not available for long periods of work, for example, transients and people with chronic health problems.[18]

POLICY ISSUE—WORK SHARING

During the sharp 1981 to 1982 recession, employers in the United States cut the workweek by over one-half hour. But they resorted to substantial layoffs, too: The number of unemployed workers who had lost their jobs rose from 3.7 to 7.5 million. The popular feeling that employers' incentives to reduce hours rather than employment are insufficient has led other countries, such as Germany, to institute programs to induce employers to spread work rather than lay off workers. In the United States, similar proposals have been introduced in Congress, and California has actually instituted a limited program.[19] Under this program and the proposed federal legislation, workers can receive partial unemployment benefits if they lose part of a week's work because of a reduction in hours. Thus a plant that puts its workers on a 4-day week would pay 80 percent of their normal weekly pay; they would get another 10 percent (since unemployment benefits are normally 50 percent of wages) from the government.

Workers will be more satisfied, and may be willing to work for lower wages if they know they will not lose their jobs entirely during bad times. Employers will thus have an incentive to participate in a work-sharing plan of this sort even if the benefits paid out are entirely financed by payroll taxes on the employer. If they are not financed that way, or if payroll taxes pay only part of the costs occasioned by the employer's workers who receive the benefits, the incentive is still greater. Indeed, if employers finance none of these costs, they are surely better off: Their workers receive a higher weekly income on average than if the program did not exist, yet their costs are no higher. In return they will have either a more satisfied work force or one willing to work for less.

These incentives guarantee that work will be shared more than otherwise. But will the same number of worker-hours be used? So long as businesses as a whole must bear the cost of the program through higher payroll taxes, the program amounts to a higher labor cost. The average employer will demand fewer worker-hours, although those who can take advantage of the program will use more. With fewer worker-hours employed, output will decrease. Whether this reduction and the lower per capita real income it entails is a price worth paying for the increased equity in distributing the burden of recession among more workers is mainly a political issue.[20]

THE DEMAND FOR OVERTIME HOURS AND SHIFT WORK

Much of any adjustment of hours must necessarily take the form of a change in the number of overtime hours used. Adding overtime hours involves paying premium rates, the statutory time and a half, or in some union contracts double or even triple time. It may also involve losses of efficiency resulting from fatigue, increased

[18] For a more detailed account of the development of temporary help agencies, see Mack Moore, "Historical Development, Operation, and Scope of the Temporary Help Service Industry," *Industrial and Labor Relations Review* (18): 554–569 (1965).

[19] These proposals and their potential effects are discussed in Fred Best, *Work Sharing: Issues, Policy Options and Prospects,* Upjohn, Kalamazoo, Mich., 1981.

[20] Frank Reid, "UI-Assisted Worksharing as an Alternative to Layoffs," *Industrial and Labor Relations Review* (35): 319–329 (1982), makes this argument in discussing an experimental Canadian program.

absenteeism, and larger amounts of leisure taken on the job. On the other hand, the alternative to increasing overtime when product demand rises, which is adding new employees, entails fixed costs of employment. Although the overtime premium on wages is 50 percent, it is usually less than 50 percent of total compensation per employee hour.

The choice between adding overtime hours and adding additional workers depends on the relative sizes of fixed costs and overtime premiums. During the period since World War II, the use of overtime in manufacturing, the only sector on which there are good data available, has risen by 1 percent per year.[21] Overtime reached a peak of 3.8 hours per week per manufacturing production worker in 1973; even at the trough of the 1981 to 1982 recession average overtime hours in manufacturing stood at 2.3 hours, compared to only 2 hours in the less severe 1958 recession. One possible explanation for this increase is that the fixed costs of employment may have become larger relative to premiums for overtime work, which have generally been constant. Since fixed costs are more important for skilled than for unskilled employees, the rising average level of skill contributes to the rise in the importance of fixed costs.

During postwar recessions in the United States, average overtime hours in manufacturing have fallen by roughly 30 percent from the cyclical peak to the cyclical trough. If variations in the amount of overtime worked depended mainly on the supply behavior of workers, we would expect overtime hours to rise in a recession: The income effect resulting from the lost labor income of unemployed family members would induce those still employed to seek additional pay by working more. Some of this may occur, but the cyclical decline in the use of overtime suggests that demand effects predominate.

An alternative to the use of additional overtime during cyclical expansions is the addition of additional shifts of workers. This avoids the premium pay required for overtime work, although it does require the (usually smaller) wage premiums associated with shift work. Such a response to increased product demand is usually likely only in heavy manufacturing, where product demand is quite cyclical and there is a substantial investment in capital equipment that is more profitable, the more intensively the equipment is utilized.[22]

POLICY ISSUE—DOUBLE TIME FOR OVERTIME

Employers' use of overtime even during a severe recession is a continuing irritant to organized labor and to citizens sympathetic with its goals. Why should the burden of a recession be so uneven that some people are unemployed, whereas others receive premium wages for overtime hours? This feeling has repeatedly been embodied in proposed legislation that would increase the premium pay rate for overtime work to 100 percent from the current 50 percent. Bills for this purpose were introduced in the early 1960s, during the late 1970s and early 1980s, and will undoubtedly be introduced in any future severe recession.

[21] Ronald Ehrenberg and Paul Schumann, *Longer Hours or More Jobs?* New York State School of Industrial and Labor Relations, Ithaca, N.Y., 1982, p. 11.

[22] See Frank Stafford, "Firm Size, Workplace Public Goods, and Worker Welfare," in John Siegfried (ed.). *The Economics of Firm Size, Market Structure and Social Performance,* Federal Trade Commission, Washington, 1980.

These proposals, like work sharing, seek to change employers' incentives to substitute hours for workers, thereby reducing the use of overtime hours and increasing the number of people employed. The central economic question is the extent to which employers will make this substitution. Many studies have addressed this question. The estimates vary widely, indicating that forcing employers to pay double time for overtime could increase employment by as little as 0.5 percent to as much as 3 percent, *if total worker-hours remain constant.*[23]

Total hours worked will not remain constant, however, because the increase in the overtime premium is equivalent to an increase in the cost of employing additional labor. So long as labor demand schedules are not completely inelastic, the cost increase will reduce total hours worked, just as the cost of unemployment compensation reduces total hours demanded under a work-sharing program. Since the double-time proposal is quite specific, one can calculate its potential impact on the demand for labor services. Double-time represents an increase in the cost of overtime of 33 percent. With overtime representing roughly 3 percent of hours worked in the entire labor force, the proposal implies an increase in labor costs of 1 percent per hour. Assuming a demand elasticity of 0.5, not far from what Chapter 4 showed was a reasonable estimate, total hours would fall by 0.5 percent. This could be enough to offset the entire increase in employment produced by employers substituting workers for overtime. Even if employment does rise, this implies that total production would decrease, for the economy's capital stock would be combined with fewer worker-hours of labor services. This reduction in output, and thus real income, would be the efficiency cost of the attempt to achieve greater equity by inducing employers to spread work hours among more workers.

SUMMARY

Under nearly every form of product-market structure, the firm's demand for labor will be negatively related to the wage rate it must pay. In most cases firms that do not have profit maximization as their central motive will react to imposed wage changes by changing employment in the opposite direction. Some examples of pathological labor-market structure suggest this effect will not occur; but the empirical importance of such cases is evidently fairly minor.

Fixed costs of employment, any costs that rise less than proportionately with the wage bill as the hours of a given work force are increased, are large and greater for more skilled workers. Their existence explains why unemployment rates are lower and cyclical employment fluctuations in unemployment are smaller among skilled workers; why employers respond to changes in product demand by changing hours per worker before they change employment; and why labor productivity falls during recessions. The trend toward higher fixed employment costs in the United States has resulted in an increase in employers' reliance on overtime work, because the relative price of an overtime hour has fallen.

[23] The available literature is summarized in Ehrenberg and Schumann, op cit., p. 26; estimates for 1976 are provided in *Ibid.*, p. 29.

three

LABOR MARKETS

chapter 6

Supply and Demand Together: The Search Process

The analysis of many markets can safely be confined to the forces that determine supply and demand, and little attention need be paid to the mechanics of the market itself. This is not true of labor markets, even highly competitive ones. Labor services, unlike goods, are embodied in people, which has important consequences for the nature of labor markets.

People do not like to have their wages cut, so that nominal wages are rigid downward. This means that labor markets for specific skills often do not clear—do not reach an equilibrium. Quantity demanded can be less than quantity supplied, with the difference represented by unemployed job seekers. Investment in people takes much longer than it takes to make most capital goods, so that the supply of particular kinds of labor can be very slow to adjust to changes in wages. Finally, people care about their working conditions, so that wages do not uniquely determine whether a job is attractive. This makes searching for a job more difficult and time-consuming than search in most commodity markets.

We shall deal in detail with these matters in Chapter 8. Nevertheless, many labor markets do eventually reach, or at least approach, an equilibrium in which wages balance the quantities demanded with quantities supplied. For this reason it is useful to begin our discussion of labor markets by a brief review of the operation of the market for a particular good.

SUPPLY AND DEMAND: A BRIEF REVIEW

Figure 6.1 depicts the market for cassettes. The supply curve slopes up because, with a given structure of costs and technology, suppliers' profits rise when the price increases, leading them to increase output. The demand curve slopes down, for with

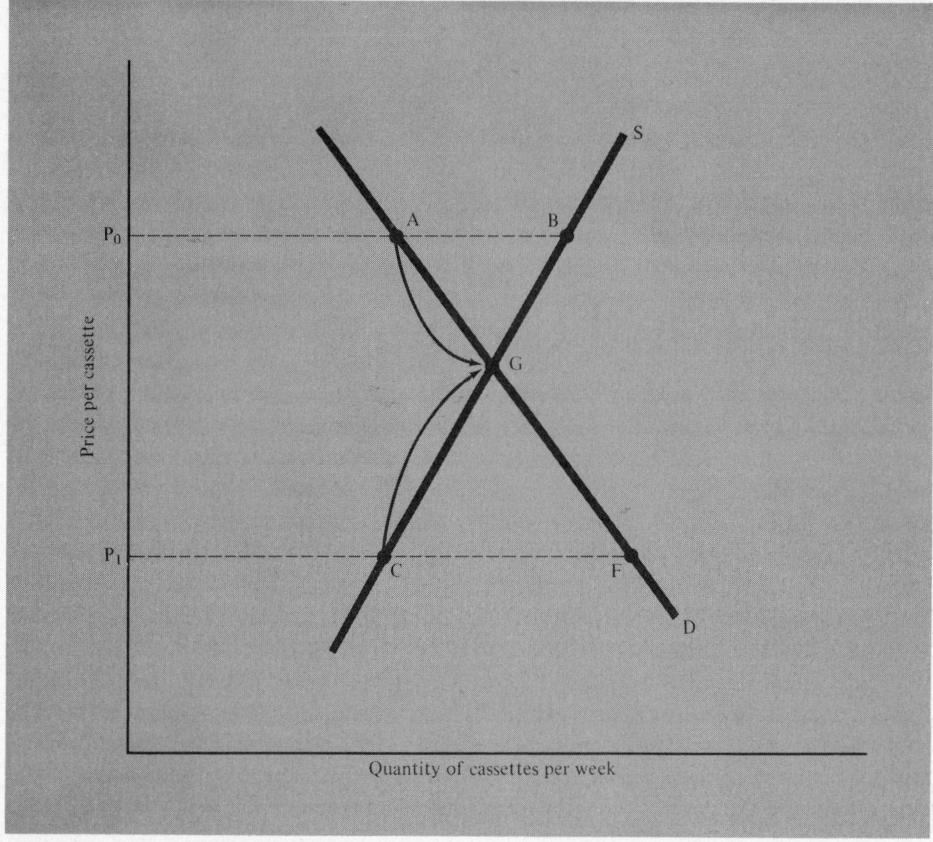

Figure 6.1 The market for cassettes.

a fixed income, and given other prices and tastes, consumers will want more cassettes if they become cheaper.

If the price of cassettes is P_0 in Figure 6.1, there is an excess supply of cassettes of an amount AB. Suppliers, attempting to sell the cassettes they have produced, will cut prices. As they do so, consumers will begin buying more cassettes, for they become more attractive relative to other goods at the lower price. So long as there is an excess supply, the price will keep falling. Only when the market is at point G, with demand and supply equal, will there be no reason for suppliers to reduce prices further. If the quantity demanded adjusts instantly for each drop in price, the market price and quantity will move from A to G along the demand curve. If, however, the quantity demanded adjusts slowly in response to the drop in price, the market price and quantity will move along a path like the arrow between A and G. Instead of moving along demand or supply curves, which show the quantities desired or offered at each price that has prevailed for some time, observed quantities and prices move off the curves due to the slow adjustment of actual supply and demand to their long-run levels. The slower the adjustment in quantity demanded is, the greater will be the pressure on sellers to cut the prices in order to move the unsold output.

The opposite case is one of excess demand. If the price is for some reason at P_1, people will want to buy more cassettes than are being produced; there will be a shortage of CF. The depletion of inventories signals suppliers that they can sell more cassettes and still charge a higher price. The price begins to rise; it continues rising until there is no excess demand. If the amount supplied adjusts instantly to each price, the market moves to the equilibrium at point G. If supply adjusts slowly, perhaps because suppliers learn only slowly that the higher prices are permanent, or because it is initially difficult to obtain the raw materials used in producing cassettes, the market will adjust along a path like the arrow between C and G.

HOW SUPPLY AND DEMAND DETERMINE WAGES AND EMPLOYMENT

As in the market for a particular commodity, so, too, in many labor markets supply and demand forces combine to determine the quantity sold (amount of labor employed) and the price (the wage rate). The fact that they do so is of little interest in and of itself: Knowing that supply and demand combine, for example, to produce an equilibrium wage of $5 per hour for an equilibrium employment level of 100,000 worker-hours per day may be useful, but it says nothing about how the market will respond to the changes that continually buffet it. The discussion of the last five chapters allows us to answer the more interesting question: How will wage rates and employment be affected by changes in the determinants of the quantity of labor demanded or supplied? When we can answer this question, we can gauge the impact of a wide range of changes that occur naturally in the labor market or are imposed upon it by government policy. Even where supply and demand do not determine an equilibrium characterized by a shortage or a surplus, *shifts* in supply or demand will change observed wages and employment in predictable directions. Thus the discussion is relevant for all labor markets, even those that do not clear.

In the general case, the demand curve for labor in a particular market is neither horizontal (infinitely elastic) nor vertical (completely inelastic), but is instead negatively sloped. So, too, the supply curve of labor to the market may be quite elastic but is unlikely to be horizontal (have an infinite elasticity). The effects of shifts in demand or supply can be seen if we examine some real-world examples. Figure 6.2 depicts the labor market for production workers in manufacturing. The real wage, the actual wage adjusted for the price level, is on the vertical axis. The supply curve is shown as being very flat. The study on which the figure is based estimated that the elasticity of labor supply to manufacturing is 5.30—other things equal, each 1 percent rise in real wage rates induces an additional 5.3 percent increase in the number of workers seeking manufacturing jobs.[1] The demand curve is depicted as having a much steeper slope; the estimated elasticity of labor demand in this study is −0.55. If the market for manufacturing workers were competitive, the supply and demand curves would produce an equilibrium at point A, with a wage rate W_0 and equilibrium employment of E_0.

One of the conditions held constant along the supply curve to manufacturing

[1]Richard Freeman, "Employment and Wage Adjustment Models in U.S. Manufacturing, 1950–1976," *Economic Forum* 11: 1–27 (1980).

or new machines acquired, that can usually be done within 1 or 2 years. Workers are likely to perceive changed conditions more slowly; and in many occupations years of training are required before a fully qualified work force is available. (That is what produced the difference between the short- and long-run supply curve to an occupation shown in Figure 3.9.) The difference in the length of time it takes supply and demand to adjust affects how employment and wages change during the movement from the initial to the final equilibrium when a change in some underlying condition shifts the demand or supply schedule. In both Figures 6.2 and 6.3 the relatively slow adjustment in supply leads employers to bid wages up sharply as they compete for the same employees to meet the excess demand for labor. Wages rise along paths like the light curved segments between A and C. The sharp rises in wages speed the adjustment to equilibrium at C. Indeed, the adjustment of supply may be so slow that the real wage may rise above equilibrium for some time, as in Figure 6.2.

Lags in supply are especially important in markets where new entrants must commit themselves to long periods of training, which will yield returns years later when market conditions may have changed drastically. As an example, take the market for lawyers. The decision to attend law school is made during a college student's senior year or before; the new lawyer does not enter the job market until the end of a 3-year legal curriculum. Consider what happens if the salaries of new lawyers are temporarily high at W_0 in Figure 6.4. This high salary induces a large enrollment of new law students, and three years later, a large supply of fledgling lawyers, shown by point B. For these people to find jobs the average starting salaries of new lawyers must fall relative to other wages, or law firms would not hire them. There is a surplus of lawyers at the wage W_0. Thus all the new lawyers may be employed (point C in Figure 6.4), but a majority will receive a lower wage than they expected, with the average real wage being only W_1. This drop in average legal salaries affects the decisions of college juniors and seniors; fewer seek to enter law school, shown by the distance between points C and F in Figure 6.4. When this new small crop of lawyers enters the market 3 years hence, there will be a temporary shortage of new lawyers. The excess demand will raise the average salaries offered to new lawyers.

This "cobweb" (so-called because the lines connecting points A, B, C, and F resemble a spider web) exists in many professional occupations in which there is a lag between the decision to train for the occupation and the time when the formal training is completed. An extra 10 percent increase in the crop of new lawyers depresses starting salaries by 4 percent within a year. The same increase in the number of new physicists causes a 2-percent drop in the average salaries of physicists.[4] The lagged responses mean that salaries in these markets fluctuate in cycles of lengths that are roughly equal to the time it takes to acquire the formal training specific to the occupation. Salaries fluctuate between W_0 and W_1 in Figure 6.4 (of course, in reality around a rising trend). This will occur in any market where there is a long training period and where supply decisions are based on current market conditions rather than on good forecasts of future patterns of changes in the returns to that training. The fact that forecasts are not very good is demonstrated by

[4]Richard Freeman, *The Overeducated American,* Academic Press, New York, 1976, p. 126, and Richard Freeman, "Supply and Salary Adjustments to the Changing Science Manpower Market: Physics, 1948–1973," *American Economic Review* (65): 33 (1975).

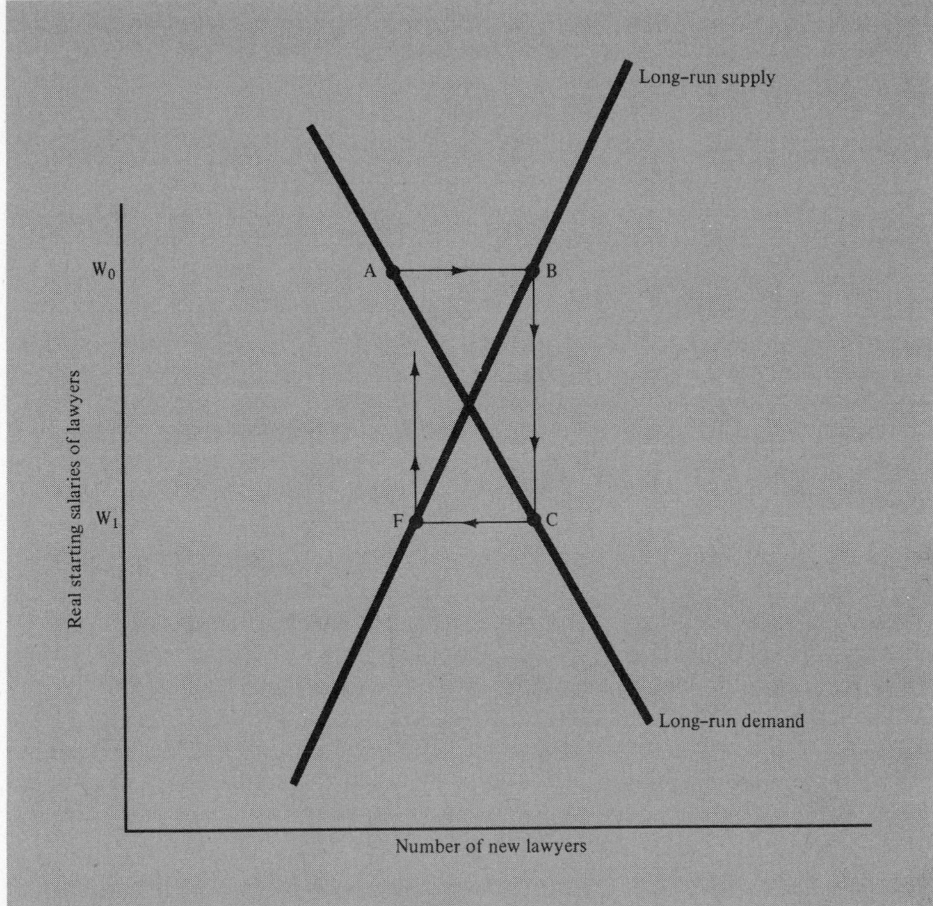

Figure 6.4 The cobweb in the market for lawyers.

independent evidence on how entrants to professional occupations and employers of professionals form expectations about salaries.[5]

The importance of information about salaries and job opportunities is underlined by the cobweb phenomenon. If college students' expectations about future wages were *rational* (based on the entire past history of wages), fewer of them would choose to enter an occupation, for example, law, in response to a current high salary. They would realize that today's high salary indicates salaries will be relatively lower when they graduate. That cobwebs exist indicates students' expectations about wages are not fully rational. If expectations could be made more accurate, the cycle in lawyers' salaries would be smoothed. This would lead to a more desirable allocation of resources, as students invested in occupation-specific training based upon its

[5] Keith Leffler and Cotton Lindsay, "How Do Human Capital Investors Form Earnings Expectations?" *Southern Economic Journal* (46): 591–602, (1979); and Jonathan Leonard, "Wage Expectations in the Labor Market: Survey Evidence on Rationality," *Review of Economics and Statistics* (64): 157–161 (1982).

returns over their entire lifetimes rather than upon the salary that happened to prevail when they made their investment decisions. For example, one study estimates that if college seniors realized that today's high wages for new lawyers lead law firms to reduce the number demanded, enough seniors would shift their occupational choices so that the total present value of the earnings of all of them would rise by 2 percent.[6] Those who enter reap the higher return because the cycle is smoothed out; those who do not enter choose an alternative that has a current salary that is nearly as attractive as that of new lawyers and which need not be subject to the same cobweb-type fluctuation. The increase in economic welfare resulting from increased information about wages and employment suggests the importance of examining how such information is acquired, which we do in the rest of this chapter.

As we stressed earlier, markets for workers are fundamentally different from markets for commodities. Because workers are often unwilling to accept cuts in nominal wage rates, the market response to declines in demand may be very slow. If price inflation is occurring simultaneously with a drop in demand in an individual labor market, that market's adjustment to a new equilibrium at a lower real wage could be more rapid (for nominal wages need only rise less rapidly than otherwise; they need not decline). If the price level is not rising, and current workers refuse to take wage cuts, the only way the market can adjust is if new entrants to the market, who are not used to the high nominal wage that prevailed earlier, accept employers' offers of a lower nominal (and thus real) wage. This process is also likely to be slow, as it depends on retirements and other infrequent causes of workers leaving the occupation or industry in which the drop in demand has occurred. Nonetheless, in the long run labor markets will tend toward a new equilibrium in response to changes in supply or demand, including those that dictate a lower real wage. The duration of this equilibrium process may, though, be quite long indeed, as we shall discuss in Chapter 15.

POLICY ISSUE—THE INCIDENCE OF PAYROLL TAXES

In the United States, as in many developed countries, employers must pay taxes based on the size of their payrolls. Some of these taxes are fixed percentages of each worker's earnings, whereas others vary with the worker's earnings or with other factors. These taxes pay half the costs of Social Security programs in the United States, and essentially all the costs of unemployment insurance and worker's compensation. Payroll taxes amounted to 8.6 percent of total wages and salaries in 1980. This is far below that in some other developed nations: In 1979 in Sweden, the average payroll tax bill was 36 percent of wage and salary costs.[7]

These taxes appear on the surface to present a tremendous burden to the employer, but a more careful consideration suggests that employers may not bear much of the burden. Consider the situation in the economy described in Figure 6.5(a). Initially the hourly wage is $8. The government imposes a payroll tax of $3 per hour. Employers will not continue to employ E_0 hours of labor unless total labor costs remain at $8 per hour; that is, unless they can cut the real wage by $3 per hour. Their demand shifts from D_0 to D_1, which is $3 lower than D_0. When the demand shifts, though, the returns to work drop.

[6]John Freebairn and Glenn Withers, "Welfare Effects of Salary Forecast Error in Professional Labor Markets," *Review of Economics and Statistics* (61): 234–241 (1979).

[7]The data on Sweden are from Bertil Holmlund, "Payroll Taxes and Wage Inflation: The Swedish Experience," *Scandinavian Journal of Economics* (85): (1983). In press.

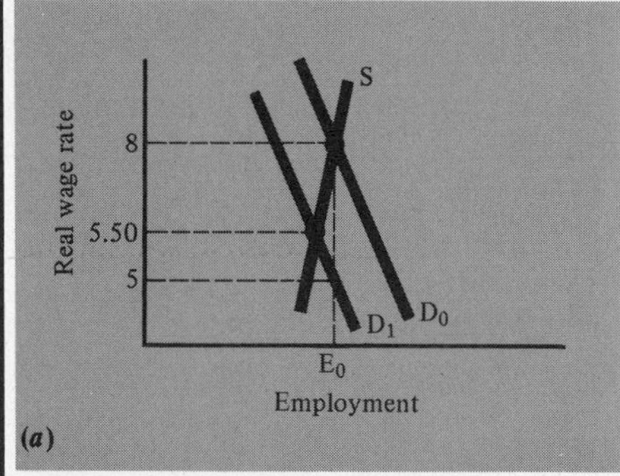

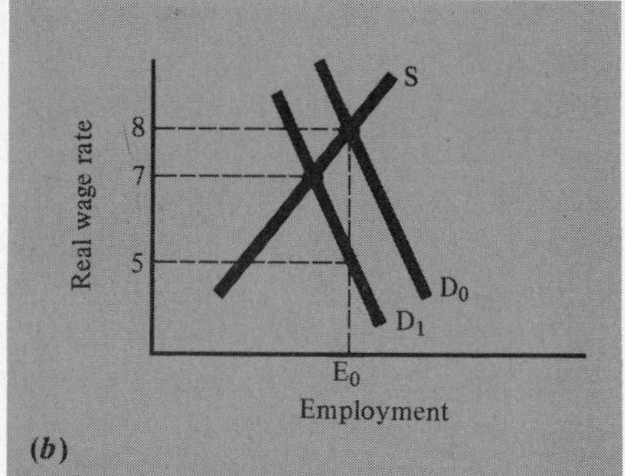

Figure 6.5 (a) Effect of a payroll tax—inelastic labor supply; (b) effect of a payroll tax—elastic labor supply.

In Figure 6.5(a) the elasticity of hours supplied is sufficiently low that the supply curve S is nearly vertical. For that reason the *incidence of the payroll tax* of $3 is mostly on labor: The wage rate must eventually fall to $5.50 if those workers who set a low value on their leisure are to remain employed. Average labor costs rise only by 50 cents to $8.50 (the wage of $5.50 and the tax of $3). If labor supply were more elastic, as in Figure 6.5(b), the story would be different. The burden of the tax would fall less on labor, with wages falling only to $7 and labor costs rising by $2.

The incidence of the payroll tax determines the cost per worker. If exchange rates are not completely flexible, a country's competitive position in world markets will also be affected, so it is important to examine the issue. If the supply elasticities characterizing adult males listed in Chapter 2 characterize the economy as a whole, Figure 6.5(a) is a good description of the economy. With a nearly vertical supply curve, workers bear most of the burden of a payroll tax increase in the form of a wage rate that is lower than would otherwise exist. If the elasticities characterizing married women are more typical, the situation depicted in Figure 6.5(b) is relevant. Employers must bear much of the burden in the form of higher labor costs per worker and employment drops substantially.

Substantial effort has been expended to estimate what actually happens to wage rates when payroll taxes are increased. This is still a very controversial area of research by labor economists. Recent evidence from Great Britain and Sweden, both countries that experienced rapid increases in payroll taxes in the 1970s, indicates that within a year after a payroll tax increase about half of the rise in labor costs had already been offset by wages that are lower than they otherwise would have been.[8] Their situation seems to be between those in Figures 6.5(a) and (b), perhaps closer to Figure 6.5(a).

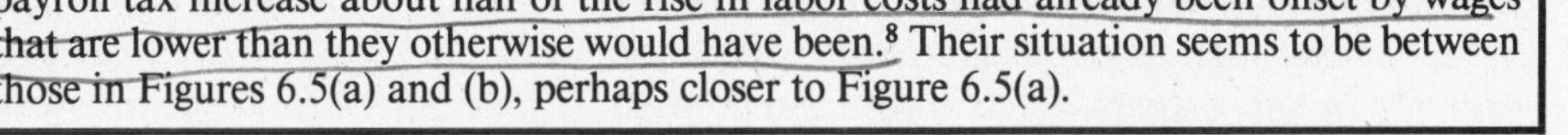

SEARCH IN THE LABOR MARKET

The process described in the previous section is very mechanical. Somehow when demand increases, wages rise and the number of workers supplying labor to the market increases. As Kenneth Arrow has asked, though, if all firms and workers are price takers (as we assume they are in competitive markets), how can any one of them raise the wage offered (or asked) and get the labor market to equilibrium at the new, higher wage rate?[9] The answer lies in the theory of employers' and workers' search for the best available alternatives in the labor market. Standardized goods or

[8] Great Britain is studied in Charles Beach and Frederick Balfour, "Towards Estimation of Payroll Tax Incidence," *Economica* (50): 35–48 (1983); Sweden is examind by Holmlund, loc. cit.

[9] Kenneth Arrow, "Toward a Theory of Price Adjustments," in Moses Abramovitz (ed.). *The Allocation of Economic Resources,* Stanford University Press, Stanford, Calif., 1959, pp. 41–51.

securities are often traded in organized markets, such as stock or commodities exchanges, where prices fluctuate freely so as to clear the market at all times. Markets for less homogeneous commodities or services are characterized in varying degrees by differences in the prices asked or offered by different sellers or buyers at a given time; there are also differences in quality or terms of sale that correspond in part to these price differences. Participants in such markets must engage in search in order to get good terms.

Search takes place in labor markets for two main reasons. First, even within one occupation there are many important differences among both workers and jobs. These differences are complex, multidimensional, and often difficult to quantify or to describe. Second, the fixed costs of employment discussed in Chapter 5 ensure that in most cases a person holds a job for a substantial period of time. A hiring transaction is therefore a large transaction for both parties, more like buying a car than like buying a loaf of bread; for the worker the transaction is one that is not frequently repeated. A large, nonrecurring transaction will involve more search than a small, frequent one. It requires new search on each occasion, since what has been learned in looking for one's last job is usually not still relevant. Moreover, the absolute differences in terms offered by different sellers or buyers may be large, justifying substantial outlays on search in order to improve the terms of the transaction.

Search by Unemployed Workers

Consider the case of experienced unemployed workers who are looking for jobs in their usual occupations. A number of employers may be hiring workers with their competence and offering different wages to them. Workers who accept the first offer received are unlikely to be making the best possible bargain. They will therefore look into a number of possibilities—a process that involves costs. The most important of these costs is the workers' own time; by prolonging the period of unemployment to search further they sacrifice the income that could have been earned during the search period, less any offsetting unemployment insurance benefits. There may also be direct costs such as carfare, postage, employment agency fees, or placing advertisements in newspapers. Each additional contact with another employer thus costs unemployed workers something, often both time and money; the marginal cost of an additional contact is clearly greater than zero.

The search begins with the most promising possibilities, such as firms known to pay good wages and the establishments closest to workers' homes. As the number of openings investigated increases, the probability decreases that a new offer will be better than any previously received. Before investigating additional openings, workers have the option of taking the best jobs investigated up to that time. If they choose not to take those jobs, and instead contact other employers, they are giving up the wages they could have gotten as well as paying the other costs we have discussed. Because delay in accepting an offer increases the likelihood that an attractive opening will already have been filled, the opportunity cost of an extra search rises the more contacts have been made. This is depicted in Figure 6.6 by the increasing marginal cost of an additional contact, shown along the curve MC_0. Choosing to

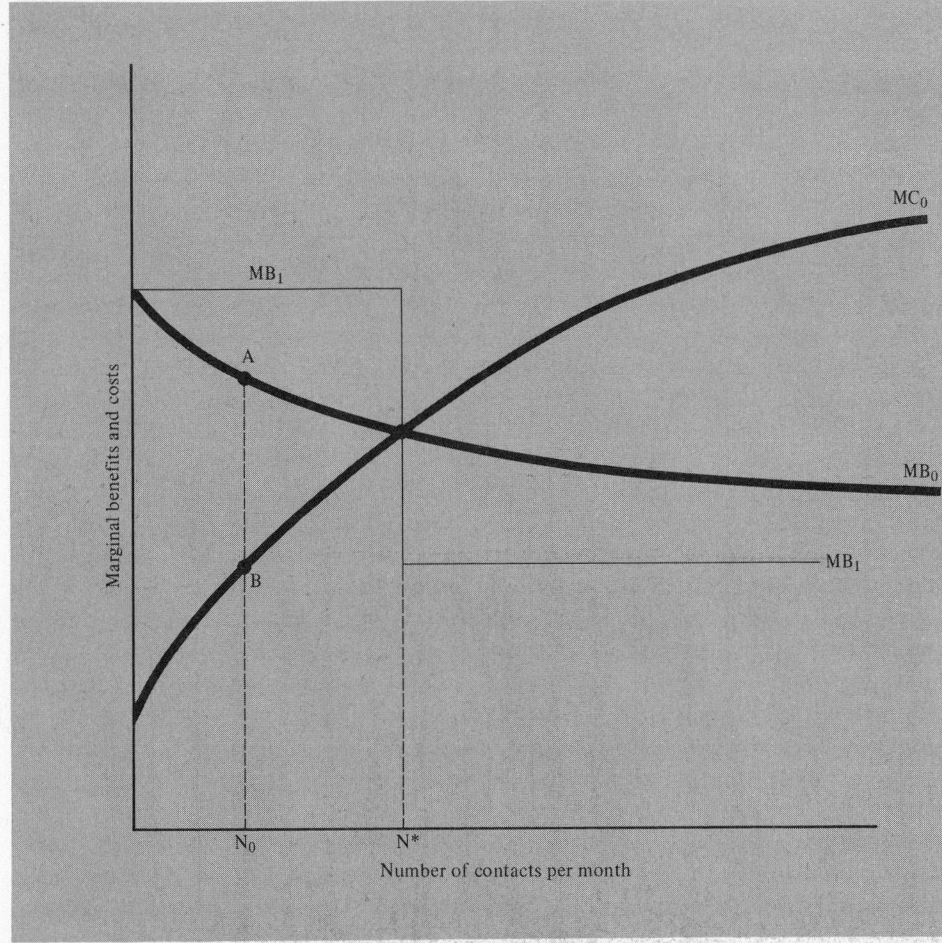

Figure 6.6 Benefits and costs to search.

contact one more employer is an increasingly costly endeavor for the typical unemployed worker.

The fact that the likelihood of finding a better job if one more employer is contacted decreases means that the benefit to contacting an additional employer is lower, the more searching has already been done. This is shown by the declining marginal benefit of search curve, MB_0, in Figure 6.6. Consider people who have contacted N_0 employers; should they contact yet another one, or should they take the best offer found thus far? With only N_0 employers contacted, the benefits of investigating another opportunity exceed the costs of that extra contact by an amount AB; they should search out another opportunity. If they have already contacted N* employers, they would be wise to take the best offer found up to that time. Although an additional contact may yield a very fine offer, the chances of that are slim. By failing to take the best offer already found, they are forgoing the certainty of a fairly high wage and also spending more time and money looking for work. The rational unemployed worker will search out job opportunities until the marginal benefit, the expected higher wage that might result from another contact, equals the marginal cost of making the contact. In the example in Figure 6.6 it does not pay to search more than N* employers.

The marginal benefit and cost curves in Figure 6.6 are smooth, reflecting the opportunities that an average worker can expect during an average period of search. For any individual worker, though, the marginal benefit curve is not likely to be smooth. Workers may receive no offers despite having made many contacts; on contact N* they may find an excellent job. At that point the marginal benefit to another contact, which had been constant because no offers had been obtained, falls sharply, as shown by MB_1 in Figure 6.6. It falls so far that the marginal benefit from another contact is below the marginal cost, and the worker takes the job offered. This case is more realistic than that depicted by the smooth marginal benefit and cost curves. Yet it still shows that additional search reduces the marginal benefit from still further search, although perhaps not at a steady rate, for the chance of finding one's first offer increases the more contacts one has made.

Unemployed workers do contact substantial numbers of employers in their efforts to find work, and they do spend a lot of time in the process. The data in Table 6.1 show that the typical male worker who has been unemployed for at least 1 month has spent 20 hours in the past month looking for work and has contacted six employers. Fifteen percent of the unemployed spent at least 70 hours looking for work, equivalent at least to the time spent by a worker employed halftime. The fact that such large amounts of effort are devoted to looking for work reflects the importance of work in people's values and the long-term nature of the jobs people expect to find. Unemployed female workers in the sample spent 12 hours searching and contacted five employers. This lower amount of search may reflect many women's high value of time, because of childcare responsibilities and other household work. It may also stem from the expectation that, for whatever reason, the job she eventually finds will not last as long as that found by the typical unemployed male worker.

The marginal benefits to search vary among labor markets, at different times, and for different people depending upon their circumstances. For example, the

Table 6.1 HOURS SPENT LOOKING FOR WORK, AND EMPLOYER CONTACTS BY UNEMPLOYED PERSONS, FOUR WEEKS APRIL–MAY 1976, PERCENT DISTRIBUTIONS

Hours	Men	Women	Employers contacted	Men	Women
10 or less	29	47	0	14	15
11–20	23	22	1–2	12	20
21–40	20	17	3–5	19	23
41–75	11	8	6–10	23	19
76–100	10	5	More than 10	23	23
More than 100	6	2			
Total	100	100	Total	100	100
Median hours	20	12	Median contacts	6	5

Source: Calculated from Bureau of Labor Statistics, *Job Search of the Unemployed,* May 1976, Special Labor Force Report No. 210, p. 41.

higher the level of unemployment in an area or occupation is, the greater the risk becomes that a job not taken will be filled by someone else. In terms of Figure 6.6 this means that the marginal benefit curve decreases very rapidly and the marginal cost curve rises very rapidly. Thus if unemployment is very high, workers may accept the first offers received, thinking it unlikely that they will get better ones and very likely that these openings will be promptly filled by someone else if they do not accept them at once. Under these circumstances they may also have to search for some time before they receive any offers at all. This suggests that the number of contacts made need not be closely related to the calendar time elapsed.

The costs of search will also vary with the density of the labor market. In a larger labor market, where many employers are in close proximity, the cost of an extra contact is lower, for it takes less extra time and money to investigate another opportunity. In such markets, workers can be expected to engage in more search before they accept a job. Indeed, unemployed workers who reside in metropolitan areas in the United States contact significantly more employers during a month of unemployment than do otherwise identical unemployed workers who do not live in urban environments.[10]

POLICY ISSUE—UNEMPLOYMENT BENEFITS AND JOB SEARCH

Unemployment benefits are paid in the United States to qualified job losers who must have been unemployed (in most states) for at least 1 week before they receive benefits. In 1981 nearly $16.3 billion of benefits were paid. One of the conditions for the receipt of benefits is an active search for work; recipients must demonstrate to local officials that they have contacted employers. In most states benefits are paid out of the same office that houses the state employment service, the public job-matching agency; thus additional job search is expected to be conducted as part of the physical process of collecting unemployment benefit payments. All these requirements should increase the amount of search undertaken by beneficiaries of this transfer program, allowing them to become reemployed more quickly. The benefits may also provide unemployed workers who have no other source of income and very little savings with the means to finance the transportation and other money costs of looking for work. This, too, could enable workers receiving benefits to contact more employers and find work sooner than otherwise. This view implies that the marginal cost of searching is reduced by unemployment insurance, so that more search will be undertaken in each period of time.

On the other hand, unemployment benefits provide a means of support that reduces incentives to look for work. Recipients know that they will receive benefits, and thus have after-tax incomes often 50 percent or more of what they had been earning. This reduces the marginal benefit from contacting another employer. With a reduced benefit from searching, the amount of search undertaken during each period of unemployment will decline.

The discussion shows that the receipt of unemployment benefits has conflicting effects on the recipients' search behavior. The net effect must be determined by examining how unemployed workers actually react. The answer seems quite clear: They search less hard than do unemployed workers with the same demographic characteristics and the same reason for having lost their jobs. Accounting for these other factors, the average unemployment insurance beneficiary in 1976 searched 1.6 hours fewer per week than the unemployed worker who did not receive benefits. This represents a difference in search

[10]Robert Chirinko, "An Empirical Investigation of the Returns to Search," *American Economic Review* (72): 498–501 (1982).

effort of over 30 percent.[11] Unemployment benefits may entail requirements for search, and they may provide the means to finance search; but the disincentive to taking another job so reduces the amount of search that the net effect of the program is to diminish weekly search effort by unemployed workers.

Search by Employed Workers

Not all the workers who look for jobs are unemployed. In May 1976, 4.1 percent of employed men, and 4.3 percent of employed women actively looked for other work.[12] Workers who are dissatisfied with their jobs for any reason may look for other positions while retaining their present ones. Economic factors are quite important in determining the benefits to search while employed. Persons who want to work more hours per week than they can on their current jobs are nearly twice as likely to search while employed. Those whose current job pays less than the wages of other workers with the same objective characteristics also search more.[13] Both effects raise the marginal benefit curve in Figure 6.6; not surprisingly then, we find they increase the amount of time each week devoted to searching.

The major cost of searching while employed is the loss of leisure time rather than the loss of employment income. The cost of search will be reduced if people retain their jobs rather than quitting first and then searching for new positions. This clear-cut incentive is recognized by workers: Nearly two-thirds of job changes take place without any intervening period of unemployment.[14] But if leisure is more valuable, employed workers will be less likely to search. (In terms of Figure 6.6, the marginal cost of search is shifted to the left.) People with school-aged children, who presumably must spend substantial amounts of time in child-rearing activities, do search much less while employed than those without young children.[15] Another problem is that the danger of losing one's current job before an alternative is found, coupled with rigid work schedules, raises the cost of search while employed. This may reduce the number of contacts made per time period.[16]

Wages and Job Search

This account has implicitly assumed that workers come into the market with no particular ideas about their work and that they form such ideas from the offers made to them. An alternative view, often closer to the truth, is that workers enter the market with strong notions of what they want, based on their pay in their last or current jobs and general information obtained from friends and relatives. These

[11] John Barron and Wesley Mellow, "Search Effort in the Labor Market," *Journal of Human Resources* (14): 399 (1979).

[12] Bureau of Labor Statistics, *The Extent of Job Search by Employed Workers,* Special Labor Force Report No. 202, 1977.

[13] Matthew Black, "An Empirical Test of the Theory of On-the-Job Search," *Journal of Human Resources* (16): 132 (1981).

[14] J. Peter Mattila, "Job Quitting and Frictional Unemployment," *American Economic Review* (64) 235–239 (1974).

[15] Black, op. cit., p. 132.

[16] Some indirect evidence on this is provided by Lawrence Kahn and Stuart Low, "The Wage Impact of Job Search," *Industrial Relations* (21): 53–61 (1982).

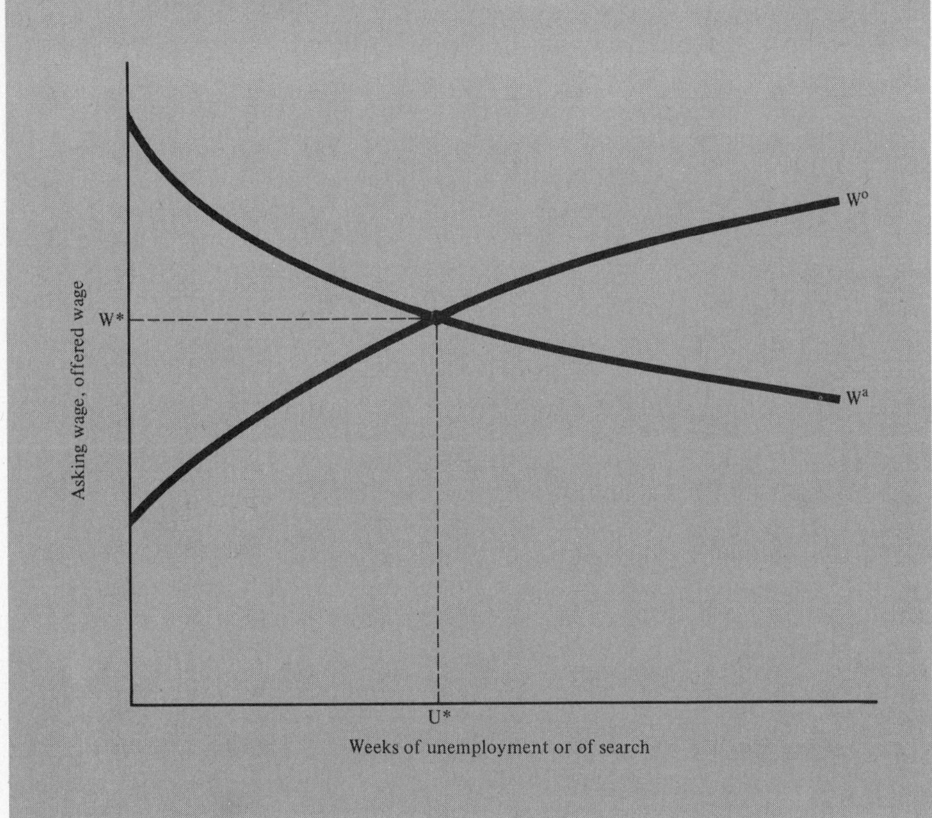

Figure 6.7 Asking and offered wage and time spent unemployed.

notions are the basis of an asking wage—the lowest wage a worker will consider accepting.

The asking wage is revised during the search to be more consistent with offers received. Most workers begin their search with overly optimistic views about what might be available for them. As they contact more employers they acquire more realistic information about their alternatives and their asking wage drops. Assuming the number of contacts per period does not change greatly with the time elapsed since the search began, the asking wage will also be related to the duration of unemployment (or of search while employed), as shown in Figure 6.7. In one sample of unemployed workers, the asking wage fell by 1.3 percent during the first month of unemployment. It fell only 0.7 percent during the seventh month of a worker's spell of unemployment.[17] As shown in Figure 6.7, workers engaged in job search learn quickly what the relevant range of job offers for them might be. After that they are

[17] William Barnes, "Job Search Models, the Duration of Unemployment, and the Asking Wage: Some Empirical Evidence," *Journal of Human Resources* (10): 235 (1975). The earliest available estimate of the relation between the asking wage and the amount of search, by Hirschel Kasper, "The Asking Price of Labor and the Duration of Unemployment," *Review of Economics and Statistics* (49): 165–172 (1967), finds that the asking wage declines by between 0.3 and 0.7 percent per month of unemployment.

unwilling to cut their asking wages as rapidly, perhaps because their search effort has convinced them that their revised asking wage is within the range of offers they are likely to receive in any additional contacts with employers.

In Figure 6.7, W^o denotes the highest wage offered by the employers a job searcher has contacted. It rises with time spent searching for reasons already discussed. When workers have searched long enough that their asking wage has dropped and the best offer received has increased to equal the reduced asking wage, they will stop searching and take the best available job. In Figure 6.7, this means they will take a job paying W^* after U^* weeks of unemployment (or of search while employed).

The asking wage schedule in Figure 6.7 differs among workers. Those whose previous wage (current wage if they are searching while employed) was higher will start the job search with greater expectations, believing that their last or present wage is a rough indication of what they might receive from the employers they contact. So, too, the wage offered, W^o, will be higher. Higher unemployment benefits shift the asking wage schedule upward. They reduce job searchers' incentives to lower their asking wages to levels that are consistent with finding work quickly. Married men's asking wages fall more rapidly than those of otherwise identical single men, because family responsibilities require them to be more realistic about available jobs so they can become reemployed more quickly. People who have had more stable employment, and who presumably seek such employment in the jobs they search over, have asking wages that fall less rapidly.[18]

We have discussed job search as if workers were concerned solely with the wage on the new job. In assessing job offers, though, workers are interested in factors other than the wage, such as job security, costs of commuting, opportunities for advancement, fringe benefits, interesting work, congenial colleagues, and many similar factors. Therefore, workers will not necessarily choose the job that offers the highest starting wage. Even where money wages are very important, a lower starting wage may be offset by better opportunities for subsequent wage increases or job promotion.

Employers with vacancies to fill also engage in search. If they find vacancies hard to fill, they will improve their wage offers or lower their hiring standards until the vacancies can be removed. Large employers hiring for occupations in which they employ substantial numbers of people are less likely to change their wage offers in response to information obtained in the search process. Often their wage level is set by collective bargaining or by company policy over which personnel managers in particular plants have no control. In these cases, if vacancies are hard to fill, the adjustments will be made entirely by widening the area of search, by using more costly methods of search, or by lowering hiring standards and applying them more flexibly.

Employers who offer low wages will have to search longer and harder than employers who offer high wages, and they will often have to use more expensive

[18] Nicholas Kiefer and George Neumann, "An Empirical Job-Search Model, with a Test of the Constant Reservation-Wage Hypothesis," *Journal of Political Economy* (87): 99 (1979), and John Warner, J. Carl Poindexter, and Robert Fearn, "Employer-Employee Interaction and the Duration of Unemployment," *Quarterly Journal of Economics* (94): 224 (1980).

channels of recruiting.[19] High-wage employers can choose among the many good applicants who may present themselves as soon as it becomes known that there are vacancies to be filled. Thus high wage costs are to some extent offset by lower costs of recruitment, screening, and training. But there is no reason to expect the offset to be complete, particularly where the high-wage employers are required by collective bargaining agreements to pay more than they would choose to pay in the absence of unions.

Like workers, employers must decide how long to continue their search. If none of the applicants for openings quite measures up to their standards, they must weigh the cost of relaxing the standards against both the costs of securing additional applications and those of keeping the vacancies unfilled. The latter costs may include lost output or the costs of overtime payments to present workers. If the probability of getting better applicants seems small and the costs of keeping the jobs vacant are high, they will take the best of the applicants who are still available, not necessarily the ones who applied last. The lower the unemployment rate is, the greater will be the probable cost of rejecting an applicant in the hope of finding a better one.

Employers who initially search outside their own organization to fill vacancies above the starting level may eventually decide instead to fill the positions by promotion from within, thus creating new vacancies at a lower level. If a vacancy is filled by hiring a person already employed elsewhere, a new vacancy will usually be created in another firm. Thus the filling of a vacancy at a high level can lead to a chain of mobility, internal or external to the firm, ending when a vacancy in the chain is filled by someone who is not already employed, either an unemployed person or a new entrant to the labor force.

Just as workers consider opportunities for promotion in deciding which offers to accept, employers must consider suitability for promotion in selecting new employees. In hiring for a "dead end" job, only the applicant's ability to perform the initial job need be considered. But where a job is the first step in a promotional ladder, the employer will select the workers who seem to have the most potential for advancement.

employers
unemployed
employed

Equilibrium in the Labor Market

Search by employers and by unemployed or employed workers is the force that brings about a new equilibrium in a competitive labor market when underlying demand or supply forces change, or when quits or retirements create vacant jobs that the employer wishes to fill. Search is the process that leads wages in competitive markets to change; it is the solution to the conundrum posed by Arrow that we referred to at the start of this section. Consider the responses to an outward shift in

[19] This hypothesis that the employer can substitute search costs for wages was first advanced by George Stigler in "Information in the Labor Market," *Journal of Political Economy* (70) S94–S105 (1962). Some empirical results that tend to confirm the hypothesis are in Albert Rees and George Shultz, *Workers and Wages in an Urban Labor Market*, University of Chicago Press, Chicago, 1970, pp. 207–210. William Goodwin and John Carlson, "Job Advertising and Wage Control Spillovers," *Journal of Human Resources* (16) 80–93 (1981), show that when employers cannot raise wages as rapidly as underlying market conditions would normally lead them to (because of wage controls), they rely more heavily on newspaper help-wanted advertising.

employers' labor demand schedules that is caused by an increase in product demand. Employers find that the wages they are offering induce only enough acceptances to replace employees who are leaving the firm. Finding an insufficient flow of new workers, employers will raise the wage offer somewhat. This induces some workers to take the jobs offered; others, though, finding that the quality of offers has increased, will increase their asking wages and continue searching. Eventually part of the additional demand for labor is met, and part is choked off by the higher wages employers must pay. The system is back in equilibrium, with higher wages, more workers employed, and a higher asking wage of those workers engaged in job search, reflecting the now higher distribution of wages being paid.

The process works similarly if some event changes the supply of labor to a particular market. Assume that the supply decreases because of an increase in wages in occupations that workers regard as alternatives to those used by employers in this market. For example, the supply of economists may decrease if lawyers' salaries rise. Employers will find that too few of their wage offers are being accepted to maintain their work forces. The same process of higher offered wages, increased acceptances of jobs by workers who are searching, and so forth will occur as takes place when the demand for labor rises. The new equilibrium will be established with a higher distribution of wage rates offered in the market and a higher level of asking wages by workers who are engaged in search. Because the amount of labor demanded has dropped due to the rise in wages relative to other factor prices, employers will search for fewer workers each month than before the average wage offer was forced up by the reduction in supply.[20]

CHANNELS OF JOB SEARCH

The process of search in labor markets takes place through a number of channels of employment, formal and informal, whose importance varies from place to place and by type of job. Informal channels include referrals from present employees. Another informal channel is *gate hiring,* that is, applications in response to a notice of a vacancy posted on an employer's premises, such as a sign in a restaurant window, "waiter/waitress wanted" or "dishwasher wanted." The most informal method of all is the walk-in, the application not solicited in any way. The principal formal channels, or *labor market intermediaries,* are the public employment service, private employment agencies, newspaper advertisements, schools, and union hiring halls. Table 6.2 shows the channels through which a sample of workers in three quite different occupations in the Chicago labor market area found the jobs they held in 1963. Table 6.3 shows the methods used by job seekers who were interviewed in the Current Population Surveys in 1982.

As shown in Table 6.2, informal channels are by far the most important means by which unskilled and semiskilled blue-collar workers found their jobs. Similarly, Table 6.3 shows that younger workers, who often have the fewest skills, relied heavily on unsolicited applications during 1982. They were less likely than others to obtain referrals from friends and relatives, perhaps a reflection of their inexperience in job

[20] An early exposition of how the search process equilibrates markets is by Dale Mortensen, "Job Search, the Duration of Unemployment, and the Phillips Curve," *American Economic Review* (60): 847–862 (1970).

hunting. Firms paying better than average wages or firms in markets where there is substantial unemployment can usually fill all their vacancies through referrals by present workers and through unsolicited applications. This method is unsystematic, because it fails to reach the largest number of potential applicants. However, employee referrals have a variety of advantages to both employers and applicants.

Table 6.2 METHODS USED TO FIND PRESENT JOBS BY A SAMPLE OF WORKERS IN SELECTED OCCUPATIONS IN THE CHICAGO AREA, 1963

	Percentage Distribution		
Job source	Typist	Janitor	Maintenance electrician
	Informal sources		
Employee referral	23.0	34.0	26.9
Other informal referral	2.0	1.7	3.6
Gate applications	3.4	6.8	8.0
Total informal	28.4	42.5	38.5
	Formal sources		
State employment service	0.9	2.1	0.4
Private agency	20.5	1.7	1.1
Newspaper ad	10.1	2.5	5.5
School or college	1.1	—	—
Union	0.2	2.5	0.7
Other formal sources	0.5	0.6	0.7
Total formal	33.3	9.4	8.4
Rehires	5.0	4.2	5.5
Unknown	33.4	43.9	47.6
Total	100.0	100.0	100.0

Source: Albert Rees and George Shultz, *Workers and Wages in an Urban Labor Market,* University of Chicago Press, Chicago, 1970, Table 13.1. Copyright 1970 by University of Chicago Press. Reprinted by permission of University of Chicago Press.

Table 6.3 METHODS USED TO SEARCH FOR JOBS, UNEMPLOYED PERSONS BY AGE, 1982 (PERCENT USING THE METHOD)[a]

	Age							
	16–19	20–24	25–34	35–44	45–54	55–64	65+	Total
			Search Method					
			Informal					
Friends and relatives	14.3	15.5	17.5	17.1	17.1	17.7	17.5	16.3
Gate applications	82.5	79.1	76.0	75.8	75.3	71.8	70.0	77.8
			Formal					
State employment agency	15.5	26.7	27.7	27.8	26.0	21.0	16.2	24.2
Private agency	3.1	5.8	7.0	6.9	7.3	6.3	3.7	5.8
Newspaper ad	27.1	35.5	38.8	37.1	35.7	34.9	26.2	34.7
			Other					
	3.2	3.6	4.7	5.9	6.7	10.0	5.0	4.7

[a]Because many workers used more than one search method in a month, the sums of each column exceed 100 percent.

Source: Employment and Earnings, January 1983, p. 153.

Employers get some amount of screening from the referring employees, who are unlikely to make an unsuitable referral that would reflect badly on their reputation with their employers. At the same time, applicants get from the employed workers detailed information about working conditions and supervisory practices, which they cannot get through formal sources or might distrust if it were provided by the employer or an employment agency. If hired, the applicants know someone in the establishment to show them how things are done.

Among formal sources, private employment agencies are of greatest importance in white-collar markets, such as the market for typists (shown in Table 6.2), and in large cities. Most small labor markets do not generate enough transactions to support a private agency. A conspicuous characteristic of the private agencies is their willingness to make substantial expenditures on advertising to attract applicants. Furthermore, in private agencies the payment of counselors on a commission basis gives the staff a strong incentive to make placements, although it sometimes encourages unethical practices such as attempting to recruit workers previously placed. As Table 6.3 indicates, though, few of the unemployed rely on these agencies; those who do are most likely to be the more mature workers who have the skills the agencies specialize in providing.

The fee structure of private employment agencies offers clues to the way in which costs of search vary with skill level and are distributed between buyers and sellers. Agency fees tend to be a higher fraction of the wage or salary, the higher the level of the job is, with the highest percentage rates charged by professional and executive agencies. Thus costs of search seem to rise more than in proportion to salary levels. Agency fees are generally paid by employers in markets where there are many unfilled vacancies, such as clerical markets, and by employees in markets where there are many unemployed workers, such as the market for unskilled male labor. How these fees actually affect wage rates (what their incidence is) depends, as in the case of the payroll tax, on the elasticities of demand and supply in the particular labor market.

Newspaper advertisements, used mostly by employers, reach a wide audience at relatively low cost; Table 6.3 shows they produce a large flow of applicants, none of whom has been screened. They are therefore used mostly in markets where labor is scarce and by large employers with personnel departments that can carry out screening. Some amount of preselection can be achieved by careful choice of newspapers. For example, employers who wished to recruit blacks used to advertise in newspapers serving the black community, whereas those who discriminated against blacks used neighborhood papers in all-white neighborhoods.

Among formal sources, the public employment service has two great advantages. It charges no fees to either the employer or the employee, and it generally has the largest pool of information about unemployed workers and job vacancies. These advantages should give it a more central role in the labor market than it has yet attained. One of its handicaps has been that the long and close association of the employment service with the unemployment insurance program has tarnished its image for skilled and white-collar workers and for some employers. The latter feel that the service is more interested in placing the recipients of unemployment insurance benefits than in meeting employers' requirements. Some evidence of this is provided by comparing the relatively small percentage of workers in Table 6.2 who found their jobs through the employment service to the large percentage of the unemployed who reported (in Table 6.3) using this method.

The benefits of increasing the efficiency of labor-market intermediaries would come in the form of a better matching of job seekers and vacancies. This would result in both employers and workers spending less money and time searching. In addition to these reduced search costs, the faster equilibration of markets when underlying supply or demand conditions change means that the costs of being out of equilibrium, in terms of deviations of the value of marginal product from wages that reduce profits and total income in the economy, will not persist as long as before.

POLICY ISSUE—IMPROVING THE EMPLOYMENT SERVICE

One possible way of increasing the efficiency of labor-market intermediation is to allocate more tax revenues to the public employment service. If the service provides a more efficient mechanism for placing unemployed workers and filling job vacancies than the private market, logic would suggest it should be expanded to take advantage of that efficiency. Does the employment service lead applicants to higher-paying, more stable jobs than they would obtain if they used informal or private formal channels of information? One study compared people who found their jobs through the public employment service with those who contacted the service but found their jobs through other sources.[21] The results, adjusted for numerous demographic differences and the individuals' pre-unemployment earnings, shed an interesting light on the effectiveness of the employment service. Those people who found their jobs through the service had the same annual earnings in the first year after they got the jobs as did people in the other group of unemployed workers. However, those aided by the service were employed more steadily than those in the other group. We may infer that the service succeeded in encouraging the unemployed to take steadier jobs offering lower wage rates rather than take higher-paying unstable jobs. Whether this represents a success for this public activity is unclear. What is evident, though, is that the benefits of the employment service go beyond the number of unemployed workers placed to the quality of those placements, both in terms of initial wages and retention on the job.

For many years a serious problem with the public employment service was that available information on job openings and applicants could not be scanned quickly and thoroughly with the manual search methods then in use. It was thought that this difficulty would be overcome by the introduction of computerized data banks. In fact, however, computerization does not seem to have made a great difference in performance. Speed of access to data has been improved, but at the cost of the loss of specialization by employment service personnel.[22]

SUMMARY

Competitive labor markets move toward equilibrium through a process of workers and employers revising the wages they seek or offer. When the market is tight, employers raise their offered wages and induce workers searching for jobs to take them earlier than they otherwise would have. When markets are loose, employers,

[21] Arnold Katz, "Evaluating Contributions of the Employment Service to Applicant Earnings," *Labor Law Journal* (28): 472–478 (1977).

[22] See Joseph Ullman and George Huber, *The Local Job Bank Program,* Heath, Lexington, Mass., 1973.

finding that their job offers are being accepted more readily, offer wages below what they had planned or raise the quality standards for hiring. Any change in demand or supply conditions will change the search behavior of workers and employers. Search behavior entails frequent revision of wages that are offered and sought, even when market conditions are not changing. Workers who have been unemployed for a while will lower their asking wages; employers with vacancies that have remained unfilled will raise their wage offers or reduce hiring standards.

Even during boom periods, both employed and unemployed workers engage in substantial amounts of search activity. The information upon which search is based comes from a variety of formal and informal sources. In general, formal sources are more important in markets for white-collar workers, whereas informal sources, such as referrals by other employees, are relied upon more in markets for blue-collar labor. More experienced workers are less likely than others to rely on gate applications and more likely to use formal sources.

chapter 7

Migration and Mobility

Migration between geographical areas, and mobility between jobs, are the primary manifestations of the search process. Although many of the considerations that motivated the discussion of search underlie the analysis of these forms of mobility, there are issues that are specific to this topic. In this chapter we examine some of these, showing in particular how the theory of investment in human capital that we discussed in Chapter 3 affects these decisions.

THE CAUSES OF MIGRATION

The migration of labor is a somewhat more restricted topic than the migration of population. We shall not consider children who move with their parents or people who move at or after retirement. The migration of the retired and the migration of active workers are governed by quite different considerations. The retired often seek more pleasant climates and low living costs that will augment the real value of their pensions and Social Security benefits. They may frequently return to their place of origin, which they left earlier to pursue their careers.

Even within the working-age population, though, the amount of migration—geographic mobility—is very large in the United States. As the upper panel of Table 7.1 shows, nearly one-fourth of the population aged 25 to 44 moved to a new county in the 5-year period, 1975 to 1980. The fact that much of this migration is for economic reasons is suggested by studies of individual migrants' decisions; these indicate that between 70 and 80 percent of migrants move for economic reasons. Nearly 30 percent of those moving change occupations as well as jobs.[1]

[1] Ann Bartel, "The Migration Decision: What Role Does Job Mobility Play?" *American Economic Review* (69): 776 (1979), and Larry Schroeder, "Interrelatedness of Occupational and Geographical Labor Mobility," *Industrial and Labor Relations Review* (29): 407 (1976).

Table 7.1 GROSS MIGRATION RATES BY AGE, 1975–1980, AND HISTORICAL DATA, 1955–1980, IN PERCENT

	Males	Females
By age, 1975–1980		
25–34	33.3	31.6
35–44	21.1	16.9
45–54	12.9	11.4
All ages 5 and over		
1955–1960	18.1	16.9
1965–1970	17.7	16.4
1970–1975	17.5	16.7
1975–1980	19.9	18.8

Source: Bureau of the Census, *Geographical Mobility: March 1975 to March 1980,* Current Population Reports, P-20, No. 368, Table 5; *Mobility of the Population of the United States: March 1970 to March 1975,* Current Population Reports, P-20, No. 285, Table 4; *Census of Population, 1970,* PC(1)-1D, Table 196; *Census of Population, 1960,* PC(1)-1D, Table 164.

It is immediately apparent that economic motives are important in migration decisions where there are gross disparities in income levels. The tremendous flow of immigrants to the United States from southern and eastern Europe before World War I is a conspicuous example, as are the flows from Puerto Rico to the mainland United States and from the West Indies, Pakistan, and India to Great Britain after World War II. Many such migration flows would have been far larger or continued much longer had they not been restricted by rigid control of immigration by the receiving countries. The flows after World War II also illustrate the role of costs; in many of these cases a prewar trickle became a large postwar stream when air transport became available at fares far below those of passenger ships. Yet it would be incorrect to give the impression that only economic forces govern the international migration of labor. Many migrants are refugees from war or from political, religious, or racial persecution. Sometimes refugees blaze a path that is then followed by others whose motives are more largely economic.

The analysis of workers' migration decisions is formally similar to the analysis of investment in schooling in Chapter 3. Consider workers whose possible streams of future earnings are shown in Figure 7.1. They will earn a stream indicated by the profile E_0 if they remain in their current locations; if they migrate to their best alternative locations, their earnings will follow the profile E_1. The costs of migrating include forgone earnings, denoted by the nearly triangular segment ABC. Even though many migrants line up jobs before they move, many do not, so that the forgone earnings may be substantial. Furthermore, Figure 7.1 also describes the decision-making process of people who consider migration but choose not to move; that choice may in many cases be made because of the prospect of substantial earnings that would be forgone. The returns to migration are represented by the area between E_1 and E_0 to the right of point C. As in the analysis of investment in education, here too, we must discount the costs and returns back to the present. The

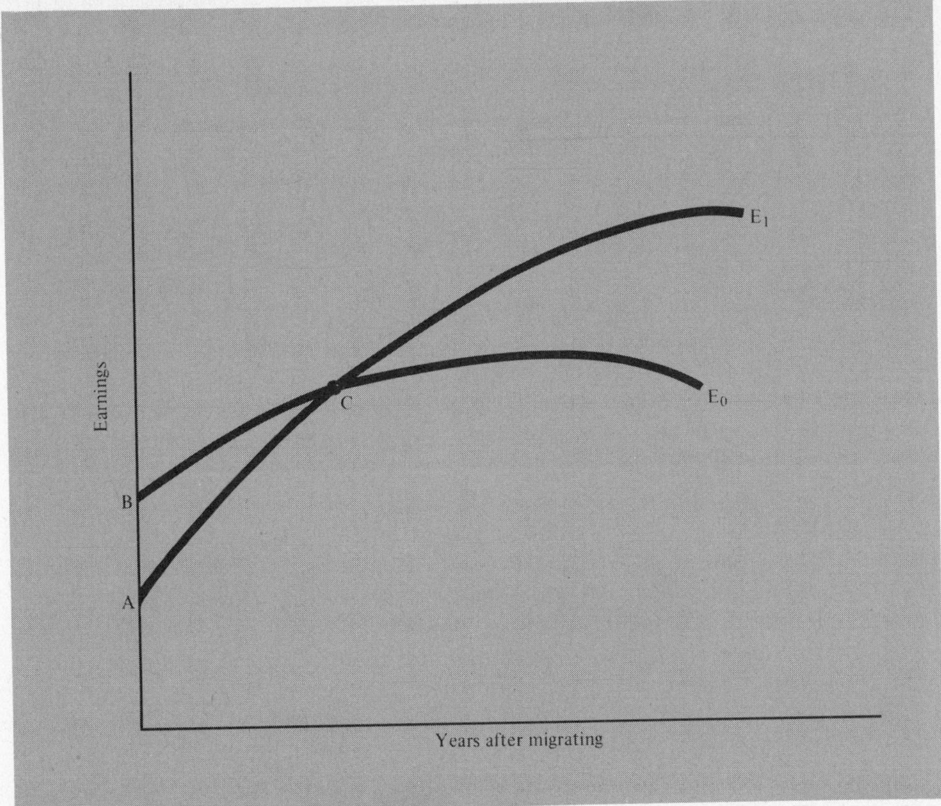

Figure 7.1 The individual's migration decision.

out-of-pocket costs of migration—transportation, costs of searching for employment, and others—must also be included in the benefit-cost calculation. If the present value, the discounted returns minus the discounted costs, exceeds zero, workers should migrate. In an alternative calculation, they should migrate if the internal rate of return on the investment exceeds their rate of preference for income now versus income in the future (their subjective rate of time preference).

In a formal sense this short exercise solves the problem of workers' migration decisions. It is, moreover, rich in empirical implications. The likelihood of migration will be greater among young workers, for they can expect more working years during which to enjoy higher earnings in the new location. This prediction is borne out by the data in the top panel of Table 7.1. Migration rates drop off sharply from a peak rate early in the work life; one-third of the people in their late twenties migrate, but only one-eighth of the people in their late forties and early fifties do so. The reduction in migration rates with age is not due to differences in earnings streams resulting solely from a longer horizon. If we hold these earnings differences constant, we still find that older workers are less likely to migrate.[2] The reduction is also the result of

[2]Solomon Polachek and Francis Horvath, "A Life Cycle Approach to Migration," *Research in Labor Economics* (1): 103–149 (1977).

the psychic costs of leaving families, friends, and familiar surroundings for a strange and hostile environment. The psychic costs of breaking ties with the home community increase rapidly with age, so that the purely economic return to migration increasingly overstates workers' perceived rates of return as they age.

Greater income differentials, the distance between E_1 and E_0 in Figure 7.1, increase the amount of migration. If potential migrants were certain of jobs in their destinations, we should expect a \$1 increase in expected income there to have the same positive effect on migration as a \$1 decrease in income in the current location. Any migration, though, is fraught with uncertainty about economic prospects, so that declines in income in potential destinations may have a sharp deterrent effect on the probability of migration. Indeed, a \$1 decrease in the present value of income in an area reduces the amount of migration into that area by several times as much as it raises the outflow of workers from that area.[3] This suggests that workers attach substantially greater uncertainty to income prospects in other areas than to those in their current homes and that these uncertainties modify their calculations of the present value of the benefits and costs of migration.

The degree of uncertainty is enhanced by the possibility of unemployment in the potential destination, as we should expect: The unemployment rate of migrants not only is higher than that of nonmigrants, but it varies more with changes in business conditions. A small reduction in demand could cause only a slight increase in the unemployment of established workers, yet cause a great reduction in new hires. The amount of new hiring in an area is in fact a far better predictor of migration into that area than is the unemployment rate.[4] Workers migrate to places where jobs are available; the amount of competition for those jobs is itself less of a deterrent to migration. Nonetheless, unemployment in potential destinations is important, too. The sensitivity of rates of migration to business conditions in the destination areas is sometimes quite startling.[5] Even where the risk of unemployment is in fact reasonably small, it may be exaggerated in the mind of the potential migrant.

Variations in expected incomes and changes in the probability of obtaining those incomes (through changes in unemployment and hiring rates) both affect the streams of returns presented in Figure 7.1. Uncertainty about these conditions in potential migrants' destinations gives any variations in them a far larger impact on the likelihood of migration than is produced by variations in income and unemployment at home. Migration to twentieth-century America has been much more a "pull" than a "push": Migration rates respond chiefly to fluctuations in economic conditions in destination areas, less so to fluctuations in home areas.

The psychic costs of entering a new area can be reduced by migrants' own behavior. The most obvious way for migrants to reduce these costs is to congregate in particular neighborhoods in the destination cities and to establish stores, bars, clubs,

[3] John Vanderkamp, "Migration Flows, Their Determinants and the Effects of Return Migration," *Journal of Political Economy* (79): 1012–1031 (1971); Gary Fields, "Place-to-Place Migration: Some New Evidence," *Review of Economics and Statistics* (61): 21–32 (1979); and Stephen Farber, "A Directional Flow Migration Model," *Southern Economic Journal* (45): 205–216 (1978).

[4] Fields, op. cit., p. 28.

[5] For example, from 1907 to 1908 the estimated unemployment rate in the United States rose from 1.8 to 8.5 percent. The number of immigrants declined from 1,285,000 to 783,000. See U.S. Bureau of the Census, *Historical Statistics of the United States,* Series D-47 and C-88.

and churches that reflect their special tastes. To some extent the concentration in slum neighborhoods is enforced by poverty and racial discrimination, but it goes beyond what can be explained on these grounds. It is true of white migrants from South to North as well as of black, so much so that particular blocks in Chicago and Detroit may be almost entirely occupied by white migrants from one Tennessee or Kentucky county. Obversely, factors that reinforce ties with one's home area reduce one's desire to migrate: The presence of relatives nearby makes workers less likely to migrate than their otherwise identical neighbors.[6]

Despite the efforts to replicate home institutions in the destination area, many migrants return home, disappointed with life in their new location. The probability that migration will end in a reverse move also lowers the a priori return, for it reduces the expected stream of benefits from moving ($E_1 - E_0$ beyond point C in Fig. 7.1). Even for those who remain in the new area, the costs of transportation are more than the cost of the first trip. The cost of later visits home at times of illness or death in the family or for holidays must also be counted. Increased awareness of these costs as time passes helps account for the high rates of return migration that exist: In Canada, for example, return migration accounted for as many as half of all moves in some of the years between 1947 and 1966. Not surprisingly, since recent migrants are likely to be among the first to lose their jobs during a cyclical downturn, return migration is especially pronounced during recessions.[7]

The psychic costs of migrating long distances can be used to explain why the power of income differentials to induce migration is sharply diminished by increases in distance between origin and destination. One study found that in 1960 it took an additional difference between the present values of earnings streams E_1 and E_0 of \$4.62 to offset the deterrent effect of an extra mile of distance between a worker's place of origin and a potential destination.[8] This far exceeds the money cost of moving, and is far greater even than the amounts likely to be spent on transportation during return visits.

The remarkably large deterrent effect of distance may be due to workers' lack of information about more distant labor markets. People may have a good idea about conditions in labor markets in the same region as their current location, for they have contact with the residents and access to news media from nearby locations. More distant labor markets, even within the same country, may be largely unknown. The importance of the role of information is suggested by examining how the response of migration to distance varies with the educational attainment of the migrant. More educated workers, who presumably have better access to information about labor-market conditions, are less deterred from migrating by greater distances than are less educated workers. On the other hand, distance has only slightly greater deterrent effects on migration among older people. Since psychic costs rise with age, as we have seen, they do not account for the effect of distance on migration as well as lack of information does.[9]

[6] Polachek and Horvath, op. cit., p. 138.

[7] Vanderkamp, op. cit., p. 1022.

[8] See Larry Sjaastad, "Income and Migration in the United States," Doctoral Dissertation, University of Chicago, 1961, and Vanderkamp, op. cit., p. 1026.

[9] Aba Schwartz, "Interpreting the Effect of Distance on Migration," *Journal of Political Economy* (81): 1153–1167 (1973). Any effects of education that work directly through changing wages are already removed because migration flows have been adjusted for income differentials across regions.

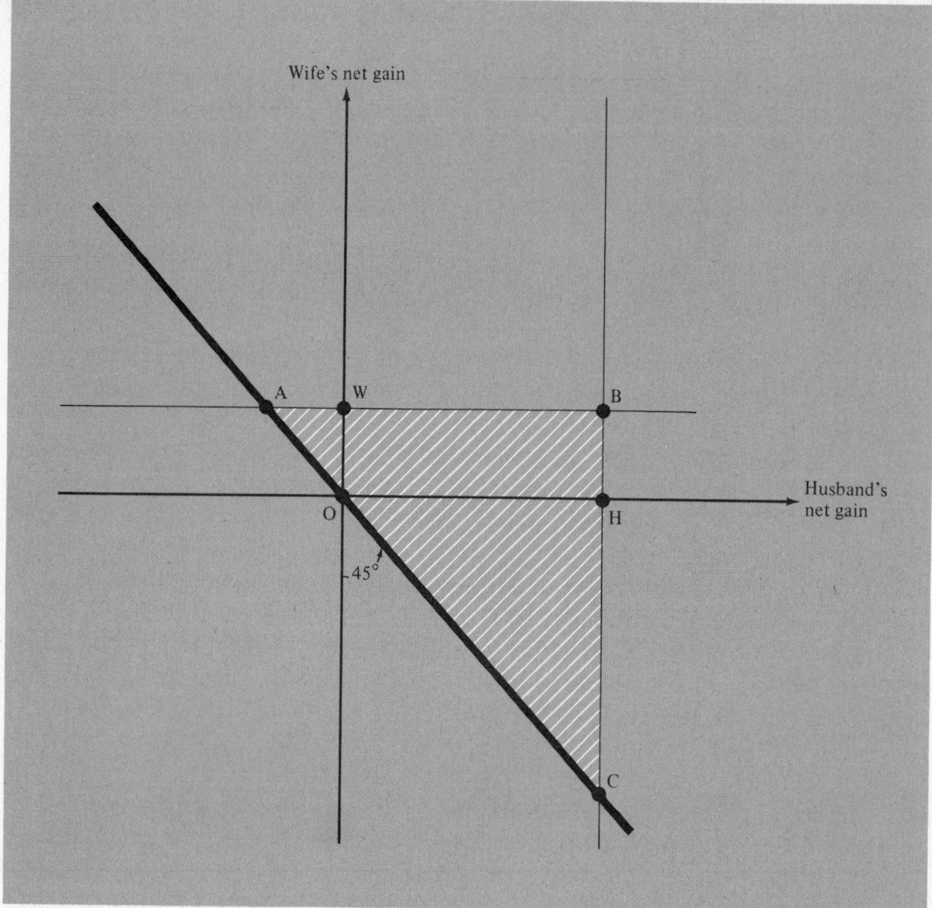

Figure 7.2 The family's migration decision.

This discussion has treated migration as though it resulted from one person's decision about the economic advantages resulting from a move, modified by the psychic costs and uncertainty we have noted. This is a narrow approach, for it ignores the *joint decision making* by a husband and wife considering migration. Although some of their decision-making process may be noneconomic, much will be based on a joint attempt to maximize their economic well-being. As with labor supply decisions that we discussed in Chapters 1 and 2, this is likely to be increasingly important over time with the increased commitment of married women to the labor market.

The conditions determining the typical family's decision are shown in Figure 7.2. The husband's net gain from migration, the present value of the differences between earnings streams E_1 and E_0 in Figure 7.1, is shown on the horizontal axis; his wife's is shown on the vertical axis. Because the average woman's wage is below her husband's, the maximum net gain in her lifetime earnings, OW, falls short of her husband's, which has a maximum of OH. Assume the family decides to migrate if the total net gain, the sum of the husband's and wife's net gains, is positive; in Figure 7.2, any combination of husband's and wife's net gains to the right of the 45° line indicates a positive sum of the net gains. However, because the wife's maximum gain is limited to OW, and the husband's to OH, only those points below the horizontal line AB and to the left of the vertical line BC are possible. Thus the only sums of net gains that are both positive and possible are shown by the shaded triangle ABC.

Migration will be economically beneficial to both spouses' economic prospects only for net gains in the rectangle WOHB. In a few cases, indicated by the triangle AOW, the family will move and the husband's labor-market position will be worse; in a larger number of cases, shown by the large triangle OCH, the family will move and the wife's labor-market position will be worse. Because men's wages are higher and their attachment to the labor force is stronger than those of their spouses in most cases, a family's decision to migrate is quite likely to raise the family's income, but to reduce the wife's labor-market opportunities. This is exactly what occurs: Among American families that moved between 1967 and 1971, earnings of the husbands increased substantially on average, whereas earnings of the wives who moved with them fell. Similarly, among Canadian families that moved between 1965 and 1971 the wife's earnings were sharply reduced by the move.[10] Points in the triangle OCH appear to be more common than those in the rectangle WOHB. As women become more attached to the labor market, though, and if women's wage rates move closer to those of men, there will be more cases of migration in which the husband's labor-market opportunities are worsened by the move. This can be seen by considering the effects of an upward shift in the line AB in Figure 7.2, indicating a greater net gain to the wife from migration; the triangle AOW becomes larger, whereas OCH is unchanged.

Where one spouse's labor-force attachment is very weak, the net change in that spouse's lifetime earnings resulting from migration will be small. But where both spouses are closely attached to the labor force, it is much more likely that one spouse will gain a little, and the other will lose a lot if the couple migrates. The two-worker family will therefore be less likely to migrate than a similar family in which only one spouse works regularly outside the home. For example, among couples in which the husband was between ages 35 and 44, 1.8 percent that had both spouses working moved across state lines in each year 1966 to 1971; among similar couples in which the wife did not work, 3 percent moved each year.[11] Married men move less frequently than single men, and this is especially so, as the analysis in Figure 7.2 suggests, when the wife works.

POLICY ISSUE—MIGRATION TO COLLECT WELFARE BENEFITS

We have defined the income streams of migrants and those who remain behind in terms of earned income. This may be too narrow a view. Other kinds of income also may be higher in the destination areas, especially unemployment insurance benefits and welfare

[10] Steven Sandell, "Women and the Economics of Family Migration," *Review of Economics and Statistics* (59): 410 (1977), and E. Kenneth Grant and John Vanderkamp, "The Effects of Migration on Income: A Micro Study," *Canadian Journal of Economics* (13): 381–406 (1980).

[11] Jacob Mincer, "Family Migration Decisions," *Journal of Political Economy* (86): 759 (1978).

payments. Migrants are not immediately eligible for all such benefits, but eventually they qualify. This should not be interpreted as suggesting that people migrate solely to get on welfare, although some people may. Rather, the existence of a more generous welfare and unemployment insurance system in the destination area reduces the cost that is attached to the probability of unemployment after the initial period of getting established.

To the extent that differential welfare and unemployment benefits do affect migration patterns, it means that the allocative role of migration—workers responding to differences in employment opportunities by supplying their labor services where they command the highest pay—is reduced. Where differences in the levels of these transfer payments are a major factor in the decision to migrate, substantial pressures arise to hold down the cost of transfer payment programs by reducing benefits (and thus in-migration). These reductions hurt migrants who might move for other reasons, as well as current residents who must rely on these transfers for part of their income. It is thus important to know whether, and to what extent, people migrate in response to higher transfer payments in potential destination areas, and whether migrants are more or less adept at obtaining such payments than persons native to the area.

Among black migrants in the late 1950s migration (mostly from the South) was partly determined by the levels of welfare benefits obtainable in different northern cities. The effects were quite small, though, suggesting that migration to collect welfare was not a major motivating factor in the decision to move. Interregional migration in the late 1960s does not seem to have been affected significantly by differences in the levels of welfare benefits or of benefits paid as unemployment insurance.[12] There is, unfortunately, no convincing evidence on the effects of these transfer payments on migration within states or between neighboring states. However, migrants are not especially successful at obtaining these transfer payments once they have moved. In 1975 people who had immigrated to the United States and their families were much less likely than natives to have obtained payments from welfare programs, and their income from such social insurance (Social Security and unemployment benefits) was roughly the same as that of otherwise identical natives. Recent immigrants received less from both types of programs.[13]

In general, economic forces are a major determinant of patterns of migration; but welfare and unemployment benefits, although they have some impact, play only a small part in affecting the direction and amount of flows of migrants. This evidence suggests that state governments need not be concerned that migration from other states will rise sharply if they increase the levels of transfer payments. Rather, those levels can be based upon political and economic factors that are internal to the particular state. So, too, immigrants to the United States do not come here chiefly to avail themselves of our liberal social welfare programs. Thus immigration policy can be based upon other criteria, such as labor-market conditions or humanitarian feelings, rather than considerations of how such policy might interact with welfare and social insurance programs.

EFFECTS ON THE MIGRANT

Having made a decision to migrate, the worker in the new location must use the human capital accumulated in the original location. That process is a difficult one. Migrants cannot be sure of doing so well in the destination area as otherwise similar nonmigrants do. Employers give preference to local workers whose references are easily checked and who are less likely to quit because of homesickness or family

[12] Fields; David Kaun, "Negro Migration and Unemployment," *Journal of Human Resources* (5): 191–207 (1970).

[13] Francine Blau, "The Use of Transfer Payments by Immigrants," *Industrial and Labor Relations Review* (37) (1983). In press.

emergencies that call them back. Even after an initial period of unemployment has ended, migrants may be more exposed to the possibility of future unemployment than nonmigrants. And they may have to accept lower wages because they do not yet have some of the specialized skills that explain part of the high average earnings in the new area. Indeed, the rate of return to schooling among foreign-born Americans in 1970 was only 80 percent of that of natives. The rate of return to on-the-job training received before migration is still further below that to training acquired in the United States.[14]

Offsetting this is the migrants' innate ability. If intelligence is at all definable, it must have at least something to do with the ability to adapt to, and even thrive in new situations, and to learn previously unfamiliar tasks quickly. That migrants left their home regions or countries, where economic conditions presumably were quite poor, whereas otherwise similar people did not, suggests they have more initiative and motivation than the average person in the area of origin. For both these reasons we should expect migrants who acquire the same training, both formal and informal, as natives to be more successful in the labor market. Because of the monetary and psychic costs involved, the migration process on average selects workers who are inherently more able in ways that produce success in the labor market.

These advantages eventually help migrants overcome their somewhat inappropriate training and lack of familiarity with the new environment. Eventually typical immigrants earn more than otherwise identical natives. Indeed, comparing natives and foreign-born Americans with identical education, geographic location and years of experience, immigrants earn roughly 3 percent more than their native counterparts. The difference is greater still for those foreign-born Americans who came from the British Isles and whose schooling and experience acquired abroad is presumably nearly as well suited to the U.S. labor market as skills acquired here.[15]

EFFECTS ON THE LABOR MARKET

Migration affects labor markets themselves as well as the individual migrant; and the size of the impact can be substantial. Even the United States, which from the 1920s until today has not encouraged immigration, has added between 0.2 and 0.3 percent of its population each year through legal immigration. This addition represents nearly one-fourth of the net increase in population that occurs in the United States each year. As the distribution of migrants by age in the lower part of Table 7.2 makes clear, the impact on the labor market is likely to be even greater than these figures suggest. Immigrants are heavily concentrated, as the theory of migration predicts, among persons who are just beginning their work lives.

Migrants affect the labor market they enter in a number of ways, depending largely upon the skills they supply to that market. Overall the supply of labor is increased, and the returns to native labor are bid down. Insofar as migrants are concentrated among skilled workers, as U.S. immigration policy explicitly required

[14] Barry Chiswick, "The Effect of Americanization on the Earnings of Foreign-born Men," *Journal of Political Economy* (86): 908 (1978), and Jacob Mincer and Haim Ofek, "Interrupted Work Careers: Depreciation and Restoration of Human Capital," *Journal of Human Resources* (17): 20 (1982).

[15] Chiswick, op. cit., p. 908.

Table 7.2 LEGAL IMMIGRATION TO THE UNITED STATES, BY ORIGIN AND AGE, 1951–1978

	Fiscal years			
	1951–1960	1961–1970	1971–1975	1978
	Immigrants/year (thousands)			
Total	251	333	387	601
	Source area			
Europe, Canada, and Oceania	173	156	104	94
Mexico	30	46	63	93
Other Western hemisphere	32	85	96	153
Asia	15	43	118	249
Africa	1	3	6	11
Age			**Percent distribution**	
<16		25.5	27.5	25.4
16–39		55.5	54.8	54.7
40–59		14.9	13.0	14.4
60+		4.1	4.7	5.5

Source: U.S. Department of Justice, *Annual Report of the Immigration and Naturalization Service,* 1970, Table 10; 1977, Table 10; 1978, Tables 10, 13.

in the 1960s and 1970s, and still requires to a somewhat lesser extent, the effects are more diverse. The influx of skilled workers reduces the real wages of native skilled workers, making them worse off. The expansion in output induced by the increase in the number of skilled workers raises the demand for unskilled workers. This bids up their real wages, although the effect is partly offset by substitution toward industries that rely on skilled labor. Unskilled workers are thus likely to be made better off if immigration is restricted to skilled workers. Owners of capital will clearly be made better off by such immigration. Because capital and skilled labor work together in production, an influx of skilled labor increases the demand for the limited supply of capital, thus raising its rate of return, as well as expanding output.

These effects overstate the detrimental impact migration has on the economic returns to native labor. Although the human capital acquired before migration is not entirely applicable to the new country, it does raise migrants' productivity somewhat above what it would be without the investment. Taxpayers in the new country paid nothing to finance migrants' premigration investments in human capital; yet, because their productivity is higher as a result of it, migrants earn more and pay higher taxes. Migration gives taxpayers, both employers and workers, in the receiving country a windfall of human capital for which they have not paid, but from which they reap returns.

The situation is different in countries that are net exporters of labor. Most countries regard the outflow of unskilled labor tolerantly, and most restrict its inflow. But attitudes become quite different toward international flows of highly skilled labor such as scientists, engineers, and physicians. The concern of the countries of origin is expressed in the common term "brain drain." Professional workers who change countries usually get higher incomes and frequently better working facilities and opportunities for advancement. But the home country, which seldom views the permanent emigrants as part of the group whose welfare it seeks to maximize, is concerned that it has invested in their education and does not share the returns.

As the top part of Table 7.2 shows, immigration flows can be quite substantial. In the 1960s, for example, the United States received 1.6 million immigrants from Europe and English-speaking countries. This flow represented a substantial loss of prior investment in human capital that had been made in and partly financed by other citizens of the countries whose workers emigrated. The only compensation is that the loss of workers by such countries should raise the real wage rate there, for the supply of labor has been reduced.

The direction of net migration is in accord with the predictions of economic theory. But economic theory also predicts that the migration of labor, together with the reverse migration of capital, will bring the incomes of different areas into equality (within a country or region of free migration and capital movement), and this they have not yet done. The disparity arises because the traditional theory is designed to deal with a system in equilibrium that is disturbed by a single shock, although most disequilibria are not caused by single events. In the case of a one-time disturbance, any positive rate of net migration in the direction of the area with higher income would eventually close the income gap. But the dynamic disturbance caused by a growth rate of population of working age that exceeds the growth rate of employment can be alleviated only by a rate of migration larger than the difference between the two growth rates. Despite heavy out-migration, some areas can therefore have continuing surpluses of unskilled labor. Like the Red Queen, they must run very fast just to stay in the same place.

Despite the tremendous amount of internal migration in the United States, interarea differentials in real wage rates (money wages adjusted for differences in area living costs) have not been equalized. Accounting for the union status, age, and sex of workers, there was almost a 30 percent range in real wage rates among the 30 largest metropolitan areas in the mid-1970s.[16] Migration clearly has eliminated some differences in wages among areas, though, especially between the South and the rest of the United States. In 1950 median income of full-time year-round male workers in the South was 79 percent of the median in the entire nation; in 1980 it was 92 percent. Thus the migration of the 1950s and 1960s did produce an effect that is in the direction predicted by the theory; but it did not fully equalize wages among areas. This is due partly to the continuing shocks that prevent any economic system from coming to rest at an equilibrium, partly to other factors that we shall discuss in Chapter 12.

POLICY ISSUE—ILLEGAL MIGRATION

Although Table 7.2 shows that immigration policy in the United States has become increasingly liberal since the 1950s, that policy still rations entry to the U.S. labor market. Restrictions (so-called preferences) are imposed on the types of workers admitted according to their skill level and to their relationship (or lack thereof) to American citizens. The bias against unskilled migrants, and the very high wages for unskilled workers in the U.S. compared to those in the nearby developing countries, create tremendous incentives for migrants to try to enter the country illegally. Although the Immigration and Naturalization Service devotes substantial resources to preventing illegal entry to this country, many

[16]George Johnson, "Intermetropolitan Wage Differentials in the United States," in Jack Triplett (ed.). *The Measurement of Labor Cost,* University of Chicago Press, Chicago, 1983.

people do work here without citizenship or legal admission as temporary or permanent residents. Estimates in the late 1970s of the number of such undocumented aliens ranged from 3 to 12 million, that is, between 1.5 and 6 percent of the population.[17] Since most illegal aliens are drawn by labor-market opportunities, we may infer that a disproportionate number are of working age, so that they represent an even larger percentage of the labor force.

Proposals for dealing with the presence of this large group of workers and with the continuing inflow of additional illegal aliens range in the 1980s from amnesty and opening up borders, to massive efforts to deport aliens and increase surveillance to prevent new illegal workers from entering. Consider the impact of a policy that allowed an increase in the stock of illegal workers. The bulk of these workers would be very unskilled, as are today's illegal immigrants. To the extent their labor is competitive with that of any U.S. citizen, it is competitive with the labor of unskilled native workers. Since migrants are especially close substitutes for less recent migrants and for the second-generation Americans, the competition with them would be most severe.[18] This suggests that such a policy might hurt the economic status of some other workers, especially those recent migrants whose few skills make them most similar to the illegal migrants who would enter the country as restrictions are relaxed. If the economy is booming and real wages of unskilled workers are not artificially maintained by a minimum wage that is held constant in real terms (a nominal minimum wage that rises with price inflation), the policy will result in lower real wages of all unskilled workers. If, however, jobs are scarce because of a recession, or if real wages cannot drop, new migrants will compete for the scarce jobs with other unskilled workers; unemployment among all workers in the unskilled group will increase. Regardless of whether the adjustment is in wages or employment, however, the labor market position of the typical native unskilled worker will be hurt by this policy.

The less similar that the skills of native workers are to those of the additional illegal aliens who enter the country, the less will be the competition with them, and the smaller will be the loss. We saw in Chapter 4 that skilled and unskilled workers are complements. Thus the increased supply of very unskilled labor represented by the new illegal workers will increase the demand for skilled labor. Domestic skilled workers will receive higher wages as a result of this hypothetical policy change. Because the average real wage will fall, employers will, at least temporarily, reap higher profits. It may even be that the illegal immigrants have few skills as compared even to the lowest-skilled workers in the native labor force.[19] If that is true, the illegals' labor may be complementary with that of native unskilled workers, and even their wages will rise.

This analysis suggests that different interest groups will have very divergent attitudes toward liberalization of the policies that restrict the entry into the United States of unskilled migrants. Employers will welcome such changes; representatives of groups of low-skilled workers will oppose them vigorously if they believe that the illegals compete with unskilled citizens. Unions of skilled workers are likely to be torn by their recognition that the policy helps their constituents yet may injure less fortunate native workers. The analysis suggests that the benefits (or harm) from illegal immigration are ambiguous. If illegal immigrants are qualified only for jobs that require less skill than native labor has to offer, American workers and employers are better off after the immigrants' entry to the country. If, however, illegal immigrants compete with unskilled American workers, the desirability of illegal immigration depends on one weighing the gains and losses of different groups in the labor market.

[17] Walter Fogel, "Illegal Alien Workers in the United States," *Industrial Relations* (16): 243–263 (1977).

[18] Jean Grossman, "The Substitutability of Natives and Immigrants in Production," *Review of Economics and Statistics* (64): 596–603 (1982).

[19] *Wall Street Journal*, December 6, 1982, p. 1.

VOLUNTARY MOBILITY WITHIN A LABOR MARKET

Although migration is an important force in affecting wage and employment determination among labor markets, it represents only a small part of the labor mobility that occurs in an economy. For example, less than one-third of workers who leave their jobs migrate; and less than one-quarter of those whose job changes involve changes in occupation migrate.[20] Workers sometimes change jobs without changing locations because they must—they have been dismissed for misconduct or poor performance or have been made superfluous by technological change or shifts in demand. Other workers choose to change jobs because they are dissatisfied with their present ones or expect to do better elsewhere. The first kind of mobility, *involuntary mobility*, often forces the worker to take a lower-paying job, whereas *voluntary mobility* ought to result in an improvement of the worker's position. Our present concern is with the determinants of voluntary mobility; the layoffs that give rise to most involuntary mobility are discussed in Chapter 8.

If all labor markets were initially in equilibrium, voluntary mobility would occur only when some change caused one set of jobs to become more attractive through a rise in its relative wages or an improvement in its nonpecuniary advantages. Such changes would induce a flow of labor toward the jobs that had become more attractive. However, labor markets are usually not in equilibrium. For many jobs the compensation is always above that needed to attract recruits, and there is ordinarily an excess supply of applicants, many of whom are already employed at less attractive jobs. Such situations result from high wages set through collective bargaining or from declines in demand where real wages are rigid downward. In such cases voluntary mobility will occur whenever there are openings in the high-wage jobs, without the need for further improvement in their relative wage.

Workers who change jobs within a labor market can change occupation, industry, employer, or any combination of these. Particular kinds of moves are characteristic of different kinds of workers. Unskilled workers may change occupation frequently, working first as dishwashers, then as laborers, then as messengers. Clearly skilled workers would not voluntarily make such shifts, for they would earn much less if they worked outside their usual trades. Nevertheless, there are a few common patterns of occupational change among the highly skilled, particularly the shift of lawyers, engineers, and accountants into management. Such shifts are usually made without changing employers and may involve a very gradual change of duties and responsibilities.

Voluntary mobility may be a way in which workers acquire information about the labor market. Although search can take place without workers changing jobs, information about employers is often inadequate unless a job is actually tried out for a while. Voluntary mobility may be part of workers' strategies of "job shopping," finding out which employers and occupations are most suitable to their skills, interests, and habits.[21] This is especially likely to be important for young workers, particularly those whose lack of formal education has left them very ignorant about

[20] See Bartel, op. cit., p. 776, and Schroeder, op. cit., p. 407.

[21] William Johnson, "A Theory of Job Shopping," *Quarterly Journal of Economics* (92): 261–278 (1978), develops this idea.

Table 7.3 ANNUAL RATES OF JOB QUITTING, MEN, 1967–1973 (PERCENT PER YEAR)

	Years of tenure on the job					
Total years of experience	**0–1**	**1–3**	**3–5**	**5–9**	**9–15**	**15+**
0–4	24	20				
5–9	24	21	13	5		
25–29	10	—	11	5	2	1
30–34	10	6	5	4	4	3
35–39	9	5	5	5	4	1

Source: Calculated from Jacob Mincer and Boyan Jovanovic, "Labor Mobility and Wages," in Sherwin Rosen (ed.). *Studies in Labor Markets,* University of Chicago Press, Chicago, 1981, p. 25.

how their preferences fit the characteristics of different jobs that are offered by employers. As the data in Table 7.3 show, the probability of quitting is very high among inexperienced workers.

Firm-specific training—fixed costs that make trained workers more valuable to their present employer than to others—automatically creates a deterrent to voluntary mobility. So long as workers share part of the returns to the training in the form of compensation higher than they could obtain elsewhere, their incentives to quit the firm are reduced. Employers, seeking to reduce turnover costs, thus have an incentive to share these returns by paying higher wages than they might in the absence of training costs, or by offering more extensive fringe benefits. Where on-the-job training, which is usually partly general and partly specific, is more extensive, we will observe less voluntary mobility among firms. The evidence in Table 7.3 shows that mobility is reduced by experience with the current employer, independent of the amount of total experience. Since tenure on the job is likely to be correlated with the amount of investment in firm-specific training, these data illustrate the importance of the effects of such training on mobility.

Perhaps the most firmly established fact about voluntary mobility is that it declines sharply with age; this can be seen by reading down the columns in Table 7.3. Psychic costs of moving rise with age; the remaining length of working life sets an outer limit on the period during which returns can be received, and the marginal amounts of information from additional job shopping diminish the more shopping has already been done. The natural impediments to voluntary mobility of older workers created by family responsibilities and the decline of the spirit of adventure are reinforced by the growth of specialized skills. In part, too, this is because it is harder to "teach an old dog new tricks" (although not impossible, as the proverb would have it); in part, it is because there is not enough time left in which to perform them.

Experience, age, and length of tenure with the employer all raise wages, as the discussion of investment in human capital in Chapter 3 showed. Not surprisingly, then, an examination of the relationship between quitting and wages shows that workers earning high wages are less likely to quit their jobs than are other workers. Much of this relationship is due to the effect on wages of the factors we have already discussed. Part, however, results from the independent effect of wages alone:

Table 7.4 **QUIT RATES IN PERCENT, MONTHLY AVERAGES, 1979 AND 1981, SELECTED INDUSTRIES**

Industry	Year 1979	1981
Durable goods manufacturing	1.7	1.1
Furniture and fixtures	3.2	1.9
Electric and electronic equipment	1.7	1.0
Nondurable goods manufacturing	2.5	1.7
Food products	3.3	2.1
Chemical and allied products	0.8	0.7
Mining	2.7	3.0
Telephone communications	0.4	0.3

Source: Employment and Earnings, March 1980, Table D-2, and March 1982, Table D-2.

Workers who receive wages above what others with comparable experience and job tenure receive are less likely to quit their jobs.[22]

There is little difference between black and white workers in the likelihood of quitting a job. Indeed, allowing for black-white differences in wages, educational attainment and other measures of skill, blacks are less likely to quit a job than are otherwise identical whites. Even though women have higher propensities to quit their jobs than men, this difference is solely a reflection of the opportunities they face: Once their lower wages and shorter labor-market experience are accounted for, there is no difference between men and women in the probability of quitting a job.[23] Thus there appear to be only minor differences by race and sex in the way workers react to the underlying stimuli—differences in compensation and nonpecuniary returns—that induce voluntary mobility.

A remarkably large amount of voluntary mobility across employers exists in the U.S. economy. Published data on quit rates—the percentage of a typical employer's work force that leaves the plant each month—imply voluntary turnover on the order of 2 percent per month in manufacturing, as Table 7.4 shows. Within this figure there is very substantial variation, as the data suggest, due partly to differences in amount of firm-specific training. Telephone communications is a good example of an industry in which the skills are industry-specific and, although decreasingly so, firm-specific, too, because of one firm's dominance in the industry. The comparisons between food and chemicals and between furniture and electrical equipment show that quit rates are usually higher in low-wage industries.

Table 7.4 shows that in all industries except mining the quit rate was lower in 1981 than in 1979. The drop is a reflection of the reduced job opportunities caused by the recession of 1981 to 1982: In 1979 the average unemployment rate was 5.8

[22] John Pencavel, *An Analysis of the Quit Rate in American Manufacturing Industry,* Industrial Relations Section, Princeton University, Princeton, N.J., 1970. Table 1 partly demonstrates this by adjusting quit rates for differences in age.

[23] Francine Blau and Lawrence Kahn, "Race and Sex Differences in Quits by Young Workers," *Industrial and Labor Relations Review* (34): 563–577 (1981), and W. Kip Viscusi, "Sex Differences in Worker Quitting," *Review of Economics and Statistics* (62): 388–398 (1980).

percent; in 1981 it was 7.6 percent. Even the rise in quits in mining may reflect improved labor-market conditions, occasioned by an expansion in the demand for coal. Workers respond very strongly to a decline in job opportunities: A 1 percent drop in the rate of job vacancies induces an even larger decline in the rate of job quitting. This may reflect workers' risk aversion: Why quit even an unpleasant job when the chance of getting another is low? Workers may be aware that leaving jobs when few others are available sharply increases the likelihood that they will spend some time unemployed before obtaining work.[24]

There appears to be a downward trend in the quit rate in manufacturing. Accounting for the changes in job opportunities and the demographic mix of the labor force, the quit rate declined by over 10 percent between 1950 and 1980.[25] This decline may be a reflection of an increase in the fixed costs of employment, including firm-specific training, over the period, an increase that may not be fully reflected in higher wages. On the other hand, improved transportation and the growth of a national market in information should have offset some of the inhibitory effects of greater fixed costs.

POLICY ISSUE—JOB MOBILITY AND THE VESTING OF PENSIONS

With an increasing fraction of workers covered by pension plans, it is likely that qualification for pension rights will increasingly affect workers' decisions about changing jobs. Under some plans pension rights are immediately *vested* in workers: They may collect pensions on retirement based on these rights even if they have left the firm before retirement. Under other pension plans, vesting occurs later. The Employee Retirement Income Security Act of 1974 (ERISA) imposed requirements on pension plans, stipulating maximum years of employment after which contributions by employers must be vested. For many plans this meant a reduction in the average tenure required before a worker's pensions became vested. How do the shorter vesting periods affect voluntary mobility? More generally, what is the effect of pensions upon voluntary mobility?

Among manufacturing industries in 1959, those in which fringe benefits formed a greater percent of total compensation exhibited lower quit rates. This was due partly to the effect of employer contributions for pensions: Quit rates were lower in those industries in which employers paid a greater fraction of wages into employee pension plans.[26] These results would suggest that the growth of private pensions has inhibited mobility and may have contributed to the apparent downtrend in quit rates in the United States since World War II.

This finding does not necessarily imply that the continued growth of pensions will restrict mobility; the changing structure of pensions, especially that imposed by ERISA, may produce an offsetting effect. In particular, if pensions are vested earlier, fewer workers will lose their pension rights if they quit. With the costs of quitting reduced, more workers are likely to change jobs when the current returns to working elsewhere become more attractive. Comparing similar workers in the age cohort 45 to 54, one finds that each $10 of additional vested pension benefits per month raises the probability of quitting by 2 percent.

[24] Donald Parsons, "Quit Rates Over Time: A Search and Information Approach," *American Economic Review* (63): 399 (1973). John Barron and Stephen McCafferty, "Job Search, Labor Supply and the Quit Decision: Theory and Evidence," *American Economic Review* (67): 689 (1977), show that the fraction of quitters who enter unemployment falls as the vacancy rate rises.

[25] James Ragan, "Uncovering the Trend in the Manufacturing Quit Rate," Unpublished Paper, Department of Economics, Kansas State University, 1981.

[26] Pencavel, op. cit., Table 7.

On the other hand, a young worker who can obtain a vested pension fairly quickly may be less likely to quit than one for whom vesting is a distant possibility. Young workers in firms in which vesting requirements are more stringent (more years of service are required before a pension vests) are more likely than other young workers to quit.[27] The inhibition to mobility is likely to be especially great in the period immediately preceding the date of vesting, for the cost of leaving during that period is particularly large.

This discussion suggests that the effects on voluntary mobility of requiring earlier vesting of pensions under ERISA are ambiguous. Earlier vesting will raise the mobility of some experienced workers because their pensions become vested sooner; but it will reduce mobility among inexperienced workers by increasing the costs of leaving during the (shorter) period before a pension becomes vested. The legislation may or may not increase interfirm mobility. So, too, the growth of private pension plans has varying effects on voluntary mobility. Simply having a pension is not an inhibition to mobility; its effects depend on the characteristics of the pension, particularly what rights are granted if the employee leaves the firm.

THE BENEFITS FROM VOLUNTARY MOBILITY

Unless workers have very poor information, we should expect that they improve their overall job satisfaction as a result of a voluntary move. Since economic gains are a major contributor to improved job satisfaction, this suggests that their economic returns from work will also increase. Among young workers, the evidence shows this is the case: Workers who quit their jobs experience more rapid wage growth later on than they would have if they had stayed with their old employer. This does not mean, though, that all young workers would be better off quitting; indeed, young workers who remain on their job appear to do better than they would have if they quit.[28] Both decisions—quitting and staying—appear to reflect a rational calculation of the returns to remaining with the present employer as compared to the returns available elsewhere. Among older workers there is less evidence that workers gain from voluntary mobility, perhaps because economic considerations are less important, or because voluntary mobility rates are so low among older workers that it is difficult to discern the effects on wage gains.

Employers have generally regarded voluntary turnover as an evil to be combated. By definition there cannot be a highly competitive market for workers with specific training, since the training is only useful in the firm where it was provided. This underscores the importance of employers' efforts to reduce turnover and to minimize fixed costs of employment per hour of labor by spreading them over a long job tenure. The frequency of articles in management journals designed to instruct employers in methods of reducing turnover suggests the problem is one that has substantial effects on firms' profitability. Given the size of the fixed employment costs that we presented in Chapter 5, this should not be surprising.

The traditional model of economists, on the other hand, views with approval workers who quit their jobs to gain a slight advantage. Such mobility creates the

[27] Bradley Schiller and Randall Weiss, "The Impact of Private Pensions on Firm Attachment," *Review of Economics and Statistics* (61): 369–380 (1979).

[28] George Borjas and Sherwin Rosen, "Income Prospects and Job Mobility of Younger Men," *Research in Labor Economics* (3): 172 (1980).

competitive labor market that tends to ensure that workers are used where they are most needed by the economy. The view is that fixed employment costs, by reducing mobility, detract from the ability of the labor market to allocate labor where it is most productive. Implicitly the amount of voluntary mobility in the economy is taken to be too low. This view ignores the long-run costs of a policy that seeks to encourage greater mobility among firms. Any such policy will of necessity lower the return on employers' investments in specific training. That in turn will lead to reduced investment and lower productivity of workers while they stay with a firm. Reducing fixed costs does make the labor market more responsive to change, and for that reason mobility should be encouraged. On the other hand, when underlying conditions are not changing, higher fixed costs, if they reflect additional firm-specific training, add to labor productivity and thus to per capita incomes. There is a trade-off between the gains in economic efficiency that result from flexibility in response to change as compared to the gains that result from specialization under a fixed set of demand conditions. It is not clear that voluntary mobility in the United States today errs too much on the side of specialization at the expense of an insufficient ability to allocate labor quickly to new uses when conditions in product markets change.

SUMMARY

Mobility of workers among jobs and labor markets is a manifestation of the job search process that benefits both the workers who move and in many cases the labor market as a whole. Workers considering moving compare the costs, in terms of forgone income and the psychic losses attendant upon moving, to gains in terms of higher incomes in new locations or jobs. Thus we find that larger wage differentials induce more migration, and higher wages on workers' current jobs make them less likely to change jobs. Because workers consider the entire stream of future gains from mobility, older workers have a much lower likelihood of changing jobs, especially when the change might require a geographical move as well.

Insofar as mobility leads workers away from employers or areas where wages are depressed, it benefits the workers who remain behind by raising their wages. This effect is less pronounced if the labor of those migrating is a complementary input in production with that of the workers who remain. Also, workers in locations in which society had made substantial investments in the human capital embodied in the departing workers will be worse off as a result of their migration. In areas receiving net inflows of workers, those workers already there will be hurt to the extent that the new labor competes with them. Other workers, whose labor is complementary to that of the immigrants, will be helped by their entrance to the new labor market. All workers will benefit from the import of human capital that was financed elsewhere. Taken together, the impacts of interfirm and interarea mobility are so complex that it is impossible to say if there is too much or too little migration or job-changing. Rather, the impact on mobility of each particular institution or policy must be analyzed individually to determine how it affects the ability of the labor market to remain flexible while still generating high-paying jobs.

chapter 8

The Structure of Employment, Vacancies, and Unemployment

INTERNAL LABOR MARKETS AND LIFETIME JOBS

We have seen that the existence of fixed costs introduces a rigidity into labor markets that makes them very different from markets where both suppliers and demanders are constantly searching to improve their positions. Mobility among firms and across geographical areas is concentrated among the young. As workers age, their chance of leaving a job decreases, so that many workers in their thirties will hold their current job for the rest of their working lives. The data in Table 8.1 bear this out: Both women and men hold an average of 10 jobs over their lives; but 9 of these are held before age 45, and 7 before age 30. The picture of tremendous mobility in the labor market that was implied by the discussion of voluntary mobility is thus incomplete; whereas mobility is very high for some people, many other workers have a steady long-term relationship with a single employer.

The patterns of mobility implied by the data in Table 8.1 are not new; in industrial societies youths have always shopped for jobs, whereas older workers have generally remained with their employer for long periods of time. Nor are these patterns restricted to the United States; data from sources like those underlying Table 8.1 show similar patterns of long duration jobs in the United Kingdom.[1] This behavior has led to, and has also partly resulted from, the growth of wage-setting and hiring arrangements sometimes described as an *internal labor market.*[2] Recognizing

[1]Brian Main, "The Length of a Job in Great Britain," *Economica* (49): 325–333 (1982).

[2]The operation of internal labor markets was first pointed out by John Dunlop, "The Task of Contemporary Wage Theory," in George Taylor and Frank Pierson (eds.). *New Concepts in Wage Determination,* McGraw-Hill, New York, 1957. Peter Doeringer and Michael Piore, *Internal Labor Markets and Manpower Analysis,* Heath, Lexington, Mass., 1971, develop the concept further.

Table 8.1 JOB-HOLDING PATTERNS BY AGE, UNITED STATES, 1978

Age group	New jobs per year	Cumulative number of jobs held	
		Women	Men
16–17	0.394	0.7	0.8
18–19	0.534	1.8	1.9
20–24	0.425	3.8	4.1
25–29	0.309	5.2	5.8
30–34	0.240	6.4	7.0
35–39	0.192	7.4	7.9
40–44	0.167	8.3	8.7
45–49	0.126	9.0	9.3
50–54	0.096	9.4	9.8
55–59	0.076	9.8	10.2
60–64	0.054	10.0	10.5
65–69	0.032	10.2	10.7
70+	0.010	10.2	10.8

Source: Robert Hall, "The Importance of Lifetime Jobs in the U.S. Economy," *American Economic Review* (72) (1982), Tables 3, 6.

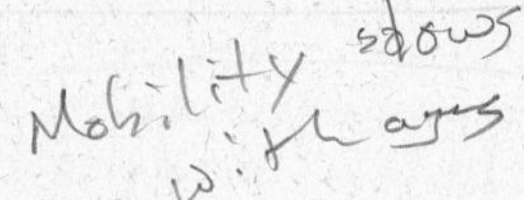

that older workers are less likely to quit, employers respond by investing more in the specific training of workers in these markets. This investment creates a larger gap between workers' VMP with their employers and their VMP elsewhere, making it even less likely that they will quit the firm. This mutually advantageous arrangement is particularly important among blue-collar workers. In some industries, such as basic steel and petroleum refining, there are long chains of progression extending into highly skilled jobs. Training for each job takes place through working at the next lower job. In such cases the firm hires from the external labor market only for the lowest job level, or *port of entry*.

The existence of internal labor markets means that seniority rights are beneficial to management and would exist in many cases in the absence of unions. Unions and workers favor seniority on grounds of equity and because they do not trust management to apply other criteria, such as ability, in an objective way. The unions therefore tend to get customary seniority rights embodied in written agreements and try to increase the weight given to seniority in promotion. But the interests of union and management conflict only to the extent that seniority and ability are uncorrelated; where experience with an employer is valuable, the correlation is often high.

Even where the correlation is not high it may be in both workers' and employers' best interest to set low wages for entry-level workers and have wages rise as workers move up the seniority ladder. Wage progression gives younger workers an incentive to work hard. High wages for senior workers can induce younger workers to exert themselves to show the employer that they are worthy of retention and advancement. In terms of Figure 8.1, workers would produce only VMP_0 if they were paid a wage equal to the value of their marginal product each year. Employers recognize this and structure wages so that they move along the line W_1W_1, starting low for workers with little experience, reaching a peak for the most senior workers, who retire after T_1 years. This induces all workers to produce more, so that the value

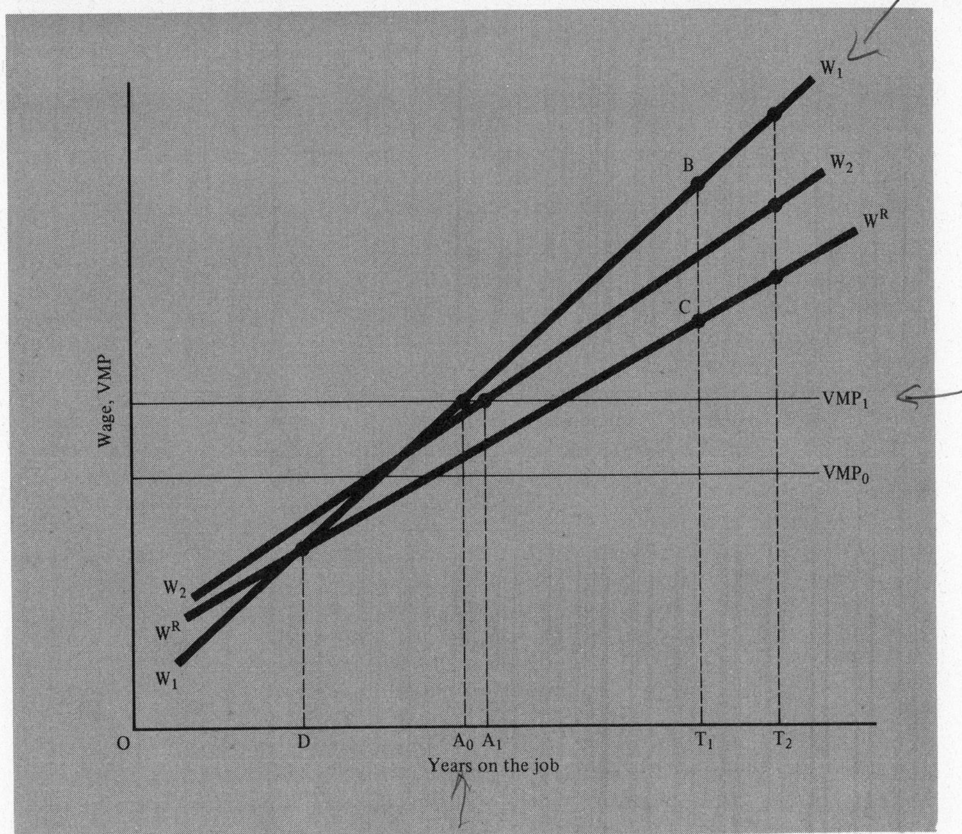

Figure 8.1 Wage growth productivity and retirement.

of marginal product is VMP_1. The employer gets more output from his work force because of this arrangement (since the productivity of each worker is higher). Workers receive higher lifetime earnings (the area under W_1W_1 exceeds that under VMP_0); they can bargain with their employer for some of the increased profits generated by their extra effort.[3]

Earnings progression with seniority also characterizes executive employment, and for much the same reason. In that case, though, the differences in salaries are more exaggerated: The company's president may earn three times what each of the vice presidents earns. It is unlikely that the president's productivity is three times that of other executives. Rather, the tremendous return to attaining the top job is like winning the first prize in a tournament. Only one vice president can win, and that makes all of them work harder. The high earnings received by a top executive are often the reward for hard work in the past that has shown the corporation's board that the executive is marginally more productive than others.[4]

[3]This diagram is based on Edward Lazear, "Agency, Earnings Profiles, Productivity and Hours Restrictions," *American Economic Review* (71): 606–620 (1981).

[4]Edward Lazear and Sherwin Rosen, "Rank-Order Tournaments as Optimum Labor Contracts," *Journal of Political Economy* (89): 841–864 (1981).

When firm-specific training insulates the worker from the external labor market, the setting of specific wage rates for individual jobs becomes more subject to managerial discretion. It is not merely a matter of comparing VMP at one point in time to the cost of labor in the external market. To cope with this difficulty, employers have devised a variety of methods that make the wage scale rise with seniority, yet allow what seems like an objective determination of relative rates of pay. Jobs are evaluated by industrial engineers in terms of their complexity and responsibility, with points (and higher wages) assigned to increasingly complex tasks. Rather than setting wage rates individually for each job in plants that have long progressions based on seniority, employers set wages for a *key job,* often an entry-level job for which some comparable external market exists. Wages in *job clusters* around the key job are set by using evaluations made by engineers or agreed on in collective bargaining.

POLICY ISSUE—THE EFFECT OF LIMITING MANDATORY RETIREMENT

Under the 1978 Amendments to the Age Discrimination and Employment Act most workers cannot be forced to retire before their seventieth birthday. This could have a substantial effect on the number of older people employed: In 1973, 37 percent of employed male workers aged 62 to 64 were in jobs in which they would be subject to mandatory retirement; this represented 25 percent of the male population in this age group.[5] How many workers would choose to stay on until age 70 among those who would otherwise retire earlier? What would be the impact of this change on job opportunities for younger workers? More important, what would happen to the structure of wages paid to workers of different ages? Indeed, why is there mandatory retirement at all?

The last question can be answered by using Figure 8.1, assuming one can relate years on the job to age. The optimal wage structure for both workers and employers is depicted by the line W_1W_1, which is upward-sloping to provide the incentives that induce the higher productivity indicated by VMP_1. For firms to break even on workers' lifetime productivity, the discounted wage must equal the discounted VMP. Thus there is some point A_0 at which the wage equals VMP_1. Beyond this age, wages exceed productivity; before it, they fall short of productivity. Despite this excess, it does not pay employers to drive wages of older workers down to VMP_1. If they did, younger workers would soon stop producing so much, VMP would fall, and the employers would be worse off.

Without mandatory retirement, workers whose reservation wage is indicated by the line W^R would not wish to leave the firm beyond their age at point D, for their wage exceeds their reservation wage; at age T_1 the excess is substantial, an amount BC. Yet if they stay until T_1, their lifetime earnings just equal the value of their marginal product; if they stay beyond T_1, as they would like, they cost the firm more than they produce. Mandatory retirement is thus a way of getting workers to leave the firm who would otherwise stay. It maintains the upward-sloping wage structure that induces most workers to work harder in order to qualify for higher wages later in their work lives.[6]

Raising the age of mandatory retirement gives some of today's older workers a windfall gain, for their lifetime earnings exceed what they expected when they entered the firms they have worked at for most of their working lives. It also changes the incentives facing firms and workers, incentives that give rise to the progression of wages with seniority. With a higher mandatory retirement age, say, at T_2, younger workers have a

[5] Richard Burkhauser and Joseph Quinn, "Is Mandatory Retirement Overrated? Evidence from the 1970s," *Journal of Human Resources* (18) 337–358 (1983).

[6] Edward Lazear, "Why Is There Mandatory Retirement?" *Journal of Political Economy* (87): 1261–1284 (1979).

greater incentive to work hard, for they can expect to be with the firm longer. There is thus less need to have wages rise so rapidly with seniority. Also, because workers will remain longer, and lifetme wages must still equal lifetime productivity, the worker will be older before wages equal VMP_1. The wage-seniority profile will look like W_2W_2—flatter than W_1W_1. Lifetime earnings will rise, but future generations of older workers will receive lower wages each year than if the age of mandatory retirement had not been raised.

Some evidence suggests that raising the mandatory retirement age to 70 may sharply lower the rate of labor force withdrawal of those older men who would otherwise have stayed at work only until required to leave at age 65. One estimate indicates that the annual rate of labor force withdrawal would be decreased by one-fifth among such men. However, the overwhelming majority of men who are subject to mandatory retirement leave before the mandatory date, attracted to retirement by Social Security and pension benefits. It has been estimated that raising the age of mandatory retirement to 70 would induce only a 2 percentage point increase in labor-force participation rates of men in their sixties.[7] This very small increase in the number of older workers is unlikely to have much effect on wages or job opportunities for younger workers.

LAYOFFS

Employment in firms with well-developed internal labor markets is constantly buffeted by drops in demand for the firm's product. Some of these are seasonal; in most industries there is a peak demand period and a time when demand is somewhat slack. Seasonal variations in product demand are expected by both workers and firms, for they have (by definition) been regular occurrences in the past. Fluctuations in product demand occur from year to year as well; their timing may not be predictable, but at least they are not a complete surprise. In this case, too, firms and workers, knowing that variation in output is inevitable, will structure employment practices in the internal labor market to reflect this variability.

When product demand declines, the demand curve for labor shifts leftward. If wage rates were free to adjust they would decline, as workers accepted pay cuts in order to remain employed. This does not occur in the United States or in most other developed countries. In Japan, though, the institution of "lifetime employment"—known as the *nenkō* system—has produced a set of employment practices that are consistent with employer profit maximization and maintenance of employment during declines in product demand. Annual bonuses amounting to over one-fourth of earnings are paid in manufacturing industry. This provides a substantial cushion for reducing labor costs when product demand falls. And, in fact, the greatest year-to-year variation in bonuses is in those industries where product demand varies most over the cycle.[8]

There is no institution like the *nenkō* system in North America or Western Europe, and no institutionalized method of reducing hourly labor costs when demand drops that will induce employers to maintain the size of their work forces. Wages are not reduced and indeed may even rise in real terms. Employment is reduced through layoffs that are viewed as temporary by both workers and em-

[7]Burkhauser and Quinn, loc. cit.

[8]Masanori Hashimoto, "Bonus Payments, On-the-Job Training, and Lifetime Employment in Japan," *Journal of Political Economy* (87) 1102 (1979).

ployers. One may wonder why workers are not willing to take wage cuts during periods of seasonal slack, or during recessions, to avoid being laid off. In a unionized environment, in which layoffs are made in inverse order of seniority, only a fraction of the workers are hurt by a policy of wage rigidity that produces layoffs; but all workers would be hurt by a policy of accepting wage cuts. The median worker, who determines policy through a vote for the union leadership, will prefer rigid wages and layoffs for the least senior workers, since most employment can be maintained without a wage cut. It is thus understandable that unionized firms reduce employment instead of cutting wages when product demand drops, for this approach does not hurt the interests of the majority of union members.

In nonunionized firms there is much more year-to-year variability in wages, and less variability in employment, than in unionized firms. Among unionized employees, real wage rates actually rose by 0.13 percent along with each 10 percent drop in production during the period 1967 to 1974; their average weeks worked dropped by 0.11 percent in response to this drop in product demand. Nonunion workers, on the other hand, experienced a 0.12 percent decline in real wages in response to a drop in product demand of 10 percent. Although their real wage rate did fall during slack times, the decline was insufficient to induce employers to maintain employment levels: Their average weeks worked declined 0.5 percent when product demand dropped by 10 percent.[9]

Why don't wages fall enough to keep employment from falling during periods of reduced demand for the output of nonunion firms? After all, the employer is free to vary wages without interference. The most likely answer lies in the same considerations that lead to the profit-maximizing wage structure implied by the upward-sloping wage relation W_1W_1 in Figure 8.1. By offering more senior workers the prospect of employment at a high wage, free of the risk of layoff, the employer induces both younger and older workers to work harder. Output per worker over the years is higher than if wages were cut sufficiently to maintain employment. Younger workers accept the layoffs caused by reduced product demand knowing that they will soon have enough seniority to be protected from the vicissitudes of the product market. Layoffs in nonunion firms can thus be viewed as part of an *implicit contract* between workers and employers. The relationship reduces the risks of demand fluctuations for most workers and creates a system of incentives that leads to levels of output that are above what they would otherwise be. The political process in unionized plants that produces the same outcomes is itself partly a formalization of the same set of customs, partly a reflection of the greater attention paid to seniority in union plants: Young unionized workers are more likely than young nonunion workers to be laid off permanently from their jobs when demand drops.[10]

Temporary layoffs account for a substantial fraction of people who are unemployed because they lost their jobs (as opposed to labor-force entrants or voluntary quitters). Although only a few are on layoffs of known durations, as Table 8.2 shows, many more are on indefinite layoff. Such layoffs are a larger fraction of total

[9] John Raisian, "Cyclic Patterns in Weeks and Wages," *Economic Inquiry* (17): 487 (1979).

[10] Francine Blau and Lawrence Kahn, "Unionism, Seniority and Turnover," *Industrial Relations* (23): (1983). In press.

Table 8.2 PERCENTAGE DISTRIBUTION OF JOB LOSERS, MARCH 1974

	All persons	Men 25–64
Type of job losers		
Fixed duration layoff	10.1	13.0
Indefinite duration layoff	27.3	27.4
No job	61.4	58.1
New job starting within 30 days	1.2	1.5
Total	100.0	100.0
Job losers as percent of unemployed	49	73

Source: Martin Feldstein, "The Importance of Temporary Layoffs: An Empirical Analysis," *Brookings Papers on Economic Activity,* 725–744 (1975).

unemployment among prime-age men than among all the unemployed, for most adult men are job losers rather than new entrants to the labor market who are unable to find work. Table 8.2 describes the pool of laid-off workers at a single point in time, but it understates the importance of temporary layoffs among people entering unemployment, because workers on layoff remain unemployed for a much shorter time than other unemployed workers. During March 1974, a month of approximately full employment, temporary layoffs of persons expecting to be rehired represented 56 percent of all job losses and 60 percent of job losses among men aged 25 to 64.[11]

Blacks are more likely to be laid off than whites: Even accounting for differences in total experience and tenure on the job, occupation, and industry, the average black male worker is at least 5 percent more likely to be laid off than an otherwise identical white male; among females the difference is at least 15 percent. These racial differences seem to reflect pure discrimination, since any effects resulting from differential years of experience and tenure, or variations across industries in the extent of fluctuations in product demand, are accounted for. White women, on the other hand, are at most half as likely to be laid off as white men with the same tenure and experience, and in the same occupation and industry, and black women are also less prone to layoff.[12] This surprising difference may be due to the location of women within a given industry in jobs that are less sensitive to fluctuations in demand. Women are more often part of the "overhead labor" that is necessary to keep the firm operating even when production is cut.

POLICY ISSUE—LAYOFFS AND UNEMPLOYMENT INSURANCE

In the United States, unemployment benefits are financed almost exclusively by payroll taxes on employers. These taxes, whose levels are determined by statute in each state, are *experience-rated:* The more layoffs, and thus the more unemployment benefits a particular firm has generated in the past, the higher its current tax rate will be. If the labor market consists of many firms, the imposition of taxes exactly equaling benefits paid to each firm's unemployed workers will have no effect on employment in any firm. In Figure 8.2 the wage (which the competitive firms take as given) falls from W_0 to W_1; workers are

[11] Martin Feldstein, "The Importance of Temporary Layoffs: An Empirical Analysis," *Brookings Papers on Economic Activity:* 733 (1975).

[12] Francine Blau and Lawrence Kahn, "Causes and Consequences of Layoffs," *Economic Inquiry* (19): 283 (1981).

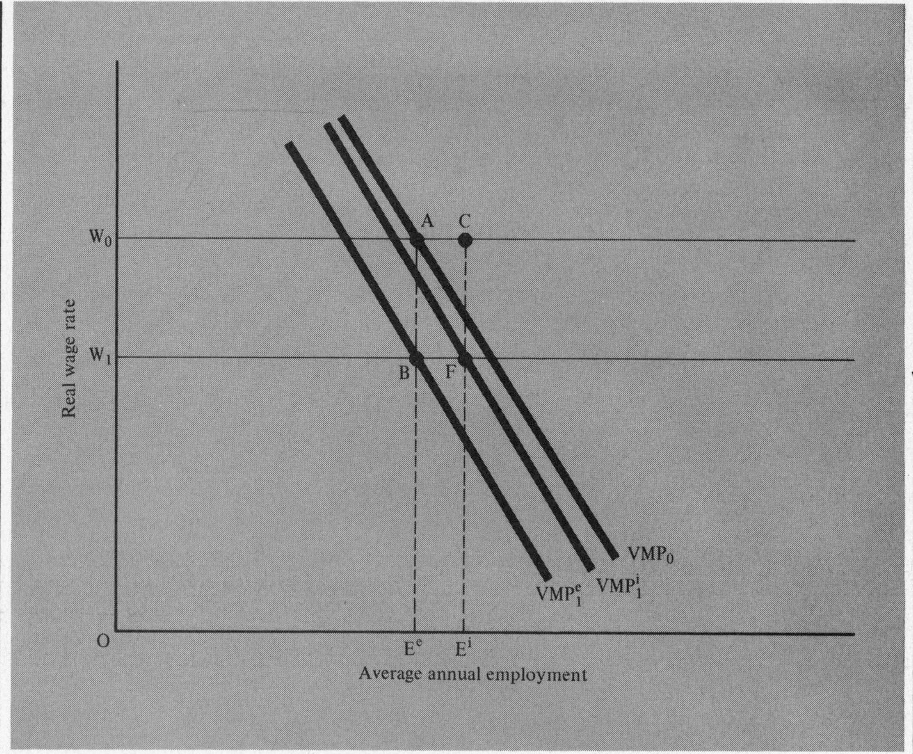

Figure 8.2 Employment under payroll-tax financed unemployment benefits.

willing to supply their labor at a lower wage rate, because their hourly return now includes the unemployment benefits. Employers' demand for labor drops from VMP_0 to VMP_1^e, for the VMP is reduced by the tax that must be paid. Since the tax equals the benefit and any extra benefits raise the tax by an equal amount, VMP falls exactly to B, leaving employment at E^e. The wage bill is OW_1BE^e; unemployment benefits (and taxes) are W_0W_1AB.

In fact, there is a limit on tax rates; employers can consistently be paying the highest tax rate and still pay less in taxes than is paid in benefits to their workers who are on layoff. A system of unemployment insurance financed by taxes that are incompletely experience-rated changes the incentives facing a firm and its workers. Workers will be compensated by unemployment insurance during any layoff resulting from reduced demand due to fluctuations in output. If workers expect this, they will be willing to supply their labor for less to firms that experience regular, often seasonal variations in output demand than to firms in more stable industries. With fewer hours at work, their income from the labor market (wages and unemployment benefits) and the value of the additional leisure could exceed what they would get from firms where employment is stable and no unemployment insurance would be received. Employers' wage costs per hour worked will be lower; but because of the limit on the payroll tax imposed by incomplete experience rating, this reduction in the total labor cost per hour need not be completely offset by higher payroll taxes. In terms of Figure 8.2 the wage drops to W_1 as before; but the demand falls less, since the firm's tax does not completely cover the unemployment benefits paid to its workers. This firm receives a subsidy from other firms, one that encourages it to expand employment to E^i, and thus expand average production during the year above what it would otherwise be. The partial experience rating induces a shift in production toward firms that exhibit greater fluctuations in output, since their instability is subsidized by taxes on other firms. Employment in those other firms is reduced, because their tax bill exceeds the benefits their workers receive that induce those workers to offer their labor for a lower wage. This tax structure encourages the subsidized firms to increase layoffs. By doing so they can share a larger subsidy, in the form of the difference between unemployment benefits received by their workers and taxes paid by them, with their employees who are subject to seasonal layoffs. Since workers on seasonal layoff represent as much as one-third of the recipients of unemployment insurance at cyclical peaks, this effect could be substantial.[13]

In states where the payroll tax rate reaches a higher maximum, layoff rates in manufacturing industries are lower. The degree of seasonal fluctuation in employment in manufacturing also is greater, other things equal, in those states where the tax structure allows more workers to receive unemployment benefits that do not result in higher taxes for their employers. The estimates vary, but removing the ceiling on unemployment tax rates could reduce the layoff rate in manufacturing by one-third.[14] Given the importance of layoffs in the pool of unemployed, this could reduce the unemployment rate in the United States by as much as 0.5 percentage points (500,000 people). Moreover, by making firms that generate unemployment pay for it in the form of higher taxes, which are presumably passed on to consumers in the form of higher prices, the U.S. government can achieve a more equitable tax burden. Those consumers who want products whose production involves seasonal fluctuations in employment must pay more to satisfy their tastes. Broadening the range of experience-rated unemployment insurance taxes would both reduce unemployment (increase efficiency) and shift the burden of taxes to those who benefit from seasonal fluctuations in output (increase equity).

VACANCIES

Layoffs or reductions in compensation are responses to reductions in product demand. When product demand rises, the opposite responses must occur: Workers must be hired, and wages may have to be increased to attract them. The rise in wages will itself choke off some of the increased demand for labor, if prices of the product and other inputs to production fail to rise proportionately. In establishments characterized by long wage progressions and an internal labor market, the rise in product demand is met by a process of promotions that leaves vacancies at ports of entry into the firm. Hiring is done into lower-paid jobs.

Most vacancies that open up are for low-skilled work, even in those firms in which the internal labor market is less well developed. Even if hiring is being done only to replace workers who have left voluntarily, the very strong negative correlation between quit rates and wage levels that we noted in Chapter 7 ensures that the incidence of vacancies will be disproportionately in low-skilled positions. Low-skilled vacancies will not represent so large a fraction of the pool of vacancies open at a particular time, though, for the *duration of vacancies* increases with the level of skill required for the vacant job. This occurs partly because the pool of job applicants

[13]Charles Warden, "Unemployment Compensation: The Massachusetts Experience," in Otto Eckstein (ed.). *Studies in the Economics of Income Maintenance,* Brookings Institution, Washington, 1967.

[14]Frank Brechling, "Layoffs and Unemployment Insurance," in Sherwin Rosen (ed.). *Studies in Labor Markets,* University of Chicago Press, Chicago, 1981, p. 201; Terrence Halpin, "The Effect of Unemployment Insurance on Seasonal Fluctuations in Employment," *Industrial and Labor Relations Review* (32): 353–362 (1979); andRobert Topel, "On Layoffs and Unemployment Insurance," *American Economic Review* (73): 541–559 (1983).

Table 8.3 THE VACANCY-UNEMPLOYMENT RELATION

	Date				
	1963	1968	1973	1978	1982
United States					
Unemployed per vacancy	6.0	1.3	3.7	7.0	—
Unemployed rate (%)	6.6	4.0	5.5	7.0	—
United Kingdom					
Unemployed per vacancy	4.5	2.8	2.7	8.5	25.1
Unemployment rate (%)	2.6	2.5	3.0	5.8	11.8
West Germany					
Unemployed per vacancy	0.4	1.0	0.3	5.2	11.3
Unemployment rate (%)	0.8	1.4	0.8	4.5	6.7

Source: Katharine Abraham, "Structural/Frictional Versus Deficient Demand Unemployment: Some New Evidence." *American Economic Review* (73) 721 (1969), Table 4, and OECD, *Main Economic Indicators,* various issues.

consists mainly of low-skilled people, enabling employers to fill low-skilled jobs faster. Partly, though, the duration of vacancies increases with skill because the greater fixed costs of specific training of a newly hired skilled worker give employers an incentive to search more carefully for such workers.

Obtaining information on the structure and number of job vacancies in the United States is very difficult. Most employers do not list vacancies with the state employment service; and there is no monthly survey comparable to the Current Population Survey of households that provides data on employers' job vacancies (although such data were collected from manufacturing firms from 1969 to 1973). The results of one attempt to circumvent this deficiency are presented in the first two rows of Table 8.3. These vacancy data show that there are usually more unemployed workers than vacant jobs available. The data from manufacturing from 1969 to 1973 corroborate this inference, as do data from several states that continued the federal program to collect vacancy statistics after 1973. However, many vacancies probably go unreported, because employers often fill jobs without formally advertising them. This suggests that, when the measured number of unemployed workers per vacancy approaches one, we may be fairly sure there are at least as many actual vacancies as there are unemployed workers. Along with the low vacancy rate there is a very low average duration of vacancies: Even during the boom year 1968 the best estimate is that the average vacancy stayed open only 2 weeks.[15]

Many European countries require employers to register vacant jobs with the government, enabling a more precise count of vacancies. Unfortunately, the corresponding measures of unemployment are not comparable to those based on the household surveys that generate North American unemployment statistics. Nonetheless, the comparisons of the number of job seekers per vacancy and the unemployment rate in West Germany and the United Kingdom, shown in the bottom four rows of Table 8.3, provide useful information. They show that in the United

[15] Katharine Abraham, "Structural/Frictional Versus Deficient Demand Unemployment: Some New Evidence," *American Economic Review* (73) 721 (1969), Table 4.

Kingdom, as in the United States, the number of vacant jobs does not approach the number of unemployed workers. Experience in West Germany is more mixed; as in the United States, however, it is likely that vacancy data are less complete than are the counts of the unemployed.

TYPES OF UNEMPLOYMENT

Unemployment can be divided into two basic types: unemployment that results from deficient aggregate demand and all other unemployment. The latter in turn is often divided into frictional, structural, and seasonal unemployment. These latter forms of unemployment are the focus of discussion in the rest of this chapter; we leave the discussion of cyclical unemployment and its causes to Chapter 15.

We saw in Chapter 6 that unemployment and unfilled vacancies exist simultaneously because it takes time to match jobs and workers appropriately. The unemployment that accompanies this matching process is *frictional unemployment,* which, strictly defined, is unemployment that corresponds to unfilled vacancies in the same occupations and the same places. All the factors that affect the matching process of firms' and workers' search, such as unemployment benefits and the existence of efficient labor-market intermediaries, will affect the amount of frictional unemployment. More stubborn frictions result when the unemployed are mismatched with job vacancies because they do not have the right skills or live in the wrong places. Such mismatching creates *structural unemployment,* a concept that will be examined in more detail later. Finding jobs for the structurally unemployed requires more than searching in local markets; wages must become more flexible, workers must be retrained, or jobs or workers must move to new locations. The term *seasonal unemployment* is self-explanatory. Seasonal unemployment occurs in activities such as construction, agriculture, canning, and the tourist trade, in which weather or the calendar determine when production can be carried on or govern the level of demand. For purposes of measuring the strength of demand in the labor market, it is usual to use unemployment statistics that have been seasonally adjusted. This adjustment does not remove the seasonal component of unemployment from the total; it merely spreads it evenly over the year.

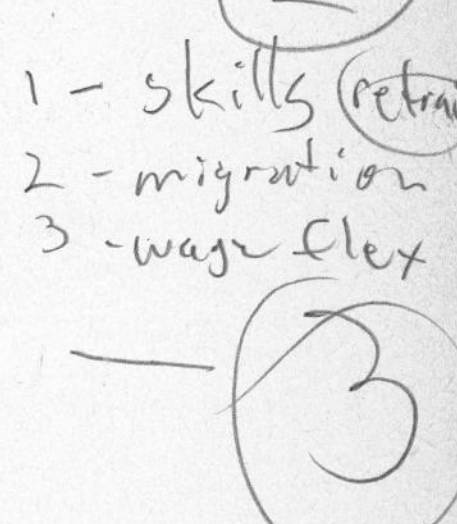

In contrast with all of these, we define *demand-deficiency unemployment* as unemployment that occurs when there is not enough aggregate demand to provide work for the whole labor force no matter how it is trained or deployed. This implies that in the economy as a whole there are more unemployed workers than vacant jobs when both are accurately measured.

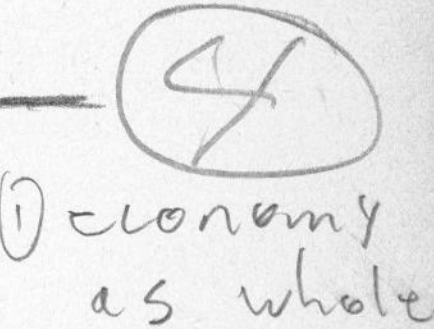

In the United States, the annual average unemployment rate (unemployment as a percent of the civilian labor force) over the period 1948 to 1982 has fluctuated between a low of 2.9 percent in 1953 and a high of 9.7 percent in 1982. Average rates below 4 percent occurred in 1948, 1951 to 1953, and 1966 to 1969. These were years of tight labor markets and most of them were during the Korean and Vietnam wars. All unemployment in these years can safely be considered frictional, structural, or seasonal. Rates above 6 percent occurred in 1958, 1961, 1975 to 1978, and 1980 to 1982. All these were years of recession or recovery, and the unemployment of these years includes a component caused by deficient demand.

A second way of classifying unemployment is to divide it into *voluntary and involuntary unemployment.* The basic idea of the division is that workers are voluntarily unemployed when they have been offered a job for which they are qualified and that pays the going wage, but they continue to search for a better job at a higher wage rather than accept the offer. Workers are involuntarily unemployed when they would be willing to accept a job for which they are qualified at the prevailing wage or below it, but cannot find any such job. Thus voluntary unemployment is essentially frictional, whereas involuntary unemployment indicates demand deficiency.

These definitions conceal a number of serious problems. Even when there is substantial unemployment, some unpleasant, low-wage jobs may remain unfilled because no one wants them. If skilled workers lose high-wage jobs and turn down low-wage jobs while searching for work at their old trades, are they voluntarily or involuntarily unemployed or both at once? Some writers say that they are voluntarily unemployed and that therefore all unemployment even in depressions is voluntary.[16] But this view involves an aggregation fallacy. If a job is unpleasant and badly paid, 100 workers might turn it down. Yet if any one of them took it, the vacancy open to the other 99 would disappear. The common view therefore relates involuntary unemployment to the numerical balance between vacancies and unemployment workers.

THE RELATION BETWEEN UNEMPLOYMENT AND VACANCIES

The data for the United States, the United Kingdom, and West Germany in Table 8.3 indicate that the number of vacancies falls as the number of unemployed workers rises. The general form of this relationship is shown in Figure 8.3. For any given structure of the labor market, vacancies and unemployment are negatively related along a curve such as the one marked AA.[17] Improvement of the functioning of the labor market, or reductions in structural unemployment achieved by retraining or the relocation of workers or jobs, will shift the curve toward the origin, producing a new curve such as BB. Along it there are fewer vacancies and less unemployment for any given level of aggregate demand. Increases in aggregate demand result in movements to the left along the curve representing a given market structure. Decreases in aggregate demand produce movements to the right along such a curve.

All positions at which the number of unemployed workers is equal to the number of vacancies lie on the 45° ray from the origin. This ray forms one common basis for distinguishing between full and less than full employment. To the right of this ray there is said to be demand deficiency, because the number of unemployed exceeds the number of vacancies; to the left there is no demand deficiency. This implies that there is more than one possible position of full employment; indeed, there is a different one for each possible structure of the labor market.

[16]See, for example, Robert Lucas and Leonard Rapping, "Real Wages, Employment and Inflation," *Journal of Political Economy* (77): 721–754 (1969).

[17]For Great Britain for 1949–1966 Anthony Thirlwall has estimated the relation to be linear, with each 1 percentage point higher vacancy rate reducing the unemployment rate by a 0.9 percentage point. See "Types of Unemployment with Special Reference to 'Non-Demand Deficient' Unemployment in Great Britain," *Scottish Journal of Political Economy* (16): 20–49 (1969).

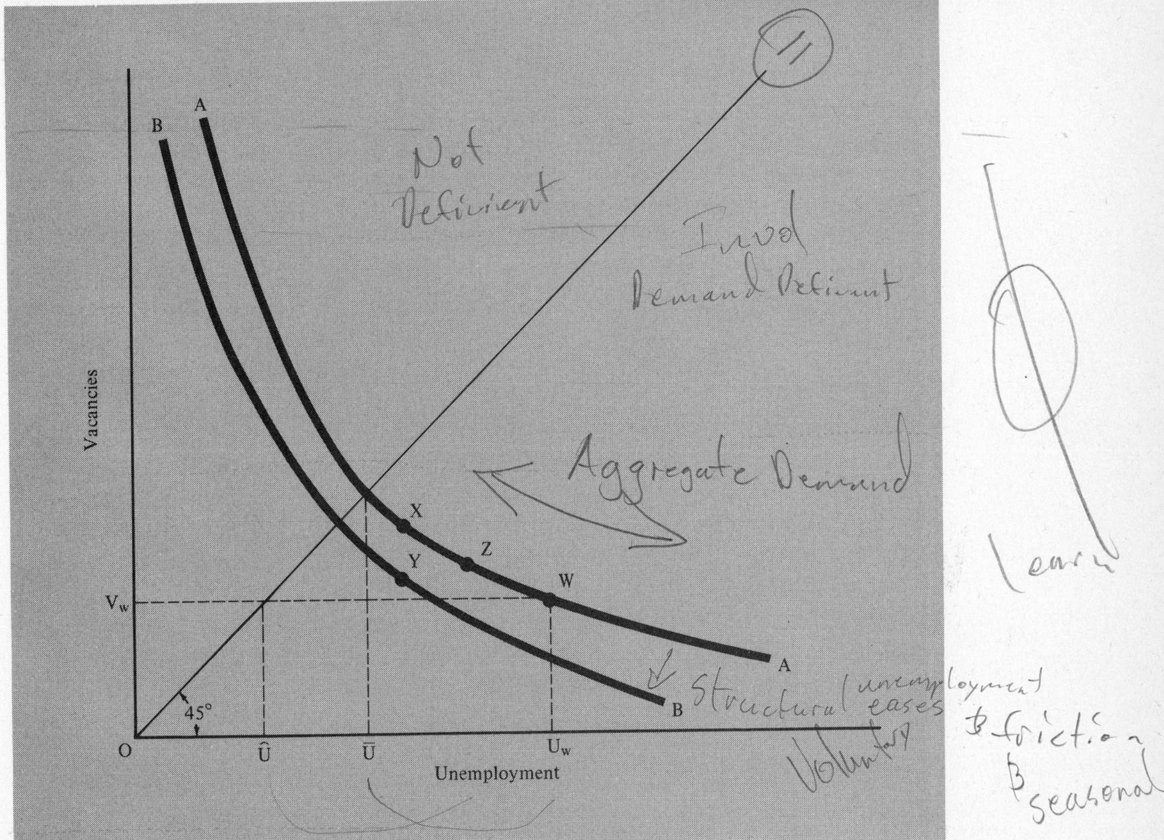

Figure 8.3 The relationship between unemployment and job vacancies.

When there are no comprehensive statistics on unfilled vacancies, as in the United States, it is especially hard to distinguish increases in unemployment resulting from a decline in aggregate demand from increases resulting from greater structural imbalance. Where vacancy statistics are available, the former would be indicated by a movement such as that from X to Z, with vacancies decreasing as unemployment increased. The latter would be indicated by a movement such as that from Y to Z. In the absence of vacancy statistics, the second type of movement might be identified by the increasing dispersion of geographical and occupational unemployment rates, since growing structural imbalance would involve constant or falling unemployment in sectors where the number of vacancies was increasing, and rising unemployment in other sectors. An increase in unemployment with no change in vacancies (a horizontal shift to the right from an initial position in Figure 8.3) represents a simultaneous increase in structural and demand-deficiency unemployment.

Figure 8.3 can be used to explore ways in which a given total of unemployment can be broken down into two components, one of which represents demand deficiency, and the other frictional, seasonal, and structural unemployment. Suppose that we are at point W on curve AA, with unemployment of U_w and vacancies of V_w. If we accept the definition that there is no demand deficiency when the total number of vacancies equals the total number of unemployed, then a first approximation is to subtract V_w from U_w and call the difference demand-deficiency unemployment. This would put the boundary between the components at $\hat{U}$, with the distance $0\hat{U}$ equal to the frictional and structural component. However, it is clear from the diagram that the distance $\hat{U}U_w$ overstates the number of jobs that need to be created by increasing demand. If demand is increased with no change in the market structure, the point describing the state of the market will move leftward along AA, and equality between unemployment and vacancies will be reached at the unemployment level $\bar{U}$, along the 45° line. At this point the frictional and structural component, $0\bar{U}$, is larger than $0\hat{U}$. The increased demand for labor has not consisted entirely of demand for people with the skills and in the locations represented by the unemployed, and the number of unfilled vacancies has therefore risen.

Figure 8.3 does not provide any basis for distinguishing among frictional, seasonal, and structural unemployment. It should be noted, however, that if frictional unemployment is defined as unemployment matched by vacancies in the same market, then the boundary between frictional and seasonal unemployment and structural unemployment depends on how markets are defined. The greater the number of different occupations and localities that are considered as separate markets, the smaller will be the frictional and seasonal components of unemployment and the larger will be the structural component.

THE STRUCTURE OF UNEMPLOYMENT

Unemployment rates at any time have a pronounced structure by place, industry, occupation, and type of worker. The structure can be related to a number of factors already considered. Selected unemployment rates for 1979 are shown in Tables 8.4 and 8.5. This is the most recent year when the U.S. economy approached the 45° line in a graph like Figure 8.3 that would relate actual, as opposed to measured, vacancies to unemployment. These rates are the percentages of the civilian labor force in each group who are unemployed. The structure of rates shown is broadly similar to that of other years in which there was little demand-deficiency unemployment. We are explicitly examining patterns only of seasonal, structural, and frictional unemploy-

Table 8.4 UNEMPLOYMENT RATES BY AGE, SEX, RACE, AND ETHNICITY, 1979

	Males			Females		
Age	White	Black	Hispanic	White	Black	Hispanic
16–17	16.1	37.6	23.4	15.9	42.9	30.5
17–18	12.3	31.8	13.8	12.5	36.9	16.1
20–24	7.4	18.4	9.0	7.8	22.4	8.0
25–54	3.0	7.4	5.0	4.7	8.9	8.0
55 and over	2.6	5.3	5.0	3.0	4.5	7.6
All ages, 16 and over	4.4	11.2	6.9	5.9	13.2	10.4

Source: Employment and Unemployment During 1979: An Analysis, Special Labor Force Report No. 234, Table 51.

Table 8.5 UNEMPLOYMENT RATES BY OCCUPATION GROUP, 1979

White-collar workers	
Professional and technical workers	2.4
Managers, proprietors, and officials	2.1
Clerical workers	4.6
Sales workers	3.9
Total white-collar	3.3
Blue-collar workers	
Craft and kindred workers	4.5
Operatives	7.7
Nonfarm laborers	10.8
Total blue-collar	6.9
Service workers	
Private household workers	4.8
Other service workers	7.3
Total service	7.1
Farmers and farm laborers	3.8

Source: Employment and Training Report of the President, 1980, Table A-23.

ment, although in fact patterns of demand-deficiency unemployment are not very different.

A number of features of these tables are consistent with the theory of fixed costs of employment, which predicts lower unemployment where the investment in the employee is greatest. Unemployment rates are generally higher for women than for men, which is probably a result of the less continuous participation in the labor force by women and their need to search for new jobs when they reenter the labor market. Unemployment rates are substantially lower in the occupations that require high levels of skill and education. This reflects the greater stability of employment created by higher fixed costs. It may also indicate that those skilled workers who do become unemployed usually have an easier time finding new jobs, perhaps because other employers are willing to offer slightly less-skilled jobs to these workers.

The high rate of unemployment of teenage workers also is consistent with the fixed-cost hypothesis. Young workers have little specific training and are usually employed in relatively unskilled jobs, where they can be among the first dismissed if demand decreases. Many move in and out of the labor force frequently, because they are in school most of the year and must search for a new job at the time of each entry. Even those teenagers who have left school are shopping for jobs, often quitting those that do not turn out to be agreeable and then looking for new ones.

The high teenage unemployment rate of the United States is not found in most European countries. In part, this is a result of the usually tighter labor markets in Europe, but more specific factors are also at work. Labor-market institutions in Europe may be better designed to facilitate the transition from school to work by providing school-leavers with vocational training and information about the labor market. Some countries (e.g., Great Britain) have an explicit system of youth or juvenile wage rates, which start substantially below the adult rate and rise with each year of age. This makes the teenager a "good buy" for employers in jobs that can be learned quickly. In the United States, teenagers usually receive the same rates as adults in a given job, except perhaps for a few months at a lower trainee or probationary rate. The importance of labor market policy in affecting the unemployment rate of youths is also shown in Sweden, where the unemployment rate of males aged 16 to 19 rose sharply relative to the adult rate during the 1960s and 1970s, due partly to policies that made it much more difficult to lay off workers.[18] These changes converted wage costs into fixed employment costs, which reduced employers' willingness to hire new workers.

The unemployment rate in 1979 for married men was 2.7 percent, which was well below the average for all men. This is the counterpart of the higher labor-force participation rate of married men, discussed in Chapter 1. Again, the chain of causation may be complex. Whatever causes men to remain bachelors or makes their marriages unstable could also make it harder for them to find jobs. As we saw in Chapter 6, the greater financial pressures on married men induces them to engage in more intensive job search and to end it more quickly by accepting the best opening discovered. A married man is also less likely to quit a job than a single man, and employers prefer married men for this reason.

The ratio of black to non-Hispanic white unemployment in 1979 was somewhat above 2. This ratio has been slightly above 2 since the mid-1950s and has not yet been brought down appreciably by government policies designed to eliminate racial discrimination in employment. To some extent the unemployment rates reflect racial differences in educational attainment, though; as we showed in Chapter 3, those have decreased sharply. Blacks are still overrepresented in less skilled occupations and on average have slightly fewer years of schooling than do whites. Blacks are disproportionately represented in such occupations as laborers, domestic servants, and service workers, where much employment is casual and there is little on-the-job training. However, differences in unemployment rates by race are also present even within occupations and even when differences in experience, education, and the amount of formal on-the-job training are accounted for.[19] These differences reflect direct discrimination in the hiring process rather than the indirect effects of discrimination in other forms.

Particularly striking and disturbing in Table 8.4 are the very high unemployment rates for black youths, even at a time when there was little demand-deficiency unemployment. As we saw in Chapter 4, only a small part of this high unemployment rate is due to the unwillingness of employers to hire young blacks at jobs that must be paid the minimum wage. Part may stem from a high degree of voluntary quitting by young blacks that leads them from employment to unemployment and then back to another job. Still more may come from differences in asking wages: Unemployed black teens in 1979 had asking wages that were higher than those of unemployed white teens, relative to the average wages offered.[20]

[18] Linda Leighton and Siv Gustafsson, "Differential Patterns of Unemployment in Sweden," *Research in Labor Economics* (6) (1984). In press.

[19] Compare estimates for blacks and whites in U.S. Department of Labor, *Manpower R and D Monograph,* No. 15 (1975), Tables 2A-13 and 2A-14, and No. 16 (1977), Table 6A-6.

[20] Harry Holzer, "Black Youth Nonemployment: The Determinants of Its Duration," Doctoral Dissertation, Harvard University, 1983.

Table 8.6 UNEMPLOYMENT RATES IN SELECTED STATES, 1968 AND 1979

State	1968	1979
California	4.5	6.2
Colorado	3.0	4.8
Illinois	3.0	5.5
Massachusetts	4.1	5.5
Michigan	4.3	7.8
New Mexico	5.1	6.6
New York	3.5	7.1
South Carolina	4.3	5.0
Texas	2.7	4.2
Utah	5.2	4.3
West Virginia	6.4	6.7
United States total	3.6	5.8

Source: Manpower Report of the President, 1971, Table D-4; *Employment and Training Report of the President,* 1980, Tables A-1 and D-4.

The unemployment rates of Hispanic youths are much higher than those of non-Hispanic whites. As Hispanics accumulate experience, however, their unemployment rates begin to approach, but never attain, the low rates of non-Hispanic adult whites. During the later years of their work lives, the unemployment rates of Hispanics begin to rise again relative to unemployment rates of blacks and of non-Hispanic whites.

In addition to the demographic and occupational differentials in unemployment shown in Tables 8.4 and 8.5, there are important differentials in unemployment rates by geographical area. Table 8.6 lists unemployment rates in 2 years when demand-deficiency unemployment was low or nonexistent. Some concentrations of unemployment are long-lived, reflecting the decline of localized industries or the large-scale displacement of labor by technological change. Thus West Virginia, in which problems of structural unemployment arose after World War II because of the decline in coal mining, still exhibited above-average unemployment as late as 1979. Persistent unemployment above the national average may also reflect a labor force whose skill and demographic mix is weighted more heavily toward groups that exhibit high unemployment rates; New Mexico, with a large Hispanic population, is one such example.

Geographical differences in unemployment, although often very persistent, can also be eliminated by the workings of the market. In some depressed communities the combination of unemployed labor and vacant factories attracts new industry. The growth of employment in plastics, electronics, and other light industries has helped reduce to reasonable levels the unemployment rates in some of the old New England textile towns. This explains why Massachusetts, where the unemployment rate was above average in 1968, had below-average unemployment in 1979. Changes in the regional flows of consumer and government spending can stimulate demand in a local economy that previously contained many unemployed workers. This is especially likely when the educational attainment of local workers increases sharply, with the growing skilled work force attracting capital investment. This may explain the switch of South Carolina and Utah from above- to below-average unemployment between 1968 and 1979.

Although there are some problems of comparability in the data between the 2 years, the comparisons nonetheless are in accord with other observations on the economy. The overall picture conveyed by the data in Table 8.6 is one of flux. There is some persistence of unemployment among states or regions, but differentials are eliminated over time. States that exhibit high unemployment in one decade may well have below-average unemployment in the next.[21]

POLICY ISSUE—INCREASED STRUCTURAL-FRICTIONAL UNEMPLOYMENT

In discussing Table 8.6, we described the 3.6 percent unemployment rate in 1968 as indicating the absence of demand-deficiency unemployment; yet we also suggested that a 5.8 percent unemployment rate represented mainly structural-frictional unemployment in 1979. This view is standard among macroeconomists: Most believe that the amount of structural-frictional unemployment rose slowly from the late 1950s until the late 1960s in the United States, then rose sharply after that to a peak in the late 1970s. One expert has placed the "full-employment" unemployment rate at 4.3 percent in 1957, 4.9 percent in 1968, and 5.6 percent in 1979.[22] Others place the change even higher, perhaps 1.6 percentage points between 1957 and 1979.

One source of this increase is clear: The demographic mix of the labor force during the period tilted away from groups that always exhibit low rates of unemployment. Thus in 1957 males aged 25 to 54 accounted for 46 percent of the U.S. civilian labor force; in 1979 they represented only 36 percent. The relative decline was due to the growth of the teenage labor force, stemming from both the baby boom of the 1950s and increased teenage labor-force participation, and to the rapid increases in adult female labor-force participation. If the structure of the labor force in 1979 had been the same as it was in 1957, the unemployment rate in 1979 would have been only 5.0 percent. Changes in demography thus account for eight-tenths of a percentage point of an estimated 1.6 percentage point increase in the full-employment unemployment rate between the 1950s and the late 1970s.[23]

We have seen how the unemployment insurance system in the United States can induce employers to lay off more workers than they otherwise would. Since the number of firms and workers covered by unemployment insurance expanded between the 1960s and the late 1970s, the expansion of this transfer program could have caused some of the higher unemployment. One estimate suggests it accounted for half a percentage point of additional unemployment. On the other hand, the growth of other transfer programs has reduced unemployment. In Chapter 1 we showed how the growth of Disability Insurance has induced workers to leave the labor force. Because of the progressivity of benefit structures, those workers who left are likely to have been low-paid and low-skilled, with an above-average unemployment rate. The expansion of Disability Insurance (and Social Security retirement benefits too) reduced the labor force by encouraging older workers with the highest chance of being unemployed to leave. This effect is hard to measure, but it could easily have offset the impact of the expanded unemployment insurance program. On net, the growth of transfer programs probably had little if any effect on the structural-frictional unemployment rate.

The remaining 0.8 percentage points of higher unemployment can be accounted for by the tremendous shifts in industrial structure that are occasioned by the rise in energy

[21] Kevin Murphy, "An Econometric Analysis of the Geographic Distribution of Unemployment Rates," Doctoral Dissertation, Michigan State University, 1981, demonstrates this and shows that there was no trend in the dispersion of state unemployment rates between 1961 and 1978.

[22] Robert Gordon, *Macroeconomics,* Little Brown, Boston, 1981, Table B-1.

[23] Daniel Hamermesh, "Transfers, Taxes and the NAIRU," in Laurence Meyer (ed.). *The Supply-Side Effects of Economic Policy,* Kluwer-Nijhoff, Boston, 1981.

prices beginning in 1973. The expansion of industries less dependent on energy, and the shift away from U.S.-made automobiles and the materials that make them, created structural unemployment on a scale that is unprecedented in recent history. A direct estimate of the extent of this structural problem suggests it represented the 0.8 percentage point of the remaining higher structural-frictional unemployment in 1979 as compared to 1957.[24]

The higher structural-frictional unemployment of the 1970s and early 1980s meant that macroeconomic policy targets had to be selected more carefully; attempts to push unemployment below 6 percent by using stimulatory fiscal and monetary policy were likely to induce rapid inflation, as the economy moved to the left of the 45° line along curve AA in Figure 8.3. In the middle and late 1980s, though, the targets of macroeconomic policy should be achieved more readily. With the aging of the baby-boom generation the demographic mix of the labor force will tilt back toward groups with low unemployment. The impact of energy problems on structural unemployment will also lessen (even though new structural problems of great magnitude may arise). For all these reasons the amount of structural-frictional unemployment should fall. The unemployment rate at full employment should begin moving back toward where it was in the 1950s and early 1960s.

UNEMPLOYMENT—DURATION VERSUS INCIDENCE

The unemployment rate in 1979 was 5.8 percent. It could have been at that level if 5.8 percent of the labor force were unemployed all year long. In that case the *average duration of unemployment* would have been 52 weeks at year's end, assuming workers began their spells of unemployment on January 1. The *incidence of unemployment* would have been only 5.8 percent. Alternatively, the unemployment rate could have been 5.8 percent because each labor-force participant experienced a spell of unemployment in 1979. The average duration of unemployment would have been 3 weeks (5.8 percent of 52); the incidence of unemployment would have been 100 percent.

As Table 8.7 shows, neither of these extreme cases characterizes the structure of unemployment very well. The average duration of unemployment was around 11 weeks, not 52 or 3. Ignoring the fact that people move in and out of the labor force and that one person may experience several spells of unemployment during a year—this average duration implies that as much as one-fourth of the labor force experienced some unemployment during that year.[25] Accounting for these facts, perhaps one-sixth of those who participated in the labor force experienced some unemployment during the year.

The data in Table 8.7 give too pessimistic a picture of the duration of unemployment and are not to be compared to the 2-week average duration of vacancies we cited earlier in this chapter. They show the average length of time the typical unemployed worker has been out of work, that is, the average length of

[24]Computed as the change in the difference between the structural-frictional unemployment measure in David Lilien, "Sectoral Shifts and Cyclical Unemployment," *Journal of Political Economy* (90): 790 (1982), which includes this effect, and that in Gordon, op. cit., which does not.

[25]The unemployment rate (in percent) can be calculated as: $U = \frac{DUR}{52} \times \frac{SPELLS}{L} \times 100$, where DUR is the average duration of spells of unemployment, SPELLS is their number, and L is the labor force.

Table 8.7 AVERAGE DURATION OF UNEMPLOYMENT (IN WEEKS) BY AGE AND SEX, 1979

Age	Male	Female
16–19	7.9	6.9
20–24	10.1	9.3
25–34	12.5	9.8
35–44	15.7	11.3
45–54	16.8	12.1
55–64	19.2	14.1
65 and over	19.3	10.3
All ages 16 and over	12.0	9.6
Whites, 16 and over	11.4	9.0
Blacks, 16 and over	14.2	11.3
Hispanics, 16 and over, both sexes		9.3
Married	13.4	9.1
Single	10.5	9.1
Other	15.6	11.6

Source: Employment and Unemployment During 1979: An Analysis, Special Labor Force Report No. 234, Tables 18, 52.

Table 8.8 THE DISTRIBUTION OF COMPLETE SPELLS OF UNEMPLOYMENT, 1968 AND 1978 (PERCENT)

	Length of complete spells (weeks)						Average duration of spells		
Year	<5	5–10	11–14	15–26	27+	Total	Complete	Incomplete	Unemployment rate
1968	74.1	16.7	3.2	4.1	1.9	100.0	4.5	8.4	3.6
1978	60.2	23.6	6.1	6.7	3.4	100.0	6.3	13.1	6.0

Source: Calculated from George Akerlof and Brian Main, "Unemployment Spells and Unemployment Experience," *American Economic Review* (70) (1980), Table 1.

incomplete spells of unemployment. The average length of *complete spells,* the time the worker who is completely attached to the labor force spends between jobs, is of greater interest in evaluating the hardship faced by the typical unemployed worker. There are very many spells of unemployment that are quickly over, as shown in Table 8.8 for 2 years in which demand-deficiency unemployment was not very great. Only a few people are unemployed for a long time and keep being counted as having long spells when they are included in the monthly Current Population Survey. Thus one can infer that in the United States the average length of complete spells of unemployment in 1979 was less than the 11-week figure that is the average of the duration data for men and women in Table 8.7. Even accounting for those workers who experience more than one spell of unemployment, the average American worker who is unemployed at some time in a year of little demand-deficient unemployment probably spends no more than 10 weeks out of work during that year.[26]

The duration of unemployment is somewhat higher among blacks than among whites, although not by an amount sufficient to account for the much higher black

[26]George Akerlof and Brian Main, "Unemployment Spells and Unemployment Experience," *American Economic Review* (70): 885–893 (1980).

unemployment rate. This implies that the incidence of unemployment is also higher among black workers. Interestingly, Hispanics have a lower average duration of unemployment than do all whites. Other evidence shows this to be the case for all three of the largest Hispanic groups—Mexican-Americans, Cubans, and Puerto Ricans.[27] Their higher average unemployment rate, shown in Table 8.5, thus is due entirely to a greater incidence of unemployment.

The pattern of the duration of unemployment by sex is consistent with patterns of labor-force participation. Average duration is higher among males than females; since unemployment rates among males are lower, this means the incidence of unemployment among males is much lower than among females. The unemployed male does not usually drop out of the labor force after being unemployed for some time. Unemployed females are more likely to drop out of the labor force (and thus cease being counted as unemployed), for in many cases their past attachment to the labor force has not been very strong.

The duration of unemployment generally rises with age; since unemployment rates generally fall with age, this means the incidence of unemployment decreases very sharply as a person ages. Both patterns reflect the greater firm-specific human capital embodied in older workers that makes them less susceptible to layoffs, and the inclination of younger workers to intersperse job-shopping with periods out of the labor force (at school full time, or at leisure). Married men are unemployed longer than single men; their lower unemployment rate implies, though, that their likelihood of being unemployed is much lower than that of single men. This too reflects the investment in firm-specific training that produces few layoffs of married workers, the married workers' lower likelihood of quitting work, and their greater commitment to the labor force should they become unemployed.

Examining data on the duration and incidence of unemployment also sheds light on the serious problem of black teenage unemployment. In 1976 black teens were three times as likely as white teens to move from employment to unemployment, and only one-third as likely to move from unemployment to a job. Also, they were no more likely than white teens to drop out of the labor force if unemployed. Black teens, therefore, had much longer spells of unemployment than did whites—80 percent longer for males, 60 percent longer for females.[28] Part of the high black youth unemployment rate is reflected in a very high incidence of unemployment; part is shown in a relatively long average duration of unemployment.

More educated unemployed workers are out of work for shorter periods of time than are their less educated counterparts. In 1959 workers with some college education were unemployed 20 percent fewer weeks than workers who dropped out of high school. This difference mostly reflects the higher average wage offers available to more educated workers: Once differences in wages are accounted for, differences in education produce only slight effects on the duration of unemployment in data from 1975. The theory of search also explains other differences among workers in the

[27] Gregory DeFreitas, "Ethnic Differentials in Unemployment Among Hispanic Americans," Unpublished Paper, Barnard College, 1982.

[28] Kim Clark and Lawrence Summers, "The Dynamics of Youth Unemployment," in Richard Freeman and David Wise (eds.). *The Youth Labor Market Problem: Its Nature, Causes and Consequences,* University of Chicago Press, Chicago, 1982, p. 217.

duration of unemployment. Workers facing a more dispersed range of wage offers have longer spells of unemployment. Because the chance of finding a high-paying job is greater if the range of wage offers shows more variance, such workers search longer.[29]

The duration of unemployment in 1979 was appreciably shorter for those who were on layoff from a job to which they expected to return than for others who had lost their jobs. About 14 percent of the first group had been unemployed 15 weeks and over as compared to 31 percent of the second group. Among those who are searching for new jobs, we saw in Chapter 6 how the existence of adequate unemployment insurance benefits can lengthen the duration of unemployment by making job seekers less willing to take undesirable jobs. Indeed, each 10 percent increase in unemployment benefits in the United States appears to increase the duration of spells of unemployment by about 2 percent.[30] This should not be too disturbing, for one of the purposes of an unemployment insurance system is to make possible a longer and more thorough search for work. (As we saw in Chapter 6, however, the receipt of unemployment benefits reduces the intensity of search efforts, although it may increase total search effort by lengthening the time spent unemployed.) However, liberalization of benefits does tend to have the effect of raising the level of frictional unemployment.

In the United States, the pattern of unemployment by duration and incidence is different from that in other Western nations. In 1979, for example, the Canadian unemployment rate was 1.29 times that in the United States; the average duration of unemployment was 1.38 times as long. In 1968 the unemployment rate of males in the United States was 2.6 percent, whereas in Sweden it was only 2.3 percent. Yet the average duration of spells of unemployment among males in the United States was only 6.5 weeks, whereas in Sweden it was 13.7 weeks. In 1972 British males aged 25 to 39 experienced a 4.4 percent unemployment rate; those who were unemployed, though, were out of work an average of 16 weeks.[31] Structural-frictional unemployment rates in the United States have generally exceeded those in other developed countries. The difference is due to a much higher incidence of unemployment; the average time spent unemployed is actually lower in the United States than it is elsewhere.

POLICY ISSUE—ECONOMIC WELFARE AND THE INCIDENCE OF UNEMPLOYMENT

There is good reason to be concerned about whether a nation's unemployment rate arises from many short spells of unemployment or from fewer long ones, for the seriousness of unemployment to the worker depends on how long a spell of unemployment lasts. Most workers can survive a short period of unemployment with little difficulty. Some lost

[29] Arnold Katz, "Schooling, Age and Length of Unemployment," *Industrial and Labor Relations Review* (27): 602 (1974); DeFreitas, loc. cit.; Robert Feinberg, "Risk Aversion, Risk, and the Duration of Unemployment," *Review of Economics and Statistics* (59): 269 (1977).

[30] See Alan Gustman, "Analyzing the Relation of Unemployment Insurance to Unemployment," *Research in Labor Economics* (5): 69–114 (1982).

[31] *Employment and Earnings,* June 1979, Tables A-1 and A-18; Statistics Canada, *The Labor Force,* May 1979, Tables 34 and 35; Nancy Barrett, "The U.S. Phillips Curve and International Unemployment Rate Differentials," *American Economic Review* (65): 216 (1975); and Stephen Nickell, "A Picture of Male Unemployment in Britain," *Economic Journal* (90): 780 (1980).

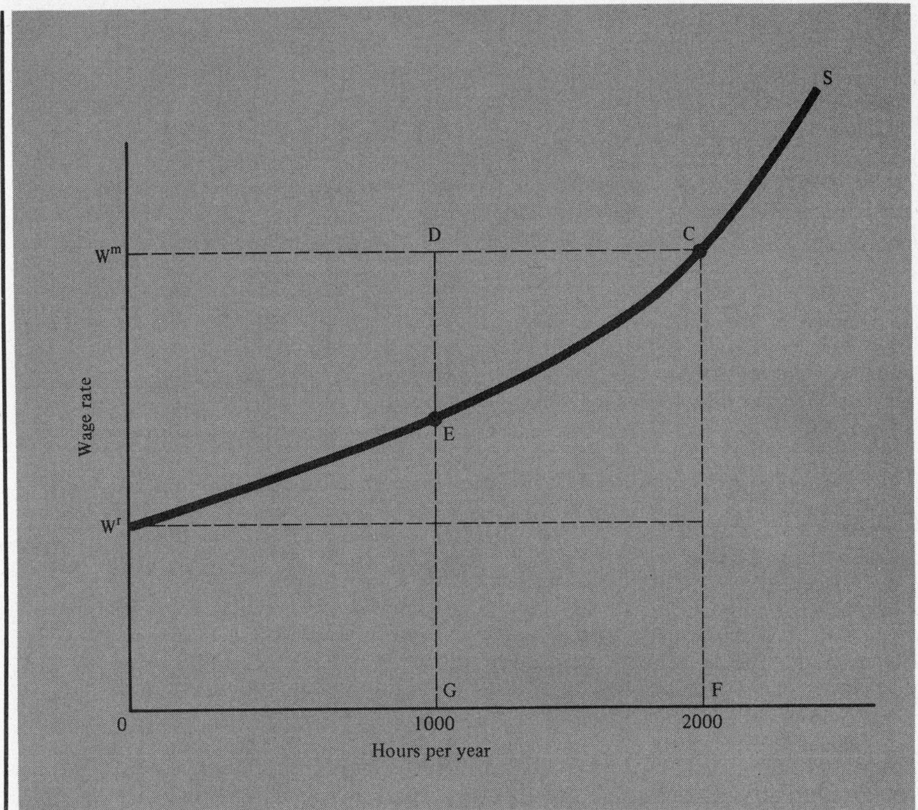

Figure 8.4 The burden of unemployment.

income will frequently be replaced by unemployment insurance benefits. Living standards can in many cases by maintained by drawing down savings or by borrowing. The longer unemployment persists, the more serious the consequences will be. Eligibility for unemployment insurance benefits is eventually exhausted, savings are used up, and creditors are unwilling to extend further credit. In very long spells of unemployment, work skills can deteriorate from disuse.

Consider an economy consisting of many workers, each of whom has the labor supply curve S in Figure 8.4.[32] The horizontal axis shows the number of hours per year each is willing to supply at a given wage; obversely, the wage at each hour of labor supplied is the reservation wage for that many hours, showing the value of an extra hour of leisure. At a market wage of W^m the typical worker wishes to supply 2000 hours per year. The difference between W^m and the supply curve at each point shows the gain from working that hour. Assume demand is high enough to provide employment for all but 2000 of the total hours supplied to the economy. Those 2000 hours of unemployment could all be borne by one worker, who would be employed the entire year. Ignoring search costs, which we assume are the same during each hour of unemployment, the monetary loss to that worker is the lost wage income, $0W^mCF$. The true loss is W^mW^rC, though, for the worker derives some value from the leisure that is consumed. Even at zero hours of work, an hour of leisure has a value equal to the reservation wage W^r.

[32] This argument and figure expand upon Michael Hurd, "A Compensation Measure of the Cost of Unemployment to the Unemployed," *Quarterly Journal of Economics* (95): 225–244 (1980).

If the burden of the 2000 hours of unemployment is split between two workers, each works 1000 hours per year and is unemployed 1000 hours. The lost wage income for each is shown by the rectangle DGFC: For both together the loss is the same as the wage loss if one person bore the entire burden of unemployment. The true loss per worker is the triangle DEC; the total loss is twice this, which is less than $W^m W^r C$, the loss experienced by the one worker who bore the entire burden of 2000 hours of unemployment. The reason is that the first few hours spent out of work yield more enjoyment as leisure and do not entail substantial financial adjustments.

This discussion helps explain why the relatively high structural-frictional unemployment in the United States is tolerated when it would probably not be so easily accepted in other Western countries. The relatively short duration of unemployment in the United States spreads the burden of unemployment much more widely. The average loss in utility to each unemployed worker is less in the United States than elsewhere. The burden of unemployment is mitigated further by the high incidence of two-earner families: At the trough of the 1981 to 1982 recession, 58 percent of the unemployed were in households in which at least one other family member was employed.

SUMMARY

In contrast to the high mobility of young workers, many older workers remain with the same employer for decades. This close attachment leads to the development of long lines of promotion, substantial investments in firm-specific human capital, wage structures that induce workers to produce more, and rules governing mandatory retirement. When product demand drops, employers in Western countries respond by laying off workers. When product demand rises, vacancies are created. These vacancies are often filled by promotion; the ensuing vacancies at entry-level jobs are filled by hiring workers away from other employers or by hiring from the pool of unemployed workers or new labor-force entrants. The rate of vacancies is higher when unemployment rates are lower. Only at low unemployment rates, though, are the two rates equal (there is no demand-deficiency unemployment).

Unemployment rates are higher among women and minorities than they are among white males; they are generally lower among adult workers than among youths. Women and youths have shorter spells of unemployment than adult men, although the chance of a female or young worker becoming unemployed is much greater than that of an adult male. Even though unemployment rates in the absence of demand-deficiency unemployment are higher in the United States than in other Western countries, the average duration of unemployment is lower.

four

UNIONIZED LABOR MARKETS

chapter 9

Unions: Growth and Goals

So far our discussion of labor markets has considered the behavior of individual workers and employers, with only passing reference to trade unions. This neglect must be remedied, for unions and collective bargaining play a major role in the determination of wage levels and wage structures, as well as in the many other aspects of the employment relation. Between 20 and 25 percent of nonagricultural employees in the United States have been members of unions or employee associations in recent years, and the effects of collective bargaining extend beyond its impacts on union members.

Our discussion will focus on the economic functions of the trade union to the exclusion of its role as a social and political institution. Even within the area of collective bargaining, such topics as grievance machinery and seniority will not be considered. Although these areas are extremely important, the kind of analysis that is useful in dealing with them is very different from the economic analysis used here.[1] In this chapter we examine the economic determinants of the incidence and growth of trade unionism and discuss the possible employment and wage goals that a union might pursue and achieve. Chapter 10 analyzes the methods unions use to obtain their goals. The process of collective bargaining and its occasional result—strikes—can be studied fruitfully by using economic analysis, as can the methods employed to settle those disputes. In Chapter 11 we consider the impact of unions on those outcomes—wages, employment, and mobility—whose determination in competi-

[1] Additional information on the institutions of collective bargaining can be found in Marten Estey, *The Unions: Structure, Development, and Management,* Harcourt Brace Jovanovich, New York, 1976; D. Quinn Mills, *Labor-Management Relations,* McGraw-Hill, New York, 1982; or Thomas Kochan, *Collective Bargaining and Industrial Relations,* Irwin, Homewood, Ill., 1980.

tive markets was the focus of our attention in Chapters 6 to 8. These impacts provide some evidence of the unions' ability to achieve the goals we discuss here.

UNION GROWTH

Institutional economists have sought to explain the growth of trade unionism in industrial economies by a variety of theories.[2] The best known theory, the "job-scarcity" hypothesis, views unions as a response of workers to fears of layoff or insufficient work to provide employment for all the members of the work group. This notion explains much of today's political efforts by unions. In the United States, for example, trade union support for higher overtime premiums and programs to share work (see Chapter 5) can be seen as attempts to spread what is viewed as a limited supply of jobs. One problem with this view is that it assumes workers believe that the demand for their labor is very inelastic, so that there is little trade-off between wages and employment goals. As we see later in this chapter, there is good evidence that workers, or at least the unions that represent them, are more sophisticated than this.

An extension of this hypothesis views workers' demands for unionization as a response to their current and recent economic status. When unemployment is high, indicating workers have been forced to accept layoffs, their desires to protect themselves against additional losses of employment, and their resentment at managers exercising discretion over employment, will lead them to seek unionization. Unemployment thus spurs workers to seek a change in the work rules governing employment as a way of protecting their jobs. On the other hand, management resistance to unionization may be stronger when unemployment is high, for there are more workers to substitute for those who wish to unionize and profits are low or nonexistent.

Whether management resistance is strong enough to overcome workers' pressure is an empirical question. The traditional view among students of the institutions of collective bargaining is that recessions hurt the growth of unionism. Yet some statistical studies of union growth in English-speaking countries suggest that there was a weak positive correlation between that growth and the unemployment rate. In the United States between 1909 and 1960, each additional percentage point of unemployment resulted in an increase in the growth rate of the unionized work force of 0.25 percent. Although most of this relationship reflects union growth during the Great Depression, the relationship existed before and after the 1930s also. In the United Kingdom between 1893 and 1970, each 1 percentage point increase in unemployment raised the growth rate of the unionized work force by 0.05 percent. In Canada, each 1 percentage point increase in unemployment raised the growth rate of the unionized work force by 0.5 percent between 1925 and 1966.[3]

[2] See Mark Perlman, *Labor Union Theories in America,* Row, Evanston, Ill., 1958.

[3] Orley Ashenfelter and John Pencavel, "American Trade Union Growth: 1900–1960," *Quarterly Journal of Economics* (83): 434–448 (1969); George Bain and Farouk Elsheikh, *Union Growth and the Business Cycle,* Blackwell, Oxford, 1976; Michael Abbott, "An Econometric Model of Trade Union Membership Growth in Canada, 1925–1968," Working Paper No. 154, Princeton University Industrial Relations Section, Princeton, N.J., 1982. The first study accounts for the fraction of Democrats in the U.S. House of Representatives, thus at least partly abstracting from political determinants of the growth of unionism that may be correlated with its economic determinants.

Table 9.1 U.S. UNION MEMBERSHIP, SELECTED YEARS 1930–1978

Year	Number (000)	Percent of nonagricultural employment
1930	3,401	11.6
1935	3,584	13.2
1940	8,717	26.9
1945	14,322	35.5
1950	14,267	31.5
1955	16,802	33.2
1960	17,049	31.4
1965	17,299	28.4
1970	19,381	27.3
1975	19,611	25.5
1980	19,898	21.9

Source: Handbook of Labor Statistics, 1980, Table 165. 1980 figures are based on 1978 and 1980 data from this and from Bureau of National Affairs, *Directory of U.S. Labor Organizations, 1982–83,* Bureau of National Affairs, Washington, 1982.

Much of the inconsistency between the traditional view and the more recent statistical evidence on union growth before 1970 is due to the very rapid growth of unionism in the late 1930s. Table 9.1 shows the history of union growth in the United States. (Statistics that include employee associations would be several percentage points higher but would show the same trends.) The passage of the National Labor Relations Act (Wagner Act) of 1935, which made union organizing much easier, was coincident with a period of very high unemployment. The fact that unionism expanded only slightly between 1930 and 1935 suggests that the impact of the new law was more important than the high unemployment was.

The argument that cyclical increases in unemployment induce an expansion of unionism is not easily extended to the data shown in Table 9.1 for the post-World War II period. Indeed, since 1974 unemployment has been persistently high by postwar standards, yet unionization has declined relative to nonfarm employment more rapidly than before. (If we excluded government employment, where union membership grew rapidly after 1965, the decline would appear even more pronounced.) Although the higher unemployment of the late 1970s and early 1980s might engender a spurt of unionization, it has not yet happened. This suggests that, at least for the recent past, the correctness of the traditional view that higher unemployment is associated with a falling extent of unionism unless government policy becomes favorable to union growth.

The importance of political and institutional factors also can be seen by comparing the extent of unionism in the United States with that elsewhere. In 1977 to 1978, for example, union membership as a percent of nonfarm employment was 80 percent in Sweden, 52 percent in the United Kingdom, 44 percent in the Netherlands, and 38 percent in West Germany.[4] Although the figures are not strictly comparable across countries, they strongly suggest that the United States is relatively nonunion as compared to most developed Western nations.

[4]Calculated from John Windmuller, "Concentration Trends in Union Structure: An International Comparison," *Industrial and Labor Relations Review* (35): (1982), Table 1, and International Labor Organization, *Yearbook of Labor Statistics,* 1979.

If unemployment cannot explain the decline in unionization, what can? The most likely answer is the expansion of the economy in those areas, occupations, and industries that have historically had the smallest extent of union membership. Thus the South, white-collar work and the service sector have expanded at the expense of the Northeast, blue-collar work and extractive and manufacturing industries. Although there has been some decline in the extent of unionization within industries, the changing industrial mix of the economy has accounted for much of the lessened percentage of union membership in the work force.

Other factors affect the growth of unionization, too. Even if wages are flexible, so that declines in product demand, or increases in the costs of other inputs, result in lower real wages, workers will view a decreased real wage as a worsening of their position and will attempt to prevent it by organizing to determine wages collectively rather than individually. Slower growth in money wages should have no effect on the desire to organize a union so long as price inflation moderates and the employed worker's real rewards do not drop. In the United States between 1909 and 1960, each 1 percentage point rise in the rate of inflation raised the growth rate of the unionized work force by 0.6 percent.[5]

POLICY ISSUE—VOTING AGAINST UNIONIZATION

One might think that, as a response to the declining share of the American work force that is unionized, organized labor would redouble its efforts to organize additional workers. In fact, as the first column of Table 9.2 shows, that has not been the case. The total vote in *representation elections* conducted by the National Labor Relations Board (NLRB), one of whose most important responsibilities is the conducting of such elections, has decreased steadily as a percentage of nonunion employment. Organized labor is not only contesting elections involving a smaller part of the nonunion work force, it is also winning a steadily smaller fraction of the elections it does contest and of the votes cast in those elections, as shown by the data in the second and third columns of Table 9.2. In addition, although only 0.1 percent of unionized employees *decertified* unions as collective bargaining agents and returned to nonunion status, that rate has risen steadily, quadrupling in the past 25 years. What has caused these changes?

Table 9.2 PARTICIPATION AND OUTCOMES OF REPRESENTATION ELECTIONS, UNITED STATES, 1955–1980

Fiscal year	Total votes as a percentage of nonunion nonfarm employment (1)	Percentage of elections won (2)	Percentage of votes cast for unions (3)
1955	1.2	67.6	74.0
1960	1.1	58.6	64.1
1965	1.0	60.2	62.4
1970	1.0	52.4	57.7
1975	0.8	46.2	49.5
1980	0.6	43.9	43.8

Sources: Calculated from National Labor Relations Board, *Annual Reports.* Council of Economic Advisors, *Economic Report of the President,* 1983, Table B-29; and Table 9.1 (this edition).

[5] Ashenfelter and Pencavel, loc. cit.

One possibility that union leaders suggest is that those groups that are most readily unionized had become covered by 1955, so that additional gains had become increasingly difficult. This suggestion is consistent with unions' optimal allocation of scarce resources: First concentrate on those easy targets in which the probability of successful organizing efforts is high, then move to increasingly more difficult targets. Also, if there are alternative uses for these resources, unions will shift them out of organizing as the returns to organizing diminish. This is consistent with the data in column (1) of Table 9.2. Union leaders also argue that employers have become more adept in dealing with the NLRB election procedures. Employers' resistance is increasingly served by an industry of specialists who offer consulting services that are designed to ensure the employer a victory in a representation election. A third argument put forward by union leaders is that workers have forgotten the Depression and now take unions for granted. Stated differently, this means that the high unemployment of the 1930s led to union growth then and in the next decade, perhaps because of lingering fears of another depression. By the 1950s those fears had mostly dissipated, swept away by the entry of a new generation of workers and by a decade of sustained low unemployment. The relatively low unemployment of the 1960s and early 1970s could have reinforced these beliefs and made unions appear less relevant: Job scarcity is not likely to be an important motive to form unions when jobs have not appeared to be scarce. Whether this long trend in the outcomes of representation elections will be affected by the period of higher unemployment from 1975 on is unclear. But the first signals that the trend toward decreasing importance of unionism in America is reversing will be an upswing in the unions' share of votes in these elections and a greater effort by unions to contest representation elections.

WHO BECOMES UNIONIZED?

Having examined the growth of unionization since 1930, let us now consider the determinants of differences in the extent of unionization at a point in time. Some of the causes result from differences in the product market and can be viewed as reflecting the supply of union jobs. Others stem from differences among workers—their tastes, wages, and personal characteristics—that determine the demand for union jobs. If the union is successful in raising wages, the demand for union jobs will exceed the supply; there will be a queue of workers seeking them.[6] As in the case of the minimum wages (see Fig. 4.9), the difference must be rationed. Part of the function of the union is to determine how unionized jobs are allocated to workers in the queue. Anything that increases the supply of union jobs will increase the extent of unionism that we observe. Anything that increases the demand for union jobs will raise the extent of unionism only if the wage advantage of unions is reduced; otherwise, the queue will merely be longer.

On the supply side, a firm's product-market power gives it the ability to obtain profits that exceed the competitive return on capital. Individual employees cannot demand a share of these excess profits, for they lack the bargaining power that can make a threat to the employer's position seem serious. Collectively, though, workers can hope to obtain some of the excess profits by threatening to withhold their labor (strike), thus reducing the firm's profits. Unionization becomes a way in which workers can share in their employer's power in the product market. In the United

[6] Jacob Mincer, "The Economics of Wage Floors," *Research in Labor Economics* (6) (1984). In press.

States in 1960, manufacturing industries in which the four top firms accounted for all sales had a 15 percentage-point greater incidence of unionism than did industries in which the top four firms accounted for only 50 percent of sales.[7]

Organizing a workplace takes substantial effort by both the workers themselves and the union organization that seeks to represent them. Even after a representation election has been won and a contract has been negotiated, administration of that contract requires substantial resources. Both activities are likely to be characterized by some degree of economies of scale. Thus, from the standpoint of becoming and remaining unionized, the supply of union jobs will be greater in larger plants. Indeed, in 1974 the average establishment in heavily unionized industries had five times as many employees as did the typical establishment in other industries.[8]

The structure of labor demand can also affect the supply of union jobs. Its effects can be inferred from our discussion of Marshall's laws in Chapter 4. If labor accounts for a large share of total costs, the employer has a greater incentive to resist unionization (is less likely to supply union jobs). Similarly, if the demand for labor is quite elastic, the employer can realistically threaten to reduce employment should the workers organize and seek to raise wage rates. Among manufacturing industries in the United States in 1972, the estimated elasticity of labor demand in nonunion establishments was −1.03; that in union establishments was −0.81. Employers are also less likely to be able to resist the organizing attempts of blue-collar workers if they are less able to threaten to substitute white-collar workers and capital for blue-collar workers if the workers succeed in organizing the plant. In fact, blue-collar labor is substantially less substitutable for white-collar labor and capital in those manufacturing establishments that are unionized.[9] Part of these differences may be imposed by union work rules that reduce labor-demand elasticities by limiting management flexibility; but part may also stem from unions' greater success in organizing where the flexibility is inherently less.

One of the reasons that establishments are large is that the industry requires a capital-intensive technology to achieve the lowest average cost; establishment size and capital intensity are often found together. Capital intensity exerts an independent effect on workers' demands for unionism even in the absence of large scale, however. Where employers have invested in large amounts of capital equipment, they will institute rigid work rules that are designed to protect the equipment and ensure that their investments yield a high return by being utilized continually and efficiently. In 1973, firms in heavily unionized industries employed 50 percent more capital per worker than did firms in industries with a below-average extent of unionization. Workers who stated they worked with machines most of the time had a 24 percentage-point greater likelihood of being unionized than did other workers with the same demographic characteristics. Workers who stated they were not free to determine their work schedules were 20 percentage points more likely to be union-

[7]Orley Ashenfelter and George Johnson, "Unionism, Relative Wages, and Labor Quality in U.S. Manufacturing Industries," *International Economic Review* (13): 488–508 (1972).

[8]Daniel Mitchell, *Unions, Wages, and Inflation,* Brookings Institution, Washington, 1980, p. 84.

[9]Richard Freeman and James Medoff, "Substitution Between Production Labor and Other Inputs in Unionized and Non-unionized Manufacturing," *Review of Economics and Statistics* (64): 220–233 (1982).

Table 9.3 COLLECTIVE BARGAINING COVERAGE BY INDUSTRY AND OCCUPATION, UNITED STATES 1980 (PERCENT OF EMPLOYED WAGE AND SALARY WORKERS)

Industry	White-collar	Blue-collar
Agriculture	2.7	8.1
Mining	10.2	47.1
Construction	12.2	39.6
Manufacturing	12.3	46.9
Transportation and public utilities	38.4	62.6
Wholesale trade	4.6	28.9
Retail trade	8.5	21.3
Finance and services	20.5	20.8
Public administration	36.3	41.0
Total	18.5	41.4

Source: Earnings and Other Characteristics of Organized Workers, May 1980, Bulletin No. 2105, Table 7.

ized than other workers; and workers in jobs requiring more physical effort were also more likely to be union members than other workers.[10] Although unions do institute work rules, greater capital intensity itself induces the rigid scheduling that increases workers' demands for unionism. A good example of this is the automobile industry before 1938.

Many of the factors that affect the supply of and demand for union jobs coexist. Firms that use a capital-intensive technology are likely to operate large establishments and to sell in concentrated product markets. It is thus difficult to infer the separate impacts on interindustry differences in unionization of each of the supply and demand factors we have discussed. Table 9.3 shows the pattern of *union coverage* (percentage of workers whose wages and working conditions are subject to collective bargaining). It is quite consistent with most of these considerations. Manufacturing and transportation and public utilities are both characterized by firms with substantial product-market power and the use of capital-intensive methods of production. Mining too has become increasingly capital-intensive and increasingly concentrated. The industries with below-average unionization—wholesale and retail trade and finance and services—have relatively little product-market concentration. Only construction, a very competitive industry, does not fit the theory well.

Industries do not just become unionized; individual workers, exercising their right to organize and voting in government-run representation elections, choose to have their compensation and work rules determined by collective bargaining. Workers' demands for unionization reflect partly the net gain in satisfaction that they expect to obtain if the plant becomes unionized. The greater the expected gain is, the more likely workers are to vote for unionization. Much of this net gain is in the form of higher wages. In a sample of union elections in 1972 and 1973, those workers whose wages were furthest below the average within the plant were most likely to

[10] Mitchell, op. cit., p. 84, and Frank Stafford and Greg Duncan, "Do Union Members Receive Compensating Wage Differentials?" *American Economic Review* (70): 367 (1980).

Table 9.4 UNIONIZATION BY DEMOGRAPHIC CHARACTERISTIC (PERCENT OF GROUP)

	1980, Union membership	
	Men	**Women**
White	30.3	17.5
Nonwhite	36.6	27.4
	1978, Males, union coverage	
	Age: 16–24	**25–64**
	Region	
Northeast	19.8	37.7
North central	20.4	38.1
South	9.6	21.1
West	19.4	32.6
	Education	
College	12.1	16.8
High school	21.2	35.5
Grade school	9.3	37.5

Source: Calculated from Harry Holzer, "Unions and the Labor Market Status of White and Minority Youth," *Industrial and Labor Relations Review* 35 (1982), Tables 3, 4, and *Earnings and Other Characteristics of Organized Workers,* May 1980, Bulletin No. 2105, Table 4.

vote for a union, even accounting for seniority and demographic differences. Also, in those plants in which, other things such as skill levels being equal, there was a greater dispersion of wages, workers were more likely to vote for a union. Unionization is one way in which workers respond to what they perceive as management arbitrariness in the form of different compensation for workers with the same objective characteristics and to their own desire for more equal outcomes.[11]

Pervasive discrimination against black workers has resulted in their receipt of lower wages than white workers, and may also take other forms. To the extent black workers perceive unions as a force for stopping discriminatory nonwage practices, they will be more likely to vote for union representation than will similar white workers. Black workers do in fact vote for a union more frequently than whites. As the top part of Table 9.4 shows, they are also more likely than whites to be union members; their preferences for unionism are, at least to some extent, satisfied.

More educated workers have usually acquired skills that enable them to avoid the worst effects of any management arbitrariness. Formal education inculcates many skills, one of which may be an ability to "get by." Accounting for the differences in wages that we know are generated by differences in education, more educated workers may still have a good reason not to be anxious for the protections that unionization may offer. More educated workers vote less frequently for unionization when confronted with the opportunity; moreover, as Table 9.4 shows, except

[11] The discussion here and in the next three paragraphs is based upon Henry Farber and Daniel Saks, "Why Workers Want Unions: The Role of Relative Wages and Job Characteristics," *Journal of Political Economy* (88): 349–369 (1980).

among youths, the more educated are less likely to be in establishments covered by collective bargaining.

Female workers are more likely to vote for unionization when given the chance. To the extent that they, like blacks, benefit more from the rules (grievance machinery) instituted under union representation, this is a reasonable response. The *incidence* of unionization among women, unlike their willingness to *vote for* unionization, is less than that of men. Table 9.4 shows that white women were only two-thirds as likely as white men, and black women only three-quarters as likely as black men to be in unionized plants.

The sharp difference between votes and the incidence of unionization by sex shows that the demand for unionization and actual outcomes need not coincide. The reason is that a worker may prefer to join a union, but unless the majority of her coworkers agree, and unless she has access to a supply of union jobs, she will not be in a unionized workplace. Among a random sample of workers observed in 1977, women were more likely than men to express a demand for union representation; but women who expressed the desire to be in a union job were less likely than men who sought a union job to obtain one. This view also helps clarify the position of nonwhites vis-à-vis unions. Nonwhites are far more likely (83 versus 58 percent among whites) to desire a union job; yet, because nonwhites who seek such jobs are less likely than whites to obtain them, the racial difference in the fraction unionized is, as Table 9.4 shows, not so large.[12] The supply of union jobs to blacks and females is smaller, relative to their demands, than it is for white males. Implicitly, their queue for such jobs, which unions and employers must ration, is relatively longer than that of white males.

Table 9.4 shows sharp interregional differences in the incidence of unionism. Workers in the South are much less likely than others to be unionized, and workers in the West are less frequently covered by collective bargaining than are their counterparts in the Northeast and north central areas. Other data show that southern workers are less likely than other workers to demand union jobs (49 percent as compared to 58 percent for workers elsewhere). This difference is too small to account by itself for the much lower incidence of unionism in the South. Rather, their lack of interest in becoming unionized combines with employers' resistance to unionization to produce the very low fraction of southern workers who are unionized.

POLICY ISSUE—RIGHT-TO-WORK LAWS

Under the Taft-Hartley Act individual states are free in effect to amend the federal law by passing so-called "right-to-work" legislation. Such laws prohibit *union shops* that make union membership compulsory in a particular plant once a new worker has held the job longer than at most a few months. As of 1982, 20 states had right-to-work laws on the books. Eleven of these states were in the South, four were in the West, five were in the north central region. Have these laws produced the low incidence of unionism in the South that we observed in Table 9.4, as union leaders have claimed; or would the unions' relative

[12]Henry Farber, "The Determination of the Union Status of Workers," *Econometrica* (51): 1417–1437 (1983), presents this and the following evidence of workers' desires for unionization.

inability to organize southern plants have occurred even if the Taft-Hartley Act had never allowed states to exercise this option?

Without a doubt, states that have right-to-work laws have a lower incidence of unionism than do other states. Even accounting for the demographic and industrial mix of the state's work force, those states *within a geographic region* that had such laws had a 5 percentage-point lower incidence of union membership in their work force than did other states.[13] This could be because the laws have discouraged union membership. However, low union membership and the laws themselves could be both reflections of workers' lack of interest in unionization and the strength of employers' opposition.

The coexistence of right-to-work laws and a low incidence of unionization reflect correlation rather than causation. The difference in the fraction of workers unionized between states that later adopted right-to-work laws and other states was as big in 1939, before the laws were passed, as it was in the 1950s and 1960s. Also, the passage of right-to-work laws is affected very strongly by many of the same individual characteristics that make workers less interested in becoming unionized. When one accounts for this effect, the apparent impact of the laws on the incidence of unionization disappears. Workers in right-to-work states also have less demand for unionism, even lower than otherwise identical workers in the same region of the United States.[14] Their demand is sufficiently below that of workers elsewhere to lead to queues for the smaller number of union jobs that are no longer than queues elsewhere. Although unionization is lower in right-to-work states, the policy and the outcome are both reflections of underlying attitudes and conditions that affect the demand and supply of union jobs.

UNION OBJECTIVES WHEN EMPLOYERS CONTROL EMPLOYMENT

Whatever models of union goals we construct, the union must deal with management. It is thus convenient to analyze union goals under two different classes of models of union-management wage and employment setting. The first class implicitly assumes that the union sets the wage rate, allowing the employer control over the amount of labor used in production—*demand models*. The second assumes that unions have some control over both wages and employment—*bargaining models*. All the models assume that the union has some monopoly power in the market for labor of the type used by the firm that the union has organized. In this section we examine union goals in the context of a model in which the union sets the wage rate and the employer determines the amount of labor to use.

Although Samuel Gompers, long-time president of the American Federation of Labor, answered "More" when asked what unions want, no union can consistently get more of everything it desires. The difficulty in analyzing the decisions facing the leadership of a union is made clear if we consider the role of unions in affecting wages and the level of employment. A union's concern with the total amount of employment is part of its broader concern with job scarcity and job

[13] Barry Hirsch, "The Determinants of Unionization: An Analysis of Interarea Differences," *Industrial and Labor Relations Review* (33): 158 (1980).

[14] Keith Lumsden and Craig Petersen, "The Effect of Right-to-Work Laws on Unionization in the United States," *Journal of Political Economy* (83): 1237–1248 (1975); Ronald Warren and Robert Strauss, "A Mixed Logit Model of the Relationship Between Unionization and Right-to-work Legislation," *Journal of Political Economy* (87): 648–655 (1979); Walter Wessels, "Economic Effects of Right to Work Laws," *Journal of Labor Research* (2): 55–75 (1981); and Henry Farber, "Right-to-Work Laws and the Extent of Unionization," Working Paper No. 1136, Cambridge, Mass., National Bureau of Economic Research, 1983.

security. The term *job security* includes the union's concern for the distribution of employment among members and for the job tenure of the individual members. In formal models, however, the focus is limited to the less inclusive goals of increasing total employment and expanding union membership; thus the models represent what may be an excessively narrow view of the union's concern with employment.

The starting point for discussing the demand for labor in Chapters 4 and 5 was the model of the profit-maximizing firm. In analyzing firm behavior, specialists in industrial organization often modify this model, especially for large firms whose policies are directed by managers rather than by owners. Nevertheless, the concept of profit maximization as a point of departure for analysis has great value.

It is much more difficult, if not impossible, to analyze union behavior by constructing a simple model of a trade union as a maximizer of anything, which implies a single goal that is common to the entire organization. Far more than the firm, the union is both an economic and a political entity. Although ultimate power nominally rests with stockholders in the corporation and with members in the union, both corporate management and union leadership play critical roles in determining policy. But in many unions, wage bargains must be taken back to the membership for ratification, and leadership decisions are not always routinely endorsed. As a tactic in negotiation with management, leaders may sometimes send agreements back for ratification, knowing that they are unacceptable; at other times they are genuinely surprised by the repudiation of a bargain they firmly believed to be the best obtainable. In contrast, corporate management and directors have full authority to negotiate wages without consulting the stockholders. In the long run they may suffer if they make a bad bargain, but in the short run their decisions will not be challenged.

Furthermore, union leaders face greater risks than corporate directors when they seek reelection. In corporations the rule of one share, one vote makes it very expensive to challenge management by soliciting proxies where management controls large blocks of stock. In contrast, the one person, one vote rule of unions, although it does not eliminate the advantages of incumbents, poses greater potential threats. In recent years such major American unions as the American Federation of Teachers, the United Mine Workers, and the American Federation of State, County and Municipal Employees have replaced their presidents in elections that the incumbents lost.

The sharing of power in the union between leadership and membership creates difficulties in constructing a formal model of union behavior because there may be differences in aims or emphasis between leaders and the rank and file. Leaders want to head large and stable organizations and to expand the membership; they may become interested in extending their personal influence in the larger labor movement or on the national political scene. The members, on the other hand, are interested primarily in job security, higher wages, and good working conditions. Union leaders pursue these goals as well as their personal goals for two reasons—they believe in them and their own jobs may be threatened if they do not pursue them.

A second source of difficulty in constructing a formal model of union behavior is that the gains won by unions in collective bargaining do not go to the organization as such but to the individual members directly, and there is no mechanism for the secondary redistribution of these gains. This reduces the control that union leaders can exercise over the allocation of the gains that result from their efforts. This is in sharp contrast to the corporation, where profits go to the firm before there is any distribution to stockholders. Some profits, often a major part of the total, are not distributed at all, and profits made in one establishment or activity within the corporation can be used in expanding another.

Keeping these difficulties in mind, let us consider possible formal models of union goals. One approach to unions' maximization assumes that they *maximize rents.* The union seeks the highest total receipts for its membership in excess of the earnings they would obtain if they were all employed at the best wage they would receive in nonunion employment. In Figure 9.1(a) that alternative wage is denoted as W_s; the line labeled S is a horizontal supply curve of labor to the firm. The firm's demand curve for labor is DD, determined by the factors that were considered in Chapters 4 and 5. MR is the union's *marginal revenue* curve corresponding to DD, which shows the addition to the total wage bill produced by lowering the wage just enough to permit the employment of one more worker. Following the analog of the product-market monopolist, the union would seek to set the wage W_0, at which marginal revenue is equal to the supply price of labor. (For a product-market monopolist the analogous price would maximize profit.) The employer, taking this wage W_0 as given, will set the marginal revenue product equal to the wage and employ E_0 workers.

The problem with this solution of the union's choice of goals is that maximizing the rent (the rectangle W_sW_0AC) fails to solve the question of how to allocate the gains the union is capable of achieving. Compared to a wage slightly above W_0, rent-maximization is not so attractive a solution for those workers who would retain their jobs were the wage higher than W_0. It is also less attractive, compared to a lower wage, to those workers, $E_1 - E_0$ of them, who do not obtain jobs in this unionized firm; were the wage slightly above W_s, they would be employed in the firm and earn more than in their best nonunion alternative. A wage below W_0, though, makes the workers who would be employed in the firm anyway worse off. Since the wage loss and the employment gain do not accrue to the same people, it is of little use to treat wages in excess of the supply price as a fund to be maximized. The union leader must balance pressures by unemployed members for work against pressures for higher wages, weighing the political importance of each group. This balancing will not lead to the rent-maximization solution, except by mere chance.

An alternative rule that is sometimes suggested is that unions try to *maximize the wage bill*—total wages paid by the firm to union labor.[15] The wage bill, defined as employment times the wage rate, is shown in Figure 9.1(a) as a rectangle such as OW_0AE_0. The largest such rectangle possible is OW_1BE_1, formed when wages are W_1 (halfway between W_2 and zero), employment is E_1, and MR is zero. This solution, too, fails to reconcile the conflicting interests of members who would retain their jobs and thus would benefit from a wage higher than W_1 with those of members who would like a wage even lower than W_1 so that they could obtain union work.

[15] The wage-bill maximization hypothesis was first proposed by John Dunlop, *Wage Determination Under Trade Unions,* Augustus Kelley, New York, 1950.

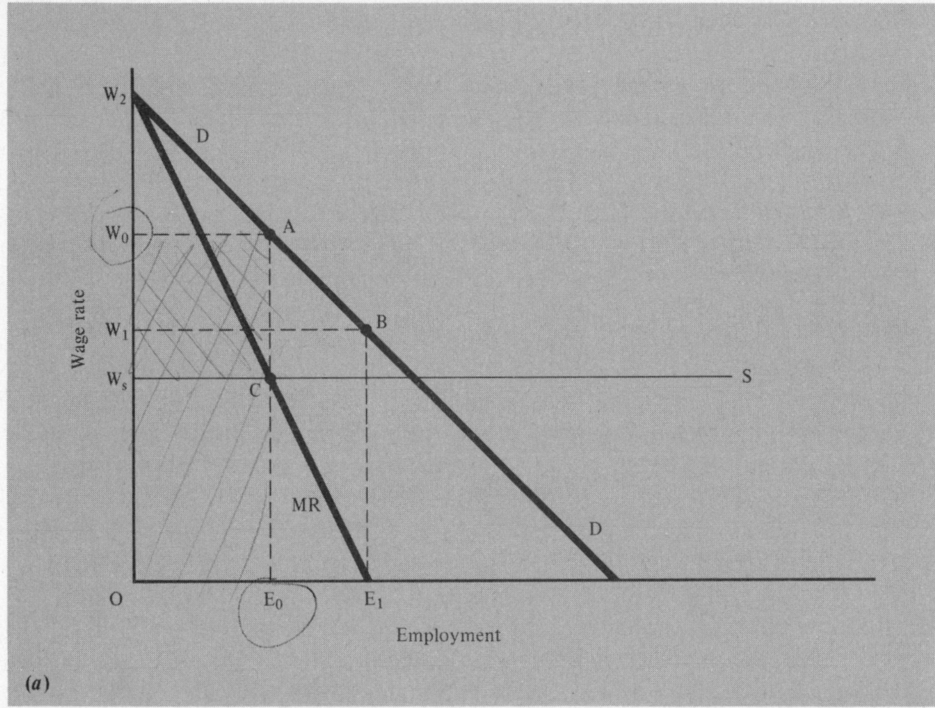

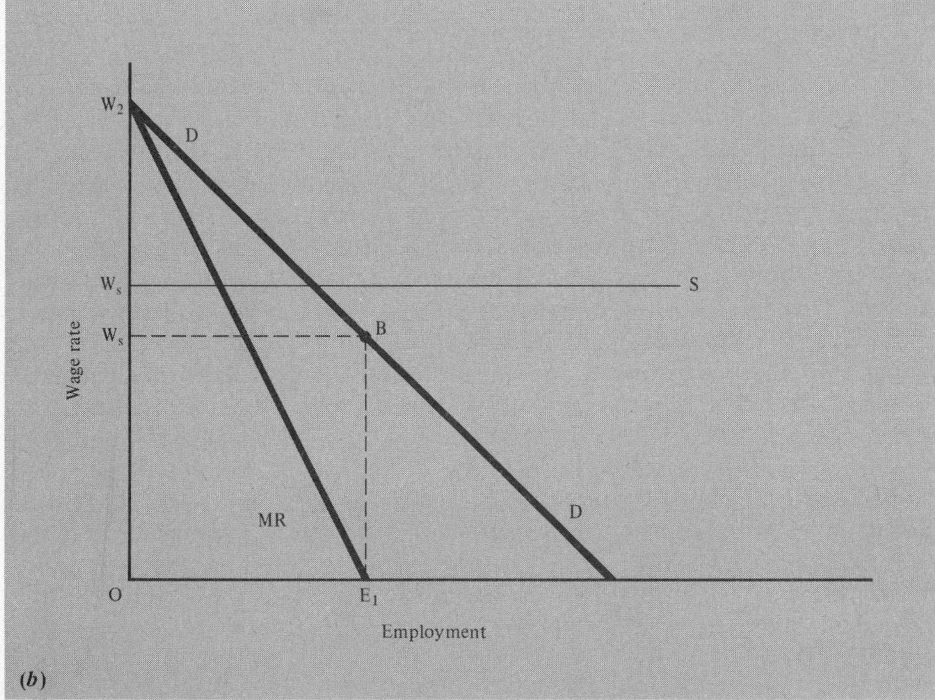

Figure 9.1 (a) Rent and wage bill maximization by unions; (b) wage bill maximization that hurts workers.

An even greater problem with wage-bill maximization is that it rests on arbitrary assumptions about the supply price of labor, the nonunion wage W_s. In Figure 9.1(b) we reproduce the demand curve DD, the marginal revenue curve MR, and the wage-bill maximizing wage W_1 that were shown in Figure 9.1(a). Assume now that the supply of labor to the firm (determined by the wage available to union members in nonunion firms) is S; the supply price of nonunion labor is thus W_s. In this case, maximizing the wage bill would involve setting a wage lower than the supply price of labor, that is, lower than the wage in the absence of a union. It is impossible to see why any union membership or honest union leadership would want such a solution. Nor would employers want it. They would be unable to recruit labor, for workers could obtain nonunion jobs at a wage W_s.

An interesting example shows how membership and employment are alternative and sometimes conflicting goals of the union. Some major firms in the meat-packing industry in the early 1960s threatened to close a number of unprofitable unionized plants unless the unions agreed to wage reductions. The local unions concerned reacted differently to these threats, depending on local labor market conditions. The Amalgamated Meat Cutters and Butcher Workmen influenced its local unions to accept wage reductions, because it had organized many small plants, especially in the South, that faced competition from low-wage, nonunion firms. It felt that it could grow only through a wage policy of moderation. In contrast, the United Packinghouse Workers influenced its locals to refuse the wage cuts and to accept the plant shutdowns. It was interested in organizing large, new, independent packing companies in the Midwest and felt that it could best do so by a policy of militance.[16] If the case of the United Packinghouse Workers were analyzed as a choice between wages and employment, it would appear that employment had no weight in the union's preferences. When employment is replaced by membership as the second element affecting preferences, both elements play a role.

The difficulties inherent in both maximization models can also be illustrated by considering the case of an industrial union that includes two distinct classes of members—a small group of craft workers and a large group of operatives. In the United States, the United Auto Workers union is a good example. We assume, based on the discussion in Chapter 4, that the demand for craft workers is quite inelastic and that the demand for operatives is more elastic. The solution that maximizes rents is to have marginal revenue in each market equal to the common marginal cost or supply price, which implies paying a higher wage to the craft workers for whom the demand is less elastic. (The product-market analog is the case of the discriminating monopolist selling the same product in two separate markets. Such a monopolist maximizes profits by charging a higher price in the market where demand is less elastic.) But if the union achieves large wage gains for its craft members and small ones or none for the more numerous operatives, it has no way to channel part of the rents to the operatives. Such a policy will therefore put the union leaders in severe political trouble. They are forced to settle for a smaller total gain more equitably distributed, and there is good evidence, both for specific crafts and for a random

[16] Hervey Juris, "Union Crisis Wage Decisions," *Industrial Relations* (8): 247–258 (1969). The two international unions in the meat-packing industry have since merged.

sample of craft workers, that for this reason craft members of industrial unions sometimes fare badly.[17]

A more general formulation of union goals appears to describe behavior better than do hypotheses of wage-bill or rent maximization. An examination of wage (and thus employment) setting by a number of locals of the International Typographical Union suggests that unions value *both* higher wages and expanded employment but that they are not willing to trade-off wages for employment in a way that keeps the wage bill constant. So, too, they do not simply try to achieve the highest rent regardless of the consequences for employment.[18] Unions that set wages and allow employers to determine the amount of union labor to be used are aware that higher wages lead to fewer jobs for their members; but their wage policy cannot be described by any simple hypothesis that involves maximizing a single sum, such as rent or the wage bill.

Unions' ability to achieve higher wages with little loss of membership or employment depends critically on the elasticity of demand for union labor. With a lower elasticity, the rent- or wage-bill maximizing wages, W_0 and W_1 in Figure 9.1(a), can both be pushed higher. That elasticity can be kept low only if the union can restrict the use of nonunion substitutes for products made with union labor. Thus most unions are very concerned to organize all firms within an industry. In the 1980s, for example, the United Auto Workers have made major efforts to organize workers who are employed by Japanese auto manufacturers that have built plants in the United States. This is, as we should expect from our discussion of the incidence of unionism, fairly easy when the establishments operate on a large scale. But when there are many small establishments it becomes much more difficult, to the detriment of the position of unionized workers. This is shown by the continuing problem of "runaway shops"—firms leaving the unionized garment manufacturing centers of the East Coast for smaller towns—which have tended to erode the position of the International Ladies Garment Workers Union.

POLICY ISSUE—UNION GOALS AND ANTITRUST POLICY

Under the antitrust laws of the United States, unions are explicitly exempt from prosecution for being combinations in restraint of trade. Nonetheless, unions' actions in conjunction with certain employers can be viewed as a restraint of trade. In the case of *United Mine Workers v. Pennington* in 1965 the Supreme Court ruled that the union was guilty of colluding with some employers to raise wage rates to harm another group of employers.[19] How can the union help itself by colluding with some employers to raise wages throughout the industry? Why not just impose different wage increases on different firms?

[17] Albert Rees and George Shultz, *Workers and Wages in an Urban Labor Market,* University of Chicago Press, Chicago, 1970, chap. 10, and Jody Sindelar, "Intraunion Redistribution of Economic Rents," Unpublished Paper, University of Chicago Graduate School of Business, 1983.

[18] James Dertouzos and John Pencavel, "Wage and Employment Determination Under Trade Unionism: The International Typographical Union," *Journal of Political Economy* (89): 1162–1181 (1981).

[19] The discussion is based upon Oliver Williamson, "Wage Rates as a Barrier to Entry: The Pennington Case in Perspective," *Quarterly Journal of Economics* (82): 85–116 (1968).

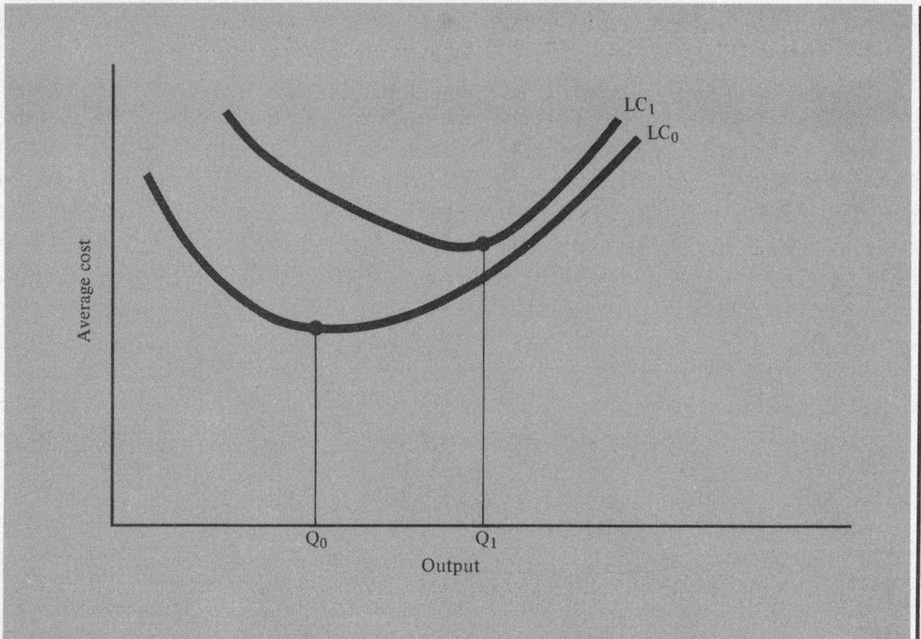

Figure 9.2 Cost, capital intensity, and union wages.

The answer can be seen in Figure 9.2. LC_0 is the long-run average cost curve in the industry before the union imposes the wage increases. It shows the per unit cost of producing at each output level in the long run—after the firm has had time to adjust its capital and labor inputs to produce as efficiently as possible at a particular output. With the configuration of costs (including wages) that prevailed, the efficient size of a firm in the industry (the lowest average cost) was at an output of Q_0. The imposed wage increase raised costs for all firms; even nonunion firms had to raise wages to attract or retain their work force. Because larger firms used more capital-intensive methods of production, the increased wage represented a smaller increase in costs per unit of output for them than for small firms. The long-run average cost curve rose to LC_1; the efficient scale of operations increased from Q_0 to Q_1.

The union benefited from this change in two ways. First, union workers employed in large firms received a wage increase; more important, though, competition for the product of their labor from employees in small firms was reduced, because the smaller firms became relatively less profitable. Second, the United Mine Workers, like other unions, had had repeated difficulties in maintaining union organization in small companies. The wage gains that benefited employees in the larger firms reduced employment of some union miners in the small firms; but they functioned as a substantial barrier to entry into the industry for new small companies that the union leadership felt would be difficult to organize and would compete with the larger, unionized firms.

UNION OBJECTIVES WITH SHARED CONTROL OVER EMPLOYMENT

Pushing Beyond the Demand Schedule

We have been assuming thus far that the union formulates its wage demands in collective bargaining on the expectation that employers will be free to adjust employment in response to whatever wage is agreed on. This amounts to assuming that the final position will lie on the demand curve for labor. Some unions, however, succeed in imposing rules that force employers to use more labor than they would like at the union wage; in other words, employers are forced off the demand curve to the right. The labor-demand schedule arises from employers' decisions about maximizing profits; thus the union can only be successful in forcing employers to hire more workers than they would like at a given wage if employers can operate with the extra workers and remain in business. If there are no excess profits to be extracted from the employer, any attempt by the union to force the employer to use more labor than is implied by the demand curve will eventually result in the employer leaving the industry.

Assume the unionized employer does have some product-market power, so that a powerful union can force the employer to the right of the labor-demand curve. (Alternatively, assume a powerful union organizes an entire industry whose product demand is not completely elastic.) The employer's labor-demand schedule, DD from Figure 9.1(a), is reproduced in Figure 9.3, as is the supply schedule of nonunion labor

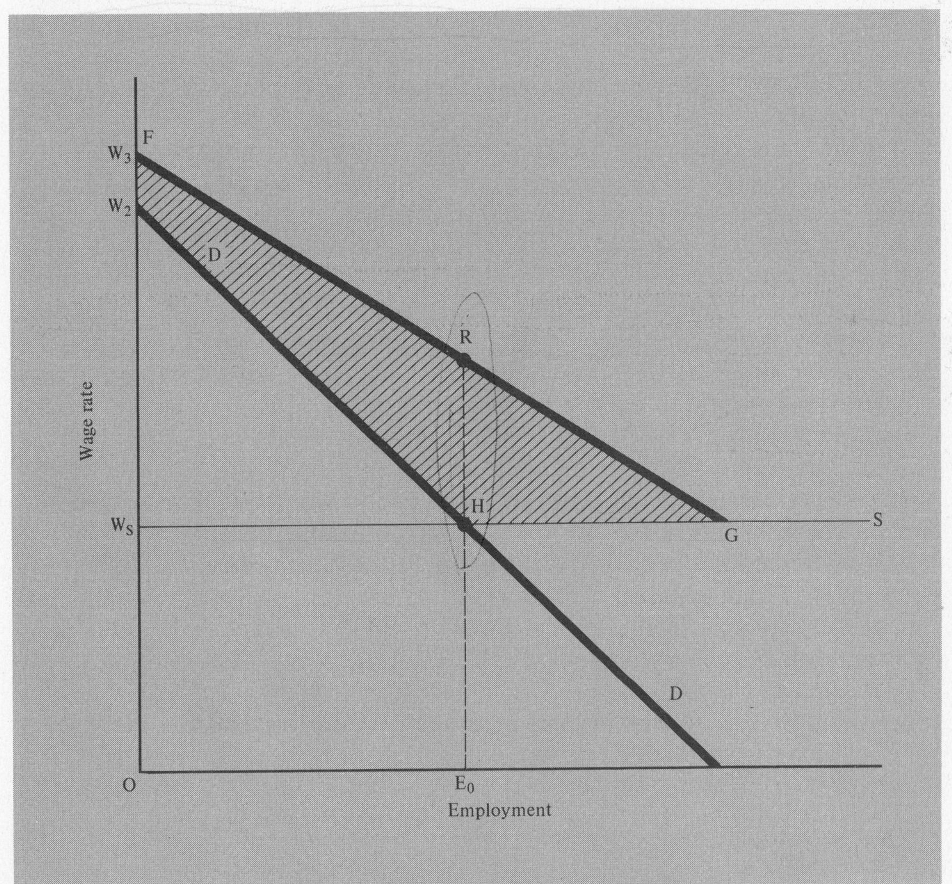

Figure 9.3 The range of bargainable employment levels and wage rates.

to the firm, S. As we saw before, no honest union will set a wage below W_s. But if the firm makes positive economic profits (profits in excess of a competitive rate of return), the union could raise the wage as high as W_3 and the employer could still earn a competitive rate of return. The line FG indicates the maximum amount of labor the firm could pay for at each wage and still earn a competitive rate of return.

If the union alone sets the wage and determines how many workers the employer must hire, it will choose from among combinations of wage rates and employment along FG. It cannot pick a point to the right of FG; if it does, the employer will shut down. It would be foolish to pick a point to the left of FG, for more employment and/or higher wage rates can be attained on FG. In this case, as in the previous section, the union's choice between higher wage rates or more employment determines the outcome. The only difference is that more of each can be attained.

In reality few unions have ever exerted sole control over both wage rates and employment; rather, control is shared by the union and the employer, and *both* wages and employment are determined through the process of collective bargaining. Indeed, that process can be viewed as the determination of where in the irregularly shaped area W_2FGH in Figure 9.3, the *contract range,* the wage and employment outcome will lie. The area W_2FGH represents the range of bargainable outcomes; where in this range the outcome actually occurs depends on the bargaining power and tactics of the union and the employer.

If the union could reallocate the gains from bargaining among its members in a way consistent with their influence in the union's political process, it could achieve the same employment level, E_0, as would be attained if the firm were nonunion and took the competitive wage, W_s, as given. Any point on the line RH is in the set of *efficient wage-employment bargains.* At any other points in W_2FGH the level of employment differs from what a competitive labor market would produce.[20] Only on RH does the marginal revenue product of labor equal the opportunity cost of a worker's time, as measured by the competitive wage. The vertical distance RH is an amount over which the union and management can bargain if employment is set at the competitive level. Despite the possibility that a unionized firm could duplicate the competitive outcome and not induce an inefficient allocation of resources, it is not likely that this will happen, for precisely the reasons stressed in the previous section. The union has no easy way of allocating the gains among its members so as to make all of them better off than they would be at an outcome not on RH. Thus any point in W_2FGH is possible, depending on the union's political structure and its members' preferences. The determinants of the outcome will be discussed in more detail in Chapter 10 in the context of analyzing bargaining behavior.

Regardless of what we assume about the nature of the union's preferences, the contract-range view of union goals seems more closely supported by data for craft-type unions than is the view expressed in the demand models, which imply that the union moves along the employer's demand schedule. Newspapers that employed members of the International Typographical Union between 1945 and 1973 did not

[20] Wassily Leontief, "The Pure Theory of the Guaranteed Annual Wage Contract," *Journal of Political Economy* (56): 76–79 (1946).

move along a well-defined demand curve in response to wage changes imposed by the union; rather, there was a range of wage and employment outcomes from which the union chose given its members' preferences and the other input-market conditions facing the employers. Similarly, in school districts where teachers' unions in the 1970s had greater control over class size, teachers also received higher wages. Rather than having their higher wages forcing school districts to use fewer teachers, in those districts where the unions were more powerful they obtained both higher wages and greater employment opportunities for their members than in other districts.[21]

One must not infer from this discussion that powerful unions can always raise both wages and employment. Once a point in W_2FGH is reached, if the bargaining power of the union and the firm do not change, the only way the union can obtain a higher wage rate for its members is to sacrifice employment. Even if the union can force the employer to the right of the demand curve, the union leadership must still solve the political problem of choosing between higher wages for a few members and lower wages for a larger membership. The contract range hypothesis merely implies that a more powerful union can obtain both higher wage rates and greater employment for its members than a less powerful union facing an employer with equal bargaining power and the same contract range.

Featherbedding

The means by which unions try to create additional employment are called *restrictive working practices* or, more commonly, *featherbedding*. Such practices are formalized into rules largely among craft unions, although informal equivalents exist at the plant level in some industrial unions. Featherbedding takes a number of closely related forms. The unions may require the employment of workers who do no work. For example, musicians unions may require the employment of a local "standby" band when a well-known traveling band is engaged.[22] They may require unnecessary work to be performed. For example, the "bogus" rules of some locals of the International Typographical Union made necessary the subsequent resetting of advertising material printed by newspapers from papier-mâché matrices received from outside the shop.[23]

In other cases a union may refuse to permit the introduction of technological changes; thus many locals of the typographers unions long resisted the setting of type by computers. Finally, the union may require that more workers be used to do particular work than the employer thinks are needed. This is perhaps the most general form of restrictive work practice; an example is the musicians unions' rules on the minimum size of orchestras.

[21] Thomas McCurdy and John Pencavel, "Testing Between Competing Models of Wage and Employment Determination in Unionized Markets," Unpublished Paper, Stanford University, 1983, and Randall Eberts and Joe Stone, "On the Contract Curve: A Test of Alternative Models of Collective Bargaining," Unpublished Paper, University of Oregon, 1983.

[22] For a discussion of working rules of the American Federation of Musicians as of 1948, see Vern Countryman, "The Organized Musicians," *Chicago Law Review* (16): 56–58, 239–297 (1948). Reprinted in Paul Weinstein (ed.). *Featherbedding and Technological Change,* Heath, Boston, 1965.

[23] For a classic discussion of this long-standing practice, see George Barnett, "The Printers," *American Economic Association Quarterly,* Third Series (10, no. 3): 435–819 (1909), partly reprinted in Weinstein, loc. cit.

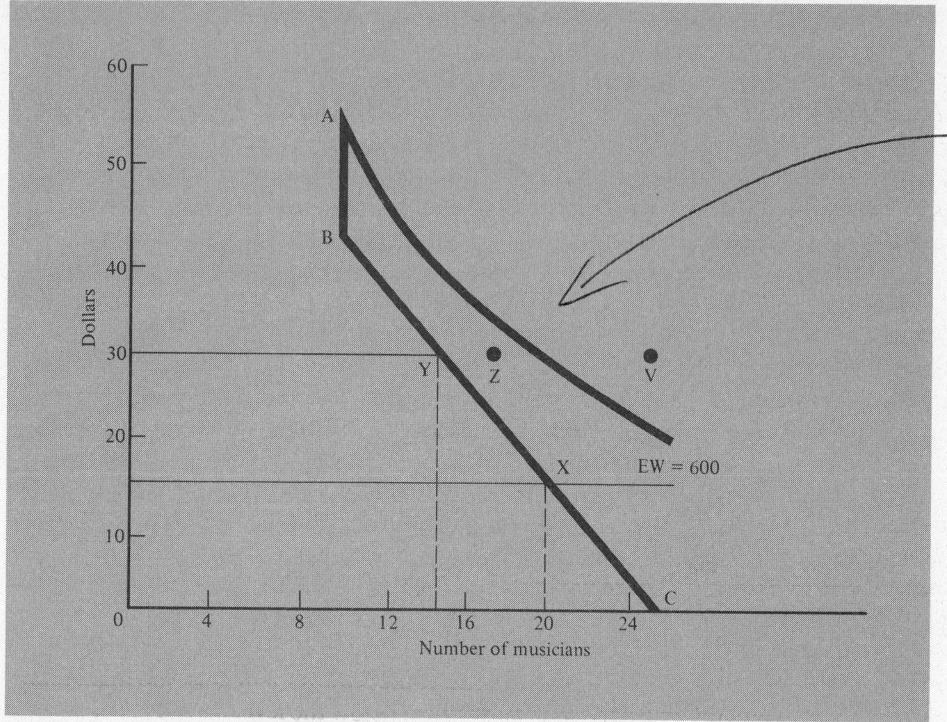

Figure 9.4 An example of a featherbedding rule.

The case of requiring a minimum number of workers for a task is analyzed in Figure 9.4, using as an example the requirement once enforced by the Chicago local of the musicians union that an orchestra for a musical show must consist of at least 18 musicians.[24] The diagram shows the number of musicians who would be employed at each performance of a musical show at various wage rates. We assume that the musical would not be produced with an orchestra of fewer than 10; the demand curve is line ABC, which is vertical at an employment of 10 when the wage is $45 per performance or higher. The supply curve of competent musicians to any one producer in the absence of the union is assumed to be horizontal at a wage of $15 per performance. In the nonunion case the producer would choose point X, using an orchestra of 20. If the union simply imposed a wage of $30 per performance, with no further requirements, the producer would choose point Y, using only 15 musicians in the orchestra. By combining a union wage of $30 with the requirement that the orchestra consist of at least 18, the union forces the producer to point Z, which lies to the right of the demand curve.

The union's ability to force the employer to spend more on the orchestra by a combination of wage demands and working practices must have a limit like FG in Figure 9.3. At some point, the show would not be produced at all. In the diagram this limit is represented as a budget constraint consisting of a portion of the rectangular

[24]Countryman, op cit., p. 31, fn. 43.

hyperbola, EW = \$600, where E is employment and W is the wage. The producers would accept any point to the left of this rather than not produce the show; to the right, the cost of the orchestra would consume such a large portion of the expected gross revenue that the production would be unprofitable. Thus if the producers were confronted by a requirement that they use 24 musicians at \$30 a performance (point V), the show would not be produced. The area above the supply curve at the wage 15 and lying between the demand curve and the budget-constraint hyperbola is the contract range.

It is important to note that by specifying employment per task, the union does not determine the total amount of employment of its members for either the industry or the individual employer. Nor does the union specify the ratio of employment of its members to all other inputs.[25] In general, the union requires that its members be employed in fixed proportion to some subset of other inputs, and there may be substitution against this whole subset. At the industry level the union's employment requirement will raise costs and prices and therefore will lower output (the quantity of product demanded). In the preceding example these forces can be represented by both a reduction in the number of shows produced and a shortening of runs (number of performances), since a larger proportion of seats must be filled to justify extending a run. There will be a tendency to use larger houses for musical shows (a change in factor proportions), which will also contribute to shorter runs. For these reasons a requirement of a specified number of musicians per performance is not guaranteed to increase total employment. If the requirement is set too high, total employment at any union wage could be reduced below the level that employers as a group would offer in the absence of the requirement. A clearer case of the failure of a union work rule to fix factor proportions is represented by the rules of railroad unions on the size of freight train crews, which specify the number of workers per train. The ratio of capital to labor can be increased (and has been) by having more and larger cars per train.

Since true featherbedding represents a conspicuous waste of resources, it is understandably condemned by management, economists, and the general public. In some cases, however, unions defend practices that appear to be featherbedding as necessary to protect the safety of workers or the public. A long debate between unions of airline cockpit personnel and airlines' management over the requirement that there be a third person in the cockpit to take over the aircraft should both other fliers suddenly become incapacitated eventually resulted in the elimination of the third seat in smaller commercial jets.

The protection of union members from work hazards is an entirely legitimate union objective, and practices that in fact provide such protection should not be called featherbedding. An economist would nevertheless be inclined to insist, as in the case of occupational licensing that we discussed in Chapter 3, that the added safety produced by these practices be obtained at reasonable cost; that is, it should

[25] This suggests that much of the diagrammatic analysis of cases in which the union is said to specify either the level of employment or the ratio of employment to all other inputs is of little relevance to existing restrictive practices. For example, see the articles by Weinstein and by N. J. Simler in Weinstein, loc. cit.

meet the test of a careful benefit-cost analysis. The union is more likely to argue that life and health are priceless, to be guarded at any cost.

This issue arose in the case of railroad firemen. The unions argued that these workers were essential to the safety of other workers, but in 1963 the railroads won the right to operate trains without including firemen in the train crews. Employment of firemen dropped 50 percent by 1967. Simultaneously, however, derailments rose 60 percent, and total accidents rose 50 percent. This was not just a coincidence: A disproportionate amount of the increase in accidents occurred on those railroads that had reduced the input of hours of firemen the most.[26] Although unions' claims that safety is impaired if employment in some activity is reduced may often be self-serving, this case demonstrates that safety can be reduced by management-imposed cuts in staffing.

Featherbedding is the means by which the union pushes the employer off the demand curve. In many cases it is a response to a technical change that sharply reduces the demand for union labor in a particular craft while at the same time increasing the profitability of the firm. (The introduction of smaller commercial jets is one such example.) The technical change induces a struggle between management, which seeks to reap the profits from the improvement, and the union, which wishes to maintain employment for its membership. In some cases both parties can be satisfied and the fruits of technical change can be shared with workers who might lose their jobs. For example, the agreement negotiated by the International Longshoremen's and Warehousemen's Union that became effective in 1961 provided employers the freedom to automate at their discretion, subject to each current employee being guaranteed pay for 35 hours per week during the life of the contract.

Often attempts at featherbedding find their initial impetus in the expansion of a competing industry. Thus television has reduced employment in the motion picture industry, and the automobile and airplane have increasingly reduced employment in railroad passenger service. Unions in the declining industries have struggled to maintain employment by imposing restrictions on employers' attempts to economize on their inputs of labor. These may be successful in the short run, for they are backed up by the threat of a total shutdown during a strike, but in the long run they are usually unsuccessful. The reason is clear from the preceding discussion: The employers do not have any excess profits that the union can extract. In such cases it is not a matter of pushing the employer to the right of the demand curve. Rather, the union must accommodate a demand curve for labor that is shifting leftward because of the decline in demand for the industry's output.

FACTORS INFLUENCING WAGE POLICY

Taking the goals of higher wages and increased employment or membership as central to any union, consider the different ways in which unions may try to achieve these goals. One important feature of union wage policy is the critical role of the current money wage. A union will almost always insist on maintaining the current

[26] Franklin Fisher and Gerald Kraft, "The Effect of the Removal of Firemen on Railroad Accidents, 1962–1967," *Bell Journal of Economics and Management Science* (2): 470–494 (1971).

wage even at the cost of severe contraction in employment, whereas it would not insist on increasing the money wage if the consequences for employment were nearly as severe. In other words, the weight given to the size of membership or employment is much smaller for wage cuts than for wage increases. There have been no general reductions in money wages in any important industry since the early 1930s, although there have been several moderately severe recessions and a number of major industries have had declining employment.

Unions have occasionally agreed to wage reductions at the firm or establishment level when there has been a threat that an establishment would shut down or be relocated or that a firm would go bankrupt, and the promise that a wage reduction would avert this. In the case of Chrysler in 1980, the wage reduction was the price the workers paid for the firm's obtaining federal loan guarantees that helped keep it operating. Such a position will seem credible only when taken by a management with whom the union has had good relations. Even in such cases, the union can agree only if the concession to one firm does not provide an occasion for other unionized employers to demand similar treatment. For this reason a union cannot make wage concessions to one employer in a group engaged in multiemployer bargaining or where the bargain struck with one firm sets the pattern for others: After the Chrysler concessions General Motors and Ford were quick to demand similar concessions, though they did not get them. To avoid this difficulty a union can try to help one employer improve productivity by providing technical assistance or reducing restrictive work practices, a much less visible kind of concession.

Unions protect their members' real wages against rising prices by including escalator clauses or cost-of-living allowances (COLAs) in collective bargaining agreements, particularly agreements with a duration of more than one year. Such clauses provide for periodic changes in money wages during the life of the agreement based on changes in the Consumer Price Index. By 1982, 57 percent of workers covered by major collective bargaining agreements in the United States (those covering 1000 workers or more) received wage increases under escalator clauses. This percentage rose from 28 percent in 1971, spurred by the sharp inflation of the early 1970s, reaching a peak of 61 percent in 1977. It fell steadily from 1977 to 1982. These changes illustrate that members' pressures on the union leadership to achieve different goals depend very much on changes in economic conditions.

The wage demands of any one union are strongly influenced by comparisons with other groups of workers with whom there have been traditional parities or differentials. The logic of such comparisons is often open to question, for wage comparisons can be made in many directions. The unions will, of course, try to make those most favorable to a wage increase, whereas the management will make those least favorable. But once a particular comparison has been long accepted as equitable, it becomes difficult to change. One author has referred to these relations as *orbits of coercive comparison.*[27] For example, in both the United States and Great Britain, there are cities with a long tradition that police and firefighters receive the same salary. At this equal salary it has sometimes been difficult to recruit police, although there has been a long queue of candidates for posts in the fire department. Some

[27] Arthur Ross, *Trade Union Wage Policy,* University of California Press, Berkeley, Calif., 1948.

public employers have reacted to this by trying to give a differential increase to police, but in several cases they have eventually been forced to extend the wage increase to firefighters as well. The shortage of police could be alleviated only by increasing the excess supply of firefighters.[28]

Nevertheless, established wage relationships sometimes change even among unionized workers. Where a traditional differential has been established in absolute terms (cents per hour) rather than in percentage terms, its relative value is eroded by rises in the general level of money wages until it no longer is sufficient compensation for the extra training or responsibility of the more skilled group. In such cases the more highly paid group may exert pressure to widen the absolute differential. Where the situation arises within one union, these efforts may take the form of attempts or threats to form a separate union. The special increases given to skilled craft workers in some general wage settlements in the automobile industry are cases in point.

Demands of a particular group of union workers to achieve parity with a more highly paid group doing comparable work often have particular force because worker sentiment is mobilized around a concrete goal rather than simply a demand for "more." The force of such definitions of equity in wage structures in forming union goals should be contrasted with the outcome of maximization models in which there is no room for concepts of equity. The successful drive of Canadian automobile workers for wage parity with the American employees of the same companies is an example of such a goal (where parity was defined as the same number of dollars per hour in the two national currencies for the same work).

In the long run the weight given by employers, the public, and other unions to claims for relative wage increases is likely to be influenced by labor-market conditions. For example, the claim of organized schoolteachers that their pay is inadequate to compensate them for their long training was more convincing when there was a shortage of labor in this profession in the 1960s than when there was a surplus in the late 1970s. But it is also true that a rather wide range of relative wages may be consistent with adequate supplies of workers to each of the trades concerned. These issues will be considered further in Chapter 12.

SUMMARY

Less than 25 percent of the American work force are members of trade unions. The growth in union membership in the United States and other Western countries has usually been spurred by high unemployment and favorable political circumstances and has usually fallen during periods of prosperity. Unionized workers are more likely to be found in firms in concentrated industries that use a capital-intensive technology in large-scale operations. Nonwhites are more likely than whites to be union members; women are less likely to be unionized than men, although their demand for union jobs exceeds that of men. The South contains relatively few

[28] H. A. Turner, "Inflation and Wage Differentials in Great Britain," in John Dunlop (ed.). *The Theory of Wage Determination,* Macmillan, London, 1964, p. 124, and E. J. Devine, "Manpower Shortages in Local Government Employment," American Economic Association, *Proceedings* (59): 543 (1969).

unionized establishments, both because workers there have relatively little interest in joining unions and because employers offer fewer union jobs.

Unions pursue a variety of goals, including higher wages and the maintenance of union membership. What may seem like political goals are often the union leaders' way of meeting the perceived wishes of the membership. No single conception of the goal, such as maximizing the wage bill or achieving the greatest excess of earnings above the nonunion sector, characterizes unions' actions very well. Wage goals that are often sought include protection from nominal wage cuts and from inflation (through cost-of-living allowances). Employment goals are attained by attempts to prevent employers from reducing the amount of union labor demanded in response to union-imposed wage increases. Featherbedding practices typify unions' efforts in this direction, as do attempts to organize nonunion firms that might sell products that compete with the output of firms employing union members. The former represent unions' attempts to gain a share of employers' excess profits; the latter represent their efforts to shift the demand for labor schedule to the right and to reduce its elasticity.

chapter 10

Union Methods: The Bargaining Process

In this chapter we examine the ways in which unions pursue their goals, including higher wages and more employment of union members. Wages and employment in the union sector are outcomes of collective bargaining between unions and management, and it is important to understand the bargaining process. Because the bargaining process occasionally breaks down and results in strikes, investigating why such breakdowns occur and what their effects are can give us a better understanding of unionized labor markets.

THE SOURCES OF BARGAINING POWER

The power of unions to wrest concessions from employers, to raise wage rates above the nonunion wage, or to force employers to use additional union labor is based almost entirely on the threat of a strike—the concerted withdrawal of labor by all or some of the members of a union. Occasionally a slowdown or partial strike is used in place of an ordinary strike. Union members "work to rule" and reduce normal output by scrupulous observance of all regulations, or they refuse to perform certain functions that are normally part of their job, even though they continue to perform others. The purpose of strikes and slowdowns is, of course, to impose costs on employers through loss of output, profits, and customers if they do not accede to union demands. At the same time, a full strike, as distinguished from a slowdown, also involves costs to the union, because members do not receive wages while on strike and the strike benefits sometimes paid in lieu of wages come from union funds.

The alternative sources of union power are political action, boycotts, and control of labor supply. Some government unions win wage gains through influence in Congress or in the state legislatures. Consumer boycotts have generally been weak weapons for unions, although they were used with success by the United Farm Workers in the 1960s and 1970s in organizing California agriculture. The secondary labor boycott is really a strike by a union that is not involved in the bargaining. True union control of labor supply through control of all opportunities to learn a skill is very rare, if it exists at all. Even where unions have apprenticeship programs, many craft workers learn their skills in nonunion shops. In most cases unions prevent nonunion members from working for union employers through an implicit threat to strike if nonunion members are employed.

On the employer's side there are three possible sources of bargaining power that permit employers to win some strikes. The strongest is the ability to replace strikers with other workers, called *strikebreakers* or *scabs* by the unions. This is now a rare practice among large employers but may still be used at times, especially by small employers in areas where unions are weak. A more common practice is to carry on production operations, perhaps on a somewhat limited scale, by using managerial, supervisory, and clerical workers outside their usual occupations. This method has been used by utility companies, petroleum refineries, and retail stores. Where a company cannot carry on operations during a strike, its bargaining power depends largely on its financial resources, that is, its ability to survive the losses imposed by the strike. The ultimate threat is that the strike will force the company to move its operations or even shut down permanently. This threat is especially convincing where the struck employer accounts for a large fraction of local employment, thus leaving few alternative jobs that strikers could obtain.

As all this implies, the balance of bargaining power differs greatly in different bargaining situations. At one extreme is the typical situation of the construction craft unions, where struck employers can have their jobs closed down for months while the strikers are working at good wages in some other nearby towns. In such a case the fragmentation of bargaining units works to the advantage of the union. At the opposite extreme is the telephone company or electric utility where management and supervisory personnel can carry on the bulk of normal operations for months while strikers are out of work. Between these extremes lie the more usual cases in which strikes impose relatively equal losses on both parties. This discussion suggests that we can define each side's *bargaining power* as its relative ability to impose costs on the other side.

Some employers may agree to union demands without ever engaging in negotiations. In the early days of unions this occurred when employers acquiesced in a pay scale proposed by the union. Today it usually occurs when a union extends a bargain reached elsewhere to employers who were not party to it. These employers regard it as certain that the union will strike if they do not accept the terms of the *pattern bargain* and regard the costs of a strike as clearly in excess of the probable gains from holding out. The automotive industry, where one of the Big Three manufacturers is chosen as the strike target, is the best known example of this pattern bargaining.

THEORIES OF BARGAINING

The Bargaining Problem

Economists have long been interested in formulating models of the bargaining process, or bargaining theories, that are applicable to union-management negotiations. This has proved to be an extremely difficult task. The factors that determine the outcome of the collective bargaining process are so varied and complex that it is exceedingly hard to devise models that are both realistic and manageable.

There are important differences between collective bargaining and the situations considered in more general bargaining models used in economic theory. For example, it is an important aspect of many general bargaining models that the parties may permanently cease to deal with each other if the outcome is unsatisfactory to one of them. Suppose that the Smiths put their house up for sale at $50,000 and that the Joneses offer them $45,000. They may then bargain over the difference, with two possible outcomes—a sale is or is not agreed upon. If the Joneses are secretly prepared to go as high as $48,000 and the Smiths are really willing to accept $47,000, then there is a zone of $1000 within which the bargaining can go on; the exact terms of the sale will depend on the bargaining skill and tactics of the negotiators. However, if the Joneses have a firm upper limit of $46,000 and the Smiths are completely unwilling to accept less than $49,000, then no transaction will take place. The Smiths will find another buyer or continue to occupy their house. Much of general bargaining theory consists in determining the limits at which parties will break off negotiations altogether.

This kind of bargaining model has only partial relevance to collective bargaining, where the parties are generally forced to deal with each other permanently on some terms. Occasionally a small employer will go out of business rather than reach an agreement with a union. Occasionally a union may be broken by a strike and the employer will operate with nonunion labor, as was the case with the air traffic controllers in 1981. But the vast majority of negotiations must result, either before or after a strike, in an agreement that both parties accept. In this sense the zone of indeterminacy is enormous, because the option of no exchange is almost nonexistent.

Much of general bargaining theory deals with the division of a fixed stock, or of a flow of constant size, between two parties. Such models also are not usually applicable to collective bargaining. One of the most common reactions of employers or industries to wage settlements is to raise the price of the final product, which passes on some of the cost of the settlements to third parties. Or the employers may adjust the level of employment as a result of a settlement. Thus the terms of the settlement themselves influence the size of the revenue flow to be shared. In the terminology of the theory of bargaining, union-management negotiations are not a *zero-sum* game. These arguments are one more reason that the so-called efficient bargain, the line RH in Figure 9.3, is not likely to be the location of the outcome of the bargaining process.

Most bargaining theory also deals with cases in which there are only two parties to the bargain, whereas in collective bargaining there are almost always, in reality, more than two. We noted in Chapter 9 that the goals or tactics of union leaders are not always acceptable to the members; leaders may find themselves bargaining with the employer in one direction and with their own membership in the other. In addition, the public is often an interested party because either a strike would harm or inconvenience users of the product or service produced or a generous settlement would lead to price increases. Such effects can bring about government intervention in negotiations, which often becomes another active force in the determination of the outcome.

POLICY ISSUE—UNION DEMOCRACY AND UNION MILITANCE

A number of federal laws and programs enacted since World War II have instituted changes that could affect unions' bargaining power by affecting internal relations within the union, particularly the relationship of the union leaders and their constituents. Most important, the Labor-Management Reporting and Disclosure Act (Landrum-Griffin Act) of 1959 required among other provisions that elections of union officers be held on a regular and not too infrequent schedule. The likely effect of such legislation on workers' militancy, and thus on the ability of union negotiators to threaten a strike, is not clear; but union members, often not so well informed about the management's problems, may be more militant than the leadership. They may in that case press for an even stronger negotiating position than the leadership would have taken; and increased union democracy may encourage the leadership to respond more readily to the members' wishes.

Greater union democracy appears to increase unions' militancy, as measured by indexes of strike activity. Accounting for numerous other factors that might affect strike activity, one study found significantly more strikes between 1959, when the Landrum-Griffin Act was passed, and 1967 than before. The effect seemed to be attenuated somewhat in the 1970s but was still there.[1] We may conclude from the evidence on the Landrum-Griffin Act that workers are more militant than their leaders, and their militance becomes effective when internal union politics become more democratic.

The kind of bargaining model that is most easily expressed in precise terms deals with only one magnitude among the terms of settlement, such as a wage. Even in the simple contract range model of Chapter 9, however, both wages and employment were jointly determined by the union and the management. In reality collective bargaining is frequently multidimensional, and a concession in one area of bargaining, such as union security, may be traded for a concession in another, such as wages. It also helps to make a bargaining model manageable if one assumes that the nature and outcome of bargaining in one period do not affect the outcome in the next. Again, this condition does not hold in collective bargaining. If a union that negotiates annual contracts has a long strike in one year, it will regard a new strike the following year as more costly, since its members will not want to go without wages repeatedly. On the other hand, the threat of a strike may not seem credible if strikes never occur. Thus a successful strike, by convincing the employer that the union is strong, can produce gains that last over more than one bargaining period.

Despite these formidable difficulties, some of the propositions of formal bargaining theory are applicable to union-management negotiations over wages, although they are less applicable to negotiations over other issues that may be

[1] Orley Ashenfelter and George Johnson, "Bargaining Theory, Trade Unions and Industrial Strike Activity," *American Economic Review* (59): 35–49 (1969), and Bruce Kaufman, "The Determinants of Strikes in the United States, 1900–1977," *Industrial and Labor Relations Review* (35): 473–490 (1982).

regarded as matters of principle. The central proposition of the theory is that each party to the bargain compares its probable gain from a strike with the costs it perceives and is willing to strike (or accept a strike) rather than settle if the present value of the expected gain over the contract period exceeds the expected cost. However, since bargaining always involves an attempt by each party to conceal its true position from the other and thus to create uncertainty, the expected gains and costs cannot be known in advance with any precision. In wage negotiations a particular kind of parity or coercive wage comparison will sometimes be regarded by one of the parties as so much a matter of principle or equity, or will involve such a firm prior commitment, that they will strike (or accept a strike) even when the expected present value of this behavior is negative for the current bargaining period.

One of the purposes of the statistics on wages, profits, and so forth, so often mentioned in wage negotiations, is to inform the other party of the strength of commitments of this kind.[2] For example, a union might present figures showing that its members are paid less than employees of other firms doing similar work. The purpose of these figures could be to convince employers that they will not be at a competitive disadvantage in the sale of their products if they accept the union demands. In most cases, however, their purpose is to show that the union is prepared to strike rather than accept a settlement it considers unfair. By increasing employers' estimates of the probability that it will strike, the union thus increases the amount employers will offer to avoid a strike.

To Strike or Not to Strike?

The union's expected gain from a strike is the discounted value of the difference over the contract period between the most it thinks the management will offer without a strike and the expected settlement that could be won by striking. For management the gain from taking a strike is the discounted value of the difference between the minimum it believes the union will accept without a strike and the expected settlement after a strike. The two parties will not expect the same settlement nor will they ordinarily expect a strike of exactly the same duration. A difference in the expected duration of the strike will produce a difference between the two parties' estimates of the probable costs of a strike to each of them. It is this difference in perceptions of the other party's costs and of the size of the eventual settlement that causes a strike to occur. If both sides were rational and were certain of the duration of a strike and its outcome, they would settle for that outcome and avoid the costs of a strike.[3]

A strike is thus more probable, the greater the amount of uncertainty is about the other side's resources and behavior, for then the parties are more likely to differ in the perceptions of the costs of a strike. This conflict is more likely in new collective

[2]Carl Stevens, "On the Theory of Negotiation," *Quarterly Journal of Economics* (72): 77–97 (1958).

[3]A model with these implications is in J. R. Hicks, *The Theory of Wages,* 2d ed., Macmillan, London, 1964, chap. 7. For a criticism of this model, contending that it gives insufficient weight to uncertainty, see G. L. S. Shackle, "The Nature of the Bargaining Process," in John Dunlop (ed.). *The Theory of Wage Determination,* Macmillan, London, 1964, pp. 299–305.

bargaining relations, when the parties' expectations about each other's behavior are not well formed. So, too, when both parties perceive the costs of a strike as being relatively small, a strike is more likely to occur. If one or both parties perceive the costs as being huge, perhaps threatening the existence of the parties, a strike is far less probable.

During a strike two forces tend to bring the positions of the parties closer together. First, the costs per day of a strike to each party are almost certain to increase as the strike continues. Second, if negotiation goes on during the strike, it improves each party's knowledge of the true position of the other and thus reduces uncertainty. The combination of rising costs and improved information eventually leads to a settlement.

The costs of a short strike to a union may be very low if the members have previously been working steadily. They can draw on savings for living expenses during the strike and can buy some necessities on credit. Some members may be tired of work and have things they want to do around the house. As a strike goes on, savings are depleted, creditors become less willing to extend further credit, and the union's fund for strike benefits is drawn down. The most important projects around the home that use free time productively have been completed. Thus the costs of continuing the strike become higher in each succeeding week.

The costs of short strikes to employers who produce a commodity rather than a service will be low if they or their customers can build up inventories in anticipation of a strike and draw them down during the strike. Higher inventories have been associated in the United States since World War II with longer strikes.[4] As the strike goes on, inventories are depleted and sales stop. Customers turn to alternative sources of supply, with the danger that they will find them to their liking and not come back to their former supplier when the strike is over.

Although the costs of a strike to both parties rise with time, there are many cases in which the costs rise faster for the union. This will be particularly true where the employer is a large corporation with great financial resources and where the strike involves all the members of a union rather than a small group who can be supported by those still working. The greater staying power of the large corporation has led to the generalization that unions tend to win short strikes and management tends to win long ones, and the recommendation that managements must occasionally accept long strikes to establish important matters of principle.[5]

The discussion thus far has been concerned with the private and possibly temporary costs of strikes to firms and their employees. The social cost of a strike, the lost output resulting from a strike, is undoubtedly far less than the amount of wages lost by the strikers or output not sold by the firm. To the extent that customers find other suppliers, economy-wide production will be reduced by less than the struck firm's lost output. The buildup of inventories before a strike and the replenishing of inventory stocks after a strike also reduce the net loss to society. Economy-wide wage losses are also smaller than the losses to strikers during the strike. The extra wages

[4]Melvin Reder and George Neumann, "Conflict and Contract: The Case of Strikes," *Journal of Political Economy* (88): 867–886 (1980).

[5]E. Robert Livernash, "The Relation of Power to the Structure and Process of Collective Bargaining," *Journal of Law and Economics* (6): 10–40 (1963).

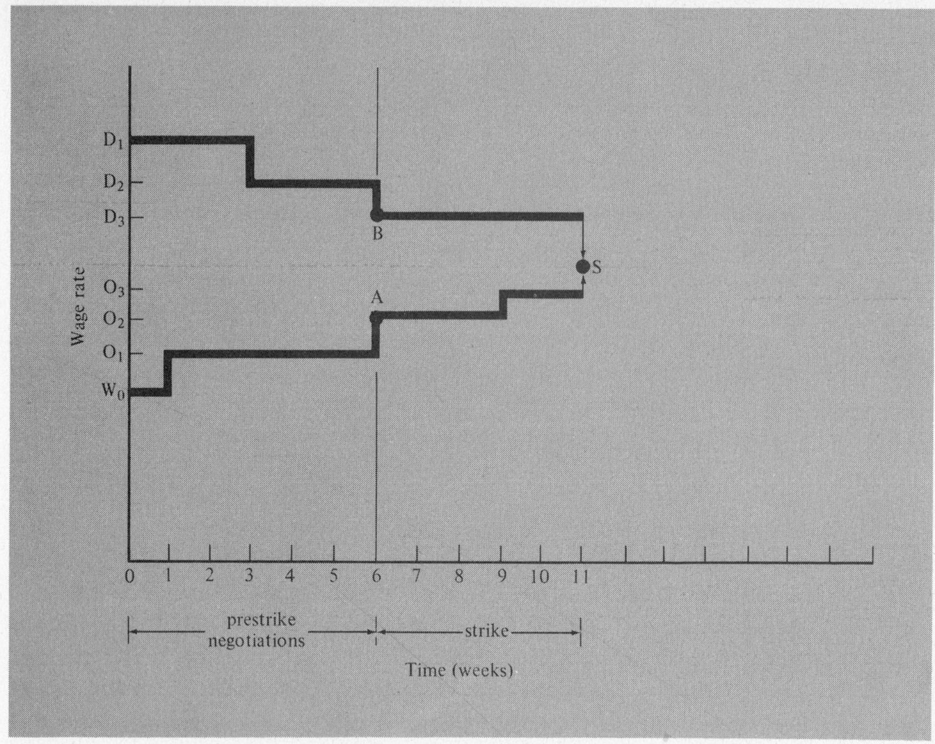

Figure 10.1 A diagrammatic representation of wage negotiations.

received during the inventory buildups before and after a strike and the wages received by employees of the struck firm's competitors both offset in part the lost earnings of the strikers. Case studies of strike situations suggest that these considerations are important and that newspaper accounts of the "cost" of strikes vastly overstate the true social cost. Evidence from U.S. manufacturing from 1958 to 1977 showed no significant effect of strikes on output in 38 of 63 industries; in the others, strikes resulted in lost output equal to only 0.2 percent of annual production.[6]

THE BARGAINING PROCESS AND OUTCOMES

Some of the preceding arguments are summarized in Figure 10.1, a diagrammatic representation of the course of the parties' positions during a hypothetical wage negotiation.[7] Wages are measured on the vertical axis, with the old wage denoted by W_0. Time is measured on the horizontal axis. Negotiations are assumed to begin in

[6]Neil Chamberlain and Jane Metzger Schilling, *The Impact of Strikes, Their Social and Economic Costs,* Harper, New York, 1954, and George Neumann and Melvin Reder, "Output and Strike Activity in U.S. Manufacturing: How Large Are the Losses?" *Industrial and Labor Relations Review* (37) (1984). In press.

[7]This diagram bears some resemblance to the well-known diagram in Hicks, op. cit., p. 143. The most important difference is that Hicks measures the expected length of the strike *ex ante,* whereas we measure the actual length *ex post.* Thus the diagram here is not intended to have any predictive value.

week 0, six weeks before the expiration of the previous agreement. The union makes an initial wage demand, D_1. A week later management makes its first counteroffer, O_1. These initial demands and offers are almost always further apart than the serious positions of the parties and are intended to stake out the general area within which bargaining will take place. The strength of the tradition that initial offers are understated may be illustrated by a well-known court decision concerning the General Electric Company. For a long time the company followed a pattern of making a well-publicized initial offer and refusing to modify it during negotiations, a practice now called *Boulwarism* after the executive who was the company's chief negotiator. This conduct was held by a U.S. Court of Appeals to constitute lack of good faith in bargaining, and therefore illegal under the National Labor Relations Act.

After two more weeks of negotiation, the union reduces its demand to D_2. Nothing happens for three weeks until the night before the contract is due to expire and the strike is scheduled to begin. At that time each side, recognizing that the other side is serious about its willingness to accept a strike and is not merely bluffing, and realizing that maintaining its position raises the expected cost of a strike, changes its position. The management raises its offer to O_2, hoping to avoid the loss of customers during a strike and attempting to induce the union to lower its wage demand still more. The union lowers its wage demand to D_3, the lowest wage settlement that the leadership believes its membership will accept in the absence of a strike.

Last minute bargaining is typical of union-management negotiations. Strike votes are often taken, but previously "hard and fast" positions are abandoned immediately before the strike deadline. This type of behavior is quite rational. The party that is more successful in convincing the other side of its willingness to bear the costs of a strike will be more successful in inducing the other side to change its demand or offer. With the strike deadline near, each party, afraid that a strike may be more costly than the potential gains it might produce, abandons its steadfast position and changes its negotiating position.[8]

Despite the last minute flurry of bargaining, the sides fail to reach an agreement and a strike begins at the contract expiration date. Three weeks after the start of the strike, management improves its offer to O_3. Although the union does not accept this offer, the remaining gap is now narrower. A final compromise is reached in the fifth week of the strike at wage S, somewhat above O_3.

Clearly the number and timing of these moves or plays in the negotiation process will vary greatly from one negotiation to another. The positions of the two parties need not converge continuously. For example, management might make offer O_3 before contract expiration on condition that it be accepted without a strike; if this offer is not accepted, management could return to O_2. A study of eight bargaining situations involving 1500 or more workers each in 1966 and 1967 showed that the management concedes gradually and steadily throughout the duration of the strike. The management's offer curve, AS in Figure 10.1, is much more like a diagonal line between those points than like the step function shown in the figure.

[8] John Cross, *The Economics of Bargaining,* Basic Books, New York, 1969; and Mario Bognanno and James Dworkin, "Time and Learning in the Bargaining Process," Industrial Relations Research Association, *Proceedings* (30): 294–302 (1977).

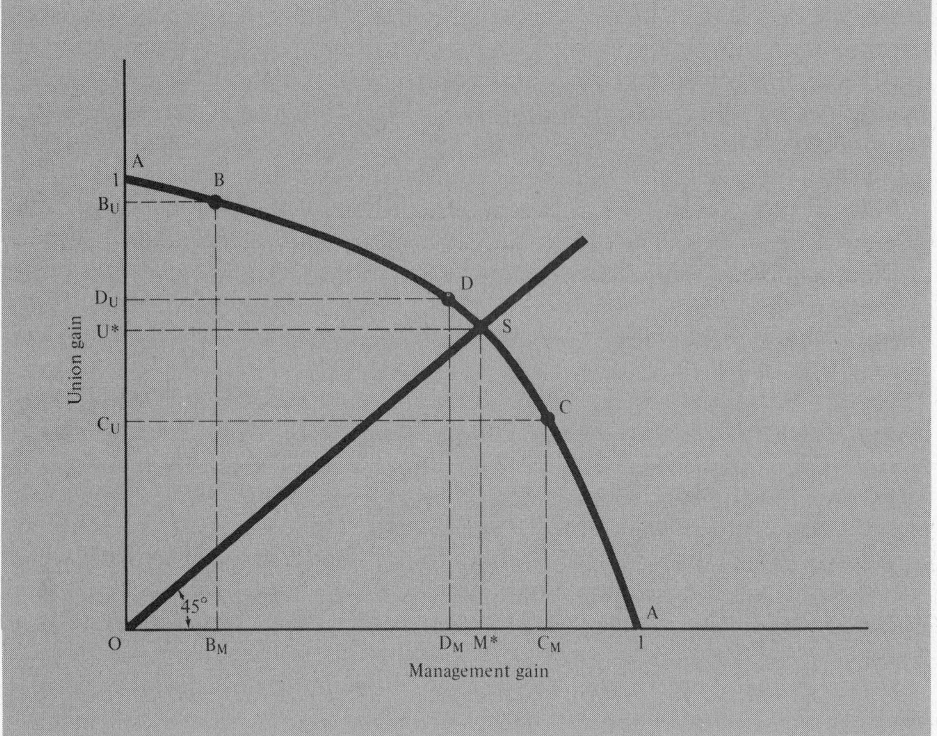

Figure 10.2 The outcome of bargaining.

The union's demands change little during most of the strike but fall sharply shortly before the strike is over. The line BS shown in Figure 10.1 appears to characterize the typical union's negotiating position quite well. The evidence also shows that the union's rate of concession in a sample of 10 bargaining situations between 1954 and 1970 was more rapid when wage-price guidelines were in effect. It was less rapid in those firms in which the share of labor in the firms' total costs was highest.[9] This latter finding is consistent with the observation that the union has more power in such cases. It is more difficult for management to keep the plant operating, and management is not fully aware of the union's power. (If it were, it would concede more rapidly.)

Figure 10.1 describes only the rates at which the parties to the negotiations concede. It cannot describe the process that determines which of the parties concedes at which time, nor does it provide any insight into what is probably the most important question in bargaining, namely, who "wins" in the negotiations. Some insight into these questions can be derived from considering Figure 10.2.[10] The

[9]Yochanan Comay, Arie Melnik, and Abraham Subotnik, "Bargaining, Yield Curves, and Wage Settlements: An Empirical Analysis," *Journal of Political Economy* (82): 303–313 (1974), and Henry Farber, "Bargaining Theory, Wage Outcomes, and the Occurrence of Strikes," *American Economic Review* (68): 262–271 (1978).

[10]The model originated in Frederick Zeuthen, *Problems of Monopoly and Economic Warfare,* Routledge, London, 1930. It was expanded upon and generalized by John Nash, "The Bargaining Problem," *Econometrica* (18): 155–162 (1950).

vertical axis shows the union's gain, the excess of the settlement over the perceived cost of the strike. No gain for the union is that settlement that leaves it indifferent between striking, or continuing a strike, and settling. Similarly, a zero gain for the management is that settlement that makes it indifferent between settling and bearing or continuing to bear a strike. The origin in Figure 10.2 thus shows the loss to each party if the strike starts or continues.

The curve AA shows the range of possible settlements of the negotiations. If the union wins everything it receives 1, and the management receives nothing, settling for the amount that just offsets the costs of continuing the impasse, and conversely, if the management wins everything. If there is no settlement, the solution is at the origin of the graph, with both sides bearing the costs of continuing the impasse. The curve is bowed outward, indicating that the negotiations are not a zero-sum game; at any points on AA except its endpoints on the axes, the sum of the parties' gains exceeds 1. We assume that the union's preferences are well-defined and that it can allocate the gains from bargaining among its members to satisfy those preferences. As we saw in Chapter 9, this is a highly questionable assumption; nonetheless, it allows us to draw specific inferences about bargaining behavior that are useful in explaining observed phenomena.

Assume the negotiations start off with management offering an outcome indicated by point C and the union demanding an outcome shown by point B. (These are equivalent to O_1 and D_1 in Figure 10.1.) The relative difference between what the management suggests for itself and what the union suggests exceeds the relative difference between what the union suggests for itself and what management offers, $(B_U - C_U/B_U)$. Management would fare relatively worse under the union demand as compared to its position if its own offer were accepted than the union would fare if it acceded to management's suggestion. Management, having more to lose by accepting the union demand, remains intransigent, whereas the union, having less to lose, lowers its demand to point D. Now the relative difference between its offer to management and management's suggestion for itself is $(C_M - D_M/C_M)$; this is more than $(D_U - C_U/D_U)$, the union's gain under its new demand relative to its gain under the management's offer. The union is now going to become intransigent and threaten a strike (or a prolonged strike) if the management fails to revise its offer. The management, not wishing to incur or prolong a strike, does concede. The process continues, with each side that is making the less conciliatory offer conceding, until the solution is reached at point S.

The outcome of the bargaining process at point S has a unique characteristic among all points along AA: It is the only one at which each party to the negotiations obtains the same gain beyond what it would obtain if a strike occurred or continued. This result is not accidental; it occurs because of the assumption that the party whose wage offer or demand leaves relatively less for the other party is the one that moderates its offer. An outcome at point S implies that the parties split the gains from bargaining evenly; and because AA is bowed outward (the bargaining process is a *positive-sum* game), the sum of the parties' gains is at a maximum. Thus although the parties do not cooperate, their behavior, described by their alternative concessions, leads them to the point where the total value of the settlement (the sum of the excess of each party's value of the settlement less the cost of continuing the impasse) is greatest.

This view of bargaining contains the explicit prediction that the results will reflect an even split of the gains to concluding negotiations peaceably or to settling a strike. If it is correct, neither party should "win" more than the other in bargaining. Although it is very hard to test this prediction, an even split in wages does not appear to be what happens. In a study of 43 negotiations in the public sector between 1968 and 1970, the average wage gain was 12 percent, the average initial union demand was 23 percent, and the average initial management offer was 8 percent. A study of bargaining by 16 unions with the Tennessee Valley Authority between 1960 and 1975 found that the settlements averaged 6 percent, the initial union demands averaged 12 percent, and the initial management offers averaged 3 percent.[11] In both cases the clear implication is that the union gets far less than half the difference between its initial demand and management's initial offer.

That the union appears to do worse than management in the typical bargaining situation ignores the possibility of bluffing. The management cannot realistically offer a zero-wage increase or a wage cut except in times of severe financial distress when it is faced with the possibility of bankruptcy. This usually puts a floor of zero on its initial offer. The union, on the other hand, is free to attempt to bluff management by staking out an exorbitant demand as its initial position. For example, in 1981 the Professional Air Traffic Controllers proposed wage parity with the much higher-paid airline pilots. The possibilities for bluffing thus favor the union, especially insofar as the union leadership feels obligated to bluff in order to retain the support of the membership. This means that the typical outcome may in fact reflect an even split of the potential gains, even though it lies closer to management's first offer than to the demand the union announces initially.

The outcome is not sensitive to government wage controls or guidelines, presumably because those programs modify both employers' offers and unions' demands. The outcome is closer to the union demand when unemployment is higher and inflation is more rapid.[12] Since it is highly improbable that higher unemployment enhances the union's bargaining power, we can infer that it reduces the union's initial demand by more than it reduces management's initial offer.

STRIKE ACTIVITY

One might conclude from the discussion thus far that strikes are a frequent occurrence in collective bargaining. As column (1) of Table 10.1 makes clear, this would be an erroneous inference. Only a tiny fraction of the work hours supplied in the United States are lost to industrial disputes. Even in 1959, the year that the greatest fraction of work time was lost to strikes since 1948, only 0.5 percent of workdays were lost, and the fraction of time lost has been decreasing. Moreover, only a small fraction of employed workers are involved in strikes in any particular year, as column (2) shows. Even accounting for the relatively low incidence of unionism in

[11] Daniel Hamermesh, "Who 'Wins' in Wage Bargaining?" *Industrial and Labor Relations Review* (26): 1146–1149 (1973), and Roger Bowlby and William Schriver, "Bluffing and the 'Split-the-difference' Theory of Wage Bargaining," *Industrial and Labor Relations Review* (31): 161–171 (1978).

[12] Jan Svejnar, "Bargaining Power, Fear of Disagreement and Wage Settlements," Working Paper No. 285, Cornell University Department of Economics, Ithaca, N.Y., 1982.

Table 10.1 WORK STOPPAGES, SELECTED YEARS, 1948–1981

Year	Percent of total work time lost (1)	Workers involved (percent of total employed) (2)	Average duration (days) (3)
1948	0.30	4.7	25.6
1955	0.22	5.2	18.5
1960	0.14	2.4	23.4
1969	0.24	3.5	22.5
1973	0.14	2.9	24.0
1975	0.16	2.2	26.8
1979	0.15	1.9	32.1
1980	0.14	1.5	35.4
1981	0.11	1.1	[a]

[a]Not available.

Source: Analysis of Work Stoppages, 1980, Table 1; U.S. Bureau of the Census, *Statistical Abstract of the United States, 1982–83,* p. 410.

the United States (below 25 percent), strikes are rare. In each year between 1979 and 1981, fewer than 10 percent of union members took part in a strike or were locked out by their employers.

The fraction of total work time lost to industrial disputes is determined by the numbers of workers going on strike and the average duration of strikes. The average duration appears to have increased somewhat in the last 20 years, suggesting that the picture of increasing industrial peace conveyed by the declines in work time lost and in the fraction of the unionized work force involved in strikes is not entirely correct. The average duration of strikes listed in the table is somewhat misleading, however, for the distribution of the duration of strikes is highly skewed. Between 1953 and 1974, 13 percent of strikes lasted only 1 day, and 38 percent lasted 5 days or less; only 13 percent lasted more than 50 days.[13] A large fraction of the strikes that do occur thus impose very little hardship on either party. They can be viewed more appropriately as extensions of the last minute bargaining that precedes the strike deadline than as the kind of strike analyzed in Figure 10.1.

POLICY ISSUE—UNEMPLOYMENT BENEFITS AND THE DURATION OF STRIKES

Nowhere in the United States can strikers receive unemployment benefits immediately after a strike or work stoppage begins. In two states, however, strikers become eligible for benefits after a strike has lasted some time, seven weeks in Rhode Island, eight weeks in New York. The payment of benefits incenses employers, who view themselves as subsidizing their bargaining opponents' losses (because their taxes finance the benefits). Union leaders, on the other hand, argue that after eight weeks the issue should be treated as one of lack of job availability for workers desiring employment, so that at that time strikers should be treated like any other unemployed workers.

The interesting economic question is what the payment of benefits after eight weeks does to the likelihood that a dispute will be settled. Once the ninth week of a strike begins, the willingness of the union membership to accept a settlement decreases, for the costs of

[13]John Kennan, "Pareto Optimality and the Economics of Strike Duration," *Journal of Labor Research* (1): 87 (1980).

continuing a strike are reduced. The provision of unemployment benefits changes relative bargaining power in the union's favor. Whether it prolongs strikes depends upon whether the bargainers perceive this change correctly. If they do, it will make the settlement more favorable to the union, but the likelihood of settling will be unaffected. If not, the law will retard the rate at which an agreement is reached.

Examining this by comparing strike duration between New York and the rest of the United States, one study found that strikes in New York that had already lasted eight weeks had a much lower probability of being settled each week thereafter than strikes elsewhere. One may infer that the payment of benefits increased the length of long-duration strikes. On the other hand, fewer strikes in New York than elsewhere lasted eight weeks or more. On average, no more days were lost to strikes in New York than in the rest of the United States, although the cost of strikes was probably higher because the proportion of long-duration strikes was greater.[14] Apparently some firms correctly perceive how the law will affect bargaining power after eight weeks of the strike have occurred, and settle before then, presumably giving up more than if the law did not exist. Other firms apparently do not perceive the changed costs correctly and take a still longer strike.

There is a truly remarkable diversity in strike behavior among industrialized countries, as Table 10.2 shows. In some countries, Italy and Sweden, for example, a large fraction of the work force is involved in strikes each year. However, neither there nor elsewhere is more than 0.5 percent of possible work time lost to industrial disputes; by inference, where the incidence of strike activity is high, the average duration of strikes is very short. Indeed, given the relatively small fraction of the work force involved in strikes in the United States (and in Canada also), the percent of work time lost is quite high. This implies that although strikes are relatively uncommon in North America, those that do occur are not quickly settled, as compared to Europe and Japan.

As the data in Table 10.1 suggest, strike activity in the United States is procyclical: The fraction of the work force involved in strikes is higher when unemployment is lower. The result generalizes to many other industrialized coun-

Table 10.2 INTERNATIONAL COMPARISON OF STRIKE ACTIVITY, 1980

Country	Percent of total work time lost[a]	Workers involved (percent of total employed)
United States	0.14	1.5
Canada	0.34	4.1
Japan	—	1.0
France	0.03	2.4
West Germany	0.002	0.2
Italy	0.32	67.2
Sweden	0.42	17.6
United Kingdom	0.20	3.4

[a]Assumes 250 workdays per year.

Source: Calculated from International Labor Organization, *Yearbook of Labor Statistics,* 1981, Tables 3, 28.

[14]John Kennan, "The Effect of Unemployment Insurance Payments on Strike Duration," in National Commission on Unemployment Compensation, *Unemployment Compensation: Studies and Research,* NCUC, Washington, 1981.

tries, including Canada, Australia, and the United Kingdom.[15] The fact that unions' bargaining power is procyclical is hardly surprising: When unemployment is low, employers have few alternative sources of labor other than their current workers. Why this greater bargaining power translates into more strikes, though, is not clear. If management correctly perceives that its bargaining power diminishes during a boom, it will grant more concessions to the union, but will be no more likely than at another time to take a strike. The fact that strikes are procyclical implies that the gap in perceptions of the other party's relative strength increases as the labor market tightens. Either the union overestimates the increase in its power, management underestimates the increase, or both. Since the union is the one that actually calls the strike, one may infer that it is overestimating the increase in its power.[16]

Cyclical indicators other than the unemployment rate are also positively correlated with strike activity. Indeed, if one accounts for firms' inventory accumulation, the impact of unemployment on strike activity is quite small.[17] Clearly, firms build up inventories in response to a strike threat by the union; larger inventories may reflect workers' as much as firms' behavior. Nonetheless, this result suggests that the procyclicality of strikes is in part the result of firms' and workers' misperceptions of how changing conditions in the product market rather than in the labor market alter relative bargaining power.

The pressure placed by union members on their leadership may also reflect the members' satisfaction with the gains they have made in prior negotiations and during the life of the current contract. To the extent that real wages are rising more rapidly, the leadership will feel less obligated to press for a large wage increase, as members are not pressuring the leadership for such increases as strongly as they might if inflation had eroded the purchasing power of the wages previously gained. If management, not perceiving the extent of the reduced pressures on union leaders, continues to bargain as if nothing had changed, the area of disagreement between the parties will be reduced. That this occurs is suggested by the lower strike activity, other things equal, in the United States and the United Kingdom in those times in the first half of the postwar period when real wages were rising more rapidly. Since 1965, however, the negative relationship between real wage increases and strike activity has broken down.[18]

Periods of wage controls or guidelines, such as those in effect in the United States from 1962 to 1966 and 1971 to 1974, reduce the range of possible wage outcomes over which unions and management can bargain. Although it is not clear that this reduction reduces the potential for differences in perceptions of the costs of a strike to the other party, this does seem likely. With the government suggesting an

[15] For the United States see Albert Rees, "Industrial Conflict and Business Fluctuations," *Journal of Political Economy* (60): 371–382 (1952); Ashenfelter and Johnson, loc. cit., and Kaufman, loc. cit. The foreign studies are John Vanderkamp, "Economic Activity and Strikes in Canada," *Industrial Relations* (9): 215–230 (1970); John Pencavel, "An Investigation into Industrial Strike Activity in Britain," *Economica* (37): 239–256 (1970); and Philip Bentley and Barry Hughes, "Cyclical Influence on Strike Activity: The Australian Record, 1952–1968," *Australian Economic Papers* (9): 149–170 (1970).

[16] Rees, loc. cit.

[17] Reder and Neumann, op. cit., p. 878.

[18] Ashenfelter and Johnson, loc. cit., and Pencavel, loc. cit.; contrary evidence is provided by Kaufman, loc. cit.

Table 10.3 WORK STOPPAGES BY INDUSTRY, 1980

Industry	Percent of total work time lost	Average duration (days)
Manufacturing	0.34	39.7
Agriculture, forestry and fisheries	0.03	12.0
Mining	0.73	23.2
Construction	0.43	20.2
Transportation, communications, and public utilities	0.14	16.0
Wholesale and retail trade	0.03	25.1
Finance, insurance, and real estate	0.005	46.3
Services	0.09	47.6
Government	0.06	13.9

Source: Analysis of Work Stoppages, 1980, Table 14.

acceptable wage increase, the possibilities for bluffing are reduced. The evidence suggests that this is what happens: The wage guidelines of 1962 to 1966 reduced strike activity, as did the various programs of wage controls in effect between 1971 and 1974.[19]

The discussion of the incidence of strike activity over time masks a great diversity in strike behavior among industries. Even accounting for differences in the extent of unionization this variety is truly enormous, as Table 10.3 shows. Strikes are far more common in mining, construction, and manufacturing than in other industries, and the number of days lost per unionized worker is higher there, too. Where the industry is heavily unionized (see Table 9.3), and where there are substantial investments in firm-specific skills, there is little chance that customers can find nonunion substitutes or that employers can readily substitute new employees for strikers. In other industries, such as services, finance, and wholesale and retail trade, nonunion substitutes are more readily available for union-provided services and products whose flow is interrupted by a strike. Also, new workers can be trained fairly quickly because there is little firm-specific investment. The only exceptions to these generalizations are government, transportation and utilities, which are relatively heavily unionized, yet there is little strike activity. A probable reason for the comparative absence of strikes is the existence of laws prohibiting strikes in government and of mechanisms designed to aid the parties in these industries in reaching a settlement without a strike.

This discussion and the data in Table 10.3 show that where the union's relative bargaining power is greater, the incidence of strikes is also greater. Why their greater power should induce more strikes, rather than simply resulting in employment, wage, and other outcomes more favorable to the union, is not clear. By inference, employers' awareness of the greater power of the unions that their workers form falls

[19] Ashenfelter and Johnson, loc. cit., and David Lipsky and Henry Farber, "The Composition of Strike Activity in the Construction Industry," *Industrial and Labor Relations Review* (29): 388–404 (1976).

further short of the unions' perceptions than in other industries. This does not explain why the incidence of strikes differs, however; it merely pushes the question back to a deeper level of ignorance.

THIRD-PARTY INTERVENTION IN NEGOTIATIONS

We have been assuming that strikes end because of rising costs to one or the other of the parties, and this is usually the case. In some cases, however, the costs to the public or to other third parties rise much faster than those to the parties involved in the labor dispute. This is particularly true when the output of the struck enterprise or industry is a service or a perishable product rather than a durable product. A strike against automobile producers could go on for months without seriously inconveniencing the public, which holds a large stock of usable cars. On the other hand, a strike of bus drivers has an immediate impact on the public, for there is no way of using stocks to buffer the impact.

When the costs of a strike to third parties become very high, government or other neutral intervention in the dispute usually occurs. Three kinds of neutral intervention are used—in increasing order of forcefulness—mediation (or conciliation), fact-finding, and binding arbitration.

The role of a *mediator* in a wage negotiation is often to discover through private talks with each party separately a position that is acceptable to both that they have been unwilling to reveal to each other. Essentially the mediator reduces uncertainty in the negotiations by giving each side a better understanding of the other's position. Since we saw earlier that imperfect information about the other party's costs of striking leads to strikes in the first place, mediation can reduce the chance of a strike occurring or shorten an ongoing strike. Another important function of a mediator is to help get talks started again when they have been broken off. Mediation in labor disputes is routinely provided by the federal government and many state governments without cost to the parties.

Sometimes the parties cannot reach a settlement through negotiation even with the aid of a mediator, and they may then resort to neutral *fact-finding* with public recommendations. The fact finder's job is to issue a public report detailing the conditions surrounding the dispute and suggesting an appropriate settlement. This step is included in the procedures of a number of states with laws regulating collecting negotiations for public employees. Fact-finding is invoked if mediation fails to resolve an impasse. In general, the weaker party to a dispute may be anxious to have third-party intervention such as fact-finding because of the hope that the recommendations will bolster its cause, although the stronger party may resist intervention as long as possible. Attitudes of the parties toward intervention may depend also on how the fact finder or arbitrator is to be chosen. Thus unions may favor fact-finding if a mayor or governor who is elected with union support is to choose the fact finder.

The term fact-finding is something of a misnomer, since fact finders cannot in the limited time available justify a wage recommendation by making a detailed investigation of the underlying economic positions of the parties, without reference to their bargaining positions. Usually they inquire into the attitudes of the parties in attempts to reach compromises that might be acceptable to both sides if they were presented to them by a neutral. Both parties may sometimes be willing to accept fact finders' awards because they do not have to take responsibility for them. For example, a union leader can tell the members that a fact finder's award is too small but that a strike against accepting the award would not be successful.

The last resort in the case of failure to reach agreement is *binding arbitration,* in which the parties agree in advance that the arbitrator's decision will be adopted. Because this involves giving up their freedom of action, the parties rarely consent to such a procedure. However, in some bargaining situations in which the social cost of a strike is viewed as high, such as police and fire protection, it is often stipulated by law that arbitration rather than resort to strikes will be used to resolve disputes.

The effects of third-party procedures on outcomes—wage increases and the incidence of strikes—are unclear. One study shows, however, that wages are between 0 and 6 percent higher in public employment where compulsory arbitration is the final stage of dispute resolution.[20] The problem in all such third-party procedures, but especially in arbitration, is to maintain the incentives for both parties to make concessions during negotiations, rather than to remain intransigent and to hope the arbitrator will split the difference between them. The arbitrator becomes one more party who relies on the informational signals that are conveyed by the negotiators, and thus one more party who may be bluffed into allowing a settlement more favorable to one party to the dispute. This is also possible even in fact-finding. The regular recourse to emergency boards in wage disputes under the Railway Labor Act has resulted in a situation in which the parties make few concessions in negotiations and collective bargaining has almost been destroyed. This resulting "narcotic effect" of third-party intervention has also been noted in negotiations by police and firefighters.[21] Its existence suggests that the outcomes of bargaining are less likely to reflect the underlying profit and utility-maximizing outcomes that the parties initially desired when third-party procedures are used. This view is supported by evidence on negotiations in both the private and public sectors in Canada: Wage settlements were less responsive to labor-market conditions in those negotiations that involved third-party procedures.[22]

POLICY ISSUE—FINAL OFFER ARBITRATION

As one way of restoring incentives for negotiators to make concessions, final offer arbitration has been used.[23] This ingenious scheme requires the arbitrator to choose one or the other of the two sides' final positions. By preventing the arbitrator from splitting the difference between final offers, supporters of the scheme hope it will induce negotiators to

[20] Craig Olson, "The Impact of Arbitration on the Wages of Firefighters," *Industrial Relations* (19): 323–339 (1980).

[21] Thomas Kochan and Jean Baderschneider, "Dependence on Impasse Procedures: Police and Firefighters in New York State," *Industrial and Labor Relations Review* (31): 431–439 (1978). Richard Butler and Ronald Ehrenberg, "Estimating the Narcotic Effect of Public Sector Impasse Procedures," *Industrial and Labor Relations Review* (35): 3–20 (1981), use complex methods to analyze the same issue and find a narcotic effect only in the first few years after the arbitration option became available.

[22] Douglas Auld, Louis Christofides, Robert Swidinsky, and David Wilton, "The Effect of Settlement Stage on Negotiated Wage Settlements in Canada," *Industrial and Labor Relations Review* (34): 234–244 (1981).

[23] Carl Stevens, "Is Compulsory Arbitration Compatible with Bargaining?" *Industrial Relations* (5): 38–52 (1966).

reduce bluffing and reach agreement more quickly, and more often, on their own. Final offer arbitration has been used in state statutes governing dispute settlement, particularly in negotiations involving police and fire protection and in professional sports.

There are two questions of interest in this scheme: Does it reduce conflict and result in quicker settlements? Does it consistently favor one side or the other to the bargaining? There is little direct evidence of the first question. On the second question, in New Jersey in 1978, 1979, and 1980, the union won over two-thirds of the final offer arbitration awards that were made. Whether this means the union was favored by the process or merely that the process affected its final offer more than that of management cannot be determined. The propensity of the arbitrators to select the union offer may have induced a decrease in the use of the procedure: Fewer cases went to final offer arbitration in 1979 and 1980 than in 1978. Similarly, in final offer arbitration between a professional baseball player and club owners, the player's offer is more likely to be selected, other things equal; and club owners have responded by reducing their reliance on the procedure.[24] The available evidence suggests that either final offer arbitration favors the unions, which seems difficult to believe, or it induces a greater moderation in their bargaining behavior than in that of management. Perhaps the union, recognizing that its past reputation for bluffing is greater than management's, moderates its position more in order to win the award.

GOVERNMENT AS A SOURCE OF UNION POWER

The entire discussion thus far has ignored the effects government can have on the bargaining power of the negotiating parties. This is clearly a gap, especially as we saw in Chapter 9 how political attitudes can effect the growth of unionization and presumably union power. In this section we first examine whether unions in the public sector have relatively more or less power than they would have if the same function were carried out privately, and then discuss ways in which private-sector unions try to obtain government help to enhance their bargaining power.

Until the 1960s, bargaining in government employment in the United States was rather different from bargaining in the private sector because government employees were not legally permitted to strike. The main bargaining power of government unions was exerted through political processes—lobbying and efforts in behalf of candidates favorable to union positions. This is still the general situation in the federal government, although there have been a few strikes and slowdowns on the part of postal employees and air traffic controllers.

In state and local employment, strikes are increasingly being used despite legal prohibitions and even fines and jail sentences for union leaders. Organizations of government employees that are not affiliated with the AFL-CIO, such as the National Education Association and the Patrolmen's Benevolent Association, have become like true trade unions. Most states provide by law for collective bargaining of public employees. In a few states, legal prohibitions on strikes have even been removed and replaced with a limited right to strike.

A government service financed by taxes (as distinguished from a government enterprise, like a transit system, that charges fares or similar prices for its services) has one great advantage over a private employer. Its flow of revenue is not halted by a

[24]Orley Ashenfelter and David Bloom, "Models of Arbitrator Behavior: Theory and Evidence," Working Paper No. 1149, National Bureau of Economic Research, Cambridge, Mass., 1983; and James Dworkin, *Owners versus Players: Baseball and Collective Bargaining,* Auburn House, Boston, 1981, pp. 166–173.

strike; taxes are collected as usual. On the other hand, government negotiators face a number of important disadvantages. The union can use political pressures as well as the threat of a strike to win its demands. Government officials may partly owe their jobs to the political support they received from the unions with which they negotiate. The government cannot move to another location to escape union demands nor can it go out of business if union demands are completely unreasonable. Indeed, a number of government enterprises in such areas as transit were originally taken over by government because previous private owners could not operate profitably and pay union wages. All these considerations suggest that unions in the public sector face a demand schedule that is less elastic than that facing unions in the private sector, although the evidence on this is by no means clear. (Compare, e.g., the demand schedules in Figs. 6.2 and 6.3.) Unions in the same industry in the public sectors may have more bargaining power than if the function is transferred to the private sector. Only slightly higher wages are received in government-owned unionized local transit lines than in those operated privately. On the other hand, unionized municipal sanitation workers receive much higher wages than do those in private firms.[25]

Unions in the private sector are also heavily and increasingly involved in activities with government. Until the 1920s the American trade union movement practiced a philosophy of *voluntarism*, shunning aid from government in the belief that on net legislation would be detrimental to union interests. With the increased role of the government in the U.S. economy, this philosophy has long since been abandoned, and lobbying and support to political candidates in the form of contributions of money and volunteer time are made by union members. In the 1981 to 1982 biennium in the United States, union members donated $20.8 million to congressional candidates alone, mostly through political action committees. Although a large amount, this was much less than business groups provided; unions' more important contributions were the volunteer efforts of their members.

As with most other political donations, unions' contributions are not merely charity provided with no hope of return. Candidates thought to support prounion positions are given extra help; and the help is provided in the hope that the candidate will, if elected, oppose legislation that the union opposes and be more amenable to prounion legislation. Unions have recently lobbied heavily against efforts to restrict *common situs* picketing—the ability of construction craft unions to set up picket lines at a large construction site and halt work by craft workers in many trades when only one trade is involved in a dispute. Such picketing expands the power of an individual craft by enabling it to impose higher costs on the employer. Attempts to prevent the passage of right-to-work laws, and to repeal those already passed, are designed to reduce the possibility of competition from nonunion output. Union political activity often consists of efforts to push legislation restricting competition from low-wage, nonunion labor or from imports. Higher minimum wages, which we saw in Chapter 4 reduce the competition from young workers (who are unlikely to be

[25] Daniel Hamermesh, "The Effect of Government Ownership on Union Wages," in Hamermesh (ed.). *Labor in the Public and Nonprofit Sectors,* Princeton University Press, Princeton, N.J., 1975, and Linda Edwards and Franklin Edwards, "Wellington-Winter Revisited: The Case of Municipal Sanitation Collection," *Industrial and Labor Relations Review* (35): 307–318 (1982).

unionized), is probably the most obvious example. Unions' financial support for candidates was associated with a greater likelihood of a prounion vote on the minimum wage amendments of 1974; and states that are more heavily unionized are more likely to have a state minimum wage law, and one with a high legislated minimum.[26]

POLICY ISSUE—THE DAVIS-BACON ACT

Some of the most intense defensive lobbying by unions in the United States in recent years has been in support of the Davis-Bacon Act of 1931. This law requires the payment of "prevailing wages" to workers employed by contractors who are engaged on construction projects financed by the federal government. Supporters of the legislation argue that this takes labor out of competition among contractors bidding on government projects; it prevents the federal government from trying to act like a monopsonist in the market for construction labor.

The difficulty with the legislation lies in the concept of prevailing wages in a craft within a labor market. The "prevailing wage" is determined by the U.S. Department of Labor according to various formulas. The determination is not based on the average wage in a craft in a locality: One study found that over 90 percent of determinations equaled the union wage rate in the area (although nonunion construction accounted for large fractions of total construction work in many areas). Another set of estimates suggests that Davis-Bacon determinations are 4 percent higher than average wages in commercial construction and 9 percent higher than the average in residential construction.[27] This difference is consistent with formulas based on union wages, since commercial construction is more heavily unionized than residential construction.

Rather than acting as a monopsonist in the market for construction labor, the federal government goes to the opposite extreme under the administration of the Davis-Bacon Act. Federally supported construction projects usually pay wages as high or higher than those paid elsewhere in the labor market to workers of the particular craft. Aside from raising the cost of federally supported construction, this raises costs in the private sector as well through spillovers of wages from high-wage government construction. The difficulty in reforming the system is to find a middle ground that would prevent monopsonistic exploitation while at the same time preventing the policy from being used, as it now is, to support union wages in construction. Determinations of prevailing wages should be based on what an average wage would be in the absence of the government-supported project. Finding this middle ground is not easy, and union leaders fear that abandonment of the present system will mean a move to the other extreme of paying the lowest wage in government construction.

SUMMARY

Union-management bargaining is best understood as a continuing relationship involving the two parties, the union members, and increasingly the government. The greater the ability of the union is to inflict damage on management by reducing

[26] Jonathan Silberman and Garey Durden, "Determining Legislative Preferences on the Minimum Wage: An Economic Approach," *Journal of Political Economy* (84): 317–329 (1976), and James Cox and Ronald Oaxaca, "The Political Economy of Minimum Wage Legislation," *Economic Inquiry* (20): 533–555 (1982).

[27] A summary of these studies is provided by Robert Goldfarb and John Morrall, "The Davis-Bacon Act: An Appraisal of Recent Studies," *Industrial and Labor Relations Review* (34): 191–206 (1981).

profits, the greater will be its power; the more that management can reduce the range of alternative sources of income to union members, the greater will be the likelihood of management achieving its goals during bargaining. Although the relative strengths of the parties determine what compensation will be compared to that in similar nonunion situations, they do not determine the path of negotiations nor whether they will be settled peacefully. That depends on each side's reactions to the other's demands, and in general, on the ability of each to discern correctly what the other side is really seeking when it makes its demands.

Despite the attention focused on strikes, they are relatively rare in industrialized countries. In the United States, fewer than 10 percent of unionized workers go out on strike in most years and far less than 1 percent of available work time is lost. The cost of strikes to society is far less than the loss in wages or output in the struck firm. The outcomes of strikes and of collective negotiations that do not result in a strike can be affected by third-party procedures that are designed to resolve industrial conflicts. Whether these procedures benefit society by reducing the resources lost to industrial conflict is not known.

chapter 11

Unions' Effects on Labor Markets

AN OVERVIEW

In the previous two chapters we examined the motives that lead different workers to join unions and studied the methods unions use to achieve the goals of their members. Prominent among these goals is higher wages. This chapter will examine the extent to which unions achieve this goal, how their success has varied over time, and how much the wages of different union members are improved by unionism. As we saw in Chapters 1 to 8, changes in labor costs change employers' incentives to hire labor and workers' incentives to remain with the firm. We therefore examine the extent to which union-imposed changes in relative wages affect employment and mobility.

Let us first consider the data in Table 11.1 (based on the May 1980 Current Population Survey). The table lists for a standard workweek the average earnings of workers classified by industry or occupation and whether or not their wages are determined by collective bargaining. The last column is headed M, the symbol we use for the unadjusted effect of unions on relative wages. M is the percentage difference between columns (1) and (2):

$$M = 100 \times \frac{W_u - W_n}{W_n}$$

Overall, as the bottom line of the table shows, unionized workers do have higher weekly earnings than nonunionized workers. Through the bargaining process, backed by the use or threat of the strike, unions raised the wages of their members relative to other workers. Yet using the figures for M presented in the table is likely to give a very inaccurate picture of the effect of unions. It is difficult to believe, for

Table 11.1 AVERAGE USUAL WEEKLY EARNINGS OF FULL-TIME EMPLOYEES, MAY 1980

Occupation or industry	Represented by a union (1)	Not represented by a union (2)	M (3)
Occupation			
Professional, etc.	$349	$371	−6
Managers and administrators	450	400	12
Clerical	281	215	30
Craft	369	309	19
Operatives	295	221	34
Nonfarm laborers	290	202	43
Service workers	255	174	47
Industry			
Construction	405	284	42
Manufacturing	303	309	−2
Transportation, communications, and public utilities	359	330	9
Wholesale and retail trade	292	222	32
Services	291	255	14
Public administration	348	311	12
Total	320	278	15

Source: Earnings and Other Characteristics of Organized Workers, Bulletin No. 2105, Tables 10, 11.

example, that unions actually lower the relative wage rates of unionized manufacturing workers, as the figure −2 percent in column (3) of Table 11.1 would suggest. This highly anomalous number indicates that a much more careful study of the effects of unions on wages is required than is provided by simple calculations of M such as those in Table 11.1.

MEASURING UNION-NONUNION WAGE DIFFERENTIALS

The basic difficulty in estimating unions' impact on earnings arises because we cannot observe what the earnings of unionized workers would be if they were not in a union and in the absence of unions anywhere else in the economy. The *wage gain* that could result from such a comparison would be the best measure of how unions affect the wage received by the individual worker. It cannot be observed because we cannot perform the experiment of suddenly imposing unions on some sectors of a previously nonunion economy and measuring what happens to the wages of the workers who become unionized. Failing this, we attempt to measure the adjusted union *wage gap,* the percentage difference between the wage rates of two otherwise identical union and nonunion workers. The trick in measuring this gap is to adjust for as many differences as possible between union and nonunion workers, other than union status, that might affect their wage rates.[1]

[1] The distinction between the wage gain and gap is analyzed by H. Gregg Lewis, in *Union Relative Wage Effects: A Survey,* Unpublished Manuscript, Duke University, 1982, chap. 2.

Threat and Spillover Effects

Even if we account for all such differences, however, the adjusted wage gap is unlikely to measure the wage gain very accurately. A number of factors may cause the adjusted wage gap to underestimate the wage gain. Some nonunion employers may raise their wages because unionized workers have won wage increases. Usually, nonunion employers raise their wages to reduce the probability that a union will organize their employees. In some cases they will pay their workers the full union rate and yet will prefer to remain nonunion, because this gives them greater flexibility in personnel policies and because their plants can operate while union plants are on strike. There is a similar gain from the absence of strikes to the workers in the nonunion plant. They also save the cost of union dues, although they lose the services the union provides in such areas as processing grievances and establishing and enforcing seniority rights. The positive effect of unions on nonunion earnings is called the *threat effect,* a term that indicates the threat of successful organization of the nonunion employer whose wages lag. Such direct threats are not the only way in which union wage gains can raise the wages paid by nonunion employers. In a tight labor market, nonunion employers may raise wages in response to increases in the union rate in order to compete with union employers in recruiting labor.

If we attempt to estimate the impact of collective bargaining by comparing wages in union and nonunion establishments in the same industry and locality, we will certainly underestimate it because of the threat effect; we may even find it to be zero. We are therefore forced to make wider comparisons, perhaps among cities, which leads to a greater need for corrections for differences between the groups of employees being compared. Even this device does not remove threat effects entirely, for employers in one city might feel threatened by the growth of unions in another.

The discussion thus far has suggested that estimates of the union wage gap are likely to be smaller than the true gain. However, not all the biases run in this direction. When unions impose high wages on employers, the employers respond in part by selecting workers who are better qualified than those they could attract at the lower wage. Much of the difference in quality cannot be measured when we try to estimate the adjusted wage gap. Some characteristics of workers that make them more attractive to employers—such as education or experience (and hence general on-the-job training)—are easily measured and available in the sets of data that economists use to standardize wage differences among workers. Other factors that make one group of workers more attractive to employers than another are not readily measurable. Chief among these are the indications the workers provide of such personal traits as native intelligence, willingness to work, and punctuality. All of these, when they are apparent to the employer, add to workers' productivity and justify hiring workers with these traits when unions impose a higher wage, yet none can be observed by economists who use statistical data to adjust M.

For the economy as a whole a higher union wage may actually reduce the nonunion wage, also causing the estimated adjusted wage gap to overestimate the wage gain to unionism. We have seen how threat effects can cause nonunion firms within an industry or a product market to respond to higher union wages by raising the wages they offer. The opposite effect can also occur among firms that are in entirely separate product markets or in geographical areas far from the unionized firms on which a wage increase has been imposed. In Figure 11.1(a) we show the impact of unionization on employment in union firms (or in nonunion firms that raise wages because of the threat effect). The real wage is increased from W_0 to W_u; the downward-sloping demand for labor ensures that employment in the affected firms falls from E_0 to E_u. This increases the supply of labor to the rest of the economy by an amount shown by the horizontal distance AB in Figure 11.1(a). In terms of the discussion in Chapter 9 of the demand and supply for union jobs, CR is the length of the queue that must be rationed. The workers who would otherwise have been employed in unionized firms seek jobs in nonunion establishments, shifting the supply curve in Figure 11.1(b) from S to S′. Their competition with workers who are already working or seeking jobs in the nonunion sector checks the rise in nominal wages there, driving real wage rates in the nonunion sector down from W_0 to W_n.[2] (This decline will occur as long as the supply curve is not horizontal.) This *spillover effect* means that when we calculate the wage gap as $100 \times (W_u - W_n/W_n)$, the percentage difference in wages between the two sectors, we overstate the true wage gain, which is $100 \times (W_u - W_0)/W_0$.

Whether the threat effect and the other effects that cause the measured wage gap to understate the wage gain exceed the effects of wage spillovers and the unmeasured workers' characteristics that induce an upward bias to the estimated wage gap is unclear. All we can know is that all these potential effects do exist and that estimates of $\overline{M}$, the *adjusted union wage gap,* that account for them are likely to be better than those that do not. By the very nature of the problem, though, no estimate of $\overline{M}$ will measure the union wage gain precisely, for none can account for all the potential biases we have discussed.

Simple Techniques for Measuring Wage Gaps

Three simple approaches to estimating $\overline{M}$ using cross-section data have been developed. The *intercity method* examines the wages of workers within an occupation in different cities among which the extent of unionization in the occupation differs. In such studies other factors that affect the general level of wages in the cities are accounted for. The *aggregate method* examines the average wage rates of unionized and nonunionized plants within an industry, or compares wages in heavily unionized industries to those in industries in which the extent of unionism is less. Similar studies are based upon occupations rather than upon industries. Such studies also account for other factors that affect wage differences among industries. Thus, for example, differences in education must be considered in adjusting the value of M (minus 6 percent) that is shown in Table 11.1 for professional workers. Undoubtedly those who are unionized in this occupation have less schooling than nonunion professional workers. Among professional workers very few doctors and lawyers are unionized, whereas some nurses and other workers who have not gone beyond

[2]Some evidence of a spillover effect is in Lawrence Kahn, "The Effect of Unions on the Earnings of Nonunion Workers," *Industrial and Labor Relations Review* (31): 205–216 (1978).

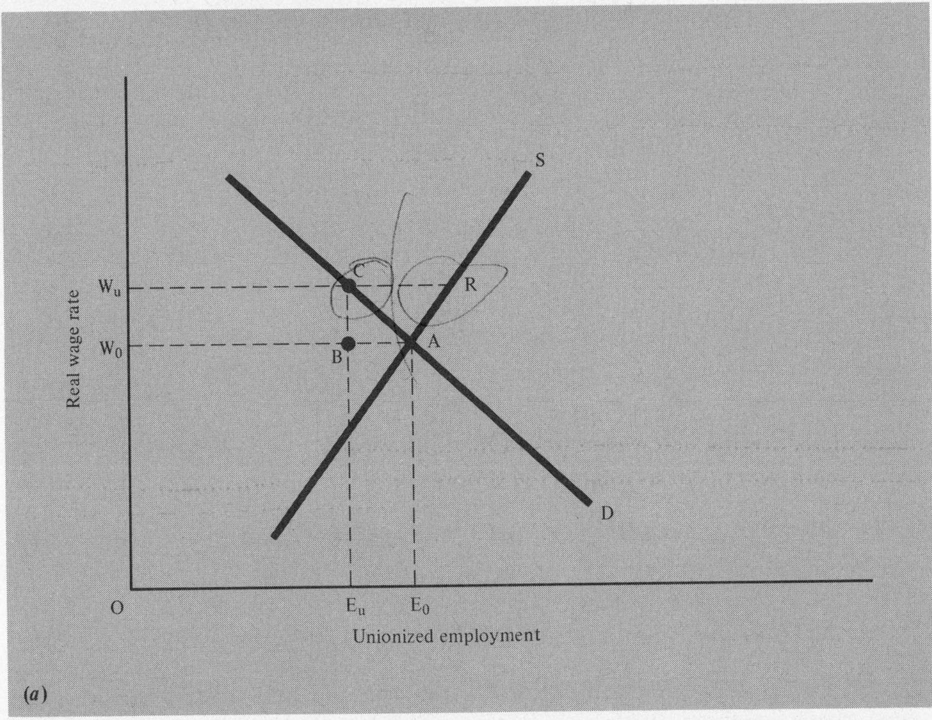

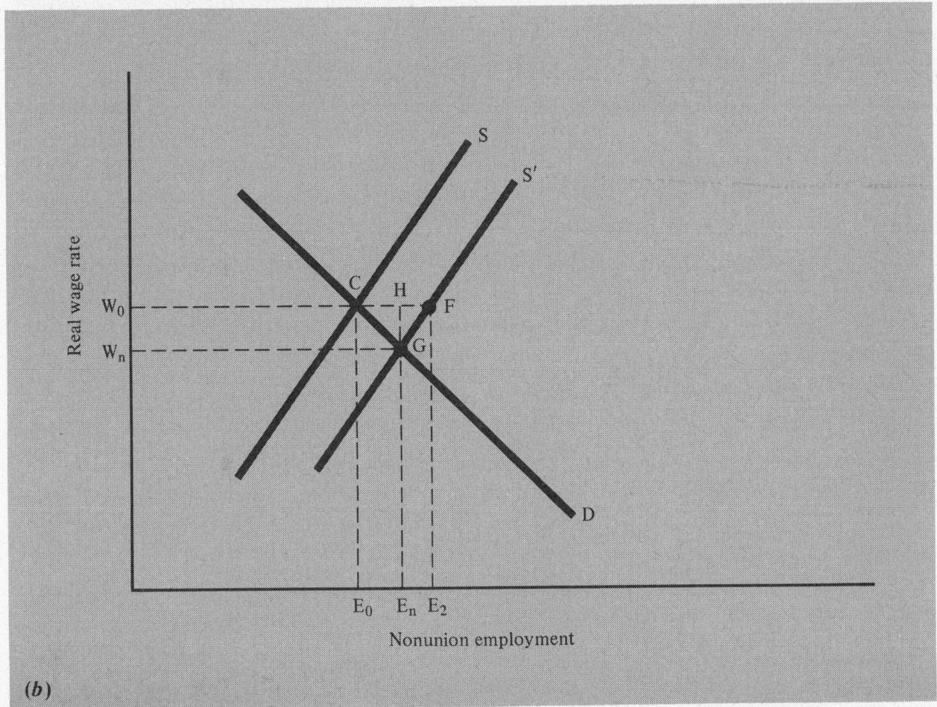

Figure 11.1 (a) Wage spillovers—the union sector; (b) wage spillovers—the nonunion sector.

college are union members. The third approach, the *individual method,* obtains data on the characteristics of large numbers of individuals, information that includes whether or not they belong to a union or have their wages determined by collective bargaining. This approach has been used most recently, as massive samples of data on individuals have been collected, and as the decreasing cost of analyzing these samples using computer technology has made the approach feasible.[3]

Among these three approaches to measuring wage gaps using cross-section data, the individual method is likely to be the most reliable. The intercity approach will often produce estimates that are contaminated by spillovers from wages in heavily unionized cities to wages in less heavily unionized cities. The aggregate method is also inherently incapable of accounting for the extent of spillovers. The individual method does not completely avoid inducing biases to the estimates of $\overline{M}$ because of spillovers, but this problem is reduced.

Widely differing estimates of $\overline{M}$ have been obtained by researchers using these three simple approaches.[4] Obviously the estimates will differ, depending on such factors as what industries or occupations are being analyzed, the year when wages are measured, and the demographic composition of workers who form the samples used in the third approach. Nevertheless, for the United States the estimates of $\overline{M}$ using data covering a broad range of workers (mostly utilizing the aggregate and individual methods) cluster between 10 and 25 percent. Not accounting for all the potential biases that may cause the adjusted wage gap to differ from the wage gain, we may infer tentatively that these simple methods show that the typical union in the United States raises wages by at least 15 percent. This conclusion should be modified, though, to account for the biases we have discussed if more complex methods allow us to resolve the problems with the simple approaches to estimating $\overline{M}$.

Estimates of $\overline{M}$, using these same three simple approaches, have been made for countries other than the United States. One study estimated that the adjusted wage gap in Canada in the early 1970s was 16 percent. Studies using the aggregrate approach to analyze data for the United Kingdom from various time periods show that the adjusted wage gap is between 10 and 30 percent. Only for West Germany is there no sign of a positive wage gap.[5] This may be because unions in continental Europe are more interested in political goals than their Anglo-Saxon counterparts, so that less of their energy is devoted to achieving wages above those of nonmembers in

[3]Two studies that use the intercity approach are Melvin Lurie, "The Effect of Unionization on Wages in the Transit Industry," *Journal of Political Economy* (69): 558–572 (1961), and Joseph Scherer, "The Union Impact on Wages: The Case of the Year-Round Hotel Industry," *Industrial and Labor Relations Review* (9): 213–224 (1956). The aggregate approach is developed in H. Gregg Lewis, *Unions and Relative Wages in the United States,* University of Chicago Press, Chicago, 1963. The individual approach underlies much of the work summarized in George Johnson, "Economic Analysis of Trade Unionism," American Economic Association, *Proceedings* (65): 23–28 (1975).

[4]Lewis, *Unionism and Relative Wages . . .* , loc. cit., and Lewis, *Union Relative Wage Effects . . .* , loc. cit.

[5]Glenn MacDonald and John Evans, "The Size and Structure of Union-Nonunion Wage Differences in Canadian Industry," *Canadian Journal of Economics* (14): 227 (1981); Charles Mulvey, "Collective Agreements and Relative Earnings in U.K. Manufacturing in 1973," *Economica* (43): 419–427 (1976); David Metcalf, "Unions, Incomes Policy and Relative Wages in Britain," *British Journal of Industrial Relations* (15): 157–175 (1977); and Jan Svejnar, "Relative Wage Effects of Unions, Dictatorship and Codetermination: Econometric Evidence from Germany," *Review of Economics and Statistics* (63): 188–197 (1981).

comparable workplaces. Also, German law extends some union wage gains to nonunion firms within an industry.

Complex Techniques for Measuring Wage Gaps

The difficulty with the estimates of $\overline{M}$ based on the simple approaches is that unmeasured differences in human capital are not accounted for. One way of considering this problem is to attempt to standardize for the determinants of who joins unions. As we saw in Chapter 9, there are vast differences among demographic groups, industries, and occupations in the incidence of unionism. Being measurable, these can be accounted for when using the three simple approaches to estimating $\overline{M}$. But the unmeasurable characteristics of workers will also differ between union and nonunion workers. Employers try to improve the quality of their work force in response to union wage gaps by choosing the most capable workers from among those in the queue for union jobs. Accounting for this positive correlation of union status and worker quality should go part way to removing one of the factors that induces an upward bias in $\overline{M}$. One analysis, utilizing the individual approach to examine the wages of middle-aged men in 1969 and 1971, considered which workers obtain jobs in union workplaces and found that $\overline{M}$ is only two-thirds as large when this bias is removed. An examination of data on wage differentials, using the aggregrate approach to study data from the 1960 Census of Population, suggests a similar smaller adjusted wage gap when interindustry differences in the ways in which worker quality is related to union status are accounted for.[6]

As we noted at the outset of this section, the problem in estimating the union wage gain stems from an inability to observe the union worker's wage in the absence of unionism. Although we cannot observe union wages in the absence of unionism anywhere in the economy, recent advances in the kinds of data available permit us to go further in solving the problem of unmeasured worker characteristics. These *longitudinal data* provide information on the same individuals for a number of years, essentially following them over some segment of their work lives.[7] Since people move in and out of unionized jobs over the years, the data can be used to examine how workers' wages change when they enter unionized employment from nonunion jobs, or vice versa. Assuming underlying characteristics—particularly motivation, work effort, and other unmeasured traits—do not change when they change union status, longitudinal data on workers who leave or join unions allow us in principle to account for the upward biases in $\overline{M}$ that result from our inability to account for unmeasurable differences in characteristics among workers.

In terms of the schematic in Figure 11.2, this approach assumes that any

[6] Gregory Duncan and Duane Leigh, "Wage Determination in the Union and Nonunion Sectors: A Sample Selectivity Approach," *Industrial and Labor Relations Review* (34): 24–34 (1980), and Orley Ashenfelter and George Johnson, "Unionism, Relative Wages, and Labor Quality in U.S. Manufacturing Industries," *International Economic Review* (13): 488–508 (1972).

[7] The most widely used of these sets of data are the Panel Study of Income Dynamics, with annual information on 5000 families, beginning in 1968, collected by the Survey Research Center of the University of Michigan, and the National Longitudinal Surveys, four separate samples (of young men, young women, middle-aged women, and older men) collected, beginning in 1966, by the Center for Human Resource Research of the Ohio State University.

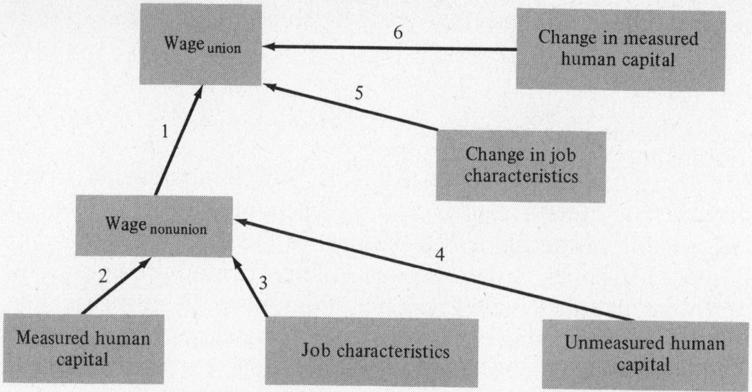

Figure 11.2 Schematic of the longitudinal approach to measuring the wage gap.

unmeasurable individual characteristics affect the workers' wages the same regardless of their union status. Thus all unmeasurable effects are reflected in the wage in a nonunion job; the only things that change when workers obtain union jobs are their measured human capital and the jobs' characteristics. Data on workers' past wages (in nonunion jobs) account for causal paths 2 to 4 in Figure 11.2. Causal paths 5 and 6 can be accounted for by examining how workers' skills and the job requirements change when they move from nonunion to union jobs. Causal path 1 in Figure 11.2 thus allows us to measure $\overline{M}$ while abstracting from unmeasured characteristics of workers. The problem is solved *if* those unmeasured traits or the returns to them do not themselves change when workers change union status. But even longitudinal studies have their difficulties. Some recorded changes may actually result from errors in the data.

Table 11.2 shows a number of estimates of adjusted union wage gaps that are

Table 11.2 UNION WAGE GAPS (IN PERCENT)

Group (1)	Years observed (2)	Method of estimating $\overline{M}$: Individual data (3)	Method of estimating $\overline{M}$: Longitudinal data (4)
Men 14–24 in 1966	1969–1971	21	12–13
White men 45–59 in 1966	1969, 1971	8–9	2–4
Nonfarm workers	1977–1978	20–21	7
Men age 65 or less	1967–1977	22–34	7–9

Source: Based on H. Gregg Lewis, *Union Relative Wage Effects: A Survey,* Unpublished Manuscript, Duke University, 1982, chap. 5. The underlying studies are: Row 1: Gary Chamberlain, "Panel Data," Working Paper No. 8209, Social Science Research Institute, Madison, Wisc., 1982; Row 2: Jacob Mincer, "Union Effects: Wages, Turnover and Job Training," Working Paper No. 808, National Bureau of Economic Research, Cambridge, Mass., 1981; Row 3: Wesley Mellow, "Unionism and Wages: A Longitudinal Analysis," *Review of Economics and Statistics* (63): 48–49 (1981); and Row 4: William Moore and John Raisian, "Unionism and Wage Rates in the Public and Private Sectors," Unpublished Paper, Miami University, 1981.

produced by using the microdata and longitudinal methods. Most of these estimates account for measurable changes, such as in occupation or industry, that accompany a change in union status and that are shown in paths 5 and 6 in Figure 11.2. Comparing the estimates in column (4) to the estimates of $\overline{M}$ in column (3) that are produced by the simple individual method, we find that the former are in general much lower than those estimates of the wage gap that do not standardize for unmeasured characteristics. The picture that emerges from columns (3) and (4) is that the *true adjusted union wage gap for male workers in the American economy is probably between 5 and 10 percent.* This is lower than the estimates of $\overline{M}$ that are usually produced by the three simple approaches. Apparently unionized firms compensate for imposed wage increases by hiring workers with more desirable unobserved traits.

As we noted, the longitudinal approach is valid only to the extent that unmeasurable characteristics do not change when the worker switches between the union and nonunion sectors and that the payoff to the unmeasurable characteristics is the same in both sectors. Although the first of these assumptions obviously cannot be tested, the second has been examined by using data on young men in 1969 and 1971 (the same data on which the study in row 1 of Table 11.2 is based). Accounting for the possibility that unmeasured factors have different effects in the union and nonunion sectors apparently induces only tiny changes in the estimates of $\overline{M}$ that are produced by using longitudinal data.[8]

This discussion seems to suggest that there is one wage gap that is applicable to each industry or occupation regardless of the union's success in organizing the workers. This is not likely to be the case; there is reason to suppose that the adjusted wage gap is related to the fraction of workers in the occupation or industry who are organized. The nature of this relation is shown in Figure 11.3. When the portion of the market organized is very small, the union will generally have little effect. If wages are an important element in costs, attempts to raise the wages paid by the few union employers much above the level paid by their competitors will put union employers at a severe disadvantage in selling their product. This will both strengthen their resistance to union pressure and encourage the union to moderate its demands. In such cases the union has relatively little bargaining power. At the opposite end of the horizontal scale, the union will approach its maximum effect on relative earnings well before it reaches 100 percent organization because of the strength of the threat to organize the few remaining nonunion firms. It is in the middle range of extent of organization that the most rapid gains in relative wages are likely to occur as the percent of workers in the industry or occupation who are unionized increases. Thus in 1973 to 1975 unionized manufacturing production workers in industries that were completely unionized received wages 15 percent above those paid to similar workers in union establishments in industries that were almost entirely nonunion.[9]

[8] Mark Stewart, "The Estimation of Union Wage Differentials from Panel Data: The Problem of Not-so-Fixed Effects," Unpublished Paper, Princeton University, 1983.

[9] Sherwin Rosen, "Trade Union Power, Threat Effects, and the Extent of Organization," *Review of Economic Studies* (36): 185–196 (1969), and Richard Freeman and James Medoff, "The Impact of the Percentage Organized on Union and Nonunion Wages," *Review of Economics and Statistics* (63): 561–572 (1981).

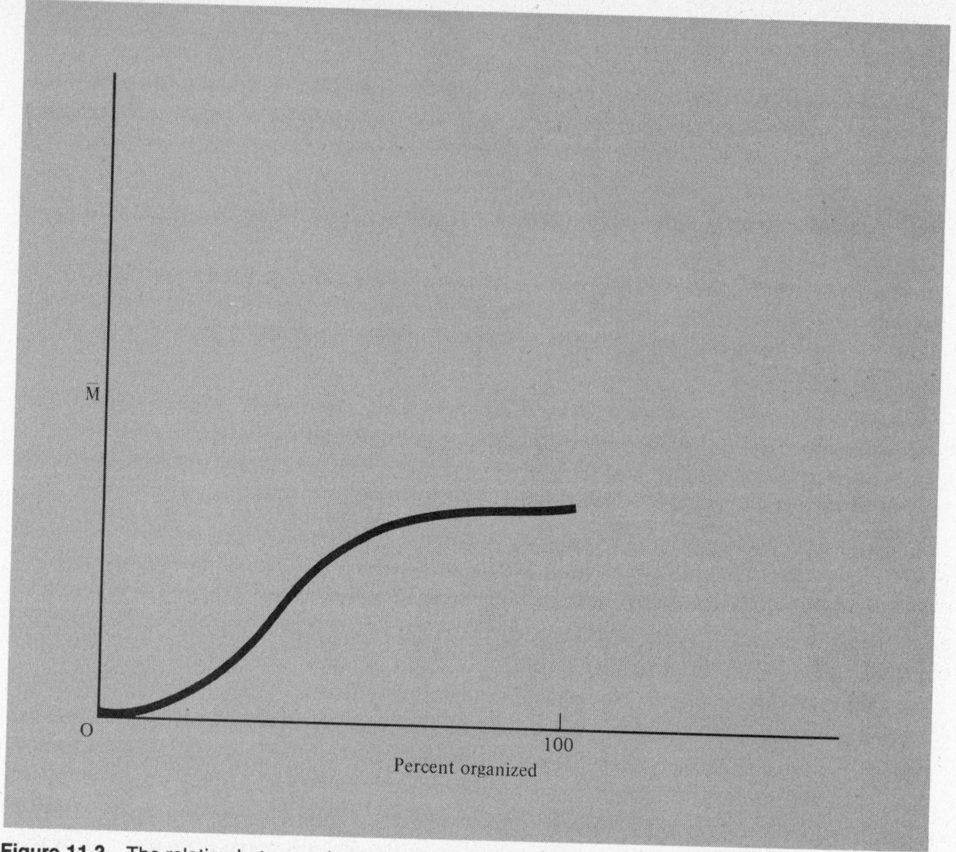

Figure 11.3 The relation between degree of organization and the adjusted union wage gap.

POLICY ISSUE—DO UNIONS RAISE PROFESSORS' WAGES?

In the United States, a large number of college and university professors have their wages and working conditions determined by collective bargaining. In the academic year 1976 to 1977, for example, nearly one-sixth of the over 1200 schools examined in one study had faculty wages determined through collective bargaining. The adjusted union wage gap, calculated by using the intercity approach, ranged in the sample of schools between 3 and 10 percent in 1970 to 1976.[10] Although smaller than the estimates of the economy-wide adjusted union wage gap that we have discussed, these estimates are large enough to suggest a substantial payoff to professors who become organized.

As with the estimates for the economy as a whole, so, too, among professors there may be unmeasured, productivity-increasing characteristics whose incidence is correlated with the likelihood of being unionized. Unlike most industries in the United States, the growth of unionism in higher education came fairly recently. This permits the collection of data before and after unionization occurred. These longitudinal data on four-year colleges and universities show that schools at which professors were better paid than professors with identical measured characteristics at other schools in the same region were more likely to

[10]Richard Freeman, "Should We Organize? Effects of Faculty Unionism on Academic Compensation," Working Paper No. 301, National Bureau of Economic Research, Cambridge, Mass., 1978.

have become unionized in the late 1960s or early 1970s. (This seems to contradict the general findings on the determinants of the extent of unionism that we discussed in Chap. 9.) Accounting for the incidence of unionization in relation to salaries before unionization, we find that the adjusted relative wage gap is between 0 and 5 percent. The gains to unionization are far smaller than simple methods of calculation would suggest.

VARIATION THROUGH TIME IN UNION WAGE EFFECTS

The effects of unions on earnings are not uniform through time. Collective bargaining not only raises wages, but it makes them more rigid by fixing them for definite periods. The length of the typical American collective agreement is from one to three years. Many agreements of more than one year provide for annual reopenings for adjustment of wages only or provide during the life of the agreement for wage increases whose size is determined in advance (deferred increases). As we saw in Chapter 10, other agreements base increases on movements in the Consumer Price Index (contain COLAs).

The existence of long-duration contracts has quite different consequences at different phases of the business cycle. In some circumstances it holds union wages up. During the early phases of a depression, collective bargaining agreements can keep union wages constant while wages elsewhere are falling. In periods of moderate prosperity and stable prices, unions may win more frequent wage increases than are offered by nonunion employers. On the other hand, in booms and periods of rapid inflation the rigidity of union wages that are not indexed to the cost of living becomes a disadvantage, and nonunion employers may raise wages more frequently than union employers. This disadvantage is overcome if, as in the late 1970s, the indexation of union wages is widespread. Indeed, if the inflation is accompanied by slow economic growth (stagflation), unionized workers may improve their relative position. In general, if the size of the union relative wage gap is considered normal or average in periods of moderate prosperity and generally stable prices, then it tends to be abnormally large in depressions. If the extent of inflation or deflation is correctly anticipated at the time of contract agreements by the parties to wage negotiations, then the size of wage changes can be adjusted to correct for their infrequency. Even if inflation is not anticipated, indexation of contracts provides many unionized workers protection of their relative wage advantage over nonunion workers in times of rapid unanticipated inflation.

Table 11.3 presents estimates of the adjusted union relative wage gap for five-year periods, beginning in 1920, along with the unemployment rate for each period. The estimates for 1920 to 1954 are based on time-series data that show variations in the relative wage rates between two broad groups of industries, one highly unionized for much of the period and the other always substantially nonunion. For 1955 to 1982 the estimates of $\overline{M}$ are based on comparisons of changes in relative wages to the rates of unionization by industry. (Essentially the aggregate method of measuring the wage gap is used to produce all the estimates presented in Table 11.3.)

The table shows a dramatic increase in the size of the union wage effect during the depression of the 1930s. No doubt this stemmed from the downward wage

Table 11.3 ESTIMATES OF THE EFFECT OF UNIONS ON RELATIVE WAGES, 1920–1982

Period	$\overline{M}$	Unemployment rate
1920–1924	17	7.3[a]
1925–1929	26	5.0
1930–1934	46	16.4
1935–1939	22	16.8
1940–1944	6	6.5
1945–1949	2	3.9
1950–1954	12	4.0
1955–1959	17	5.0
1960–1964	17	5.7
1965–1969	11	3.8
1970–1974	14	5.4
1975–1979	23	7.0
1980–1982	27	8.1

[a] 1922 to 1924 only.

Source: $\overline{M}$: George Johnson, "Unionism in a Macroeconomic Context," Unpublished Paper, University of Michigan, 1983. Unemployment Rate: Before 1940, from Robert Coen, "Labor Force and Unemployment in the 1920s and 1930s," *Review of Economics and Statistics* (55) (1973), Table 2; and 1940 to 1982, Current Population Survey data.

ridigity in union contracts, coupled with the drop in the level of prices that helped lower nonunion nominal wages. The table also shows a sharp decline in the union effect during World War II and the immediate postwar period. This seems to reflect the failure of unions and management to anticipate fully the duration of the wartime and postwar inflation and the absence of contracts with escalator classes. After 1950 the estimated effect of unions grew, reaching 17 percent in 1955 to 1959. During the period of relatively high unemployment in the early 1960s, the relative wage gap increased again, but with the accelerating inflation of the late 1960s and early 1970s it fell slightly.[11] The long-term nature of union contracts, underestimates of the rate of inflation, and the small number of indexed contracts caused union wage rates to rise more slowly than nonunion wages. In the late 1970s, unemployment remained relatively high even during the cyclical recovery, union members' expectations of inflation caught up in part with the higher inflation, and indexed contracts protected many union members against unexpected inflation. These factors all caused the wage gap to continue its rise. The data for the early 1980s show that the high unemployment of that period and the existence of many indexed contracts caused the union wage gap to rise still further.

It is interesting to compare the changes in $\overline{M}$ in the past 20 years with the changes in the extent of union membership (shown in Table 9.1). During this period, as $\overline{M}$ has increased, the unionized sector has shrunk, and the shrinkage has been

[11] This same trend is apparent even if wage gaps are estimated by using the individual approach and are adjusted for changes in the relative human capital of union and nonunion workers. See George Johnson, "The Wage Structure in the U.S.," in Saul Hymans (ed.). *The Economic Outlook for 1982,* University of Michigan Department of Economics, Ann Arbor, 1982.

most rapid in those times when $\overline{M}$ has been highest. Part of the shrinkage may have been due to external forces that have reduced the demand for products of unionized firms. Part, though, may reflect the decreased competitiveness of unionized firms that has been induced by the increase in $\overline{M}$. Implicitly unions have chosen a combination of higher wages and lower employment (a point farther northwest in the area W_2FGH in Fig. 9.3).

Even in the absence of macroeconomic fluctuations, adjusted relative wage gaps will vary over time with the state of the labor market in particular occupations. For example, one study estimated $\overline{M}$ for teachers in 1974 as 7 percent, but found it to be 23 percent in 1977.[12] Although the change is quite large, it is consistent with the evidence in Table 11.3 and with the very sharp deterioration in the market for teachers that accompanied the reduced school enrollment in the United States in the late 1970s. It, too, suggests that unions will sacrifice their employment goal to their wage objectives when the demand schedule for unionized labor shifts leftward.

WAGE GAPS BY TYPE OF UNION AND LEVEL OF SKILL

We have been considering the average effects of unions on the relative earnings of their members. Undoubtedly there is considerable dispersion of the effect of unions around this average beyond that produced by differences in the extent of organization. Thus one might expect differences by type of union (craft versus industrial) and by the level of skill of the employees organized. There may also be differences that depend on the structure of the product market; we examine these in the next section.

It is often thought that unions of skilled craft workers have greater effects on relative earnings than do industrial unions.[13] The bases of this expectation are Marshall's laws of derived demand that we discussed in Chapter 4. A union whose jurisdiction is well-organized will generally set higher wage goals in bargaining, the less elastic the demand for the labor of its members is, since inelastic demand means smaller percentage reductions in employment for given percentage increases in wages. In the short run, at least, there are not likely to be any good substitutes in production for skilled craft workers, and the union thus has more to fear from substitution in consumption than from substitution in production. But in this case, as we saw in Chapter 4, it is desirable to be "unimportant." If the wages of members of one craft are a small part of total cost, then even a large wage increase will add only a small percentage to the total cost of a unit of output. A price increase that reflected this would cause only a small reduction in quantity demanded and hence in employment.

For example, let us assume that the wages of carpenters make up only 10 percent of the cost of a house and that no substitution in production is possible. (The isoquant is like that in Fig. 4.7(a).) Then a wage increase of 20 percent for carpenters would add only 2 percent to the cost of a house, which would probably have little effect on the number of houses built. If, however, the wages of carpenters were half

[12] William Baugh and Joe Stone, "Teachers, Unions, and Wages in the 1970s: Unionism Now Pays," *Industrial and Labor Relations Review* (35): 368–376 (1982).

[13] See, for example, Milton Friedman in David Wright (ed.). *The Impact of the Union,* Harcourt Brace Jovanovich, New York, 1951, p. 208.

the cost of a house, a 20 percent wage increase would add 10 percent to costs, which would have a larger effect on the volume of home building.

The cases in which this set of factors works to the union's advantage are those in which one craft bargains completely independently of others (e.g., airline pilots). On the other hand, where all crafts bargain together or where one craft sets a pattern that typically spreads to the rest, then what matters is the importance of the craft group as a whole. Where this group is still fairly small relative to total costs, as in newspaper publishing, the situation remains favorable. Where the wages of all crafts are a larger part of total costs, as in residential construction, even a small craft no longer gains from being unimportant.

There remains another sense in which it may be valuable to a union to be small. If a strike of a small group of workers can tie up a large enterprise, the pressures on the employer to settle on favorable terms are greater than in a strike of the whole work force. The employer can then avert a large loss in production at relatively small total cost. But this factor, too, is important only when the settlement does not set a pattern for other employees.

Table 11.1 shows that in 1980 the unadjusted wage gap, M, was higher among laborers than among operatives, which in turn was higher than among craft workers. A large number of studies that have estimated *adjusted* wage gaps separately find the same thing: Unions have on average been less effective in raising craft workers' wages than those of other blue-collar workers. One study found estimates of $\overline{M}$ of 52 percent for laborers, 26 percent for operatives, and 24 percent for craft workers. Another estimated the wage gaps as 19, 15, and 3 percent outside construction; even in construction, where craft workers are in separate unions from less skilled workers, $\overline{M}$ is slightly higher among laborers than among skilled workers.[14]

The explanation of the inverse relation between the union wage effect and skill probably lies in the leveling effect of union wage policies. Industrial unions have frequently sought the largest percentage wage increases for the least skilled workers (e.g., by bargaining for equal absolute increases for everyone). They have also sought to eliminate interfirm and interarea differentials, and craft workers may be underrepresented in the low-wage firms and areas. Even in construction, where one might initially think the wage gap would be higher among skilled workers who bargain separately from unskilled workers, solidarity among unions organized along craft lines allows the power of skilled workers' unions to spill over to the determination of wages of unskilled workers.

Comparing blue-collar and white-collar workers, consideration of the relatively small extent of organization of white-collar workers (see Table 9.3), along with the discussion of Figure 11.3, suggests that wage gaps will be higher among blue-collar workers. With only a small fraction of white-collar workers organized, the ability of most white-collar unions to impose wages above the competitive rate for workers with comparable skills is likely to be limited. The evidence strongly supports these arguments. Every study that has examined this issue finds that $\overline{M}$ is higher among blue-collar workers. The difference between the adjusted wage gaps in the two groups

[14] Frank Stafford, "Concentration and Labor Earnings: Comment," *American Economic Review* (58): 174–181 (1968), and Orley Ashenfelter, "Discrimination and Trade Unions," in Orley Ashenfelter and Albert Rees (eds.). *Discrimination in Labor Markets,* Princeton University Press, Princeton, N.J., 1973.

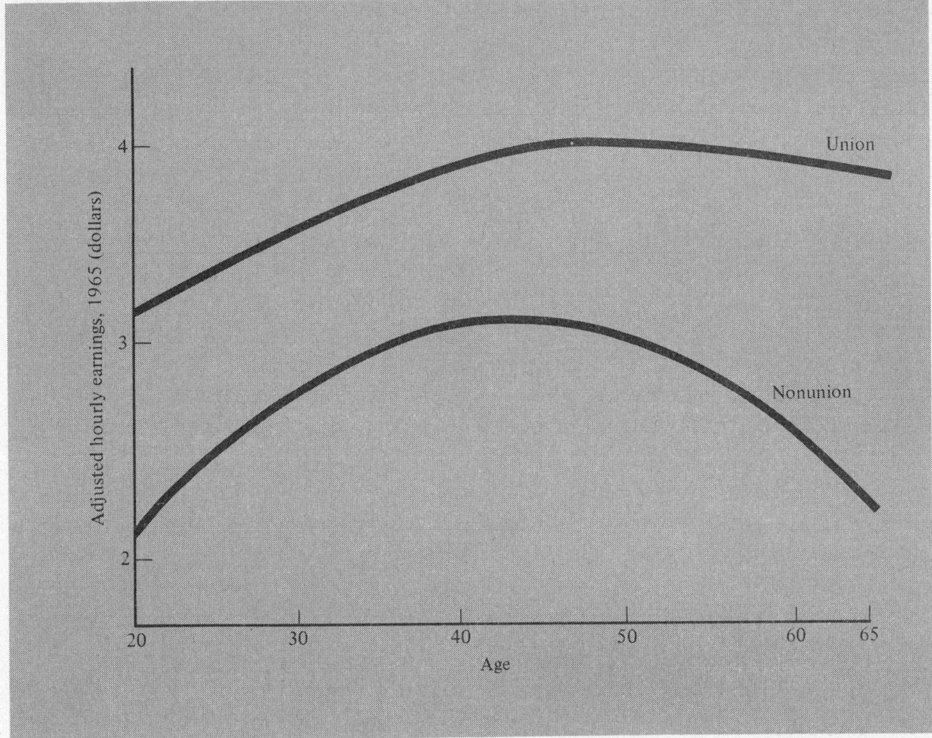

Figure 11.4 Age-earnings profiles: union and nonunion. [*Source:* Based on George Johnson and Kenwood Youmans, "Union Relative Wage Effects by Age and Education," *Industrial and Labor Relations Review* (24): 175 (1971).]

in one study covering 1976 was 10 percentage points; $\overline{M}$ estimated by the individual approach is usually not found to be above 10 percent among white-collar workers.[15]

The leveling effect of union wage policy is evident if the work force is disaggregated by the level of education. At each age in a sample of workers in 1965, $\overline{M}$ was greater among male blue-collar workers who had only completed eighth grade than among high school graduates. The leveling effect of unionism is especially pronounced when we consider how $\overline{M}$ differs by age or labor-market experience. If unions do level wages, the adjusted relative gap will be highest for young workers and workers beyond the peak of the age-earnings profile. This is exactly what we observe: As Figure 11.4 shows, the age-earnings profile among unionized workers in 1965 is raised above that of nonunion workers and flattened out.[16] The same phenomenon exists in data from the mid-1970s.[17] Undoubtedly it persists in the labor market today. This implies that $\overline{M}$ is higher the farther away the worker is from the peak of the age-earnings profile.

Since, as we noted in Chapter 9, unions are expanding only in the public sector,

[15] Lewis, *Union Relative Wage Effects . . .* , loc. cit.; Joseph Antos, Mark Chandler, and Wesley Mellow, "Sex Differences in Union Membership," *Industrial and Labor Relations Review* (33): 162–169 (1980).

[16] Richard Freeman, "Unionism and the Dispersion of Wages," *Industrial and Labor Relations Review* (34) (1980), Table 3.

[17] Antos, Chandler, and Mellow, loc. cit.

it is worth examining whether their expansion has enabled them to impose wage gaps in that sector that are larger than in other sectors. In Chapter 10 we considered reasons that the same group of workers will have more bargaining power if their product or service is made or performed in the public rather than in the private sector. Indeed, there was evidence from studies of wages of bus drivers and sanitation workers that this is the case. This does not mean that $\overline{M}$ is higher among public employees than in the private sector. By and large the services performed by government differ from those located in the private sector; thus the underlying production relations (and the derived demand elasticities) that help determine the success of unions in raising wages will differ between the two sectors. Also, supply conditions may differ; to the extent that there are fewer occupation-specific skills required in the public sector, the bargaining power of public-sector unions will be reduced by the potential competition of nonunion employees and the threat that the work could be contracted out to the private sector. Finally, the federal government and many states have laws that restrict the ability of unionized workers to strike, thus reducing the scope for withholding their labor as a means of achieving their wage and employment goals. For these reasons the adjusted relative wage gap may be lower in the public sector.

These latter considerations apparently outweigh the potential effect of union bargaining power that stems from their ability to withhold an "essential" service. One study using the individual approach estimated $\overline{M}$ for older male blue-collar workers in 1971 as 27 percent in the private sector but only 24 percent in the public sector. Another, using the same approach, estimated $\overline{M}$ for white males in 1968 as 16 percent in the private sector, but only 6 percent in the public sector. Studies of specific occupations give a similar picture: Unionized police employees earn wages that are between 4 and 14 percent higher than those of their otherwise similar nonunion counterparts. (The estimates differ depending upon the approach used to estimate $\overline{M}$.) Estimates of $\overline{M}$ among public school teachers, produced by the three simple approaches, range between 0 and 25 percent, with 5 to 10 percent being the best estimate of this effect.[18] This compares to the economy-wide $\overline{M}$ based on the simple approaches of between 10 and 25 percent that we cited earlier in this chapter. Presumably if unmeasured differences could be accounted for by using longitudinal data, we would find that the estimated adjusted wage gap in the public sector would be below the best estimates of the economy-wide wage gap.

POLICY ISSUE—UNION WAGE GAPS AND THE EXTENT OF UNION CONTROL

During debate on the Taft-Hartley Act of 1947, the United States Senate came within one vote of passing the Ball Amendment. This would have restricted unions from bargaining on behalf of workers in workplaces in different metropolitan areas. Effectively

[18] David Shapiro, "Relative Wage Effects of Unions in the Public and Private Sectors," *Industrial and Labor Relations Review* (31): 193–204 (1978); Daniel Hamermesh, "The Effect of Government Ownership on Union Wages," in Hamermesh, (ed.). *Labor in the Public and Nonprofit Sectors,* Princeton University Press, Princeton, N.J., 1975, Table 12; Ann Bartel and David Lewin, "Wages and Unionism in the Public Sector: The Case of Police," *Review of Economics and Statistics* (63): 53–59 (1981); and Donald Frey, "Wage Determination in Public Schools and the Effects of Unionization," in Hamermesh, loc. cit.

this would have meant the demise of national unions in the United States; local unions alone would have remained. It is interesting to speculate about how this provision would have affected union bargaining power, as measured by union relative wage gaps, had it been enacted.[19]

Most national unions of craft workers in the United States consist of very strong local unions that bargain with employer groups in one locality. In construction this bargaining structure is the result of the product market being effectively limited to the metropolitan area. Outlawing national unions would probably not have much effect on the relative bargaining strengths of workers and employers who are organized this way because of the relative lack of opportunity for competition from nonunion construction in areas with weak local unions. The union wage gap of craft workers would probably not be affected severely by such a change. Industrial unions by definition cover workers of all skill levels in as much of an industry as can be organized. In many cases the bargaining structure is national, with much of the determination of wages and fringes taking place at the national level. Legislation like that rejected in 1947 would disrupt bargaining completely; and with the easy substitution of output produced by plants where the local union is relatively weak, the power of relatively strong local unions would be nullified. Since industrial unions in manufacturing consist disproportionately of operatives, such legislation would probably reduce the union wage gap among operatives. The equalization of wage rates shown by the evidence on wage gaps by skill level would be reduced.

UNIONS AND COMPETITION IN PRODUCT MARKETS

A difficult question is whether unions win larger gains when the product market is monopolized than when it is competitive, assuming in both cases that the union has fully organized the market. The discussion in Chapter 9, where we showed that product-market power is a precondition for the union to raise employment and wages above their nonunion levels, implies a positive answer to this question. A positive answer is also suggested by looking at manufacturing industries, where the unions that seem to be strongest are in industries such as basic steel and automobiles, in which a large fraction of total output is produced by a small number of firms. On the other hand, outside manufacturing there are many strong unions in unconcentrated industries such as construction, trucking, and bituminous coal mining.

The assumption underlying the view that unions gain more in noncompetitive industries is that unions can somehow succeed in capturing monopoly profits. This view considers them, in J. K. Galbraith's terms, as having *countervailing power* that offsets the monopoly power of the employer. The opposite view sees unions in unconcentrated industry as having original power. By raising costs the unions can raise the price of the product to the general level where a successful product-market monopolist would have set it in the first place. Instead of capturing monopoly profits from the employer, they create wage gains by their own strength. Monopolists might also be willing to spend some of their profits to stave off unionization, or to weaken the union that has organized their workers. This, too, would lower union power and lead to a wage gap that is smaller in concentrated industries.

The idea implicit in Figure 9.3 that unions can capture monopoly profits suggests that monopolists will not raise prices by the full amount of wage increases

[19] See the discussion in H. Gregg Lewis, "The Labor-Monopoly Problem: A Positive Program," *Journal of Political Economy* (59): 277–287 (1951).

imposed by unions, but will, instead, pay part of the increases out of their previous profit margins. This would generally be true of profit-maximizing monopolists, although the precise answer depends on the elasticity of demand for the product. In contrast, the price charged by a competitive industry would in the long run have to rise by the full amount of the increase in labor costs.

If we consider the possibility that many monopolists or oligopolists do not maximize profits in the short run, we see that it is possible for monopolists to allow some of their profits to be "captured" by the union. Oligopolists may not maximize profits, for example, when they are following wage-price guideposts set by the government, or when they fear the imposition or reimposition of price controls. In such circumstances, prices may be held below the level that clears the market. The automobile and basic steel industries followed such pricing policies in the period 1946 to 1948, as shown by the existence of *gray markets* for cars and steel in which sales took place above list prices. In these circumstances wage increases won by unions were used as the occasion to raise prices by more than the increase in labor costs, so that the new prices are closer to the market-clearing level. Far from sharing profits with the union, the employers in question make the union bear the onus of raising profits closer to their target levels when increases in nonlabor costs have been eroding them.[20]

The evidence on how $\overline{M}$ varies with the extent of product-market concentration, as measured by the percentage of sales in the industry accounted for by the top four firms, is mixed. One study found no difference in $\overline{M}$ among industries where the top four firms had less than 70 percent of sales, but estimated that $\overline{M}$ is higher in those very concentrated product markets in which the top four firms account for at least 70 percent of sales.[21] However, another study that accounted for differences in plant and firm size showed that $\overline{M}$ in the late 1970s was 7 percentage points lower in industries where the top four firms had more than 70 percent of sales than where they had 30 percent or less.[22] The alternative effects we have discussed apparently balance each other off. We saw in Chapter 9 (Fig. 9.3) that unions in firms with product-market power could raise both wages and employment as compared to unions that deal with competitive firms. This negative evidence on their effects on wages suggests they may produce positive effects on employment.

Where product markets are characterized by oligopolies, union workers can maintain a relative wage advantage over nonunion workers in other industries by relying on the lack of competition in the product market. Where an industry is more competitive, though, how can unionized firms survive competition from nonunion firms that do not have to pay the higher union wages? One possibility is that unions provide firms a number of advantages that reduce costs sufficiently to compensate for the higher wages received by otherwise equal unionized employees. All these can

[20] Albert Rees, "Wage-Price Relations in the Basic Steel Industry, 1945–48," *Industrial and Labor Relations Review* (6): 195–205 (1953).

[21] Wallace Hendricks, "Labor Market Structure and Union Wage Levels," *Economic Inquiry* (13): 401–416 (1975), and see also Leonard Weiss, "Concentration and Labor Earnings," *American Economic Review* (56): 96–117 (1966).

[22] Wesley Mellow, "Employer Size and Wages," *Review of Economics and Statistics* (64): 495–501 (1982), and see also Farrell Bloch and Mark Kuskin, "Wage Determination in the Union and Nonunion Sectors," *Industrial and Labor Relations Review* (31): 183–192 (1978).

be lumped under the heading of productivity-increasing impacts of unionism on the workplace. For example, unions may reduce turnover costs (see the next section). By providing workers an outlet for grievances and for frustrations in general, they may also increase worker morale and thus productivity. (However, unionized workers report less satisfaction with their jobs, other things equal, than do nonunion workers.[23]) Also, management may for a time be shocked into operating more efficiently; the effects of such shocks on labor demand were discussed in Chapter 5.

Whether the net effect of unions on worker productivity is positive, let alone sufficiently large to compensate for the higher wages paid to otherwise similar union employees, is very much an open issue. One study of data for manufacturing industries in 1972 that used a method like the aggregate approach to measuring adjusted relative wage gaps found that there is a *relative productivity gap* of 22 percent favoring unionized firms. This is about the same size as the relative wage gaps that were estimated by using this approach. It suggests that productivity rises by enough to offset the higher union wages, allowing union firms the same cost and thus the ability to compete with nonunion firms. On the other hand, a detailed study of the cement industry that used both cross-section and time-series data on the physical output of cement found only 6 to 8 percent greater output per worker in unionized plants. This is far less than the adjusted relative wage gap for most industries, including cement, suggesting that productivity improvements are insufficient to allow unionized firms to compete effectively. Another study finds no effect of unions on productivity in data covering the 1970s for over 900 individual product lines.[24]

The ability of unionized firms to survive is best indicated by their overall profitability. The same problems of measurement arise here as exist in measuring union wage gaps: How can one account for unobserved differences in the causes of profitability that may be correlated with union status? Despite these problems one estimate shows that unionized establishments earned a lower rate of return on investment than did nonunion establishments making the same product line. Another study shows that, holding other factors constant, the value of shares of stock in a firm whose workers vote to unionize declines as a response to that vote. Implicitly the market signals its belief that unionization reduces profitability.[25]

The results are consistent with a union relative wage gap in excess of any positive impact of unions on productivity. They imply, however, that unionized establishments will gradually account for smaller shares of output in industries where both union and nonunion establishments compete, for the more profitable nonunion establishments will attract customers by selling more cheaply. In the aggregate, they suggest that the only way the union sector can maintain its share of

[23]George Borjas, "Job Satisfaction, Wages, and Unions," *Journal of Human Resources* (14): 21–40 (1979).

[24]Charles Brown and James Medoff, "Trade Unions in the Production Process," *Journal of Political Economy* (86): 355–378 (1978); Kim Clark, "Unionization and Productivity: Micro-Econometric Evidence," *Quarterly Journal of Economics* (95): 613–640 (1980); and Kim Clark, "Unionization and Firm Performance: The Impact on Profits, Growth and Productivity," Working Paper No. 990, National Bureau of Economic Research, Cambridge, Mass., 1982.

[25]Clark, "Unionization and Firm Performance . . . ," loc. cit.; Richard Ruback and Martin Zimmerman, "Unionization and Profitability: Evidence from the Capital Market," Unpublished Paper, Massachusetts Institute of Technology, 1983.

output is by continuing organization of new firms to replace the declining, unionized firms that have difficulty competing. The fact that this has not happened in the United States in the past 25 years is shown by the discussion of union growth in Chapter 9 and by the data in Table 9.1.

EFFECTS ON EMPLOYMENT AND TURNOVER

Union-imposed wage increases will result in reductions in employment in the union sector as long as there is a downward-sloping demand curve for union labor. These negative gross employment effects are indicated by the horizontal distance AB in Figure 11.1. The gross effect exceeds the net employment effect, which is HF in Figure 11.1(b). (Notice that AB in Fig. 11.1(a) is equal to CF in Fig. 11.1(b).) The net effect is smaller because some workers who do not find jobs in the union sector find work, although at a lower wage, in the nonunion sector. The net effect is negative—total employment is reduced—as long as the supply curve of labor to the market slopes upward (as long as some of the workers forced into the nonunion sector find the reduced wage available to them to be less than their reservation wage).

Unfortunately, there are no estimates of the net effect of unionism on employment in the United States (or any other industrialized nation). To the extent that we believe, as the discussion in Chapter 2 suggested, that the supply of labor to the market is quite inelastic for most workers, we may conclude that the net employment effect is likely to be fairly small. Gross employment effects, though, are a different matter; they depend only on labor demand elasticities, which we showed in Chapter 4 can be quite substantial for individual firms and even for entire sectors of the economy. One study compared employment in heavily unionized industries (mining, construction, manufacturing, transportation, etc.) to that in the rest of the U.S. economy between 1919 and 1958. The estimates suggest that each 1 percent increase in the relative wage gap reduced relative employment between the two broad subdivisions of the economy by 1 percent.[26] Thus if the unionized sector were three-quarters covered by unions, and the true relative wage gap were 10 percent, employment in that sector would be 7.5 percent lower relative to that in the nonunion sector than it would be in the absence of any union wage effect.

Studies of individual industries also indicate substantial gross employment effects. Estimates for the bituminous coal industry, in which the relative wage gap widened rapidly after World War II to as much as 35 percent by the late 1950s, show that this large effect reduced employment roughly 20 percent below what it would have been just by inducing substitution toward capital along a production isoquant.[27] These studies indicate that union members and their leaders are right to be concerned about employment effects when they bargain. As discussed in Chapter 9, the union usually cannot simply impose a wage increase, but must instead weigh its consequences for employment against the benefits it will produce for those members who retain their jobs.

[26] H. Gregg Lewis, "Relative Employment Effects of Unionism," Industrial Relations Research Association, *Proceedings* (16): 104–115 (1963).

[27] Ibid.

How does unionism affect job mobility? As we showed in Chapter 7, higher wages that reflect greater investment in firm-specific training reduce the likelihood that a worker will leave a job voluntarily. Indeed, among a large sample of workers observed between 1968 and 1974, union members' probability of quitting was only 5.8 percent per year, whereas nonunion workers' was 9 percent. Part of this difference is due to the higher wages received by union members, but part results from an independent effect of unionism: Even accounting for differences in wages and demographic characteristics, union workers had a substantially lower likelihood of quitting a job in any given year. Another way of looking at this phenomenon is to examine job tenure. Union workers in this sample had averaged 8.8 years on the job, compared with only 6.6 years for nonunion workers. Adjusting for differences between the two groups in wages, schooling and demographic characteristics, union workers had been on the job for one year more than their nonunion counterparts.[28]

The difference in quit rates between union and nonunion workers cannot be explained by the union wage effect alone, for it is still present when that effect is accounted for. One explanation is that the unionized employer selects workers who are more stable in ways that are not measurable using available data on workers' demographic characteristics. This selection mechanism would be a profit-maximizing response by the employer to the imposed relative wage increase. It is part of the same response that makes it so difficult to find a satisfactory estimate of the adjusted relative wage gap. This does not appear to provide the entire explanation of the union-nonunion difference in quit rates. Young workers who took union jobs had the same quit rate as similar workers before they took the union job; afterward, the union joiners had a 13 percent lower quit rate even adjusting for the wage gap between the two groups. A final explanation is that the union provides services to its members that reduce the nonwage disadvantages that induce workers to quit. Dissatisfaction over working conditions may be reduced by union work rules; and it is true that quit rates are lower in those union plants that have a less restrictive grievance procedure.[29]

POLICY ISSUE—DOMESTIC CONTENT LEGISLATION AND AUTO WORKERS' EMPLOYMENT

In response to the very sharp decline in employment in the U.S. automobile industry (from 330 thousand production workers in 1977 to 210 thousand in 1982), a number of bills were introduced in the U.S. Congress in the early 1980s requiring that imported autos contain certain minimum percentages of American-made components.[30] Because imports had obtained an increased share of the U.S. market (from 18 percent in 1978 to 27 percent in 1981), part of the decline in employment was attributed to competition from imports. The proposals represent an attempt to shift the demand schedule for labor in the automobile industry from D′ to D in Figure 11.5, where it was before the large influx of imports. Assuming the legislation is enacted and is effective in reducing the value of imported

[28] Richard Freeman, "The Exit-Voice Tradeoff in the Labor Market: Unionism, Job Tenure, Quits, and Separations," *Quarterly Journal of Economics* (94): 643–674 (1980).

[29] Henry Farber, "Unionism, Labor Turnover, and Wages of Young Men," *Research in Labor Economics* (3): 33–53 (1980); Jacob Mincer, "Union Effects: Wages, Turnover, and Job Training," Working Paper No. 808, National Bureau of Economic Research, Cambridge, Mass., 1981; and Freeman, "The Exit-Voice Trade-off . . . ," loc. cit.

[30] For example, S.707, 98th Congress, introduced by Donald Riegle of Michigan.

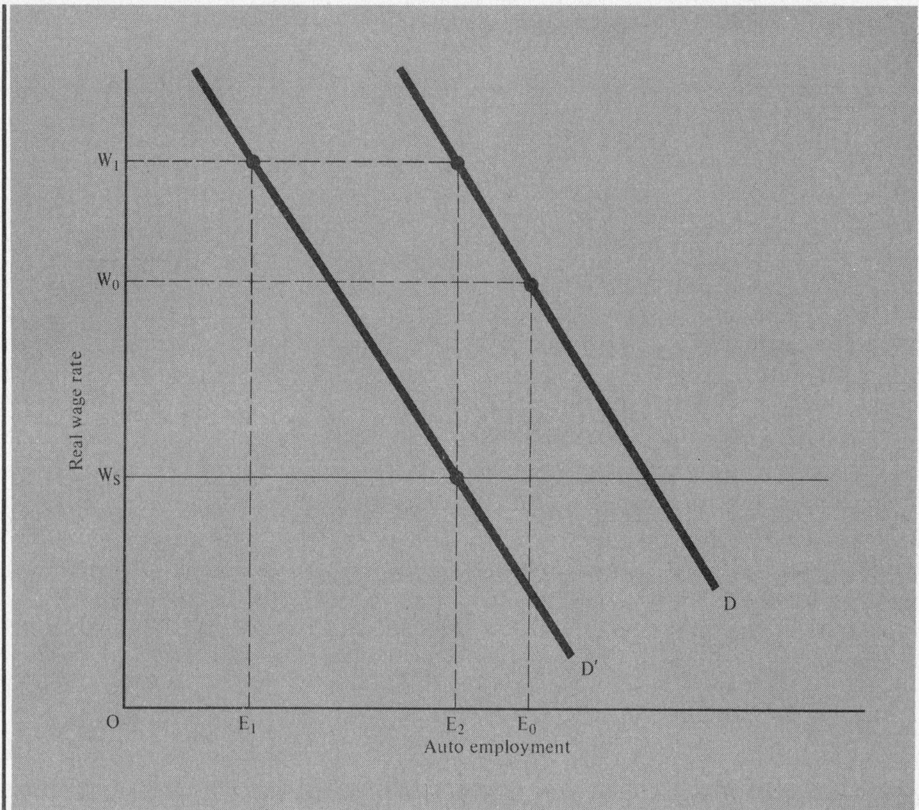

Figure 11.5 Domestic content legislation and auto employment.

components of cars sold in the United States to earlier levels, would it restore the reductions in employment in the auto industry (the negative gross employment changes)?

The evidence presented in Table 11.3 suggests that the adjusted wage gap in the United States grew in the late 1970s and early 1980s. This would suggest that the leftward shift in the demand schedule for labor in the American auto industry was only partly responsible for the decline in employment. Assuming capital costs did not change relative to the competitive wage, W_s, the decline also resulted from employers substituting capital for labor in response to the increase in relative wages paid to auto workers. Shifting the demand schedule back to D via the proposed legislation would restore part of the lost employment (an amount $E_2 - E_1$). The rest could be restored only if union wages (actually union compensation) fall relative to the cost of capital.

UNIONS AND RESOURCE ALLOCATION

Because unions change relative earnings, they also affect the allocation of labor among sectors of the economy. Figure 11.6 shows one way in which this reallocation can be viewed. It is essentially a composite of Figures 11.1(a) and (b), except that we now assume the economy has a fixed supply of homogeneous labor, S, that is unaffected by changes in relative wages. This means that there will be no net employment effect of unions. This assumption allows us to concentrate on the

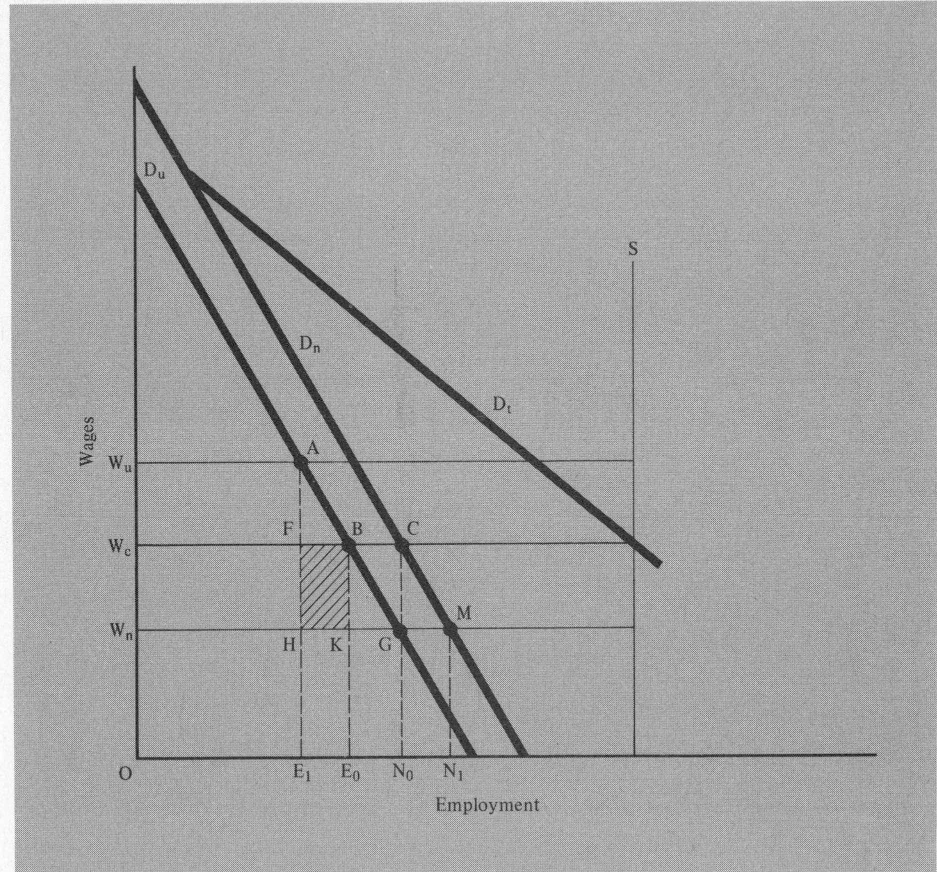

Figure 11.6 The effects of union wage differentials on resource allocation.

potential for misallocating resources that is produced by the gross employment effects.

We assume that the economy is divided into two sectors, U and N, both originally nonunion. The demand for labor in these sectors is represented by the parallel lines D_u and D_n, which sum horizontally to D_t, the total demand for labor. (See Chap. 4 for conditions under which it is appropriate to draw a downward-sloping demand curve for labor for the economy as a whole.)

Initially the wage is set competitively at W_c, the same in both sectors. It is determined by the intersection of D_t and the vertical labor supply curve S. Employment is E_0 in sector U and N_0 in sector N. Sector U is then organized by unions, which through collective bargaining set the wage in this sector at W_u. We assume that employers determine the number of workers to be hired. Employment in the union sector falls to E_1, as employers and consumers make substitutions against union labor and union-made products. If we assume that the workers who have lost their jobs prefer working at the nonunion wage to remaining unemployed, the supply of labor to the nonunion sector increases to N_1. Wages in that sector, still determined competitively, fall to W_n.

The welfare loss, the loss in total output, arises because the workers who have moved from the union to the nonunion sector are now being used where their productivity is lower than before. The union sector has become more capital-intensive, and the nonunion sector has become more labor-intensive. (Remember that the demand schedule shows the VMP of each additional worker employed in the sector.) Thus the area under each demand schedule up to the level of employment in that sector is the total product of the sector. The decrease in output in the union sector is the trapezoid ABE_0E_1; the increase in output in the nonunion sector is the trapezoid CMN_1N_0. Under the assumption that the net employment effect is zero, the horizontal distances E_1E_0 and N_0N_1 are equal. Since the demand curves are parallel, the triangles ABF and CMG are equal. The net loss in output is therefore the difference between the two trapezoids, which is the shaded rectangle FBKH. Even though total employment does not change, total production, and thus real living standards, decrease.

This analysis is highly abstract and could be modified in many ways to make it more realistic. The labor in the two sectors need not be of the same original quality, and the two demand schedules need not be parallel (more precisely, need not have the same elasticity). In particular, if the demand schedule is flatter in the nonunion sector, as evidence of demand elasticities indicates, the shift of labor from the union sector reduces VMP only slightly in the nonunion sector.[31] Triangle ABF would then exceed triangle CGM, so that rectangle FBKH would overstate the lost output in the economy. (If D_n were flat around employment of N_0, the only loss in output would be the triangle ABF.) If the nonunion labor markets are not perfectly competitive, the transfer of workers from the union sector also reduces VMP less, again implying that the rectangle FBKH in Figure 11.6 overstates the lost output. On the other hand, if the supply curve S has a positive elasticity (is not vertical), some of the workers leaving the union sector will cease working entirely. Their contribution to output will drop from W_c to zero, a far larger loss in output than is implied by the reduction in wages from W_c to W_n. The rectangle FBKH may also understate the lost output if workers who lose jobs in the union sector experience prolonged spells of unemployment before they obtain work in the nonunion sector.

The net impact of all these modifications of the discussion of Figure 11.6 is unclear. Under the assumption that the adjusted wage gap is 15 percent, one estimate places the output loss in 1957 in the United States at 0.14 percent of GNP. Another estimate that was based on slightly different methods found the effect to be 0.33 percent for the 1950s, again assuming that the adjusted wage gap is 15 percent.[32] Today the adjusted wage gap, as measured by the simple approaches, is above 25 percent (see Table 11.3). On the other hand, the results using the longitudinal approach to estimating the wage gap showed the gap is not much more than 10 percent. If that is a better estimate of the wage gap, we may infer that the lost output is

[31] Richard Freeman and James Medoff, "Substitution Between Production Labor and Other Inputs in Unionized and Non-Unionized Manufacturing," *Review of Economics and Statistics* (64): 220–233 (1982).

[32] Albert Rees, "The Effects of Unions on Resource Allocation," *Journal of Law and Economics* (6): 69–78 (1963), and Harry Johnson and Peter Mieszkowski, "The Effects of Unionization on the Distribution of Income: A General Equilibrium Approach," *Quarterly Journal of Economics* (84): 560 (1970).

below the 0.14 or 0.33 percent figures suggested by the available estimates of this effect. In any case, the impression remains that the lost output caused by the misallocation of labor to areas where it is less productive is relatively small. The losses resulting from restrictive work practices or from unemployment that occurs when a unionized plant can no longer compete are likely to be substantially larger.

SUMMARY

It is impossible to measure the true effect of unionism on the wages of unionized workers because we cannot observe what their wages would be in the absence of unionism anywhere else in the economy. Estimates of the difference today between the average union worker's wage and that of the average nonunion worker with the same observable characteristics fall mostly between 10 to 25 percent. Once differences in unmeasured characteristics are accounted for, the estimated wage difference is often below 10 percent. The wage difference rises in recessions and falls in booms but has shown a steady upward trend since the late 1960s. Despite some evidence that unionism raises productivity, that effect is insufficient to offset the higher wages paid to unionized employees. This makes it difficult to understand how unionized firms survive the competition from nonunion firms in the same industry or from substitute products produced by nonunion labor.

Because labor demand schedules slope down, higher union wages induce employers to decrease their use of labor. This gross employment effect is fairly substantial; but the net employment effect is small, for the relative inelasticity of labor supply leads most workers who would have obtained union jobs to find work at lower wages in the nonunion sector. This shift of resources results in a small loss of output for the economy, as labor is shifted from its most efficient use to a nonunion sector that is crowded with labor working with relatively little capital.

five

DIFFERENCES IN PAY

chapter 12

Compensating Differences and Fringe Benefits

AN OVERVIEW

The basic forces that affect the structure of pay have been reviewed in Chapters 1 through 11. We turn now to an examination of the outcomes produced by these forces and to more specific factors that govern structures of particular kinds. There are many structures of pay differentials: by occupation, by industry, by location, by race, by ethnicity, and by sex, to list only a few. Since groups of workers who differ in one of these dimensions are unlikely to be the same in all others, particular differentials are seldom observed in pure form. In order to measure the differences in pay between groups that result solely from the way they are classified in one structure, we must standardize for differences in their other characteristics.

In this chapter we describe the determinants of a number of these pay differences, including those resulting from differences in skills embodied in workers and from heterogeneity in their tastes for nonpecuniary aspects of work. Because pay consists of both wages and fringe benefits, we examine the determinants of the division of compensation between these two basic forms. In Chapter 13 we discuss pay differences resulting in part from discrimination—by race, ethnicity, and sex. These differences have been the focus of much attention by economists and policymakers; a better understanding of their causes can help policymakers to ameliorate some of the discrimination. Taken together, all these differences produce a distribution of earnings that implies a degree of inequality in the returns to work within a work force. In Chapter 14 we examine differences over time and within occupations in the extent of inequality in the distribution of earnings and present additional theories designed to explain this distribution. The determinants of the total amount of compensation received from a particular level of output—labor's share of income—are also discussed.

THE SOURCES OF PAY DIFFERENTIALS

From a purely statistical point of view, one could start standardizing the wage distribution anywhere to isolate particular differentials, but the economic significance of some wage structures is greater than that of others. Occupational differentials are perhaps the most basic of all, since they reflect differences among workers in levels and kinds of skill and in conditions of work. In a perfectly competitive market in equilibrium one might expect to observe almost no industry differentials beyond those that arise because industries use different mixes of occupations. (The qualification "almost" is needed because the nonpecuniary advantages or disadvantages of work may be related to industry rather than to occupation. For example, a secretary might prefer to do the same general kind of work in an insurance office rather than in an office that is part of a steel mill or an oil refinery.) We shall therefore start the discussion of wage structure with occupational wage differentials.

The forces that determine the level of pay in an occupation change substantially depending on the length of the period being considered. In the very short run the number of people qualified for all but the least skilled occupations is fixed; if there is an increase in the demand for labor in an occupation, its compensation will therefore rise. Thus in the short run the supply is inelastic and largely determines the number of people in the occupation, whereas demand largely determines their wage. Given adequate time for training, including in some cases time for the establishment of new training facilities, the number of qualified people in an occupation can be increased and the number who enter will depend on tastes, training costs, and expected career earnings. Thus in the long run the supply of labor to an occupation could be highly elastic. This is exactly what we saw in the synthesis on labor supply in Chapter 3: the long-run supply curve of labor to an occupation is much flatter than the short-run supply curve. The height of the supply curve would largely determine compensation, whereas the strength of demand would largely determine the number of workers employed. It is the determinants of the long-run structure that are of most interest.

The basic outlines of the problem can be seen by making some limiting assumptions. Consider an economy with only two occupations, U and S. Occupation U is unskilled and can be entered at age 18 with no further training. Occupation S requires four years of formal training beyond age 18; it thus requires workers to forgo earnings for four years. (The people who train others to work in an occupation can be considered as members of that occupation to avoid introducing a third occupation, teachers.) If all workers had both the same tastes and the same expectations about future earnings in the two occupations, and if all workers discounted future earnings at the same rate of discount, the supply of labor to S in the long run would be perfectly elastic at some constant *compensating differential* above pay in U. If the nonpecuniary advantages of the two occupations were equal, this constant differential, when discounted back to age 18 at the uniform interest rate, would be just sufficient to cover the cost of the investment in training. For example, if all workers retire at age 68, the market rate of interest in equally risky investments is 11 percent, and the wage in U is \$5 per hour, the wage in S would be \$7.75, as shown in Figure 12.1. If the nonpecuniary advantages were not equal and workers preferred occupation S, the differential in pay would be less than enough to cover training

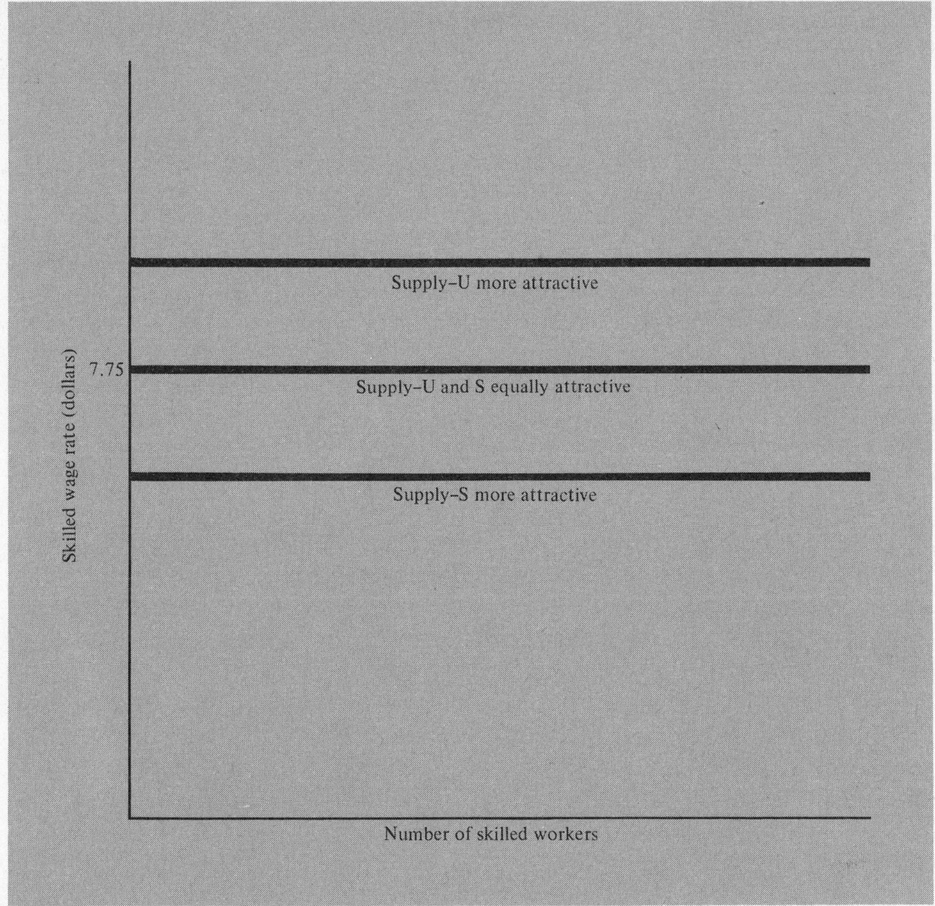

Figure 12.1 Homogeneous tastes and occupational wage differentials.

costs; the supply curve would still be horizontal, but at a lower wage. If, on the other hand, workers would prefer U if the wage were the same as in S, the differential would have to be more than enough to cover training costs; the supply curve would be horizontal at a wage above $7.75.

Role of Tastes

Differences among workers in tastes and expectations will cause the long-run supply curve for the skilled occupations to depart from the horizontal position it occupies in the case just considered. Where tastes differ, a small wage differential will suffice to attract into occupation S those with the strongest preference for this occupation, those who discount future earnings at the lowest rate, and those with the most optimistic expectations about the future size of the differential. Larger and larger differentials would be needed (for constant training costs) to attract additional entrants whose tastes and expectations differed increasingly from those just mentioned. The long-run supply curve to the occupation would therefore slope upward, as in Figure 3.9.

Discussion of the role of tastes in determining the long-run wage level of an occupation goes back to Adam Smith, who wrote:

> The whole of the advantages and disadvantages of the different employments of labor and stock must, in the same neighborhood, be either perfectly equal or continually tending to equality. If in the same neighborhood there was any employment evidently either more or less advantageous than the rest, so many people would crowd into it in one case, and so many would desert it in the other, that its advantages would soon return to the level of other employments.[1]

The nature of advantages and disadvantages of different employments must be specified to avoid the circularity involved in defining them after the fact as those things that make people change occupations. Smith, of course, went on to specify them so that his argument gives rise to testable hypotheses.

The advantages of an employment include not only the pay and any perquisites or amenities that go with it, but the prestige in which it is held and the satisfactions of working in it. If an occupation is disagreeable or held in low esteem, Smith argued, its pay must be higher to compensate for this. Moreover, this will be true even in long-run equilibrium, so that there will be no tendency for such compensating differentials to be eliminated by mobility. In a very real sense the worker purchases prestige and agreeable work by accepting a wage lower than could be gotten on a less prestigious and less agreeable job.

Smith wrote as though all workers had the same tastes, so that everyone disliked being a butcher or an executioner to the same extent. In such cases the size of the differential needed to compensate workers for doing disagreeable work is entirely independent of the strength of demand. However, if tastes differ, this proposition will no longer be true. Suppose that all but 1 percent of the labor force considers being a butcher more distasteful than working in other occupations requiring the same amount of training but that the remaining 1 percent does not. If the number of butchers demanded at a wage that does not include any compensating pay differential is 1 percent of the number of people demanded in all occupations taken together, it will be possible to fill all the openings for butchers at this wage from among those workers who do not dislike the occupation. In that case there would be no pay difference between butchers and other workers who incurred the same costs of training.

The Market for Disamenities

Even this extension of the theory of compensating differentials is too simplistic. The labor force cannot simply be disaggregated into those who mind working in what is commonly viewed as an unpleasant occupation and those who do not. As with

[1] Adam Smith, *The Wealth of Nations,* Random House, New York, 1937, Book 1, chap. 10. See also the discussion in Albert Rees, "Compensating Wage Differentials," in Andrew Skinner and Thomas Wilson (eds.). *Essays on Adam Smith,* Clarendon Press, Oxford, 1975.

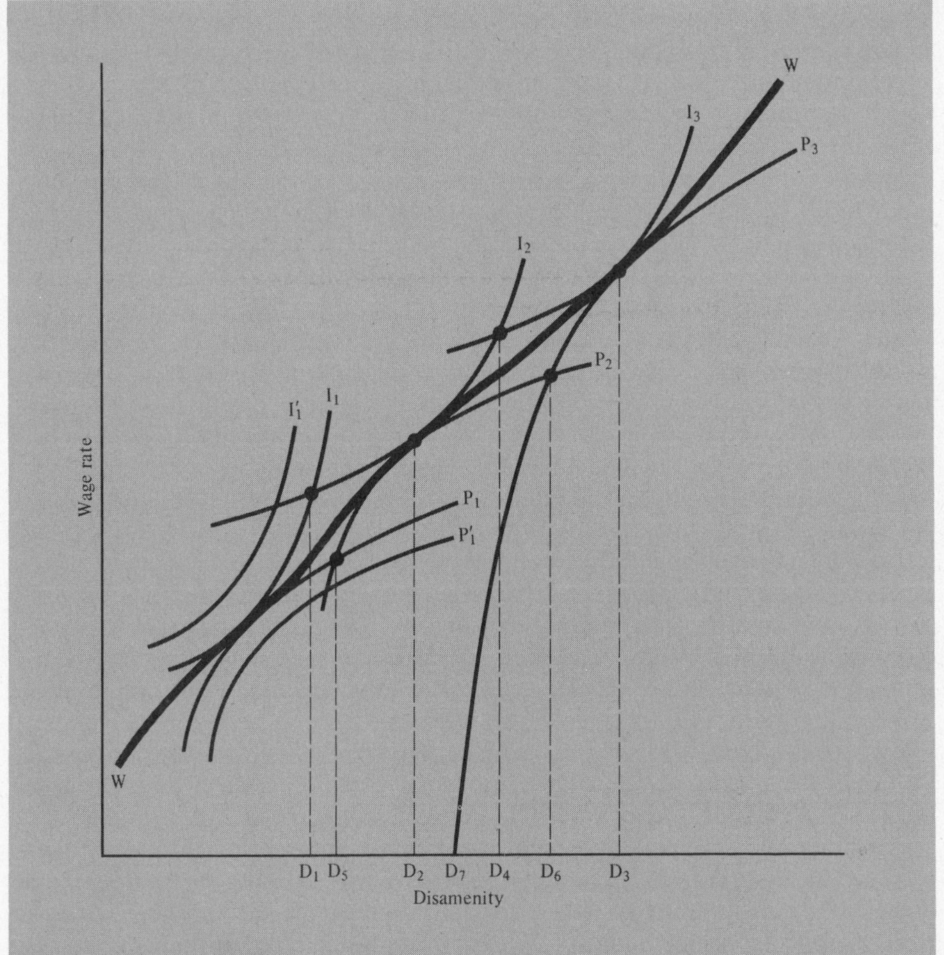

Figure 12.2 The market for a disamenity.

nearly everything else in economic life there is a trade-off: At a sufficiently high rate of pay even those who are appalled at the sight of blood would leave their current occupation and attempt to become butchers. Obversely, if the rate of pay is not so high as that in other occupations requiring the same amount of training, even those professing no distaste for the gorier aspects of the job may be unwilling to enter the occupation. Consider the indifference curve I_1 in Figure 12.2.[2] It shows the combination of pay, and the extent of a disamenity that goes with the receipt of pay, as viewed by one particular worker, say, worker number 1. The disamenity could be anything —risk of injury, dirtiness of the work, temperature at the workplace, repetitiousness of the production process, and so on. Indifference curve I_1 slopes upward, for the worker requires more pay to compensate for more of the disamenity. It slopes up at

[2]This method of analysis originated in Sherwin Rosen, "Hedonic Prices and Implicit Markets," *Journal of Political Economy* (82): 34–55 (1974).

an increasing rate because increasingly higher pay is required to offset extra amounts, for example, of dirtiness, the more of the disamenity the worker bears. Indifference curve I_1' describes another set of combinations of pay and the disamenity, all of which keep the worker equally well off. The worker prefers I_1' to I_1: More pay is received along I_1' at each value of the disamenity.

Worker 1 is only one of many workers in the market in this particular occupation. Worker 2 is another, whose tastes for pay and the disamenity are described by indifference curves like I_2. In some sense worker 2 is less bothered by the disamenity than worker 1. Worker 2 can be compensated for a small increase in the disamenity from D_1 with a much smaller pay increase than is required to keep worker 1 equally satisfied. (I_2 is flatter than I_1 at D_1.) Similarly, worker 3 is even more willing to accept small increases in the disamenity; moving right from D_4, worker 3 can be kept equally happy with a much smaller increase in pay than is required by worker 2 at that point. Note that we have drawn only one indifference curve each for workers 2 and 3; there are in fact infinitely many such curves for each worker, with movements to the northwest in Figure 12.2 denoting higher utility, as in the case of worker 1.

Workers not only have different tastes for the disamenity and different degrees of willingness to trade pay for the disamenity, but employers have different abilities to offer combinations of pay and the disamenity. To some extent available technology dictates that some jobs will be less agreeable than others along certain dimensions. (Steel manufacture is necessarily dirtier than retailing.) But employers of workers in a particular occupation can also vary the disamenity by devoting resources to its removal. Employers of butchers, for example, can provide an antiseptic environment, or they can allow their employees to work in a slightly less clean, but less costly workplace. Thus profits of employer 1 in Figure 12.2 are the same at all points along P_1. The curve P_1 slopes up because the employer can offer greater pay to workers, due to the fact that less is spent on removing the disamenity. Removing a bit of the disamenity is more costly, the more the disamenity has already been removed; to keep profits the same, therefore, the employer must cut the pay more, the smaller the amount of the disamenity that is left in the workplace. Thus P_1 is steeper as one moves to the left in Figure 12.1. Employer 1 has other of these *isoprofit curves.* P_1' is one of these, and the employer prefers it because less pay can be offered at the same amount of the disamenity.

Other employers in this occupation have different abilities to remove the disamenity. (They may need differing combinations of workers to be in a different location from employer 1.) Those like employer 2 can remove the disamenity only at higher cost for each level. At an amount D_5, their profits, as shown by the isoprofit curve P_2, can only be maintained by a sharper cut in pay than that made by employer 1 as the disamenity is reduced. Employer 3 is still less able to maintain profits at low amounts of the disamenity. Indeed, as the isoprofit curve P_3 is drawn, there is no positive rate of pay that is consistent with a reduction in the disamenity below D_7.

What does equilibrium in the labor market in this occupation look like? People like worker 1 will find jobs offering only small amounts of the disamenity. They will work for an employer like employer 1, who finds it fairly easy to operate a workplace that is relatively free of the disamenity. Workers 2 and 3 will be employed in firms that are less able to reduce the amount of the disamenity and maintain a reasonable profit. Workers with the least dislike for the disamenity will be matched by the market with employers who have the greatest difficulty in removing the disamenity. The market will be observed offering a greater reward to those otherwise identical workers whose workplace eliminates less of the disamenity. In Figure 12.2 the market trade-off between pay and the disamenity is shown by the heavy line WW. All workers are as well off as they can be, given that the competitive market produces zero economic profits. Each firm is making the best return on investment it can, given the need to attract workers to the job by offering sufficient pay to compensate for the disamenity. Equilibrium occurs where each firm is making normal profits (a competitive rate of return on capital).

The trade-off WW is much flatter than would be required if all workers were like worker 1. Very large pay premia would have to be offered by firms like employer 3 in order to induce workers to accept jobs that involve large amounts of the disamenity. Other things equal, the greater workers' distastes are for a disamenity, the greater will be the pay premium associated with that disamenity, and the smaller will be the amount of the disamenity that is present. If all employers were like employer 1, we would also observe less of the disamenity in the market.

This discussion may seem to contradict reality. After all, the dirtiest, most dangerous jobs are not associated with the highest pay. Professors and lawyers usually earn more than sanitation and construction workers. These gross pay differentials, however, do not standardize for other factors, such as the amount of formal training embodied in the different workers. Professors and lawyers incur much greater costs of schooling than do sanitation and construction workers, perhaps enough to account for their higher pay. The theory of compensating differentials only states that pay premia for disamenities will exist in the long run among otherwise identical people—identical along such dimensions as training, education, and other observable characteristics.

Other Effects on Occupational Pay Differences

It should also be noted that one may not observe compensating differentials in the short run. If the general level of demand for labor in all occupations is low enough (i.e., if there is substantial demand-deficiency unemployment, or substantial unemployment among particular groups such as immigrants or racial minorities), market conditions can cause a reversal of the usual differentials. Among the least agreeable occupations are many that require little skill. Disadvantaged minorities and the long-term unemployed may bid down relative pay in such occupations. Alternatively, employers may reduce their efforts to decrease the levels of disamenities facing workers in these occupations. The pay for disagreeable work may be less than that for agreeable work requiring no more skill, which is opposite to the result Smith predicted; but the composition of the work force in the two sets of occupations will be noticeably different. A return to tight labor-market conditions would produce shortages of labor in the disagreeable occupations and eventually lead to a reappearance of compensating pay differentials.

A second component of occupational pay differentials is the premium for accepting the risk of low income. This risk can arise because workers in the occupation are subject to frequent periods of unemployment, or because individuals are uncertain when they enter the occupation how well they will do in it. (We deal with these issues of risky earnings in a section later in this chapter.) So long as these workers, drawn into the occupation by the chance of a large income, are unwilling to leave because of the sunk costs of investment in their training, the occupation will look risky to the next generation of prospective entrants.

Occupational pay differences may also be made up of *rents* to scarce natural talents. These rents, which are pay over and above that required to compensate the worker for the costs of training, are more important in some occupations than in others. Clearly, in the case of professional athletes, actors, artists, and musicians, such rents make up most or all the differences in earnings between the most successful members of the profession and the average member. If average earnings in these professions are above those in other occupations requiring as much training but less native ability, this average difference also consists of rents. But it is not clear that in general there will be such rents. That depends upon whether the large differentials in pay among members in the occupation and the risk implied by these differentials repel more prospective entrants to the occupation than they attract.

The most important basic component of occupational wage differentials is the one mentioned at the beginning of this discussion—the return on investment in acquiring skills. If a skilled occupation is to attract new entrants, the private costs of the training needed to enter it must be recouped over the recruit's working life. The rate of return must be equal to the return on other equally risky investments, or equal to the subjective rate of discount used by entrants in making their decision. Thus as we saw in Chapter 3, pay differentials will exist among workers who are distinguished by the amounts of formal and informal training they have undertaken.

RISKS AND HAZARDS ON THE JOB

Work is dangerous. In the United States in 1980, over 4000 workers were killed on the job, and over 5 million cases of on-the-job injury were reported. As Table 12.1 shows, the distribution of work-related injury and illness is by no means uniform among industries. Construction and mining are much more dangerous than finance and services. For example, in 1980 each 100 workers in construction lost 117.0 workdays due to occupational injury; the same number of workers in finance lost only 12.2 days because of work-related injuries. The substantial differences shown in Table 12.1 hide even greater differences among industries that are disaggregated more finely. In primary lead manufacturing 591.93 workdays per 100 workers were lost due to work-related injury or illness; each worker could expect to lose five days per year because of on-the-job injuries. Among employees of nondeposit trust companies, the rate was 0.8 days per 100 employees. This tremendous diversity of experience suggests that there is room for substantial differences in pay to compensate for the large differences in risks from work.

Comparisons across the columns in Table 12.1 give the impression that the rate of work-related illness and injury increased during the 1970s. This may be the case,

Table 12.1 LOST WORKDAYS FROM OCCUPATIONAL ILLNESS OR INJURY, INCIDENCE PER 100 FULL-TIME WORKERS, BY INDUSTRY, SELECTED YEARS

Industry	Year			
	1973	1975	1979	1980
Agriculture, forestry, and fishing	68.0	73.8	83.7	82.7
Mining	119.6	113.0	150.5	163.6
Construction	98.1	100.8	120.4	117.0
Manufacturing	68.2	75.4	90.2	86.7
Transportation and public utilities	82.5	88.2	107.0	104.5
Wholesale and retail trade	37.6	39.6	49.0	48.7
Finance, insurance, and real estate	10.2	11.4	13.3	12.2
Services	27.5	32.4	38.1	35.8
Total private sector	53.3	56.1	67.7	65.2

Source: Handbook of Labor Statistics, 1980, Table 175, and *Occupational Injuries and Illnesses in the United States by Industry, 1980,* Bulletin No. 2130, Table 1.

although that conclusion must be tempered by recognition that the methods of collecting these data were new in the early 1970s, so that trends are somewhat harder to infer than is usually the case. Also, work-related fatalities decreased during the 1970s (comparing the business-cycle peaks 1973 and 1979) in the United States and in the other leading industrialized nations.[3] With rising real incomes, this reduction in work-related deaths should continue. Wealthier workers seek out safer workplaces; thus increasingly affluent workers can be expected to take part of the wage gains generated by their increased productivity in the form of improvements in workplace safety.[4]

POLICY ISSUE—LEGISLATING WORKPLACE SAFETY

We have not yet developed the tools to analyze the economic effects of the Occupational Safety and Health Act (OSHA) enacted by the federal government in 1970. We can, though, examine whether this program, under which the federal government issues standards specifying limits on various workplace hazards, has been successful in reducing injury rates on the job. Given the substantial rate of work-related injuries, it is worth knowing whether the major federal response to this perceived problem has been successful. Because the U.S. government spends substantial resources enforcing this legislation (employing over 2000 people in its field staff), its success is also related to the problem of efficiency in government.

There are difficulties in assessing how successful the program is in reducing injuries, for those firms that produce more accidents are more likely to be inspected by OSHA personnel. This is a sensible allocation of resources, putting the greatest emphasis on high-accident plants where presumably the marginal impact will be greatest. Accounting for this difficulty by examining annual accident rates in plants inspected early in the calendar year, for which most of the annual experience could be affected by the inspection, and those plants inspected late in the year, one study found that inspections had a slight effect in 1973, but had none in 1974. An update of this study found no effects of inspections in 1976 to 1978, despite sharp increases in the average penalties assessed against employers

[3]International Labor Organization, *Yearbook of Labor Statistics, 1981,* Table 27B.

[4]W. Kip Viscusi, "Wealth Effects and Earnings Premiums for Job Hazards," *Review of Economics and Statistics* (60): 408–416 (1978).

who were found not to be in compliance with OSHA standards.[5] This evidence does not prove the program was ineffective—the threat of inspection may induce equal increases in safety among all firms because of the deterrent effect of OSHA inspections and penalties. It does, however, cast doubt on the efficiency of the standards-inspections program as a way of reducing workplace injuries and fatalities.

Pay Differences Due to Dangerous or Unpleasant Work

That there are substantial differences among industries in the rates of work-related death and injury does not necessarily mean that pay differences will be associated with these rates. As we saw in the previous section, if enough workers do not mind what others view as a disamenity, there may be no premium attached to jobs with that characteristic. Although very few workers welcome the possibility of being killed or maimed on the job, their attitudes toward these risks vary substantially. Perhaps there are enough workers who are not too bothered by dangerous jobs so that the premia paid on these jobs do not need to be very large.

Substantial effort has been devoted to measuring the extra compensation provided for the risk of being killed on the job. The evidence is overwhelming that workers facing a higher probability of death on the job receive higher pay than otherwise identical workers. The size of this compensating differential for the risk of death varies in studies using data from the 1970s of between $200 and $3500 of extra pay per year for each one-thousandth increase in the probability of being killed.[6] Comparing an occupation that is completely safe to one where there is a 1 percent chance of being killed on the job, otherwise identical workers in the second occupation would earn between $2000 and $35,000 extra per year.

Pay premia for the risk of injury on the job are likely to be smaller and more difficult to discern than the compensating differentials for the risk of death on the job. The evidence does suggest, however, that workers' aversion to risk requires employers to pay extra if workers are more likely to suffer injuries. One study of six manufacturing industries between 1947 and 1973 finds pay premia of between 0.2 and 2 percent associated with each 10 percent increase in the accident rate. Among otherwise identical workers in 1969, those working in industries in which the risk of injury was 10 percent above the average received wages that were 1 percent above average.[7] The market does compensate workers, at least in part, for the possibility of being injured on the job by inducing employers whose workplaces are dangerous to offer compensation above that offered in safer workplaces.

Assume that the disamenity in Figure 12.2 is workplace danger. Data on the characteristics of workers in different jobs and the pay premia they receive allow us to infer what kinds of workers correspond to the individuals whose indifference curves

[5]Robert Smith, "The Impact of OSHA Inspections on Manufacturing Injury Rates," *Journal of Human Resources* (14): 145–170 (1979), and David McCaffrey, "An Assessment of OSHA's Recent Effects on Injury Rates," *Journal of Human Resources* (18): 131–145 (1983).

[6]Robert Smith, "Compensating Wage Differentials and Public Policy: A Review," *Industrial and Labor Relations Review* (32): 339–352 (1979).

[7]Hal Sider, "Work-Related Accidents and the Production Process," Working Paper No. 117, U.S. Bureau of Labor Statistics, Office of Research and Evaluation, Washington, 1981, and Viscusi, loc. cit.

are described by I_1, I_2, or I_3. Workers with more human capital, as measured by years of education and extent of experience, are located in safer and healthier jobs. Inferentially, the indifference maps that are further out on the WW line in Figure 12.2 are those of workers who are less skilled. Married males receive greater pay premia for on-the-job risks than do unmarried males, and nonwhites receive higher premia for risks than do whites.[8] Whether this is because married men and nonwhites are more risk averse than others, or because they are more likely to locate in jobs that are less safe and therefore provide above-average risk premia, is unclear.

In addition to the risk of death or injury, other aspects of work are also disamenities. Noise, stress, heat or cold, requirements of physical strength, lack of freedom to set one's own hours, and others may fall in this category. There is no clear evidence like that for workplace safety that these characteristics generate pay premia among otherwise identical workers, either in a broad sample of occupations or within a specific occupation.[9] Consideration of requirements for physical strength suggests why these effects might be small or absent. The supply of physical strength could well exceed employers' needs for workers to fill jobs that require this attribute. That being the case, no pay premium will exist. The argument is less plausible for stress and heat or cold, but their inherently subjective nature makes it difficult to evaluate how the labor market will reward those who accept these disamenities. One person's stressful job may suit another worker perfectly.

It is well known that large plants and firms pay higher wages than do smaller plants in the same industry. Workers of the same demographic characteristics and who embody the same human capital received 6 percent higher wages in 1979 if they worked in a plant employing more than 1000 workers than others in a plant employing fewer than 25 workers. Given plant size, workers in larger firms also received higher wages than other workers.[10] These wage differences may reflect compensating differentials for the disamenity of working in the more rigid environment that often characterizes larger firms and plants. If not, we must infer that the larger plants and firms are more productive (to justify the higher wages), for the wage differences are standardized for differences in firms' product-market power.

Workplace Standards

Having discussed the economics of occupational safety, we can now examine the effect of the workplace standards that have been set by the agency that is responsible for enforcement of OSHA. The effect of this legislation on workers' well-being in a competitive labor market can be seen from Figure 12.3. Typical workers receive a

[8] Greg Duncan, "Earnings Functions and Nonpecuniary Benefits," *Journal of Human Resources* (11): 462–483 (1976); Richard Thaler and Sherwin Rosen, "The Value of Saving a Life: Evidence from the Labor Market," in Nestor Terleckyj (ed.). *Household Production and Consumption,* Columbia University Press, New York, 1975.

[9] Charles Brown, "Equalizing Differences in the Labor Market," *Quarterly Journal of Economics* (94): 113–134 (1980); Albert Rees and George Shultz, *Workers and Wages in an Urban Labor Market,* University of Chicago Press, Chicago, 1970, pp. 110–112.

[10] Stanley Masters, "An Interindustry Analysis of Wages and Plant Size," *Review of Economics and Statistics* (51): 341–345 (1969); and Wesley Mellow, "Employer Size and Wages," *Review of Economics and Statistics* (64): 495–501 (1982).

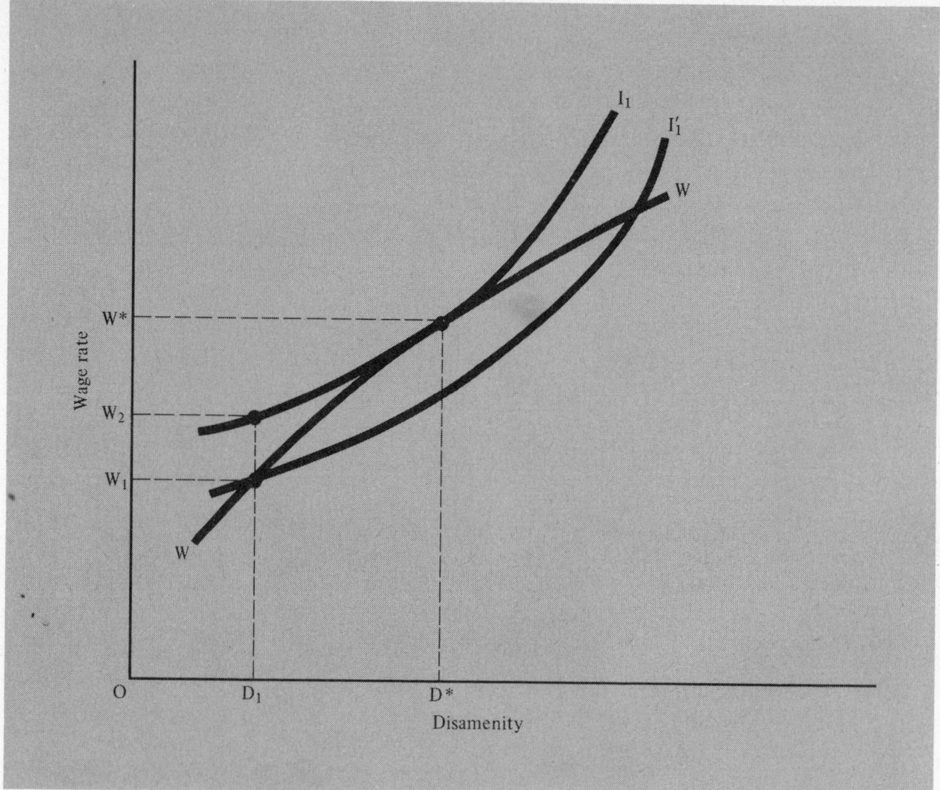

Figure 12.3 The impact of a workplace standard in a competitive market.

wage rate of W* and work in an environment that is characterized by an amount D* of the disamenity. Given the structure of firms' costs, I_1 is the highest indifference level they can attain. Suppose a standard is imposed requiring firms to operate with no more than D_1 of the disamenity. The wage rate will drop along the WW line from W* to W_1, as employers reduce pay in order to devote expenditures to reducing the disamenity while still retaining normal profits. Typical workers can now only attain indifference level I_1', a lower level than they reached in the absence of the standard. $W^* - W_2$ represents the reduction in pay that workers would be willing to take in order to obtain a reduction in the disamenity from D* to D_1, for they can remain on indifference curve I_1. The distance $W_2 - W_1$ represents a loss to the workers, who are forced to take a larger cut in pay than they would be willing to offer for the reduction in the disamenity from D* to D_1.

This argument assumes that the labor market is described by competition among both workers and employers.[11] To the extent that this assumption is incorrect, workers might be made better off by the imposition of a standard. For example, as we saw in the previous section, persistent unemployment may drive workers into risky jobs and so reduce pay premia for risks that the imposition of standards will

[11] A detailed discussion of the process of standard setting and its problems is contained in Robert Smith, *The Occupational Safety and Health Act: Its Goals and Its Achievements,* American Enterprise Institute, Washington, 1976.

make workers better off. In the long run at least part of the unemployment will be eliminated, but substantial time may pass before this occurs. In the short run the standards would improve workers' well-being. A more important potential cause of a failure of the market to pay an appropriate differential for unsafe work is insufficient information about the nature of the risks. The evidence we presented before shows workers receive some compensation for workplace risks. Whether these premia are enough to reflect all the safety and health risks of the job cannot be inferred. It is likely, though, that the premia compensate better for safety than for health risks. Workers have good information on frequent and observable events, such as work injuries. Information is probably much worse on the extent to which chemicals, dust, or asbestos in the workplace turn out to be carcinogens that produce an above-average rate of cancer up to 30 years after initial exposure to them. This consideration suggests that the market for occupational health will work less well than that for industrial safety. Health standards set by the government can improve the well-being of workers if the government has better information about the nature of the hazards than workers do.

POLICY ISSUE—"TAXING" EMPLOYERS FOR WORK-RELATED INJURIES

Table 12.2 shows the number of occupational injuries per 100 workers in 1980 among firms of different size. In the United States, there is a very pronounced inverse U-shaped relation between employer size and the frequency of work-related employee injuries. This phenomenon is not merely due to aggregation across major industries. Even within one major industry, manufacturing, as column (2) of Table 12.2 shows, the same relationship exists. What causes this unusual phenomenon?

Table 12.2 OCCUPATIONAL INJURY RATES PER 100 FULL-TIME WORKERS, BY SIZE OF EMPLOYER, 1980

Number of employees	Private sector (1)	Manufacturing (2)
1–19	3.6	7.8
20–49	8.3	13.9
50–99	10.9	16.6
100–249	12.1	16.2
250–499	11.7	14.1
500–999	9.9	11.1
1000–2499	8.0	8.2
2500+	6.5	5.8

Source: Occupational Injuries and Illnesses in the United States by Industry, 1980, Bulletin No. 2130, Table 5.

In the United States, employers are required to compensate injured workers according to schedules that are set by law in each state. Many firms cover the risk that the cost of these payments imposes by paying premiums to insurance companies that specialize in this business. To some extent the premiums are experience-rated: Employers that have generated more frequent and severe accidents in the past pay higher insurance rates now. However, the structure of insurance premiums makes this relation very weak except among firms having at least 500 employees.[12] This helps to explain the lower injury rates

[12] Louise Russell, "Safety Incentives in Workmen's Compensation Insurance," *Journal of Human Resources* (9): 361–375 (1974).

observed in larger firms. Large employers have an incentive, in the form of reduced insurance premiums, to operate safely. This is especially true among very large firms that generally self-insure: They pay the entire cost of workers' compensation. The low injury rates in small firms are not explicable by the structure of the workers' compensation system, since insurance premiums for small employers are not well experience-rated. Perhaps the more intimate nature of the small workplace induces employees to be more careful; or perhaps small firms with their lower base of capital per worker provide fewer opportunities for injury, because there are fewer repetitive tasks that induce boredom and carelessness.

The differences in experience rating by firm size suggest not only that there is an incentive for larger firms to reduce injuries but that this incentive affects firms' behavior. One study that examined individual states in the United States between 1900 and 1940 (a period when many states adopted workers' compensation laws) shows that making employers liable for accidents reduced injury rates below what they otherwise would have been. Consistent with this observation is evidence from 1970 that the provision of workers' compensation benefits reduces compensating wage differentials for the risk of industrial fatality (by making workers more willing to bear risks).[13] Together with the evidence on the relation between firm size and the extent of experience rating of insurance premiums, this finding strongly supports the view that "taxing" injuries—assessing higher costs on those employers who generate more injuries—is a good way to reduce injury rates. If compensating differentials are insufficient because the market for safety is imperfect, a properly structured workers' compensation system can improve workers' well-being. Taxing employers for work-related injuries may be a better way to reduce injuries than setting safety standards for the workplace.

LOCATIONAL AMENITIES

In Chapter 7 we showed how interregional migration tends to eliminate pay differences among workers having the same skills but located in different areas. In the United States, for example, this process has resulted in a substantial narrowing of the divergence of real wages between the North and South. The difference has not completely disappeared, though: Even in 1980 nominal earnings were 8 percent lower in the South than in the rest of the country, and real earnings probably were, too. Within occupations that are classified very narrowly, wages are lower in the South than in other regions of the United States.[14] This may merely reflect a continuing disequilibrium in the labor market, but it may show that interregional pay differences among workers of identical skills reflect compensating differentials for permanent differences in the amenities associated with locations.

Which of these views is correct is shown by the same considerations that underlay the analysis of compensating differentials for risk. To the extent that workers' views of differences in the characteristics of jobs among locations are similar, the disamenity on the horizontal axis in Figure 12.2 can be something that differs among areas. Characteristics such as extremes of temperature and precipitation may be viewed as disamenities by most workers. Employers will then be forced

[13] James Chelius, *Workplace Safety and Health: The Role of Workers' Compensation,* American Enterprise Institute, Washington, 1977, pp. 75–80; and Richard Arnould and Len Nichols, "Wage-Risk Premiums and Workers' Compensation," *Journal of Political Economy* (91): 332–340 (1983).

[14] Robert Goldfarb and Anthony Yezer, "Evaluating Alternative Theories of Intercity and Interregional Wage Differentials," *Journal of Regional Science* (16): 345–363 (1976).

to offer pay premia if the jobs they offer are located in areas where value of the disamenity is high. The market for the locational disamenity will be characterized by the same heavy WW line in Figure 12.2 that characterizes the market for any disamenity.

The importance of pay premia for locational disamenities is illustrated especially well by the market for professors. This is a market that is at least nationwide, and one in which employers have little choice about location. A Nobel prize-winning Harvard physicist was approached about a job by a large public university in a small city in the Southwest. When asked about living in a hot climate away from the urban amenities of Boston, he answered that the heat appeared to be less of a problem the more he heard about the salary he would be offered. One Big 10 university pays substantially less in most fields than the others, yet it has continued to attract some of the leading scholars in many disciplines. The administrators at that university argue that salaries that are 10 percent lower than elsewhere are a price people must pay to enjoy the beautiful scenery and pleasant environment.

These considerations do not deal with the supply side of the market for the disamenity. If employers located in areas that workers would rather avoid must pay more, how can they compete with employers located elsewhere who have lower labor costs? If they are free to relocate their business, they will move to the area of lower labor costs. In fact, though, employers in many industries are not free to relocate, or do so at the expense of higher costs for nonlabor inputs into production. Minerals must be mined where they are located: Appalachian coal cannot be mined by workers living in Florida. Less directly, the total cost of producing steel may be lower if the plants are located between Chicago and Pittsburgh, even though labor costs may be higher, because iron ore can be transported cheaply to those cities. A location that suffers from what workers view as disamenities must be more productive in some respects, otherwise no firm would produce there. Thus employers have the same kinds of isoprofit curves for locational disamenities that we saw in Figure 12.2.

Whether in fact locational characteristics do produce pay differences is essentially an empirical question. It depends on the ability of employers to relocate away from what is viewed as a disamenity by workers and on differences among workers in their distastes for the disamenity. Some evidence on the importance of locational disamenities as they affect pay premia is shown in Table 12.3. For each of the three studies there are listed the percentage differences in earnings between otherwise identical workers located in a city having an above-average value of the disamenity compared to a city in which the disamenity is at its average for the sample of cities under study. Pay premia clearly exist in cities having higher crime rates or greater pollution levels. This should not be surprising, for it is unlikely that many workers would prefer locating in areas having more crime or pollution. The existence of compensating differentials for variations in climate is less clear. Cold weather is apparently disliked by most workers: More heating-degree days, more snow, and a lower average temperature in January all produce positive pay premia. On the other hand, the two studies that examine the effect of locating in a rainy area offer conflicting evidence on its effects on earnings; and although more sunny days induce a greater supply of labor to the area, as shown by the negative pay premium, a higher average temperature in July does not require employers to offer higher wages.

Table 12.3 PERCENTAGE EFFECTS OF LOCATIONAL AMENITIES AND DISAMENITIES ON EARNINGS[a]

Amenity or disamenity	Male workers, 18 cities, 1973	Male workers, 19 cities, 1970	Teachers, 1419 school districts, 1970
Crime or assault rate	4.8	13.3	0.9
Air pollution (particulates)	2.2	10.7	
Heating-degree days	9.0		
Total snowfall	1.7		
Sunny days		−43.8	
Rainy days or rainfall		6.9	−8.8
January temperature[b]			−2.7
July temperature[b]			−0.7

[a]Compares the city with a value of the amenity twice the average to the city with the average value of the amenity. Differences in personal and job characteristics are accounted for, as are cost of living differences.

[b]Compares the city with a value of the amenity 10 percent above the average to the city with the average value.

Source: Computed from Jennifer Roback, "Wages, Rents and the Quality of Life," *Journal of Political Economy* (90): 1270 (1982), cols. 1, 2; Sherwin Rosen, "Wage-Based Indexes of Urban Quality of Life," in Peter Mieszkowski and Mahlon Straszheim (eds.). *Current Issues in Urban Economics,* Johns Hopkins University Press, Baltimore, 1979, p. 99, cols. 7, 28; and Lawrence Kenny and David Denslow, "Compensating Differentials in Teachers' Salaries," *Journal of Urban Economics* (7): 201 (1980).

Relative to the locational structure of jobs in the United States, workers must be compensated for living where there is more crime and pollution, and where there is more cold and snow, although not necessarily where it is rainier or hotter in the summer. This means that so long as the location of jobs continues to be conditioned partly by differences in nonlabor costs, these disamenities will produce interregional differences in pay among otherwise identical workers. These compensating differentials reflect an equilibrium of workers' tastes and employers' costs; they will not be eliminated by interregional migration.

RISKY EMPLOYMENT AND INCOME

Imagine a worker confronted with the choice between two jobs, one offering a $5 wage rate and guaranteed employment, the other offering a $10 wage rate but a 50 percent chance of being unemployed half the time. One might guess that most workers would prefer the certainty of the $5 per hour job to the risky prospect of a $10 per hour job. This preference can be demonstrated for typical workers, using the same analysis that led to our conclusions about labor-force participation and the choice of hours of work in Chapters 1 and 2. In Figure 12.4 typical workers can choose combinations of leisure and income along the budget line OAB. In the absence of any restrictions on the hours they may work, the workers choose to work H* hours; point P along indifference curve I_1 is the best they can do. Assume they are now faced with the possibility of being able to obtain only H_1 hours during half the weeks of the year. In those weeks they would be located at point Q in Figure 12.4. To be as well off in those weeks as they are in the weeks they can work H* hours, they would have to be at point R; to be there they would require a higher wage rate, shown by the slope of the segment AR. The average wage rate over the year is the slope of the line that bisects the angle BAR; alternatively, it is shown as the slope of the line

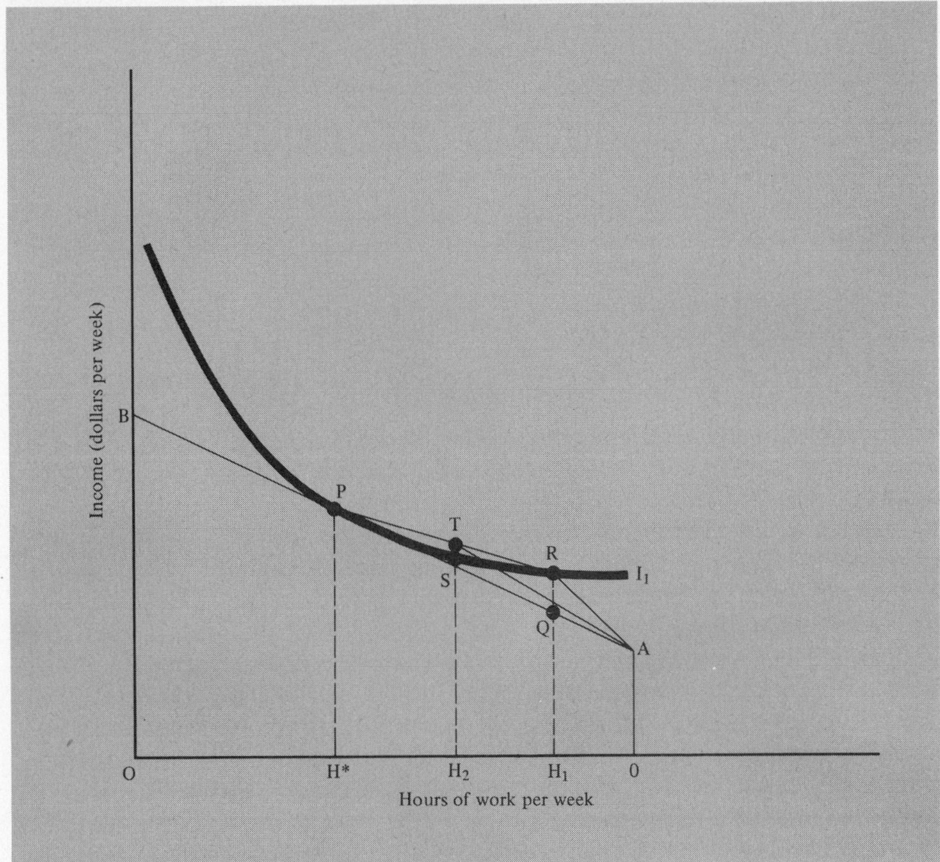

Figure 12.4 Uncertainty about hours of work.

connecting A and point T, the middle of the line segment PR. If the workers could obtain H_2 hours per week with certainty, they could remain on indifference curve I_1 if the wage rate equals the slope of AS. Since AT lies above AS, the wage rate associated with the risk of being unemployed must exceed the wage rate associated with a job that has no such risk. Since expected hours are the same if they work H_2 each week, or work H* and H_1 each half the time, earnings must be higher the greater is the risk of variation in hours if they are to maintain indifference level I_1.

This discussion shows that the typical worker will view the risk of unemployment as something that must be compensated for by higher pay. As with any other disamenity, workers' distastes for it will differ, so that workers will be arrayed according to their distastes as in Figure 12.2. Because of workers' tastes, employers will have an incentive to avoid variations in hours of work. Avoiding them is costly, though: Employers would have to maintain their work force in a time of slack product demand, or refrain from using overtime during cyclical booms. This makes employers' isoprofit curves in the market for the disamenity of risky employment look like those in Figure 12.2. Taken together, employers' and employees' behavior will produce an increasingly positive pay premium, the greater the risk of unemployment in the job is. The premium will be another reflection of the implicit contract between workers and their employer that we discussed in Chapter 8.

Without a doubt, real wage rates are higher where the unemployment rate is higher. One study of workers in 12 large cities in 1966, a year in which there was little demand-deficiency unemployment, found that each 1 percentage-point higher unemployment rate was associated with a 2 percent higher real wage rate. Estimates of the effect on nominal wage rates using data for 1970 and 1973 range from nearly 0 to as high as a 5 percent wage premium associated with each additional 1 percentage point of unemployment.[15] These observed pay premia may partly reflect employers' moving up their demand schedules for labor. The higher real wage will reduce the number of workers demanded; if labor-force participation is relatively insensitive to the probability of obtaining work, a positive correlation between real wages and unemployment rates will be produced. This correlation need not indicate the existence of a compensating differential for unemployment. Nonetheless, its existence even in years when there was little demand-deficiency unemployment provides some evidence of such a compensating differential.

Better evidence is provided by the analysis of data from 1970 to 1975 that allow us to infer workers' desired hours of work per week and the hours they actually work. The average worker received a wage rate that was 3 percent higher than that received by otherwise identical workers who worked exactly the hours they desired. This compensating differential for more variable employment differs if there are nonmarket mechanisms that compensate workers for the risk of unemployment. Thus higher unemployment insurance benefits reduce the pay premium associated with the risk of unemployment, and do so on a nearly one-for-one basis.[16] This offsetting effect suggests that, as with pay premiums for the risks of work-related injuries or fatalities, the labor market provides some of the compensation that government programs offer; and the introduction of those programs reduces the compensation offered by the market.

As we saw in Chapter 3, greater risk in the prospects for earnings in an occupation reduces the supply of labor to that occupation. Pay premia are associated with greater dispersion of earnings within a particular occupation: Although some workers may view as an attractive gamble entry into an occupation where a few do very well while most do badly, the majority of workers require a pay differential to compensate for uncertainty about lifetime earnings.[17] This result and the evidence on the effect of unemployment on wage differentials underscore the conclusion that

[15]Robert Hall, "Turnover in the Labor Force," *Brookings Papers on Economic Activity*: 732 (1972); Sherwin Rosen, "Wage-Based Indexes of Urban Quality of Life," Peter Mieszkowski and Mahlon Straszheim (eds.). *Current Issues in Urban Economics,* Johns Hopkins University Press, Baltimore, 1979; and Jennifer Roback, "Wages, Rents and the Quality of Life," *Journal of Political Economy* (90): 1257–1278 (1982).

[16]John Abowd and Orley Ashenfelter, "Anticipated Unemployment, Temporary Layoffs and Compensating Wage Differentials," in Sherwin Rosen (ed.). *Studies in Labor Markets,* University of Chicago Press, Chicago, 1981, p. 160.

[17]See Allan King, "Occupational Choice, Risk, Aversion, and Wealth," *Industrial and Labor Relations Review* (27): 586–596 (1974); Richard Evans and Robert Weinstein, "Ranking Occupations as Risky Income Prospects," *Industrial and Labor Relations Review* (35): 252–259 (1982); and William Johnson, "Uncertainty and the Distribution of Earnings," in F. Thomas Juster (ed.). *The Distribution of Economic Well-Being,* Ballinger, Cambridge, Mass., 1977.

Table 12.4 INDEXES OF UNION SKILL DIFFERENTIALS, SKILLED TO UNSKILLED UNION WAGE RATES, 1907–1980

	Comparison		
Date	Bricklayers and Bricklayers' tenders (1)	Machinists and press assistants (2)	Local truck drivers and helpers (3)
1907	172	—	—
1917	165	128	—
1927	152	106	—
1937	138	109	113
1947[a]	121	97	108
1957[b]	113	96	101
1967	100	100	100
1977	99	99	100
1980[c]	99	103	101

[a] 1948 for printing.
[b] 1958 for printing.
[c] 1978 for printing; 1979 for truck driving.
Source: Union Wages and Benefits, Building Trades, July 1, 1980, Bulletin No. 2091, Table 2; *Union Wages and Benefits, Printing Trades, September 1, 1978,* Bulletin No. 2049, Table 2; and *Union Wages and Benefits, Local Truck Drivers and Helpers, September 3, 1979,* Bulletin No. 2089, Table 1.

most workers are very averse to bearing risks that involve their incomes and that they must be compensated in order to do so.

THE CHANGING SKILL DIFFERENTIAL

The return to investments in acquiring skills, independent of any risks associated with occupational choice or the workplace, produces a higher wage rate for the skilled than the less skilled worker. Historically, there has been a clear tendency for occupational wage differentials to narrow in percentage terms. Evidence of the narrowing of skill differentials can be assembled by taking the ratios of earnings in skilled occupations to those in unskilled occupations and observing the movement of such ratios through time. This method is the easiest to understand and the most frequently used, although the results may be influenced by the particular occupations chosen for comparison.

An example of the narrowing of skill differentials using the ratio method is given in Table 12.4. Column (1) shows the ratio of indexes of skilled to unskilled wages in two trades in construction; column (2) shows similar indexes for two trades in printing, whereas column (3) is for local transport. The first two imply a rapid narrowing of skill differentials in the first three decades of this century. All three columns in Table 12.4 suggest that this narrowing continued at least until the 1940s; in construction, and less so in local transit, the trend continued through the 1950s. A similar trend exists in the relative wages of maintenance workers within cities since 1952.[18]

[18] Robert Schoeplein, "Secular Changes in the Skill Differential in Manufacturing," *Industrial and Labor Relations Review* (30): 314–324 (1977).

The ratio method is necessarily confined to selected trades and may give a biased picture for that reason. To avoid this possibility one can examine changes in the coefficient of variation, a measure of relative dispersion, computed across all the occupations in an industry.[19] The historical narrowing of relative differentials is also apparent when this method is used.

Most studies of occupational wage differentials have dealt with skilled and unskilled manual occupations, where good data are available over a long period. Equally striking evidence of narrowing can be found by comparing the movement of earnings in white-collar and blue-collar occupations. In 1899 the annual earnings of nonproduction workers in manufacturing were 2.5 times as large as the annual earnings of production workers (wage earners). By 1980 this ratio had fallen to 1.5. The drop occurred despite the great increase in the proportion of professional and technical workers among the nonproduction workers. Given the size of union relative wage gaps, only a small part can be explained by the growth of blue-collar unions during this period. Since many nonproduction workers are clerical workers and the basic clerical skills are literacy and facility with figures, we may surmise that the fall in the private cost of primary and secondary education has been a basic force in narrowing the relative differentials.

The fall in the private costs of training has been of two kinds. First, the rise in the legal school-leaving age and the prohibition of child labor have largely eliminated juveniles between the ages of 12 and 15 from the full-time labor force. Since by remaining in school people in this age group no longer sacrifice potential full-time earnings, their forgone earnings have ceased to be a private cost of secondary education. However, these earnings are still a social cost, because society has decided to sacrifice current output in order to increase its investment in education. Second, more and more of the direct costs of secondary and, especially, higher education are paid by government or by the educational institutions rather than by students themselves and their families.

As we showed in Chapter 3, the fall in the private costs of secondary and higher education has contributed to the tremendous increase in the number of people receiving it. The result has been a sharp rise in the fraction of the labor force with the basic educational qualifications for professional, managerial, and clerical work. The same forces have also reduced the private costs of learning skilled manual trades. Apprentices can now enter apprenticeship at a later age, take fewer years to become journeymen, and earn a higher fraction of a journeyman's wage during their apprenticeship.

This argument implies that if all the costs of training needed to acquire skill were paid by the public through a system of grants, occupational wage differentials would become much smaller and be based entirely on compensation for nonpecuniary disadvantages of occupations and on rents to scarce abilities. These factors might be sufficient to justify some of the ordinary rules of wage and salary administration, such as the rules that supervisors should receive more than the people they

[19] Paul Keat, "Long-run Changes in Occupational Wage Structure, 1900–1956," *Journal of Political Economy* (68): 584–600 (1960). The coefficient of variation is the standard deviation divided by the mean.

supervise or that additional responsibility justifies additional pay. The reward for extra responsibility could be based on the assumption that scarce natural ability is involved in good supervision or that, other things equal, most people dislike taking responsibility.

A second major force that has lowered skill differentials in the United States during this century has been fluctuations in the rate of immigration. As we saw in Chapter 7, if immigrants are mainly unskilled workers, a rise in the rate of immigration will raise the skill differential by increasing the relative supply of unskilled labor. Indeed, accounting for historical changes in the average educational attainment of the work force, we note that the skill differential in a variety of construction trades fell less rapidly in those periods when the rate of immigration was higher.[20]

Since 1923 immigration laws have usually kept total immigration low and within this total have encouraged the immigration of those with skills. The role played by the European immigrant has since that time been played to some extent by migration from farm to city. Like the last wave of European immigrants, the internal rural migrant has reached the cities with little schooling and no industrial experience. The force of this migration in keeping skill differentials wide in nonfarm employment must now be getting weaker with the declining size of the remaining farm population. The increased rate of immigration in the 1970s that we noted in Chapter 7 may help reverse the narrowing of the skill differential, especially if it is accompanied by reductions in the share of the costs of education and training that are borne by government.

DIFFERENCES BY INDUSTRY: THE PUBLIC SECTOR

We noted at the beginning of this chapter that in competitive markets there will be no long-run pay differentials among industries except those arising from interindustry differences in the mix of occupations. An additional requirement is that industries do not differ in the hazards and risks offered to workers in the same occupation. Even accounting for these possibilities, though, pay differentials can persist in the long run if markets are not competitive. We saw in Chapter 4, for example, that employers who operate in more concentrated product markets offer higher pay to otherwise identical workers. Monopsony might also produce pay differentials among industries, to the extent that some industries are more likely than others to be located in monopsonistic labor markets. In Chapter 5, however, we noted that such markets are not likely to be of major significance in the long run in developed economies.

Nonprofit firms and governments need not minimize costs, so that the pay they offer may differ from that offered in the for-profit sector to equally qualified workers in equally risky jobs. Consider the data presented in Table 12.5, showing the ratio of earnings of full-time civilian government workers—federal, and state and local—to the average for the entire U.S. economy. Federal government employees earn substantially more than workers in the private sector. Their relative advantage has fallen recently, though, after rising very sharply in the late 1950s and the late 1960s.

[20] Eliot Orton, "Changes in the Skill Differential: Union Wages in Construction, 1907–1972," *Industrial and Labor Relations Review* (30): 16–24 (1976).

Table 12.5 RATIO OF EARNINGS OF FULL-TIME PUBLIC EMPLOYEES TO ALL FULL-TIME EMPLOYEES' EARNINGS, 1956–1981

Year	Federal civilian workers	State and local general government
1956	1.19	0.92
1961	1.30	0.98
1966	1.31	0.99
1971	1.42	1.04
1976	1.40	1.00
1981	1.34	0.95

Source: U.S. Department of Commerce, *Survey of Current Business,* selected July issues, Table 6.9B, July 1982.

State and local government workers, on the other hand, earn no more than workers in the private sector. Indeed, today their relative earnings are slightly less, after having risen steadily during the 1950s and 1960s.

The ratios presented in Table 12.5 are gross differentials, unadjusted for the many other differences that may distinguish both workers and jobs in the public and private sectors. Consider first the federal sector that, although only one-fifth as large as the state and local sector in the United States, is important both because of its pervasiveness and because wage determination is controlled centrally. The first row of Table 12.6 presents an analysis of this issue for the federal sector. The gross differentials are quite close to those shown in Table 12.5, although Table 12.6 is based on the information from the Current Population Survey rather than from the national income accounts that form the basis for Table 12.5. The adjusted differentials are based upon techniques that account for differences in human capital (education and experience), demographic characteristics, occupation, location and union status, and the rewards to these characteristics in the two sectors. After all these adjustments a substantial wage differential still remains, suggesting that an identical average worker receives more in the federal government than in the private sector. Assuming the adjusted differentials in Table 12.6 fell along with the gross differentials shown in Table 12.5, we can infer that federal workers still received a wage premium of at least 10 percent in 1981.

Although this is true for the average federal worker, other data suggest that among the top civil servants, the wage premium may be zero or negative. Among elected or appointed federal officials, the premium is negative: These people sacri-

Table 12.6 ANALYSIS OF PUBLIC-PRIVATE WAGE RATIOS, 1975

	Males		Females	
	Gross	Adjusted	Gross	Adjusted
Federal	1.39	1.15–1.18	1.46	1.21–1.24
State	1.08	0.89–0.97	1.22	1.01–1.02
Local	1.03	0.91–0.96	1.30	1.01–1.02

Source: Calculated from Sharon Smith, *Equal Pay in the Public Sector: Fact or Fantasy,* Princeton University Industrial Relations Section, Princeton, N.J., 1977, p. 63.

ficed to take high-level public jobs. That "sacrifice" was really an investment, however. Their wages after leaving government far exceeded the earnings they obtained before they entered government.[21]

A number of factors that we have already shown produce compensating wage differentials and that are not considered in the adjustments in Table 12.6 could produce a compensating wage differential for federal employees. However, none of the explanations works out. Federal workers are less likely to indicate that their jobs are repetitive, offer bad working conditions, and require physical strength than are private-sector employees. Federal workers also were more likely to work year-round than were private-sector workers in 1970.[22] Thus the risks of the workplace and the risks of unemployment were lower for the federal worker. The existence of compensating differentials for these risks suggests that the true wage differential is somewhat higher than that presented in Table 12.6. Fringe benefits are a greater percentage of payroll in the federal sector; thus the adjusted wage differential does not reflect a compensating differential for a less attractive set of fringe benefits in the federal sector.[23] In short, all possible adjustments suggest there is a substantial difference in pay between otherwise identical federal and private workers.

In state and local government the situation is quite different. Although these workers did receive slightly higher wage rates than private-sector employees in 1975, the gross differentials are at least fully accounted for by differences in the workers' and jobs' characteristics. Adjusted pay differentials are below one for male employees in state and local government, and only slightly above one for female employees. The true pay differential may be slightly more favorable to state employees than is indicated by Table 12.6, for their working conditions are somewhat less onerous than those of private workers. The opposite is true among local employees: Their jobs appear somewhat riskier and more subject to undesirable working conditions than the average private-sector job.[24]

On net there is a slight advantage to government work averaged over all levels, perhaps a 5 percent pay differential. Although this may not be universal, it is not just an American phenomenon: The same adjusted differential exists for public employees in Canada.[25] There are differences in pay between public and private sectors in the United States, but they vary by level of government. Federal workers receive substantially more than otherwise equal private workers, state government employees receive about the same as their private-sector counterparts, and local government workers receive slightly less. The reasons for the decrease in the pay differential with the level of government are undoubtedly partly political. Partly, though, it may be due to the nature of competition in the market for public services. Local

[21] Arnold Weber and George Burman, "Compensation and Federal Executive Service, Survey and Analysis," in *Staff Report to the Commission on Executive, Legislative and Judicial Salaries,* U.S. Government Printing Office, Washington, 1977.

[22] Joseph Quinn, "Wage Differentials Among Older Workers in the Public and Private Sectors," *Journal of Human Resources* (14): 41–62 (1979), and Sharon Smith, *Equal Pay in the Public Sector: Fact or Fantasy,* Princeton University Industrial Relations Section, Princeton, N.J., 1977, p. 57.

[23] Ibid., p. 27.

[24] Quinn, loc cit.

[25] Morley Gunderson, "Earnings Differentials Between the Public and Private Sectors," *Canadian Journal of Economics* (12): 228–242 (1979).

governments that offer costly services because they pay more for equal-quality labor will find their citizens leaving. This creates substantial incentives for local officials to minimize labor costs; movement between localities within a state is quite easy and may not even require a change in job. Movement among states is somewhat more difficult and less frequent; emigration from the United States is even less frequent.

FRINGE BENEFITS

Compensation consists of two components: money wages and fringe benefits. Throughout this book, and in this chapter thus far, fringe benefits have been brushed aside. The discussion of pay structure has dealt entirely with the structure of money earnings. To remedy this deficiency we examine the structure of compensation in terms of its division between current money earnings and fringe benefits. We do not include as fringe benefits the value of paid leave, such as vacations, holidays, and sick leave. We regard these as reductions in hours of work, which we considered in Chapter 2. The corresponding definition of money earnings is then earnings per hour at work rather than the more common "earnings per hour paid for."

Fringe benefits are any part of compensation not paid currently in money to individual employees, but paid by the employers on behalf of employees, either individually or collectively. This concept does not include those nonpecuniary benefits of a job that involve no explicit cost to employers. Nor does it include costs incurred in the reduction of disamenities, such as the choice of a more expensive but safer technology. However, it is somewhat broader than the national income accounting concept "supplements to wage and salaries," because that concept excludes expenditures on providing such amenities as subsidized cafeterias or recreation facilities. Some fringe benefits are required by law in the United States; the two most important are unemployment insurance and old-age, survivors, disability, and health insurance (Social Security). Others are provided unilaterally by employers or are determined by collective bargaining.

Fringes: Growth and Variety

Compensation *in kind* has long been common in some occupations, for example, the provision of a parsonage to ministers or the provision of room and board to farmhands or domestic servants. Today payment in kind usually takes the form of provisions of the employer's product at a discount or even gratis: Airline employees receive cheap or free flights, some college professors receive reduced tuition for their families, and auto salespeople have access to demonstration models at reduced prices. Nonetheless, with the growth of industrialization these traditional forms of payment in kind have become less important as a part of all compensation. In industrial societies compensation increasingly came to be paid currently in cash, a tendency that seems to have reached its peak in the United States during the 1920s. Since then there has been rapid growth of newer forms of noncurrent or nonmonetary compensation, as shown in Table 12.7. The main task of this section is to explore some of the reasons for this rapid growth.

The growth in fringe benefits has been concentrated particularly in the provision of protection against the risks of sickness, death, and unemployment, and in the provision for retirement. Thus, as Table 12.8 shows for a sample of large firms, life

Table 12.7 FRINGE BENEFITS, TOTAL AND AS A PERCENTAGE OF TOTAL COMPENSATION, SELECTED YEARS, 1929–1982[a]

Year	Supplements to wages and salaries ($ billions)	Supplements as a percent of compensation
1929	$ 0.7	1.3
1939	2.2	4.6
1949	6.5	4.6
1959	21.0	7.5
1969	55.1	9.8
1979	220.7	15.1
1982	295.8	15.9

[a]Supplements include employer contributions to social insurance and employer payments for private health, welfare, pension, and insurance plans. Compensation adds these to wages and salaries.

Source: Council of Economic Advisors, *Economic Report of the President,* 1983, Table B-21.

Table 12.8 EMPLOYEE BENEFITS BY TYPE, 1981 (PERCENTAGE OF PAYROLL)[a]

	All companies	Manufacturing	Nonmanufacturing
Legally required payments	9.0	10.1	7.8
Old-age, survivors, disability, and health insurance	6.3	6.4	6.1
Unemployment compensation	1.2	1.5	0.9
Workers' compensation	1.4	2.1	0.8
Other	0.1	0.1	0
Not legally required	12.7	12.9	12.7
Pensions	5.6	4.5	6.0
Life and health insurance and death benefits	6.0	7.3	5.4
Other agreed-upon payments[b]	1.1	1.1	1.3

[a]Data are based on a survey of 994 reporting employers and cover the employer's share of benefits only. Since the reporting employers tend to be large, the percentages shown may be higher than for all firms. Payment for time not worked, profit-sharing plans, and bonuses are included in the original table and are excluded here.

[b]Includes separation pay, meals furnished, discounts on goods purchased, disability pay, and miscellaneous payments.

Source: Adapted from Chamber of Commerce of the United States, *Employee Benefits 1981,* Table 4.

and health insurance, and provision for retirement, both legally required and privately chosen, totaled nearly 20 percent of payroll. A broader sample of employers in Canada in 1976 showed nonrequired health and pension costs equaling 9.3 percent of payroll, only slightly smaller than the percentage paid by the large employers in the United States, whose costs are shown in Table 12.8.[26]

Market Effects on Fringes

The great advantage of current cash compensation is that it maximizes workers' freedom to spend their income how and when they like and to make such provision

[26]Statistics Canada, *Canada Year Book, 1980–81,* Table 7.28.

for contingencies and risks as they think proper. In contrast, other forms of compensation determine part of their consumption pattern for them and, at worst, may be entirely useless. For example, group life insurance may have little value to single workers without dependents. Single college professors do not benefit at all from free tuition provided for members of the immediate family. More important, employees whose families are generally healthy benefit relatively little from the comprehensive health insurance that they may receive.

In general, a worker will prefer a dollar of after-tax earnings to a dollar of fringe benefits tied to the provision of a particular commodity or service. Consider workers like those whose behavior is depicted in Figure 12.5. They receive after-tax compensation of OC. They can take this all as earnings, or they can choose to spend some of it on a particular fringe benefit. Their tastes between dollars received as earnings and dollars received in the form of the fringe benefit are shown by their indifference curves. These have the usual shape (see Chap. 1), because increasing amounts of the fringe benefit yield successively less additional satisfaction. They choose to buy an amount OA of the fringe benefit, for I_0 is the highest indifference level they can attain. Assume now that the employer offers fringe benefits in an amount OB (also equal to CR) without reducing the wage. The budget line shifts out to CRF; workers

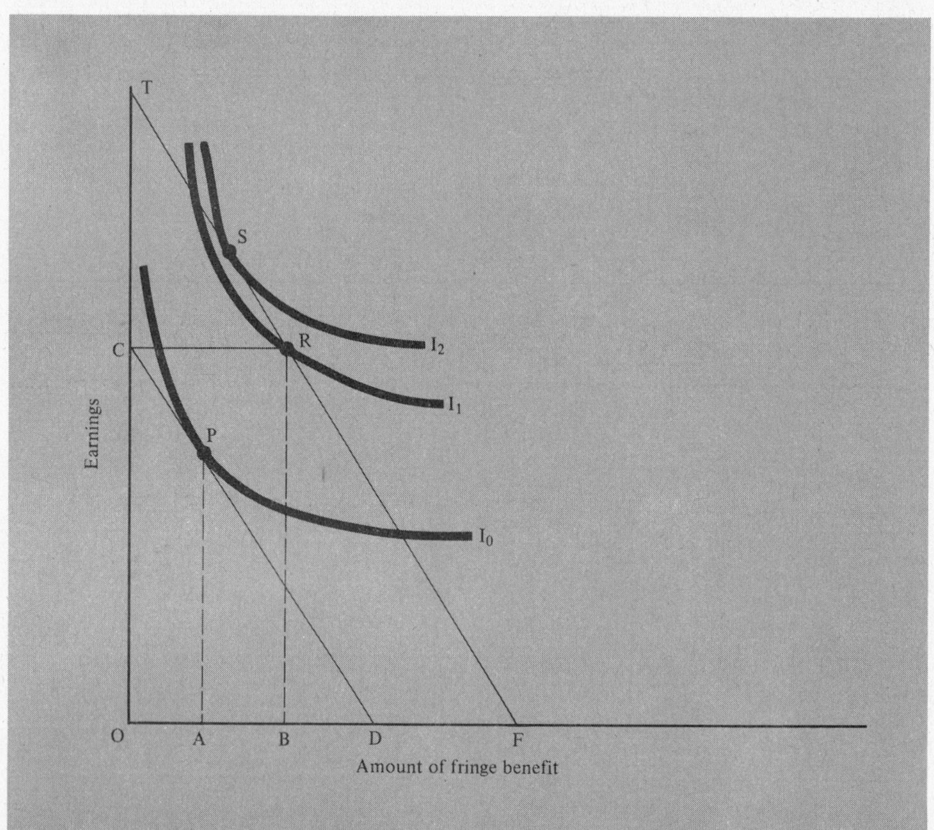

Figure 12.5 The value of fringe benefits.

can now obtain any amount of the fringe up to B without reducing other consumption or savings. As shown in Figure 12.5, the indifference map is such that they do exactly that, achieving the highest satisfaction at point R. Had the employer given them an amount OB in cash, though, the budget line would have been TF; all the points in the triangle CTR would have been available to them, but they are not within the budget if the employer provides the fringe. In this example the workers would have been better off with the cash, for they could have attained their highest indifference level at point S on I_2, consuming less of the fringe and spending the income on something else. Each dollar of fringe benefit beyond an amount OA is worth less to the worker than a dollar of earnings.

Despite employees' inherent preferences for earnings instead of fringes that are imposed upon them, offsetting considerations make fringes attractive for both employers and employees. A dollar of fringe benefits received by the worker may cost the employer less than $1 paid as wages. There are substantial economies of scale in purchasing such services as insurance. Because of savings in administrative costs, insurance carriers may issue group policies at much lower cost than individual ones, but they would not permit individual employees to opt out of the group for fear of creating an adverse selection of risks. Economies of scale in providing nonmonetary compensation can permit an employer to cater to tastes of particular groups in the work force so as to lower the costs of recruiting and holding workers. For example, employers in a warm climate who are the first in their areas to provide a free employee swimming pool may find that this expenditure does more to attract new workers than an equivalent sum spent in raising wages. However, the attraction is only for people who like to swim. If more and more employers tried to follow this example, a point would be reached where pools were being provided for nonswimmers and additional funds would be better spent on cash wages.

Employers may sometimes want to influence employee consumption patterns by providing income in kind in particular forms thought to be beneficial to the firm. In Britain it is common for employers who do not operate staff canteens (cafeterias) to give white-collar workers luncheon vouchers as a fringe benefit. These vouchers are accepted at restaurants in full or part payment for lunch. The company that operates the voucher scheme stresses in its advertising that employees do better work after a good lunch, although a more important reason for the scheme may be to permit employees to escape income taxation on a portion of their income. A study of the *truck system* (payment in kind in nineteenth-century British mining communities) concluded that employers' desires to influence consumption patterns (in particular, to limit expenditures on drink) were an important reason for the system.[27]

Employers who give their employees freedom of choice in insuring against disability or providing for their income after retirement must refrain from aiding those who fail to provide for themselves. If employers relied on workers to purchase individual annuities to furnish income in their old age but were then moved by sympathy to provide later for those employees who did not do so, this provision would weaken the incentives to save on the part of the employees who had not yet retired. On the other hand, to force the retirement of long-service employees who

[27]George Hilton, *The Truck System*, Heffer, Cambridge, Eng., 1960.

have no source of income (or only an inadequate one) might reflect badly on employers or cause them to feel distress. Since even educated and intelligent workers may lack foresight in providing for the distant future or in insuring against unlikely misfortunes, governments and employers generally consider some compulsion to be a lesser evil than complete reliance on individual choice.

Nonmarket and Other Effects

Most forms of fringe benefits either escape income taxation entirely or are taxed on more favorable terms than cash wages. The personal income tax on employer contributions to pensions is deferred until the pension is received, when the worker will usually be in a lower tax bracket. Employer-paid health insurance premiums are not taxed, nor are premiums paid by the employer for workers' life insurance. The personal income tax has grown greatly in importance since the 1920s and is highly progressive with respect to wage and salary income. Tax considerations go a long way in explaining both the growth of fringe benefits through time and their positive correlation with the level of earnings. For example, earnings fell as a fraction of compensation of office employees in large manufacturing establishments from 0.92 to 0.88 between 1966 and 1974. The rise in the marginal income tax rates facing workers, coupled with changes in their pretax incomes, accounts for two-thirds of this drop. Among manufacturing workers with the same earnings, but with different tax rates because of unearned or spouse's income, those facing higher tax rates are more likely to work for employers who incur greater expenditures for pension and health insurance benefits. In the context of collective bargaining, the behavior of members of the United Mine Workers implies they value a dollar of employers' contributions to their health and welfare funds 40 percent more than they value a dollar of earnings.[28] This difference reflects very closely the tax rate that the workers face on additional (taxable) earnings.

The final force to be considered in the trend toward higher fringe benefits is the role of unions. Higher fringes may be paid in unionized firms for two reasons. First, unions may be better judges than employers of what employees want, and employees may want increasing amounts of security while at work. A possibly more important reason is that negotiated fringe benefits permit product differentiation by union leaders. The leader who first negotiates a new form of benefit, such as dental insurance for dependents of workers, is a popular innovator. The equivalent gain in cash wages would seem routine and in some cases insignificant.

Unionized workers are more likely to receive most of the major fringe benefits than are nonunion workers with the same demographic characteristics working in the same industry. In the late 1960s and early 1970s a unionized worker was 8 percent more likely to have health insurance coverage and 29 percent more likely to have pension coverage than a similar nonunion worker. Evidence for the late 1970s shows the effect of unions on fringes was especially strong in smaller firms. Even

[28] Stephen Woodbury, "Substitution Between Wage and Nonwage Benefits," *American Economic Review* (73): 166–182 (1983); William Alpert, "Manufacturing Workers' Private Wage Supplements," Unpublished Paper, Lehigh University, 1980; and Henry Farber, "Individual Preferences and Union Wage Determination: The Case of the United Mine Workers," *Journal of Political Economy* (86): 923–942 (1978).

where both were covered, the programs received by unionized workers were more generous. These considerations imply that the growth of unionization from the 1920s until the 1950s was partly responsible for the increased fraction of compensation accounted for by supplements. They also suggest that adjusted union wage gaps understate the adjusted union compensation gap. If the adjusted union wage gap for otherwise identical workers is 10 percent, the adjusted compensation gap may be 12 percent.[29]

In addition to these factors, the growth of fringe benefits has been partly due to the apparent income elasticity of workers' demands for them. This is particularly true for pension coverage, less so for health and life insurance coverage.[30] Taken together, all these factors have meant that the rapid growth of private fringe benefits has provided increasing security for those who are already most secure—the better paid workers in the larger companies and the members of the stronger unions. The development of social insurance has been necessary to provide a modicum of security for workers in small enterprises and workers with casual employment.

POLICY ISSUE—TAXING FRINGE BENEFITS

The Internal Revenue Service and federal officials interested in increasing revenues and achieving a more equitable burden of the income tax regularly suggest that employer contributions for fringe benefits be taxed as income to the employee. There is no doubt that this would initially achieve its goals of increased tax revenue and the payment of a greater share of that revenue by higher-income workers (among whom, as we have seen, fringe benefit coverage is more generous). In the long run, though, would it actually affect the distribution of after-tax incomes?

The answer to this question depends on whether or not there are compensating wage differentials that offset higher fringe benefits, leaving after-tax compensation unchanged. For example, taxing fringe benefits may merely induce new workers to require higher wages in order to supply their labor to firms that previously offered unusually generous fringe packages. Some evidence suggests this is at least partly what happens. In a sample from the private sector in 1969, among otherwise identical workers, earnings were roughly $1 lower for each $1 increase in employers' costs of pensions. Among otherwise similar police and firefighters in 1973, earnings were lower where the city offered more generous pension coverage.[31] These pieces of evidence imply that after-tax compensation is raised by less than $1 for each extra dollar of employer-paid fringe benefits. They show, too, that taxing fringes will not have so big a redistributive effect as would be implied by consideration of the short-run effects on after-tax incomes.

SUMMARY

Characteristics of work that employees generally find distasteful are compensated for by higher pay. The extent of the compensation depends on the extent of workers'

[29] Richard Freeman, "The Effect of Unionism on Fringe Benefits," *Industrial and Labor Relations Review* (34): 503–504 (1981); Freeman, "Unions, Pensions and Union Pension Funds," Unpublished Paper, National Bureau of Economic Research, 1983.

[30] Woodbury, loc. cit.

[31] Bradley Schiller and Randall Weiss, "Pensions and Wages: A Test for Equalizing Differences," *Review of Economics and Statistics* (62): 529–538 (1980); Ronald Ehrenberg, "Retirement System Characteristics and Compensating Wage Differentials in the Public Sector," *Industrial and Labor Relations Review* (33): 470–483 (1980).

distastes for the characteristics and on employers' costs of ameliorating the offending characteristics compared to the cost of paying the higher wage. The same worker would receive higher pay for a job that was unsafe or that offered worse prospects for stable employment and income. Among all workers, though, those with greater skills spend some of their potential earnings by seeking and obtaining jobs that are safer and more stable. Thus unless one accounts for differences in skills, there is a negative association between workers' earnings and their likelihood of being in risky jobs.

Pay differences also reflect compensating differentials for risk and rewards for skill, although these latter have decreased in the twentieth century as the public provision of education and training has expanded. Most workers in federal employment are paid more than comparable private employees, but this is not generally true of state and local public employees. Earnings differentials understate differences in total compensation, for higher-skilled workers receive a greater part of their compensation in the form of fringe benefits. This is due to the nontaxation of fringe benefits, to underlying preferences, and to differences in the extent of unionization. All these factors have helped to induce rapid growth in fringe benefits as a fraction of total compensation in the United States in this century.

chapter 13

Pay Discrimination

THE EXTENT OF DISCRIMINATION

In the United States, as in many other countries, differential treatment of persons distinguished by race, religion, sex, or ethnicity begins at birth. Fewer resources may be devoted to the care of infants of different groups; and preschool children receive amounts of early education that differ depending upon their race, ethnicity, or sex. Educational attainment differs among groups, as does the quality of the education obtained. When workers finish school they may receive pay that differs from that of otherwise similar workers or be employed in different jobs. All these differences constitute forms of discrimination. Only the last represents *labor-market discrimination,* although the existence of discrimination in the labor market affects the amount of discrimination experienced at earlier stages of life. In most of this chapter we concentrate on labor-market discrimination and assume that the productivity of workers in different groups is equal. That assumption is often incorrect, but the treatment of discrimination outside the labor market is beyond the scope of discussion here. Rather, we show how pay differences among equally productive workers of different race or sex can arise.

At the outset it is useful to get some notion of the size of earnings differentials by race, sex, and ethnicity in the United States. Table 13.1 presents measures of annual earnings in 1980 for all persons who worked in that year and for those who worked full time and at least 50 weeks. Comparisons of earnings in the latter group are fairly good proxies for wage rates, since they are not confounded by differences between groups in the incidence of unemployment and part-week or part-year work. Among steady workers, men earn substantially more within each race or ethnic group. This difference is especially pronounced among all workers, because women

Table 13.1 MEAN EARNINGS BY WORK STATUS, RACE, ETHNICITY AND SEX, 1980

	All workers		Full-time year-round workers	
	Male	Female	Male	Female
White	$16,308	$7,595	$21,023	$12,156
Black	10,656	7,455	14,709	11,230
Spanish origin	11,840	6,510	15,660	10,504
All persons	15,770	7,592	20,521	12,038

Source: U.S. Bureau of the Census, *Current Population Reports,* P-60, No. 132, Table 58.

are more frequently part-time workers. White males earn more than Hispanic males, who earn more than black males.[1] Among women, the differences in earnings by race and ethnicity are much smaller. None of these differentials is standardized for differences in the amount of skill embodied in workers belonging to different groups. After discussing some of the channels of discrimination and theories about how discrimination operates in the labor market, we compare earnings that have been standardized for skill differences among groups.

In this discussion and throughout this chapter, the available data restrict us to comparing workers' earnings. Although the appropriate comparison is of compensation among groups in the labor market, the picture conveyed by earnings comparisons is unlikely to be too biased. Fringe benefits, even though of increasing importance, are less than one-fourth of earnings per hour worked. Also, some evidence suggests that otherwise identical women receive only slightly higher fringe benefits relative to their earnings than do men; no comprehensive evidence is available comparing blacks and whites on this criterion.[2]

The most common forms of discrimination are refusing to employ women or minorities in jobs for which they are qualified, employing them only at lower wages, or insisting on higher qualifications where they are employed at the same wages as others. Discrimination in the United States now seldom takes the form of paying lower wage rates to minorities than to whites or to women than to men working in the same job in the same workplace, in part because such practices are clear violations of federal law. Even in the nineteenth century, when there were no laws on this issue, this was already true.[3] The common forms of discrimination are demanding higher qualifications for members of the minority group for doing the same work, or excluding members of the minority groups from the better-paid jobs. When different employers in a market offer different wages for the same occupation, as is almost always the case, members of minorities will be overrepresented in the work forces of the employers who pay the lowest wage.[4]

[1] The U.S. Bureau of the Census defines Hispanics as individuals who identify themselves as such. Thus both the nonwhite and white categories contain individuals who are also Hispanics.

[2] B. K. Atrostic, "Alternative Pay Measures and Labor-Market Differentials," Working Paper No. 127, U.S. Bureau of Labor Statistics, Office of Research and Evaluation, Washington, March 1983, Table 3.

[3] Myra Strober and Laura Best, "The Female/Male Salary Differential in Public Schools: Some Lessons from San Francisco, 1879," *Economic Inquiry* (17): 218–236 (1979).

[4] Albert Rees and George Shultz, *Workers and Wages in an Urban Labor Market,* University of Chicago Press, Chicago, 1970, pp. 161–166.

Data on the distribution of workers by occupation and color show a lower representation of blacks and Hispanics, the higher one goes up the occupational scale. The underrepresentation of blacks and Hispanics in the best-paid occupational groups is to some extent a reflection of differences in educational attainment, but it is much greater than can be explained on this ground alone. Table 13.2 shows the substantial differences among whites, blacks, and Hispanics in the distribution of employment by major occupational groups. Nonwhites are underrepresented among white-collar workers, craft workers and farmers, and overrepresented everywhere else. Hispanics are very much underrepresented in white-collar occupations and overrepresented elsewhere.

The differences in occupational distributions between employed males and females, which are as substantial as those by race and ethnicity, were shown in Table 3.1. Women are overrepresented in white-collar and service occupations and underrepresented in blue-collar occupations, especially in the crafts. Within white-collar occupations, they are heavily overrepresented in clerical work and have relatively few managerial and administrative jobs. A more detailed breakdown of occupations would show further differences. Although there is a somewhat higher proportion of women than of men among professional and technical workers, some professional groups, such as lawyers, medical doctors, the clergy, and accountants, are still heavily

Table 13.2 PERCENTAGE DISTRIBUTION OF EMPLOYED PERSONS BY OCCUPATION GROUP, RACE AND HISPANIC ORIGIN, 1982

Occupation group	White	Black and other	Hispanic
White-collar workers			
Professional and technical workers	17.4	14.1	8.5
Managers and administrators	12.3	5.7	6.5
Sales workers	7.1	3.1	4.2
Clerical workers	18.5	18.7	17.3
Total white-collar	55.3	41.6	36.5
Blue-collar workers			
Craft and kindred workers	12.8	8.9	13.2
Operatives	12.2	17.8	22.5
Nonfarm laborers	4.2	6.8	7.2
Total blue-collar	29.2	33.4	42.9
Service workers			
Private household workers	0.8	2.7	—
Other service workers	11.7	20.5	—
Total service	12.6	23.2	16.8
Farm workers			
Farmers and farm managers	1.6	0.3	—
Farm laborers and supervisors	1.3	1.4	—
Total farm workers	2.9	1.7	3.7
Total	100.0	100.0	100.0
Numbers of workers (millions)	87.9	11.6	5.2

Source: Employment and Earnings, January 1983, pp. 157, 177. Detail may not add to totals because of rounding.

male, whereas groups such as elementary school teachers, nurses, and librarians are still heavily female.

There are four possible sources of discrimination in labor markets. Employers may discriminate because (1) they themselves are prejudiced, (2) they believe that their employees are, (3) they believe that their customers are, or (4) government gives them incentives to discriminate. Employers' testimony about the source of discrimination is not always reliable, though, since they may be tempted to deny their own prejudice by blaming others. Because of this and the difficulty of discerning who is the source of discrimination, we treat employers as if they are discriminators, recognizing that they may only be agents for someone else's prejudice.

The term *prejudice* suggests a subjective dislike of a person or group. Discrimination can arise also from ignorance that leads employers to underestimate the productivity of those they discriminate against or from an inability to determine their productivity. This distinction is important both in analyzing discrimination and for policy: It may be easier to provide information than to remove prejudice.

THEORIES OF DISCRIMINATION

The concept of discrimination in employment has been given precise form by Gary Becker.[5] If employers can hire a woman or a minority person at the wage W, they are discriminators if they behave as though this wage were $W(1 + d_i)$, where d_i is a

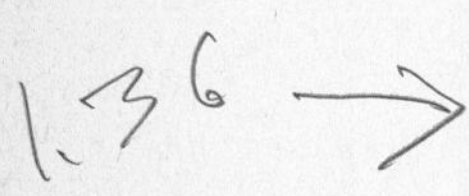

positive number called the employer's *discrimination coefficient* (the subscript identifies the employer). Employers who refuse to hire a woman or a minority person at any wage, however low, have an infinitely large d_i. If d_i is negative, the employer discriminates in favor of a particular group; this behavior is called *nepotism* if the employer is a member of this group. Obviously employers' tastes for discrimination are hard to measure; but the concept embodied in the d_i is extremely useful in identifying the factors that lead to differential labor-market outcomes by race, sex, and ethnicity.

Employers' discrimination coefficients are likely to reflect a wide range of attitudes, from the bigot to the liberal who would prefer hiring the woman or minority, other things equal. We can array employers by the number of jobs they have to offer according to their d_i, their taste for discrimination. Such an array is shown in Figure 13.1. Some small fraction of employers, indicated by the ratio of the shaded area to the total area under the curve, would prefer employing the woman or minority; the remaining employers discriminate.

This view of employers' tastes for discrimination is oversimplified. The extent to which employers discriminate in the employment of minorities not only differs from employer to employer, but also differs according to the nature of the work. (This suggests that a more complete model would specify a set of d_{ij}'s, where the subscript j identified the occupation.) Where the duties of an occupation conform to the majority view of the appropriate social role of the minority, which is often that of doing menial or servile tasks, there may be discrimination in favor of the minority by

[5] Gary Becker, *The Economics of Discrimination,* 2d ed., University of Chicago Press, Chicago, 1971.

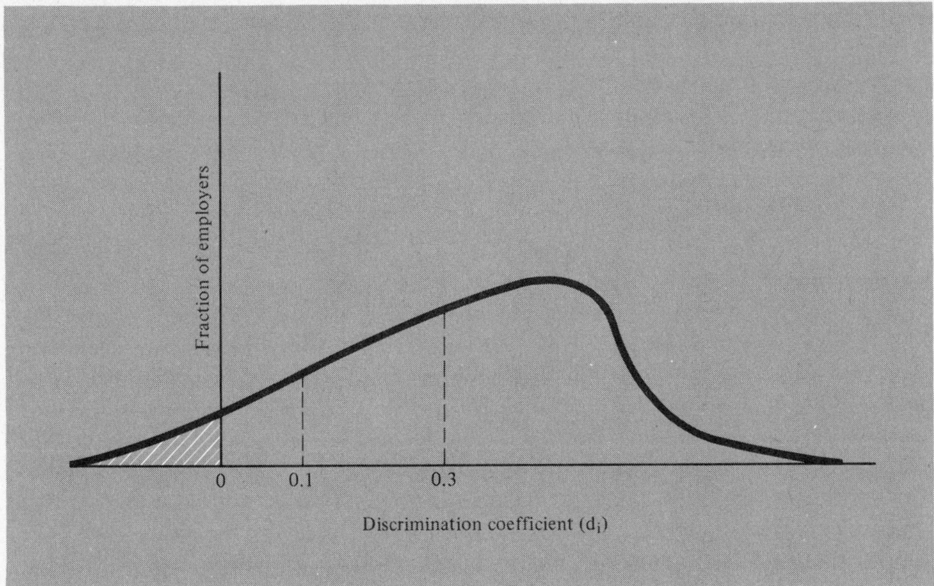

Figure 13.1 Employers' tastes for discrimination.

majority employers. For example, until the last few years those American railroads that still operated dining cars invariably employed only black waiters and white stewards, although it would seem logical to fill openings for stewards by promoting waiters. This suggests that the white employers may have had a large positive d_{ij} for black stewards and a large negative d_{ij} for black waiters. In the case of the waiters the term *nepotism*, with its connotations of kinship, is better replaced by the term *favoritism*.

This approach to discrimination can be applied to employers' decisions about hiring black or white workers, using the analysis of factor demand that we presented in Chapter 4. If black and white workers have equal productivity and are perfect substitutes in production, the typical firm's isoquants are straight lines like Q_1 in Figure 13.2(a), with OA = OB. (The assumption of perfect substitutability is an

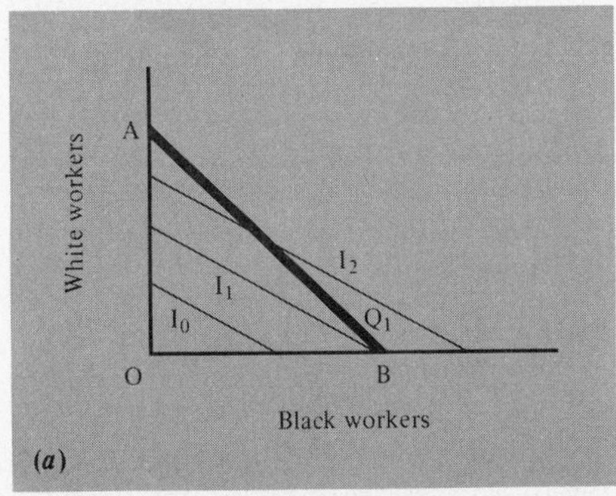

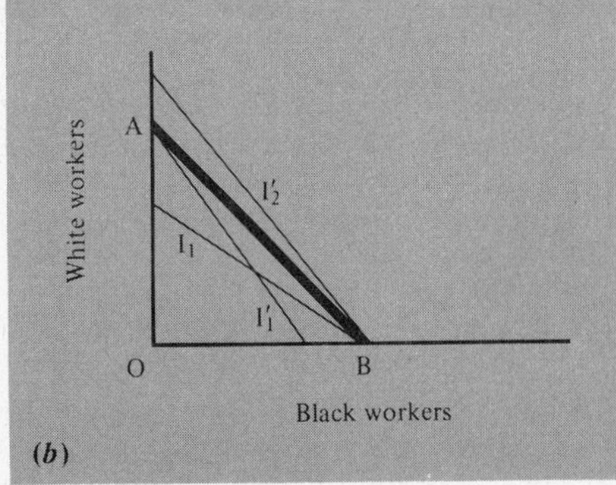

Figure 13.2 (a) The hiring decision, $d_i = 0$; (b) the hiring decision, $d_i > 0$.

extreme version of the example presented in Fig. 4.7(b). We assume employers such as those whose production is described in Figure 13.2(a) seek to produce Q_1 at the lowest cost and that they do not discriminate—their d_i equals zero. If the wage of white workers is 1, and the wage of blacks is $W_b < 1$, the typical budget constraint facing such a firm has a slope of W_b. For the same amount of money the firm can hire more blacks than whites. It will do so, minimizing the cost of producing Q_1 by spending the amount indicated by the budget constraint I_1. The firm could spend less—for example, an amount indicated by I_0—but it would not be able to produce Q_1. It could spend more—for example, the amount implied by I_2—to produce Q_1, but that would be wasteful. The nondiscriminatory firm will thus hire only blacks if blacks' wage rates are less than whites' and if the two groups are perfect substitutes.

Figure 13.2(b) reproduces the isoquant Q_1 and the budget constraint I_1. But that budget constraint is no longer relevant if employers have a positive taste for discrimination, $d_i > 0$. Each black worker costs the firm W_b in wages, which is less than the white worker's wage of 1. Employers incur an additional cost of hiring black workers because of their prejudice against blacks; the monetary equivalent of this psychic cost is $W_b d_i$. Thus for the discriminatory firm shown in Figure 13.2(b) the typical budget constraint is steeper, like I_1', with a slope of $W_b(1 + d_i)$. The slope exceeds 1, as in the figure, if the firm's discrimination coefficient more than offsets the lower wage paid to blacks. This firm could still hire OB blacks, but the "cost" would be indicated by the budget constraint I_2'. The firm instead operates along a lower budget constraint, I_1', hiring only whites at point A. Although this leads to higher wage costs than if blacks were hired, since OA = OB and whites' wages are higher than blacks', total "costs," including the employer's appraisal of the pecuniary equivalent of the firm's tastes for discrimination, are lower.

Discrimination by employers based on their own tastes and prejudices thus implies that they do not maximize money profits. Instead, they maximize utility by their willingness to sacrifice profits, paying higher wages than they need to or accepting workers less qualified than others whom they could recruit at the same wage, in order to indulge their tastes about the composition of the work force. This is in direct contradiction to the traditional Marxist analysis of discrimination, which states that capitalists discriminate against or exploit minorities in order to increase their pecuniary profits. The present analysis does not deny that some whites, or even all whites taken together, make monetary gains as a result of discrimination in employment. Rather, it asserts that the big gainers are the white male workers who get the good jobs that, in the absence of discrimination, would have gone to women or minorities. To a lesser extent nondiscriminating employers like those shown in Figure 13.2(a) also gain, for they can hire equally qualified labor at a lower wage. One leading economic consultant has acknowledged this by hiring mostly women for his company, arguing that they are better qualified than the male economists he can find and need be paid no more.

In a competitive labor market the size of the wage ratio, $W_b/1$, between equally competent black and whites will depend on two factors: (1) the shape of the distribution of employers by the extent to which they discriminate (in Fig. 13.1) and (2) the size of the minority group. The argument is depicted in Figure 13.3, which represents an occupational labor market in one labor-market area. Total employ-

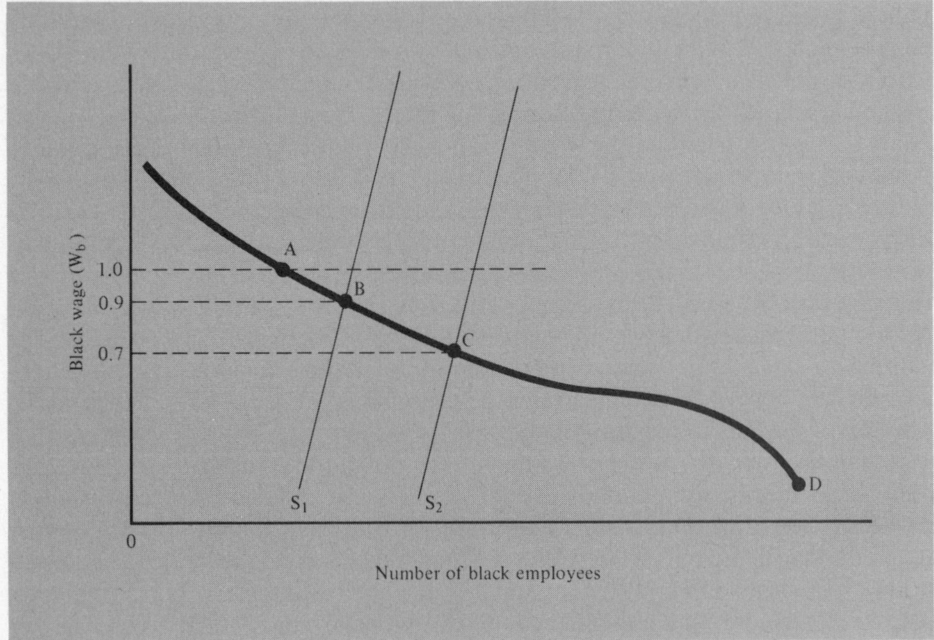

Figure 13.3 The determination of wage differentials with discrimination by employers.

ment in the occupation is assumed to be constant. We assume as before that the white wage is fixed at unity and will not be depressed by a reduction in white employment. The vertical axis shows the black wage rate, W_b.

The demand schedule for blacks, D, shows the total number of jobs that will be offered to blacks at each wage, holding the white wage fixed. It is formed from the array of employers by their tastes for discrimination presented in Figure 13.1. As implied by Figure 13.2(a), those employers with a zero or negative d_i will hire black workers even if their wage is at or above 1 (the wage paid to whites). The fraction of employers in the shaded area in Figure 13.1 determines the number of black employees hired if $W_b = 1$, so that there is no racial wage differential. It thus determines the location of point A in Figure 13.3. The D curve falls to the right of point A, because only if blacks' wages are below 1 will employers with positive discrimination coefficients be induced to hire black workers. It falls fairly slowly to the right of point C: As Figure 13.1 is drawn, a large number of employers have discrimination coefficients slightly above 0.3. If $W_b < 0.7$ the slopes of their budget constraints like I_1' in Figure 13.2(b) are below 1, and they would minimize "costs" by hiring blacks if their wages were a bit less than 70 percent of whites' wages.

The market wage ratio, $W_b/1$, is determined by the position of the supply curve. If the supply curve is S_1, the wage ratio is 0.9; if the supply curve is S_2, it is 0.7. Thus the larger the supply of minority workers is, the lower their relative wage will be. This helps explain the tendency for discriminatory pay differentials to be greatest where the minority group is a larger fraction of the total population. A striking example of this is furnished by the occupational position of Asian-Americans in the

United States in 1966. In the West, where they made up 2.5 percent of the total employment, they were underrepresented in the best-paid occupations. In the North, where they made up only 0.2 percent of the employment, they were overrepresented in these occupations in comparison with whites.[6] Presumably this led to a lower relative wage of Asians in the West. Even today the occupational distribution of Asians is less favorable in the West than in the rest of the United States. This can be viewed as a case of two markets with identical demand curves, determined by similar dispersions of employer tastes, and different supply curves, like S_1 and S_2. It might also be explained by making the tastes themselves (the level of the demand curve) a function of the numerical importance of the minority group, in which case one could get the observed result even if the demand curves in both markets were flat. The alternative explanation suggests that discrimination arises only against minorities that are large enough so that their inferior position is perceived as likely to benefit the position of workers in the majority group.

Those employers to the left of the intersection point B in Figure 13.3 will hire only blacks in this occupation, since the market wage differential is larger than is needed to overcome their desire to discriminate. Similarly, those to the right of the intersection will hire only whites. Because those employers to the left of the intersection can hire black labor of standard quality at a below-standard wage, their money profits will increase, which should encourage them to expand. If all the firms were in one competitive product market, this would eventually enable the nondiscriminators to drive the discriminators out of business. That discriminatory outcomes are still observed in developed economies suggests that product markets are less competitive than most economists believe, that the forces of competition work very slowly, or that those employers who are nondiscriminators do not compete with discriminatory employers.

Regardless of its implications for the trend in discriminatory outcomes, this analysis suggests that employers in monopolistic industries will have greater ability to pursue their tastes for discrimination, for they are insulated from competition from nondiscriminating employers. Monopolists can remain in secure positions toward the right end of the demand curve for black labor. However, evidence on whether in fact monopolistic employers pay lower wages for otherwise identical blacks (or women) is quite mixed.[7] It may be that monopolistic employers' protected positions are offset by their greater susceptibility to government pressures to offer nondiscriminatory terms of employment.

A variant of Becker's theory argues that even perfect competition in all markets is not a sufficient condition for equal wages if all employers are discriminators. In

[6]Orley Ashenfelter, "Minority Employment Patterns, 1966," Unpublished Paper, Princeton University Industrial Relations Section, 1968.

[7]Evidence in support of this proposition is presented in Walter Haessel and John Palmer, "Market Power and Employment Discrimination," *Journal of Human Resources* (13): 545–560 (1978), and William Comanor, "Racial Discrimination in American Industry," *Economica* (40): 363–378 (1973). Evidence to the contrary is in William Shepherd and Sharon Levin, "Managerial Discrimination in Large Firms," *Review of Economics and Statistics* (55): 412–422 (1973); Sharon Oster, "Industry Differences in the Level of Discrimination Against Women," *Quarterly Journal of Economics* (89): 215–229 (1975); and William Johnson, "Racial Wage Discrimination and Industrial Structure," *Bell Journal of Economics* (9): 70–81 (1978).

that case the whole demand curve lies below unity. One might object that under perfect competition black employers would enter the market and have a competitive advantage, since they could be assumed to discriminate, if at all, in the opposite direction. In fact, this kind of competition is seldom a threat in markets serving white customers, for few black enterprises have the capital and entrepreneurial skills needed to enter these markets successfully, and some white consumers may refuse to patronize them. To this extent, all competition in white markets is imperfect.

This view suggests that labor-market outcomes will be much different from those implied by the more conventional theory, especially if employers' discrimination coefficients differ greatly depending upon the occupation. Black workers will be "crowded" into occupations where white employers have low d_{ij}. This increases the relative supply of blacks to these occupations, so that even in them the wage paid to blacks may be less than that received by whites if all black workers are to be employed. Even if they are not, *occupational crowding* implies that blacks will be in lower-paying occupations and will on average receive lower wages than whites with the same formal training. Blacks and whites in the same narrowly defined occupation may receive equal pay, but blacks' wages will be lower in the aggregate because they are crowded into less desirable occupations by employers' relative distaste for hiring them into better-paying occupations.[8]

Both Becker's theory and its occupational crowding variant imply that discriminatory outcomes can be removed only by actions that change the tastes of the discriminatory agents or that raise the cost of discrimination. In terms of Figures 13.1 to 13.3, this means inducing enough employers to reduce their d_i to zero so that the market supply of blacks can be employed at the same wage as whites. Whether this is done by persuasion or by compulsion, the analysis of its potential impact is the same. Alternatively, it means penalizing discriminatory employers sufficiently so that they change their relative demands for black and white workers.

An entirely different view of discrimination in the labor market is based on employers' differential ability to discern the true productivity of white males as compared to minority or female workers. No employer is assumed to have a taste either for or against minority or female employees. Rather, it is assumed that employers have more difficulty discovering the true productivity of these workers than that of white males. This *statistical discrimination* is shown in Figure 13.4, which relates the worker's productivity (VMP) in a typical occupation to his or her score on a test that may be used in screening new employees for that occupation. (Instead of a test score, which may be more relevant in discussing discrimination against minorities, the length of the applicant's prior work record may be used as an indicator in discussing discrimination against women.)

Assume black and white workers are on average equally productive in the occupation, with an average productivity of VMP*, shown in Figure 13.4 as OB. Assume that the test used in screening predicts perfectly the ability of a white worker to perform on the job; the relation between the test score and VMP is shown by the 45° line. The average black worker scores as well as the average white worker, G*.

[8] Barbara Bergmann, "The Effect on White Incomes of Discrimination in Employment," *Journal of Political Economy* (79): 294–313 (1971).

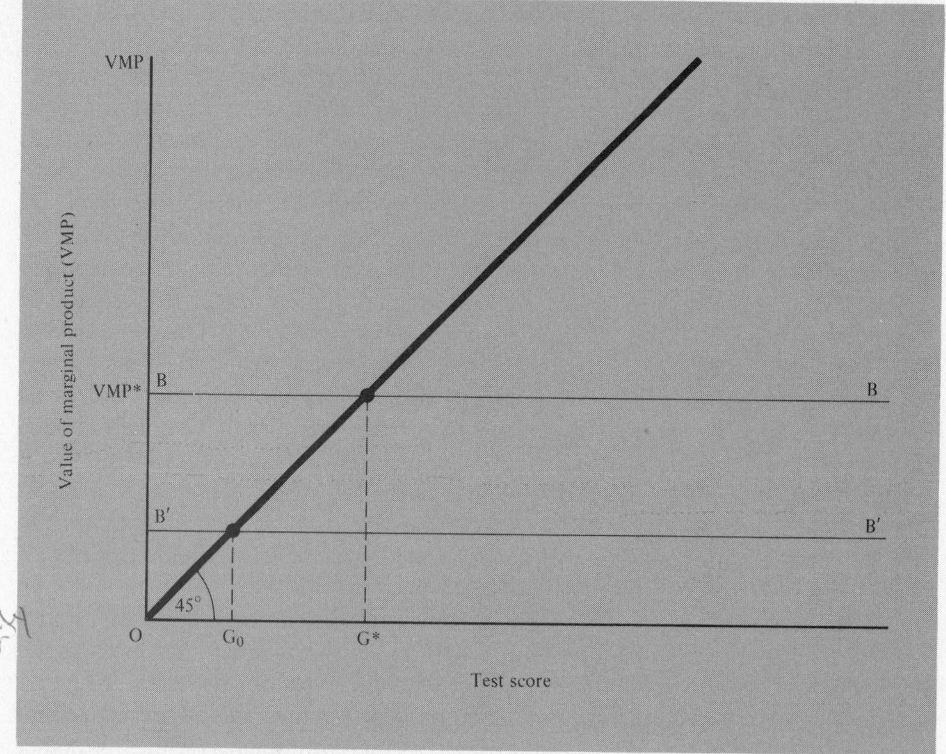

Figure 13.4 Statistical discrimination.

But the test is such a poor indicator of blacks' productivity that employers cannot distinguish at all between blacks with high or low scores.[9] (So long as the tests are better predictors for whites than blacks, the conclusions of this model will hold.) The relation between test scores and ability among blacks is shown by the line BB.

If employers do not mind bearing risks, they will hire blacks in preference to whites if both have below-average scores: Employers know the white will have below-average productivity on this job, although they infer that the black will be average. Obversely, they will hire whites in preference to blacks if both have above-average test scores. This would imply that the average black and white workers will earn the same amount, which is not consistent with observed wage differences. If employers do not like bearing the risk of hiring a black who may not be as productive as VMP*, they will give preference to whites with test scores below those of blacks. Thus B′B′ shows the relation between blacks' test scores and productivity discounted for the risks employers must bear. With employers' risk aversion, only those blacks scoring below G_0 will be given preference over whites. Most blacks will receive lower wages than equally able whites to compensate employers for the risk that the black

[9]Edmund Phelps, "The Statistical Theory of Racism and Sexism," *American Economic Review* (62): 659–661 (1972), and Dennis Aigner and Glen Cain, "Statistical Theories of Discrimination in Labor Markets," *Industrial and Labor Relations Review* (30): 175–187 (1977). The latter article also contains a discussion of the evidence on racial differences in the reliability of tests.

worker will be unproductive, a risk the employer cannot circumvent because the test cannot indicate the black's probable productivity. Even though blacks are as productive as whites are on average, they will earn less if the indicators used by employers to predict performance are subject to more variability when applied to blacks *and* employers do not wish to bear the risk implied by this greater variability.

One might argue that statistical discrimination can only affect entry-level wages, for employers will soon determine each worker's true productivity and be forced to pay accordingly. This ignores the many instances where each individual's productivity is difficult to determine even after many years of employment. (Measurement problems provide one reason that, as we discussed in Chapter 2, piece-rate work is relatively uncommon.) It also ignores the fact that the screening process is vital in determining which workers obtain access to the on-the-job training opportunities that provide them with a higher path of earnings over the remainder of their working lives.

Competition among employers will not eliminate discrimination resulting from a differential ability to predict the productivity of white male workers as compared to that of minorities and women. Only better predictors, or the complete prohibition of the use of predictive devices that are less reliable for the group that is discriminated against, will suffice to reduce the extent of observed discrimination. However, since employers will always try to obtain information on prospective employees to avoid incurring the cost of training workers with little aptitude for the job, they have very large incentives to develop alternative predictors, which may be just as discriminatory as those that are outlawed.

The discussion in this section has been based mostly on the case of discrimination against nonwhites. Although important, that form of discrimination is used here only as an example to illustrate general principles. In the following sections we discuss the extent of and changes in discrimination against various groups, both in the United States and elsewhere, and relate these to the alternative views of discrimination presented here.

POLICY ISSUE—JOB-RELATED TESTS

Employers use a variety of tests and other criteria as screening devices in the selection of employees. Although there is no federal legislation regulating the use of these tests, a case law has arisen that implicitly does this. The lead case, *Griggs* et al. *v. Duke Power Company* (1971), requires employers to show that tests that have an adverse impact on minorities are job-related. Later cases refined this doctrine by imposing requirements on how tests should be validated.[10]

The restrictions on the kinds of screening criteria employers may use have interesting implications for discriminatory outcomes. Partly they prevent direct employer discrimination—the imposition of employers' tastes for discrimination—by preventing employers from using invalid tests as a catspaw for those tastes. Because it is often difficult to validate a test, employers will respond to the strict application of the case law by abandoning or reducing their use of tests in selecting new workers or in deciding promotions. In the context of the theory of statistical discrimination, this could reduce discrimi-

[10] A detailed discussion of the legal issues in testing is provided by Sheldon Zedeck and Mary Tenopyr, "Issues in Selection, Testing and the Law," in Leonard Hausman et al. (eds.). *Equal Rights and Industrial Relations,* Industrial Relations Research Association, Madison, Wisc., 1977.

natory outcomes by removing an instrument that is a less perfect indicator of blacks' potential productivity than it is of whites'. With less information about *both* blacks and whites, risk-averse employers will have a reduced incentive to prefer the white employees whose productivity the tests predicted better; and society could reap the benefits of having workers receive wages more closely reflecting their productivity.[11] It may be, though, that the less formal screening devices they substitute are even worse predictors for blacks relative to whites than are formal tests. If so, the case law could have the unintended effect of increasing discriminatory outcomes that result from employers' greater inability to obtain information on blacks' than on whites' potential productivity.

DISCRIMINATION AGAINST BLACKS

In each case of potential discrimination we begin with an attempt to *standardize* the unadjusted earnings ratios implicit in Table 13.1 to account for differences in productivity between groups. These differences do not necessarily reflect discrimination by employers. Instead, they may reflect differences in the amount of skill acquired before entry into the work force or in the amount of skill acquired on the job. What is left after earnings differences are adjusted for other differences between groups is a standardized wage difference, a measure of market discrimination. Although we use these differences to indicate the amount of discrimination, even they may be biased. To the extent the studies upon which the discussion is based fail to adjust for all the relevant productivity differences between groups, the standardized earnings differences will usually overstate the amount of discrimination. Conversely, studies that adjust for differences that result indirectly from discrimination in the labor market will conclude that the amount of labor-market discrimination is less than in fact exists.

From Table 13.1 it is apparent that black workers earn less than white workers. The data in Table 13.1 imply that the unadjusted ratio of earnings of year-round black workers to that of whites was 0.70 for males and 0.92 for females. In Table 13.3 we present standardized hourly wage rates for white and black males based on the Current Population Survey from March 1980. These data show wage differences among otherwise identical whites and blacks: Marital status, geographic location, veteran status, and differences in the likelihood of working in the public sector are accounted for. The study upon which the estimates are based is an especially convenient one to use to demonstrate patterns in the standardized wage differences, but many other studies show similar patterns.

Role of Human Capital

Among male workers who only finished high school, the results in Table 13.3 show that whites earned more than otherwise identical blacks at all age levels. However, for college graduates this is true only for those older than 30: Young black college graduates earned more in 1980 than did their white counterparts. This rather surprising difference implies that the rate of return to college education for blacks

[11] Shelly Lundberg and Richard Startz, "Private Discrimination and Social Intervention in Competitive Labor Markets," *American Economic Review* (73): 340–347 (1983).

Table 13.3 HOURLY WAGES, SELECTED AGE AND SCHOOLING LEVELS, WHITE AND BLACK MALES, MARCH 1980[a]

	Years of school			
	12		16	
Age	Whites	Blacks	Whites	Blacks
22	$5.72	$5.17	$ 5.99	$ 7.07
27	6.89	5.74	7.64	8.38
32	7.55	6.38	8.86	8.76
37	7.54	7.16	10.26	10.08
42	7.68	6.96	10.45	9.80
47	7.82	6.76	10.64	9.52
52	7.96	6.57	10.83	9.26

[a]Married, living in a center city in the West, nonveteran, private-sector worker.

Source: Calculated from Saul Hoffman and Charles Link, "Selectivity Bias in Male Wage Equations: Black and White Comparisons," *Review of Economics and Statistics* (66) (1984). In press.

may now be as high or higher than that for whites. Although there is labor-market discrimination against older and less-educated blacks, there is little if any against young blacks who completed college in the 1970s.

Comparing the small differences in standardized wages shown in Table 13.3 to the substantial unadjusted differentials in earnings of year-round workers implied by Table 13.1, we can infer that the characteristics that increase productivity differ by race. In 1980 the median educational attainment of black males was 0.4 years less than that of white males. More important, there is also substantial evidence that the quality of schooling that the average black worker has received is inferior to that received by whites.[12] The differences in the quantity of education account for a large part of the unadjusted earnings differential implied by the data in Table 13.1. The difference in quality helps explain part of the standardized differences in Table 13.3 for most workers, for the study could not standardize for the quality of education. Finally, productivity may differ by race even among year-round full-time workers because of differences in the amount of skills acquired in the past through on-the-job training. Black males who worked full time all year in 1980 are less likely to have worked full time all year for their entire work lives than are white males. As we showed in Chapters 1 and 8, black males' participation rates are lower than whites', and blacks have higher unemployment rates than do whites. This means that at any age their labor-market experience is less; since experience is in general a good measure of productivity, otherwise identical black workers will have less human capital than white workers at the same age. Racial differences in participation and unemployment thus induce differences in productivity, even among year-round full-time workers.

We have shown that some labor-market discrimination still remained in the United States in 1980 and that there is substantial discrimination in the process of acquiring human capital. It is important to note that the United States is not unique in this problem. In the United Kingdom in 1972, for example, nonwhite immigrants

[12]Finis Welch, "Black-White Differences in Returns to Schooling," *American Economic Review* (63): 893–907 (1973).

earned only 78 percent of the earnings of white immigrants with the same education and labor-market experience.[13] Direct evidence of employers' tastes for discrimination is provided by a British study that used pairs of fictitious job applications for work in accountancy. Nonwhite workers were not only less likely to be contacted by employers receiving the applications than were white Britons, but they also fared worse than non-English-speaking white immigrants. This direct evidence of labor-market discrimination against blacks was not present in a similar U.S. study, confirming the absence of labor market discrimination against young, educated workers, as shown by the standardized wage differentials in Table 13.3.[14]

The existence of labor-market discrimination by race at most age and education levels feeds back into workers' decisions about the amount of human capital that it pays a worker to acquire. If the rate of return to training is lower among black workers, they will acquire less. Black men aged 18 to 64 in 1976 were less likely to have received formal on-the-job training than otherwise similar white men. Even more important, there is less complementarity between formal schooling and on-the-job training among black men than among whites.[15] As we showed in Chapter 3, this complementarity is an important source of earnings growth over the life cycle. The racial differences in it help explain why the standardized white-black wage differentials in Table 13.3 are greater among older workers, especially more educated ones. Younger whites, especially those with college degrees, are more likely than young blacks to have low current wages because they are investing in training. This training pays off in increasingly higher wages as they acquire more experience.

Despite differences in the amount of education and on-the-job training that have been acquired, blacks are no more likely than whites to quit their jobs.[16] This raises the questions of why employers fail to invest as much in training black workers as they do in whites, and why blacks do not invest in their own training. The second question can be answered by pointing to blacks' lower incomes and their unwillingness to sacrifice current low living standards in order to reap higher rewards in the future. The behavior of employers is more difficult to explain; perhaps, even though economists have shown there are no black-white differences in voluntary quits, employers do not perceive this. Their (incorrect) perception of blacks' quit behavior leads them to expect blacks to remain with the firm for shorter periods than whites; the employers respond by investing less in training blacks than whites.

Feedback mechanisms will affect the acquisition of education if the rates of return differ by race. Although the rate of return today is perhaps even higher for young blacks than for whites, that was not true as recently as the late 1950s.[17] Thus

[13] Barry Chiswick, "The Earnings of White and Colored Male Immigrants in Britain," *Economica* (47): 81–87 (1980).

[14] Michael Firth, "Racial Discrimination in the British Labor Market," *Industrial and Labor Relations Review* (34): 265–272 (1981), and Jerry Newman, "Discrimination in Recruitment: An Empirical Analysis," *Industrial and Labor Relations Review* (32): 15–23 (1978).

[15] Greg Duncan and Saul Hoffman, "On-the-job Training and Earnings Differences by Race and Sex," *Review of Economics and Statistics* (61): 601 (1979).

[16] Robert Flanagan, "Discrimination Theory, Labor Turnover, and Racial Unemployment Differentials," *Journal of Human Resources* (13): 187–207 (1978), and Francine Blau and Lawrence Kahn, "Race and Sex Differences in Quits by Young Workers," *Industrial and Labor Relations Review* (34): 563–577 (1981).

[17] Giora Hanoch, "An Economic Analysis of Earnings and Schooling," *Journal of Human Resources* (2): 322 (1967).

older blacks acquired less schooling than whites because the payoff to schooling was lower. The change in the rate of return to schooling implicit in the standardized wage rates in Table 13.3 for young black and white men classified by educational attainment may be responsible for the very rapid increase in schooling attainment of blacks in the 1970s. If the earnings ratios among young workers remain high and the earnings ratios of the 1970s college-educated cohort hover around 1 as the cohort ages, we may infer that the rate of return to education for blacks equals that for whites. Schooling attainment of blacks should equal that of whites by the end of the century, as young blacks respond to the higher return by obtaining more education.

Wage discrimination also reduces labor-force participation. Assuming no differences by race in the reservation wage, labor-market discrimination makes it more likely that the market wage will be below the reservation wage for blacks than for whites. As we saw in Chapter 1, participation of black males is lower than that of whites. This lower participation itself reduces the incentive to acquire human capital, and thus produces lower wages.

In all these facets of labor-market behavior—the acquisition of human capital through education and on-the-job training, voluntary turnover, and labor-force participation—labor-market discrimination induces blacks to make decisions that produce racial differences in the characteristics that enhance productivity. Only if labor-market discrimination is eliminated—if standardized wages do not differ by race throughout the entire life cycle—will there be an incentive for employers and workers to change their behavior so as to raise the productivity of black workers and thus reduce the unadjusted earnings differential implicit in Table 13.1.

Trends and the Effect of Federal Policy

Whether and, if so, why discriminatory labor-market outcomes have been reduced in the United States has occupied much of the attention of labor economists in the 1970s and early 1980s. Ideally one would like to construct data like the standardized wage differentials in Table 13.3, covering the entire post-World War II period; the absence of sufficient data makes this impossible. Instead, we must rely upon an examination of unstandardized earnings differentials and whatever other evidence is available. The unstandardized differentials are shown in Table 13.4 for selected years

Table 13.4 NONWHITE-WHITE EARNINGS RATIOS, 1939–1980[a]

	All workers		Year-round full-time workers	
Year	Males	Females	Males	Females
1939	0.41	0.36	0.45	0.38
1955	0.59	0.43	0.63	0.57
1960	0.60	0.50	0.67	0.70
1965	0.57	0.60	0.64	0.71
1970	0.62	0.84	0.69	0.82
1975	0.66	0.98	0.74	0.96
1980	0.66	1.00	0.71	0.95

[a]Ratios of medians of wage and salary incomes.

Source: U.S. Bureau of the Census, *Current Population Reports,* P-60, Nos. 23, 37, 51, 80, 105, 132.

since 1939. They show a remarkable convergence of blacks' and whites' earnings, a change that was concentrated mostly in the years between 1965 and 1975. Since 1975 there has been a slight reversal of this gain, but black-white earnings differences are still far smaller than they were in the mid-1960s. This is especially true for female workers.

The unstandardized differentials in Table 13.4 do not account for changes in the composition of the work force. During the 1960s and 1970s labor-force participation rates of whites rose relative to those of blacks. To the extent that it was the least educated and skilled blacks who ceased participating, the unadjusted earnings ratio between blacks and whites in the labor force would have risen because of this change in composition. Part of the increase shown in the table probably stems from this source; but the magnitudes of the increase in the ratio and of the changes in participation are such that we can infer that black-white earnings ratios for workers with the same education and skill have risen since the 1960s.[18]

Part of the convergence of earnings reflects a reduction in occupational segregation. The percentage of white workers holding white-collar jobs increased from 46.1 in 1960 to the 54.3 shown in Table 13.2 for 1981; among blacks, the percentage grew from 16.5 to 40.5. Similarly, the percentage of whites holding craft jobs declined from 15.0 to 13.0, whereas among blacks it rose from 7.0 to 9.2.

The apparent reduction in occupational segregation and the possible reduction in wage discrimination within each occupation reflect the improved status of younger blacks in particular; little improvement has occurred in the relative earnings of older blacks and whites as they have aged. This difference by age cohort is suggested by the data in Table 13.3. It is demonstrated more directly by comparisons over time. Between 1960 and 1970 the earnings ratio of black and white high school graduates with 16 to 20 years of experience in 1960 fell from 0.71 to 0.70; but in 1970, relative earnings of black high school graduates with 16 to 20 years of experience in 1970 were 0.75 that of whites, substantially higher than for workers born 10 years earlier. Among college graduates, and among high school graduates in different age cohorts, a similar pattern prevails.[19] There is no question that discriminatory labor-market outcomes have been reduced since the early 1960s. The reduction has occurred through the replacement of earlier age cohorts who experienced substantial labor-market discrimination throughout their working lives by later cohorts of black workers against whom discrimination has been less from the start of their working lives.

It is important to know whether this improvement has resulted from the efforts of government to improve the labor-market position of blacks or whether it would have occurred anyway. This knowledge will help us both to understand recent history and to guide future policy. In the mid-1960s the federal government undertook a variety of new programs that could have affected the earnings and occupational status of blacks relative to whites. The Civil Rights Act of 1964 established the

[18] Richard Butler and James Heckman, "The Government's Impact on the Labor Market Status of Black Americans: A Critical Review," in Hausman et al., loc. cit.; and Charles Brown, "Black-White Earnings Ratios Since the Civil Rights Act of 1964: The Importance of Labor Market Drop-Outs," *Quarterly Journal of Economics* (98) (1983). In press.

[19] James Smith and Finis Welch, "Black-White Male Wage Ratios: 1960–1970," *American Economic Review* (67): 323–338 (1977).

Equal Employment Opportunity Commission (EEOC), whose budget, which increased rapidly from 1965 to 1975, is spent partly on cases involving unequal pay for equal work and on unequal access to promotion. At the same time, Executive Order 11246 required federal contractors (most large employers) to file *affirmative action plans* showing how they intended to increase the employment of minorities and women in higher-paying jobs. At the state level, expenditures of fair employment practice commissions increased seventeen-fold between 1964 and 1975.

The explosion of federal and state efforts to equalize labor-market outcomes between blacks and whites was coincident with the rapid increase in black-white earnings ratios. At the same time that the programs were becoming effective, however, the least skilled blacks were leaving the work force and black educational attainment was increasing; both factors also would have produced an increase in black-white earnings ratios. The programs do, though, appear to have been partly responsible for the increased earnings ratios. Employers reported that they changed their recruitment practices as a result of these programs. Accounting for the supply changes, EEOC expenditures were correlated with the increased earnings ratios.[20] A very careful study of affirmative action programs found that black male employment increased significantly in those firms that were federal contractors (and thus were obligated to file affirmative action plans that were subject to review by federal officials).[21]

Whether the reduction in discriminatory outcomes would persist if federal pressures on employers were relaxed is unclear. On the one hand, the evidence just discussed suggests that the reduction would not have taken place without that pressure. On the other hand, having at least partly broken the feedback relationship between labor-market discrimination and the acquisition of human capital, government policy may no longer be required. Employers themselves may have sufficient incentives, in the form of a supply of more educated blacks, to maintain the improvements in earnings ratios. Also, having achieved greater representation in white-collar jobs, blacks may have reduced employers' uncertainty about their productivity (shifted up and tilted the B′B′ line in Fig. 13.4), thereby reducing statistical discrimination against them. Only experience with the apparent reductions in federal antidiscrimination efforts in the early 1980s will tell which answer is correct. We do know, however, that most of the gains made by black workers have persisted through the higher unemployment of the 1970s: This is demonstrated by the relatively small declines between 1975 and 1980 in the ratios in Table 13.4 and by more detailed research that standardizes earnings for some of the other factors that changed during this time.[22]

DISCRIMINATION BY ETHNICITY—HISPANICS AND OTHERS

Table 13.2 shows that the Hispanic work force is about one-half the size of the black work force in the United States, as measured in the Current Population Survey. The

[20] Richard Freeman, "Black Economic Progress After 1964: Who Has Gained and Why?" in Sherwin Rosen (ed.). *Studies in Labor Markets,* University of Chicago Press, Chicago, 1981.

[21] James Heckman and Kenneth Wolpin, "Does the Contract Compliance Program Work? An Analysis of Chicago Data," *Industrial and Labor Relations Review* (29): 544–564 (1976).

[22] Richard Freeman, "Have Black Labor Market Gains Post-1964 Been Permanent or Transitory?" Working Paper No. 751, National Bureau of Economic Research, Cambridge, Mass., 1981.

Table 13.5 HOURLY WAGES BY AGE, HISPANICS AND NON-HISPANIC WHITE MALES, 1975[a]

Age	Non-Hispanic whites	Mexican whites	Puerto Rican whites
22	$4.54	$4.47	$4.07
27	5.33	4.96	4.71
32	6.11	5.42	5.29
37	6.81	5.84	5.76
42	7.38	6.22	6.08
47	7.77	6.54	6.21
52	7.96	6.79	6.16
57	8.02	6.95	5.91
62	7.65	7.02	5.50

[a]Nonveteran, native-born, private-sector worker in good health, speaks good English, and has received 12 years of schooling.

Source: Calculated from Cordelia Reimers, "Labor-Market Discrimination Against Hispanic and Black Men," *Review of Economics and Statistics* (65) (1983), Table 5. In press.

diversity of the Hispanic population requires that it be disaggregated into subgroups when we examine labor-market discrimination. The two largest subgroups—Mexican-Americans and Puerto Ricans—have quite different cultural backgrounds and are most heavily concentrated in different parts of the United States. Other groups—Cubans, Central Americans, and still others—are included in this variegated but important minority in the work force.

The unadjusted earnings data in Table 13.1 show that Hispanics, even year-round full-time workers, earn less than do all whites. The unadjusted earnings ratios for these workers are 0.74 for men and 0.86 for women. As with blacks, the greater extent of discrimination, both in wages and in the acquisition of skill, is against men. To isolate the amount due to pure labor-market discrimination, we present in Table 13.5 the adjusted hourly wage rates of Mexican-American, Puerto Rican, and non-Hispanic white males. Among the dimensions by which these wages are standardized, there are education, ability to speak English (especially important for this group), and whether or not the man is native born.[23] (This is important, too, for as we saw in Chap. 7, the returns to schooling acquired outside the United States by men working in the United States are less than the returns to schooling acquired here.)

The data show that Hispanics' wages are below those of non-Hispanic whites even after adjusting for numerous differences that affect productivity. The differences are much greater for Puerto Ricans than for Mexican-Americans; they are the smallest early and late in the work life. The Hispanic-white earnings ratio is U-shaped over the life cycle. There are two ways of explaining this interesting fact. If Hispanics invest less in on-the-job training, their earnings will be relatively higher during the period early in the work life when whites are investing heavily; their earnings will fall relatively as non-Hispanic whites reap the returns on their larger investments in training and will rise again near the end of the work life when the investment in training depreciates. An alternative explanation for the relatively small standardized earnings differentials among young workers is that discrimina-

[23]Cordelia Reimers, "Labor-Market Discrimination Against Hispanic and Black Men," *Review of Economics and Statistics* (65) (1983). In press.

Table 13.6 STANDARDIZED EARNINGS RATIOS, SELECTED MINORITIES, 1969[a]

Group	Males	Females
Japanese	0.89	1.02
Chinese	0.83	0.91
Filipinos	0.80	0.97
American Indians	0.81	0.80

[a]Standardized for age, education, hours worked, location, English-language ability, and whether first- or second-generation American.

Source: Calculated from James Gwartney and James Long, "The Relative Earnings of Blacks and Other Minorities," *Industrial and Labor Relations Review* (31) (1978), Table 4.

tion against younger cohorts of Hispanics is less than that against older cohorts. Without detailed studies of the progress of different cohorts over time, we cannot distinguish between the two hypotheses.

Although annual data on the earnings of Hispanics that are comparable to those shown in Table 13.4 are only available since the mid-1970s, we can use these and decennial census data to examine the economic progress of Hispanics. The census data show substantial progress of Puerto Ricans between 1959 and 1969, but little gain for Mexican-Americans in the unadjusted earnings ratios as compared to non-Hispanic whites. Once one standardizes these ratios for changes in the relative amounts of skill embodied in the various groups, a different picture emerges: Male workers belonging to these two Hispanic groups received wages in 1969 that were only 14 and 9 percent, respectively, below those of otherwise identical non-Hispanic whites. In 1959 the standardized wage differences were 40 and 23 percent, respectively.[24] As with blacks, labor-market discrimination against Hispanics was reduced sharply during the 1960s, presumably during the late 1960s. A comparison of census data on earnings in 1969 with data for 1975 from the Current Population Survey indicates this improvement continued through 1975. There was, however, no change in the unstandardized earnings ratios for Hispanics as compared to non-Hispanic whites between 1975 and 1980. This, too, parallels the changes we observed for blacks in the previous section.

The diversity of ethnic groups in the United States precludes an analysis of labor-market differentials or discrimination characterizing each group. Nonetheless, it is worth noting in Table 13.6 the extent of discrimination, as measured by standardized earnings ratios (minority to white) in 1969, against a few of these groups. The ratios show that substantial discrimination existed against male workers in these small minorities, although less labor-market discrimination existed against women minority workers. These differences by sex parallel the differences for blacks and Hispanics as shown in Tables 13.1 and 13.4. The ratios are probably slightly higher today, assuming that the same pattern of reduced discrimination in the early 1970s, and no change in the late 1970s, prevailed for them as for blacks and Hispanics. Other data show that in 1969 Jewish men with parents who emigrated to

[24]James Gwartney and James Long, "The Relative Earnings of Blacks and Other Minorities," *Industrial and Labor Relations Review* (31) (1978), Table 5.

the United States had earnings 16 percent above other whites with the same education and experience, and in the same occupation. Much of the difference was due to a greater rate of return on schooling and a greater amount of investment in on-the-job training.[25]

One cannot generalize from ethnic discrimination in the United States to discrimination elsewhere. The patterns of discrimination, whether pure labor-market discrimination or discrimination in access to activities that enhance productivity, differ across countries and, as we have shown, within a country among different minorities. Nonetheless, one would suspect that employers' tastes for discrimination against minorities, and their frequent inability to predict the performance of minority workers as well as that of majority workers, make ethnic discrimination as pervasive elsewhere as in the United States. For example, bilingual French-speaking natives earned 4 percent less than bilingual English-speaking natives in Canada with the same education, experience, immigrant status, and living in the same size city and in the same region.[26]

POLICY ISSUE—COMPETITION AMONG MINORITIES

Federal antidiscrimination programs aim at increasing the employment and wages of a broad range of protected groups, including both blacks and Hispanics. Given limitations on the budget for enforcement of antidiscrimination laws, a continuing political decision must be made, either explicitly or implicitly, about which groups should be targeted most closely. There is also an economic question underlying choices about targeting antidiscrimination efforts: Will successful attempts to help one group be made only at the cost of worsening the labor-market position of other groups? More specifically, does affirmative action for blacks result in unemployment or lower wages among Hispanics, and vice versa?

The answer to these questions depends on whether the various minorities are viewed as complements or substitutes by employers who use their labor. If they are complements, aiding one group increases the demand for another minority group, creating jobs and raising wages of its members, too. If they are substitutes, programs aiding one group will reduce the demand for the labor of members of another group, thus reducing their employment, their real wages or both. Evidence for 1975 suggests an optimistic conclusion about this question, at least in the case of Hispanics and blacks. In labor markets in which there are relatively more blacks, the wages of Hispanics are higher than elsewhere; similarly, blacks' wages are higher where Hispanics constitute a greater proportion of the working-age population.[27] Where black workers are in greater demand, so that their wages are higher, Hispanic workers are also in greater demand, leading to higher wages for them, too. The two groups thus appear to be complements in production. This may be the case, for example, because blacks and Hispanics are employed in complementary production processes or because they work in industries producing goods and services that are complements in consumption. These results suggest that there is no necessary economic trade-off in targeting antidiscrimination efforts to one or the other of these groups. Indeed, aiding one group aids indirectly members of the other group as well.

[25] Barry Chiswick, "The Earnings and Human Capital of American Jews," *Journal of Human Resources* (18):313–336 (1983).

[26] Geoffrey Carliner, "Wage Differences by Language Group and the Market for Language Skills in Canada," *Journal of Human Resources* (16) (1981), Table 2.

[27] George Borjas, "The Substitutability of Black, Hispanic and White Labor," *Economic Inquiry* (21): 93–106 (1983).

DISCRIMINATION AGAINST WOMEN

Based on the data on earnings of year-round full-time workers in 1980 shown in Table 13.1, the female-male earnings ratios are 0.58 for whites, 0.76 for blacks, and 0.67 for Hispanics. In standardizing these earnings ratios, we find that a number of extremely difficult issues arise, all of which involve distinguishing between sex differences that reflect discrimination and those that would imply differences in productivity even in the absence of discrimination. Since the educational attainment of women and men in the United States is essentially the same, that cannot be a major source of nonlabor market discrimination. The quality of the education also probably differs little by sex, since boys and girls generally are in the same classrooms. The only sex difference in educational attainment is that women are more likely to complete high school, whereas men are more likely to obtain college or advanced degrees. Even this difference is much smaller today than it was in the 1960s. We can thus rule out education as an important source of differences in productivity.

Fewer women than men have the strength to do very heavy physical work; but the increasing mechanization of materials handling and similar activities has greatly reduced the importance of this factor. Even without these trends in technology, though, it is not likely that slight differences in physical strength will affect wages greatly. We showed in Chapter 12 that the compensating pay differential on jobs requiring physical strength is small or zero. Laws designed to protect women's (and children's) health do limit the weight they can lift, and if the limits are set unreasonably low, the effect is to keep women out of jobs that they could perform and that may be high-paying. Here, too, however, this possible source of institutionalized discrimination that should be considered in standardizing the earnings ratios is of decreasing importance, as these laws have been repealed in many jurisdictions.

Role of Labor-Market Experience

The most difficult issue is that of labor-market experience. In presenting the standardized wage rates in Tables 13.3 and 13.5, we were nearly correct to compare men by race or ethnicity at a given age, for age is a good measure of the work experience of men who spend nearly full time in the labor force after they finish school. Age does not measure experience very well for women. The interruption of careers by child-rearing means that at any given age married women are likely to have had less labor-force experience than men, and hence less investment in on-the-job training. Estimates for 1966 and 1967 indicate that married women lost two years of work experience per child.[28] We standardize for differences in experience by sex in order to isolate labor-market discrimination, although we realize that these differences are often the result of sex stereotyping.

[28] Ronald Oaxaca, "Sex Discrimination in Wages," in Orley Ashenfelter and Albert Rees (eds.). *Discrimination in Labor Markets,* Princeton University Press, Princeton, N.J., 1973, and Jacob Mincer and Solomon Polachek, "Family Investments in Human Capital: Earnings of Women," *Journal of Political Economy* (82): S76–S108 (1974).

Table 13.7 HOURLY WAGES BY TENURE AND EXPERIENCE, WHITE MEN AND WOMEN, 1975[a]

	No prior experience		Ten years' prior experience	
Years on current job	Men	Women	Men	Women
0	$4.24	$3.25	$4.74	$3.64
5	4.79	3.67	5.35	4.11
10	5.40	4.15	6.04	4.65
15	6.10	4.69	6.81	5.25
20	6.88	5.30	7.69	5.93

[a]Twelve years of school; non-South; average days of absenteeism; no work limitations, part-time work, or interruptions between jobs or between school and work; living in an area with a city of 500,000 people.

Source: Calculated from Mary Corcoran, "The Structure of Female Wages," American Economic Association, *Proceedings* (68) (1978), Table 1.

The responsibilities of caring for families also contribute to a somewhat higher average rate of absenteeism for women than for men. A survey of earnings of manual workers in Great Britain for September 1968 showed that 22 percent of women lost pay because of absence for all or part of one or more days, as compared with 15 percent of men, even though men had a somewhat higher rate of approved absences.[29] This difference must also be standardized for, because a greater rate of absenteeism from the workplace indicates a lower rate of acquiring on-the-job training for each year of job experience.

Table 13.7 presents standardized hourly wage rates for white men and women with the same amount of experience on their current jobs and in jobs held before the current one. Since these calculations are based on actual work experience, they circumvent the problems introduced by the weak correlation between a woman's age and her work experience. Taking ratios of women's to men's wages in the categories in Table 13.7, we see that these adjusted ratios are about 0.77. Compared to the unadjusted earnings ratios for year-round full-time white workers of 0.58, they imply that about one-half the wage differences between white women and men can be explained by differences in experience, in absentee rates, and by other differences that affect productivity. A substantial amount of labor-market discrimination exists against women in the United States today. This penalty is beyond that inflicted by the lesser attachment of women to the work force.

The fact that wage differentials exist between men and women with the same amount of prior experience is not surprising. A woman who has the same amount of prior experience as a man is usually older and probably dropped out of and then reentered the labor force several times. Longitudinal data show that women who drop out of the labor force receive a lower real wage upon reentry than they received before. The on-the-job training they received depreciates somewhat when not used. Even though their wages rise fairly rapidly when they are reemployed, three inter-

[29] *Employment and Productivity Gazette,* September 1969, p. 824.

rupted three-year spells of employment do not lead to so high a wage rate as does one continuous nine-year spell.[30]

Wage differentials between men and women with the same current job tenure can be explained by the theory of investment in training, together with statistical discrimination. Employers, viewing a woman's chance of staying with the firm as highly uncertain, will be less willing to invest in her firm-specific training. Thus years of tenure on the job will reflect a smaller amount of firm-specific training and will produce a lower wage for women than for men.

These effects produce feedback relations among wages, turnover, and investment in training. Wage discrimination induces greater turnover and a reduced labor-force participation rate; these induce employers to invest less in female employees, which reduces their wages below those of males. Pay discrimination also reduces a woman's incentives to invest in her own general training.[31] With a lower rate of return to education because of time spent out of the labor force, she is less likely to choose those fields that yield a high payoff. Similarly, she will be less willing to invest in on-the-job training. Both choices reinforce the behavior that produced them, and consequently she will receive lower wages than men of the same age and even with the same experience.

Although it is very difficult to solve the chicken-and-egg problem that is implicit in a feedback relationship of this kind, it is worthwhile trying to do so, as its solution can enable us to understand the source of the discrimination. One study showed that individual women's wages are relatively lower in industries in which women's rates of quitting are relatively high. Another study has attempted to solve this problem by using longitudinal data for the years 1976 to 1979. Women who in 1976 expected to drop out of the labor force received the same wages as otherwise identical women; but lower wages were found to induce a greater rate of actual dropouts. Women's work plans do not affect their wages, but low wages affect their plans and decisions on staying at work. This striking difference suggests that the source of the discrimination is the lower wage offered to women, not their response to that wage in the form of reduced investment in training and a greater rate of exit from the labor force.[32]

This discussion suggests that much of the labor-market discrimination against women results from their relegation to occupations in which the skill requirements are less than in those that are dominated by otherwise identical male workers. This is not true if workers are classified only by broad occupations—professionals, clericals,

[30] Jacob Mincer and Haim Ofek, "Interrupted Work Careers: Depreciation and Restoration of Human Capital," *Journal of Human Resources* (17): 3–24 (1982). See also Mincer and Polachek, loc. cit.; Steven Sandell and David Shapiro, "The Theory of Human Capital and the Earnings of Women," *Journal of Human Resources* (13): 103–117 (1978); and Mary Corcoran, "The Structure of Female Wages," American Economic Association, *Proceedings* (68): 165–170 (1978).

[31] Marianne Ferber and Helen Lowry, "The Sex Differential in Earnings: A Reappraisal," *Industrial and Labor Relations Review* (29): 377–387 (1976), show that education has a greater impact on earnings in those narrowly defined occupations that are predominantly male.

[32] James Ragan and Sharon Smith, "The Impact of Differences in Turnover Rates on Male/Female Pay Differentials," *Journal of Human Resources* (18): 343–365 (1981), and Reuben Gronau, "Sex-Related Wage Differentials and Women's Interrupted Labor Careers—The Chicken or the Egg," Working Paper No. 1002, National Bureau of Economic Research, Cambridge, Mass., 1982.

and so on; only one-sixth of the shortfall of the standardized earnings ratio from complete equality resulted from broad occupational differences during the late 1960s. If one defines occupations more narrowly, though, occupational segregation looms more important. Within one large firm, for example, there was no difference in pay between men and women in each job category, but women with the same experience and education as men earned 10 percent less on average because they were disproportionately represented in those jobs in the firm that paid less.[33] This suggests that occupational crowding plays a part in explaining why the standardized earnings ratios are below 1.

The tied family migration decisions that we noted in Chapter 7 also reinforce existing patterns of discrimination. With lower wages, wives' labor-market prospects are more likely to be hurt by a move than are those of their husbands. This, too, induces them to invest less in training, which in turn makes them more susceptible to earnings losses when the family moves again. Even if the family does not move, women are often tied by their husbands' jobs to a particular job market and cannot accept the best job that they might otherwise obtain. Also, women who never married may be the victims of crowding into "women's jobs"; in metropolitan areas in which their labor-supply elasticities are lower, their earnings relative to those of otherwise identical men are also lower.[34]

After all these adjustments are made, however, substantial differences in wages between men and women remain. Part of these may reflect differences in personality traits that workers bring to the market and which are rewarded by employers. One study using data for 1972 found that 6 percentage points of the remaining adjusted earnings ratio between women and men are accounted for by differences in such traits as sociability, desire for domination, emotional stability, and so on.[35] The fact that women do not have these traits to as great an extent as male workers merely implies that labor-market discrimination is less than the data in Table 13.7 suggest. The differences in traits may not be innate, but instead may result from sex stereotyping at an early age.

As with discrimination by race and ethnicity, sex discrimination is not confined to the United States. In the United Kingdom in 1975, for example, the unadjusted earnings ratio between single women and men was 0.97; the standardized ratio was 0.91. (Standardized earnings ratio being below the unadjusted ratio indicates that single women had better job qualifications than did single men.) Even within the workplace in Britain the same kind of occupational segregation exists as in the United States: Otherwise identical single women averaged 16 percent lower, 9 percent lower, and the same earnings as single men in three establishments in different British industries. In Canada in 1970, the unadjusted earnings ratio for all

[33] Randall Brown, Marilyn Moon, and Barbara Zoloth, "Incorporating Occupational Attainment in Studies of Male-Female Earnings Differentials," *Journal of Human Resources* (15): 1–28 (1980), and Burton Malkiel and Judith Malkiel, "Male-Female Pay Differentials in Professional Employment," *American Economic Review* (63): 693–705 (1973).

[34] Lucy Cardwell and Mark Rosenzweig, "Economic Mobility, Monopsonistic Discrimination and Sex Differences in Wages," *Southern Economic Journal* (46): 1102–1117 (1980).

[35] Randall Filer, "Sexual Differences in Earnings: The Role of Individual Personalities and Tastes," *Journal of Human Resources* (18): 82–99 (1983).

Table 13.8 FEMALE-MALE EARNINGS RATIOS, 1939–1980[a]

Year	All workers: Whites	All workers: Nonwhites	Year-round full-time workers: Whites	Year-round full-time workers: Nonwhites
1939	0.61	0.53	0.61	0.51
1955	0.52	0.38	0.64	0.58
1960	0.49	0.41	0.60	0.63
1965	0.50	0.53	0.60	0.66
1970	0.38	0.51	0.59	0.70
1975	0.39	0.58	0.58	0.75
1980	0.45	0.68	0.58	0.76

[a]Ratios of medians of wage and salary workers.

Source: U.S. Bureau of the Census, *Current Population Reports,* P-60, Nos. 23, 37, 51, 80, 105, 132.

men and women with earnings was 0.60. Accounting for hours worked as well as demographic characteristics and experience, we find that the standardized earnings ratio was 0.83, not much different from what Table 13.7 implies exists in the United States.[36]

Trends and the Effect of Federal Policy

A long and consistent series of standardized female-male earnings ratios is not available. In its absence, Table 13.8 shows unadjusted earnings ratios for both whites and nonwhites. Among whites there is a striking lack of a trend; the unadjusted female-male earnings ratio has hovered around 0.6 as far back as the available data go. Among blacks, though, there has been a steady narrowing of pay differentials by sex. Taken together, since whites account for nearly 90 percent of the work force, the results imply that there has been little overall change in unadjusted earnings ratios. This remarkable constancy masks an accelerating decline in the occupational segregation of workers among occupations. There was a slight reduction in a measure of such segregation during the 1960s; the reduction was three times as rapid during the 1970s.[37]

The absence of major changes in these unadjusted earnings ratios and in the occupational distributions of male and female workers does not demonstrate the absence of any change in labor-market discrimination against workers. It requires examining standardized earnings ratios, which can be calculated from the decennial census of population. A comparison of those ratios in 1960 and 1970 does not alter the implications of the data in Table 13.8. One standardization (which was not able

[36]Christine Greenhalgh, "Male-Female Wage Differentials in Great Britain: Is Marriage an Equal Opportunity?" *Economic Journal* (90): 751–775 (1980), and W. S. Siebert and P. J. Sloane, "The Measurement of Sex and Marital Status Discrimination at the Workplace," *Economica* (48): 125–141 (1981). For Canada, see Morley Gunderson, "Decomposition of the Male/Female Earnings Differential: Canada 1970," *Canadian Journal of Economics* (12): 479–485 (1979).

[37]Andrea Beller, "Trends in Occupational Segregation by Sex," Unpublished Paper, University of Illinois, 1982.

to account for sex differences in actual work experience) found that the earnings ratio fell by 0.02 during this period among whites, although it rose by 0.08 among blacks.[38]

The fact that there was little change in standardized labor-market outcomes between 1960 and 1970 may reflect the lack of government efforts in this direction. Although women's rights were mentioned in the Civil Rights Act of 1964, the major impetus behind federal efforts to aid women came in 1972, with amendments that strengthened the Civil Rights Act and others that prohibited sex discrimination in educational programs. This suggests that changes since 1972 may reflect the effect of government antidiscrimination efforts. Given the complexity of the process of sex discrimination, it may be some time before these efforts produce an impact on earnings ratios. Nonetheless, they have had some effect: Between 1971 and 1974 the standardized earnings ratio was increased by 3 percentage points by enforcement of equal opportunity laws. In the late 1970s, otherwise identical women were less likely to quit their jobs in those industries on which the greatest efforts at requiring affirmative action had been made by federal officials. Between 1971 and 1977 younger college-educated women especially increased their representation in those narrowly defined occupations that in 1960 had contained mostly male workers. Since this coincided with the passage of amendments aimed at discrimination in education, the change implies that federal antidiscrimination programs have had an effect on the occupational division of workers by sex.[39]

Statistical discrimination and occupational segregation that is decreasing only slowly explain the continuing labor-market discrimination against women. Although there has been some reduction in discrimination, the changes to date have been small and concentrated among better educated women. Whether the increased attachment of women to the labor force, coupled with government pressures on employers, will reduce discriminatory outcomes in the future is not clear. Evidence of pay discrimination against single women suggests, however, that employers must be convinced that the attachment of women to the labor force is very close before they will offer them the on-the-job training and occupational advancement that will raise their earnings closer to those of equally well-educated men.

POLICY ISSUE—COMPARABLE WORTH

Affirmative action and equal pay laws have demonstrably not produced equality of outcomes between men's and women's wages in the United States. Recognizing that this is at least partly the result of women being concentrated in occupations that have traditionally been "women's work" and that pay relatively little, advocates of women's rights have proposed pay for *comparable worth.* Jobs would be evaluated according to their inherent requirements—formal and informal training time, unpleasantness, unusual scheduling, and so on. Pay would be based upon these evaluations, eliminating situations where

[38] Calculated from Ronald Oaxaca, "The Persistence of Male-Female Earnings Differentials," in F. Thomas Juster (ed.). *The Distribution of Economic Well-Being,* Ballinger, Cambridge, Mass., 1977, Tables 1 and 2.

[39] Andrea Beller, "The Impact of Equal Opportunity Policy on Sex Differentials in Earnings and Occupations," American Economic Association, *Proceedings* (72): 171–175 (1982), and Paul Osterman, "Affirmative Action and Opportunity: A Study of Female Quit Rates," *Review of Economics and Statistics* (64): 604–612 (1982).

low-skilled men are paid more than high-skilled women who work in different occupations in which labor is equally scarce. Payment partly on the basis of comparable worth has been introduced into the setting of wages of municipal employees in San Jose, California. There, for example, the job of painter was evaluated as requiring slightly less skill than that of secretary, although painters' salaries had been well above those of secretaries.[40]

Will payment by comparable worth reduce male-female wage inequality? Is it a sensible policy that employers should be required to adopt? If the job evaluations are incorrect, substantial inefficiency will arise, as excessively high wages are paid for jobs that are rated too highly. Workers will queue for those jobs, whereas municipal employers will have difficulty hiring for those jobs that are rated too low. Even if the ratings are consistent with equilibrium wage differentials, problems can arise. The policy would remove workers' incentives to train in those occupations with equal skill requirements but in which demand is temporarily high. This would reduce the ability of competitive sectors of the labor market to adjust to the changes in demand or supply that continually buffet the economy, thus imposing higher costs on employers and reducing real output. On the other hand, it would raise wages particularly in those occupations in which unions have been unable to impose a large wage gap, for it is those where workers of comparable background receive lower pay. This would reduce the small (see Chap. 11) distortions imposed on the economy by union-imposed wage gaps. Although removing this distortion would increase allocative efficiency in the labor market, the relatively small size of the union sector in the United States makes it likely that the net effect would be to reduce efficiency.

If the policy were put into effect, it would reduce male-female wage differentials. We have seen that women's educational attainment is essentially the same as that of men in the United States, and that their years of labor-market experience are increasing to equal those of men. Imposing payment by comparable worth would reduce the adjusted wage differentials we have presented in this section by equalizing pay among jobs of equal "value" within firms. The policy has clear-cut equity arguments in its favor; its cost may be the lost efficiency, as markets fail to allocate workers toward places and occupations where labor is scarce.

THE ROLE OF FELLOW EMPLOYEES, UNIONS, AND CONSUMERS

Throughout this chapter we have discussed discrimination as if its source were solely from employers. Yet in most industrial economies one's coworkers, the union one belongs to (or is excluded from), and consumers will affect the extent of discrimination. One important case is that in which the skills of the two groups differ. For example, if most skilled workers are white and prefer to work with white rather than black unskilled workers, employers who hire blacks will have to pay skilled workers a premium. They will be willing to do this only if the wage of unskilled blacks is below that of unskilled whites.

Kenneth Arrow has pointed out a particularly interesting case of this sort arising where people at one rank or level supervise or manage those at another rank or level.[41] The prejudice of whites against having a black supervisor is undoubtedly more intense and persistent than that against having black subordinates or coworkers. There are also usually more subordinates than managers. It is therefore

[40] John Bunzel, "To Each According to Her Worth?" *Public Interest* (67): 77–93 (1982). See also Donald Treiman and Heidi Hartmann, *Women, Work and Wages: Equal Pay for Jobs of Equal Value,* National Academy Press, Washington, 1981.

[41] Kenneth Arrow, *Some Models of Racial Discrimination in the Labor Market,* RAND Corporation, Santa Monica, Calif., 1971.

expensive for employers to compensate all subordinates by enough to overcome their distaste for being directed by a black superior. Since the best-educated members of the labor force are often in supervisory or managerial positions, the distaste of most whites for being managed by a black lowers the return on education for blacks. Many educated whites are highly paid managers, whereas very few educated blacks are highly paid managers. Similarly, if men (and perhaps some women) dislike being managed or supervised by women, there will be few female managers.

Where black and white workers have identical productive capacities, prejudice by white workers need not lower black wages. The result could be simply segregation, with some employers hiring only whites and others only blacks. The presence of fixed costs of employment would prevent such an outcome from being unstable if a small wage differential should arise in favor of one group or the other. An approximation to this result can arise within a firm, where races are sometimes segregated into separate work groups to reduce contact between them. For example, a firm that does not hire black production workers may hire black janitors, who clean up after other workers have gone home.

Wage differentials by race are affected also by the attitudes and policies of trade unions. Here a sharp distinction must be made between craft and industrial unions. Many craft unions have traditionally excluded black members and to some extent still do, despite various public pressures designed to make them change. Blacks in the skilled manual crafts are therefore concentrated in the nonunion sectors of these occupations and have much lower average earnings than do whites. Industrial unions, in contrast, have not excluded black members, in part because they needed the support of black workers when they organized their industries.[42] Some industrial unions have been militant in fighting for minority rights. Even in industrial unions, however, particular locals may discriminate against minorities despite national union policy, and discrimination is most likely at the highest occupational levels. For example, in the steel industry many blacks are hired, but they are concentrated in the less skilled occupations and in the departments where the work is least pleasant.

The overall effect of unionism on black-white earnings ratios can be decomposed into two parts—the extent to which black and white workers are represented by unions and the effect of unions on the relative earnings of those that they represent. Table 9.4 showed that blacks are more likely to be unionized than whites. Estimates for 1967 suggest that for all male blue-collar workers, unions increase the earnings of black members more than those of white members. In the construction industry, however, blacks are underrepresented among union members, so that the two components work in opposite directions, and the total effect of construction unionism was to lower the earnings of black male blue-collar workers relative to whites by about 5 percent. In blue-collar occupations in other industries the effect of unionism was to narrow the black-white earnings differential. For blue-collar males outside construction, the effect of unions was to raise the average wage of blacks relative to whites by about 4 percent; for the economy as a whole the average black-white earnings ratio was raised by about 2 percentage points.[43] This effect is

[42] See Ray Marshall, *The Negro and Organized Labor,* Wiley, New York, 1965.

[43] Orley Ashenfelter, "Discrimination and Trade Unions," in Ashenfelter and Rees, loc. cit.

almost entirely due to differences among regions: Using data from 1973, one set of estimates showed little difference between whites and nonwhites in the net effect of unionism (accounting for both the wage gap and the extent of unionization) except in the South, where the impact was very large.[44] The regional difference is not surprising, because union wage policy attempts to equalize wages, and the South has historically had the largest wage differentials between blacks and whites.

The adjusted wage gap, $\overline{M}$, is higher among blacks partly because of the way in which unions change the operation of the workplace. Unionization produces a greater reduction in the propensity of otherwise identical black workers to quit a job than it does for whites. This enables black union members to acquire the specific on-the-job training that raises their earnings relative to that of whites with the same total labor-market experience.[45]

The evidence is mixed, but there is some indication that the adjusted union wage effect is greater for men than for women. Unions in those occupations and industries that have large concentrations of female workers are less successful than others in raising their members' wages relative to those of nonunion workers. Coupled with the sharply lower extent of unionization of women than of men (see Table 9.4), the net effect is that unionism reduces the female-male earnings ratio. One estimate placed the impact in 1967 at 1 percent for whites and 6 percent for nonwhites.[46]

Prejudice by consumers or buyers is important in occupations where workers are in direct contact with customers. Buyers of manufactured goods do not know the race or sex of workers in the factory where the goods were made, but they can observe the salespeople who serve them. Consumer tastes operate in both directions; indeed, black consumers may have a more intense preference for buying from black salespeople than white customers have for buying from whites. The first implication of this is that residential segregation produces segregation in employment in trade and services. Nevertheless, consumer prejudice may lower the relative incomes of blacks even though it operates in both directions. First, the policies of businesses that serve all neighborhoods, such as downtown department stores, may be dominated by the tastes of the white majority. Second, whites have higher per capita purchasing power, so black influence on the employment policies of retailers is less than the number of black consumers would suggest.

Consumer preferences were probably also responsible for some conspicuous instances of occupational segregation by sex. Until the 1960s, most passengers on domestic airlines were men, and almost all flight attendants were young women. Since the passage of the Civil Rights Act of 1964 there has been an increase in the number of male flight attendants. The abolition of age restrictions for flight attendants has resulted in an increase in the number of female attendants over age 30.

[44]Nicholas Kiefer and Sharon Smith, "Union Impact and Wage Discrimination by Region," *Journal of Human Resources* (12): 521–534 (1977).

[45]Duane Leigh, "Unions and Nonwage Racial Discrimination," *Industrial and Labor Relations Review* (32): 439–450 (1979).

[46]Calculated from Ronald Oaxaca, "Male-Female Wage Differentials in Urban Labor Markets," *International Economic Review* (14): 693–709 (1973).

SUMMARY

Pay discrimination may arise from employers', consumers', or fellow employees' unwillingness to hire, buy from, or work with persons of a minority group or of the opposite sex. These tastes induce employers to offer lower wages to the group that is discriminated against, as that group's members compete for jobs when they find themselves unable to obtain employment at the same wage as equally productive members of the majority group. Discriminatory outcomes in the labor market may also result from employers' greater inability to use standard methods of relating the background of minority or female workers to their expected productivity on the job. So long as information about the productivity of these workers is poorer than that on white male employees, and so long as employers who wish to discriminate control access to most jobs, discriminatory outcomes will persist even in a competitive economy.

Racial discrimination in pay pervades the labor market in the United States and in other countries for which detailed studies have been conducted. Similarly, Hispanics receive lower pay than otherwise identical other whites. Nonetheless, wage discrimination against younger and especially better educated blacks in the United States nearly disappeared between the mid-1960s and the late 1970s and does not seem to have reappeared. This striking structural change is at least partly due to government policy. Wage rates of female workers are still well below those of men with the same education and experience. This is due chiefly to differences in the occupational mix, with women heavily concentrated in occupations in which the returns to experience and education are lower. There has been little change over the past 20 years in the extent of pay discrimination against women except for younger and better educated women. Unions help reduce discrimination against blacks, chiefly through the policy of equal pay for equal work.

chapter 14

The Distribution of Earnings and Income

SIZE AND FUNCTIONAL DISTRIBUTIONS OF EARNINGS AND INCOME

The distribution of income by size is a topic of vital importance for both economics and public policy. The massive systems of progressive income taxes and transfer payments that are operated by modern governments are partly designed to alter the size distribution so that income after taxes and transfers is distributed less unequally than before and poverty is alleviated. All of this topic cannot be viewed as part of labor economics, since total income includes income from capital (rents, interest, dividends) and income from self-employment, which includes a component of income from capital. Our first concern in this chapter will be with the distribution of wage and salary income. However, this is more closely related to the total distribution than might be imagined.

In the United States in 1980, the mean before-tax income of all families was $23,974. Of this $18,319 came from wages and salaries; self-employment income contributed about $1500, transfers about $2800, and property income about $1300. Wages and salaries constituted over one-half the income of every income class above $10,000 of total income. (Below $10,000, other income sources, largely social security and public assistance, were more important.) A second way of seeing the importance of labor income in total income is to look at the differences in total income of families by number of earners. In 1980, families with no earners had median incomes of $8560, those with one earner had median incomes of $16,714 and those with two or more earners had median incomes of $27,121.

This focus on the *size distribution* of income ignores the basis for the payment of most income, namely, as rewards for different kinds of services in production. Until the nineteenth century one could analyze the size distribution of income by

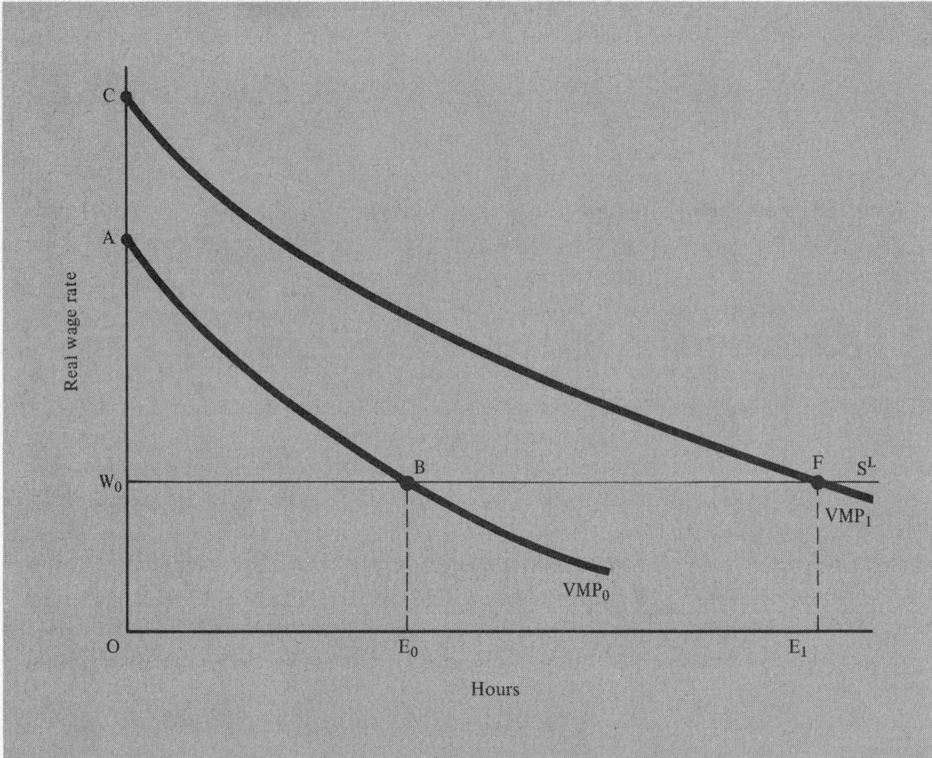

Figure 14.1 The distribution of income in a two-factor world.

using the same tools as those used to analyze the *functional distribution,* how national income is divided according to income producers' functions as owners of factors of production. In describing a preindustrial economy, one can for simplicity assume that land and labor were the only factors. The demand for labor can be described, as in Figure 4.3, by the VMP relation shown again as VMP_0 in Figure 14.1. In this type of economy conditions may have been such that any increase in wages above a subsistence level W_0 merely encouraged expansion of the population (and hence the work force). This assumption means that the long-run supply of labor was horizontal at W_0, described by the supply curve S^L.

With workers having only their agricultural labor to sell, each would receive only the wage W_0. The size distribution of earnings would be degenerate—all workers receiving the same earnings once differences in hours of effort are accounted for. The functional distribution would also be described simply: Labor income is the rectangle OW_0BE_0 in Figure 14.1; landowners' income (rent) is the triangle AW_0B, the excess of each worker's contribution to output above what is paid out as wages. The size distribution of income would thus show some inequality, but solely because of income differences between workers and landowners.

As we showed in Chapter 4, technical improvements shift the labor-demand schedule, VMP_0, to the right, to VMP_1 in Figure 14.1. In the long run no change is produced in the size distribution of earnings; the population expands, but each worker still receives only W_0. The functional distribution may change, depending upon how the VMP schedule shifts to the right. If the shift is parallel, no change occurs; otherwise the distribution will change. The size distribution of income may change even if the functional distribution does not. For example, if the population of landowners does not increase as much as the laboring population, rents per landowner rise, and the inequality in the size distribution of income increases.

This model shows the relation between the size distributions of earnings and income and the functional distribution of income in a world that is much less complex than any industrialized economy today. Labor is no longer homogeneous; its heterogeneity means that the size distribution of earnings is not all concentrated at one hourly wage rate. Also, one cannot make a clear distinction between workers who receive only wages and landowners (or capitalists) who receive only rent (or interest). Workers receive nonlabor income through ownership of capital directly and through their pension plans. Capitalists also work; we showed in Chapter 1 that essentially all adult males aged 30 to 34, for example, are in the labor force, so that at least part of the income received even by those who are owners of capital can be viewed as the return to effort. For these reasons and others the easy identification of how changes in one distribution relate to changes in another is no longer possible. The size distribution of earnings and the functional distribution of income must be discussed separately today. We thus consider the size distribution of earnings (and income) first, and then examine the functional distribution of income.

THE SHAPE OF SIZE DISTRIBUTIONS

Size distributions of earnings have a characteristic shape. They have a single mode to the left of the mean and a long tail to the right; that is, they are positively skewed. Figure 14.2 shows such an earnings distribution for full-time year-round male workers in 1981. The frequencies at low incomes would be larger if part-year workers

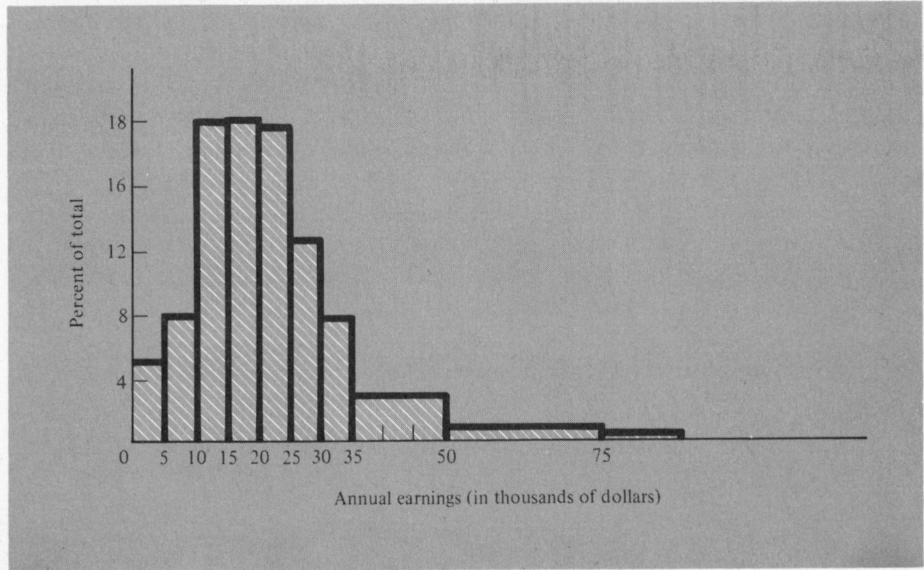

Figure 14.2 The distribution of wage and salary income of male full-year workers, 1981.

were included; with only full-year workers included, the lower tail contains fewer observations. More generally, the distribution of annual earnings reflects two components—the number of hours worked during the year and the amount earned per hour. Each of these components is affected by both demand and supply forces. Workers can to some extent choose the number of hours worked and the type of work done, and thus affect annual earnings. However, the demand for workers' services sets limits to that area of choice; as we saw in Chapter 2, it may not pay to work more hours if the hourly wage on second jobs is low.

The earnings distribution shown in Figure 14.2 does not reflect the distribution of all the returns to work received by full-time male workers in 1981. Like other workers, these men also received fringe benefits, which can form a significant fraction of labor income. If these were added to earnings and the figure redrawn, its shape would not show much change; the same positive skewness would still be there. But the skewness would be a bit more pronounced, for men with above-average earnings receive disproportionately large amounts of their compensation in the form of fringe benefits.[1] This results from factors such as attitudes toward risk and reactions to a progressive tax structure, which we showed in Chapter 12, affect the amount of fringe payments included in the compensation package.

Figure 14.2 shows the earnings of individuals rather than those of families. Yet labor income is consumed by members of the family in amounts that are determined by the preferences of the members of the household; not all labor income is spent by its direct recipients. To discover the distribution of economic welfare produced by wage and salary income, one should examine the distribution of earnings by families, not by individuals. This change would also increase (although only very slightly) the skewness in the distribution of earnings. Two opposite effects make the distribution of husbands' earnings a rough approximation to the distribution of family earnings. On the one hand, men with a higher earnings potential tend to marry women with a higher earnings potential; on the other hand, income effects on the supply of labor mean that in most industrial societies a wife whose husband earns more supplies fewer hours per year to the labor market. The evidence suggests that these effects nearly offset each other or that the second is somewhat larger.[2] Together they result in a size distribution of family earnings that is shaped similarly to the distribution of earnings of full-time male workers. The distribution of total family incomes has a similar shape as well.

Throughout the discussion of the size distribution of earnings (or income) the issue of inequality is paramount. Unfortunately, though, the amount of inequality implicit in *histograms* such as the one in Figure 14.2 cannot readily be summarized. Instead, alternative summary measures of inequality have been used. One such

[1] Timothy Smeeding, "The Size Distribution of Wage and Nonwage Compensation: Employer Cost vs. Employer Value," in Jack Triplett (ed.). *The Measurement of Labor Cost,* University of Chicago, Chicago, 1983.

[2] James Smith, "The Distribution of Family Earnings," *Journal of Political Economy* (87): S163–S192 (1979); Richard Layard and Antoni Zabalza, "Family Income Distribution: Explanation and Policy Evaluation," *Journal of Political Economy* (87): S133–S162 (1979); Jacob Mincer, *Schooling, Experience, and Earnings,* Columbia University Press, New York, 1974, pp. 123–125; Reuben Gronau, "Wives' Labor Force Participation, Wage Differentials and Family Income Inequality," Working Paper No. 668 National Bureau of Economic Research, Cambridge, Mass., 1981.

measure is the *variance* of the logarithms of income, the average squared deviation around the mean; the difficulty with this measure is that it implies a very large degree of inequality is present in those cases where there are a few persons or families with extraordinary earnings or income. Another measure is the *relative interquartile range.* The population is arrayed, for example, by its earnings, with the lowest earner at the bottom, the next lowest earner next, up to the highest earner. The measure is the difference between the earnings of the worker at the 75th percentile of the population and the earnings of the worker at the 25th percentile, all divided by the earnings of the median worker. If the measure is zero, the earnings distribution is essentially perfectly equal. A higher relative interquartile range denotes greater inequality.

A third measure, which takes into account the distribution of earnings in the entire population, also begins by arranging the population by earnings, from lowest to highest. A box such as that in Figure 14.3 is drawn. The amount of earnings (or

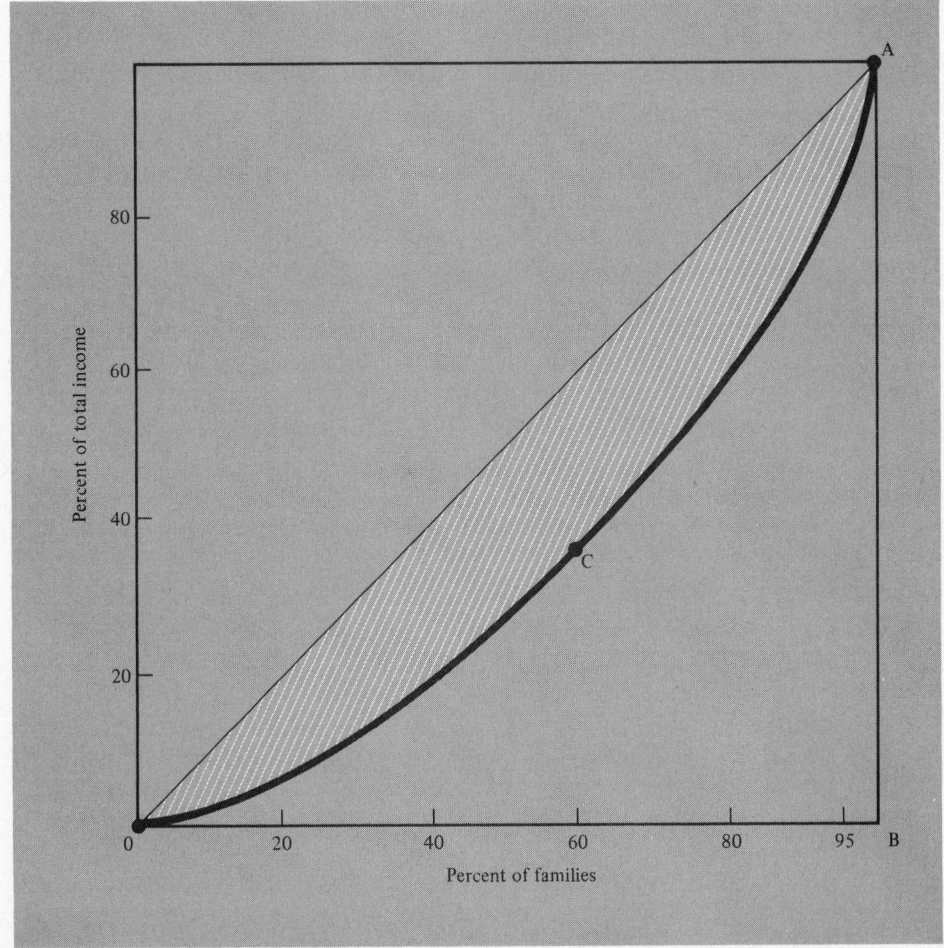

Figure 14.3 Cumulative distribution of family incomes, whites, 1980.

income) accruing to the lowest fraction of earners (or families) is graphed. In Figure 14.3, we have graphed the percentages of all the income received by white families. Of this, 5.6 percent goes to the 20 percent of white families with the lowest incomes. The cumulative percentage of total income received up to the next cutoff point (in Fig. 14.3, by the lowest 40 percent of families) is then graphed, and so on. This process produces the *Lorenz curve* OCA in Figure 14.3. The *Gini coefficient* is the ratio of the shaded area, between OCA and the diagonal OA, to the triangle OBA. In the case of the distribution shown, the Gini coefficient is 0.365. If each white family received identical incomes, the Gini coefficient would be zero, because the Lorenz curve would coincide with the diagonal; if all but one family received nothing, and one family received all the income, the Gini coefficient would be 1, because the Lorenz curve would be the edge of the box, OBA. A higher Gini coefficient denotes more inequality.

None of these measures of inequality, nor any of the many other measures we have not presented, is necessarily correct for all purposes. Each provides a different way of summarizing the information about the extent of inequality contained in distributions like that in Figure 14.1. Therefore, when making statements comparing inequality in distributions, one should be aware that the comparison may differ if alternative measures of inequality are used. Similarly, conclusions about the determinants of inequality in earnings or income distributions must be tempered by the recognition that the results may depend upon the measure of inequality that is employed in the analysis. A change in one part of the distribution could imply an increase or a decrease in inequality depending on the measure used. In most cases, though, such a change will cause most measures of inequality to move in the same direction.

POLICY ISSUE—EARNINGS OR INCOME INEQUALITY?

The distribution of earnings has not become more equal in the United States in the last 30 years. One measure, the Gini coefficient of earnings of males, rose from 0.40 to 0.44 between 1958 and 1977.[3] On the other hand, Table 14.1 implies that the distribution of income has become more equal, especially when one considers the shares of the bottom 20 percent and the top 5 percent of families. This trend would be quite pronounced if we could include the value of services received from such rapidly growing in-kind transfer programs as Food Stamps, Medicaid, and Medicare.[4] Can we infer from the earnings

Table 14.1 PERCENTAGE DISTRIBUTION OF FAMILY INCOMES, 1950–1980

Year	Lowest fifth	Second fifth	Middle fifth	Fourth fifth	Highest fifth	Top 5 percent	Gini coefficient
1950	4.5	12.0	17.4	23.4	42.7	17.3	0.365
1960	4.8	12.2	17.8	24.0	41.3	15.9	0.354
1970	5.4	12.2	17.6	23.8	40.9	15.6	0.364
1980	5.1	11.6	17.5	24.3	41.6	15.3	0.379

Source: U.S. Bureau of the Census, *Current Population Reports,* P-60, No. 132, Table 19.

[3]Robert Plotnick, "Trends in Male Earnings Inequality," *Southern Economic Journal* (48): 724–732 (1982); see also Martin Dooley and Peter Gottschalk, "Earnings Inequality Among Males in the U.S.," Unpublished Paper, McMaster University, 1982.

[4]Morton Paglin, *Poverty and Transfers In-Kind,* Hoover Institution Press, Stanford, Calif., 1980.

distribution that disparities in earning power have not been reduced? If so, should we rest content with the decline in the dispersion of incomes?

The two distributions are not independent of each other. By offering transfer payments, such as unemployment insurance, Social Security retirement benefits and Disability Insurance benefits, the government has retarded the narrowing of the distribution of earnings. As the example of Disability Insurance in Chapter 1 showed, these programs induce workers with the lowest potential earnings to earn disproportionately less than their potential. Because replacement rates under these programs are greater for low-wage workers, and because these workers have higher labor-supply elasticities, they have been most likely to reduce their supply of effort to the market. The rapid expansion of transfer payments in the United States (from 8.2 percent of disposable income in 1960 to 16.5 percent in 1981) has made the distribution of earnings less equal, yet it has equalized the distribution of income. People who supported this expansion should feel it achieved its goals and should not be upset at the failure of distribution of earnings to become more equal; this was partly the result of the policies they endorsed.

THEORIES OF THE SIZE DISTRIBUTION

The typical shape of size distributions of earnings gives rise to a problem that has concerned economists and statisticians for a long time. Many human characteristics, such as height, are distributed according to the familiar symmetrical "bell curve" (normal distribution). This type of distribution is usually assumed to fit many kinds of ability, including mental ability, although the evidence on this point is by no means clear. (Some material suggests that the normal distribution of IQ scores is an artifact of test construction rather than a characteristic of the population being tested.[5]) But if we assume a symmetric distribution of ability, why should heterogeneity in the labor force give rise to a skewed distribution of earnings? Such a bewildering variety of answers has been given to this question that the problem is no longer that of finding an answer, but, rather of choosing judiciously among the competing alternatives.

The alternative theories of the size distribution of earnings can be classified into two main groups: *stochastic process* theories and economic theories. The former, which we shall not consider here, generates skewed distributions of earnings from normal distributions of ability by the cumulative effect of random variation in fortunes through time. In other words, they view the actual distribution of earnings essentially as a result of chance, like the process that would produce winners and losers at a fair roulette wheel. There is apparently substantial random mobility of individuals between earnings classes; the stochastic theories have the virtue of depicting these random movements.[6] Because they are mechanical, though, they lack the ability to relate differences in demographic or social characteristics to differences in the extent of inequality among economies or in the same economy in different periods of time. Economic theories of the size distribution include many separate themes. For our purposes, however, they can be classified into the human capital approach and those other theories that are based on interactions of different abilities or on the hierarchial structure of large organizations.

[5]Harold Lydall, *The Structure of Earnings*, Clarendon, Oxford, 1968, pp. 76–79.

[6]Mary Bane and David Ellwood, "Slipping Into and Out of Poverty: The Dynamics of Spells," Unpublished Paper, Harvard University, John F. Kennedy School, 1982.

HUMAN CAPITAL AND THE SIZE DISTRIBUTION

Effect on Earnings Inequality

Suppose at the outset that all people have the same ability and that there are no nonpecuniary advantages or disadvantages in any employment, so that in the absence of investment in human capital all workers would receive the same earnings. Then let us examine the effects of the heterogeneity in the work force that is produced by investment in human capital in the form of schooling beyond the minimum school-leaving age. To simplify matters we assume also that there are no out-of-pocket costs of investing in education and that no work in the market is performed while people are at school. As we showed in Chapter 3, otherwise identical individuals who have access to loanable funds will invest in human capital up to the point where the returns on the investment are equal to the rate of return on equally risky investments in physical capital.

These assumptions are sufficient to introduce inequality into the distribution of earnings. Consider a society made up of three different groups of workers, each of whom works until age 68: clerks who acquire 12 years of schooling and work from 18 on; auditors who attend school for 16 years and work from age 22 on; and economists who attend school for 20 years. Viewed at age 18, workers in each occupation will receive the same discounted lifetime earnings. Yet, because those with more education receive earnings during shorter work lives *and* must be compensated for postponing the receipt of earnings (must receive a positive real rate of return on their investment in schooling), earnings at any age will differ. Table 14.2 shows the extent of these differences at any age between 26 and 68 (when people in all three groups are working), assuming in each case that clerks earn $10,000 per year. The real rates of return are in the range of 5 to 14 percent which, as we showed in Chapter 3, bracket the real rate of return to schooling. Two facts stand out from this table: (1) Differences in the amount of investment in human capital produce substantial inequality in the distribution of annual earnings; (2) The degree of inequality increases, the greater is the rate of return to schooling.

Effect on Earnings Skewness

This simple example shows clearly why there is inequality in the distribution of earnings; it does not, however, explain why there is skewness. To do this we need to

Table 14.2 HYPOTHETICAL ANNUAL EARNINGS IN THREE OCCUPATIONS REQUIRING DIFFERENT AMOUNTS OF SCHOOLING

Real rate of return (percent)	Occupation (years of schooling)		
	Clerks (12 years)	Auditors (16 years)	Economists (20 years)
5	$10,000	$12,461	$15,106
8	10,000	13,869	19,287
11	10,000	15,562	24,249
14	10,000	17,519	30,706

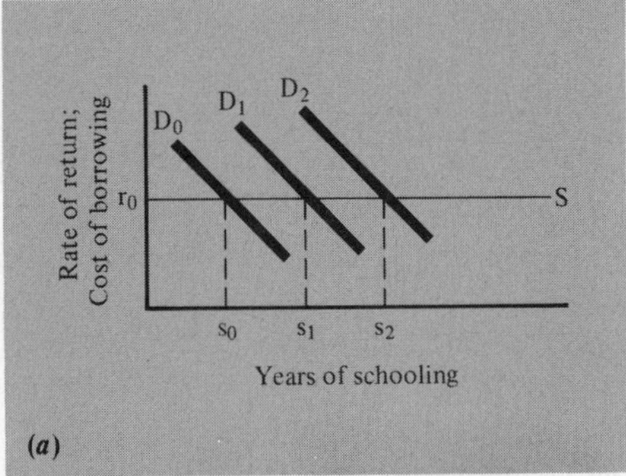

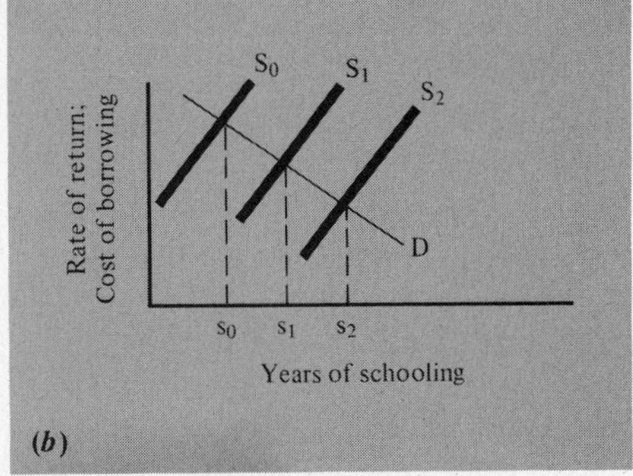

Figure 14.4 The market for funds for investment in schooling: (a) ability differences; (b) liquidity differences.

explain why relatively few people are in those occupations that require substantial investments in human capital, and thus yield high annual earnings. Two explanations are possible; each depends on the nature of the demand for schooling by students and their families and on their ability to finance their investments by borrowing, drawing down savings, or obtaining government subsidies (in other words, on the supply of funds that are available for investment in schooling).[7] One possible case is shown in Figure 14.4(a). All workers are assumed to have equal access to funds to finance investments in schooling at the market rate of interest r_0; but because students differ in their ability to benefit from schooling, they have different demand curves for those funds. Assume, for example, that the distribution of ability is symmetric, such as the bell curve. Sixty percent of the population has average ability, 20 percent is below average, and 20 percent is above average. Then 60 percent of the people will obtain s_1 years of schooling, and 20 percent each will obtain s_0 and s_2 years of schooling.

If the rate of return is 11 percent, and the three levels of schooling are 12, 16, and 20 years, respectively, Table 14.2 shows that 60 percent of the work force will earn $15,562 per year; 20 percent will earn $10,000 per year, and 20 percent will earn $24,249 per year. The distribution of earnings implied in this example is shown by the histogram Figure 14.5. The three bars are connected by a smooth line to allow a better comparison to the actual distribution of earnings we presented earlier in this chapter. This figure shows the skewness that is produced by combining the assumption of a symmetric distribution of ability with individuals' utility-maximizing decisions about the amount of investment in human capital. Notice that even though educational attainment in each of two groups (the top and bottom) differs from the median by the same amount, four years, the top group's earnings exceed the median earnings by more than the earnings of the bottom group fall short of the median.

The human capital approach can also explain skewness in the distribution of earnings by differences in the ease of access to borrowed funds among people of equal

[7]See Gary Becker, *Human Capital and the Personal Distribution of Income: An Analytical Approach,* Institute of Public Administration, University of Michigan, Ann Arbor, 1967, especially pp. 3–5, 14–16.

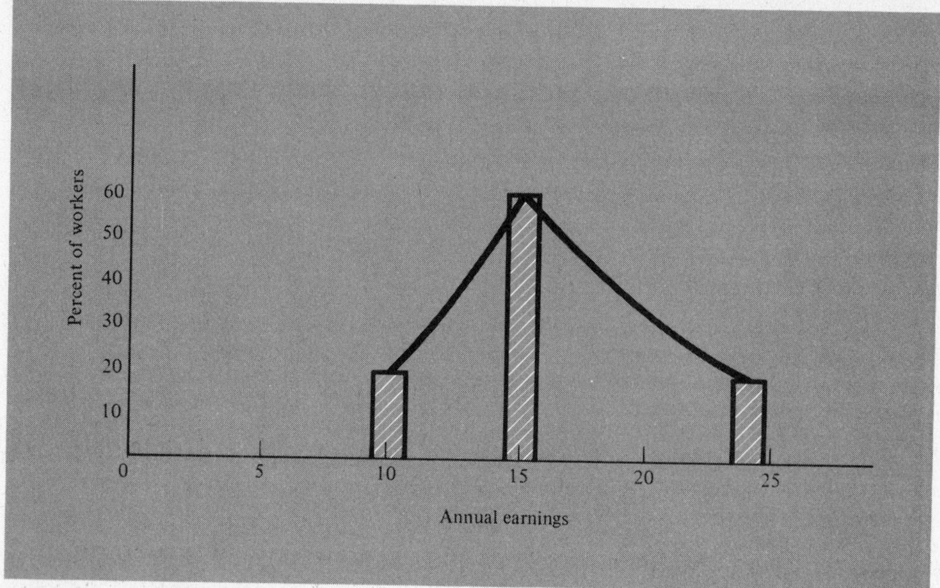

Figure 14.5 A skewed hypothetical distribution of earnings.

ability. In Figure 14.4(b) students from low-income families may have severe difficulties borrowing, and their parents may have no savings to use for their education; the supply curve of funds to finance their education is S_0. Students from better-off families will be able to finance their education more readily; for them the supply curves of funds for education are S_1, or even S_2. Assume a few people have great difficulty financing education (are on supply curve S_0), most have some difficulty (are on supply curve S_1), and a few find it very easy (are on supply curve S_2). Then most people will obtain s_1 years of schooling, whereas a few will obtain s_0 or s_2 years. As with the example in Figure 14.4(a), the dispersion in the amount of schooling obtained will produce skewness in the distribution of earnings. Those few people who obtain s_2 years of schooling will have earnings that exceed the median by more than the earnings of those who obtain only s_0 years of schooling fall short of the median.[8]

The examples in Figures 14.4(a) and (b) are each extremes. In reality differences in both ability and access to funds for investment in education affect the amount of investment in formal schooling. Indeed, if those people with greater ability to benefit from education also have easier access to funds to finance education, the results in each of the two extreme cases will be magnified and the degree of skewness in the distribution of earnings will be quite large. More concretely, to the extent that students of high ability come from better-off families, or the government offers subsidies to very able students, there will be more skewness in the distribution of earnings.

[8]This conclusion will be valid so long as the demand curve in Figure 14.4(b) is not too inelastic. If it is, rates of return on additional amounts of schooling beyond s_0 will be falling so fast that additions to earnings become successively smaller so rapidly that the tendency toward skewness is overcome.

These hypothetical examples are obviously quite artificial, although they do illustrate how the theory of the acquisition of human capital can explain the basic facts of inequality and skewness. We have ignored other aspects of investment in human capital, particularly investment in on-the-job training. We showed in Chapter 3 that investment in training produces differences in earnings in the form of the typical inverted U-shaped age-earnings profiles. Even if each worker has made the same investment in formal schooling, differences in the amount of on-the-job training would suffice to produce inequality in earnings. Since, as we showed in Chapter 3, schooling and on-the-job training are complementary, the inequality that each produces separately is reinforced when they are combined.

POLICY ISSUE—HEAD START PROGRAMS

In reality it is very difficult to distinguish between the effects of differences in ability and differences in access to funds for investment in human capital. This difficulty leads people to the hasty conclusion that there is a high correlation between ability and the ease of obtaining access to formal schooling, a correlation that, although it induces greater inequality of earnings, seems justified on grounds of efficiency. An alternative view is implicit in the legislation that created Head Start programs in the United States in the 1960s. These programs include health and nutritional services, as well as education, and are targeted at disadvantaged children. Are they successful in increasing the eventual educational attainment of participants, and do the dollars spent on the program increase the productivity of the participants more than they would raise the productivity of other young children? If so, the program would appear worthwhile, and in addition, would equalize the distribution of income.

There is little doubt about the program's success in affecting the participants' ability to perform in school. Head Start participants have generally been found to perform better on intelligence tests after completing the program and to move ahead in school more rapidly than nonparticipants with similar family backgrounds.[9] The evidence on the extremely complex issue of the heritability of intelligence suggests there is a lot of randomness between generations in levels of innate intelligence. A family that has a low income because the parents have little ability and acquire less human capital has a good chance of producing a child of above-average intelligence.[10] Taken together, this evidence implies that Head Start programs, by providing access to education to disadvantaged children, many of whom may have substantial native intelligence, equalize the distribution of earnings and can be an efficient outlet for government spending.

Role of Human Capital in Practice

The human capital approach generates several predictions relating inequality in earnings to differences in the amount of investment in schooling and on-the-job training. Substantial study has been devoted to the prediction that where there is greater variation in the amount of training embodied in the work force, there will be more dispersion in earnings. This prediction seems borne out by the facts: An examination of data from nine countries showed that earnings inequality, as indi-

[9] Congressional Budget Office, *Childcare and Preschool: Options for Federal Support,* U.S. Government Printing Office, Washington, 1978.

[10] A good summary of this literature is Christopher Jencks, *Inequality,* Harper & Row, New York, 1972, chap. 3.

cated by a measure similar to the relative interquartile difference, was greater in those nations where there was more dispersion in the level of formal schooling attained. Similarly, in 1959 those states in which there was more dispersion in the amount of schooling achieved by adult males exhibited greater variance in the distribution of adult males' earnings. At each age the distribution of earnings of white males in the United States shows less inequality than that of blacks, partly because there is more dispersion in the level of education in the black male population. Also, the distribution of earnings in the United States has changed over time with the distribution of schooling attainment. The income distribution has also been equalized when the distribution of schooling attainment has become less unequal, but the effect on incomes has been less than that on earnings.[11] This is because components of income other than wages and salaries are not so strongly affected by differences in schooling.

Taken together, differences in schooling and on-the job training account for a substantial part of the observed inequality and skewness that we showed characterize the distribution of earnings. One leading advocate of the human capital approach claims that when proper adjustments are made, these differences explained as much as two-thirds of the variance in the logarithms of earnings among workers in the United States in 1959.[12] Additional evidence for the importance of factors related to differences in the amounts of human capital is provided by a comparison of Gini coefficients for the population at a point in time to Gini coefficients for a cohort of workers over its members' work lives. The Gini coefficient for the income of the U.S. population in 1972 was 0.350; the coefficient for the lifetime incomes of people alive in 1972 was 0.199 according to one calculation.[13] Accounting for differences in yearly incomes that arise from differences in the amount of time devoted to investment in human capital explains much of the observed inequality in income.

Even the human capital approach, as its proponents admit, leaves unexplained a large fraction of the observed dispersion and skewness of the distribution of earnings. This failure is demonstrated vividly by examining the distribution of earnings among people whose age and education are quite similar. Figure 14.6 shows the 1967 earned income of the Princeton Class of 1942. Apart from the dip in the interval $25,000 to $29,999, which is probably the result of small sample size, the distribution has the typical shape of earnings distributions. The median is $23,545, and the skewness is such that 15 percent of the observations are at earned incomes more than twice the median. Yet all these men attended college at the same institution, and all were about the same age. To be sure, some went on to graduate school and others did not, and they had different kinds of on-the-job training. Family connections no doubt assisted some to achieve high earnings. But one is left with the suspicion that factors other than schooling and on-the-job training play a large role in explaining the dispersion and skewness of the distribution of earnings.

[11] Barry Chiswick, *Income Inequality,* Columbia University Press, New York, 1974, Tables 4.3, 5.5; James Smith and Finis Welch, "Inequality: Race Differences in the Distribution of Earnings," *International Economic Review* (20): 515–526 (1979); Plotnick, loc. cit.; and Barry Chiswick and Jacob Mincer, "Time-Series Changes in Personal Income Inequality in the United States from 1939, with Projections to 1985," *Journal of Political Economy* (80): S34–S66 (1972).

[12] Mincer, op. cit., p. 134.

[13] Peter Friesen and Danny Miller, "Annual Inequality and Lifetime Inequality," *Quarterly Journal of Economics* (98): 139–155 (1983).

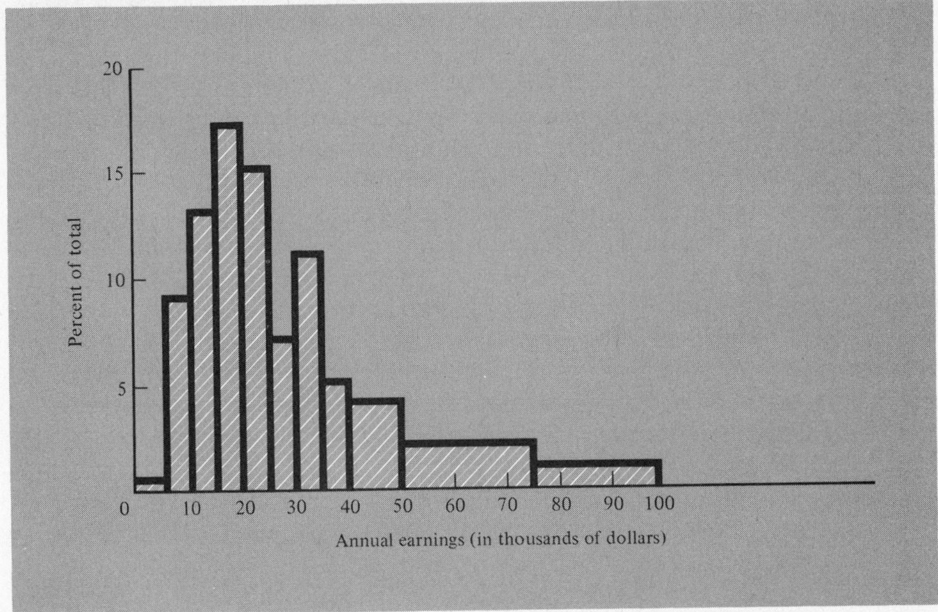

Figure 14.6 The distribution of earned incomes in 1967 of the Princeton Class of 1942. (*Source: Twenty Five Years Out,* 25th reunion yearbook of the Princeton University Class of 1942, Progress Publishing, Caldwell, N.J., 1967.)

THE ROLES OF ABILITY, RESPONSIBILITY AND RISK

The model sketched in the preceding section will explain a good deal of the dispersion of earnings, but it would require great differences in access to capital or in ability to explain the dispersion that actually exists. We therefore concentrate here on differences in ability. By *ability* we mean both genetic differences and differences produced by early childhood experiences. It is difficult to distinguish how far differences in ability affect earnings in their own right and how far they operate by shifting the demand for investment in human capital, as we assumed in the previous section. For many purposes, though, such distinctions may make little difference.

Role of Ability

Let us for now take the opposite approach from that of the previous section and turn to models that consider ability directly. Although we have been talking of ability in general terms, it is clear that several quite different kinds of abilities can affect earnings, for example, intelligence, physical stamina, and manual dexterity. It has been shown that if each of the relevant abilities is normally distributed but that if earnings vary with the multiple of several uncorrelated kinds of ability, then the logarithms of earnings rather than the earnings themselves will be normally distributed.[14] Since the distribution of earnings is skewed, the normal distribution of the

[14] A. D. Roy, "The Distribution of Earnings and of Individual Output," *Economic Journal* (60): 489–505 (1950), showed that this multiplicative process generates this *lognormal* distribution of earnings.

logarithm of earnings describes actual earnings data quite well, perhaps better than any other relatively simple distribution. However, like the models based on investment in human capital, the multiplicative model of abilities is inadequate in explaining very high earnings, which are too numerous in reality to be explained by a statistical distribution based on the logarithms of earnings. The right tail of actual earnings distributions has more people in it then can be accounted for by simply multiplying normal distributions of underlying abilities.

Surprisingly little attention has been paid to the economics of the process by which ability is translated into earnings. (In the previous section, e.g., we saw that the human capital approach merely assumed that ability defined loosely raises the return to a given investment in schooling.) The simplest case to start with is straight piecework. Consider an activity such as picking beans, where workers are paid a fixed amount per basket picked. If workers differ in only one ability (say manual dexterity) and this ability is normally distributed, and if all workers exert the same effort relative to their ability, then it follows that daily earnings will also be normally distributed. However, the operation just considered is a most unusual one because it involves no physical capital. For this reason, a grower will permit small children to work alongside their parents during the harvest even though they pick very little.

Now consider the example of a factory job (say, bench assembly) that is also paid by the piece, but on which workers produce by using their labor *and* capital equipment. Employers must make a competitive return on this equipment if they are to stay in business. Assume again that workers differ in the only relevant ability, manual dexterity, which is normally distributed. Employers will not retain the workers at the far lower tail of the ability distribution because they do not produce enough to cover the overhead of maintaining their workplace, such as the costs of capital, supervision, heat, and light. Employers may formalize this need for the worker to produce enough to cover overhead costs by setting a minimum production standard, say, 25 percent below the average. A worker who, after a fair trial, cannot produce up to this minimum standard would not be kept on the job. In this case, although we have assumed a normal distribution of a single ability, the corresponding distribution of earnings has a truncated lower tail. A worker who is so unfortunate as to be in the far lower tail of all ability distributions that are relevant to any employment will be unemployable. If any ability (say, intelligence) is relevant to all employments, a worker could become unemployable by being in the far lower tail of this distribution alone.[15]

Some specialized kinds of ability are economically valuable only in a small set of occupations, and then only when their level is much above average. For example, consider talent in music. Some amount of training in playing a musical instrument is part of many upbringings. Many of those trained must at some time have considered becoming professional musicians but had been discouraged by teachers who felt that they lacked sufficient talent. Only those in the upper tail of the ability distribution can hope to earn a living as musicians. Whether they choose to do so will depend on both the value they attach to the nonpecuniary rewards of a musical career and their probable earnings in alternative occupations.

For these reasons the occupational use of a talent will not begin at a sharply

[15] See Michael Sattinger, *Capital and the Distribution of Labor Earnings,* North-Holland, Amsterdam, 1980.

defined point in the ability ranking, assuming that ability can be ranked; some amateurs will be better than some professionals. In one major university, for example, the best attended violin concerts are given by a professor of pathology rather than by a member of the music department. The importance of alternative opportunities in selecting professionals can be illustrated by the high proportion of blacks among successful professional basketball players. This need not reflect a racial difference in the distribution of the relevant abilities. It could arise solely because greater discrimination in their alternative activities gives black basketball players a greater incentive to turn professional and to invest in further training at any level of ability that has potential market value.

Let us now return to the example of musicians. People who are very high in musical ability will continue to invest in training, but it is more the amount of ability than the length and quality of training that eventually determines their earnings. In general, the best schools and teachers will accept only the more promising pupils. People with low musical ability find this lack of ability irrelevant to earnings in other careers and turn elsewhere for employment. Suppose that somewhere in the employed labor force there are people as much below the mean in musical talent as Luciano Pavarotti is above the mean. Where should we expect to find these musical illiterates in the earnings distribution of all employed persons? From all we know, we might find them at the mean, since they may be average in all other abilities, and musicians are too small a part of the whole labor force to affect appreciably the mean of the whole earnings distribution.

We have shown so far that the process of choice of careers to accommodate different talents would tend to produce dispersion in the earnings distribution, even if all abilities were normally distributed and if abilities did not need to be used in combination in any occupation. Very able people would receive high earnings that are partly a return to the training to which their ability gave them access; partly, though, they are a rent to the specialized ability.

Differences in ability alone do not seem sufficient to explain the bunching of people in the right tail of the earnings distribution. Pavarotti earns at least 20 times what the average professional singer does; so, too, for Reggie Jackson in baseball, Mikhail Baryshnikov in ballet, and a host of other superstars in music, art, the theater, and professional sports. In these occupations, consumer demand for excellence helps determine the market value of the services of people with exceptional talent. Thus, so long as everyone agrees that Pavarotti is the best tenor, that Reggie Jackson is the best ballplayer, and so on, these men will earn rewards that are disproportionately larger than those earned by other people in the specialty, even though the differences in underlying ability are barely perceptible. Only if consumers do not agree about who is best, either because of difficulties in discerning differences in quality or because tastes for different styles of performance differ, will there be a moderation of the extreme earnings received by the one superstar in a profession.[16]

Homogeneity of consumers' tastes cannot alone explain the extreme earnings

[16] Melvin Reder, "A Partial Survey of the Theory of Income Size Distribution," in Lee Soltow (ed.). *Six Papers on the Size Distribution of Wealth and Income,* National Bureau of Economic Research, New York, 1969, pp. 216–217; and Michael Rothschild and Joseph Stiglitz, "A Model of Employment Outcomes Illustrating the Effect of the Structure of Information on the Level and Distribution of Income," *Economics Letters* (10): 231–236 (1982).

in certain professions. Why does Mick Jagger earn such fabulous amounts, whereas the best house painters (if there were consensus on quality) would probably not receive much more than the average house painter? The answer lies in the interaction of technology and demand. Mick Jagger's product can be sold, through recordings and mass performances in domed stadiums, to huge audiences. The house painters' clienteles are limited by technology to the few people whose houses they can paint during their working lives. The technology of reproducing the product in the arts and in sports (through television) expands the market for the services of the performer.

Expansion of the market comes at the cost of a reduction in intimacy and perhaps in quality. Some people would rather hear a live concert by a second-rate rock group than watch a telecast of a performance by the Rolling Stones. This quality-quantity trade-off creates a demand for the services of the less talented, allowing them to earn more than in their best alternative occupations. When an expanding market results from an increase in the popularity of the particular service rather than a change in technology, the number of performers increases. Some less talented people find they are able to satisfy some consumers' desires for live performances and earn more than they could in other occupations. The superstars even more than before the expansion, as some new consumers pay for their services by buying their records or attending their mass concerts. With more people in the profession earning barely enough to justify staying in the occupation, the extra rents of the superstars create an even more skewed distribution of earnings. The threefold combination of consumers' agreement on quality, consumers' preferences for live performances, and the technology that allows the reproduction of stellar performances for a mass audience produces great skewness in the distribution of earnings in certain occupations.[17]

Role of Responsibility and Risk

Although the examples used so far have been taken from sports and the arts, special ability may also play an important role in earnings in professions such as medicine and law and in business occupations such as sales and management. We showed in Chapter 8 how managers' salaries are structured to provide incentives to lower-level executives to work hard while competing for high-level jobs. The salary structure may also be arranged to reflect the responsibilities required at each level of management. The fat upper tail of many earnings distributions could be explained by a *hierarchical theory* of organization with the following assumptions: (1) Managers in a given grade supervise a constant number of people in the grade below them, and this constant is the same throughout the organization. (2) The salary of managers in each grade is a constant proportion (greater than 1) of the salaries of the people they directly supervise.[18] It is argued that the salary is related to the post rather than to the

[17]This discussion is based on Sherwin Rosen, "The Economics of Superstars," *American Economic Review* (71): 845–858 (1981).

[18]Lydall, op. cit., pp. 13–17, 125–129. These assumptions produce the Pareto distribution of earnings. If we let N be the number of persons with earnings above some given level X, the distribution is given by $N = AX^{-a}$ where A and a are constants. Pareto believed that a was generally in the region of 1.5, but higher values are often found. For an application of both the Pareto and lognormal distributions to recent data on earnings, see Alan Harrison, "Earnings by Size: A Tale of Two Distributions," *Review of Economic Studies* (48): 621–632 (1981).

individual; that is, executives are paid mainly for responsibility "and that this criterion of payment is, in principle, quite separate from the criterion of ability."[19] This is shown by the general rule that supervisors are paid more than their subordinates.

The hierarchical theory is vulnerable at several levels. The supposed need for a reward for responsibility implies that people dislike taking it. This is often true, but it is also true that many other people enjoy responsibility and authority, perhaps in some cases too much. One can also question the assumption that factors other than ability have much effect on the selection for higher posts, except perhaps in family-owned businesses. The person who alone among hundreds of competing junior executives in a large corporation eventually rises to the presidency must surely have special qualities that account for this rise, although they differ from the qualities that make a successful scientist or a successful salesperson. In any event, a business that is not a monopoly would soon run at a loss if it selected executives without any regard to those kinds of ability relevant to managing a business well.

The largest rewards to executives are paid in the largest corporations. The size of these rewards may be determined by the size of the organization; but it is also true that it takes more ability to manage a larger organization. In a competitive world the most able managers will sort themselves into the largest organizations. Their ability will have its biggest effect on total productivity there, because they are able to enhance the productivity of a greater number of subordinates.[20] The reward will be correlated with the size of the hierarchy; but the size of the hierarchy merely reflects the ability of the manager, and the reward is for ability, not for supervision. Some evidence for this view is provided by the common career path of managers who, having proved successful in smaller companies, are recruited to manage larger firms.

The most important difficulty with the theory is that it is too special, since it applies only to hierarchical organizations. Many earners of high salaries are not in such organizations. In the distribution of wage and salary incomes for 1980 of males who worked 50 to 52 weeks during the year, 442,000 men (1.1 percent of the total) had earnings of $75,000 and over, the highest earnings class tabulated. However, only 207,000 of these were managers and administrators. There were 109,000 professional and technical workers with salaries of $75,000 and over and 51,000 sales workers. In both of these occupational groups, individual ability seems more important on the whole than managerial responsibility.

Distributions of earnings with a fat right tail can also be found within groups working in rather small organizations. Figure 14.7 shows the distribution of earnings of medical doctors in the United States in 1979. Few doctors presided over large numbers of subordinates, yet the right tail of the distribution looks very much like that predicted by the theory of earnings in hierarchies. Differences in ability and work effort are better candidates to explain the nature of this earnings distribution than is the hierarchical theory.

One final factor that produces dispersion and skewness in the earnings distribution is the willingness to take risk. Some careers involve much greater risks than others; in general, owning a business, or self-employment in professional practice,

[19] Lydall, op. cit., p. 126.

[20] Sherwin Rosen, "Authority, Control, and the Distribution of Earnings," *Bell Journal of Economics* (13): 311–323 (1982).

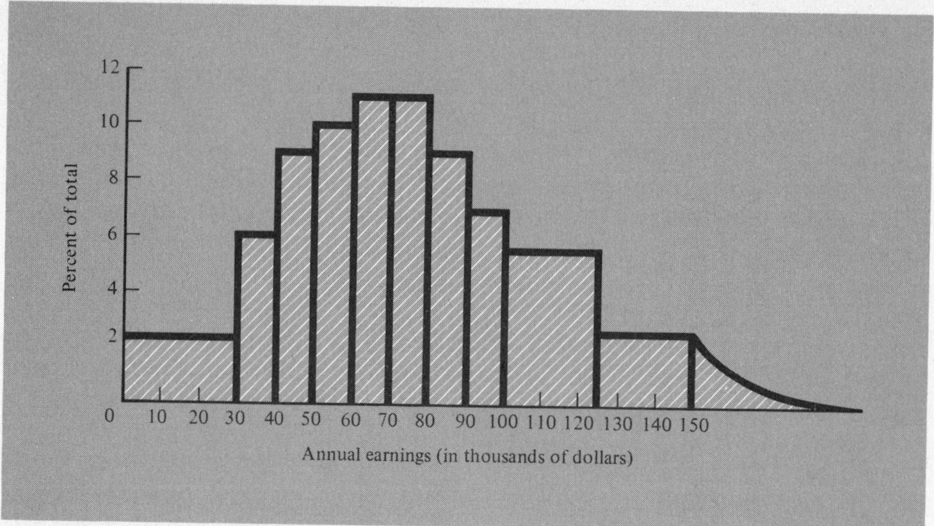

Figure 14.7 The distribution of earnings of M.D.'s, 1979. [*Source:* Calculated from *Medical Economics* (57): 190–191 (January 19, 1981).]

will involve greater risk than being a salaried employee. The greater is the willingness of people in general to take risks, the lower will be the average return in such occupations, and the greater will be the dispersion of the earnings distribution. We should expect to find in the lower tail of the earnings distribution many self-employed people who have been attracted into self-employment by the small chance of making a great gain. Balancing these will be the few who are highly successful. This is exactly what happens: Among white male employees who worked full time in the private sector throughout 1980, the median earnings were $19,648; mean earnings were 10.0 percent above this. Among white male full-time self-employed workers, median earnings were $12,924; mean earnings were 35.4 percent above this, suggesting much greater skewness. Clearly, ability plays a part in determining who succeeds, but chance also may play some part. To the extent that low income results from the deliberate assumption of risk through occupational choice, it may give somewhat less cause for social concern than when it results entirely from forces beyond the control of the individual.[21]

THE FUNCTIONAL DISTRIBUTION OF INCOME IN AN INDUSTRIALIZED ECONOMY

For purposes of discussing the functional distribution, *income* can be defined as output during a particular time period (usually a year) minus the portion of this output that is needed to maintain the initial stock of real capital, that is, minus an appropriate allowance for depreciation and depletion. In other terms, income is the

[21] A much more extensive and formal treatment of this point is in Milton Friedman, "Choice, Chance and the Personal Distribution of Income," *Journal of Political Economy* (61): 277–290 (1953).

Table 14.3 THE DISTRIBUTION OF NATIONAL INCOME, SELECTED YEARS, 1929–1981, IN PERCENT

	1929	1939	1949	1959	1969	1979	1981
Compensation of employees	60.2	67.3	66.2	69.8	73.5	74.1	75.1
Proprietors' income							
Farm	7.2	6.2	6.0	2.8	1.9	1.6	1.0
Business and professional	10.4	10.4	11.0	9.2	6.7	5.1	4.3
Rental income of persons	5.8	3.7	2.9	3.4	2.5	1.4	1.5
Net interest	5.6	5.0	1.2	2.5	4.5	7.9	10.0
Corporate profits	10.8	7.4	12.7	12.3	10.9	9.9	8.1
Total	100.0	100.0	100.0	100.0	100.0	100.0	100.0

Source: Council of Economic Advisors, *Economic Report of the President,* 1983, Table B-21.

amount that a society could consume during a period without having less real capital at the end of the period than it had at the beginning. If actual consumption is less than this, the difference is an addition to capital that constitutes both savings and investment. For individuals the concept of income is the same except that the definition of capital includes financial assets such as money, bonds, and stocks. These are claims of some individuals on others that cancel out for an economy as a whole.

In considering the personal or size distribution of income, one ordinarily includes only the part of corporate income that is distributed to stockholders as dividends, although in fact stockholders may also have unrealized capital gains that result in part from undistributed earnings. In considering the functional distribution, however, we include corporate profits whether or not they are distributed. The functional distribution also considers only income arising in production, before there has been any redistribution through taxes and transfer payments.

The property share of income includes the rent of land, interest, and profit. In a modern industrial economy the rent of unimproved land is a very small part of total income; most of what is entered as rent in national income accounts is actually a charge for the use of structures and improvements. We shall therefore treat the nonlabor share of income as though it were all a return to physical capital. Later on, monopoly profit will also be considered briefly.

Table 14.3 shows the functional distribution of income in the United States as reported in the national accounts. The compensation of employees (wages, salaries, and supplements to wages and salaries) makes up 75 percent of the total today. *Labor's share* has been rising fairly steadily in the United States, as reported in the official data on the national accounts. Increases in labor's share also occurred between 1960 and 1979 in Canada, the United Kingdom, France, West Germany, and Japan. The increases in the last three years in these nations were larger than those in the United States during this period.[22]

There are two reasons for believing that the increases in Table 14.3 overstate the true increase in labor's share. The less important of these is the increasing share of economic activity performed by government. No return on government capital is included in national output or national income, although government activities do

[22]Calculated from United Nations, *Yearbook of National Accounts Statistics,* vol. 1, 1980.

use capital; the whole output of government is represented by the compensation of its employees. The growth of government thus automatically raises labor's share of national income because of this accounting convention.

The more basic reason for distrusting the data on compensation of employees as a measure of labor's share has to do with self-employment. The data on proprietors' income, or income from self-employment, include a return on the labor of the self-employed and their families. To estimate the movement of labor's share, one should add this return to employee compensation. Since self-employment has been declining, the amount to be added to labor's share for this reason has been declining over time. This means that a corrected measure of labor's share has been growing less rapidly through time than employee compensation alone. Even after full allowance is made for the labor component of self-employment income, though, estimates of changes in the functional distribution show a rise in labor's share. A simple way of seeing this is to assume two-thirds of proprietors' income represents a return to work effort. Adding this fraction of proprietors' income to compensation, labor's share would have been 71.9 percent in 1929 and 78.6 in 1981. Using three more complex methods to construct data on labor's share in the United States from 1900 to 1963, one study found that even with these adjustments, labor's share rose substantially during this period.[23]

A THEORY OF FUNCTIONAL DISTRIBUTION

The dominant tradition explains factor shares from the side of production.[24] In its simplest terms it says that labor's share is the hourly compensation of workers times the number of hours of labor used in production. Capital's share is the return to a unit of capital services times the number of units of capital services used. The prices or returns to a unit of each factor are equal to their marginal products. Under certain conditions, of which the most important is constant returns to scale, the payment to each factor of its marginal product would exactly exhaust the total product. If these conditions were not fulfilled there would be a residual (positive or negative) that would alter the share of the enterprise owners.

We have already looked at the division into factor shares of the output in a single production process (see Fig. 14.1). The apparent simplicity of that approach to factor shares conceals many difficult problems; it is sometimes argued that these problems make the approach useless or circular. The income share of a factor can vary because either the quantity of it that is used changes autonomously relative to the quantity of the other factor or its price (marginal product) changes relative to the price of the other factor, which will induce changes in relative quantities. However, it is often difficult to separate factor incomes into quantity and price components. In the case of labor we have a measure of quantity (hours of work), although it is an

[23] Irving Kravis, "Income Distributions: Functional Share," in David Sills (ed.). *Encyclopedia of the Social Sciences,* vol. 7, Crowell Collier and Macmillan, New York, 1968, pp. 132–145.

[24] An alternative approach sees functional shares as determined by differences between workers and capitalists in marginal propensities to consume and by the Keynesian equilibrium condition that ex-post savings must equal investment. A very lucid exposition of the model is in Nicholas Kaldor, "Alternative Theories of Distribution," *Review of Economic Studies* (23): 83–100 (1955).

unsatisfactory one if differences in the quality of labor are not taken into account. In the case of capital it is impossible to obtain physical measures of inputs at an aggregate level and often even at the level of the firm, so that it is necessary to resort to proxies such as energy consumption. Financial measures of the quantity of capital are either based on historical costs, which may not be relevant to current value, or they are themselves influenced by the market rate of return on capital. (An asset yielding a perpetual net income stream of $1 is worth $20 when the interest rate is 5 percent but is worth only $10 when the interest rate is 10 percent.) This is awkward when one wants to decompose changes in the value of capital services into quantity and price components.

When we examine historical changes in factor shares, we are not examining merely the effect of changing the quantity of inputs with a constant production function. Technical progress is continually shifting the function so as to permit the production of more output for given quantities of conventional inputs. Almost all such progress is labor saving; much of it is capital saving as well.

Aside from technical progress, capital-deepening has occurred. Physical capital per worker has increased rapidly by any measure used, which is what we would expect from casual observation of changes in production processes. Based on one official measure of the stock of business capital equipment and structures, the real value per full-time equivalent employee rose by 2.7 percent per year between 1950 and 1975.[25] Other things equal, this increase would lead us to expect an increase in the property share of national income if labor were homogeneous and supplied at a subsistence wage, since there is now a larger proportion of capital in the input mix. But this is just the opposite of what has occurred.

A number of forces would resolve this paradox, of which two seem like the best explanations. Each is based on our discussion of the demand for factors of production in Chapter 4. The first explanation is that capital deepening has shifted the economy from point C to point F on a relative demand curve for capital and labor like that shown in Figure 14.8. The relative increase in the amount of capital has lowered the price of new capital relative to that on labor. (The relative price in question is the price of a piece of capital equipment of given productive capacity, relative to the wage of a given grade of labor.) If firms cannot substitute capital for labor very easily (the elasticity of substitution is relatively low), the only way the relative increase in capital could have been absorbed is through a sharp drop in the price of capital, relative to that of labor, from R_0 to R_1. The share of capital, relative to that of labor, is shown by the area under the relative demand curve at the going relative factor prices. Thus before the capital deepening occurred, the relative share of capital is indicated by the rectangle OR_0CA; afterward, by the rectangle OR_1FB. The latter rectangle is smaller, showing that the sharp fall in the relative price of capital induced by capital deepening led to a decline in capital's share of national income.

A second important explanatory force is the familiar one of investment in

[25]The capital stock data are from Allan Young and John Musgrave, "Estimation of Capital Stock in the United States," in Dan Usher (ed.). *The Measurement of Capital,* University of Chicago Press, Chicago, 1980, Table 1.A.3. Data on full-time equivalent employees in the private sector are from the U.S. Department of Commerce, *Survey of Current Business,* July 1952 and July 1977.

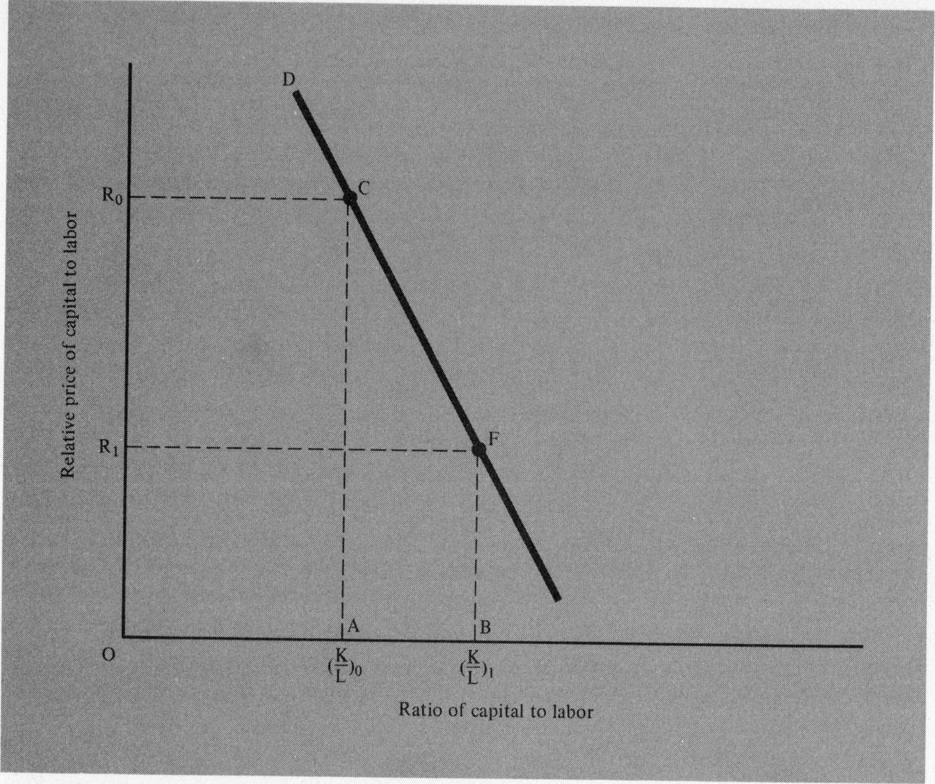

Figure 14.8 The effect of capital-deepening on factor shares.

human capital. Return on such investment, is of course included in labor income in the national accounts. The distinction between human capital and unskilled labor in production, and the concept of the complementarity of human and physical capital, are of use here.[26] Even though physical capital per worker has been rising, human capital per worker may have been rising even more rapidly. If so, at constant relative prices the share of national income going to labor, composed both of returns to unskilled labor and returns to human capital, could have risen.

Since we lack precise measures of inputs of human and physical capital, we cannot be sure that inputs of human capital have been rising relative to those of physical capital. But it seems likely, given the rapid growth of technical, professional, and managerial employees as a percentage of the labor force and the declining importance of common labor (see Table 3.1). Moreover, the complementarity of human and physical capital implies that the same technological changes that bring new forms of physical capital into use generally call for greater investment in human capital. In terms of Figure 14.1 this means that even though the VMP curve may

[26] P. R. Fallon and Richard Layard, "Capital-Skill Complementarity, Income Distribution, and Ouput Accounting," *Journal of Political Economy* (83): 279–302 (1975), show how complementarity will affect the functional distribution.

have shifted out in a parallel fashion, the growth of human capital has meant that the share of labor—untrained labor and human capital together—has increased.

THE EFFECTS OF UNIONS, MONOPOLIES, AND DISCRIMINATION ON INCOME DISTRIBUTION

Our discussion has proceeded as though the prices of factors and the quantities of factors used were determined entirely by market forces. Clearly, this is not always the case. The compensation of labor is often determined by collective bargaining, with possible effects on both the size and functional distributions of income. Product-market monopoly affects the return to capital, the quantity of capital used and its share, and hence labor's share in national income. Finally, even though we saw in Chapter 13 that discrimination can exist in competitive markets, its effects on earnings distributions can be analyzed in much the same way as those of unions and monopolies.

Effects of Unions

How trade unions affect the size distribution of earnings depends on: (1) The extent of unionism by earnings level and (2) The union wage gap at each point of the earnings distribution. If union membership is most heavily concentrated among workers who would be in the right tail of the earnings distribution in the absence of unionism anywhere in the economy, and if those workers achieve the greatest relative wage gain, unionism will have a disequalizing effect on the distribution of earnings.

Unfortunately, as with attempts to gauge the true effect of unions on relative earnings, one cannot estimate their true effect on the distribution of earnings because one cannot observe what the economy would have looked like in the absence of unionism. Because of this difficulty, we are thrown back on less than satisfactory empirical evidence. In Chapter 11 we showed that union relative wage gaps are at least as high among laborers as among craft workers, suggesting an equalizing effect on the distribution of earnings. Also, union policies of equal pay for equal work can be expected to reduce the dispersion of earnings within plants and within industries that are organized across many plants. This does occur: Wage dispersion is lower within unionized plants as compared to otherwise identical nonunion plants; and earnings are more equally distributed in otherwise similar cities and industries in which the extent of unionization is greater.[27]

In the opposite direction, however, there is the indication that industries that would pay high wages even in the absence of unionism have a higher incidence of unionism and a greater relative wage gap, both of which disequalize the distribu-

[27] Richard Freeman, "Union Wage Practices and Wage Dispersion Within Establishments," *Industrial and Labor Relations Review* (36): 3–21 (1982); Thomas Hyclak, "The Effect of Unions on Earnings Inequality in Local Labor Markets," *Industrial and Labor Relations Review* (33): 77–84 (1979); Barry Hirsch, "The Interindustry Structure of Unionism, Earnings and Earnings Dispersion," *Industrial and Labor Relations Review* (36): 22–39 (1982). But see William Brown and Courtenay Stone, "Academic Unions in Higher Education: Impacts on Faculty Salary, Compensation and Promotions," *Economic Inquiry* (15): 385–396 (1977), for the opposite result in one industry.

tion.[28] With these conflicting effects, the net impact of unionism on earnings inequality is still an open question. The only study that considered the potential ways in which unions affect the earnings distribution found that on net they reduced the dispersion of earnings in the United States.[29] The tentative conclusion must be that unions do equalize the distribution of earnings.

It has long been one of the stated objectives of the labor movement to raise labor's share through collective bargaining, and thus to reduce the share of property. Whether the attempt has been successful is exceedingly difficult to answer. All the problems that arise when one attempts to measure the influence of unions on earnings are compounded when one tries to measure their effects on labor's share, because fresh sources of disturbance occurring on the side of property income must be allowed for. The general answer is that no union influence on labor's share can be detected. Analyses that relate changes in the extent of unionization by industry to changes in labor's share of income originating in the industry find no effect in the United States and only a weak effect in the United Kingdom; one that uses more complex methods that account for the nature of production in the union and nonunion sectors finds the same answer for the United States: The gains of unionized labor come at the expense of nonunion labor rather than of owners of capital.[30]

There is no contradiction between the findings that unions raise the relative wages of their members and that unions fail to raise labor's share, even within particular industries where they are powerful. One of the most common management responses to higher labor costs is to increase the capital intensity of production methods, that is, to invest in labor-saving equipment. This means that the percentage increase in the wage bill will be smaller than that in the wage rate. Indeed, in some cases the long-run effect of a wage increase would be to *decrease* the wage bill; these are the cases in which the elasticity of demand for labor is greater than unity. The substitution of capital for labor also means an increase in outlays on capital services, for the new equipment must earn a reasonable rate of return. The combination of these effects may result in a labor share that is smaller, rather than larger, after long-run adjustment to a wage increase. This seems to have occurred in the bituminous coal industry, where higher wages have contributed to a rapid expansion of mechanization and the use of less labor-intensive methods of production, such as strip mining.

Effect of Monopoly and Discrimination

Monopoly in product markets can also be expected to affect labor's share, but here the direction of the effect is less ambiguous. Successful monopolists will earn a

[28] H. Gregg Lewis, *Unionism and Relative Wages in the United States,* University of Chicago Press, Chicago, 1963, chap. 8.

[29] Richard Freeman, "Unionism and the Dispersion of Wages," *Industrial and Labor Relations Review* (34): 3–23 (1980).

[30] See Clark Kerr, "Labor's Income Share and the Labor Movement," in George Taylor and Frank Pierson (eds.). *New Concepts in Wage Determination,* McGraw-Hill, New York, 1957; N.J. Simler, *The Impact of Unionism on Wage-Income Ratios in the Manufacturing Section of the Economy,* University of Minnesota Press, Minneapolis, 1961; Keith Cowling and Ian Molho, "Wage Share, Concentration and Unionism," *Manchester School of Economic and Social Studies* (50): 99–115 (1982); and Harry Johnson and Peter Mieszkowski, "The Effects of Unionization on the Distribution of Income: A General Equilibrium Approach," *Quarterly Journal of Economics* (84): 539–561 (1970).

monopoly profit over and above the going rate of return on the capital they use, and this should decrease labor's share. However, monopoly profit is not, strictly speaking, a return on capital; it is a rent arising from the legal or technological position that created the monopoly and that prevents other firms from entering the protected market. For this reason increased monopoly profit, unlike higher wages won by unions, does not necessarily mean that inputs will be used in proportions that are different from those that would prevail if all markets were competitive. In the national income accounts, monopoly profit cannot be distinguished from profits that are a normal rate of return on equity capital or from the short-run gains that can arise when a competitive market is in temporary disequilibrium.

If a competitive industry were suddenly transformed into a profit-maximizing monopoly, protected from foreign competition by tariffs and with no fear of government interference with its position, one would expect prices to rise relative to marginal costs. Physical output and the use of all inputs would decline, the *value* of total output could fall or rise, and labor's share of income would decline. The effect on labor's share need not be much different if the competitive industry were to become a regulated monopoly held to some "reasonable" rate of return on its total assets by the regulatory body (although in this case, as we noted in Chapter 4, factor proportions might change). Whenever such an industry could borrow funds at less than the permitted rate of return on total assets, it would have an incentive to use more capital, and labor's share could decline for this reason.

All this suggests that a possible logical reason for the historical rise of labor's share in national income could be a secular decrease in the extent of monopoly in product markets. However, there is no evidence that such a decrease has actually occurred. We are therefore left with the decline in the relative price of capital goods and the increase in investment in training and education as the two most probable causes of the slow, steady rise in labor's share of national income.

Racial discrimination will affect labor's share in a manner that depends on the underlying production function and on which group is the source of the discrimination. For example, if employers discriminate and pay for their tastes for discrimination by accepting a rate of return that is below the market rate, the impact is opposite that of product-market monopoly. Labor's share of income will be increased, presumably because white workers' earnings rise by more than black workers' earnings fall. If white employees are the source of discrimination, the effects are more difficult to disentangle. No studies exist to shed empirical light on this complicated issue.

To the extent that discriminatory outcomes result from occupational segregation, we should expect that they increase the dispersion in earnings between groups. The segregation of black workers into low-paying occupations raises the wage of workers in other occupations (which were already the better-paying ones) by reducing the supply of labor to them. The crowding of blacks into lower-paying occupations reduces earnings there still further. One observes that the Gini coefficient of the income distribution of whites is higher in those areas in which the black-white income ratio is lower (and presumably there is more labor-market discrimination against blacks).[31] It is not clear whether this difference stems from discrimination or

[31] Michael Reich, "Who Benefits from Racism? The Distribution Among Whites of Gains and Losses from Racial Inequality," *Journal of Human Resources* (13): 524–543 (1978).

correlation of greater dispersion in the determinants of earnings in the white population with other factors in those areas where there is greater racial discrimination.

SUMMARY

There are many forces in the labor market that can help explain the shape of the earnings distribution, and all may play some part. Those that seem most important are differences in training and in ability. Dispersion in the amount of schooling achieved by members of the work force has an important effect on the dispersion of earnings. Small differences in ability often generate huge differences in earnings, especially in those occupations in which the worker sells a service that can be replicated for a mass audience. The distribution of earnings in the United States is made slightly more equal by the activities of trade unions.

Labor's share of national income shows the fraction of income resulting from production that accrues to individuals as workers rather than as owners of property. In the United States and other developed countries, this share has been rising slightly during the past half century. The increase has not been caused by the growth of unions, for unionized workers win their gains at the expense of nonunion workers, leaving labor's share unchanged; nor has it resulted from a decline in the monopolized portion of the economy. The best explanation is that the stock of human capital has grown more rapidly than the stock of physical capital. Labor's share, which partly reflects returns to human capital, has grown accordingly.

six

Labor in the Macroeconomy

chapter 15

Wages, Inflation, and the Business Cycle

The topic of this chapter once would have been thought to lie wholly outside the realm of labor economics, but in recent years it has become more important in the labor economics literature than any other topic. Until the 1930s most economists accepted the view that the labor market determines the pattern of relative wages—wage differentials—and the general level of real wages, insofar as these are affected by the size of the labor supply. However, the general levels of money wages and prices were thought to depend entirely on changes in the quantity of money and its velocity of circulation rather than on anything that happens in either labor or product markets. In other words, in this view the economy can be decomposed into two separate sectors—the first monetary and the second real—with labor markets forming part of the real sector. All relative prices and the quantities of all real outputs and inputs (and hence all real incomes) are determined in the real sector. The monetary sector merely determines the nominal units in which prices are stated.

This view has now been abandoned; but no substitute has come forth in its place to explain the behavior of wages over the business cycle in a way that captures the approval of most economists. Instead, there are a variety of views, each of which is internally consistent, but none of which can explain all the phenomena that merit consideration. This intellectual disarray characterizes the field of macroeconomic theory in general. Its importance for labor economics is that the facts that the theories try to describe, and the behavior underlying the theories and facts, stem from the analysis of the labor market.

In this chapter we present the salient facts with which a satisfactory theory of the labor market must contend. Some of these—such as the cyclical behavior of the labor force and of productivity and the relationship between vacancies and unemployment—have been dealt with before (see Chaps. 1, 5, and 8, respectively). Here we present facts on wage inflation during the course of the business cycle and on changes in the structure of unemployment and wages over the cycle. We then examine the various theories of the adjustment of the labor market and consider how that adjustment in turn may affect the rate of inflation. Finally, we examine the prospects for government intervention aimed at improving the macroeconomic performance of the labor market.

CYCLICAL WAGE AND UNEMPLOYMENT VARIATION—THE FACTS

As we noted in Chapter 8, the rate of unemployment that one might denote as being consistent with "full employment" in the United States changes through time and increased by about 1.5 percentage points between 1960 and 1980. Variations in the demographic structure of the labor force and in the size of the incentives offered by a variety of government programs prevent one from equating all increases in unemployment with business-cycle downturns. Let us define the *unemployment gap* as the deviation of actual unemployment, as measured in the Current Population Survey, from the full-employment unemployment rate prevailing at the time.[1] Although different observers of the labor market measure the full-employment unemployment rate differently, and many would disagree with the measure we use, most would acknowledge the need to measure cyclical variations by changes in some form of the unemployment gap.

Table 15.1 shows the unemployment rate and unemployment gap at cyclical peaks and troughs (as dated by the National Bureau of Economic Research) since 1957. The gap increases by 2.2 percentage points on average as the economy moves from peak to trough (2.7 percentage points if one counts the period from 1979 and 1982 as one long downturn). Because of the growth in population, the rise in the unemployment gap has been accompanied in most recessions by only a small decrease, or even an increase in total employment. During post-World War II recessions the discouraged-worker effect has been too small to reduce the supply of labor by enough to offset the reduced demand for workers.

The structure of unemployment also changes over the business cycle, in ways that are consistent with the determinants of employers' and workers' behavior that we discussed in Chapters 7 and 8. As can be seen in Table 15.2, the percentage of unemployed workers who are job losers rises during recessions. The percentage who are job leavers (who have quit) falls sharply, for when good alternative jobs are not available few people quit the positions they have. The average length of time those currently unemployed have been without work rises, although not in proportion to the increase in the aggregate unemployment rate. This is true also for the completed spells of unemployment that we discussed in Chapter 8. (Some evidence of this is shown by comparing data for 1968 and 1978 in Table 8.8.) These facts imply that the

[1] Michael Wachter, "The Changing Cyclical Responsiveness of Wage Inflation," *Brookings Papers on Economic Activity*: 115–159 (1976), discusses ways of measuring the unemployment gap.

Table 15.1 UNEMPLOYMENT, EMPLOYMENT AND PAY CHANGES, BUSINESS CYCLES, UNITED STATES, 1957-1982

Peak and trough years of cycle	Unemployment rate (1)	Unemployment gap (2)	Civilian employment (3)	Hourly earnings index, percentage change (4)
1957	4.3	0	64.1	5.0
1958	6.8	2.5	63.0	4.2
1960	5.5	1.1	65.8	3.4
1961	6.7	2.3	65.7	3.0
1969	3.5	−1.5	77.9	6.7
1971	5.9	0.8	79.4	7.2
1973	4.9	−0.5	85.1	6.2
1975	8.5	3.1	85.8	8.4
1979	5.8	0.2	98.8	8.0
1980	7.1	1.5	99.3	9.0
1981	7.6	2.0	100.4	8.9
1982	9.7	4.1	99.5	6.8

Source: (1) Council of Economic Advisors, *Economic Report of the President, 1983,* Table B-29; (2) Ibid., and Robert Gordon, *Macroeconomics,* Little Brown, Boston, 1981, pp. XVI–XVII; (3) Council of Economic Advisors, op. cit., Table B-29; (4) Council of Economic Advisors, op. cit., Table B-38.

incidence of unemployment increases in recessions. The percentage of long-term unemployed workers, for whom the hardship associated with being unemployed is presumably greatest, increases sharply. Since we showed in Chapter 6 that a longer duration of unemployment suggests a lower asking wage, the indication is that asking wages of unemployed workers will on average decline, or will rise less rapidly, during a recession.

Table 15.2 UNEMPLOYMENT BY REASON, AND DURATION OF UNEMPLOYMENT, BUSINESS CYCLES, UNITED STATES, 1957-1982

Peak and trough years of cycle	Rate	Percent of unemployed who are: Job losers	Percent of unemployed who are: Job leavers	Duration: Average (weeks)	Duration: Percent >26 weeks
1957	4.3	—	—	10.5	8.4
1958	6.8	—	—	13.9	14.5
1960	5.5	—	—	12.8	11.8
1961	6.7	—	—	15.6	17.1
1969	3.5	35.9	15.4	7.9	4.7
1971	5.9	46.3	11.8	11.3	10.3
1973	4.9	38.8	15.6	10.0	7.9
1975	8.5	55.3	10.4	14.2	15.2
1979	5.8	42.9	14.3	10.8	8.7
1980	7.1	51.7	11.7	11.9	10.7
1981	7.6	51.6	11.1	13.7	14.0
1982	9.7	58.7	7.9	15.6	16.6

Source: Council of Economic Advisors, *Economic Report of the President, 1983,* Tables B-34, B-35.

POLICY ISSUE—EXTENDED UNEMPLOYMENT INSURANCE BENEFITS

In each recession except that from 1979 to 1980 on which data are presented in Tables 15.1 and 15.2, the U.S. government has enacted emergency legislation, extending the maximum duration of receipt of unemployment benefits. Their announced purpose has been to alleviate hardship. In several of the recessions the extensions were for an extra 13 weeks of benefits beyond the usual (although not universal) 26 weeks to which unemployed workers are normally entitled. In the 1973 to 1975 recession the extension provided for as much as an extra 39 weeks of benefits (13 of which were automatically triggered by previous legislation). In the 1981 to 1982 recession extended benefits up to 29 extra weeks (13 of which were triggered by previous legislation) were available.

Unemployment benefits go to people whose incomes would otherwise be temporarily low; but whether the benefits help people maintain consumption above what it would otherwise be is a different question. To the extent that unemployed workers expect cyclical layoffs and have accumulated savings toward this eventuality, they can maintain consumption by drawing down savings while on layoff. Even if they have no savings, they may be able to borrow while unemployed. If either of these actions occurs, they will treat extended unemployment benefits like any other income flow, spending most of them and adding the rest to savings. Only if they have no savings and cannot borrow will they spend each dollar received. The evidence suggests that about one-half all unemployment benefits go to recipients who do not have sufficient savings, or cannot borrow enough, to prevent a drop in consumption.[2] Among long-duration unemployed workers, though, one would expect a higher fraction of benefits that are received to be spent immediately. Extended benefits probably do reduce hardship fairly efficiently, for they are targeted toward those workers whose consumption would otherwise be reduced sharply because of a lack of access to savings or borrowing.

Table 15.1 also shows the annual percentage change in an index of hourly earnings. This wage measure is adjusted for changes in the amount of overtime hours worked and in the mix of employment by industry. As Table 15.1 makes clear, there is little evidence of any consistent peak-to-trough variation in this measure of the rate of change of nominal wages. However, nominal wage growth has been more rapid in the most recent three cycles than it was in the previous three.

We can get additional insight into the pattern of changes in nominal wages by considering the scatter diagram in Figure 15.1, which plots the relation of changes in hourly earnings to the size of the unemployment gap. The scatter of points for the whole period 1954 to 1982 looks completely random, like the results of throwing darts at a board. If, however, we separate the points into two periods, 1954 to 1973 and 1974 to 1982 (denoting the former by dots and the latter by x's), two distinct patterns emerge. The curve P fits the points from 1954–1973 fairly well; the straight line P′ provides the best fit to the points from 1974–1982. More complex relationships, which account for the effects on wage changes of factors other than the unemployment gap, show a similar pattern.[3]

The relationships between wage changes and the unemployment gap depicted in Figure 15.1 are *Phillips curves.* It is apparent from the figure that no one curve

[2]Daniel Hamermesh, "Social Insurance and Consumption: An Empirical Inquiry," *American Economic Review* (72): 101–113 (1982).

[3]James Medoff and Katharine Abraham, "Unemployment, Unsatisfied Demand for Labor, and Compensation Growth, 1956–1980," in Martin Baily (ed.). *Workers, Jobs and Inflation,* Brookings Institution, Washington, 1982.

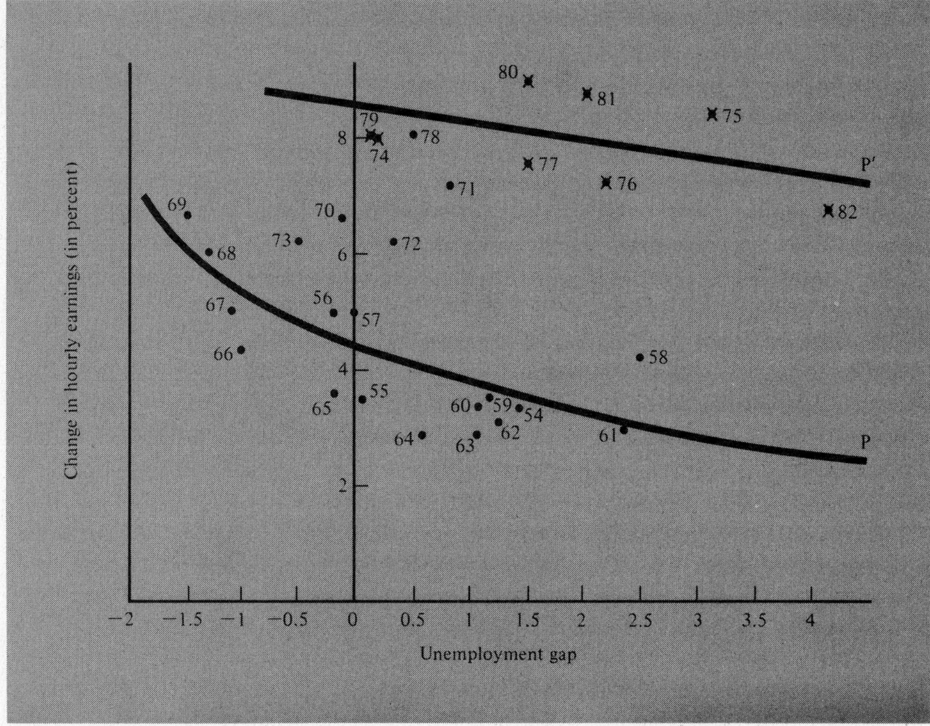

Figure 15.1 The relation between changes in hourly earnings and the unemployment gap in the United States, 1954 to 1982.

describes the wage change–unemployment relationship for the postwar United States. As we have shown, though, subperiods since World War II can be characterized by separate Phillips curves. Long periods of history until the 1970s, in both the United States and, as Phillips showed in his study (which gave the name to this relationship), in the United Kingdom, seem to be described fairly well by curves like P.[4] As in the United States, the Phillips curve seems to have shifted outward in the 1970s in many of the countries for which this relationship has been studied. In other countries there is no evidence that a downward-sloping line like P′ can even be drawn to fit the points characterizing the wage change–unemployment relationship since the early 1970s.[5]

These observations have led economists to examine in more detail the mechanisms that determine the relation between wage inflation and unemployment. Is the

[4] A. W. Phillips, "The Relation Between Unemployment and the Rate of Change of Money Wage Rates in the United Kingdom 1861–1957," *Economica* (25): 285–299 (1958), is the original study in this entire area. An historical Phillips curve for the United States is shown in Otto Eckstein and James Girola, "Long-Term Properties of the Price-Wage Mechanism in the United States, 1891–1977," *Review of Economics and Statistics* (60): 323–333 (1978).

[5] Among the many studies of the Phillips curve outside the United States and the United Kingdom are William Craig Riddell, "The Empirical Foundations of the Phillips Curve: Evidence from Canadian Wage Contract Data," *Econometrica* (47): 1–24 (1979), and for Sweden, Robert Flanagan, "The U.S. Phillips Curve and International Unemployment Rate Differentials," *American Economic Review* (63): 114–131 (1973).

relation stable over time? If not, why does it shift outward, as in the early 1970s? If it is stable, so that over a long period of time a curve like P describes the data, we may infer that the Phillips curve is a "menu for policy choice."[6] Those who control economic policy could, if they had the political will, pick any combination of wage inflation and unemployment along the Phillips curve that they wished and be assured that the economy would exhibit those rates of wage inflation and unemployment. If the curve is not stable, such an attempt would be futile.

The second, related question is whether the labor market is inherently self-righting; obversely, the issue is whether substantial amounts of unemployment can reflect equilibrium in the labor market, in the sense that the unemployment will persist for some time. If such an equilibrium does exist, is it permanent, or is it of relatively short duration; and what are the forces that move the labor market from short-run to long-run equilibrium? The answer to this question lies partly beyond the scope of labor economics, since it is really the question that underlies the debate in macroeconomics that has raged on and off since Keynes's *General Theory* was published in 1936. However, it is also a question for labor economists, for there are aspects of labor market behavior that are central to answering this basic macroeconomic question, on which we have already shed some light on in earlier chapters.

A VERTICAL LONG-RUN PHILLIPS CURVE

Several explanations have been presented, stating that the apparent instability of the Phillips curve reflects movements of a short-run Phillips curve up or down a vertical long-run curve. If the long-run curve is vertical, policymakers cannot choose a combination of wage inflation and unemployment. Instead, they can only determine the rate of nominal wage inflation (by changing the rate of growth of the supply of money). In the long run the rate of unemployment at equilibrium is determined solely by the structure of the labor force and labor-market institutions, including all the institutions, workers' and firms' characteristics, and government programs that, as we showed in Chapters 6 to 8, affect search, mobility, and the duration of unemployment. This rate, the *natural rate of unemployment,* is for our purposes identical to what we have been calling the full-employment unemployment rate. Many of the explanations hinge on workers' expectations about future wages and prices. These explanations, by arguing for a vertical Phillips curve in the long run, hark back to the classical dichotomy between real and monetary effects that we noted at the outset of this chapter.

None of these explanations provides a fully satisfactory description of the process of adjustment of labor markets to the changes that continually buffet them. None implies behavior that can be reconciled with all the major patterns of unemployment and wage inflation that have occurred in the United States and elsewhere since 1929. Nevertheless, each has received substantial attention from labor economists and economists generally. More important, each provides some insights into the very complex issue of the fundamental determinants of the aggregate unemployment rate and the rate of change of nominal wage rates over the business cycle.

[6]Albert Rees, "The Phillips Curve as a Menu for Policy Choice," *Economica* (37): 227–238 (1970).

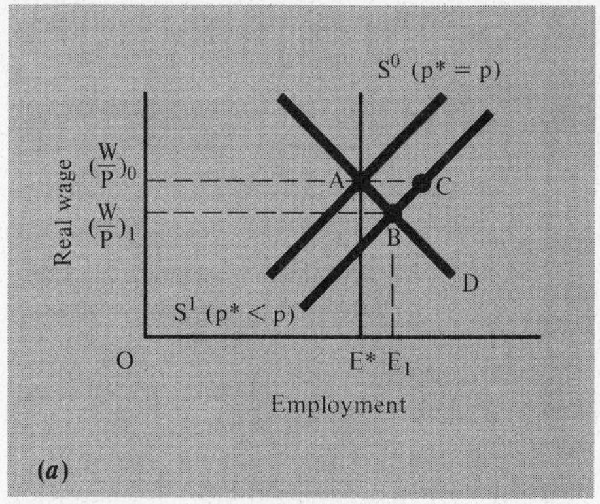

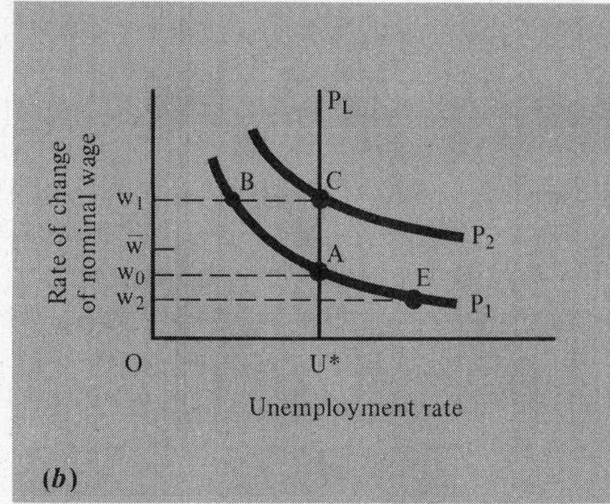

Figure 15.2 (a) The labor market and unexpected inflation; (b) a vertical long-run Phillips curve.

Role of Price Expectations

Consider a labor market in which employers perceive the real wage, determined in terms of the prices of their own products, and thus observe the real cost of employing an hour of labor, perfectly. Assume, however, that workers base their labor-supply decisions on imperfectly perceived real wages, determined by comparing the nominal wage they are offered, W, to the perceived level of consumer prices, P*. Since employers are concerned only about prices of their products, they should have better information on them than do workers who shop infrequently for the wide variety of products that make up a broad-based price index such as the CPI. Assume further that workers' expectations about inflation adjust slowly to an increase in the measured rate of inflation. An acceleration of wage and price inflation temporarily leads workers to believe their real wage has risen, since W rises faster than P*. Eventually, as their perceptions of inflation catch up to the actuality, workers become aware that their real wage has not in fact changed.

The labor market depicted in Figure 15.2(a) illustrates these differences. Employers' demands for labor are shown by the usual downward-sloping curve D, based on a comparison of the real wage to the VMP. Workers' labor supply is assumed to be upward sloping but is based on the perceived real wage, which differs from the actual real wage if price expectations are slow to adjust to changes in prices.[7] If inflation has been constant for some time, workers' expectations are probably correct; labor will be supplied along the curve S^0, along which actual and perceived inflation, p and p*, are equal. If the rate of price inflation accelerates, perhaps because the government increases the rate of growth of the money supply, nominal wages and prices will rise more rapidly. Workers seeing these changes will perceive their real wage as having risen, because they see the rise in nominal wages without fully perceiving the rise in prices. At any true real wage, for example, the equilibrium $(W/P)_0$, they supply more labor. The supply curve shifts out from S^0 to S^1, with AC more labor supplied at the old equilibrium real wage. Since employers perceive real

[7]Robert Lucas and Leonard Rapping, "Real Wages, Employment and Inflation," in Edmund Phelps (ed.). *Microeconomic Foundations of Employment and Inflation Theory,* Norton, New York, 1970.

wages correctly, this increased supply of labor lowers the real wage employers pay and induces an increase in employment. In Figure 15.2(a) this is represented by a movement from A to B. Assuming that the potential labor force remains unchanged, the increase in employment from E* to E_1 reduces unemployment. In terms of Figure 15.2(b), an increase in the rate of change of wages is associated with a decreased unemployment rate; the economy moves from point A to point B in that figure, too.

If price inflation is held at the new higher rate, workers' expectations about inflation will eventually catch up to the reality; they will perceive that their true real wage has not risen and will reduce their supply of labor. The supply curve will shift back from S^1 to S^0. Equilibrium will be restored at A in Figure 15.2(a), with the same real wage rate and the same level of employment. With the same employment, unemployment also returns to its previous rate. But the rate of increase of both wages and prices is now higher; the economy has moved back to the natural rate of unemployment U*, from B to C in Figure 15.2(b). A temporary increase in employment (and thus output) has been purchased at the cost of an acceleration in the rate of inflation.

Curves P_1 and P_2 in Figure 15.2(b) are different *short-run Phillips curves.* Curve P_1 reflects the behavior of the labor market before workers' expectations have begun catching up to the acceleration in inflation; P_2 reflects the behavior of the labor market when the expected inflation rate is higher. Policymakers cannot choose a point like B; eventually workers' expectations of inflation adjust, and the economy moves back to the vertical *long-run Phillips curve,* P_L, at the same rate of inflation as at point B. The only choice for macroeconomic policy is the rate of wage (and price) inflation; the unemployment rate is in the long run determined by labor-market institutions.

The strongest support for this view of the labor market comes from the evidence we have given of the instability in the short-run Phillips curve. The points in Figure 15.1 could not all lie on the same downward-sloping curve. It is hard to avoid the conclusion that between the 1960s and the 1970s the Phillips curve shifted upward, unless one is prepared to argue instead that there is no longer a meaningful relation between unemployment and inflation even in the short run.

This view of the vertical long-run Phillips curve is called the *expectations* theory or the *intertemporal substitution* hypothesis. The former term refers to its basis in the deviation of perceived from actual price inflation; the latter refers to its dependence on workers temporarily increasing their labor supply in response to short-run changes in perceived real wages. The evidence against the hypothesis confronts its underpinnings in price expectations and the response of labor supply. The depression of the 1930s persisted for a decade, and the Consumer Price Index was lower in 1939 than in 1929. It is very difficult to believe that it took that long to realize that prices were not going to rise.[8] Yet to explain the high unemployment of the thirties by this theory, one must argue that the extraordinarily low employment of the period resulted from workers believing real wages had fallen, when in fact they

[8]Albert Rees, "On Equilibrium in Labor Markets," *Journal of Political Economy* (78): 306–310 (1970).

had risen, and maintaining that belief for 10 years. Independent evidence covering more recent periods suggests that expectations about price inflation adjust more rapidly than this, although forecasts of price changes do exhibit substantial errors.[9] High unemployment also persisted from 1975 to 1983 (with the exception of 1978 and 1979); this also implies that a theory based on very slow adjustment of workers' expectations about price inflation fails to explain the historical facts.

Ignoring the issue of whether workers' price expectations adjust slowly enough to be the source of persistent high unemployment, the theory also requires labor supply to be very responsive to short-run fluctuations in perceived real wages. Yet all the evidence suggests the actual response is quite small. In the context of the life-cycle model of labor supply, one study found a short-run supply elasticity for adult men of below 0.5. A study of time-series data for the United States and the United Kingdom since World War II showed that fluctuations in employment and unemployment were not consistent with an increasing supply of labor when expected price inflation lagged behind actual price inflation.[10]

The logic of the expectations argument is compelling; one must admit that workers' inflation expectations will eventually adjust to reflect past changes in prices. Even if they are fooled for a while, workers are unlikely to be fooled forever into believing that their real wage has risen merely because nominal wages have increased. The argument fails, however, to explain the persistence of high rates of unemployment over a long period of time. Whether the Phillips curve is vertical in the long run seems less important than the observation that, if it is vertical, the adjustment to it (e.g., between points B and C in Figure 15.2(b)) is very slow.

Role of Job Search

An alternative justification of the vertical long-run Phillips curve rests on the theory of job search by workers and employers that we discussed in Chapter 6.[11] The argument assumes that there is some average rate of unemployment, determined by the incidence and duration of spells of unemployment. (These are in turn determined by labor-market institutions that affect how easily workers' skills are matched to firms' job vacancies.) Assume the economy is at an unemployment rate at which vacancies and the number of unemployed workers are equal. (This is a point on the 45° line in Fig. 8.3.) In such a situation typical employers can maintain work forces of a given size by many combinations of wage offers and hiring standards. By paying more they can attract more workers and maintain employment at a higher minimum skill requirement. Firms choose the least-cost combination of wages and hiring standards.

For some reason, perhaps because of expansionary fiscal or monetary policy,

[9] For example, see Stephen Figlewski and Paul Wachtel, "The Formation of Inflationary Expectations," *Review of Economics and Statistics* (63): 1–10 (1981).

[10] Thomas MaCurdy, "An Empirical Model of Labor Supply in a Life-Cycle Setting," *Journal of Political Economy,* (89): 1059–1085 (1981); and Joseph Altonji, "The Intertemporal Substitution Model of Labour Market Fluctuations: An Empirical Analysis," *Review of Economic Studies* (49): 783–824 (1982).

[11] Dale Mortensen, "Job Search, The Duration of Unemployment, and the Phillips Curve," *American Economic Review* (60): 847–862 (1970).

employers find they can charge higher prices for their products. This raises the VMP in each firm. Attempting to expand employment, an employer will offer higher nominal wages or reduce hiring standards to attract more workers. With these changes in the employer's hiring policies, workers will spend less time searching; employment will rise, and unemployment will fall. Coincident with the drop in unemployment, though, is a rise in the growth rate of nominal wages. The economy moves leftward along a short-run Phillips curve, such as P_1 in Figure 15.2(b), from a point like A to one like B.

Recognizing that all firms have raised their wage offers, workers will raise their asking wages. As we showed in Chapter 6, this will lead them to search longer than before. Eventually their asking wage will be rising as rapidly as employers' wage offers. Since labor is no longer a bargain, employers will bring hiring standards back to their equilibrium level. Employment will be the same as before, but wage offers and asking wages will be rising more rapidly than before. The economy will have moved from point B to point C in Figure 15.2(b).

The result of the search-theoretic approach is the same as that of the intertemporal substitution hypothesis: In the short run increases in employment are positively correlated with higher growth rates in nominal wages. This approach, too, provides an internally consistent explanation of cyclical fluctuations in wage growth and employment. It agrees with the observation that the duration of unemployment decreases in good times. Unfortunately, there is no evidence on whether the amount of time actually spent searching increases in a recession. The rise in the number of persons who report themselves as too discouraged to search that accompanies a recession suggests that longer-duration unemployment need not imply that more time is devoted to search. That being the case, it is not clear that the facts are consistent with the predictions of this theory.

Role of Implicit Contracts

Both of these approaches are essentially theories of voluntary unemployment. Under the intertemporal substitution hypothesis, workers are counted as unemployed because they choose not to work when their nominal wage has failed to rise as rapidly as their perception of price inflation; under the search approach, cyclical unemployment is observed because workers choose to spend more time searching. An entirely different approach is based on the theory of long-term employer-employee relations (implicit contracts), which we discussed in Chapter 8.[12] Assume the product demand in the typical firm varies randomly between zero and some maximum, shown along the horizontal axis in Figure 15.3. We assume the average output is halfway between zero and the maximum. The typical firm's wage bill, its wage rate times its employment, is shown on the vertical axis.

The firm has two choices. It can vary the wage continually, as in an *auction market,* to keep employment constant. In Figure 15.3 this is shown by movements of

[12] Costas Azariadis, "Implicit Contracts and Underemployment Equilibria," *Journal of Political Economy* (83): 1183–1202 (1975); Martin N. Baily, "Wages and Employment Under Uncertain Demand," *Review of Economic Studies* (41): 37–50 (1974); and Herschel Grossman, "Risk Shifting and Reliability in Labor Markets," *Scandinavian Journal of Economics* (79): 187–209 (1977).

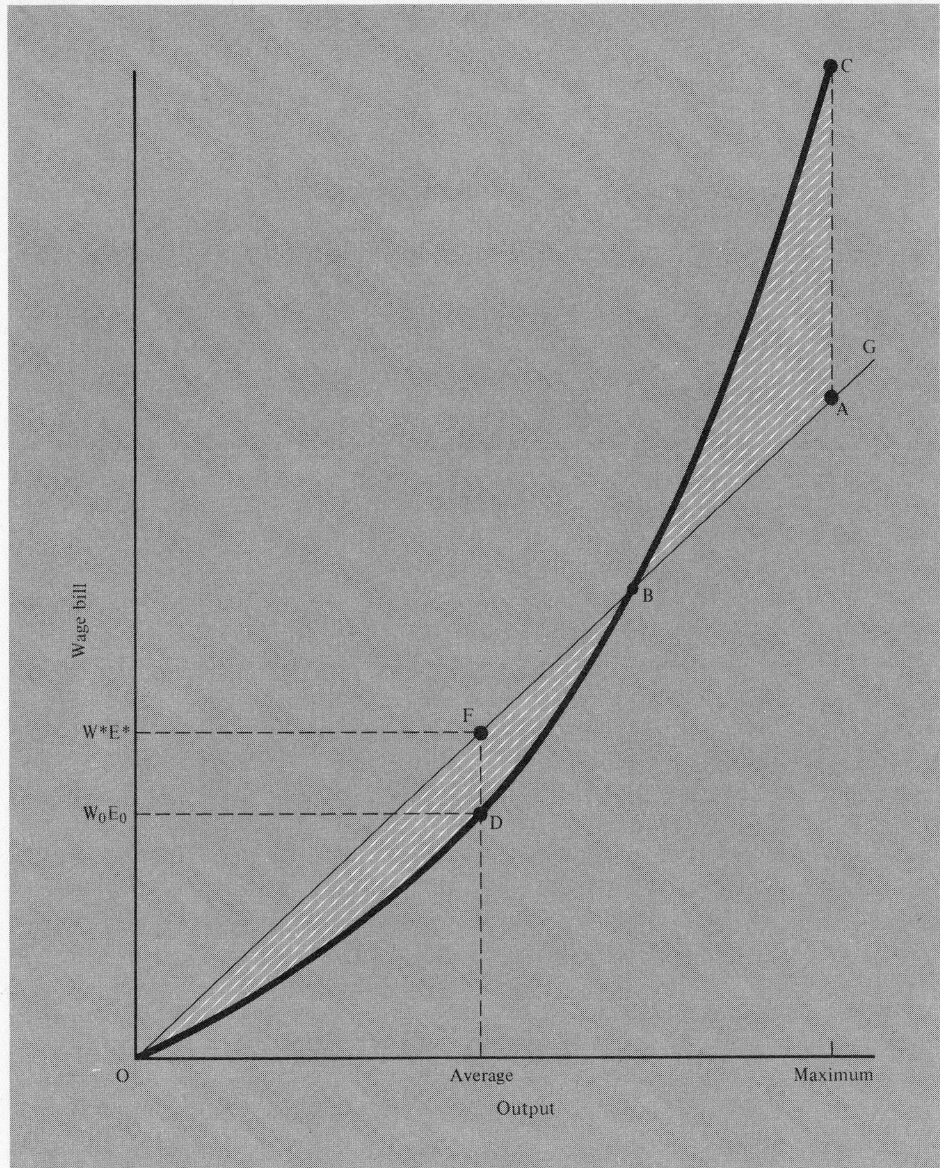

Figure 15.3 Implicit contracts and wage rigidity.

the wage bill along OC. When product demand is low, increases in it require that employers offer only small increases in wages to keep their workers from quitting. Since demand at other firms is also likely to be low, there are few alternatives for each employer's workers, and thus little need to raise wages to retain them. Because the wage falls as output demand drops, VMP can be kept equal to the wage without any reduction in employment. At higher rates of output, increased demand requires larger increases in wages. The alternatives open to the typical worker are improving rapidly, as product (and hence labor) demand elsewhere is probably also higher than before. With a constant level of employment (full employment), the acceleration of wages as output demand rises implies that the wage bill will also rise increasingly rapidly. The firm's second choice is to offer an implicit contract that will keep the worker's nominal wage constant at W*. This requires firms to lay off workers when product demand falls, for their VMP then declines below the fixed wage. The wage bill is shown by the straight line OG.

The typical firm will be indifferent between an implicit contract offering a fixed wage W* and a variable wage if the wage bills are the same on average. If wages are variable, the wage bill over the cycle is the area under OC. If wages are fixed at W*, the wage bill over the whole cycle is the area under OG. The two are equal if the shaded area OFBD equals the shaded area BCA. If that happens, though, the typical worker will prefer the fixed-wage contract. At the average point in the output cycle, if wages are fixed at W*, the wage bill exceeds the wage bill that the employer would pay if the wage rate fell low enough to justify keeping all the workers employed. Wages are higher by an amount $W^* - W_0$. Although employment is lower than the full-employment level E_0, total labor income is higher by FD. This means that workers will prefer cyclical fluctuations in employment to cyclical fluctuations in nominal wages. Employers are willing to pay the higher fixed wage W* because their average profits are the same as if they paid an auctioned wage. Workers are better off, however. So long as they are averse to risks (as we assumed, e.g., in the discussion of compensating differentials in Chap. 12), they prefer the fixed wage to the large fluctuations in wages that would occur if they received an auctioned wage. The *contracting* hypothesis predicts that nominal wages will be sticky over the output cycle because of workers' and employers' preferences. That stickiness will generate fluctuations in employment.

Because output demand never drops to zero, not all workers will be laid off when it does fall and the fixed nominal wage requires layoffs. But all workers would experience wage cuts when output demand fell if wages were flexible. As we saw in Chapter 8, internal union politics, or customary relationships among workers in nonunion establishments, make the risk of job loss very low for most workers. This increases their willingness to have the burden of fluctuations in output borne in the form of layoffs rather than in the form of reduced wages.

The contracting hypothesis has the virtue of being able to explain the facts of employment fluctuations, unemployment above the frictional rate, and nominal wage ridigity. It is consistent with evidence from U.S. manufacturing that wage rates diverge from the VMP in the short run by more than they do in the long run.[13] The difficulty is its inability to explain the persistence of high unemployment, such as prevailed in the 1930s and for most of 1975 to 1984. With high rates of unemployment persisting for a long time, contracts, either explicit (in unionized establishments) or implicit (in nonunion plants), will be revised to account for the state of the labor market. In the United States, union contracts rarely are longer than three years; in many other countries, union wages are renegotiated even more frequently.

[13] James Brown, "How Close to an Auction Is the Labor Market? Employee Risk Aversion, Income Uncertainty, and Optimal Labor Contracts," *Research in Labor Economics* (5): 189–235 (1982).

Nonunion wages in the United States are changed much more frequently than are union wages.[14] The fact that such frequent wage setting would continuously ignore the presence of high unemployment is not credible. In the face of continuing high unemployment, employers have substantial incentives to break implicit contracts by reducing nominal wages. If employers believe demand is stuck, for example, at the average in Figure 15.3, they can save an amount FD by breaking the implicit contract and cutting the wage from W* to W_0. If this is so, unemployment would fall as employment rose from E* to E_0. This hypothesis, like the others, implies a faster approach toward equilibrium unemployment (reduction in cyclical unemployment) than is consistent with the facts.

SLOW ADJUSTMENT

All the justifications for a long-run vertical Phillips curve imply a faster adjustment to it than is consistent with the real world. Rationalizing the observed slowness of adjustment has recently become an objective of students of labor markets. This is not, however, a new way of looking at the labor market. The Keynesian system, with its implied underemployment equilibrium, rested upon the observation that nominal wages are rigid downward. Keynes viewed reductions in money wages as inequitable, because the money incomes of rentiers (such as bondholders) would remain constant, which would raise their relative incomes if wages fell. He saw the downward rigidity of money wages as a basic feature to be accepted and even welcomed, not as an imperfection of the economy to be overcome. This phenomenon implies that a decline in aggregate demand (whether produced by a fall in the quantity of money or by a shift in autonomous investment) cannot lower all wages and prices proportionally. Therefore, it must lower real output and employment. If some product prices are flexible downward, a decline in aggregate demand may even *raise* the real wages of those who remain employed. The real output of the system is determined by the level of aggregate demand whenever there is not enough demand to employ the whole labor force at the old level of money wages. The price level is strongly influenced by the rigid money-wage level no matter how far aggregate demand falls.

The Keynesian view of the general level of money wages in a depression is illustrated in Figure 15.4. The full-employment aggregate demand curve for labor is D_0, and the supply curve is S. It should be recalled that to draw a curve showing constant aggregrate demand at different money wages, one must assume an offsetting change in some other source of expenditure. Together the demand and supply curves determine the money-wage level, W_0, and the amount of employment, E_0. Although there may be frictional unemployment at E_0, it is balanced by unfilled vacancies; thus there is enough demand to employ all those who want to work at the prevailing wage. Assume that there is then a decline in aggregate demand (because of a fall in the money supply, a decline in government expenditures, or a shift in the

[14] Orley Ashenfelter, George Johnson, and John Pencavel, "Trade Unions and the Rate of Change of Money Wages in the United States," *Review of Economic Studies* (39): 27–54 (1972).

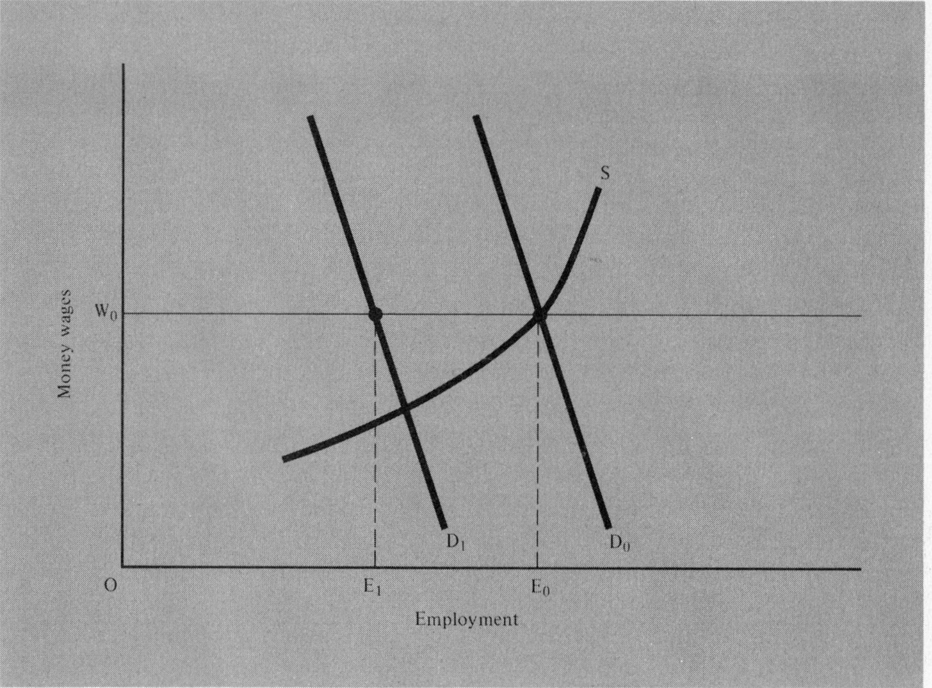

Figure 15.4 The labor market during a depression.

investment function). The new aggregate demand curve, D_1, and the old wage level, W_0, will determine the new level of employment, E_1. If we abstract from any changes in the size of the labor force, the horizontal distance E_0E_1 is the excess supply of labor, or the amount of demand-deficiency unemployment.

The money wage may be rigid downward because of trade unions—in the short run because wages are fixed by collective bargaining agreements and in the long run because union negotiators will resist wage cuts. The British economy was well-organized by unions at the time Keynes wrote, and this seems to be the reason he had in mind. Even with the high unemployment in autos and steel in the early 1980s, the much vaunted "concessions" did not in most cases mean reductions in nominal wages. Even at the trough of the 1981 to 1982 recession, major union contracts that were negotiated specified an average 2.2 percent annual wage increase over the contracts' lives.[15] Similar downward rigidity in money wages can be observed in unorganized American industries (especially those dominated by a few large firms) in the period 1929 to 1932, before the rapid growth of industrial unionism in manufacturing. For example, in the iron and steel industry from 1929 to September 1931, employee hours were reduced by more than half, whereas average hourly earnings fell only 3 percent. The picture was similar in the agricultural implement, automobile, electrical manufacturing, and rubber industries. Re-

[15]Daniel Mitchell, "Recent Union Contract Concessions," *Brookings Papers on Economic Activity*: 165–201 (1982); and *Wall Street Journal,* April 28, 1983, p. 6.

ductions in employee hours in these industries ranged from 20 to 80 percent, and hourly earnings fell no more than 3 percent.[16]

If it is true that in a depression many of the unemployed would be willing to work for less than the prevailing wage, why are nonunion employers reluctant to cut wages? The answer has at least two parts. The first relates to the specific training employers have invested in their present workers. At least in the short run the unemployed (except perhaps for those whom particular employers have laid off) are poor substitutes for the workers they have retained, and employers will tend to retain those with the most specific training. The second part of the answer applies even to workers having no specific training; workers universally regard a wage cut as an affront because they view their wage as a measure of their relative worth and of the esteem in which they are held. Nonunion employers therefore fear that wage cuts will be so resented as to cause a drop in productivity or to encourage the formation of unions. This means that during a depression the employed and the unemployed are poor substitutes in production, and the supply price of the unemployed is not relevant to determining the wage level of the employed.

Workers are less likely to be bothered by a generalized cut in real wages resulting from higher price levels that they perceive as applying to all workers than they are by a cut in their own nominal wage rate that they perceive as being limited to them and a few coworkers. Thus in an economy characterized by price inflation, nominal wages could be downward rigid, yet real wages could fall and induce employers to increase hiring. Price inflation might help overcome the rigidity in the labor market that is produced by workers' unwillingness to accept cuts in nominal wages.

An examination of the pattern of wage growth during the 1960s and 1970s suggests that *real wages* may be downward rigid, too. This observation characterized the economies of Western Europe during this period better than it did the U.S. economy.[17] Whether the differences stem from the lesser extent of unionization in the United States or from other differences in wage-setting mechanisms is not clear. Unemployment need not rise if real wages are rigid when aggregate demand declines or when a negative supply shock (such as the oil price shock of the 1970s) reduces the rate of growth of the economy's potential output. Rapid increases in productivity could be sufficient to keep the demand for labor up. But if productivity is growing only slowly, or if the negative shock is large enough, real-wage rigidity will induce unemployment. The unemployment will persist so long as real wages remain rigid downward and productivity fails to rise enough to justify the real wage that workers insist upon receiving. Real wage rigidity in Western Europe during the 1970s can explain the persistent high rates of unemployment that occurred there after the oil price shock of 1973.

Although it is easy to point out that real wages may be downward rigid and to identify the effects of their rigidity, it is much more difficult to construct a theory to explain this observation. One possibility is that the temporary rigidity induced by labor contracts can persist even beyond the length of the contracts if wage setting in

[16] Albert Rees, "Wage Determination and Involuntary Unemployment," *Journal of Political Economy* (59): 143–153 (1951).

[17] Jeffrey Sachs, "Wages, Profits, and Macroeconomic Adjustment," *Brookings Papers on Economic Activity*: 269–319 (1979).

the economy is staggered over time. Both firms and workers may be better off if they time their contract expirations differently from those elsewhere.[18] Because workers are concerned about their relative worths, those whose contracts come up for negotiation when product demand is low will base part of their wage demands on comparisons to the real wage rates received by other workers who negotiated when product demand was higher. Workers in the second group will seek, and at least in part obtain (see Chap. 10) a real wage so high that employers cannot justify retaining all members of their work force. Eventually the effect of past contracts, which produced real wages reflecting high product demand, will diminish, as employers bargain for lower real wages and workers come to base their wage demands on more recent contracts. But this process of adjustment in bargaining may take a long time, leading to substantial downward rigidity in real wages, and thus resulting in persistent unemployment in the face of declines in aggregate demand or negative supply shocks.

Even in the absence of unions real wages may be rigid downward. The same kinds of coercive comparisons that motivate union members to push for wage parity with other workers, although demand for their output has fallen, are likely to motivate nonunion workers. Customary wage differentials are important in the minds of all workers; employers who try to change them may find their firms subject to slowdowns and a general increase in worker dissatisfaction. If they maintain customary differentials by matching previous nominal wage increases received by other workers, they must reduce employment if their product demand is lower (since at the same real wage, the VMP curve has shifted to the left).[19] The maintenance of customary wage differentials in nonunion labor markets can thus lead to unemployment, which will persist until product demand increases or those customary differentials eventually break down. This latter process may take quite a long time.

THE TRANSMISSION OF WAGE INFLATION

The discussion of staggered wage setting underlines the central importance of the process by which wage increases obtained in one sector of the economy are transmitted elsewhere. When conditions in one labor market produce wage inflation there, they may generate wage inflation in other markets because workers fight to maintain customary differentials. The question is whether this process is universal, and in which directions these dynamic *wage spillovers* flow. It is difficult to believe that every worker is concerned about the wages received by every other worker in the economy. Surely there are some limits on the directions and magnitudes of wage comparisons and thus on the size of dynamic spillovers.

To analyze this issue, first consider an economy containing two labor markets of equal size. Each is characterized by a vertical long-run Phillips curve and a

[18] John Taylor, "Aggregate Dynamics and Staggered Contracts," *Journal of Political Economy* (88): 1–23 (1980), and Gary Fethke and Andrew Policano, "Determinants and Implications of Staggered Wage Contracts," Working Paper No. 82–32, College of Business Administration, Iowa City, Iowa, 1982.

[19] Daniel Hamermesh, "Interdependence in the Labour Market," *Economica* (42): 420–429 (1975), and George Akerlof, "A Theory of Social Custom, of Which Unemployment May Be One Consequence," *Quarterly Journal of Economics* (94): 749–776 (1980).

short-run Phillips curve like P_1 in Figure 15.2(b). If both sectors of the labor market are at point A on their respective short-run Phillips curves, the economy will exhibit an average rate of wage inflation of w_0. Consider, however, a second case, with one labor market having unemployment well below U*, and the other having an unemployment rate equally far above U*. The average unemployment rate in the economy is U*. In the first market, wage inflation is w_1, far above w_0, for employers in that market bid up wages very rapidly to attract workers who have skills that are specific to that sector. Some of the workers may be bid away easily from the high-unemployment sector, but others will require substantial inducements in the form of large wage increases to leave their current employers in the low-unemployment sector. Employers in the high-unemployment sector will offer a lower rate of wage increase, w_2; but it will not be far below w_0, because their workers may leave to take jobs in the high-wage sector or may reduce their effort if they are upset by the decline in their customary wage position. The average rate of wage increase is $\overline{w}$, halfway between w_1 and w_2. Even though aggregrate unemployment is U* in both cases, the greater dispersion of unemployment in the second case means that the aggregate rate of wage inflation is higher.

In terms of Figure 15.5, the aggregrate short-run Phillips curve is raised from P_0 to P_1 by this greater dispersion of unemployment. In the long run the differences in unemployment rates between sectors will be eliminated, as new workers who are not

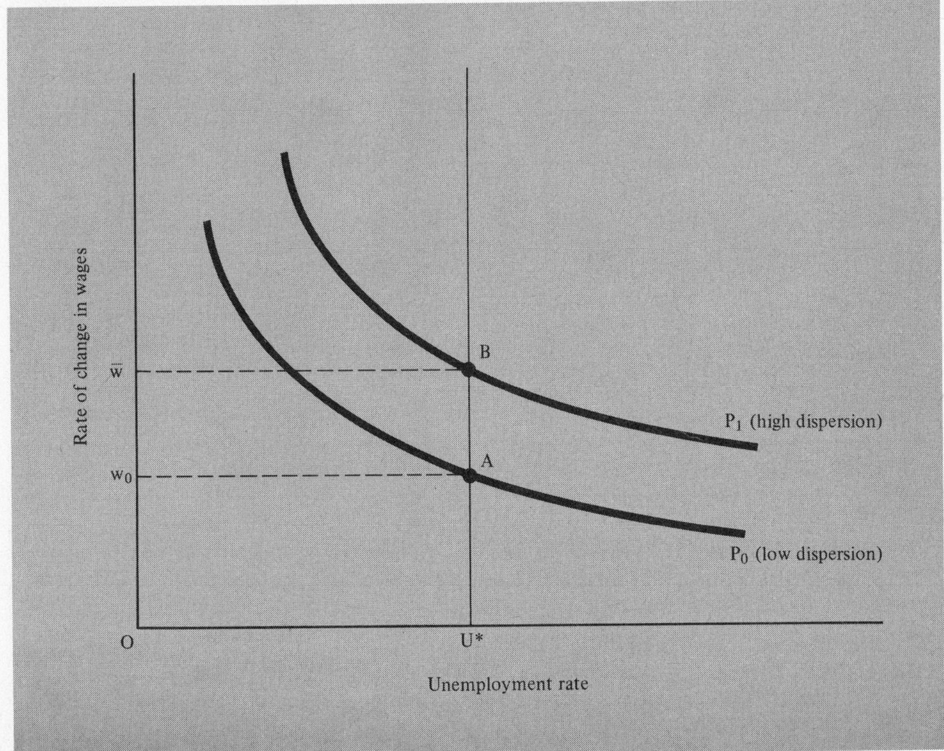

Figure 15.5 The short-run Phillips curve and unemployment dispersion.

locked in by sector-specific skills and are not used to outmoded customary wage differentials seek the most attractive position for them. In the short run, though, the structure of the labor market, in particular the dispersion of unemployment, affects the rate of aggregate wage inflation. This effect is compounded when policymakers accommodate the additional upward pressure on nominal wage growth by expanding the money supply more rapidly. The rate of wage inflation that is observed at any unemployment rate is increased. In the United States in the 1950s and 1960s, it has been estimated that dispersion of unemployment accounted for 25 percent of the inflation in nominal wages; similar estimated impacts on wage inflation have been found in the United Kingdom.[20]

The direction of spillovers between nonunion labor markets will depend on the size and direction of flows of labor, either actual or threatened. These are engendered by changes in customary wage differentials among jobs or labor markets that are classified either geographically or by skill. It is difficult to believe that a high unemployment rate in a sector, such as shown at point E in Figure 15.2(b), will prevent employers from reducing the growth rate of nominal wages if that sector offers above-average wages that result from substantial investment in skills that are specific to that sector. If, however, the high-unemployment sector is also a low-wage sector, in which there is little sector-specific human capital, low unemployment elsewhere in the economy that generates more rapid wage inflation would readily induce the low-paid workers to quit the sector. If, as we suggested in Chapters 1 and 2, the supply of low-wage labor to the market is fairly elastic, employers in the high-unemployment, low-wage sector can reduce the growth of nominal wages only slightly if they wish to retain their workers or hire substitutes for them. Thus dispersion of unemployment alone does not determine the extent of wage spillovers. Rather, wage increases flow from high-wage to low-wage labor markets when unemployment is low in the former and relatively high in the latter. In the United States between 1950 and 1969, the dispersion of unemployment affected aggregate wage inflation at each rate of unemployment; but wage inflation was especially rapid when high-wage states exhibited relatively low rates of unemployment. Similarly, between 1958 and 1978, wage inflation was more rapid when unemployment in high-wage industries was unusually low relative to unemployment elsewhere.[21] In this mostly nonunion economy the direction of wage spillovers is from tight to loose labor markets only if the tight labor markets pay higher wages than the loose ones.

POLICY ISSUE—SHIFTING THE SHORT-RUN PHILLIPS CURVE THROUGH RETRAINING

Retraining programs have been part of America's labor-market policy since the Area Redevelopment Act of 1961. Much of the focus of these programs has been on providing incomes to workers who lack useful skills or whose skills have become obsolete. Part of the emphasis, though, has been on removing skill bottlenecks that produce the dispersion of

[20]G. C. Archibald, "The Phillips Curve and the Distribution of Unemployment," American Economic Association, *Proceedings* (59): 124–134 (1969), and R. L. Thomas and P. J. M. Stoney, "Unemployment Dispersion as a Determinant of Wage Inflation in the U.K., 1925–1966," *Manchester School of Economics and Social Studies* (39): 83–116 (1971).

[21]Frank Brechling, "Wage Inflation and the Structure of Regional Unemployment," *Journal of Money, Credit and Banking* (5): 355–379 (1973), and Donald Nichols, "Effects on the Noninflationary Unemployment Rate," in Robert Haveman and John Palmer (eds.), *Jobs for Disadvantaged Workers,* Brookings Institution, Washington, 1982.

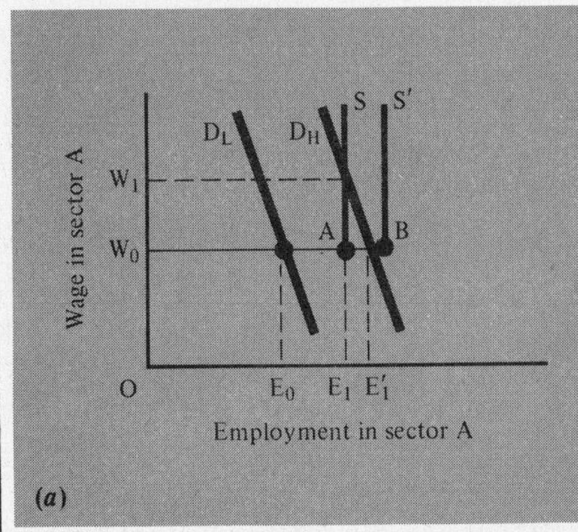

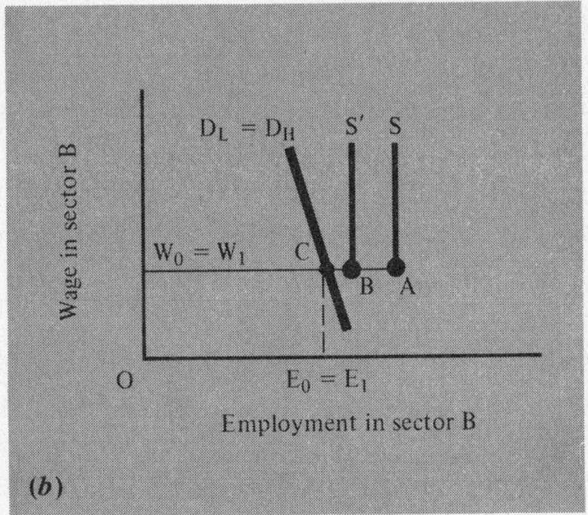

Figure 15.6 (a) The labor market in a bottleneck sector; (b) The labor market in a slack sector.

unemployment that raises the rate of wage inflation. The mechanism for ameliorating the problem is shown in Figure 15.6. In both Sectors A and B, employment and nominal wages are determined by demand and supply. The short-run supply of labor to each sector is assumed to be horizontal up to the point where all workers who have the sector-specific skills are employed [points A in Figs. 15.6(a) and (b)]. Thereafter, the supply is completely inelastic in the short run. If aggregate demand varies between a low and a high level, the demand for labor in Sector A varies from D_L to D_H. When demand is low, there is unemployment in Sector A in the amount $E_1 - E_0$ and no upward pressure on nominal wages; when it is high, there is excess demand for labor and pressures that result in wage and eventually price inflation. At the same time, we assume demand is equally low in Sector B at both times, leading to unemployment in the amount AC. When aggregate demand is high, there is still unemployment in Sector B, but wage inflation is generated in Sector A.

Solving this problem and shifting the short-run Phillips curve downward can be achieved by retraining workers from Sector B in skills that are specific to Sector A. This would shift the vertical segment of the short-run supply of labor to Sector A, to the right in Figure 15.6(a), from S to S′, and reduce the supply of labor in Sector B from S to S′ in Figure 15.6(b). Thus unemployment in Sector B would be reduced, as some retrained workers would find jobs in Sector A. Wage pressures in Sector A would be removed, for even when demand is high, no excess demand for labor exists there. Both the aggregate unemployment rate and the rate of wage inflation would be lowered.

Whether this policy makes sense depends on whether the government that sponsors the retraining can identify the sectors with skill shortages faster than individual employers and workers can. If so, the short-run Phillips curve will shift more rapidly than if the adjustment were left to the free market. Society would avoid some of the lost resources due to unemployment and the cost of price inflation that is spurred by wage inflation. If government does not have the ability, it is merely doing what the private sector would accomplish at least as rapidly on its own. The macroeconomic justification for government-sponsored retraining programs rests on the assumption that the government is better able to forecast skill bottlenecks than individual workers and employers can.

When the sectors are defined to be union and nonunion industry, the issue of the direction of spillovers becomes less clear. A number of considerations support the popular belief that unions are a source of general wage inflation, especially when unemployment is above the full-employment rate. Where the unionized sector is small and the threat of union expansion into unorganized sectors is weak, the principal effect of wage increases in the union sector will be on the pattern of relative wages. The general level of wages will be little affected by union gains. However, wage increases will be larger in the unionized sector and smaller in the nonunion sector (because of gross employment effects) than they would have been in the absence of unions. The growth of employment in the union sector will be discouraged by the widening union relative wage gap, whereas the growth of employment in the nonunion sector will be encouraged. This pattern seems to fit the experience of the United States during the 1950s.[22]

Eventually the union relative wage gap must cease rising. The employment effects of the increased gap will tend to inhibit further wage gains in the union sector, and the widened gap will encourage previously unorganized workers to join unions. The first effect weakens the wage push; the second, however, makes it become more general.

The greater the extent of union organization is and the greater the threat is that collective bargaining will spread to previously nonunion workers, the more likely union pressures are to raise the general level of money wages rather than to affect only relative wages. When most workers are organized or subject to a credible threat of organization, a rise in the general wage level could even originate in a fairly small part of the union sector and then spread by emulation to other industries or occupations. The larger the wage increases won by unions are, the higher will be the wages nonunion employers will have to offer their own workers if they hope to remain unorganized.

These arguments are convincing, but they ignore the relatively small size of the union sector, at least in the United States. It is somewhat difficult to believe that the unionized tail of the economy "wags" the entire labor-market "dog." The arguments are also inconsistent with the experience of the economy during periods, like the late 1960s, when union relative wage gaps are decreasing (see Table 11.3). During periods of rapid expansion of aggregate demand, nonunion workers, whose wages are adjusted more rapidly than those of unionized employees, receive large increases in nominal wages. When it comes time for unionized workers to renegotiate their contracts, they will seek to restore the customary relative wage gap even though demand conditions may no longer be so favorable. The experience of the United States in 1970 to 1971 seems to illustrate this process. An upward movement of wages that began in the late 1960s was originally caused by excess demand growing out of the Vietnam War and the way it was financed. By late 1969, however, output had peaked and the economy entered a mild but rather long recession. By late 1970 unemployment was well above frictional levels. Wages kept on increasing, however, as unions whose contracts expired sought to match the gains other workers had won when demand was stronger.

Spillovers of wage increases from union to nonunion industry, and vice versa, are both plausible descriptions of the transmission of wage inflation. The issue is a classic chicken-and-egg problem: For example, did the growth of nonunion wages in the late 1960s spur union wage increases in the early 1970s, as we just claimed, or did the union wage increases of the late 1950s induce nonunion employers to raise wages

[22] Adrian Throop, "The Union-Nonunion Wage Differential and Cost-Push Inflation," *American Economic Review* (58): 79–99 (1968).

more rapidly in the mid-1960s than market conditions would otherwise warrant? Does union wage setting react to deterioration in the union wage gap produced by increased nonunion wages, or does it increase the union wage gap independently?

These questions are not easily answered, and undoubtedly the answers vary among economies and over time, depending on how the institutions of collective bargaining are structured. The empirical evidence on the issue is somewhat mixed, but the preponderance of evidence for the United States suggests unions merely react to wage inflation that is generated elsewhere. One study of the United States between 1954 and 1973 found that union wage increases were substantially higher when the relative wage gap in the previous year was smaller, after adjusting for changes in labor-market conditions; nonunion wages were unaffected by the size of the gap. This suggests that unions merely try to restore the decline in their relative wage advantage over nonunion workers that is induced by wage inflation in the nonunion sector. Another study, covering 1956 to 1970, examined all changes in union and nonunion wages that were not due to variations in price inflation or in the state of the labor market (in the unemployment rate). The remaining variation in wage inflation in the nonunion sector was unrelated to what occurred in the union sector.[23]

We may conclude that the direction of spillovers does not necessarily run from union to nonunion industry. That being the case, efforts to shift short-run Phillips curves downward by reducing union power are likely to be no more successful than comparable efforts aimed at restraining inflationary pressures on nominal wages in the nonunion sector. Unionized industry is not clearly the source of wage inflation above what is produced by workers and employers reacting to changes in unemployment and the rate of price inflation. Therefore, modifying wage-setting mechanisms in the union sector is not likely to modify the rate of nominal wage inflation at a given rate of unemployment and growth in nominal aggregate demand.

WAGE AND EARNINGS DIFFERENTIALS OVER THE CYCLE

The existence of dynamic spillovers between labor markets implies that the process of wage inflation will lead to changes in the structure of relative wages over the cycle, too. This is seen most vividly if we examine one measure of the skill differential in wage rates. Table 15.3 presents the ratio of usual weekly earnings (essentially a measure of wage rates) of craft workers compared to those of nonfarm laborers. In all four business cycles on which data are available, the skill differential widened between the peak and trough of the cycle. If we were to modify the table in recognition of the possibility that the period 1979 to 1982 represented one long recession, the evidence would be even stronger that skill differentials widen in loose labor markets. More detailed evidence, based on an examination of the coefficient of variation of relative wages among manufacturing industries in the United States

[23] George Johnson, "The Determination of Wages in the Union and Non-Union Sectors," *British Journal of Industrial Relations* (15): 211–225 (1977), and Yash Mehra, "Spillovers in Wage Determination in U.S. Manufacturing Industries," *Review of Economics and Statistics* (58): 300–312 (1976). See also Robert Flanagan, "Wage Interdependence in Unionized Labor Markets," *Brookings Papers on Economic Activity*: 635–673 (1976); for contradictory evidence see Susan Vroman, "The Direction of Wage Spillovers in Manufacturing," *Industrial and Labor Relations Review* (36): 102–112 (1982).

Table 15.3 SKILL DIFFERENTIALS, U.S. BUSINESS CYCLES, 1969–1982

Peak and trough dates of cycles	Wage ratio[a]
1969	1.38
1971	1.43
1973	1.41
1975	1.45
1980:I	1.45
1980:III	1.51
1981:III	1.52
1982:IV	1.56

[a]Median usual weekly earnings of full-time craft workers, relative to nonfarm laborers. Many data only are available for the first two business cycles listed.

Source: Handbook of Labor Statistics, 1980, Table 60; and *Employment and Earnings,* selected issues.

between 1947 and 1967, showed that interindustry inequality of wages fell when unemployment rates fell.[24]

The narrowing of skill differentials during labor shortages can be explained on two grounds. The first was suggested in the discussion of compensating differentials in Chapter 12. On the whole, skilled work is more pleasant than unskilled work, and a tight labor market will reflect the true extent of the compensating differentials needed to fill the less pleasant jobs. The wide skill differentials in wages that are associated with the substantial levels of unemployment include a portion that represents the inability of the unskilled, whose unemployment rates increase most in a recession, to earn the compensating differentials they should expect under full employment.

A second explanation, and probably the more important, is based on the observation that the skill differentials observed in the statistics are those between occupations or job titles and not those between individuals of standardized abilities.[25] When skilled workers are hard to recruit, people who are not fully qualified are often promoted to skilled jobs. Some of these people will become fully qualified through on-the-job training; others may be demoted later when demand slackens. But for a time at least the quality of labor in the skilled occupation is diluted. In the completely unskilled jobs where there are few, if any, qualifications to lower, the same process cannot operate. No one can be promoted to them from below, and workers can be attracted from outside the firm only by raising entry wages. The result is a compression of differentials between job titles, but not necessarily a reduction in

[24]Michael Wachter, "Cyclical Variation in the Interindustry Wage Structure," *American Economic Review* (60): 75–84 (1970).

[25]Melvin Reder, "The Theory of Occupational Wage Differentials," *American Economic Review* (54): 833–852 (1955).

the premium paid for a constant standard of skill. The same reasoning applies even when standards for promotion and hiring are not related to qualifications for doing the work. Standards of all sorts are relaxed during periods of labor shortage, and differentials unrelated to productivity will also tend to be compressed.

Inequality in the distribution of annual earnings depends on inequality in the distribution of its two components, wage rates and the number of hours or weeks worked per year. Just as inequality in wage rates, as measured by the skill differential, rises when unemployment is high, so, too, inequality in number of weeks worked per year increases. The highest-paid workers—professionals, managers, and skilled craft workers—suffer relatively few spells of unemployment and little reduction in hours per week when aggregate demand declines. The burden is borne disproportionately by less skilled workers. The same low-skilled workers whose relative wage declines in a recession are also those whose annual hours or weeks of employment decline relatively. Earnings inequality therefore rises in recessions. The effect of changes in the inequality in weeks worked on the distribution of income is especially important: One study attributed 17 percent of the inequality in income in the United States during the recession year 1958 to the increased dispersion of weeks of work.[26]

INCOMES POLICY

Governments seeking to restrain inflation without restricting the growth of aggregate demand have used a variety of wage and price controls and related policies. From among these *incomes policies* we concentrate here on those affecting wages. The policies can take a variety of forms. For short periods they can involve a wage freeze or wage pause during which no increases in money wages are permitted. Wage freezes are most used in wartime or during a crisis in the balance of international payments. Thus the U.S. wage-price freeze of August 1971 was announced in connection with measures designed to improve the balance of payments. For the longer term most policies seek to establish some guideposts or criteria for acceptable increases in money wages. These are usually based on the trend of average productivity, sometimes with larger increases permitted where output rises result from increased skill or effort of the workers concerned, as in British productivity bargaining. Special provisions are often made for cases of equity—those of low-wage workers or workers whose wages have lagged behind those of other comparable workers. When there is already an ongoing inflation, the wage criterion may be adjusted upward to allow for it. This explains the differences among the 1962 to 1966 U.S. wage guideposts of 3.2 percent, the 1971 to 1974 pay standard of 5.5 percent, and President Carter's "real wage insurance" proposal of 1979, which implied a 7 percent criterion. The first two of these three episodes represent the major experiments in the United States with wage and price policy in a peacetime economy.

Incomes policy can be administered by a government agency; by a tripartite agency including union, management, and public representatives; or by unions and management themselves without active government participation, as in Sweden.

[26] Barry Chiswick and Jacob Mincer, "Time-Series Changes in Personal Income Inequality in the United States from 1939, with Projections to 1985," *Journal of Political Economy* (80): S34–S66 (1972).

When unions and management are opposed to the use of wage and price controls, as they usually are, the question of whether to participate in administering controls is a difficult one. By participating they appear to condone controls. This problem is especially acute for union leaders, who may seem to be working against the interests of their members and who may thus be inviting political opposition within their unions. However, by not participating they increase the danger that controls will be administered in ways that cause problems for the union, for example, by creating wage differentials that the members regard as inequitable.

Actual experience on participation by unions and management in the United States has varied. The Pay Board, which controlled wages in all industries except construction in 1971 to 1972, originally had labor and management members. However, the AFL-CIO and the United Auto Workers withdrew after a few months, and the board was recomposed of public members. Experience was different in the construction industry, where the Construction Industry Stabilization Committee continued as a tripartite organization, with the active participation of national union presidents even after union leaders from the AFL-CIO had resigned from the Pay Board. During 1971 to 1973 the Construction Industry Stabilization Committee substantially slowed the rate of increase of construction wages and fringe benefits. The continued cooperation of national union leaders appears to have been based on their realization that large wage increases won by powerful local unions had widened the union wage gap and in some cases posed threats to the maintenance of employment in the union sector of the industry.

Wage and price policies induce a number of effects on the labor markets to which they are applied. Many of these represent responses of employers and workers to the changed incentives that the incomes policy imposes on wage-setting mechanisms. For example, where there is a highly centralized trade union movement committed to an incomes policy, as in Sweden, *wage drift* may occur; actual money earnings may rise faster than the basic wage rates that are negotiated in national agreements.[27] In part, wage drift arises because employers of particular groups of workers in short supply offer them wage increases that are larger than those negotiated nationally. If such behavior is disapproved or regulated, employers may increase workers' earnings by scheduling additional overtime work, some of which adds little or nothing to output. Employers may also upgrade or hire workers into job classifications above those for which they are qualified.

Wage drift is a particularly serious problem under some kinds of piecework or incentive-pay systems. Small improvements in methods can cumulatively increase output per hour of work, with the result that earnings rise for any given amount of work effort. When labor is not scarce, management usually attempts to recapture some of such extra earnings by negotiating changes in the piecework rates, perhaps after new industrial engineering studies. When labor is in short supply, however, management may accept the high earnings as an aid to recruitment. Eventually such "methods drift" causes unrest among workers on time rates, who see less skilled pieceworkers earning more than they do. In some British industries this has led to

[27]Lloyd Ulman and Robert Flanagan, *Wage Restraint: A Study of Incomes Policies in Western Europe,* University of California Press, Berkeley, Calif., 1971.

special additional payments to time workers in lieu of the opportunities for high piecework earnings. Wage drift has never been an important phenomenon in the United States, but it has been in many European countries.

As we showed in Chapter 10, incomes policies do appear to reduce the rate of strike activity. However, even those fewer strikes that do occur can severely affect the likelihood that the policies will be successful in restraining wage inflation. The most important problem is the settlement of strikes in which demands far exceed those permitted by the wage criteria or guideposts. The economic program of the government comes in conflict with the right to strike and with the political costs to the government in power of taking strong action against unions. In both the United States and the United Kingdom, important wage settlements in excess of the criteria of incomes policy have been permitted to go unchallenged or allowed to stand over initial government objections. If this happens frequently, then incomes policy loses its credibility and must be either discarded or revamped.

Incomes policies, by substituting a norm for wage increases in place of the myriad forces that ordinarily determine the size of wage settlements, may merely rotate rather than shift the short-run Phillips curve. The wage norms may be successful in restraining wage inflation when aggregate demand is expanding rapidly; but if they establish a target for wage settlements that union members feel must be attained, union leadership, wishing to satisfy the membership, will push for the target wage increase even though the state of the labor market does not justify so large a wage increase. In the United Kingdom, where incomes policies of various degrees of stringency have been applied more often since World War II than in the United States, the short-run Phillips curve was flatter between 1947 and 1968 when incomes policies were in effect. On average, though, those policies did not shift the short-run Phillips curve downward.[28]

Another way that the changed incentives induced by incomes policies affect behavior is to change wage differentials, such as the skill differential, and thus affect the extent of inequality in earnings. The targeting of wage negotiators on the norm for wage increases will not by itself induce a change in wage differentials, for each negotiated wage rises by the same percentage. To the extent, however, that those administering the wage norms can justify making exceptions to them based on some notions of equity, the wage increases of lower-paid workers may be more likely to exceed the norm than those of other workers under an effective incomes policy. This seems to be what happened in the United States during the Korean War period of wage and price controls: The coefficient of variation of earnings among manufacturing industries was lower than at other times when the labor market and price inflation were the same. Some incomes policies explicitly mandate these results, stipulating increases in wages that are at least partly in absolute terms. With each worker receiving, for example, a $1 per hour increase, wage differentials must necessarily equalize. This type of incomes policy was in effect in the United Kingdom between 1973 and 1977 and did to some extent produce the intended equalization.[29]

[28] Richard Lipsey and J. Michael Parkin, "Incomes Policy: A Re-appraisal," *Economica* (37): 115–137 (1970).

[29] Michael Wachter, "Cyclical Variation . . . " loc. cit., and Orley Ashenfelter and Richard Layard, "Incomes Policy and Wage Differentials," *Economica* (50): 127–144 (1983).

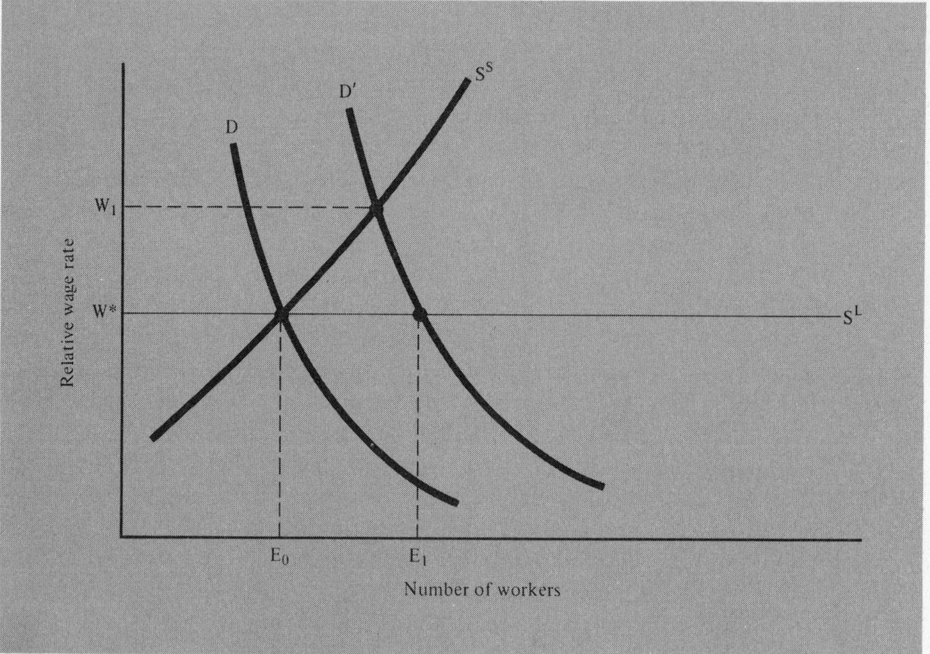

Figure 15.7 Wage norms and relative wages among industries.

Regardless of whether the wage norm is specified in percentage terms alone or partly in absolute terms, the wage increases it generates may be different among various industries from those that would arise from unfettered wage negotiating. The effects of the norms are sometimes so serious that they lead to pressures for abandoning the policies entirely. Consider an industry shown in Figure 15.7. We assume that there are no industry-specific skills or special disamenities associated with the industry, so that the long-run supply curve S^L of labor to it is flat. It is shaped this way because any temporary increase in relative wages above W*, along the short-run supply curve S^S, induces new workers to enter the industry and drives the relative wage back to W*. If demand for labor in the industry suddenly rose from D to D′, but did not change anywhere else, the wage would rise relative to wages elsewhere, from W* to W_1. With a strict incomes policy based on equal percentage increases in all industries, this cannot occur; thus the relative wage increase that would eventually attract $E_1 - E_0$ new workers also cannot occur. Instead, there is a shortage of workers of $E_1 - E_0$.

The government can circumvent this difficulty by making exceptions to its policy in those industries where demand is increasing especially rapidly. Making such distinctions is often fairly difficult, though; and it is even harder to convince union members in other industries that a government-mandated fall in their relative wages is needed to ensure the continued success of the incomes policy. Rather than take this risk, most policies rely upon private responses to the shortages that are produced. These take the form of the wage drift and additional use of overtime that we have already discussed. Also, since new workers can be paid a wage that is not limited by some previous level, excessive mobility of workers among firms is encouraged by policies that keep relative wages more rigid than they would otherwise be.

The record of incomes polices to date includes few, if any, cases in which increases in money wages have been successfully restrained over long periods. In some cases this is because the incomes policies were not accompanied by monetary and fiscal policies that contributed to restraining inflation. More often, though, the policies are abandoned when powerful political forces feel that the policy has worsened their relative position, or when the difficulties often caused by incomes policies become unbearable.

A question of some interest is whether incomes policies do shift the short-run Phillips curve down, and do so without having the curve shift up to a position that is higher than its original one after the restrictions have been removed. Examining Figure 15.1, one notices that all the points for the years 1962 to 1966 lie below the short-run Phillips curve P, drawn for the years 1954 to 1973. This simple evidence suggests that the wage-price guideposts of this period did produce a downward shift in the curve. More detailed consideration of the evidence, though, casts some doubt on this conclusion. The overhanging labor supply of workers discouraged by the long period of relatively high unemployment from 1960 to 1963, and the amount of hoarded labor (see Chap. 5) employed but not fully utilized, meant that the degree of slack in the labor market at each unemployment gap during this period was more than the measured gap suggested.[30] Whether the guideposts reduced the rate of wage inflation is still not answered satisfactorily, nor, given the range of other changes that occurred at the time, is it likely to be. We can conclude, however, that if the curve was shifted down during this period, there is no evidence that it shifted out beyond its original position after the guidepost policy was abandoned.

Between 1971 and 1974 the Nixon administration imposed a series of four different incomes policies. The brevity of each of the periods prevents one from inferring from Figure 15.1 whether the policies had any effect on the short-run Phillips curve. However, statistical evidence suggests that wage increases during the first and fourth phases of the policy (the first was a wage freeze) were below what would have been generated by similar labor-market conditions. However, in the brief periods following these two phases, wage increases were above what would have been expected based on the amount of unemployment and price inflation at the time. Although they were successful in shifting the short-run Phillips curve down, the Nixon incomes policies were soon nullified by equally large rebounds in the curve above its original position.[31]

The broader experience of Western European countries presents the same

[30] N. J. Simler and Alfred Tella, "Labor Reserves and the Phillips Curve," *Review of Economics and Statistics* (50): 32–49 (1968), and Jim Taylor, "Hidden Unemployment, Hoarded Labor, and the Phillips Curve," *Southern Economic Journal* (37): 1–16 (1970). See also the discussion by Paul Anderson, Michael Wachter, Adrian Throop, and George Perry in *American Economic Review* (59): 351–370 (1969).

[31] Frank Reid, "Control and Decontrol of Wages in the United States," *American Economic Review* (71): 108–120 (1981).

picture of diversity that is given by the briefer American experience with incomes policies. In some nations, especially those in which the incomes policy was coupled with effective demand management, wage inflation was reduced temporarily at given rates of unemployment. The best example of this was Austria in the mid-1970s, where guarantees to organized labor that job losses would be avoided where at all possible and restraints on the growth of aggregate demand caused a substantial moderation in the size of wage settlements.[32] Other countries, perhaps because of the greater diversity of the economic interests affected by incomes policies, were less successful in achieving even a temporary downward shift in the short-run Phillips curve.

Incomes policies work best when they are accompanied by aggregate demand policy that creates an environment for wage restraint by avoiding excess demand for goods and services that accelerates price inflation. To be effective incomes policies must avoid even the appearance of violability by workers in industries with the most economic or political power. Otherwise all workers will abandon their adherence to the policy for fear of seeing their relative pay reduced. The policies must, more importantly, be temporary. If not, they lead to an increasing inability of wage differentials to reflect the state of supply and demand for labor in different occupations, areas, and industries, and thus lead to increasing strains on the ability of the labor market to allocate workers where their productivity will be greatest.

POLICY ISSUE—TAX-BASED INCOMES POLICIES (TIPs)

In an attempt to provide market incentives to increase the effectiveness of incomes policies, several economists have proposed that corporate tax rates be raised on those firms whose wage and price increases exceed some specific norms. Modifications of this initial proposal for a tax-based incomes policy (TIP) have been suggested, including reductions in tax rates for firms that hold wage and price increases below the norms.[33] The general form of these ideas is shown in Figure 15.8. Having determined the norm for wage increases, in this case, w_N, the original plan specified tax rates as shown by the line BAC. The modifications would have provided a tax structure that is linked to wage increases by the lines DAC.

Whether employers will respond to the tax incentives by resisting workers' wage demands more vigorously is unclear. To the extent that employers feel they can pass on excessive wage increases and the accompanying tax increases to consumers in the form of higher prices, they are unlikely to comply with the policy. Assuming, though, that employers' resistance to wage demands is stiffened, the effects of the TIP on wage outcomes can be seen by considering the employer's wage-offer curve in the context of a bargaining situation (see Fig. 10.1). The wage-offer curve will be shifted rightward, reducing the size of the wage settlement that is eventually reached during collective bargaining. However, the reduction is purchased at the cost of a greater likelihood of a strike, or a longer strike if one would have occurred anyway.[34] The incomes policies that have been used in the United

[32] John Addison, "Incomes Policy: The Recent European Experience," in J. L. Fallick and R. F. Elliott (eds.). *Incomes Policies, Inflation and Relative Pay,* Allen & Unwin, London, 1981.

[33] Henry Wallich and Sidney Weintraub, "A Tax-Based Incomes Policy," *Journal of Economic Issues* (5): 1–19 (1971). See also Laurence Seidman, "Tax-Based Incomes Policies," *Brookings Papers on Economic Activity*: 301–348 (1978).

[34] Albert Rees, "New Policies to Fight Inflation: Sources of Skepticism," *Brookings Papers on Economic Activity*: 453–477 (1978).

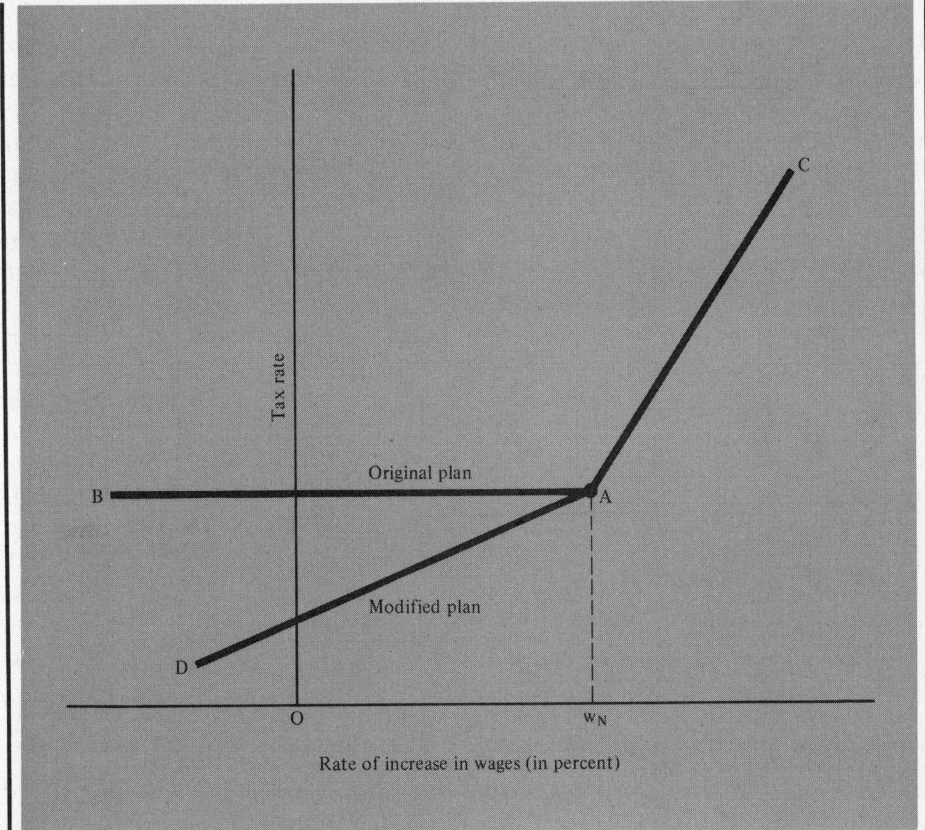

Figure 15.8 TIPS on wage increases.

States have reduced strike activity. A TIP may perhaps be more successful in moderating wage inflation than the guideposts and controls of the 1960s and early 1970s, but it would probably produce the unpleasant side effect of increasing the number and duration of strikes.

SUMMARY

There is a short-run inverse relationship between the rate of wage inflation and the rate of unemployment in an industrialized economy. In the long run the rate of inflation is determined by the rate of growth of aggregate demand, whereas the long-run equilibrium rate of unemployment is determined by the success of the institutions for matching vacant jobs and unemployed workers. However, the economy moves only slowly back toward the long-run equilibrium rate of unemployment after unemployment has risen above or fallen below this rate. The movement toward equilibrium is too slow to be explained by theories of the way in which workers form expectations about price inflation, by theories of job search, or by a theory of nominal wage rigidity produced by the existence of wage contracts, either actual or implicit. Rather, the slow movement of unemployment toward long-run equilibrium stems from the transmission of wage increases among labor markets, occupations, and industries. A wage increase obtained in a tight labor market forms part of the basis for later wage increases elsewhere, mitigating the effects of looser labor markets that otherwise would slow the rate of wage increase. Carefully constructed incomes policies can temporarily reduce the rate of wage inflation at each rate of unemployment; but the evidence shows that many of these policies have not even succeeded in doing this.

Index

84 85 86 9 8 7 6 5 4 3 2 1